RURAL POVERTY IN
THE UNITED STATES

T0329754

RURAL POVERTY IN THE UNITED STATES

EDITED BY

Ann R. Tickamyer,
Jennifer Sherman,
and Jennifer Warlick

COLUMBIA UNIVERSITY PRESS

NEW YORK

Columbia University Press
Publishers Since 1893
New York Chichester, West Sussex
cup.columbia.edu

Library of Congress Cataloging-in-Publication Data
Names: Tickamyer, Ann R., editor. | Sherman, Jennifer, editor. |
Warlick, Jennifer L., editor.
Title: Rural poverty in the United States / [edited by] Ann Tickamyer,
Jennifer Sherman, Jennifer Warlick.
Description: New York : Columbia University Press, [2017] |
Includes bibliographical references and index.
Identifiers: LCCN 2017002248| ISBN 978-0-231-17222-6 (cloth : alk. paper) |
ISBN 978-0-231-17223-3 (pbk. : alk. paper) | ISBN 978-0-231-54471-9 (e-book)
Subjects: LCSH: Rural poor—United States. | Poverty—United States.
Classification: LCC HC110.P6 R8925 2017 | DDC 339.4/60973091734—dc23
LC record available at https://lccn.loc.gov/2017002248

Columbia University Press books are printed on permanent
and durable acid-free paper.
Printed in the United States of America

Cover design: Julia Kushnirsky
Cover image: © Pete Ryan / Getty Images

CONTENTS

ACKNOWLEDGMENTS

ANN R. TICKAMYER

This book has been a long time in the making, and I wish to thank the many contributors to its completion, including the coeditors whose collective knowledge, persistence, and debate greatly enriched this volume; Columbia University Press, especially Stephen Wesley, an enthusiastic, patient, and supportive editor, Joy Wilkie, who helped keep us organized, and others at the press who have assisted along the way; and above all, the authors whose stellar scholarship is at the heart of this volume.

In addition, I would like to thank the many collaborators, colleagues, and students over the years whose work has stimulated and deepened an ongoing interest in all forms of social inequality. I particularly want to remember my late dissertation advisor, Gerhard Lenski, whose influence continues to provide inspiration and to acknowledge the lasting impact of serving on the RSS Task Force on Persistent Poverty in Rural America that set the standard for this effort.

JENNIFER SHERMAN

I wish to thank the authors and coeditors, Columbia University Press, Stephen Wesley, and Joy Wilkie for all of their hard work in making this volume come together. I also thank the important rural scholars whose work continues to inspire me, and whose support has been invaluable to my career, including Conner Bailey, Louise Fortmann, Leif Jensen, Lisa Pruitt, Kai Schafft, Gene Summers, Ann Tickamyer, and Bruce Weber. I am extremely grateful for their contributions, both to this volume and to larger understandings of rural poverty in the United States and abroad.

JENNIFER WARLICK

I thank Stephen Wesley at Columbia University Press first and foremost for recognizing the need for a multidisciplinary text investigating poverty in rural America and for inviting me to participate in this endeavor. He also proved to be a patient, able collaborator and editor. Thanks also to the other members of CUP's editorial team, especially Joy Wilkie who cheerfully provided welcomed assistance that allowed us to focus on content rather than managerial details.

I am grateful to my coeditors for sharing their perspectives as sociologists and introducing me to many important scholars in their disciplinary field. My comprehension of familiar issues has been expanded and enriched as a result.

We would not have a text were it not for our contributors. They too broadened my perspectives and provoked me to think anew. I thank them for this, as well as for their contributions and patience during the editorial process.

I am also indebted to the undergraduate students in my rural poverty course at the University of Notre Dame whose questions and comments helped me understand what students generally want and need to learn about rural poverty in America. Their overall enthusiasm for this project kept me moving forward at critical junctures. One student in particular, Ash Smith, also provided valuable research assistance. Finally, I wish to thank David Betson at Notre Dame for his valuable insights and comments about my own chapter.

Rural Poverty in the United States treats rural poverty as a uniquely important subject and set of issues. We provide a broad and multifaceted overview of the causes, consequences, and forms of rural poverty in the United States. The scope and intensity of poverty experienced by rural people are often overlooked by the public, scholars, and policy makers, yet it persists as an enduring social problem. In this book we address serious conceptual and empirical issues that are distinctive to rural poverty and that make it unique when compared to other forms of U.S. poverty, including poverty in urban and suburban areas. We include authors from multiple disciplines, including sociology, demography, economics, law, political science, public health, and education. Together this multidisciplinary group of scholars describe, interrogate, and problematize rural poverty from a variety of angles and topics.

We move thematically from more general understandings of rural poverty and its roots, forms, and impacts, to discussions of measuring it and explaining its causes, to more in-depth explorations of specific aspects of rural poverty and its effects on and interactions with particular social groups and social institutions. This enables us to first set the context and introduce the reader to the main issues and concepts and to describe the scope and depth of the problem of rural poverty. After this introduction to the big picture of rural poverty, we move on to in-depth explorations of the populations affected by rural poverty, the social structures that keep it in place, and the processes that reproduce it. We conclude by discussing possible solutions to rural poverty and its impacts and provide an understanding of the complexities inherent in addressing rural poverty from economic and policy perspectives.

Part I introduces the reader to the geography and demography of rural America. Chapter 1 describes the diversity of rural America itself, including the various types of places it includes and the populations who live in rural America. Chapter 2 then puts rural poverty in historical context, explaining both the variation in rural poverty rates over time and its concentration and persistence. In this section we familiarize the reader with the poor populations of rural America and the types of rural American communities where poverty is concentrated, providing an overview of who the poor are and where poverty is found in rural areas of the United States.

Part II explores key concepts and issues vital to understanding rural poverty, focusing on measuring and explaining rural poverty. Chapter 3 introduces the reader to the concept of poverty in detail, exploring different definitions and measurements of poverty and the contexts in which they are used. Chapter 4 goes into depth on how to understand and explain poverty, exploring theoretical understandings and the multiple dimensions of causes and consequences of rural poverty in the U.S. context. These chapters set the stage for the rest of the book by ensuring that the reader fully understands what poverty is and why it occurs in rural America.

Part III looks in more depth at the people affected by rural poverty, with examinations of vulnerable rural populations. Chapter 5 focuses on gender roles and gender relations in rural areas, examining the interplay of gender with rural poverty, and women's vulnerability to it due to both family and labor market structures. Chapter 6 looks at racial and ethnic minorities in rural areas, whose poverty rates tend to be higher than white populations due to legacies of slavery, racism, and racialized oppression. Chapter 7 investigates these issues in further depth as they pertain to immigration and the experiences of new immigrant groups, exploring the reasons for high poverty rates among rural immigrant groups.

Part IV focuses on community and social institutions affected by rural poverty. Chapter 8 looks at the roles of symbolic capital in structuring rural life, illustrating the ways in which social, cultural, human, and moral capital aid or hinder the rural poor in their daily struggles to survive. Chapter 9 focuses on old and new economies, tracing economic and labor market trends in rural America and their implications for poverty. Chapter 10 focuses on food, hunger, and homelessness and explores the intertwined conditions of food and housing insecurity for the rural poor. Chapter 11 looks in depth at the environment and health, exploring these issues from an environmental justice perspective as well as looking at access to health care for the rural poor. Chapter 12 looks at the roles of education and information in perpetuating and alleviating rural poverty.

Overviews of topics in parts III and IV are paired with brief case studies written by separate authors that illustrate the realities of the issues being discussed. The case studies help to illustrate the diverse array of causes, consequences, and faces of rural poverty across the United States. This combination of macro and micro and quantitative and qualitative studies from a variety of disciplines enables us to capture both the breadth and the depth of issues facing poor rural places and people and to showcase the richness of scholarship and knowledge from across different fields of study concerning rural poverty in the United States.

Finally, part V looks at programs, policy, and politics. Chapter 14 describes the safety net in rural areas, illustrating the ways in which the rural poor are both served and underserved by U.S. social service programs. Chapter 15 focuses on economic development and its potential for alleviating rural poverty. Chapter 16, the concluding chapter, addresses politics and policy as it affects the rural poor in the United States, exploring both opportunities and barriers to rural-focused policy and political participation.

Overall, the chapters come together to provide a comprehensive understanding of rural poverty. But why does rural poverty need its own volume? The answer isn't simply that the experience of rural poverty is distinct from the much more studied urban forms. Rural poverty is a persistent social problem that affects significant numbers of Americans. U.S. rural poverty has been persistently high and rising throughout most of the early twenty-first century, whereas metropolitan poverty (in cities and suburbs) is on the decline and consistently lower. Since America's founding, its poorest people have disproportionately lived in rural areas. They also are disproportionately ethnic minorities, and they usually suffer poverty rates considerably higher than the national average. Rural poverty, although less visible and threatening to many than urban poverty, remains a significant problem for our nation, and one that must be understood as having distinct causes and effects on individuals and families. As this volume illustrates, the depth, breadth, and persistence of rural poverty in the United States warrant it being treated as an important social issue whose causes and solutions must be looked at independently from other social problems.

What qualifies a rural American as poor? Why are some regions in rural America persistently poor? Why are their economies quicker to recess and slower to recover? What is the nature of rural poverty versus metropolitan poverty? And what approaches—economic, political, or private—might help to develop rural economies and relieve rural poverty? These are some of the questions we aim to answer. In this endeavor we have called upon some of the nation's foremost scholars of rural America and rural poverty. It is our hope that this text will help both those who have been interested in rural poverty for decades and those who are new to the topic to begin to understand and address the many different issues that surround rural poverty, poor rural communities, and poor rural individuals and families.

RURAL POVERTY IN
THE UNITED STATES

———

PART I

Geography and Demography of Rural America

The two chapters in part I set the stage for all the chapters that follow by detailing the changing demography and geography of rural America over time, explaining how poverty rates, poverty policies, and impoverished rural people have changed from the 1930s to today.

Chapter 1, "Where Is Rural America and Who Lives There?," creates a profile that provides the backdrop for examinations of poverty's influences on the viability of rural communities, the lives of rural residents, and the contributions rural America makes to the nation's material, environmental, and social well-being. Rural areas permeate the United States from coast to coast and involve agricultural (farming) lands, struggling industrial (mining and manufacturing) towns, and counties adjacent to urban areas that supply much-needed employment opportunities to commuting rural residents. The chapter also provides definitions for "metropolitan" versus "nonmetropolitan" areas, explains how rural population changes are measured, and most important, traces recent population trends and migration patterns of rural America. The chapter's unfolding demographic story reveals a rural population that is both aging and becoming more racially diverse.

Chapter 2, "Poverty in Rural America Then and Now," enriches this backdrop by focusing on changes in rural poverty in the United States from the early twentieth century to the present. Rural poverty first emerged as a policy issue in the 1930s Great Depression, and it resurfaced again in the 1960s War on Poverty. Although fifty years ago rural poverty was widespread across geographic regions and racial groups, by 2015 rural poverty had become increasingly concentrated geographically in "pockets of high poverty," and impoverished conditions had become more "self-perpetuating," especially in regions that are home to African Americans, Native Americans, and Hispanics. Today these racial/ethnic minority groups experience the highest poverty rates, and the remote rural counties in which they live are most likely to suffer persistent poverty of place and people. Persistent poverty, particularly among children, is one of the few unchanging characteristics of rural areas.

CHAPTER 1

Where Is Rural America and Who Lives There?

Kenneth M. Johnson

This chapter describes where rural America is and how the population of rural America is changing. Rural America is large and diverse. Some rural areas are growing rapidly, whereas other rural communities house far fewer people today than they did a century ago. Rural concerns are often overlooked in a nation dominated by urban interests. Yet a vibrant rural America contributes to the nation's intellectual and cultural diversity and provides most of the nation's food, minerals, clean air, and clean water. The demographic change in rural America has implications for poverty and family well-being. This chapter considers the unfolding demographic story of rural America, setting the stage for the remainder of the book. It examines how poverty influences the viability of rural communities, the lives of rural residents, and the contributions rural America makes to the nation's material, environmental, and social well-being.

Rural America is a simple term describing a remarkably diverse collection of people and places. More than 50 million people live rurally, and these areas cover nearly 75 percent of the United States. Rural America spans a broad spectrum of landscapes that includes some of the best farmland in the world. It spreads across the vast agricultural heartland of the Great Plains and Corn Belt and extends from the Canadian border deep into Texas. Rural America holds the highly productive fruit and vegetable regions of California, Florida, and the Southwest, as well as dairy regions in Wisconsin, upstate New York, and New England. But there is far more to rural America than agriculture. It includes sprawling exurban areas on the outer edges of the nation's largest metropolitan areas; the vast arid range and desert lands in the Southwest;

the deep, mountainous forests of the Pacific Northwest; the flat and humid coastal plain of the Southeast; the hardscrabble towns and hollows of the Appalachians; the rocky shorelines and working forests of New England, where rural villages look much as they did a hundred years ago; and the glaciers and fjords of Alaska.

Rural economies also depend on more than just agriculture. Some rely on auto supplier plants strung along the interstates of the auto corridor from the Great Lakes to Tennessee. Elsewhere, coal, ore, oil, and gas are extracted, processed, and shipped through a complex network of pipelines, barges, ships, and railroads to urban consumers hundreds or thousands of miles away. Warehouses and distribution centers clustered around major rural interstate interchanges facilitate the movement of goods and products. In other rural regions, struggling industrial towns facing intense global competition try to hold onto jobs and businesses. In contrast, fast-growing rural recreational areas situated near scenic mountains and inland lakes and along the Atlantic, Pacific, and Great Lakes coastlines rush to complete infrastructure improvements needed to support a growing population of amenity migrants, seasonal visitors, and the labor force needed to meet their growing demands.

The diversity of rural America is not limited to its topographical and economic features. The people of rural America also reflect the diverse strands that compose the demographic fabric of the nation. Native peoples reside in ancestral homelands scattered throughout rural areas. Many African Americans still live in the rural Southeast, even though millions moved north in the Great Migration of the early twentieth century. Hispanics are dispersing to the rural Southeast and Midwest from long-established settlements in the Southwest. Despite this growing diversity, large areas of rural America remain overwhelmingly non-Hispanic white. The rural future depends in part on the size, composition, and distribution of the rural population. Demographic change has significant implications for the people, places, and institutions of rural America. It will also influence whether rural areas remain good places to live and raise families and how many rural residents will live in poverty. The remainder of this chapter defines rural America and describes how demographers study population change; examines historical and recent rural demographic change; considers the growing diversity of the rural population by race/Hispanic origin; and explains how the Great Recession influenced rural demographic trends.

WHERE IS RURAL AMERICA AND HOW DO WE MEASURE POPULATION CHANGE THERE?

One important challenge in studying rural America is defining where it begins and where it ends. Clearly, the farm counties of the Great Plains are part of rural America, and New York City is not, but where do we draw the line in between? There is no simple answer. Even the U.S. Department of Agriculture, the federal agency with primary responsibility for rural America, has multiple definitions of which places are rural and which places are urban.

One widely used definition is based on whether a U.S. county is defined as "metropolitan" or "nonmetropolitan." Why use counties? Counties are a basic unit of government with stable boundaries that don't change over time. A great deal of demographic and economic data is collected by county.

Counties are also the basic building blocks for metropolitan areas. These metropolitan areas are the collections of cities and suburbs that are referred to as "urban areas." Counties are designated as metropolitan (urban) or nonmetropolitan (rural) using criteria developed by the U.S. Office of Management and Budget. Rural America is always changing, so definitions of rural America also change. To keep the definition of what is rural stable for this chapter, a constant 2004 metropolitan or nonmetropolitan classification is used.

Metropolitan areas include counties with an urban core (city) population of 50,000 or more residents, along with adjacent counties (the suburbs) that link to the urban core by commuting patterns. There are 1,090 metropolitan counties among the 3,141 counties in the United States. All counties that are not within metropolitan areas are grouped together and referred to as nonmetropolitan, even though they differ from one another just as dense urban cores differ from the thinly settled suburbs in metropolitan areas. Our interest is in these 2,051 counties that are not part of metropolitan America (figure 1.1). These are the nonmetropolitan or rural counties that are examined in this chapter. Here the terms "rural" and "nonmetropolitan" are used interchangeably, as are the terms "metropolitan" and "urban."

Prior research suggests that rural areas near urban areas (adjacent nonmetropolitan counties) have fared better both economically and demographically than counties that are more remote from urban areas

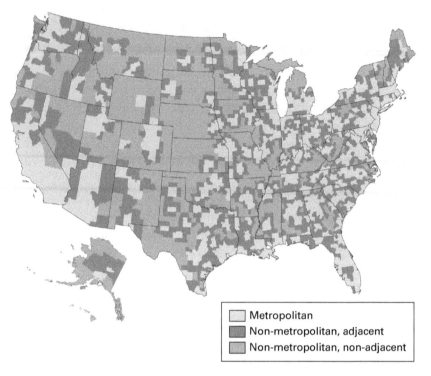

Figure 1.1 Metropolitan and adjacent counties.

Source: USDA Economic Research Service, 2004.

(nonadjacent counties). The economic activities in rural counties also differ. Some rural counties depend on farming; others have manufacturing plants; and still others attract tourists to their natural landscapes, lakes, and mountains. Subsets of rural counties are classified using typologies developed by the Economic Research Service of the U.S. Department of Agriculture (USDA, ERS), which group nonmetropolitan counties along economic and policy dimensions (for example, farm counties, manufacturing counties, recreational counties, etc).[1]

MEASURING RURAL POPULATION CHANGE

Some rural counties have gained population for decades, whereas other counties, including many in the agricultural heartland, have lost people and institutions. A key question is: How does the population of one area grow while another area declines?

Population change in rural areas reflects a balancing act between two demographic forces. The first of these is what demographers call *natural increase*. Natural increase is the difference between the number of babies born in an area and the number of people who die there (births minus deaths). In the United States as a whole, more babies have been born each year than the number of deaths, so the population has always grown from natural increase. In some parts of rural America, however, there have been times when more people have died than been born. When deaths exceed births, demographers call it *natural decrease*.

The other force that influences population change is *migration*. Migration measures the movement of the population from place to place. Migration includes both immigration (when people move between countries) and internal migration within the United States. So, how far do you have to move to be a migrant? If a person moves from one U.S. county to another, he or she is referred to as an internal (or domestic) migrant. If the person stays in the same county, he or she is a mover, but not a migrant.

Demographers are particularly interested in *net migration*. Net migration is the difference between the number of migrants moving into a county and the number of people who move out. If the number of people migrating in and out of the county is equal, there is no net migration. If one migration stream is larger than the other, then net migration will either increase or decrease the population. Young adults are more likely to migrate than any other age group. When these young adults move to an area, they bring not just themselves but the potential for future population increase through the babies many of them eventually have.

Both natural increase and net migration play important roles in rural population change, but the influence of each varies across time and space. Let's turn now to the study of the demographic changes that have reshaped rural America through their implications for rural poverty and family well-being.

HISTORICAL POPULATION TRENDS

Throughout most of American history, rural areas grew because migrants moved in and births far exceeded deaths. As the twentieth century progressed, however, these trends changed. The natural increase that sustained rural population growth earlier dwindled as rural women had fewer children. Migration patterns also changed. As the economic and social opportunities

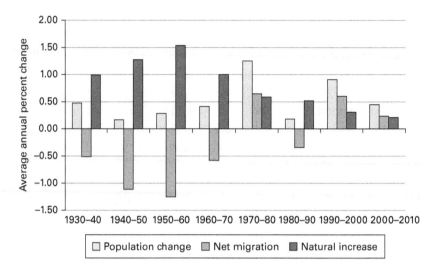

Figure 1.2   Nonmetropolitan demographic change, 1930 to 2010.

Source: U.S. Census 1930–2010 and population estimates.

in cities grew, rural areas experienced widespread out-migration (figure 1.2). The magnitude of the migration loss varied from decade to decade, but the pattern was consistent: more people left rural areas than arrived. Migration losses from some rural counties were substantial. For example, many farm counties on the Great Plains lost more than half their population from out-migration over the course of several decades. These trends changed in the 1970s when rural population gains exceeded those in metropolitan areas for the first time in the twentieth century, but this rural turnaround was short-lived, ending in the 1980s as widespread out-migration and population decline reemerged. Rural population growth rates rebounded once more in the early 1990s before slowing near the end of the decade (Johnson 2006, 2014). At the dawn of the twenty-first century, population trends in rural America remained unclear.

SOME RURAL AREAS GROW AND OTHERS CONTINUE TO DECLINE IN THE TWENTY-FIRST CENTURY

In the first decade of the twenty-first century, patterns of population growth and decline varied widely across rural America (figure 1.3). Population gains were greatest in the West and Southeast, and at the

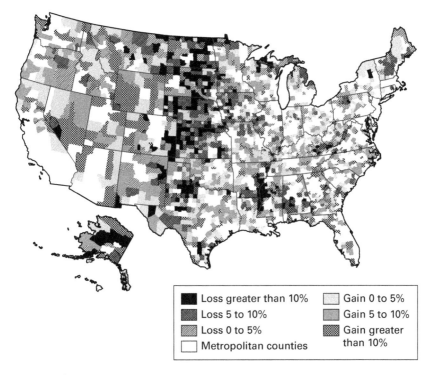

Figure 1.3   Nonmetropolitan population change, 2000 to 2010.

Source: U.S. Census Bureau, Census 2000 and 2010.

periphery of large urban areas in the Midwest and Northeast. Scattered areas of population gain were evident in recreational regions of the upper Great Lakes, the Ozarks, and northern New England. In contrast, population losses were common in the Great Plains and Corn Belt, in the Mississippi Delta, in parts of the northern Appalachians, and in the industrial and mining belts of New York and Pennsylvania.

The slowdown in rural growth has been precipitous. Nonmetropolitan areas gained less than half as many people in the 2000s as they had in the 1990s. Between 2000 and 2010, rural counties gained 2.2 million residents (4.5 percent), to reach a population of 51 million in April 2010. During the 1990s, the rural population gain was nearly twice as large at 4.1 million.

Between 2000 and 2010, population gains were greater in rural counties adjacent to metropolitan areas, just as they were during the 1990s

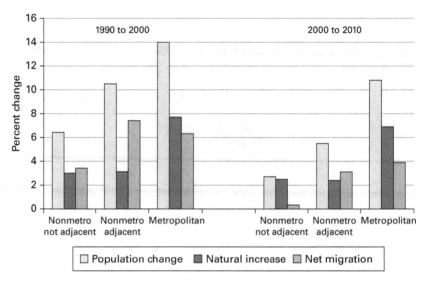

Figure 1.4   Demographic change in metropolitan and nonmetropolitan areas, 1990–2000 and 2000–2010.

Source: U.S. Census Bureau, Census 1990, 2000, 2010 and the Federal-State Cooperative for Population Estimates (FSCPE).

(figure 1.4). Adjacent counties had the advantage of proximity to urban labor markets, as suburban populations on the outer edge of metropolitan areas often spilled over into them. These adjacent counties saw a 5.5 percent population gain between 2000 and 2010. This gain was smaller, however, than it had been during the 1990s. Among more remote nonadjacent counties, the population gain was smaller (2.7 percent), and it was also smaller than during the 1990s.

Population gains in metropolitan areas exceeded those in rural areas during each period. Metropolitan areas grew by 14 percent in the 1990s and by 10.8 percent between 2000 and 2010. A key question is: Why did rural population gains diminish so much after 2000?

The primary cause of the sharply curtailed rural population growth was a slowdown in migration after 2000. During the 1990s, migration accounted for nearly two-thirds of all rural population gain. After 2000, it accounted for less than one-half of the gain. Nonmetropolitan counties gained 2.7 million residents from migration during the 1990s, but only about 1 million between 2000 and 2010. Fewer rural counties experienced migration gains. Only 46 percent of the rural counties gained migrants between 2000 and 2010 compared with 65 percent between 1990 and 2000.

Because natural increase in rural areas remained relatively stable over the two decades, this significant reduction in net migration dramatically slowed the rate of population increase. The slowdown was greatest in rural counties that were not adjacent to metro areas. Here the net migration gains were so small that they sharply reduced population growth. Migration gains in more remote areas totaled only 46,000 (0.3 percent), and just 35 percent of these counties gained migrants (Johnson and Cromartie 2006; Johnson 2014). By contrast, in adjacent rural counties, the migration gain was far more sizable at 3 percent (980,000). Overall, 53 percent of the adjacent counties gained migrants between 2000 and 2010.[2]

With little growth from net migration, natural increase became the major source of nonmetropolitan population growth between 2000 and 2010, accounting for just over half of the gain of 2.2 million rural residents. In remote rural counties, natural increase represented 90 percent of the population gain. In adjacent nonmetropolitan counties, the contributions of natural increase and net migration were more balanced—natural increase accounted for 44 percent of the population increase of 1.7 million.

DIFFERENT TYPES OF COUNTIES HAD DIFFERENT PATTERNS OF DEMOGRAPHIC CHANGE

Given the many different kinds of rural counties, it is not surprising that demographic change varied among them. Compare shifts in a county's dominant industry. Farming and mining no longer monopolize the overall rural economy, but they are still important (see Farming Counties Snapshot). Farming still dominates the local economy of 403 rural

Farming Counties: Continuing Population Loss

Rural America was originally settled by people whose livelihood depended on their ability to wrestle food and minerals from the land. The USDA defines 403 farm-dependent counties that represent this traditional rural sector. Among them are Jewell, Osborne, Republic, and Smith counties in Kansas. Situated along the Nebraska-Kansas border and straddling the boundary between the corn and wheat belts, these counties are far removed from the urban scene and have a very large proportion of their labor force engaged in agriculture.

In 1900, nearly 66,000 people lived and farmed in these four counties. The population has declined ever since. By 1990, only 20,700 people remained. The population dropped another 24 percent in the next twenty years, leaving just 15,800 people in 2010. By 2014, the population had diminished further to just 15,400 in the four counties. Young adults have historically left these farm counties in large numbers. In contrast, the older population stays. As a result, all four counties have had more people die than be born in them throughout the last four decades.

These farming-dependent counties do enjoy significant advantages. Unemployment and poverty levels are relatively low. Incomes and housing prices are moderate, producing an affordable standard of living. Residents find these farm counties appealing because they believe their neighbors will help out when needed, people get along, and residents work well together (Hamilton et al. 2008). The continuing loss of people and jobs despite strong social and community capital reflects the dilemma facing many rural farm counties. Without new economic opportunities, the potential for rising poverty levels grows, and three of the four counties have seen poverty levels rise for children in the most recent data.

counties. These counties are largely at a demographic standstill. Between 2000 and 2010, the population of farming-dependent counties grew by just 0.3 percent (figure 1.5). This minimal population gain was entirely because of a natural increase gain of 3 percent, which was large enough to offset migration loss. In contrast, in the 1990s, farm counties grew by 5 percent, from both natural increase and migration.

Mining (which includes oil and gas extraction) is a major force in another 113 counties. Mining counties did better in the 2000s than they had during the 1990s when they suffered significant migration loss. Rising oil prices and new technologies that made the extraction of shale oil financially viable contributed to an influx of energy employees to some mining areas. This resulted in a smaller migration loss and allowed for natural increase to produce a modest population gain of 2.7 percent.

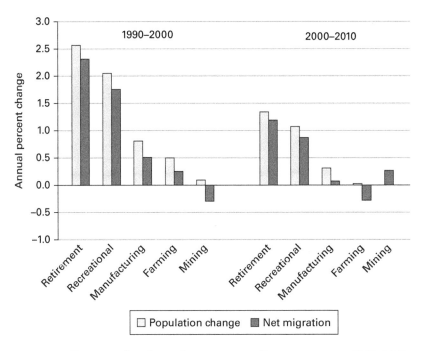

Figure 1.5   Demographic change by nonmetropolitan county type, 1990–2010.
Source: U.S. Census 1990–2010 and USDA Economic Research Service, 2004.

Counties dominated by manufacturing have traditionally been one of the bright spots of rural demographic change (see Manufacturing Counties Snapshot). For decades, efforts by states and the federal government to foster economic growth and development in rural areas focused on expanding the manufacturing base (Johnson 2006).[3] The expectation was that a growing manufacturing sector would create jobs that would encourage current residents to stay and attract others to move closer. This strategy worked in the late twentieth century. The 584 rural manufacturing-dominant counties had population gains of 8.1 percent during the 1990s, mostly as a result of migration. However, growth slowed dramatically in the new century. The net population gain was only 3.1 percent between 2000 and 2010. Natural increase accounted for 75 percent of this population gain in manufacturing counties. Migration contributed only modestly to the population growth, considerably less than it had during the 1990s. The globalization of manufacturing coupled with the

Manufacturing Counties: Economic Change and Growing Diversity

Nestled against the Virginia border in the scenic foothills of the Smokey Mountains is Surry County in North Carolina. Surry County has a long history as a rural manufacturing county, mostly in furniture-making and textiles. However, both of these sectors are fading and jobs are disappearing (Johnson 2006, 2014). Poultry processing is growing in the county, as it is in much of the rural Southeast, but jobs are still scarce. Tourism is also on the rise because of the county's beauty and its proximity to the growing urban areas to the south.

The county has had its demographic ups and downs. Surry's population grew by 16 percent during the rural turnaround of the 1970s and by 15 percent during the rebound of the 1990s, fueled almost entirely by migration. Growth has slowed down since 2000 as net migration has sharply declined.

Surry County's recent demographic change illustrates the growing diversity of rural America as well. Hispanics accounted for virtually all of the recent population gain, growing by more than 50 percent between 2000 and 2010 and now representing 10 percent of the population. Poverty is relatively high in the county as well, with nearly 25 percent of children living in families with incomes below the poverty line (Johnson 2006, 2014).

Great Recession (2007–2010) adversely affected the rural manufacturing sector as the low-skill, low-wage jobs common in some manufacturing facilities shifted offshore or disappeared altogether as technology replaced labor on the shop floor (Johnson 2006, 2014).

The demographic story is different in rural counties with natural amenities, recreational opportunities, or quality-of-life advantages (see Recreational Counties Snapshot). Counties rich in amenities have consistently been among the fastest growing in rural America. Major concentrations of these counties exist in the mountain and coastal regions of the West, in the upper Great Lakes, in coastal and scenic areas of New England and upstate New York, in the foothills of the Appalachians and Ozarks, and in coastal regions from Virginia to Florida (Johnson and

Recreational Counties: Growth Continuing, but Slowed by Recession

Michigan's Grand Traverse County exemplifies the fast-growing rec-reational and retirement destinations discussed in the text. Situated on a beautiful Lake Michigan bay, the county is well known for its crystal clear lakes, ski slopes, golf courses, restaurants, and lodging. It has a well-earned reputation as a year-round recreational center, but its economy is quite diverse.

Grand Traverse amenities attract retirees and the creative classes* seeking an alternative to the hectic pace of urban life. The result has been rapid population increase, from 39,175 in 1970 to 64,273 in 1990, a 64 percent gain in just twenty years. Growth continued in the 1990s with a population gain of 21 percent. Most of the growth came from migration, with a substantial flow from the metropolitan areas of southern Michigan and Chicago. Growth slowed after 2000 as a result of slowing migration, as it has in many recreational areas, especially as the recession deepened. Nonetheless, Grand Traverse County reached a population of 90,800 in 2014.

Grand Traverse's history of growth has expanded employment opportunities, making it easier for residents to stay and for workers from surrounding areas to move in. The economic opportunities in Grand Traverse County also contribute to low levels of poverty in the area.

* The creative classes are defined by the USDA Economic Research Service as engineers, archi-tects, artists, and people in other creative occupations.

Beale 2002; McGranahan 1999; Economic Research Service [ERS] 2015). These 299 nonmetropolitan recreational counties grew by 10.7 percent between 2000 and 2010.

This is a smaller gain than during the 1990s, but still substantial compared to farming, mining, and manufacturing counties. There is considerable overlap between these recreational counties and those that attract older adults because of the natural and built amenities that attract vacationers, owners of second homes, and retirees. These retire-ment counties, like their recreational counterparts, grew rapidly during the 2000s, and the vast majority of that growth came from migration. Some migrants are attracted to the natural and built amenities because they improve their quality of life; other migrants are attracted by economic opportunities generated by these amenity migrants and tourists. The new homes, medical facilities, restaurants, and services they need create many jobs and businesses (see Recreation, Resource Extraction, and Manufacturing Snapshot).

Recreation, Resource Extraction, and Manufacturing: Straddling an Economic Transformation

New Hampshire's northernmost county, Coos County, has a declining manufacturing and resource extraction base and a growing recreational activity base, producing an unusual demographic profile. For more than a hundred years, wood and paper products were a mainstay of the economy, with large mills employing generations of residents processing the timber of the vast northern forests. Now, nearly all of the mills are gone. Poverty levels have increased recently after decades of relatively low poverty, perhaps reflecting the economic displacements related to the loss of high-paying jobs in the mills.

Situated in a scenic region with ski areas and grand old resorts, Coos County has welcomed generations of vacationers and new amenity migrants. The county is seeking to capitalize on its growing recreational appeal through a countywide advertising effort (Dillon 2011). A great deal is riding on the success of this effort as the county attempts to adapt to the economic and demographic transformation facing rural America in the new century.

Coos County's demographic history reflects the declines in its manufacturing sector. Currently, the county has 31,700 residents, roughly 2,600 fewer than it had in 1970, and it has lost population in each of the last three decades. There were 3,000 births in Coos County between 2000 and 2010, but more than 4,100 deaths. This produced a natural population loss of 3.3 percent. Between 2000 and 2010, Coos County did gain migrants, partially because of its recreational appeal, but also because two new prisons opened in the county. It has lost migrants again recently.

MIGRATION AND AGING IN PLACE ARE MAKING THE RURAL POPULATION OLDER

Just as migration varies by place, it also varies by age. For decades, migration has drained young adults from rural areas, whereas the older population has both aged in place and grown through retirement-age migration. The combined effect of these migration trends is a reduction in the number of rural young adults and an accelerating aging of the rural population. Fewer young adults means a diminished supply of young workers and fewer children in the next generation. It also means a higher dependency ratio—the ratio of those not in the labor force (children and elderly) to those in the labor force—which puts greater pressure on workers. A growing older population puts greater demands on rural health care facilities and also increases the need for services such as senior centers and assisted living, which are more expensive and difficult to deliver in rural areas where distances are greater and populations are less dense (Chan, Hart, and Goodman 2006).

The rural population is already considerably older than that of the United States as a whole, and this trend will likely accelerate in the next several decades. Rural areas have proportionally fewer young adults and fewer children than the overall U.S. population. For example, there were 12 percent fewer people in their twenties and thirties in rural America in 2000 and 2010 than in the United States as a whole (figure 1.6). In contrast, during the same years, the rural population had 20 percent more older adults than the United States as a whole.

Rural America is older than urban America, primarily because of aging in place among those who already reside there. Rural America has a disproportionately large share of baby boomers born between 1946 and 1964, aged fifty-three to seventy-one in 2017. This group is considerably larger than the cohorts born before or after them—especially in rural America. Having a large population in late middle age has distinct advantages for rural areas right now. It means the working-age population is large compared to those either too old or too young to work. As we look to the future, however, the rural age structure presents significant challenges. As the large baby boomer cohorts continue to age over the next two decades, the number and proportion of seniors in rural America will grow.

Migration also contributes to the aging of the rural population in two distinctly different ways. Both have implications for the rural future and rural poverty. Rural areas have lost young adults through net

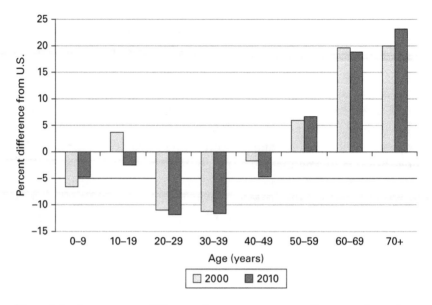

Figure 1.6   Age structure differences between nonmetropolitan counties and United States overall, 2000 and 2010.

Source: U.S. Census Bureau, Census 2000 and 2010.

out-migration in each of the last three decades (figure 1.7). This long-term loss of young migrants has been substantial. Between 2000 and 2010, rural counties lost 17.1 percent of the residents who would have been age twenty-five to twenty-nine by 2010. Rural areas sustained similar migration losses in the 1980s and 1990s and lost even greater proportions of their young adult population in the 1950s and 1960s.

The economic and social opportunities of urban areas attract rural young people. Some return later in life, but most do not. In some farm counties on the Great Plains, more than half of each generation of young adults has left over the past sixty years. The loss of so many capable young people is a serious concern in many rural areas.

Rural areas tend to gain modest numbers of older adults from migration. Migration gains were evident among those over the age of fifty, with the gains accelerating in the 1990s and 2000s. The scenic amenities, moderate weather, and leisure opportunities available in many of the recreational and retirement counties considered earlier attract older adults. Thus, although most rural counties continue to lose part of their young adult population to out-migration, the older population stays put and in

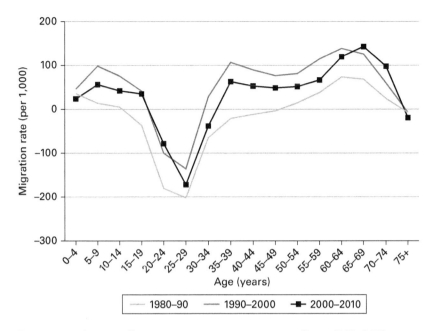

Figure 1.7   Age-specific net migration rate, nonmetropolitan, 1980–2010.

Source: Winkler et al., 2013.

some amenity counties is supplemented by an influx of older migrants. Poverty rates of older adults are significantly lower than those of children and working-age adults, so the changing age distribution in rural America has potential implications for future poverty trends.

THE GROWING DIVERSITY OF RURAL AMERICA

In 2010, 21 percent of the rural population was Hispanic or of a racial group other than white. Although these minorities represent a relatively modest share of the rural population, they accounted for nearly 83 percent of the entire rural population gain between 2000 and 2010. The rural minority population grew by 1.8 million during this decade compared with a gain of just 382,000 (less than 1 percent) among the much more numerous non-Hispanic white population. Rural America remains less diverse than urban America, but minority growth now accounts for most rural population increases, just as it does in urban areas.

Rural racial diversity is uneven (figure 1.8). Many counties remain overwhelmingly non-Hispanic white. In other rural areas, racial diversity

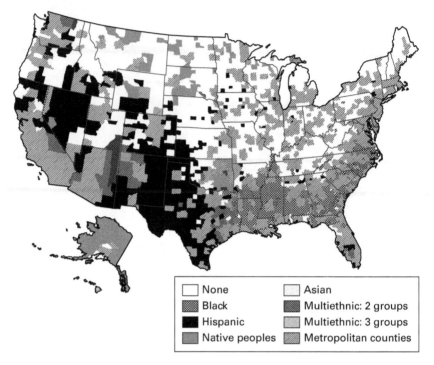

Figure 1.8   Nonmetropolitan minority population distribution, 2010.

Source: U.S. Census Bureau, Census 2010.

is substantial and increasing rapidly. Large concentrations of African Americans remain in the rural Southeast, bolstered now by a recent influx of black migrants from other regions. Hispanics are spreading out beyond their historic roots in the Southwest into the Southeast and Midwest (Johnson and Lichter 2008). About one-half of the nonmetropolitan Hispanic population now resides outside the rural Southwest (Johnson and Lichter 2008). These resettlement patterns together with Hispanic natural increase have bolstered the diversity of rural America.

Hispanics have had a substantial effect on recent rural demographic change. During the 1990s, Hispanics accounted for 25 percent of the entire rural population gain, even though they represented just 3.5 percent of the rural population. This contribution to rural growth accelerated after 2000, when Hispanics accounted for 54 percent of the rural gain although representing only 5.4 percent of the population in 2000. By 2010, the Hispanic population in rural America stood at 3.8 million,

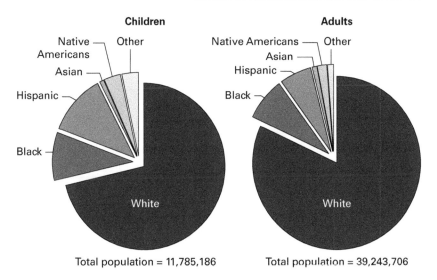

Figure 1.9   Nonmetropolitan population by race and Hispanic origin, 2010.

Source: U.S. Census Bureau, Census 2010.

or 7.6 percent of the rural population, a gain of 45 percent from 2000. Hispanic migration is now catalyzing large secondary demographic effects on fertility and natural increase (Johnson and Lichter 2008, 2010; Johnson et al. 2014). Most of the rural Hispanic population gain in the 2000s was from natural increase rather than migration (Johnson and Lichter 2008).

Children are in the vanguard of this growing diversity in nonmetropolitan areas. In rural America, minority children represented 29 percent of the population under age 18 in 2010. In contrast, only 18 percent of the rural adult population belonged to a racial or ethnic minority (figure 1.9). At more than 12 percent in 2010, Hispanics represent the largest share of this minority youth population in rural areas (Johnson and Lichter 2010). These rural patterns are consistent with national trends, although the rural population remains less diverse than the urban population.

The rural population is also becoming more diverse because the number of white children is declining. There were 940,000 (10 percent) fewer non-Hispanic white children in rural areas in 2010 than there had been in 2000. The number of African American children also declined. In all, there were 515,000 fewer children in rural America in 2010 than there were in 2000. A Hispanic child population gain of 434,000 children (45.1 percent) cushioned the overall loss. The significant loss of white children coupled with a growing Hispanic child population accelerated the diversification of the rural child population.

In 2010, 356 rural counties had more minority children than non-Hispanic white children, and another 178 counties had nearly as many minority children as white children. The concentrations of these rural majority-minority counties are in the Mississippi Delta, the Rio Grande region, the Southeast, and in the northern Great Plains. As the population of minority people grows, children will be the vanguard of this change. Because minority children have higher poverty levels than non-Hispanic white children, there are significant implications for rural poverty. If minority children continue to be at greater risk of poverty as the proportion of all children who are minority grows, child poverty levels are likely to increase significantly.

HOW THE GREAT RECESSION HAS INFLUENCED RURAL DEMOGRAPHIC TRENDS

As we have seen, the population of rural America is always changing. So, what is happening to the rural population right now? The census counts every person in the country but is completed only once every ten years. Census Bureau population estimates are not as accurate as the census, but they still provide a very good idea of how the rural population has changed recently. Data from both of these sources are reflected in the following discussion.

The recent Great Recession was the largest shock to the American economic system since the Great Depression of the 1930s. Because demographic trends are sensitive to economic change, it is important to look briefly at what happened to rural demographic trends during and after the recession. The period from 2000 to 2014 is divided into four segments: the preboom period (April 2000 to July 2004), the economic boom (July 2004 to July 2007), the recession (July 2007 to April 2010), and the postrecession period (April 2010 to July 2014). The National Bureau of Economic Research charted the Great Recession from 2007 to late 2009. The aftermath of the recession, however, is still felt in rural America's demographic trends.

Rural population growth slowed in the recession and postrecession periods. The annual population gain between 2004 and 2007 was

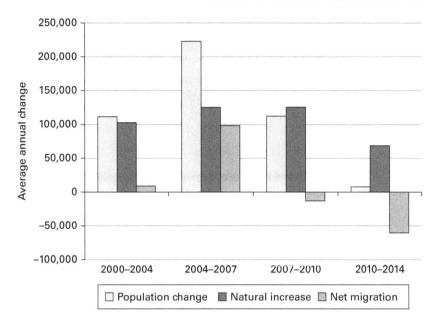

Figure 1.10   Demographic change in nonmetropolitan counties, 2000 to 2014.

Source: Census estimate, 2000–2014.

230,000. The population gain slowed to 112,000 between 2007 and 2010 and to just 8,000 between 2010 and 2014 (figure 1.10). Most of this population slowdown was due to a sharp reduction in net migration during the recession and postrecession years. During the economic boom, rural counties had a net migration gain of 98,000 per year. In contrast, they lost a net 13,000 migrants a year between 2007 and 2010 and had a net migration loss of more than 60,000 a year in the postrecession period. Natural increase also slowed as women had fewer children during the recession and are still having fewer children now. It is unclear whether these births have been delayed because of the lingering effects of the recession on employment, or whether they will be foregone entirely.

The impact of the recession on migration was spatially uneven (Johnson, Curtis, and Egan-Robertson 2016). Surprisingly, the slowdown was greater in rural counties adjacent to urban areas, where migration gains have historically been the largest due to peripheral growth and spatial sprawl. Paradoxically, in remote rural areas, where historically there has been little if any growth, the effect of the recession on migration was not as great. Remote rural counties suffered migration losses early in the decade, gained migrants during the mid-decade boom, and then, during the recession, the migration gain diminished. The net migration slowdown during the recession was far more modest in these remote rural counties. It is not clear yet whether the slowdown in births and diminished migration to rural America evident in the Great Recession and its aftermath will continue.

SUMMARY AND IMPLICATIONS

The story of demographic change in rural America in the first part of the twenty-first century is one of slowing population growth due to diminished migration and less natural increase. Rural population gains were considerably smaller between 2000 and 2014 than they were during the 1990s. Nonmetropolitan areas grew by barely half as much as they had in the last decade of the twentieth century, and growth slowed even more between 2010 and 2014.

The first decade of the twenty-first century also highlights new patterns of racial and ethnic diversity in rural America. Hispanics, in particular, represent a new source of growth in parts of rural America. The minority population represents just 21 percent of the rural population, but it produced nearly 83 percent of the rural population increase between 2000 and 2010.

Just how demographic changes in rural America affect poverty and family well-being is covered in greater detail throughout the book, but consider just one example of how rural demographic change is pertinent to rural poverty patterns: persistent child poverty. By definition, counties with persistent child poverty have had widespread poverty among their child population for at least the last three decades. Recent research documents the stubborn persistence of such child poverty in large areas of rural America, including the Mississippi Delta and Appalachia (Mattingly, Johnson, and Schaefer 2013). In all, 571 of the 706 U.S. counties with persistent child poverty (81 percent) are in rural America. More than 26 percent of the rural child population resides in counties with persistent child poverty. In comparison, only 12 percent of urban children reside in persistent child poverty counties. The recession has only made it worse, with the proportion of children in poverty rising in these already disadvantaged counties. The demographic changes in rural America over the last decade have done nothing to alleviate persistent poverty, and minority children are at greater risk of poverty than non-Hispanic white children. As we have seen, the minority child population is growing in rural America, and the non-Hispanic white child population is diminishing, increasing rural child poverty. The social and economic isolation fostered by distance and limited transportation in rural America increases the risks many of the rural poor face. Welfare reform, the expansion of government health insurance, and education reforms affect children differently in rural areas than in cities and suburbs (Lichter and Jensen 2002; Lichter and Schafft 2016). A better understanding of how the changing demographic structure of rural America influences the risk of poverty of rural children and adults is needed.

DATA AND METHODS

County population data come from the decennial census for 1990, 2000, and 2010. They are supplemented with data from the Census Bureau's Population Estimates program, which provides information on births and deaths in each county from 2000 to 2010 (U.S. Census Bureau 2010, 2015). The Census Bureau population, birth, and death estimates for 2010 to 2014 are also used. Estimates of net migration are derived by the residual method, whereby net migration is what is left when natural increase (births minus deaths) is subtracted from total population change.

Data for racial and Hispanic origin of the population are from the 2000 and 2010 censuses. Five ethno-racial groups are identified: (1) Hispanics of any race, (2) non-Hispanic whites, (3) non-Hispanic blacks, (4) non-Hispanic Asians, and (5) all other non-Hispanics, including those who reported two or more races. In some analyses, Native Americans are reported separately. To examine the spatial distribution of different racial and ethnic child populations, the number and percentage of *majority-minority counties*—those having at least half their child population from minority groups in 2010—and *near majority-minority counties*—those with between 40 and 50 percent of their children from minority populations—are estimated.

Counties were also classified as having minority concentrations if more than 10 percent of the population was from a specific minority group. Black, Hispanic, Asian, and Native American were the four minority groups that reached the 10 percent threshold in at least one county. Counties that had two or more minority groups reaching the 10 percent threshold were classified as multiethnic.

Data on whether a county is metropolitan or nonmetropolitan come from the Office of Management and Budget, and the classification of rural counties by economic type and recreational and retirement status is from the Economic Research Service of the USDA.

NOTES

1. Five types of rural counties are of particular interest here. *Farming* counties include those in which a substantial part of the local economy is based on farm earnings and employment. *Mining* counties are those in which a substantial proportion of local earning and employment comes from mining. *Manufacturing* counties are those in which a substantial proportion of earnings derives from manufacturing activity. *Recreational* counties are those in which recreational industries generate considerable earnings and employment and vacation homes are numerous. *Retirement* counties are those that receive a substantial influx of older migrants. For a fuller description, see USDA Economic Research Service, "Measuring Rurality," http://www.ers.usda.gov/data-products/rural-urban-continuum-codes.aspx.

2. Immigration contributed more to rural migration gains between 2000 and 2010 than it did during the 1990s. However, even with immigration on the rise, overall migration gains were significantly smaller in rural areas during the first decade of the twenty-first century.

3. Manufacturing is an important component of the rural economy, employing a larger proportion of the rural labor force than it does in urban areas.

REFERENCES

Chan, Leighton, Gary Hart, and David C. Goodman. 2006. "Geographic Access to Health Care for Rural Medicare Beneficiaries." *Journal of Rural Health* 22:140–46.

Dillon, Michele. 2011. "Stretching Ties: Social Capital in the Rebranding of Coos County, New Hampshire." New England Issues Brief. Durham, NH: Carsey Institute.

Economic Research Service. 2015. "Measuring Rurality: 2004 County Typology Codes Methods, Data Sources, and Documentation." Washington, DC: U.S. Department of Agriculture. http://www.ers.usda.gov/data-products/rural-urban-continuum-codes.aspx.

Hamilton, Lawrence C., Leslie R. Hamilton, Cynthia M. Duncan, and Chris R. Colocousis. 2008. *Place Matters: Challenges and Opportunities in Four Rural Americas. A Carsey Institute Report on Rural America.* Durham, NH: Carsey Institute.

Johnson, Kenneth M. 2006. "Demographic Trends in Rural and Small Town America." *Reports on Rural America* 1(1):1–35. Durham, NH: Carsey Institute.

——. 2014. "Rural Demographic Trends in the New Century." In *Rural America in a Globalizing World*, ed. C. Bailey, L. Jensen, and E. Ramson, 311–29. Charleston, SC: University of West Virginia Press.

Johnson, Kenneth M., and Calvin L. Beale. 2002. "Nonmetro Recreation Counties: Their Identification and Rapid Growth." *Rural America* 17:12–19.

Johnson, Kenneth M., and John B. Cromartie. 2006. "The Rural Rebound and Its Aftermath: Changing Demographic Dynamics and Regional Contrasts." In *Population Change and Rural Society*, ed. W. Kandel and D. L. Brown, 25–49. Dordrecht, Netherlands: Springer.

Johnson, Kenneth M., Katherine J. Curtis, and David Egan-Robertson. 2016. "How the Great Recession Changed U.S. Migration Patterns." *Population Trends in Post-Recession Rural America*. Brief 01-16. Madison, WI: Applied Population Laboratory, University of Wisconsin.

Johnson, Kenneth M., and Daniel T. Lichter. 2008. "Natural Increase: A New Source of Population in Emerging Hispanic Destinations in the United States." *Population and Development Review* 34:327–46.

——. 2010. "The Growing Diversity of America's Children and Youth: Spatial and Temporal Dimensions." *Population and Development Review* 31(1):151–76.

Johnson, Kenneth M., Andrew P. Schaefer, Daniel T. Lichter, and Luke T. Rogers. 2014. "The Increasing Diversity of America's Youth: Children Lead the Way to a New Era." Carsey School of Public Policy National Issue Brief 71. Durham, NH: Carsey School of Public Policy.

Lichter, Daniel T., and Leif Jensen. 2002. "Rural America in Transition: Poverty and Welfare at the Turn of the Twenty-First Century." In *Rural Dimensions of Welfare Reform*, ed. B. A. Weber, G. J. Duncan, and L. E. Whitener, 77–110. Kalamazoo, MI: UpJohn Institute.

Lichter, Daniel T., and Kai Schafft. 2016. "People and Places Left Behind: Rural Poverty in the New Century." In *Oxford Handbook of Poverty and Society*, ed. D. Brady and L. Burton, 317–40. Oxford: Oxford University Press.

Mattingly, Mary Beth, Kenneth M. Johnson, and Andrew P. Schaefer. 2013. "More Poor Kids in More Poor Places." Carsey Institute Policy Brief 38. Durham, NH: Carsey Institute.

McGranahan, David. A. 1999. "Natural Amenities Drive Population Change." Agricultural Economics Report No. 718. Washington, DC: Economic Research Service, U.S. Department of Agriculture.

U.S. Census Bureau. 2010. "Annual County Population Estimates: April 1, 2000 to July 1, 2009." Washington, DC: U.S. Census Bureau. http://www.census.gov/popest/data/historical/2000s/vintage_2009/index.html.

——. 2015. "Annual County Population Estimates: April 1, 2010 to July 1, 2014." Washington, DC: U.S. Census Bureau. http://www.census.gov/popest/data/counties/totals/2014/CO-EST2014-alldata.html.

Winkler, R.L., K. M. Johnson, C. Cheng, P.R. Voss and K.J. Curtis. 2013. County-specific Net Migration by Five-year Age Groups, Hispanic Origin, Race and Sex 2000–2010. *CDE Working Paper* No. 2013–04. Center for Demography and Ecology, University of Wisconsin—Madison. Madison, WI.

CHAPTER 2

Poverty in Rural America Then and Now

Bruce Weber and Kathleen Miller

RURAL POVERTY THEN (1904)

Poverty is widespread in this country. While it is possible that New York State has more poverty than other states, it is doubtful if its poverty is much greater proportionately than that of most of the industrial states. Twelve years ago I made what was practically a personal canvass of the poor in a small town in Indiana. There were no tenements, but the river banks were lined with small cabins and shanties, inhabited by the poorest and most miserable people I have almost ever seen. About the mills and factories were other wretched little communities of working people. All together the distress extended to but slightly less than 14 percent of the population, and poverty extended to not less than 20 percent of the people. I cannot say how typical this town is of other Indiana towns, but I have always been under the impression that conditions were rather better there than in other towns of the same size. In Chicago the conditions of poverty are certainly worse, if anything, than in the smaller towns, and that is also true of the poverty of New York City. On the whole, it seems to me that the most conservative estimate that can be fairly made of the distress existing in the industrial states is 14 percent of the total population; while in all probability no less than 20 percent of the people in these states, in ordinarily prosperous years, are in poverty. . . . Taking half this percentage and applying it to the other states, the conclusion is that not less than 10,000,000 persons in the United States are in poverty.

While . . . it may be thought that, although the percentage, as applied to industrial states, is fair, half that percentage, as applied to states largely agricultural, is too high. I think, however, that the figures concerning the

Figure 2.1   A beet worker's family on a Colorado farm near Starling, July 1915.
Source: Hine 1915.

number of farms rented and mortgaged would warrant the use of this percentage, if, indeed, there were not many other facts to warrant an assumption of that amount of poverty. Professor C. S. Walker said in 1897, in a
discussion before the American Economic Association, "By using all available statistics, it becomes evident again and again that, deducting rent and
interest, the American farmer receives less for his exertions than does the
laborer in the factory or the hired man on his farm."

—Robert Hunter, *Poverty*[1]

RURAL POVERTY THEN (1938)

Rural poverty has existed in considerable magnitude in the United States
for a long time. The depression served to reveal the areas in which this
poverty was most prevalent and most nearly chronic. . . .

The gradual commercialization of agriculture, while modernizing it as
an economic enterprise and making it possible for rural people to have
many social amenities that were denied their parents and grandparents,
has also thrust practically all farm families into the price and market

system and has subjected them much more directly than in the past to economic depression. Consequently, falling farm prices, mortgage foreclosures, and mounting operating costs and taxes have contributed far more heavily to recent than to earlier rural life depressions. Furthermore, alternative opportunities are not so available today as in the times of past generations. When the panic of 1873 struck, and even at a time of combined drought and depression in the 1890s, there were still "free lands" to which the ever-increasing farm populations could move with a fair promise of successful readjustment. This scene had sharply changed by 1930.

In addition to the disappearance of the frontier, which had occurred approximately two decades before the recent depression came, the fertility of the soil of many occupied areas was being rapidly depleted, and it was becoming apparent that hundreds of thousands of farm families were trying to make a living on land that should never have been subjected to cultivation. In other areas, it was apparent that farms were too small for successful economic operation. In still other areas, supplementary enterprises, especially lumbering and mining, had exhausted the natural resources and could no longer employ excess farm labor in their operations. To all of

Figure 2.2   People living in miserable poverty, Elm Grove, Oklahoma, August 1936.
Source: Lange 1936.

these changed physical conditions was added an ever-increasing number of tenants and laborers in the farm population and a steadily diminishing ownership of farm real estate equities by those who till the soil.

Sharecroppers and farm laborers have little underpinning of subsistence security to buttress them when cash farm income or wages decline. They have little in the way of livestock, poultry, or even gardens which furnish food supplies to the average owner-operator. They generally have no accrued savings or capital assets upon which they can draw, and so they quickly fall into pauperism. . . .

It is a conservative estimate that one-third of the farm families of the nation are living on standards of living so low as to make them slum families.

—Carl C. Taylor, Helen W. Wheeler, and E. L. Kirkpatrick,
Disadvantaged Classes in American Agriculture[2]

RURAL POVERTY THEN (1968)

Rural poverty is so widespread, and so acute, as to be a national disgrace, and its consequences have swept into our cities, violently. . . . Because we have been oblivious of the rural poor, we have abetted both rural and urban poverty, for the two are closely linked through migration . . . .

Rural poverty in the United States has no geographic boundaries. It is acute in the South, but it is present and serious in the East, the West, and the North. Rural poverty is not limited to Negroes. It permeates all races and ethnic groups. Nor is poverty limited to the farm. Our farm population has declined until it is only a small fraction of our total population. Most of the rural poor do not live on farms. They live in the open country, in rural villages, and in small towns. Moreover, contrary to a common misconception, whites outnumber nonwhites among the rural poor by a wide margin. It is true, however, that an extremely high proportion of Negroes in the rural South and Indians on reservations are destitute.

—President's National Advisory Commission on
Rural Poverty, *The People Left Behind*[3]

RURAL POVERTY NOW (2015)

In the United States, people living in poverty tend to be clustered in certain regions, counties, and neighborhoods rather than being spread evenly across the nation. Research has shown that the poor living in areas where poverty is prevalent face impediments beyond those of their individual circumstances. Concentrated poverty contributes to poor housing and health conditions, higher crime and school dropout rates, as well as employment dislocations.

Figure 2.3   President Lyndon Johnson in West Virginia town, 1964.

Source: Stoughton 1964.

As a result, economic conditions in very poor areas can create limited opportunities for poor residents that become self-perpetuating. . . .

Nonmetro counties with a high incidence of poverty are mainly concentrated in the South. Those with the most severe poverty are found in historically poor areas of the Southeast, including the Mississippi Delta and Appalachia, as well as on Native American lands. Pockets of high poverty are increasingly found in other regions, like nonmetro areas of the Southwest and the North Central Midwest. The incidence of poverty is relatively low elsewhere, but in general higher rates of poverty are found in the Midwest, Southwest, Pacific, and Northeast than in the past. Deindustrialization since the 1980s contributed to the spread of poverty in the Midwest and the Northeast. Another factor was rapid growth in Hispanic populations over the 1990s and 2000s, particularly in California, Nevada, Arizona, Colorado, North Carolina, and Georgia. This group tends to be poorer than non-Hispanic whites. Finally, the poverty impact of the 2007–2009 recession was fairly widespread. . . .

Areas with a high incidence of poverty often reflect the low income of their racial/ethnic minorities. Nonmetro blacks and African Americans had the highest incidence of poverty in 2013 (37.3 percent), while non-metro American Indians and Alaskan natives had the second highest rate (34.4 percent). The poverty rate for nonmetro whites in 2013 was less than half as much (15.9 percent) of both groups. Nonmetro Hispanics had the third highest poverty rate, which was 28.2 percent. The high rate of poverty for Hispanics is noteworthy as their share of the nonmetro population increased faster than other racial/ethnic groups over the last several decades.

—USDA Economic Research Service[4]

INTRODUCTION

By some measures, poverty is deeper, more persistent, and more concentrated in rural America than in urban America. This chapter provides a historical overview of the evolution of rural poverty in the United States.

The chapter begins by examining *how poverty in rural America emerged as a policy issue* over the past century and looks at the major economic and demographic forces that affected rural people during the twentieth century. Next is a description of *how and why poverty rates have varied since the 1960s,* when data on poverty first became available. The official poverty rate in rural (nonmetropolitan) America has been *higher* than

What Is Rural?

A place is rural, according to the U.S. Census Bureau, if it is not part of an urban cluster of 2,500 to 49,999 or an urbanized area with a population of 50,000 or more. The boundaries of urban and rural territory as defined in the Census do not follow county lines. Amost all of the historical data collected by governments for local areas, however, are county-level data. It is common practice to use county-based classification of "metropolitan" and "nonmetropolitan" counties to describe urban and rural areas. The Office of Management and Budget (OMB) defines as "metropolitan" (or "metro") core "counties with an urbanized area of 50,000 population or greater, plus surrounding counties that are linked to that core through significant commuting flows." OMB defines as "nonmetropolitan" all counties not included in the metropolitan definition. Following common practice, these counties are referred to in the chapter as rural or nonmetro.

the urban (metropolitan) poverty rate in every year since 1959 when the statistical series begins.

The chapter then explores how the *geography of poverty has changed during the past century.* Poverty has not been uniformly distributed across the landscape but has been concentrated in *pockets with high poverty rates*—more than one in four (26 percent) counties had a poverty rate of 20 percent or more in 2009–2013. *Many of the pockets of high poverty have strong racial and ethnic dimensions,* and this pattern has become more diffuse since 2000 due to growth in counties with concentrations of Hispanics and non-Hispanic whites outside of the Southern Highlands. One in nine counties (11 percent) is a *persistent-poverty county*, with poverty rates of 20 percent or more at the end of each decade since 1969 (that is, as measured in each decennial census since 1970), and persistent-poverty counties are disproportionately rural.

The chapter concludes with an exploration of *how concentrated rural poverty is* and how this concentration has grown since 2000.

RURAL POVERTY EMERGED IN THE GREAT DEPRESSION AND IN THE 1960S

Concern about poverty as a social problem meriting civic action has a long history in the United States. Some date this concern to the late nineteenth century and the "rapid urbanization, industrialization and a resurgence of immigration (particularly from southern and eastern European countries)" after the Civil War (Corbett 2014). This period saw the rise of the Scientific Charity movement, which attempted to study economic distress among families in a more rigorous way, and the emergence of Settlement Houses to assist the poor, many of whom were ethnic immigrants. Much of the focus of the movements and writing about poverty during this period focused on the urban centers where industrialization generated jobs for migrants from rural America and immigrants from abroad (Patterson 2000).

During the last decades of the nineteenth century, agrarian movements emerged that sought to empower farmers to correct what agrarians saw as exploitation by railroads and banks. Even though 60 percent of the nation's population lived in rural areas and almost 40 percent of the population lived on farms at the turn of the twentieth century, concern about farm conditions did not capture the attention of national policy makers.

Table 2.1 provides a selective outline of some of the forces that have affected rural poverty since 1900. The table identifies some of the notable studies that drew attention to poverty in rural areas, and it outlines the major economic forces and demographic trends that increased or reduced rural poverty, as well as the landmark legislation and programs in each period created to address poverty and rural poverty.

Around 1900, national concern about rural and farm living conditions began to coalesce. President Theodore Roosevelt appointed a Country Life Commission in 1908 to report on "the problems of farm life" (U.S. Country Life Commission 2011, 9). The commission's report has been called "the first comprehensive attempt to learn the status of farming, the traditional occupation of the United States of America, under the impact of industrialism" (Ellsworth 1960, 155–56, quoted in Peters and Morgan 2004, 296). The Country Life Commission identified six major "deficiencies" in rural life, but poverty is not among them.[5] Three of the six deficiencies were related to the economic, social, and institutional circumstances affecting farmers, farm workers, and farm women. Included were concerns about speculative landholding, monopolistic control of streams, and restraint of trade, as well as concerns about the supply of farm workers, given the seasonality, low wages, long hours, and social isolation of farm work. The commission was also concerned that the burden of the hardships of farm life "falls more heavily on the farmer's wife than on the farmer himself" and about the monotony and isolation in the life of farm women.[6]

It was not until the Great Depression that a more general national concern about rural poverty emerged, focused mostly on the population living on farms (comprising 56 percent of the rural population and 25 percent of the total U.S. population in 1930). The startling and intimate photographs of poor farm families taken by Dorothea Lange and her contemporaries funded by the U.S. Resettlement Administration revealed both the harsh economic realities confronting these families and the stoic dignity of many who lived in wretched conditions. The USDA Bureau of Agricultural Economics' "level of living" studies provided analytically rigorous statistical information about the income and expenses of different groups of farm families and the types of services available to them.

The extreme economic distress of the Great Depression led to bold federal legislation to help struggling families cope with job loss and poverty and to support large infrastructure investments that created immediate jobs in many rural areas and provided necessary support for future industry.

Table 2.1 Historical Evolution of Rural Poverty

	1900–1929	1930–1959	1960–1979	1980–present
Percent farm/ percent rural	*39.3/60.3* (1900)	*24.6/43.9* (1930)	*7.5/30.1* (1960)	*1.1/21.0* (2000)
Influential reports/ studies focused on poverty	• Hunter, *Poverty* (1904). • *Report of the U.S. Country Life Commission* (1909, published 1911).	• USDA Bureau of Economic Analysis reports. • Resettlement Administration reports (1935–1944). • Brookings Institution, *America's Capacity to Consume* (1934).	• Harrington, *The Other America* (1962). • *1964 Economic Report of the President*. • President's National Advisory Commission on Rural Poverty, *The People Left Behind* (1967).	• Murray, *Losing Ground* (1984). • Rural Sociological Society Task Force on Persistent Rural Poverty, *Persistent Poverty in Rural America* (1993).
Demographic trends affecting rural areas	• Increased immigration to the United States from southern and eastern Europe.	• Reduced childbearing in 1930s followed by baby boom (1945–1964). • Beginning in the early 1950s, male labor force participation began to decline, and female labor force participation continues to increase.	• Increased nonmarital childbearing, single parent households. • Increased female labor force participation.	• Increased immigration to the United States from Latin America and Asia. • Baby boom generation entering retirement.
Major economic forces/events affecting rural opportunities	• Closing of the frontier: end of free land and westward expansion. • Increased urbanization as industrialization draws people into cities.	• Great Depression (~1930 to ~1939) puts both urban and rural people out of work. • Overharvest of timber and minerals means fewer side jobs for farmers. • Mechanization of farms means larger farms and movement of population off farms. • Farm depression and the Dust Bowl of 1931–1939 leads to increased tenancy and sharecropping and concentration of ownership.	• Beginning in the 1960s, union membership begins a steady decline. • Technological change and associated investments in technology make workers more productive and creates an environment in which fewer workers are needed and employers can reduce wages. • Deindustrialization and movement of factories overseas. • Beginning in early 1970s, the move from fixed to flexible exchange rates leads to increased cross-country movements of capital as transnational corporations seeking low-cost labor, materials, and other inputs move operations overseas. • Beginning in the early 1970s, income inequality begins to increase.	• Each succeeding Recession since 1982–1983 has been slower in recovery, with the 2007–2009 recession taking longest. • Underemployment has increased as part-time jobs constitute a larger share of all jobs. • Jobs with nonstandard work hours make up an increasing share of all jobs, creating child-care barriers that are more challenging for rural workers.

Table 2.1 (Continued)

	1900–1929	1930–1959	1960–1979	1980–present
Landmark legislation and executive action		• Tennessee Valley Authority Act of 1933 (authorized dams for flood control, navigation, and electric power). • Social Security Act of 1935 (created Social Security, Unemployment Insurance, Aid to Dependent Children, Maternal and Child Health). • Rural Electrification Act of 1936 (authorized loans for electric power in isolated areas). • Resettlement Administration (created in 1935 by Executive Order to relocate tenant farmers and build migrant camps). • Bankhead-Jones Farm Tenant Act of 1937 (authorized federal government to buy unsuitable land and to make loans to tenant farmers to purchase land). • Farm Security Act of 1937 replaced the Resettlement Administration with the Farm Security Administration (1937–1946). • Fair Labor Standards Act of 1938 established federal minimum wage, overtime.	• Economic Opportunity Act of 1964 (created Head Start, Community Action Agencies, Job Corps, VISTA). • Food Stamp Acts of 1964 and 1977. • Social Security Act of 1965 (created Medicare—health insurance for seniors—and Medicaid—health insurance for low-income children and their relative caretakers and people with certain disabilities). • Appalachian Regional Commission Act of 1965 (created Appalachian Regional Commission). • Revenue Act of 1978 (made temporary EITC initiated in 1975 permanent).	• Tax Reform Act of 1986 (increased the EITC and indexed it to inflation). • Personal Responsibility and Work Opportunity Reconciliation Act of 1996 (changed welfare from entitlement to block grant, initiated time limits, work requirement).
New programs		• Social Security • Unemployment Insurance • Aid to Dependent Children • Maternal and Child Health • Federal Minimum Wage	• Head Start • Community Action Agencies • Job Corps • VISTA • Food Stamps • Earned Income Tax Credit (EITC)	• Temporary Assistance to Needy Families (TANF)

Public concern for both urban and rural poverty waned during the economic expansion of the 1940s and 1950s following World War II but revived in the early 1960s. Edward R. Murrow's television documentary *Harvest of Shame* in 1960 showed Americans the conditions under which migrant farm workers lived and worked. Michael Harrington's 1962 book *The Other America: Poverty in the United States* exposed the nation to the poverty that existed in urban slums, and among rural farm workers, racial minorities, and the elderly. Some credit *The Other America* with spurring the War on Poverty initiated by Lyndon Johnson in 1964. This War on Poverty focused on economic opportunity for low-income families through programs instituted by the newly created Office of Economic Opportunity and the Appalachian Regional Commission. The programs also provided financial support and access to health care and food.

Much of the attention to poverty in the 1960s focused on poverty in the nation's urban slums, but new attention was focused on the living

What Is Poverty?

Poverty is a multidimensional concept that involves insufficient income relative to need and limited access to resources such as education, health care, and social and political power. Poverty is generally measured, however, in economic terms. Except as noted, poverty is defined in this chapter using the official poverty measure (OPM) from the U.S. Census Bureau. According to the official definition, a family is considered poor if its annual before-tax money income (excluding noncash benefits such as public housing, Medicaid, and food stamps [SNAP]) is less than its poverty threshold. Poverty thresholds vary according to family size, number of children in the family, and, for small households, whether the householder is elderly. The thresholds were developed in the 1960s by estimating the cost of a minimum adequate diet for families of different size and age structures multiplied by three to allow for other necessities. The poverty thresholds are adjusted annually for inflation using the Consumer Price Index for All Urban Consumers but, apart from minor adjustments, have remained unchanged over the decades. In 2014, the poverty threshold for a single person under the age of sixty-five was $12,316. For a household with one adult and two related children under eighteen years of age, the threshold was $19,073.

conditions of the many poor households in remote rural areas. This was perhaps the first time in the nation's history that both farm and non-farm poverty in rural America were treated as a national policy concern. President Johnson created the National Advisory Commission on Rural Poverty in 1966 to study income and community problems in rural areas, evaluate current programs, and develop recommendations for both pubic and private action to increase rural economic opportunities. In its 1967 report *The People Left Behind*, the commission reminded policy makers that rural people were at much higher risk of poverty than urban residents. In the mid-1960s, the rural poverty rate was 25 percent, almost 70 percent higher than the urban rate. The commission also noted the wide geographic disparities in poverty rates, and the pockets of rural poverty in the South, Appalachia, and the Southwest.

AFTER DECLINING RAPIDLY IN THE 1960S, U.S. RURAL POVERTY HAS REMAINED RELATIVELY HIGH

Starting in the 1970s and early 1980s, demographic, economic, and technological changes; a decline in union membership; deindustrialization; globalization of capital investments; and off-shoring of jobs have led to increasing income inequality between high- and low-income households in both metro and nonmetro areas (Albrecht 2013). During this period, however, federal policy shifted away from a concern about the effects of poverty on people and communities and toward a concern about work behavior and marital and child-bearing decisions of low-income households, and the idea that federal antipoverty programs were reducing work incentives and creating dependency on government programs. The most significant legislation during the 1980s to assist the poor was the expansion of the earned income tax credit, which was available only to those who worked and thus helped only the working poor. Policies enacted during the 1990s included the repeal of some New Deal protections and programs. The clearest example of this was the Personal Responsibility and Work Opportunity Reconciliation Act of 1996, better known as Welfare Reform. Welfare Reform eliminated the entitlement to welfare payments in the Aid to Dependent Children program, and in its place created a block grant to states to fund reduced payments in the new Temporary Assistance for Needy Families (TANF) program. The new TANF program initiated work requirements for aid recipients and funded programs to encourage marriage.

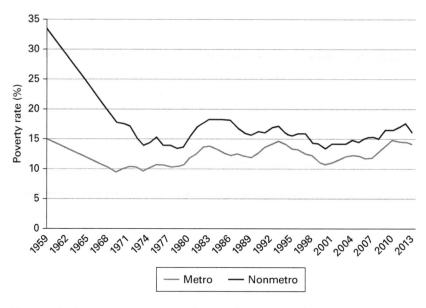

Figure 2.4   Poverty rates in metropolitan and nonmetropolitan areas, 1959–2013.

Source: Economic Research Services data calculated from the U.S. Census Bureau Current Population Survey Annual Social and Economic Supplement.

Although rural poverty declined rapidly in the 1960s, poverty, while rising and falling over business cycles, has proven to be stubbornly persistent, as shown in figure 2.4.

Rural poverty rates (using the official poverty measure developed in 1969) have exceeded metro poverty rates every year since 1959. The gap between these rates, however, has narrowed over the years from almost 20 percentage points to just under 3 percentage points, as rural poverty rates have declined from 33 percent to 16 percent, and metro poverty rates have been relatively stable at about 12 to 15 percent.

There is some controversy about whether the official poverty measure accurately captures both the resources available to households and their monetary needs. A more recently developed alternative supplemental poverty measure (SPM) adjusts the poverty threshold for the cost of housing. For the most recent years the SPM was calculated (2009–2014), the rural poverty rate has been *lower* than the metro rate due in large part to the lower cost of housing in rural areas.

The causes of poverty are multiple and interrelated, as noted in table 2.1, and changes in poverty are driven by many factors external to individuals and localities. The causes of poverty in rural America are explored in detail in later chapters.

This chapter focuses on why poverty rates have been relatively stagnant since the late 1960s even though real per capita GDP has nearly doubled. Hoynes, Page, and Stevens (2006) explore four factors to explain changes in poverty rates in the United States between 1967 and 2003: "the impact of labor market opportunities; the role of changes in family structure; the role played by government antipoverty programs; and the role of immigration" (53). In looking at labor market opportunities, they find a close relationship between unemployment rates and poverty rates, which can explain the highly cyclical pattern of both metro and nonmetro poverty rates since 1967. They also find that stagnant growth in median wages and growing wage inequality due to declines in wages for less-skilled workers explain the lack of improvement in poverty rates over the period.

Hoynes and her colleagues also find that poverty did not decline despite the growth in GDP, rising education levels, and increased female labor force participation in the 1970s. Instead, they found that "rising numbers of female-headed families may offset income gains from women's increasing labor force participation" (48).

Because the OPM takes neither noncash transfers—such as the Supplemental Nutrition Assistance Program (formerly food stamps)—nor the earned income tax credit into account in determining poverty status, the growth of these two programs is not reflected in the poverty statistics. Hoynes et al. also find the growth of antipoverty programs to be unimportant in explaining poverty rate changes.[7]

OPM statistics suggest that poverty rates have stagnated since the late 1960s, but measures that take government programs into account by constructing a historical SPM data series suggest that government programs have indeed reduced poverty. These data suggest that "trends in poverty have been more favorable than the OPM suggests" and that government policies have played an important and growing role in reducing poverty—a role that is not "evident when the OPM is used to assess poverty" (Fox et al. 2015, 567). Fox et al. found that government programs reduced the SPM poverty rate in 1967 by 6 percentage points (from 25 percent to 19 percent); in 2012, the government programs reduced poverty by 15 percentage points (from 31 percent to 15 percent). This measure suggests that government programs in 1967 cut poverty by one-quarter; in 2012, they cut poverty in half.[8]

Vignettes of Families in Poverty in Various Eras:
Excerpts from Ethnographic Research

1930s James Agee and Walker Evans. 1941. *Let Us Now Praise Famous Men.* Excerpts from Agee's reflections on the lives of the Ricketts, the Woods, and the Gudgers, white tenant farmer and sharecropper families in rural Alabama (88ff., 115ff.).

1970s Janet Fitchen. 1981. *Poverty in Rural America: A Case Study.* Excerpts from "A Day with Mary Crane," who is a wife, a state highway worker, and a mother of two children in Chestnut Valley in the mountains of upstate New York (3, 6, 8).

1990s Cynthia Duncan. 1999. *Worlds Apart: Why Poverty Persists in Rural America.* Excerpts from "Dahlia," the chapter featuring Caroline, a black single mother who supports herself and her five children through a combination of work in a sewing factory, housecleaning, and public assistance (97ff.).

2000s Jennifer Sherman. 2006. "Coping with Rural Poverty: Economic Survival and Moral Capital in Rural America," *Social Forces* 85(2): 891–913. Excerpts from Jim and Angelica Finch, a couple with three children in rural Golden Valley, California.

2010s Jennifer Sherman. 2013. "Surviving the Great Recession: Growing Need and the Stigmatized Safety Net." *Social Problems* 60(4): 409–432. Excerpts from the story of Jeff Peters and Krystal Larson, a cohabiting couple with low-wage service jobs in Riverway, a small city in Eastern Washington.

The discussion in previous paragraphs has focused on factors affecting overall poverty rates. Figure 2.4 shows that although metro and rural official poverty rates have moved roughly in parallel since the 1970s, there is a gap between metro and rural poverty rates. The gap in poverty rates between metro and rural areas averaged around 5 percent in the 1970s and 1980s and dropped to about 3 percent in the 1990s and 2000s. What explains the persistence of a poverty rate gap between metro and rural areas? Some of the factors that might explain higher poverty, such as unemployment rates and family structures, are roughly comparable between metro and rural areas. Other asssociated factors, such as labor force participation rates, education levels, and wages, are lower in rural areas and could explain the persistence of the metro–rural poverty gap.

THE GEOGRAPHY OF "FARM POVERTY" THEN (1929)

Although there were both farm and nonfarm poor households in rural areas in 1929, many of the studies of rural poverty during the Great Depression (1929 through most of the 1930s) focused on farm poverty. Farm households made up 56 percent of the U.S. rural population in 1930. By comparing the map of farm household gross income under $600 (figure 2.5) with the map of U.S. county poverty rates in 2009–2013 in figure 2.12, you can see that many of the counties with high farm poverty in 1929 also had high poverty rates eighty years later.

The map in figure 2.5 was prepared in 1938 by the Resettlement Administration and the Bureau of Agricultural Economics of the USDA to identify for program administrators the "sore spots in American rural life" and "reveal in broad outline the major factors that tend to reduce approximately one-third of the farm population of the Nation to sub-marginal standards of living" (Taylor, Wheeler, and Kirkpatrick 1938, i).

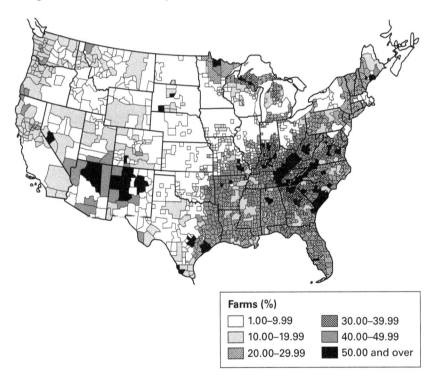

Figure 2.5 Farms with gross income under $600 as a percentage of all farms reporting, 1929.

Source: Data from U.S. Department of Agriculture, 1929.

The report selected $600 as an indicator of low income based on previous research. "It can hardly be questioned that farm families below a $600 gross income level [are low income]. An income of $600 will not meet farm operating expenses and provide the essentials for even a minimum standard of living. . . . After all farm expenses are met, there is seldom left as much as $300 for living costs, and various studies that have been made prove conclusively that this is not enough to provide the necessary elements for a minimum standard for the farm family" (7).

THE GEOGRAPHY OF "RURAL POVERTY" THEN (1960)

An imperfect sense of the enduring geography of poverty can come by way of comparing a map of the economic status of the rural population in 1960 (see figure 2.6) with the map of poverty rates in 2007–2011 (see figure 2.10).

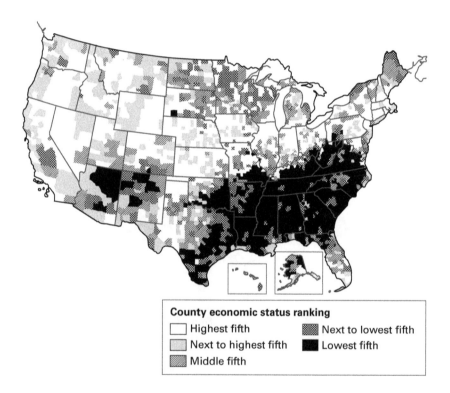

County economic status ranking

☐ Highest fifth   ▨ Next to lowest fifth
☐ Next to highest fifth ■ Lowest fifth
▧ Middle fifth

Figure 2.6   Index of economic status of rural population, by county, 1960.

Source: President's National Advisory Commission on Rural Poverty. 1967. *The People Left Behind*. Washington DC: U.S. Government Printing Office, 4.

The data presented in figure 2.6 were redrawn from a map prepared for the President's National Advisory Commission on Rural Poverty to guide the commission on the geography of economic distress in rural America. Because the federal government did not have an official poverty line when the original map was created, the Economic Research Service developed an index of economic status. The economic status of the rural population for 1960 was measured using a composite index that contained five indicators; a dependency ratio of rural children and elderly to rural working-age population; the number of rural families with less than $3,000 income; the percentage of rural families with less than $3,000 income; percentage of rural adults with less than seven years of schooling completed; and percentage of rural housing units that were deteriorating or dilapidated. The geographic spread of poverty has decreased as poverty has been reduced, but enduring pockets of rural poverty persist.

Farm Versus Nonfarm Rural Poor as Focus of Rural Poverty Concern

One might expect that the interest in farm and rural poverty would vary with the share of the population on farms and in rural areas. The overall policy interest in rural poverty, however, does not correlate well with the rural share in the population, as this share has declined steadily since the founding of the nation. Interest in rural poverty, in contrast, has waxed and waned over time, having been most intense in the Great Depression of the 1930s and after the "rediscovery of rural poverty" in the 1960s. There is some relationship, however, between the share of the rural population in farming and the relative focus on farm versus nonfarm rural people in rural poverty. During the 1930s, when farmers constituted two-thirds of the rural population (see chart), the focus of the studies of rural households was on farmers and farm workers almost exclusively and not on rural nonfarm populations. During the rediscovery of rural poverty in the 1960s, farmers were only about one-quarter of the rural population, and the focus of the President's National Advisory Committee report, *The People Left Behind,* was balanced between farm and nonfarm rural poverty. In the

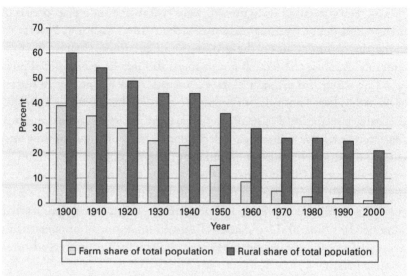

Share of the U.S. population living in rural areas and on farms.

Source: Carolyn Dimitri, Anne Effland, and Neilson Conklin. 2005. *The 20th Century Transformation of U.S. Agriculture and Farm Policy.* USDA Economic Research Service. Economic Information Bulletin No. 3. June.

current environment, in which farmers are less than 5 percent of the rural population (and only 1 percent of the total population), discussions on rural poverty focus mostly on rural nonfarm poverty and on farm workers.

RURAL POVERTY IN THE UNITED STATES IS FOUND IN GEOGRAPHIC "POCKETS OF HIGH POVERTY"

Poverty rates have changed over the past fifty years in metro and rural areas. The nation's poverty rate declined from more than 20 percent in 1960 to the 12–14 percent range between 1970 and 2000 before increasing to almost 15 percent in 2010, and the metro–rural poverty gap has shrunk from around 10 percentage points in the late 1960s to about 3 percentage points today.

Poor people, however, are not equally distributed across the country. The maps in figures 2.7 through 2.10 show how the geography of poverty has changed over this period. These maps show the official poverty rates

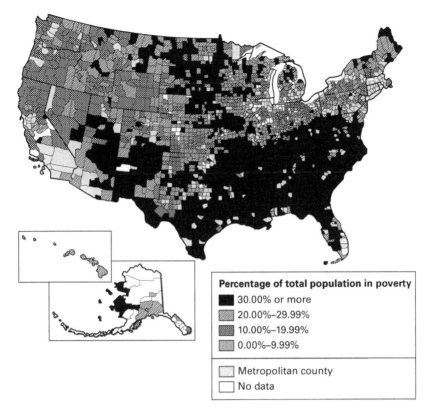

Figure 2.7 Nonmetropolitan poverty rate by county, 1959.

Source: U.S. Census Bureau, 1960 Decennial Census. Additional estimates provided by U.S. Department of Agriculture, Economic Research Service.

for rural counties in the United States for four years: 1959, 1969, 1999, and 2009 (2007–2011).[9]

The striking thing about the map in figure 2.7 for 1959 is the very large share of rural counties that have poverty rates of more than 30 percent. These are concentrated in the South, upper Great Plains, and the Four Corners states (Arizona, Colorado, New Mexico, and Utah) in the southwestern United States. These are the same regions identified by other metrics in earlier government documents on "disadvantaged classes in agriculture" (Taylor et al. 1938) and "the people left behind" (President's National Advisory Commission on Rural Poverty 1967).

There are also places scattered across the country with relatively low poverty rates (10–19.9 percent). Notable low-poverty regions include

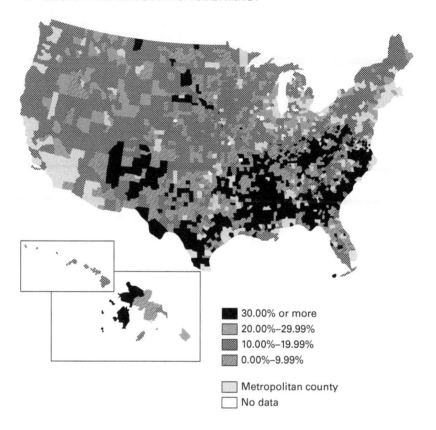

Figure 2.8   Nonmetropolitan poverty rate by county, 1969.

Source: Minnesota Population Center, National Historic Geographic Information System, version 2; 1970 Decennial Census, tables NT18, NT89.

some areas of New England and the sparsely settled Great Plains and western states. But note that none of the counties report poverty rates under 10 percent.

Figure 2.8 uses the same shading code to indicate rural county poverty rates for 1969. We can see that the number of counties with poverty rates higher than 30 percent decreased dramatically, leaving smaller pockets of poverty in the centers of the larger high-poverty areas seen in 1959. We now see many counties with poverty rates of less than 10 percent, mostly in the West, upper Midwest, and New England.

The map for 1999 (figure 2.9) shows a further decrease in the number of counties with poverty rates of 30 percent or more. The highest poverty rates are evident in the cores of high-poverty regions in Appalachia, the

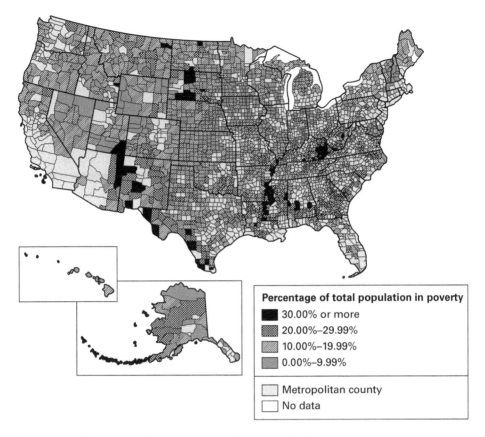

Figure 2.9 Nonmetropolitan poverty rate by county, 1999.

Source: U.S. Census Bureau, 2000 Decennial Census.

Mississippi Delta, the southern Black Belt,[10] Native American reservations in the Southwest and Great Plains, and along the Mexican border. It
also shows growth in the number of low-poverty counties in all regions of
the country. This map also reveals the dramatic expansion in the number
of metropolitan counties.

The map for 2007–2011 (figure 2.10) shows the geographic shifts in
rural poverty during the first decade of the current century. Although
there were only small increases in very high poverty counties, there was
a general darkening of the map as poverty rates in western and midwestern counties increased. The exception to this pattern was in the northern Great Plains where poverty rates declined as economic opportunity
increased with the oil boom.

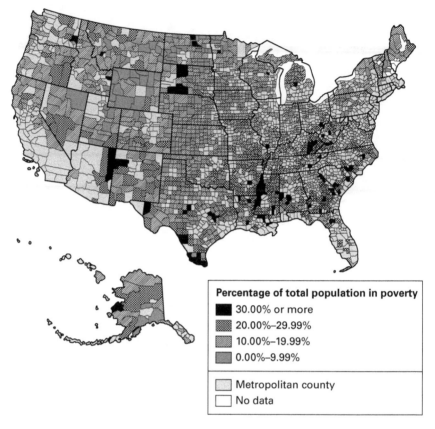

Figure 2.10   Nonmetropolitan poverty rate by county, 2007–2011.

Source: U.S. Census Bureau, American Community Survey 2007–2011 five-year estimates.

ONE-THIRD OF RURAL COUNTIES WERE HIGH-POVERTY COUNTIES IN 2009–2013

There has been a substantial increase in how many U.S. counties are considered high-poverty (rates of 20 percent or more) since 1999. Overall, one-quarter—26 percent—of all U.S. counties were high-poverty counties in 2009–2013, an increase of 70 percent from the 16 percent of all counties that were high-poverty counties in 1999. The 828 high-poverty counties in 2009–2013 are concentrated primarily in Appalachia, the southern Black Belt and Mississippi Delta, along the Mexican border, and on Native American tribal reservations.

High-poverty counties are still disproportionately rural. One-third (roughly 33 percent) of rural counties were considered "high-poverty" counties in 2009–2013 (with poverty rates of 20 percent or more). Only one-sixth (16 percent) of metro counties are classified as high-poverty. But this represents a doubling of the metro share from 1999. Less than 10 percent of the high-poverty counties in 1999 were metro. In 2009–2013, more than 20 percent (21.9 percent) are metro.

Is Poverty Greater in Rural or Urban Areas? It Depends on How You Measure Poverty

Attempts were made to estimate the rate of poverty in the United States prior to 1900, but it was not until the 1960s, as the United States was rediscovering poverty, that the federal government initiated its first attempt to estimate the share of the population that lived in poverty. Mollie Orshansky (1965), an economist at the Social Security Administration, developed a set of poverty thresholds and published an analysis of the poverty population (the population whose incomes fell below this threshold) in 1965. Her estimate of the 1963 poverty rate (the share of the total population in households with incomes below the poverty threshold) was 18.5 percent.

The first official poverty measure (OPM) for the United States was created in 1969 using Orshansky's framework. A family is poor under the OPM if pretax money income is less than the poverty threshold (the amount needed to support the basic needs of a family of that size and composition). At that time, about one-third of a low-income family's income was spent on food, so the poverty threshold was estimated by multiplying by three the estimated cost of the "economy food plan" (now called the "Thrifty Food Plan") for a family of that size.* The economy food plan was designed for "temporary or emergency use when funds are low."

Criticism of the OPM has focused on several of its perceived shortcomings. The OPM did not (1) deduct taxes and certain necessities (e.g., large out-of-pocket expenses for medical expenses or work-related costs) from resources; (2) take into account many noncash transfers (food stamps, Housing Assistance, Utility Assistance) or low-income tax credits (earned income tax credits) that had been created since the 1960s to reduce poverty and its effects; and (3) adjust the poverty threshold for geographic differences in the cost of living.

Poverty analysts generally had agreed on the need to account for geographic cost-of-living differences, but data for such a purpose are limited. Jolliffe (2006), for example, used a spatial price index based on Fair Market Rents data to account for cost-of-housing differences across metro and nonmetro areas. Because housing costs are lower in nonmetro areas, he showed a complete reversal in the metro–nonmetro poverty rankings, with metropolitan poverty incidence being higher in every year from 1991 to 2002.

In response to these criticisms, a supplemental poverty measure (SPM) was created and, since 2009, the Census Bureau releases SPM estimates each year to extend (but not replace) the OPM. The SPM adjusts both the threshold and the estimate of family resources. The SPM threshold of need "should represent a dollar amount spent on a basic set of goods that includes food, clothing, shelter, and utilities (FCSU), and a small additional amount to allow for other needs (e.g., household supplies, personal care, nonwork-related transportation)" (Short 2015, 1). This poverty threshold is adjusted to account for geographical differences in housing costs. The SPM also adjusts the family resources by adding to cash income both tax credits and noncash benefits for food, shelter, and utilities; and subtracting tax payments, work expenses, out-of-pocket medical expenses, and child support paid to others. A family is poor under the SPM if the family resources (thus determined) are less than the geographically adjusted SPM poverty threshold. Since 2009, the overall SPM poverty rate has been 0.5 to 1.0 percentage point higher than the overall OPM poverty rate. In 2014, for example, the OPM poverty rate for all people was 14.9 percent, and the corresponding SPM poverty rate was 15.3 percent.

Consistent estimates of metropolitan and nonmetropolitan poverty rates using the OPM have been available since 1959. As is seen in figure 2.4, according to the OPM, nonmetro poverty rates have been higher than metro poverty rates every year since 1959. This same pattern is clear in the figure in this box, where the nonmetro OPM poverty rate (line with triangles) is higher than the metro OPM poverty rate (line with diamonds).

The Census Bureau has produced estimates of the SPM for metropolitan and nonmetropolitan areas only since 2009, so Census Bureau estimates of SPM are available only for 2009–2014. As is seen in the accompanying figure, the metro–nonmetro poverty relationship for the SPM is the opposite of that obtained with the OPM: the nonmetro SPM poverty rate (line with crosses) is lower than the metro SPM poverty rate (line with squares) every year between 2009 and 2014. In 2014, for example, the official poverty rates for metro and nonmetro areas

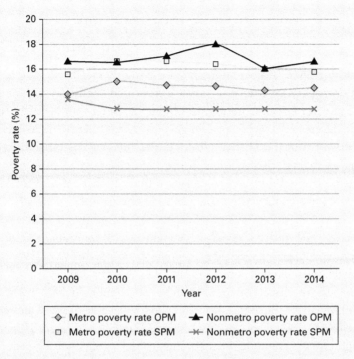

Metropolitan and nonmetropolitan poverty rates, OPM vs. SPM, 2009–2014.

Source: Short 2015.

were 14.5 and 16.6 percent, respectively. The corresponding 2014 poverty rates using the supplemental poverty measure were 15.8 percent for metro areas and 12.8 percent for nonmetro areas.

These results depend on a partial accounting of geographic cost-of-living differentials. To the extent that nonhousing costs are higher in nonmetro areas, conclusions based on a fuller accounting of metro–nonmetro cost-of-living adjustments could produce a different result about metro–nonmetro poverty-rate differentials. Census Bureau analysts are exploring geographic differences in alternative nonhousing-cost indices.

* According to Orshansky (1965), the USDA had been preparing food plans for over thirty years as guides "for estimating costs of food needed by families of different composition. The plans represent a translation of the criteria of nutritional adequacy set forth by the National Research Council into quantities and types of food compatible with the preference of United States families, as revealed in food consumption studies. Plans are developed at varying levels of cost to suit the needs of families with different amounts to spend. All the plans, if strictly followed, can provide an acceptable and adequate diet, but—generally speaking—the lower the level of cost, the more restricted the kinds and qualities of food must be and the more the skill in marketing and food preparation that is required" (5).

MOST RURAL POCKETS OF HIGH-POVERTY HAVE HIGH
CONCENTRATIONS OF RACIAL/ETHNIC MINORITIES

In 2004, Calvin Beale demonstrated the highly racialized geography of rural poverty in an article in *Amber Waves* titled "Anatomy of Nonmetro High-Poverty Areas: Common in Plight, Distinctive in Nature." In this article, he created "a typology of high-poverty counties [with poverty rates of 20 percent or more] that reflect racial/ethnic and regional differences in major characteristics like education, employment, family structure, incidence of disability, and language proficiency that are relevant to programs of poverty alleviation" (22–23). He observed that generally:

> areas of high poverty are of long standing, with conditions stemming from a complex of social and economic factors rather than from personal events, like temporary job layoffs or loss of a spouse. . . . Of the 444 rural counties classified as high-poverty counties in 2000 (based on 1999 income), three-fourths reflect the low income of racial and ethnic minorities and are classified as Black, Native American, or Hispanic high-poverty counties. The remaining quarter of high-poverty counties are mostly located in the Southern Highlands, and the poor are predominantly non-Hispanic Whites. (22–23)

Beale classified high-poverty counties (poverty rates of 20 percent or more) into types using two basic criteria: "(1) over half of the poor population in the county is from one of these minority groups or (2) over half of the poor population is non-Hispanic White, but it is the high poverty rate of a minority group that pushes the county's poverty rate over 20 percent" (23). Based on personal knowledge of these counties, Beale also made some adjustments in applying these criteria in a couple of cases when, in his judgment, the strict application of the criteria did not capture the predominant identity of a county. Figure 2.11 presents the geographic distribution of high-poverty counties identified applying these criteria to 1999 poverty data.

How has this situation changed over the past decade? We aimed to re-create Beale's analysis for 2009–2013. By slightly adjusting the criteria Beale identified, we were able to reproduce his analysis. Using these adjusted criteria, table 2.2 shows how the 647 high-poverty rural counties sorted into the Beale typology of racial/ethnic and regional concentrations in 2009–2013. Figure 2.12 maps the 2009–2013 results.

Table 2.2 Nonmetropolitan High-Poverty U.S. Counties by Dominant Racial/Ethnic Concentration, 1999 and 2009–2013

County type	1999 High-poverty nonmetropolitan counties	2009–2013 High-poverty nonmetropolitan counties	Percent change 1999 to 2009–2013
Black	210 (47%)	252 (39%)	20%
Hispanic	74 (17%)	110 (17%)	49
Native American	40 (9%)	51 (8%)	28
Southern Highlands non-Hispanic white	93 (30%)	131 (20%)	41
Other high poverty	27 (6%)	103 (16%)	281
Total[1]	444 (100%)	647 (100%)	46

[1] There were 2,308 nonmetropolitan U.S. counties in 1999, and 1,976 nonmetropolitan U.S. counties in 2009–2013. There were 3,141 U.S. counties in 2000 and 3,143 U.S. counties in 2010.

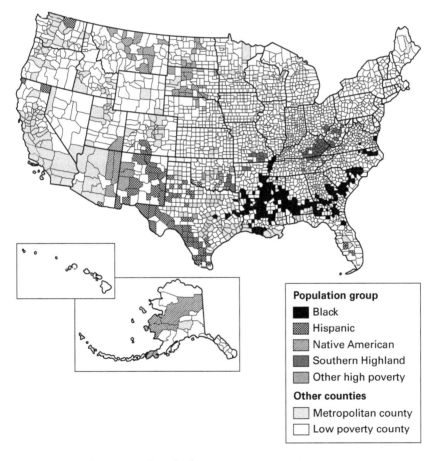

Figure 2.11 Nonmetropolitan high-poverty counties, 2000.

Source: Calvin Beale. 2004. "Anatomy of Nonmetro High-Poverty Areas: Common in Plight, Distinctive in Nature." Amber Waves 2 (1): 20–27.

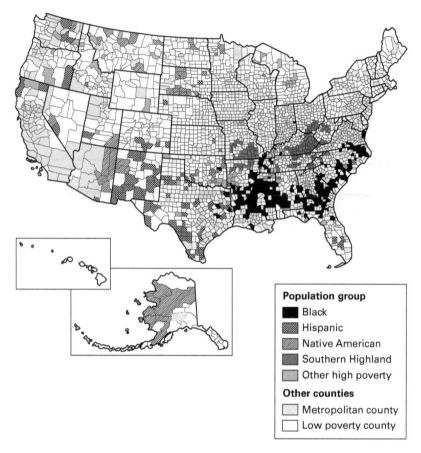

Figure 2.12   Nonmetropolitan poverty rate by county, 2009–2013.

Source: Author estimates.

As noted previously, almost all (94 percent) of the rural high-poverty counties identified in 1999 by Beale reflected the low income of either racial/ethnic minorities or residents of the predominantly non-Hispanic white Southern Highlands. By 2009–2013, however, only 84 percent of the rural high-poverty counties fit these categories. The other significant change in the racial/ethnic composition of the rural high-poverty counties is the large (49 percent) increase in the number of Hispanic rural high-poverty counties.

It is clear that poverty has spread during the first decade of the new century: there are more high-poverty counties for all of the groupings. But the largest increases in the number of high-poverty counties have been in the counties with high concentrations of non-Hispanic whites (both in the Southern Highlands and elsewhere) and Hispanics. These counties are showing up in regions where they might not be expected based on historical demographic patterns. High non-Hispanic white poverty is spreading in the Pacific Northwest and the Upper Great Lakes regions, and Hispanic poverty has spread north and west from its historic locations near the Mexican border.[11]

As one looks at the geography of high poverty in the United States over time, one sees how stable the overall geographic patterns are. There is a high degree of overlap between counties with high percentages of farm families bringing in gross incomes under $600 in 1929 (see figure 2.5) and the high-poverty nonmetro counties in 2009–2013 (see figure 2.12).

PERSISTENT POVERTY IS MOSTLY RURAL

High poverty is an enduring characteristic of many U.S. counties, and many counties show up as high-poverty counties in figures 2.7 through 2.10. One in nine (11 percent) U.S. counties (347 counties) have had poverty rates of 20 percent or more in all five of the decennial censuses since 1970.[12] These are referred to as *persistent-poverty counties.*

Figure 2.13 shows the location of the persistent-poverty counties. Persistent high-poverty is geographically concentrated in Appalachia, the southern Black Belt and Mississippi Delta, Rio Grande Valley, and on Native American lands.

SMALL AND REMOTE RURAL COUNTIES ARE MUCH MORE LIKELY TO BE PERSISTENT POVERTY COUNTIES

Rural counties are much more likely than metropolitan counties to be persistent-poverty counties (figure 2.14). More than 15 percent of rural counties are in persistent poverty, whereas only 4 percent of metro counties are persistent-poverty counties.

There is tremendous diversity in population size across different metropolitan counties and across nonmetropolitan counties. And rural counties that are adjacent to metro areas have very different opportunities than isolated rural counties. The Rural-Urban Continuum Code (RUCC) developed by the USDA Economic Research Service provides a useful classification scheme for considering the diversity of metro and rural counties along these dimensions. This nine-part classification

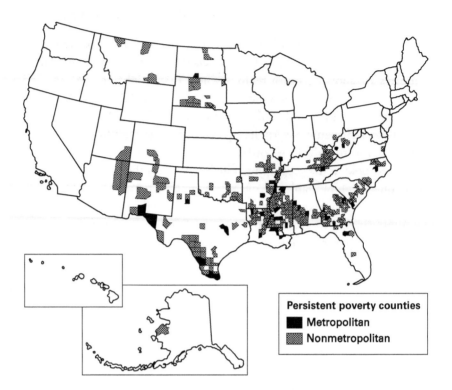

Figure 2.13 Persistent-poverty counties, 1970–2010.

Source: Kathleen Miller and Bruce Weber. 2014. "Persistent Poverty Dynamics: Understanding Poverty Trends over Fifty Years." Columbia, MO: Rural Policy Research Institute.

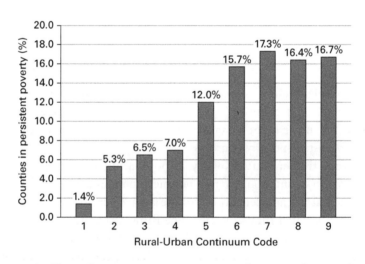

Figure 2.14 Share of counties in persistent poverty (1970–2010) across the urban-rural continuum.

Source: Author calculation.

includes three metro groupings organized by size of population (1,167 counties) and six nonmetro groups (1,976 counties) organized by size of the largest urban concentration and by whether the county is adjacent to metro counties. The largest counties (RUCC 1), for example, are metropolitan areas with a population of 1 million or more. The smallest counties (RUCCs 6–9) are nonmetro counties with a population of less than 20,000. Counties in RUCC 6 and 8 are adjacent to metropolitan areas, and RUCC 7 and 9 are not adjacent to metro areas.

Only 1 percent of large metro counties (RUCC 1) have experienced persistent poverty, and only about one in twenty smaller metro counties (RUCC 2 and 3) are persistent-poverty counties. By contrast, about one in six small town and rural counties (RUCCs 6–9) are persistent-poverty counties.

CONCENTRATED POVERTY HAS INCREASED IN RURAL AMERICA

The discussion so far has focused on high-poverty places—that is, at the location of high-poverty counties and at shares of counties with high poverty. Now the discussion shifts perspective and looks at the location of poor people and the shares of poor people in high-poverty places. How concentrated are poor people in high-poverty places? They are very concentrated. And rural poverty has become more concentrated in high-poverty counties over the past decade: almost half of the rural poor live in high-poverty counties.

Concentrated poverty is measured by the share of the poor who live in high-poverty counties. Concentrations of poverty negatively affect the opportunities of those who live there, both those who are poor and those who aren't, so how concentrated poor households are is an important measure. With the number of high-poverty counties rapidly increasing, there will be increases in the share of the poor who live in high-poverty counties and more challenging economic environments for an increasing share of the poverty population.

The last column of table 2.3 shows the share of all poor people (metropolitan and nonmetropolitan) who lived in high-poverty counties in 2009–2013. Overall, almost one out of four poor people lived in a high-poverty county. This varies dramatically by race and ethnicity. Whereas less than one in five poor non-Hispanic whites lived in a high-poverty county, more than two in five Native Americans and almost one in three poor blacks lived in a high-poverty county.

Table 2.3 Concentrated Poverty: Percent of Rural Poor by Race/Ethnicity Living in High-Poverty Counties

Racial/ethnic group	Percent of nonmetropolitan poor living in high-poverty nonmetropolitan counties, 1999	Percent of nonmetropolitan poor living in high-poverty nonmetropolitan counties, 2009	Percent change 1999 to 2009	Percent of all poor living in high-poverty counties, 2009
Black	46.9%	77.3%	64.8%	31.9%
Hispanic	31.8	48.8	53.5	22.5
Native American	47.7	69.0	44.7	41.1
Non-Hispanic white	12.5	35.6	184.8	19.1
Total	**17.0**	**45.0**	**164.7**	**22.9**

Source: Data are from the 2000 Decennial Census and American Community Survey, 2009-2013.

Rural poverty was much more concentrated than all poverty in 2009 (compare the middle column and last column of table 2.3). The share of rural poor living in high-poverty rural counties (45 percent) was twice the share of the total poor population living in all high-poverty counties (22.9 percent). The racial/ethnic disparities are even starker. More than three-quarters (77.3 percent) of rural poor blacks, more than two-thirds (69 percent) of rural Native Americans, and almost half (48.8 percent) of rural Hispanics lived in high-poverty counties. For poor rural non-Hispanic whites, more than one in three (35.6 percent) lived in a high-poverty county. Across all racial and ethnic groups, rural poverty was more concentrated than total poverty.

Rural poverty has become much more highly concentrated over the past decade. The percent of rural poor living in high-poverty counties in 2009–2013 (45.0 percent) is almost three times the percent in 1999 (17.0 percent).

Because of the very rapid growth in rural non-Hispanic white concentrated poverty, the gap in rural concentrated poverty rates between non-Hispanic whites and minorities has shrunk from 1999 to the 2009–2013 period. Whereas in 1999 rural concentrated poverty rates for blacks and Native Americans were four times the rate for non-Hispanic whites, and the rate for Hispanics was more than twice the non-Hispanic white rate, the rural concentrated poverty rates for blacks and Native Americans in 2009–2013 were only about twice the non-Hispanic white rate, and the rate for Hispanics was only about one-third greater than the non-Hispanic white rate.

SUMMARY

The main lessons of this chapter are these: (1) poverty in the United States fluctuated with changes in labor market opportunities from technology and globalization, with changes in educational levels and family structures, and due to antipoverty and other policies; (2) on average, rural poverty rates are higher than metro poverty rates using the official poverty measure, but poverty rates are lower in rural counties than in metro counties under the supplemental poverty measure, which considers the effect of noncash transfers and costs of living differentials; (3) overall poverty rates have declined somewhat since the late 1950s, but poverty rates have stagnated at between 11 and 15 percent since the early 1970s with the gap between rural and metro poverty rates declining over the past forty years from about 5 percentage points to about 3 percentage points; (4) poverty tends to persist among certain races and ethnic groups, based in part on discrimination and historical institutions, and counties with high concentrations of these groups tend to have high poverty rates; (5) poverty is particularly persistent in rural counties, and remote rural counties with small populations are particularly likely to have persistently high poverty rates; and (6) concentrated poverty rates (the percentages of the poor living in high-poverty counties) have grown rapidly since 1999 and are higher in rural than metro areas and highest among rural blacks and Native Americans.

Just as rural America is diverse, poverty is diverse across metro and rural areas. But should the policies that have been developed for the historically persistent-poverty counties and inner cities be modified to address the conditions in the new high-poverty counties? As high poverty migrates from the most densely and the most sparsely settled places to the suburban and micropolitan[13] "middle spaces," it may be time to revisit the "place-based" policies designed for the persistent-poverty regions. Many of the elements of these traditional place-based policies are still relevant: investments in locality-based economic development, local work supports, local educational systems, and collaborative institutions. What we learn about successful innovations for addressing the new suburban poverty (see Kneebone and Berube 2013) may provide guidance for micropolitan counties facing high poverty for the first time.

As Calvin Beale (2004) pointed out, the poverty population in the Southern Highlands has different barriers (disability, low educational attainment, not enough full-time work) than poor Native Americans in the Great Plains and Southwest (deep poverty, low employment rates). As Beale writes in his conclusion, "each type of high-poverty county has its own signature poverty-related characteristics. It is essential to recognize these typically deep-rooted distinctions and their significance if low-income problems are to be addressed successfully in Federal and other programs" (27).

NOTES

Several colleagues made enormous contributions to this chapter. Tracey Farrigan of the USDA Economic Research Service provided insightful comments about changes in poverty over time and the racial and ethnic dimensions of rural poverty. Richard Sandler at Oregon State University found difficult-to-locate publications and photographs that greatly enhance the chapter. Angela Johnson at the University of Missouri both produced all of the maps in this chapter and provided indispensible counsel on the categorization of high-poverty counties into racial/ethnic categories.

1. From Robert Hunter, 1904, *Poverty,* (New York: Macmillan) 59–61.

2. From Carl C. Taylor, Helen W. Wheeler, and E. L. Kirkpatrick. 1938. *Disadvantaged Classes in American Agriculture.*

3. From President's National Advisory Commission on Rural Poverty. 1967. *The People Left Behind,* ix.

4. From USDA Economic Research Service. "Rural Poverty and Well-Being." http://www.ers.usda.gov/topics/rural-economy-population/rural-poverty-well-being/geography-of-poverty.aspx; http://www.ers.usda.gov/topics/rural-economy-population/rural-poverty-well-being/poverty-demographics.aspx.

5. The word "poverty" only appears four times in the report: the first three times in connection with soil depletion and the poverty that is associated with farming depleted and infertile soil, and the fourth time in a list of hardships that fall more heavily on farm women.

6. The other three concerns were about highways, soil depletion, and health in the open country.

7. They also did not find that the fourth factor they examined—changes in the number and composition of immigrants—explained changes in poverty rates.

8. Fox et al. don't estimate the metropolitan and nonmetropolitan poverty rates, so it isn't possible to know from this study whether government programs are more effective in reducing poverty in rural or urban areas.

9. Data for 1959, 1969, and 1999 are from the Decennial Census of Population, based on a long form that was administered to a sample of the population. In the early 2000s, the decision was made to replace the long form in the Decennial Census with an annual American Community Survey (ACS). The smaller sample size of this survey requires that data be aggregated across multiple years for areas with small populations. Thus "2009" data are represented by the aggregated 2007–2011 data from ACS.

10. Wimberly and Morris (1997) identify the southern Black Belt as "a social and demographic crescent of counties containing higher than average percentages of black residents" (iii). The region includes parts of ten states: Virginia, the Carolinas,

Georgia, Florida, Alabama, Mississippi, Tennessee, Louisiana, Arkansas, and Texas. The Black Belt has also been described as "a landscape of primarily cotton agriculture and majority African American population [covering] a swath from Virginia through the Carolinas and across the Gulf South" (Tullos 2004).

11. We owe this insight to Tracey Farrigan.

12. In this analysis, persistent-poverty counties are those whose poverty rate was 20 percent or more in 1969, 1979, 1989, and 1999 (from the 1970, 1980, 1990, and 2000 censuses) and in the 2007–2011 American Community Survey (referred to as the "2009 poverty rate"). Because of county boundary and other changes, 59 counties were dropped from the dataset to allow for analysis of a consistent group of counties over the whole time period. Tabulations are based on this reduced number of counties (3,084).

13. Micropolitan counties are nonmetropolitan counties that are centered on an urban cluster with a population between 10,000 and 49,999.

REFERENCES

Albrecht, Scott. 2013. National Trends in Income Inequality. Policy Brief 11. National Agricultural and Rural Development Policy Center.

Beale, Calvin. 2004. "Anatomy of Nonmetro High-Poverty Areas: Common in Plight, Distinctive in Nature." *Amber Waves.* 2(1):20–27.

Corbett, Thomas. 2014. "The Rise and Fall of Poverty as a Policy Issue." *Focus* 30(2):3–8.

Ellsworth, Clayton S. 1960. "Theodore Roosevelt's Country Life Commission," *Agricultural History* 34(Fall):155–72.

Fox, Liana, Christopher Wimer, Irwin Garfinkel, Neeraj Kaushal, and Jane Waldfogel. 2015. "Waging War on Poverty: Poverty Trends Using a Historical Supplemental Poverty Measure." *Journal of Policy Analysis and Management* 34(3):567–92. doi: 10.1002/pam.21833.

Harrington, Michael. 1962. *The Other America: Poverty in the United States.* New York: Macmillan.

Hine, Lewis Wickes. 1915. "The summer quarters of a beet worker's family on a Colorado farm near Starling." Photograph. From the Library of Congress Prints and Photographs Online Catalog. http://www.loc.gov/pictures/item/ncl2004004208/PP/.

Hoynes, Hilary W., Marianne E. Page, and Ann Huff Stevens. 2006. "Poverty in America: Trends and Explanations." *Journal of Economic Perspectives* 20(1):47–68.

Hunter, Robert. 1904. *Poverty.* New York: Macmillan.

Jolliffe, Dean. 2006. "Poverty, Prices, and Place: How Sensitive Is the Spatial Distribution of Poverty to Cost of Living Adjustments?" *Economic Inquiry* 44(2):296–310.

Kneebone, Elizabeth, and Alan Berube. 2013. *Confronting Poverty in Suburban America.* Washington DC: Brookings Institution.

Lange, Dorothea. 1915. "People living in miserable poverty, Elm Grove, Oklahoma County, Oklahoma." Photograph. From the Library of Congress Prints and Photographs Online Catalog. http://www.loc.gov/pictures/collection/fsa/item/fsa1998021768/PP/.

Murray, Charles. 1984. *Losing Ground: American Social Policy 1950–1980.* New York: Basic.

Orshansky, Mollie. 1965. "Counting the Poor: Another Look at the Poverty Profile." *Social Security Bulletin* 28(1):3–29.

Patterson, James T. 2000. *America's Struggle Against Poverty in the Twentieth Century.* Cambridge, NJ: Harvard University Press.

Peters, Scott J., and Paul A. Morgan. 2004. "The Country Life Commission: Reconsidering a Milestone in American Agricultural History." *Agricultural History* 78(3):289–316.

President's National Advisory Commission on Rural Poverty. 1967. *The People Left Behind.* Washington DC: U.S. Government Printing Office.

Rural Sociological Society Task Force on Persistent Rural Poverty. 1993. *Persistent Poverty in Rural America.* Boulder: Westview Press.

Short, Kathleen. 2015. "The Supplemental Poverty Measure: 2014." Current Population Reports P60–254.

Stoughton, Cecil. 1964. "President Lyndon B. Johnson shakes the hand of one of the residents of Appalachia as Agent Rufus Youngblood (far left) looks on." Photograph. From Lyndon B. Johnson Presidential Library photo archives, serial number 225-9-WH64.

Taylor, Carl C., Helen W. Wheeler, and E. L. Kirkpatrick. 1938. *Disadvantaged Classes in American Agriculture.* Washington DC: U.S. Department of Agriculture, Farm Security Administration and the Bureau of Agricultural Economics cooperating.

Tullos, Allen. 2004. "The Black Belt." *Southern Spaces.* http://southernspaces.org/2004 /black-belt.

U.S. Country Life Commission. 1911. *Report on the Commission on Country Life.* NY: Sturgis & Walton.

Wimberly, Ronald C., and Libby V. Morris. 1997. *The Southern Black Belt: A National Perspective.* Lexington KY: TVA Rural Studies.

FURTHER READING

Bonnen, James T. 1966. "Rural Poverty: Programs and Problems." *Journal of Farm Economics* 48(2):452–65.

Fisher, Gordon M. 1997. "From Hunter to Orshansky: An Overview of (Unofficial) Poverty Lines in the United States from 1904 to 1965." A revised version of a paper presented October 28, 1993, at the Fifteenth Annual Research Conference of the Association for Public Policy Analysis and Management in Washington, DC. http://www.census.gov/hhes/povmeas/publications/povthres/fisher4.htm.

Leven, Maurice, Harold G. Moulton, Clark Warburton. 1934. *America's Capacity to Consume.* Washington DC: Brookings Institution.

Maddox, James G. 1968. "An Historical Review of the Nation's Efforts to Cope with Rural Poverty." *American Journal of Agricultural Economics* 50(5):1351–61.

Sherman, Jennifer. 2014. "Rural Poverty: The Great Recession, Rising Unemployment, and the Under-Utilized Safety Net." In *Rural America in a Globalizing World: Problems and Prospects for the 2010s*, ed. C. Bailey, L. Jensen, and E. Ransom. Morgantown: West Virginia University Press.

U.S. Council of Economic Advisors. 1964. *Economic Report of the President.* Washington DC: U.S. Government Printing Office.

Weber, Bruce, Leif Jensen, Kathleen Miller, Jane Mosley, and Monica Fisher. 2005. "A Critical Review of Rural Poverty Literature: Is There Truly a Rural Effect?" *International Regional Science Review* 28:381–414.

PART II

Key Concepts and Issues for
Understanding Rural Poverty

Formulation of effective strategies to reduce rural poverty must begin with an understanding of which rural residents are most likely to experience poverty and why this is so. Chapter 3 reviews the construction of alternative measures of poverty including the official poverty measure (OPM), the supplemental poverty measure (SPM), measures of relative poverty (relative deprivation/social exclusion measures), consumption-based poverty measures, and consensual or democratic survey approaches as well as the poverty counts that result from their application. Significant differences across the corresponding portraits of rural poverty underscore the importance of a reliable and valid measure of poverty that serves both scientific and political purposes. Assessing the incidence of poverty by calculating poverty rates and comparing these rates across groups, space, and time provides a better understanding of social inequality.

Chapter 4 provides a menu of theoretical perspectives that attempt to explain the stylized facts that feed the public perception of rural poverty—its absolute and relative level, its incidence and concentration, and its persistence. The theoretical frameworks fall into three major categories: individual-level theories (e.g., theories of human capital, status attainment, the culture of poverty), structural-level definitions (e.g., structural and spatial theories that consider social/economic systems), and theories that merge people–place and individual–structural explanations for poverty (e.g., intersectionality theories, social exclusion and isolation, and forms of capital). The authors prefer the third category because it demonstrates "the multidimensionality of the causes and consequences of poverty, the connections across different scales and levels of analysis, the benefit of thinking of poverty as a form of inequality and position in sets of hierarchies rather than a static condition, and the importance of access to resources whether at the individual, group, or spatial level."

CHAPTER 3

Measures of Poverty and Implications for Portraits of Rural Hardship

Leif Jensen and Danielle Ely

INTRODUCTION

Poverty is a social problem that is both universally recognized and personally experienced by all too many people in rural and urban areas. One estimate suggests that upwards of two-thirds of all Americans will experience poverty by the time they reach age eighty-five (Rank and Hirschl 1999). Poverty seems familiar to us all, and for many it is a lived experience. It touches all of our lives in one way or another. Whether it conjures up mental images of ramshackle housing tucked away in rural hollows or empty storefronts along blighted inner city neighborhoods, people think they know poverty when they see it. And most people have opinions—often strong opinions—about what poverty is, what causes it, and what, if anything, needs to be done to combat it.

Being ubiquitous, complex, and contentious, poverty is precisely the kind of social problem that first needs to be carefully defined before we can hope to pursue a rigorous and unbiased understanding. Like any measurement in the social sciences, a worthwhile measure of poverty needs to be both valid and reliable. Validity means that the measure of poverty truly captures the underlying concept it is intended to measure. "Are we measuring what we *think* we're measuring?" is the way it is often phrased. Reliability means that the measure of poverty operates in a consistent way over time and is relatively free of random error. A yardstick made from flexible material is not very reliable.

A standard operational definition of poverty—one that is both valid and reliable—serves two basic and critical purposes, one scientific and one political. First, it allows researchers to assess the prevalence of poverty through the calculation of poverty rates: the percentage of people or families that are *in* poverty. Knowing how poverty rates vary across sociodemographic groups, across space, and over time is essential for a full accounting of social inequality. That there are certain categories of people (e.g., recent immigrants or high school dropouts) or certain kinds of places (e.g., rural localities or counties in Appalachia) with high poverty rates invites scientific questions about why this is so. Assessing trends in the poverty rates for people and places over time likewise leads to intense study of the factors causing poverty rates to change. At a more micro level, analyzing survey data on individuals or families that include a variable for poverty status allows for complex statistical analyses of the correlates of poverty. If the data are collected for the same individuals at multiple points in time, social scientists can better understand the factors that give rise to the movement of people into and out of poverty over time. In short, a valid and reliable measure of poverty allows social scientists to confidently explore the complex array of factors that cause poverty, as well as its severity, nature, and consequences.

Second, a standard measure of poverty is important for social policy as well. Although the scientific study of the causes and consequences of poverty has scholarly value in and of itself, it also provides policy makers and analysts with solid information about which people and places face the greatest poverty risks and are in greatest need of attention. At the same time, by providing a dependable understanding of the causes of poverty, how the causes differ in strength, and under what circumstances they are more problematic, social science can contribute to more effective public policy. Trends in poverty rates can provide some evidence about whether or not policies are effective. Finally, a valid and reliable measure of poverty allows for policy targeting. That is, it provides an arguably fair and standardized way to assess what people or places are deserving of and qualified for various means-tested government programs.

Despite the clear value of having a standard definition of poverty, in reality, there is a wide variety of ways to define poverty. This chapter describes some of the basic definitions of poverty, with emphasis on the official U.S. definition of poverty and its strengths and weaknesses. Then, using various definitions, a brief descriptive portrait of poverty in the United States is presented that focuses on how patterns of rural and urban difference are sensitive to the definition of poverty.

ABSOLUTE DEFINITIONS OF POVERTY

Poverty can be defined in absolute or relative terms. As the term implies, *absolute poverty* refers to a situation in which individuals lack the income or resources needed to maintain even the most basic, minimally sufficient, subsistence-level standard of living (Iceland 2013). In practice, the amount of money needed to attain (purchase) this minimum standard constitutes the absolute poverty threshold (or poverty line), and those with incomes below this amount are defined as poor.

The official definition of poverty in the United States is an absolute measure. It was developed in the early 1960s by Mollie Orshansky of the Social Security Administration and, with minor adjustments, has been with us ever since (Ruggles 1990). Its logic is as follows. Recognizing that the most basic of needs is food, the official definition rests on the cost of a minimally adequate diet—sometimes referred to as a "food basket"—as determined by the U.S. Department of Agriculture (USDA). Although the USDA specified alternative food baskets that differed by ampleness, it is noteworthy that the food plan chosen as the basis for the official measure of poverty was the so-called economy food plan, which was designed for temporary or emergency use (Carlson et al. 2007) and, arguably, is nutritionally inadequate in the long run. Mid-1950s survey research on the U.S. population suggested that families spend about one-third of their income on food, so the cost of the food basket was simply multiplied by three to arrive at the poverty threshold. Different food baskets were specified for families of varying size and composition (i.e., different levels of need), so multiple poverty thresholds could be established. A process known as "equivalence scaling" allowed researchers to specify poverty lines that adjusted for family size, number of children, whether the family head was elderly, and the like. The official thresholds are expressed in annual dollars. They represent the annual pretax cash income from all sources needed to achieve the absolute minimum standard of living; families with annual incomes below this level are defined as poor. Families—people living together who are related by blood, marriage, or adoption—are considered to be the prime income-sharing unit for establishing poverty thresholds. People living alone or with unrelated individuals are essentially regarded as one-person families and assigned poverty thresholds accordingly.

In its original formulation, lower poverty thresholds were assigned to farm families who would presumably produce some of their own food, but this distinction has since been dropped. Apart from that, the only

Budget for a Family at the Poverty Level

See if you can sketch out a detailed family budget for this family of four with earnings of $2,028 per month, given the prices of necessities. Imagine where this family of four is living, and under what circumstances (e.g., employment status, housing, transportation, and so forth). Itemize all of the various expense categories, estimate the monthly cost of each, and sum these expenses for a monthly total.

Can your family "make it" at that income level? What assumptions did you need to make? If you are doing this exercise in a class, how do the budgets differ? What agreements or disagreements are there over necessities and their cost? How do the imagined circumstances of the family differ, and what does this say about what makes it easier or harder to make ends meet? Is the official poverty threshold too high, too low, or about right?

You can get the current poverty threshold from the U.S. Census Bureau, or you can adjust the 2016 threshold used here for inflation using the CPI (which you can look up) or an inflation calculator.

notable change to the original thresholds has been to adjust them for inflation, using the consumer price index (CPI). In this sense, the definition remains constant over time, which is another distinguishing feature of absolute definitions (Iceland 2013). In 2016, a family of four with two adults and two children was defined as poor if their annual pretax income was less than $24,339.

The official definition of poverty in the United States has given us a reasonably valid and reliable way to measure poverty, and as such it has served many research and policy functions. However, it has not been without its critics. In the mid-1990s, a landmark National Academy of Sciences (NAS) study provided an in-depth critical appraisal of the official definition of poverty in the United States (Citro and Michael 1995). The study criticized the official measure for failing to count noncash in-kind income (e.g., food stamps or subsidized housing) toward a family's total income, for having too restrictive a definition of the income-sharing "family" unit (e.g., not counting unrelated foster children as part of the family), for completely ignoring cost-of-living differences across space, for neglecting the disproportionate increases in the cost of nonfood necessities, for equivalence scaling that was somewhat crude and ad hoc, and for other reasons. Accordingly, the NAS study proposed an alternative poverty measure that would correct as much as possible for these short-comings. That study took place in the mid-1990s, and it is symptomatic of the inertia of official government indicators that now, a generation later, the official definition of poverty has not changed. Fortunately, in recent years the U.S. Census Bureau has begun to collect the data needed to calculate a new poverty measure based on the NAS critique, the so-called supplemental poverty measure (SPM) (Short 2015). Comparisons of rural and urban poverty rates using the official measure and the SPM are examined later in the chapter.

RELATIVE POVERTY AND OTHER DEFINITIONS

Absolute poverty exists when income is insufficient to achieve a minimally adequate standard of living. If an individual or family has an annual income just a few dollars above their poverty threshold, they are not defined as poor in absolute terms. However, as the previous exercise might have indicated, living at or just above the poverty line is often associated with having a relatively deprived standard of living. Beyond having just enough income to barely eke out a living, is having an income that is much less than aver-age meaningful? Those who define poverty in relative terms think that it is, arguing that this *relative deprivation* is associated with various forms of *social exclusion* from mainstream society and institutions (Iceland 2013). Specific definitions of *relative poverty* abound, but a typical relative defini-tion is having an annual household income that is less than one-half of the median annual household income. In 2015, the median (fiftieth percen-tile) U.S. household income was $55,775 (Posey 2016); the relative poverty threshold is computed as half of that, or $27,888. Absolute and relative poverty rates are compared in more detail later in the chapter.

The United States officially defines poverty in absolute terms, whereas in Europe relative poverty is emphasized. It is instructive to think about what is needed to bring about improvement in absolute versus relative poverty. In general, reductions in absolute poverty require a lifting up of the real (i.e., inflation-adjusted) incomes of those below the poverty line such that proportionately fewer people or families are below the line. By contrast, reductions in relative poverty require that the incomes of those at the bottom of the income distribution move closer to those in the middle. In other words, the latter requires that income be distributed more equitably. Why the United States clings to an absolute definition of poverty and European governments focus on relative poverty is a fair question to consider.

A criticism of both absolute and relative poverty measures is that by comparing income to a poverty threshold, they neglect how people spend that income. Some people may have incomes well above the poverty line but not be spending that income in ways that contribute to physical or social well-being. Others may have incomes below poverty but be living an ascetic, healthy, and fulfilling life and may not *feel* poor at all. Income-based measures of poverty capture neither actual lifestyles nor subjective self-assessments of poverty status. Another way to measure poverty uses a *consumption-based poverty measure*, which takes advantage of information gathered in surveys on detailed household *expenditures*—what they are actually spending—that can then be summed and compared to an absolute poverty threshold (Meyer and Sullivan 2012). An advantage of this approach is that in U.S. household surveys there tends to be less underreporting of expenditures than of income. A related approach commonly applied to the measurement of poverty in the developing world is to examine not the household expenditures on items but the *deprivations* a household endures. For their multidimensional poverty index, Sabina Alkire and colleagues (2015) use ten deprivations commonly captured in national-level socioeconomic and health surveys within the three domains of health (e.g., undernourishment), education (e.g., no one in the household with at least primary schooling), and standard of living (e.g., no electricity). Households reporting over a set number of deprivations are then defined as poor. A disadvantage of this technique is that the list of deprivations is specified in advance by researchers, thereby disregarding differences across cultures and countries in what constitutes a deprivation. The next approach to poverty measurement contends with this problem.

A promising consumption-based technique is the *consensual* or *democratic* approach to poverty measurement. As described by Shailen Nandy and colleagues (Nandy and Pomati 2015; Nandy and Main 2015), the consensual approach involves a two-step process. First, a representative survey of a population is conducted to assess popular attitudes about what consumption items (e.g., three meals a day) or even activities (e.g., celebrations on special occasions) are considered necessary by a majority of respondents. Second, another survey is conducted in which respondents identify whether they have each of these perceived necessities and, if not, whether this is because the household could not afford them.

Necessities that cannot be afforded are regarded as deprivations. Researchers then define as poor those households that exceed some number of these deprivations. The consensual approach is flexible and has been adapted to study poverty among children in the United Kingdom (Nandy and Main 2015) and adults in developing countries (Nandy and Pomati 2015). The method, however, is data intensive. Unfortunately, we know of no applications of this approach in the United States.

The consensual approach just described takes advantage of subjective assessments among populations regarding the necessities of life. This brings to mind the idea of *subjective poverty*. Two approaches to subjective poverty deserve brief mention. One is to ask survey questions such as "living where you do now and meeting the expenses you consider necessary, what would be the very smallest income you and your family would need to make ends meet?" (Danziger et al. 1984 as cited in Ruggles 1990). Answers to this question along with respondent characteristics can then be used to specify subjective poverty thresholds, and families with incomes below these thresholds are defined as poor. A second and admittedly crude approach to subjective poverty is simply to ask survey respondents whether they consider themselves to be poor. The sensitivities and ambiguities of asking such a question explain why researchers rarely use this measure.

Many social science concepts familiar to almost everyone, such as poverty, are deceptively difficult to define and measure. A valid and reliable measure of poverty is much needed to achieve a sufficient understanding of the depth, breadth, causes, and consequences of poverty, as well as rigorous and fair policy implementation and evaluation. A range of measurement approaches including absolute, relative, consumption-based, and subjective poverty have been reviewed here. These empirical measures differ in their official status, popularity, and the underlying conceptualization of poverty they capture. Some of these measures are used in the analysis that follows, but students of poverty need to be fully aware of all of them.

A PORTRAIT OF RURAL POVERTY TODAY USING ALTERNATIVE DEFINITIONS

INTRODUCTION AND OVERVIEW

The purpose of this section is to present a statistical portrait of the prevalence and correlates of poverty in both rural and urban America using several of the measures of poverty already defined: the official measure of poverty (and variants of it to capture "deep" and "near" poverty); the supplemental poverty measure, which corrects for some of the short-comings in the official measure; a simple indicator of relative poverty; and a quasi-subjective measure of poverty. The fundamental question is, "Who are the rural poor?" In addressing this question, it is important to pay attention to the implications of how the picture differs depending on the poverty measure used. The analysis is supplemented with conclusions drawn from the empirical literature on rural poverty in the United States.

DATA AND MEASURES

The principal data set used for analysis is the March 2015 Current Population Survey (CPS). Collected by the U.S. Census Bureau, the CPS is the nation's key source of unemployment statistics. Based on a nationally representative sample of U.S. households, the survey is conducted monthly. The CPS questionnaire contains a core set of questions that are common to each month, but in any given month the questionnaire includes supplemental questions that cover topics such as child support, volunteering, health insurance, and food insecurity. In addition to unemployment statistics then, the purpose of the CPS is to provide reliable information on the social and economic circumstances and trends among the U.S. population.

The March CPS includes the so-called Annual Social and Economic Supplement (ASEC), which contains detailed questions about income sources and amounts. The ASEC provides the basis for annual estimates of the size and composition of the U.S. poverty population. The CPS is designed to be representative of the entire noninstitutionalized civilian population. Not included are institutionalized individuals and those who are homeless and not in a shelter. Students in dormitories are only included if their information was reported in their parent's home (DeNavas-Walt and Proctor 2015). The ASEC, unlike the basic CPS, includes some individuals in the military, but only if they live in a household with at least one other civilian adult (DeNavas-Walt and Proctor 2015). The ASEC underwent a partial redesign in 2014 and transitioned completely to the new design for the 2015 data release.[1]

As noted, several measures of poverty were used in the analysis.[2] In addition, measures of deep and near poverty were used in the analysis. Deep poverty is defined as occurring when a family's income is less than half its poverty threshold (i.e., the income-to-needs ratio is less than 0.5). The near poor are those with incomes less than 150 percent of the official thresholds (i.e., the income-to-needs ratio of less than 1.5).

For comparative purposes, a simple measure of relative poverty was also computed. Based on 2014 median household income for family households and nonfamily households as reported in DeNavas-Walt and Proctor (2015), the relative poverty thresholds were set at one-half of these medians. Thus, individuals were defined as being in relative poverty if their total household income was less than $34,213 for those in family households, and $16,024 for those in nonfamily households (people living alone or with unrelated individuals). This relative poverty measure is *not* adjusted for family size or composition as is the official absolute measure.

Finally, the SPM[3] was also used in the analysis. The SPM was created in response to the legitimate criticisms of the official poverty measure. Whereas the official measure defines a family as those living together who are related by blood, marriage, or adoption, the SPM broadens this definition to include any unrelated children cared for by a family (e.g., foster children) as well as those who are in cohabiting relationships (see Short 2015 for more detail). Instead of being based on three times the cost of a minimally adequate diet, the SPM thresholds take account of actual expenditures on necessities (food, clothing, shelter, and utilities). The SPM poverty threshold is set at 1.2 times the mean (average) total expenditures on these necessities for those two-child families that fall between the thirtieth and thirty-sixth percentiles on such spending (based on consumer expenditure data). (The mean is multiplied by 1.2 to give families extra for other necessities.)[4] Whereas the official definition of poverty uses all cash income before taxes, the SPM adds in some noncash income but takes away certain expenses. Specifically, the SPM counts as income the value of food stamp (SNAP) benefits and other in-kind (noncash) resources, but it also subtracts from income things like taxes paid, out of pocket medical expenses, employment expenses, and child support. The SPM poverty thresholds differ by prevailing housing costs across some 385 different metropolitan and nonmetropolitan areas (and by whether someone is renting, owns their home outright, or is paying a mortgage) to adjust for cost-of-living differences by place of residence. Finally, whereas the equivalence scaling underlying the official measure is somewhat ad hoc, the SPM uses a formula that adjusts the thresholds consistently depending on the number of adults and children in the family and whether the head of household is a single parent. Although no measure of poverty is perfect, it is clear that the SPM does correct for significant shortcomings in the official measure. The SPM is not a measure included in the original ASEC files. However, it is made available separately and is easily merged with the ASEC data by matching the household sequence number and the unique person identification number, which was done for this analysis.

"Rural" residence is defined as living outside of a metropolitan area. In essence, metropolitan areas consist of counties with a city of 50,000 or more people (or a total urbanized area of 100,000 or more), plus surrounding counties with strong economic ties. All other counties are defined as nonmetropolitan. This analysis used the CPS variable indicating whether the household is in a metropolitan area, in a nonmetropolitan area, or is not identified.[5] A separate four-category variable was used to further subdivide metro households into those located in a principal city of a metro area or those outside of principal cities (i.e., central city versus suburban residents). Other measures are specified as they are introduced into the analysis.

Tables 3.1 and 3.2 show the prevalence of poverty using the various definitions of poverty previously described and how these poverty rates differ

Table 3.1 Poverty Rates (%) by Metropolitan Status and Region

	Total	Nonmetro	Metro all	Central cities	Non-central cities
Deep poverty	6.7%	7.4%	6.6%	8.6%	5.2%
Official poverty	14.9	16.9	14.5	18.8	11.9
Near poverty	24.2	28.0	23.5	29.4	19.7
Relative poverty	21.7	26.5	20.9	26.0	17.5
SPM poverty	15.3	12.8	15.7	20.4	13.4
$N =$	199,024	37,100	159,724	49,577	77,523

	Total	Northeast	Midwest	South	West
Deep poverty	6.7%	5.6%	5.8%	7.7%	6.8%
Official poverty	14.9	12.7	13.1	16.6	15.3
Near poverty	24.2	20.9	22.0	26.7	24.6
Relative poverty	21.7	19.0	19.6	24.6	21.1
SPM poverty	15.3	14.6	11.8	15.6	18.4
Weighted N	199,024	33,252	39,362	70,439	55,971

Data: March 2015 Current Population Survey.

Table 3.2 Poverty Rates (%) by Metropolitan Status and Race/Ethnicity

	Total	Nonmetro	Metro	Central city	Non-central city
White non-Hispanic					
Deep poverty	4.7%	5.9%	4.4%	5.7%	3.7%
Official poverty	10.1	13.8	9.3	11.2	8.0
Near poverty	17.4	23.9	15.9	17.9	14.1
Relative poverty	16.3	23.3	14.6	15.8	13.0
SPM poverty	10.7	11.1	10.6	13.1	9.4
N =	118,880	28,200	89,210	18,874	46,929
Black non-Hispanic					
Deep poverty	12.3%	15.8%	11.8%	13.3%	9.0%
Official poverty	26.3	33.5	25.4	28.6	20.1
Near poverty	38.2	48.4	36.9	41.7	29.6
Relative poverty	36.2	47.3	34.8	40.0	27.6
SPM poverty	23.1	20.5	23.3	26.2	20.0
N =	23,088	2,905	20,067	9,807	7,541
Asian non-Hispanic					
Deep poverty	5.5%	4.9%	5.5%	6.9%	4.1%
Official poverty	11.7	7.0	11.8	14.7	9.4
Near poverty	20.1	21.4	20.1	23.7	17.1
Relative poverty	17.2	16.0	17.2	20.1	14.9
SPM poverty	16.8	9.0	17.0	20.1	14.9
N =	11,313	628	10,654	4,622	4,944
Other non-Hispanic					
Deep poverty	9.0%	11.1%	8.4%	10.4%	6.3%
Official poverty	19.9	25.3	18.3	20.8	15.7
Near poverty	30.0	38.4	27.6	29.4	24.8
Relative poverty	25.0	31.1	23.2	26.9	20.0
SPM poverty	16.2	15.7	16.4	19.5	14.4
N =	7,704	2,127	5,384	1,624	2,543
Hispanic					
Deep poverty	9.8%	11.7%	9.6%	10.1%	9.0%
Official poverty	23.8	27.5	23.5	24.9	21.7
Near poverty	38.5	43.9	38.2	40.7	34.8
Relative poverty	31.7	35.9	31.5	34.1	28.5
SPM poverty	25.4	21.1	25.7	28.2	24.1
Weighted N	38,039	3,240	34,409	14,650	15,566

Data: March 2015 Current Population Survey.

by residence and race/ethnicity. These tables include all ages of individuals available, ranging from fifteen years of age and top coded at eighty-five years of age. Table 3.1 presents poverty measures by metropolitan status and region of residence. Not surprisingly, the total proportion of the population in poverty varies dramatically when comparing across the various measures. For example, in the total population, 6.7 percent are in deep poverty, 14.9 percent are under the official poverty line, and 24.2 percent are near poor (under 150 percent of the poverty line). The 14.9 percent living in poverty according to the official definition compares to 15.3 percent when using the SPM, suggesting that measured poverty is somewhat worse overall when correcting for deficiencies in the official definition. Finally, according to this crude measure, relative poverty stood at 21.7 percent.

Residential differences are, for the most part, suggestive of a rural disadvantage. Whether measured as deep, official, near, or relative poverty, individuals in nonmetro areas have higher poverty rates than their metro counterparts. A decided exception, however, is when poverty is measured via the SPM. That measure suggests that poverty is less common in nonmetro than metro areas. Although this would suggest a rural advantage rather than disadvantage, some caution is warranted. One thing that is driving the apparent improvement in rural poverty when using the SPM is the correction for cost-of-living differences across space. However, that correction is based solely on differences in the cost of housing. At present the SPM does *not* factor in the cost of necessities such as transportation, which are often more expensive in rural than urban areas. That said, although most measures of poverty give rise to a story of rural disadvantage, according to one new measure designed to be more valid and reliable than the official definition, exactly the opposite story emerges—people in rural areas have *lower* poverty rates according to the SPM.

Although not the focus of this chapter, when subdividing metro areas into principal cities versus elsewhere, the commonplace disadvantage of central cities in relation to the suburbs is clear, regardless of poverty measure used. However, the results suggest that the gross nonmetro versus metro comparison obscures disadvantages of those in central cities when compared to nonmetro residents. According to most measures, poverty is worse in nonmetro than metro places, but it is the central cities of metro areas that are the worst off (an exception being for relative poverty, which is higher in nonmetro areas than even in central cities).

The second panel of table 3.1 shows poverty rates by region and, again, except for the SPM, indicates a southern disadvantage. When using the SPM, the West has the highest rates of poverty (18.4 percent). The Northeast and Midwest have comparable poverty rates across the varying poverty measures.

Table 3.2 shows the array of poverty rates using the same set of poverty measures broken down by race and ethnicity. Specifically, poverty is examined across five racial/ethnic groups: non-Hispanics who identify as (1) white, (2) black, (3) Asian, and (4) any other race, and (5) Hispanics (who can be of any race). The results underscore persisting racial/ethnic differences in poverty risks with blacks, Hispanics, and "others" (mostly Native Americans) having distinctly higher poverty rates than non-Hispanic Asians and whites. Breaking poverty rates down by race and ethnicity also has the effect of suggesting that poverty prevalence is higher in nonmetro America than even in central cities. That is, for all but the SPM, poverty is greater in nonmetro areas than in principal cities of metro areas among whites, blacks, Hispanics, and others. Black non-Hispanics, with Hispanics and non-Hispanics, have the highest prevalence of poverty for all measures. The results for the SPM are consistent with this finding only with regard to confirming higher poverty among blacks, Hispanics, and others. Otherwise, the SPM again suggests that for all but whites, non-metro poverty rates are lower than those in metro areas.

AN ASIDE ON SUBJECTIVE POVERTY

In this descriptive portrait of poverty, virtually all of the poverty indicators are income-based. They might define what counts as income differently, or compare that income to different thresholds, but they all have income at their core. As discussed previously, other definitions of poverty are based on consumption or expenditures, and still others are more subjective in nature. One form of subjective poverty is when people define themselves as poor. Perhaps, at the very least, because it seems callous to ask, nationally representative surveys do not attempt to define poverty in this way. One survey that arguably comes close to having a subjective definition of poverty is the General Social Survey (GSS), regularly conducted by the National Opinion Research Center (Smith et al. 2016). The GSS collects data on a variety of opinions and attitudes of the U.S. population, as well as their basic sociodemographic and economic characteristics. Attitudinal items cover issues such as national spending, economics, politics, crime, and intergroup relations, among many others. Although the sample size is modest (roughly 2,000 in any given year or

Table 3.3 Subjective Class Placement

	Rural	Urban	Total (weighted)
Lower class	12.2%	7.6%	531
Working class	52.9	45.1	3,000
Middle class	34.2	44.1	2,785
Upper class	0.6	3.2	188
$N =$			6,505

Data: General Social Survey (2010, 2012, and 2014).

about twice the size of the typical political poll), the GSS is nonetheless considered nationally representative. In this analysis, the 2010, 2012, and 2014 surveys from the GSS are combined.[6]

The GSS includes the following question (Smith et al. 2016): "If you were asked to use one of four names for your social class, which would you say you belong in: the lower class, the working class, the middle class, or the upper class?" To be sure, this question does not specifically mention "poverty" as being a social class. However, given that it asks respondents to intuitively distinguish the "lower" class from higher class groups, placing oneself in the lower class may serve as a rough proxy for subjective poverty status. Of interest here is how this subjective class status relates to rural versus urban residence. Regarding the latter, the GSS includes the size of the place where the respondent lives.

As shown in table 3.3, in both rural and urban areas, Americans tend to see themselves as being in the working or middle class. In urban areas, the split between the two is rather even (45.1 percent versus 44.1 percent, respectively), whereas in rural areas, adults are much more likely to see themselves as working class than middle class (52.9 percent versus 34.2 percent). Of much greater interest here, rural adults are far more likely to place themselves in the lower class (12.2 percent) than are urban residents (7.6 percent). To the extent that lower-class identification is a valid proxy for subjective poverty, one can argue that poverty is significantly more prevalent in America's rural than urban areas.

CONCLUSION

Poverty is an all too common social problem that, even for those lucky enough to never experience it, affects us all in one way or another. As a commonplace, complex, and controversial problem, it is critically important to define poverty carefully. Measures of poverty that are valid (measure what is intended) and reliable (operate consistently over time) serve two functions. First, they allow for rigorous scientific study, which contributes to the scholarship on the causes, correlates, nature, and consequences of poverty. The second function of poverty measures is political. They allow for policy development and evaluation, and they provide a way to target policies to those most in need and to establish eligibility for support.

Poverty has been defined and measured in a surprisingly wide variety of ways. Many measures are income-based and compare income received during a particular period—usually a year—to some predetermined poverty thresholds. These thresholds can be absolute or relative. Conceptually speaking, absolute poverty means having insufficient income to buy a minimally acceptable standard of living; relative poverty means having an income that is substantially less than average. The official definition of poverty in the United States is an absolute measure developed in the 1960s, and apart from adjusting the official poverty thresholds to account for inflation, it has remained largely unchanged to this day. The official definition of poverty in the United States has come under sharp criticism for ignoring cost-of-living differences across places, for not counting in-kind income, and for other reasons. The supplemental poverty measure corrects for many of these flaws, but it has not replaced the official definition.

In addition to income-based approaches, other definitions of poverty include consumption-based measures, which use expenditures to assess poverty status; and deprivation measures, which examine the actual circumstances of people and families and assess poverty status based on the things they lack—that is, the deprivations they exhibit. The consensual approach takes this a step further by using survey research to first determine the various consumption items regarded as necessary in a population and then using that information to define a set of deprivations. Poverty status is assessed by the number of deprivations people or families endure. By relying on popular opinion to first ascertain local opinion about what families should not be expected to do without, this consensual approach begins to contend with the subjective nature of poverty. What is considered poor in some societies may not be considered poor in others. One way researchers measure subjective poverty is by asking people what they feel is the minimum income level families need to survive, and then define as poor those with incomes less than that amount. Subjective poverty can also be determined most crudely by asking people in surveys to self-identify as poor.

Using some (though admittedly not all) of these definitions, a contemporary statistical portrait of rural and urban poverty in the United States has been described that shows how patterns of inequality differ depending on the definition used. A key takeaway message is that by most definitions nonmetropolitan residents are decidedly more likely to be poor than their more urban counterparts. The glaring exception to this pattern occurs when poverty is measured by the SPM. This measure suggests that poverty prevalence is lower in nonmetro than metro areas, lower even than in the more prosperous suburbs of metro areas. Although this could be taken to mean that rural residents are *not* more likely to be poor, two caveats remain. First, the SPM's cost-of-living adjustment only accounts for the cost of housing and ignores some necessities (e.g., transportation) that may be more expensive in the countryside. Second, there is no evidence for less material deprivation in rural areas despite the presumption rural families can stretch their dollars because it is cheaper to live there (Lichter and Schafft 2016). For all but the SPM, when poverty rates are considered separately for major race and ethnic groups in the United States, nonmetro whites, blacks, Hispanics, and others (mostly Native Americans) have poverty rates higher than their counterparts in metro areas generally, and even in the central cities of metro areas specifically. Finally, a much higher percentage of rural than urban adults define themselves as being in the lower class and are arguably in a state of subjective poverty. Other chapters delve more deeply into the severity, nature, and contours of rural deprivation in the United States.

NOTES

1. The goals of the redesign to the ASEC include improving income reporting, increasing response rates, reducing errors through the use of an automated questionnaire, and updating questions related to retirement income and income from retirement accounts and other assets. More information on the redesign can be found at https://www.census.gov/library/publications/2015/demo/p60-252.html.

2. Further information on the items included in these areas can be found in the FAQs section of the Bureau of Labor Statistics at http://www.bls.gov/dolfaq/bls _ques3.htm.

3. Further information on the supplemental poverty measure can be found in Short (2015).

4. Because the SPM thresholds are set within a certain percentile range of expenditures, and because they will be continually revised with updated expenditure data, some suggest the SPM is "quasi-relative" (Iceland 2013, 32).

5. To protect the confidentiality of CPS respondents, for a small proportion of all sampled households the Census Bureau will not identify whether the household is in a metro or nonmetro area. Definitions of metropolitan and nonmetropolitan are based on OMB standards. More information on these can be found at https://www.census .gov/population/metro/about/.

6. Further, we use an adjusted weight from the final weighting variable (WTSSALL) to ensure that any analysis accounts for the over- or under-sampling of the adult population.

REFERENCES

Alkire, Sabina, Jose Manuel Roche, Suman Seth, and Andrew Sumner. 2015. "Identifying the Poorest People and Groups: Strategies Using the Global Multidimensional Poverty Index." *Journal of International Development* 27:362–87.

Carlson, A., M. Lino, W-Y. Juan, K. Hanson, and P. P. Basiotis. 2007. "Thrifty Food Plan, 2006." CNPP-19. U.S. Department of Agriculture, Center for Nutrition Policy and Promotion.

Citro, Constance E., and Robert T. Michael. 1995. *Measuring Poverty: A New Approach.* Washington, DC: National Academies Press.

Danziger, Sheldon, Jacques van der Gaag, Michael K. Taussig, and Eugene Smolensky. 1984. "The Direct Measurement of Welfare Levels: How Much Does It Cost to Make Ends Meet?" *Review of Economics and Statistics* 66(3):500–505.

DeNavas-Walt, Carmen, and Bernadette D. Proctor. 2015. "Income and Poverty in the United States: 2014." Current Population Reports. P60–252. Washington, DC: U.S. Census Bureau.

Iceland, John. 2013. *Poverty in America: A Handbook*, 3rd ed. Berkeley: University of California Press.

Lichter, Daniel T., and Kai A. Schafft. 2016. "People and Places Left Behind: Rural Poverty in the New Century." In *Oxford Handbook of Poverty and Society*, 317–40. Oxford, UK: Oxford University Press.

Myer, Bruce D., and James X. Sullivan. 2012. "Identifying the Disadvantaged: Official Poverty, Consumption Poverty and the New Supplemental Poverty Measure." *Journal of Economic Perspectives* 26(3):111–36.

Nandy, Shailen, and Gill Main. 2015. "The Consensual Approach to Child Poverty Measurement." Poverty Brief. Comparative Research Programme on Poverty. Bergen, Norway: University of Bergen.

Nandy, Shailen, and Marco Pomati. 2015. "Applying the Consensual Method of Estimating Poverty in a Low Income African Setting." *Social Indicators Research* 124:693–726.

Posey, Kirby G. 2016. "Household Income 2015." American Community Survey Briefs, U.S. Census Bureau, ACSBR/15-02.

Rank, Mark R., and Thomas A. Hirschl. 1999. "The Likelihood of Poverty Across the American Adult Life Span." *Social Work* 44(3):201–216.

Ruggles, Patricia. 1990. *Drawing the Line: Alternative Poverty Measures and Their Implications for Public Policy.* Washington, DC: The Urban Institute Press.

Short, Kathleen, 2015. "The Research Supplemental Poverty Measure: 2014." Current Population Reports, P60–254. U.S. Census Bureau. www.census.gov/content/dam/Census/library/publications/2015/demo/p60-254.pdf.

Smith, Tom W., Peter Marsden, Michael Hout, and Jibum Kim. 2016. "General Social Surveys, 1972–2014." Machine-readable data file. Sponsored by National Science Foundation. Chicago: NORC at the University of Chicago (producer and distributor).

CHAPTER 4

How to Explain Poverty?

Ann R. Tickamyer and Emily J. Wornell

INTRODUCTION

Statement 1: *Poverty is caused by bad decisions made by people who are unable to contain their desires, plan for the future, or apply themselves to tasks that may not have short-term gain but ultimately will enhance their future fortunes.*

Statement 2: *Poverty is caused by the operation of large-scale structural factors and social forces such as the state of the economy, gender and racial discrimination, and the distribution of power and resources beyond any individual's control.*

These statements represents caricatures of two different approaches to explaining the existence and persistence of poverty that afflicts an otherwise affluent society. At one extreme is an individual-level explanation that sees people as the agents of their fates and poverty as the result of their bad decisions and behavior. At the other extreme is a structural perspective in which people are pawns in social arrangements that precede their existence and over which they have very little influence or control. Although these are exaggerated expressions of different approaches—one emphasizing human agency, the other, social structure—they loosely correspond to both popular and expert theories used to understand poverty and influence policy to address it.

Poverty is a complex social phenomenon made more complicated by political, social, and religious values and beliefs about personal responsibility and the effect of social structures that lie behind the agency–structure dichotomy. Multiple theories that roughly correspond to these perspectives have been proposed to explain why poverty exists, who is most likely to experience it, and how to best address it.

In this chapter, the common theories are grouped into three categories, and the strengths and weaknesses of each approach and how it relates specifically to rural poverty are discussed. The chapter starts with a discussion of the important distinction between the poverty of place and the poverty of people, what these terms mean, and the factors associated with both. Then three categories of poverty theory are examined. The first category emphasizes individual explanations. These theories—human capital, status attainment, and the culture of poverty—are largely based on neoclassical economics and rational choice theories and view personal strengths and failings as the primary driver for economic success or poverty. The second category—structural and spatial theories—understands the primary explanation of poverty to lie in unequal social and economic systems, which make success easier for some and poverty more likely for others, regardless of their personal characteristics. The final group of theories endeavors to merge people and place and individual and structural explanations for poverty. Examples of theories in this group are intersectionality, social exclusion and isolation, and forms of capital.

PEOPLE OR PLACE?

The distinction made between individual and structural theories is mirrored by a distinction between poverty of people (based on individual characteristics) and poverty of place (based on spatial factors such as unique characteristics of regions). Thus, poverty may be explained at an individual level of analysis or at the level of aggregate and collective units. Examples of individual characteristics and explanations include demographic and social characteristics such as gender, race, ethnicity, class, and marital and family status. Spatial factors include types of places such as remote rural regions, large urban areas, deindustrialized regions, persistent poverty counties, and so forth. These different spatial units typically indicate differences in scale. Poverty theories and explanations, like many other social issues, are multidimensional, multilevel, and multiscalar.

Although sometimes presented as alternatives, these different approaches and forms of analysis are not necessarily mutually exclusive; rather, they reflect a particular perspective of interest and may be layered on each other simultaneously.

It is important not to confuse descriptive and correlational explanations with causal theories. Although individual theories of poverty may imply or mask deeper explanations of processes that associate specific factors with poverty, typically they are descriptive and correlational rather than causal. Knowing that women, racial and ethnic minorities, single household heads, and children are overrepresented in poverty populations may be transposed into a "theory" that claims that a status or circumstance, such as female single parenthood, is a causal factor in poverty. Certainly there is an empirical association, and the odds of being poor are high for people in such households, but an explanation of *why* this is true requires more than a superficial identification of individual level descriptors commonly associated with poverty. Examples of theories that seek deeper causal explanations for these empirical associations include human capital, the culture of poverty, and the persistence of patriarchy.

A more robust example of poverty theory can be found at a structural level using spatial units—such as countries, regions, states, counties, or communities—to link deindustrialization to the high poverty rates found in many rural regions. The loss of industry creates higher unemployment, higher unemployment results in loss of income, and, consequently, higher poverty rates. Here unemployment is a proximate factor, or the most immediate influence, and the loss of industry reflects deeper underlying structural changes in the economy prompted by domestic policies and global trends. Without a fully developed explanation that explicitly links these changes and trends to poverty, it remains questionable whether they are *causes* of poverty or merely correlated with it. Theories that elaborate these relationships, such as the rise of neoliberalism and the spread of global capitalism, however, have been used to provide a deeper explanation.

These examples illustrate the complexity and multidimensionality of even a seemingly straightforward social fact such as poverty. A focus on *rural* poverty further complicates matters. With individual explanations, one has to ask whether these factors differ in rural places or if they are the same regardless of location. Although place-based explanations of poverty clearly specify a spatial dimension, they must concern themselves with questions of similarity between rural and urban locations as well,[1] and whether the factors associated with poverty have the same effect in both. All social life occurs in time and space, and social processes—including poverty—are in flux and vary spatially and temporally. Theories that explicitly recognize these dimensions and the great diversity that exists across time and space are more robust and compelling.

INDIVIDUAL EXPLANATIONS

Standard explanations for rural poverty that focus on poverty of people and the individual level of analysis rely heavily on neoclassical economics and rational choice theories (Lobao, Hooks, and Tickamyer 2008; Tickamyer 2006). There are several variations, often combining elements from human capital, status attainment, and culture of poverty theories. The basic thesis of these theories is that people with lower levels of human capital—defined as education, training, and experience—are less likely to prosper in an advanced, technologically sophisticated society with a complex division of labor that rewards high skills and leaves those who lack them unable to compete in the labor market. These theories assert that investment in education and skills development will enhance attainments in a meritocratic society and, ultimately, reduce vulnerability to poverty, thus representing an informed or rational choice for behavior and action that increases human capital. Conversely, the lack of human capital creates greater economic vulnerability and risk of poverty.

Note that there is nothing specifically rural about this formulation. These theories apply to everyone, regardless of location. Empirical research is needed to specify whether the process works the same in rural and urban areas. Empirical research shows that there are lower returns for education in rural areas in the United States (Economic Research Service 2016). A number of explanations may play into this finding: rural schools may not be as good as urban educational institutions; there may be fewer opportunities for good jobs available to highly educated individuals in rural areas; or rural residents may have lower aspirations than their urban counterparts. There is some research to support each of these explanations, suggesting a need to focus on what is specific to rural areas to understand why education does not have the same payoff for rural residents.

Human capital and status attainment theories focus on the individual's ability to trade personal characteristics valued by society and the labor market into achievements that produce a satisfactory to affluent livelihood and lifestyle. A number of assumptions are built into these formulations, including the idea that meritocratic principles determine outcomes such as jobs and income; that individuals have agency, meaning they are free to make meaningful choices in whether to invest in their future or not; that people behave rationally to promote their self-interest; that a sorting process matches skills and labor market needs; and that people are mobile and can pursue opportunities and make these choices. Reality does not always match the theory. If rural schools cannot deliver the same quality of education as urban schools, for example, then individuals who attend schools that are not up to the highest standards will have fewer opportunities and perhaps lower aspirations.[2] Similarly, there are many reasons individuals are tied to place and lack the mobility necessary for advancement. There are numerous other restrictions on individual agency, some that require more exploration than there is space for here. The important point is that people live in places, and spatial constraints will influence outcomes regardless of individual actions or intentions. One variant on individual-level approaches to explaining poverty is a theory called the culture of poverty. This theory most closely aligns with statement number one from the beginning of the chapter. It has a long history of application in various contexts and an equally long history of distorted versions that bear little resemblance to the original theory developed by anthropologist Oscar Lewis (1959). The culture of poverty was originally developed to describe the difficulties of escaping generational poverty, but it was quickly reformulated and is more commonly used to blame poor people for their circumstances (Katz 1989). The extreme version of this perspective asserts that people who are too lazy, immature, or otherwise flawed will fail to invest in their futures and ultimately develop a culture of dependency on public assistance and other sources of aid. Once this dependency has developed, people will then operate in ways that run counter to the norms, values, and approved lifestyles of the larger society. These factors may include a lack of work ethic, sexual promiscuity and out of wedlock births, marital instability, family disorganization, substance abuse, and other forms of deviance or even criminality. The theory posits that these actions and lifestyles become self-perpetuating traits of a (sub)culture[3] of poverty that is then transmitted to future generations.

Embedded in the culture of poverty theory are many negative caricatures about poor people, some of which arise from the kinds of individual-level correlations previously described, such as the greater vulnerability of female single-parent households to poverty. Other caricatures are associated with popular views that the middle-class morality prevalent during the twentieth century is "proper" and "desirable" and that "nontraditional" family forms and other practices are deviant. Finally, there is a great deal of latent and overt racism and racial stereotyping in this depiction of poverty. The myth of the welfare queen is a thinly veiled racial slur used to brand single African American women as welfare cheats who game the system for benefits they haven't earned.

Although diminishing, these attitudes and stereotypes are still present in many segments of society and often drive public opinion and policy. For example, the Personal Responsibility and Work Opportunity Reconciliation Act (PRWORA)—more commonly known as Welfare Reform and adopted in the 1990s—was premised on a view of poverty that assumed safety net programs such as Aid to Families with Dependent Children (AFDC, now Temporary Assistance to Needy Families [TANF]) and Medicaid created the kinds of dependency depicted in the culture of poverty. Proponents of PRWORA argued that these safety net programs not only failed to assist the poor but victimized poor people by fostering a culture of dependence on the government that entrapped them in a vicious cycle of poverty that was difficult, if not impossible, to exit. In other words, in the view of the policy makers who adopted this legislation with much popular support, the programs designed to assist the poor perpetuate their poverty (Handler 1995; Schram 1995; Tickamyer et al. 2000).

There is, however, little evidence to support the culture of poverty theory in its popular distorted version, and there is much to refute it (Rank 2004). Furthermore, nothing in this theory suggests that poverty might vary spatially, thus it offers nothing to explain or differentiate rural poverty. In fact, there is a peculiar relationship between culture of poverty perspectives and rural poverty. The demographic and social characteristics of the rural poor are at odds with some of the most pernicious assumptions of this perspective. Historically, the rural poor are overrepresented in demographic groups that receive less disapproval and prejudice; that is, they are more likely to be white, married, and employed. Thus, they are more likely to be seen as the virtuous poor—or to be poor for reasons apart from their behavior—and to have moral capital (Sherman 2009b) even if they lack other resources. As members of the "working poor," many rural people are exempted from the negative stereotypes promulgated by culture of poverty formulations. At the same time, the existence of ethnic and racial minority poor populations located in impoverished rural places such as the Mississippi Delta, Southwest Borderlands, and on Native American reservations are either ignored or subjected to the negative stereotyping found in the culture of poverty theory. Perhaps the most contradictory example is found in discussions of Appalachian poverty. In some quarters, "hillbilly" and "white trash" are pejorative terms applied to poor Appalachians that epitomize the culture of poverty (Billings and Tickamyer 1993; Wray 2006). At the same time, because they are *white* rural poor, they are more likely to be perceived as unfortunate but not immoral. The result is an uneasy existence in a contradictory location between stigma and virtue (Henderson and Tickamyer 2009).

STRUCTURAL AND SPATIAL EXPLANATIONS

The limitations of individual explanations have made structural perspectives more attractive. Structural theories focus on how social structure, societal institutions, and spatial arrangements determine an individual's place in society. Although there are a large number of theories and perspectives, they share the understanding that human society consists of structures and processes that are more than the sum of the individual members, that outlast individual existence, and, to a large extent, that shape and constrain individual opportunity, beliefs, behavior, and outcomes. Theories of inequality and systems of stratification, including social class, race, and gender, and numerous theories of social and economic development, describe the ways that poverty is the result of systemic processes and arrangements that perpetuate disadvantage for some while simultaneously enriching others. They demonstrate how poverty, including rural poverty, is the outcome of these processes in action. Structural theories operate at different levels and units of analysis with explanations that apply to different social and demographic groups and spatial units at different levels of aggregation.

Structural approaches also receive their share of criticism. They are viewed with some suspicion for being too deterministic—for painting a picture of human existence that can appear to ignore human agency and individual volition. Although this can be a legitimate criticism, it is important to recognize that structural constraints are not an "iron cage," to echo Max Weber (1930), but rather reflect patterns maintained over time that both influence and shape individual and collective action.

Structural explanations apply to both poverty of people and poverty of place. At a structural level, poverty of people once again focuses on individual sociodemographic characteristics, but views them as part of systems of social stratification and social location. Race, gender, and class are individual attributes that are relevant to poverty because they identify systems of structured social inequality such as institutional racism, gender discrimination, patriarchy, and a number of other structures of domination and subordination determined by economic position that have been identified by Marxist and critical theories. Human capital may reflect individual decisions, but it ultimately rests on opportunity structures determined by stratification systems, which vary by location. To be relevant for explaining rural poverty, it is important to ask how these apply to rural residents and how rural and urban regions compare.

Structural explanations for poverty of place start with place-based units, such as states or counties. Rates of poverty are determined for populations located in these place-based units and are measured in the aggregate, which enables analysis to focus on larger scale processes for explanation. As the deindustrialization and unemployment example from the beginning of the chapter demonstrates, poverty rates can be "explained" by the operation of the larger economy, but a deeper understanding requires asking how economic change affects different locations differently.

Given this array of perspectives, groups of theories used to explain rural poverty can be identified. Economic development theories look at economic factors and systems, applied to both the local and the world economy, and range from modernization to internal colonialism, dependency theories, economic restructuring, globalization, and neoliberalism. All economic development theories of rural poverty were adapted from explanations of rural poverty in developing nations and applied to rural regions of the United States.

Other theories identify other forms of structural inequalities, including legacies of slavery, colonialism, institutional racism, patriarchy, and gender discrimination. Although different theories sometimes present opposing explanations for rural poverty, more typically they complement and reinforce each other or apply to specific places and populations. Many of these ideas are discussed in greater depth in subsequent chapters. An overview is provided here of how the structures that these theories describe create and sustain rural poverty.

ECONOMIC DEVELOPMENT

A popular characterization of rural poverty is that it is a consequence of people and places not benefiting from or embracing the progress of the modern world and ultimately being "left behind" (Breathitt 1967). According to modernization theory, which is heavily influenced by neoclassical economics and promulgates a widely held view of poverty in developing nations, when the rest of the country was modernizing, industrializing, and urbanizing, rural America never got off the ground. During the economic and technological revolutions of the nineteenth and twentieth centuries, rural America remained locked in a preindustrial mode of existence. In the original cross-national analysis of developing nations, the failure of poor nations to "take off" was viewed as the result of embracing traditional values and practices that prevented the adoption of economic policies, technologies, and governance structures that could guide economic and social development through a linear set of stages modeled after the United States and western Europe (Rostow 1960). Within the United States, Appalachia, "a strange land and peculiar people" (Shapiro 1966), was the poster child for this perspective (Billings and Blee 2000; Billings and Tickamyer 1993). The combined isolation and poverty of Appalachia created images of deprivation that provided much of the impetus for the 1960s War on Poverty (Tickamyer and Duncan 1990).

Rural areas in Appalachia and other regions in the United States had (and have) a disproportionate share of poverty, but it is not because of a failure to industrialize. Although the slow acquisition of infrastructure for industrial development (highways, electrification, cable, and broadband access) may retard rural economic growth, many high and persistent poverty areas are well integrated into national and even world economic systems. Appalachia, for example, has been a source of natural resources fueling the industrial economy dating back to salt extraction in colonial times, through the growth and decline of the timber industry, and the evolution of coal production from underground mining to current technologically advanced extraction processes (Billings and Blee 2000; Tickamyer and Patel-Campillo 2016). Shale gas extraction via hydraulic fracturing ("fracking") is the latest source of energy for the global economy to be produced from this and other rural regions. Similarly, the rise of corporate and industrial-scale agriculture is the norm throughout the United States, replacing the family farms dominant in preindustrial times. During the 1960s, 1970s, and 1980s, many branch manufacturing plants relocated to rural areas and provided industrial-style factory jobs—until they left to find cheaper labor overseas (Falk and Lyson 1988). As the United States has become a postindustrial, high-tech, and service economy, the places that show the most economic growth and poverty reduction are now the so-called amenity locations (places dominated by retirement and recreational industries because of their natural beauty or other environmental attractions), which have the least industrial style development.

If backwardness and lack of industrial development are not the cause of rural poverty, what is? Some Marxist, neo-Marxist, and critical theories apply variations of class analyses to argue that poverty is the outcome of power relations, exploitation, domination, and subordination pervasive to capitalism in which powerful upper-class and corporate elites exploit the labor and natural resources of rural people and places. Among the many variants of this perspective are internal colonialism, world systems theory, dependency theories, and related theories of uneven development, which view poverty as the outcome of asymmetric power relations between capital and labor, often with state collaboration or collusion. There are numerous variations on these theories, but they are all distinguished by focusing on the "development of underdevelopment" (Frank 1989) in rural economic outcomes.

A prime example of this approach is internal colonialism, which is used to explain the impoverishment of resource-rich but persistently poor rural regions. Similar to modernization theory, internal colonialism is patterned after theories originally formulated for the international arena. It hypothesizes that wealthy and powerful external elites and captains of industry gain control of the land and labor of places that are rich in natural resources and extract the wealth to enrich themselves, drawing it away from its source, and ultimately impoverishing both the people and the place. This model has been criticized for ignoring the fact that exploitation and resource extraction have often been at the hands of internal elites from the impoverished region rather than being perpetrated by external power holders (Billings and Blee 2000; Duncan 2014).

Destructive colonial exploitation certainly has played an important role in U.S. economic development, as witnessed by the persistent poverty of many rural regions whose histories include land grabs from native populations, slavery, violent repression, and a variety of discriminatory practices (Rural Sociological Society Task Force 1993). Thus, the Mississippi Delta, the southern Black Belt, and the internal colonies of the Southwest and Native American reservations provide evidence of colonial and neo-colonial power relations that have helped impoverish these regions and their inhabitants. By itself, however, internal colonialism fails as a comprehensive theory of poverty of place.

Numerous related class-based approaches acknowledge the importance of local elites as well as the state in creating areas of persistent poverty. Apart from recognition of class dynamics and power relations, a basic contribution of these approaches is the acknowledgment that many remote and persistently poor places are not places left behind by the modern world. Rather, they are poor precisely because they are part of the world capitalist system, integrated into asymmetrical economic relations and hierarchies, often on a global scale. The complexity and interconnectedness of the world economy can have profound effects on even the most isolated rural regions, especially if their economies are resource dependent and lack diversity. The specific path to poverty, however, will vary from place to place and region to region.

The lack of economic diversity of many resource-rich but persistently poor rural places is closely linked to their economic woes. Sometimes called the resource curse, primary dependence on a natural resource that can be depleted or lose its market advantage without other opportunities for economic growth and employment is linked to poor economic performance and poverty. This is particularly true if this dependency comes with heavy environmental costs, such as in mining and timber industries. Here, too, the original thesis was applied to nation states and world regions, but it has been adapted with varying results to U.S. rural regions (Betz et al. 2015; Partridge, Betz, and Lobao 2013).

Some rural places have a long history of poverty, and many others have suffered from more recent events and large-scale change. Economic restructuring and globalization gained momentum during the last third of the twentieth century and culminated in 2008 with the start of the Great Recession. Both long-term trends and shorter-term disruptions have been particularly hard on small, rural communities dependent on a single or dominant industry as their primary employer. The loss of a particular industry or firm may devastate the local labor market, whether prompted by new technologies that make old processes obsolete or industrial relocation to seek cheaper labor. The loss creates both direct economic hardship from unemployment and indirect economic hardship throughout the economy when fewer jobs means less money to spend in local businesses.

Many previously prosperous rural regions throughout the country, in both natural resource (agriculture, mining, timber, and fisheries) and manufacturing-based economies, have faced serious hardship during this economic transition. Economic cycles and processes formerly regionally and nationally constrained are increasingly subject to the world economy. Globalization moves many industries and jobs overseas as competition for cheap labor, lower taxes, less state regulation, offers of subsidies and incentives, and lower costs of production make domestic U.S. production less competitive in world markets. Further, the rise of neoliberal policies globally and nationally that push for deregulation and the reduction or elimination of barriers to trade and labor protections exacerbates these trends (Falk and Lobao 2003; Jensen and Jensen 2011; Lichter and Graefe 2011; Lobao, Adua, and Hooks 2014; Sherman 2014).

The growth of service sector jobs in some rural areas has provided new employment opportunities, but these jobs tend to be unstable and poorly paid, with few or no benefits. Good jobs in high-end services, such as those found in financial and high-tech industries, are unlikely to locate in rural communities where the necessary markets, financial and human capital, and infrastructure needs are lacking (Falk, Schulman, and Tickamyer 2003). Often the best hope for rural communities is the entry of a mass retail company such as Walmart, which residents typically welcome for its cheap goods and promise of jobs. The irony is that these stores manufacture the goods overseas, presumably replacing domestic sources and the jobs they supported, and the newly created jobs often do not supply a living wage (Irwin and Clark 2006).[4]

These economic explanations frame rural poverty as a source, outcome, and type of spatial inequality (Lobao, Hooks, and Tickamyer 2007). Thus, geography is a determinant of stratification systems and processes that allocate scarce societal resources and simultaneously is constructed by these processes. Rural poverty is a state or condition of places with certain characteristics and the outcome of larger forces such as the economic dynamics previously described. Economics plays a major role in understanding both spatial inequality in general and poverty more specifically, but it is not the only source of poverty. Other explanations are found in the institutions and organizations of rural communities, and the same reciprocal relationships hold—poverty impoverishes the institutions and organizations that in theory can help break cycles of poverty, thus reinforcing the difficulty of overcoming disadvantage. For example, schools in rural areas often cannot support the facilities or caliber of instruction of their urban counterparts, which in turn creates a poorer educational experience for rural children and reinforces the likelihood that future generations will not escape poverty (see chapter 12 for more detail). The schools, churches, public facilities, and civic groups found in rural areas may contribute to the poverty of place, and in turn are themselves weakened by the poverty they generate (Duncan 2014). The absence or poor quality of public services and the inadequacies of the safety net further reinforce poverty in many rural places (Smith and Tickamyer 2011).

SYSTEMS OF STRATIFICATION AND INEQUALITIES

Other systems of stratification are important structural sources of rural poverty. Especially prominent are those based on individual characteristics such as gender, sexuality, race, ethnicity, and age. These factors function as basic demographic characteristics of individuals while simultaneously representing social locations that determine an individual's position in stratification hierarchies that create and maintain inequalities. Here, too, it is important to identify the processes that take place in society generally, as well as those having specific dynamics that are more prevalent in rural America.

GENDER AND SEXUALITY

Feminist-inspired theories of gender inequality and patriarchy explain why women are overrepresented in poverty populations and the disadvantages women face in trying to escape poverty. Much of the story is well known. Unlike many other parts of the world, women in the United States are no longer under the legal control of men (fathers and husbands), but historical subjugation diminishes slowly, and contemporary forms of discrimination and disadvantage are still widespread. On average, women's wages still do not equal men's, and women are more likely to be employed in lower paying service sector jobs. Moreover, women still shoulder more than their share of "reproductive labor," unpaid care work and maintenance of the household and its members, even in the face of the expectation that they be full-time wage earners.

Women have made gains in some areas, and their disadvantage has been reversed in others. For example, women have increasingly higher educational attainments than men. The expected payoff for this educational attainment, however, has not kept up, and women are still underrepresented in many of the top paying and most powerful jobs and industries, most notably in executive offices, high technology industries, and politics (AAUW 2016; Council of Economic Advisors 2015). Although many gender-based disparities are diminishing, they are doing so at a disturbingly slow pace that retards progress toward equality and increases women's vulnerability to poverty. Single mothers are especially vulnerable to these trends, and it is no accident that these women and their children make up the largest shares of poor and at-risk populations (see chapter 5 for detailed information).

In rural areas, the effects of these trends are magnified because there are fewer opportunities for good employment for both women and men. The effects of economic restructuring and the changing social safety net are perhaps most evident in the economic well-being of women in rural areas. The era of economic restructuring was also marked by changing gender norms around family and work, changing family structure, and a shift away from jobs in traditionally male-dominated sectors such as agriculture, manufacturing, and natural resource extraction and toward service sector employment. All of these trends affect the distinctly gender-based poverty outcomes of women (Jensen and Jensen 2011; Sherman 2009a).

Women newly entering the workforce fill most of the positions created by the shift to the service sector (Struthers 2014). Unlike the relatively steady and full-time jobs of traditional rural industries, however, service sector work is largely characterized by low pay, part-time hours, no benefits, and general instability. High male unemployment in rural areas, coupled with a changing family structure that mirrors changes seen in urban areas—namely, higher rates of female-headed households and single-parenthood—means that rural families increasingly rely on the income of women as their primary, if not only, source of income (Sherman 2009a; Struthers 2014). When women's income comes from these unstable, low-paying, service sector jobs, the economic well-being of both women and their families suffers, and women must often take on multiple low-paying jobs or informal work to make ends meet (Struthers 2014; Tickamyer and Wood 2003). This confluence of factors in some ways forced the progression of changing gender norms that was already under way. Increasing numbers of women were entering the formal, rural workforce in the 1970s, but this trend intensified through the 1980s and 1990s in response to the Great Recession as male unemployment in rural areas steadily increased (Smith 2011; Struthers 2014).

Although women's paid work was increasing, their unpaid work at home largely stayed the same (Tickamyer and Wood 2003). Women's "second shift"—unpaid care and housework—stems from traditional notions about the role of women and men in the household and how those roles are valued in society (Hochschild 2003). Although women's formal incomes are increasingly important in rural households, help in the home may not be forthcoming, leaving women with less time for alternative economic activities (informal or self-employment) and political and community participation (Sachs 2014).

Changes to the social safety net at this time did not take into consideration the changing economic realities of rural communities. Although some research shows that the welfare-to-work system has increased the paid work of single mothers and decreased their reliance on welfare generally (Lichter and Graefe 2011), the result was not a reduction in poverty for these women, particularly in rural areas (Lichter and Jensen 2001).

The lack of well-paying, full-time employment in rural communities now has to be balanced with the new lifetime limits imposed on TANF recipients. The lack of transportation, child care options, and even grocery stores in rural areas further exacerbates women's difficulty in overcoming poverty under PRWORA. The result is to force women to "alternate between the subpoverty wages of the female labor market and the subpoverty benefits of the female welfare system" (Rural Sociological Society Task Force 1993). Even if the restructured welfare system introduced by PRWORA has reduced single mothers' reliance on welfare, it has created new hardships for rural women and their families (Tickamyer et al. 2000; Tickamyer and Henderson 2011). Chapters 5 and 8 elaborate many of these processes.

The research on lesbian, gay, bisexual, transgender, and questioning (LGBTQ) people in rural communities is somewhat limited,[5] as is the connection between LGBTQ identity and poverty more generally. New research has shown that LGBTQ adults have higher rates of poverty and food insecurity than their heterosexual counterparts (Gates 2014; Badgett, Durso, and Schneebaum 2013). Research has also shown that lesbian couples residing in rural areas are significantly more likely to be poor than their urban counterparts and that gay men are less likely to be poor if they live in large metropolitan centers than in other areas of the country (Badgett et al. 2013). What is less clear, however, is whether this correlation is a function of place, of social position, or both. The high poverty rate of rural lesbian couples, for example, may be a function of their position as women in rural places rather than as a same-sex couple. In 2010, the rural poverty rate of lesbian couples was 14.4 percent, whereas the general women's poverty rate in the same year was 18 percent (Badgett et al. 2013; Housing Assistance Council 2012). Assuming that sexual identity plays some role in the poverty status of homosexuals in rural communities, the connection likely lies in traditional notions of family values that stigmatize homosexuality, a lack of anonymity, and informal community sanctions against individuals who resist dominant cultural mores and gender norms (Sherman 2009a; Preston and D'Augelli 2013; Sachs 2014; Stein 2001).

RACE AND ETHNIC MINORITIES

The reality of minority poverty in rural areas is stark. Minorities in rural areas have higher rates of poverty than their urban counterparts as well as greater poverty than their non-Hispanic white neighbors (Brown and

Schafft 2011). Race and ethnicity serve as markers of group identities, which are associated with a social status that determines the benefits and privileges for members of that group (Green 2014). Because these hierarchies are relational, the lower status of some groups serves to *benefit* groups higher in the social hierarchy. Minority groups have always been given positions of low status in American society, and some have been more marginalized than others. The marginalization of African Americans, Native Americans,[6] and Hispanic and Latino immigrants, as seen through historical legacies of discrimination and racism, have led to lower educational attainment, poor economic outcomes, and social exclusion of these groups.

Institutional racism built into societal institutions is a major source of rural poverty for minority groups in various rural regions. The legacies of slavery, the plantation economy, sharecropping, and Jim Crow political oppression and disenfranchisement are responsible for the concentration of persistent poverty among African Americans in the Mississippi Delta and the southern Black Belt. Extreme forms of discrimination pervaded virtually all public and private institutions from schools to the criminal justice system. Indian reservations of the West and the Southwest started as concentration camps and currently make up vast rural ghettos with few economic opportunities and massive social problems associated with poverty. Diverse groups of Hispanics, including both native-born people and migrants, often endure economic hardship resulting from a variety of sources, including the historic appropriation of communal lands similar to that of Native Americans and the more recent rise of poor rural colonias, another form of rural ghetto lacking basic services. Additionally, labor practices in agricultural and food processing industries that rely heavily on a Latino labor force pay poorly and lack protections, particularly for migrant workers both documented and undocumented. Chapters 6 and 7 elaborate on these relationships, but brief overviews of diverse population groups are included here.

AFRICAN AMERICANS

The vast majority of African Americans can trace their ancestry to slavery (Green 2014). From the outset, African Americans have experienced extreme violence, exploitation, and social, political, and economic exclusion. The unequal power dynamic between African Americans and the white majority established during slavery has been replicated throughout American history and still exists today. Sharecropping, Jim Crow laws, disenfranchisement, segregated schools, illegal denial of land ownership and denial of access to credit and capital, uneven or nonexistent development in predominantly African American communities, unequally distributed punishments that imprison African American men at extreme rates, and the lack of response to environmental hazards and natural disasters have all functioned to keep African Americans in a socially, politically, and economically subjugated position (Brown and Schafft 2011; Green 2014). The outcome of systemic discrimination and exclusion is most evident in a region of the rural South called the Black Belt where high African American poverty rates have persisted for generations (Harris and Worthen 2003; Brown and Schafft 2011). This institutionalized discrimination "impedes access to labor markets" and directly limits economic opportunity and well-being (Rural Sociological Society Task Force 1993, 180–181). Individual racism and discrimination on the part of employers further limits the types and quality of jobs available to African Americans in the rural South. This division of labor has restricted African American labor to low-wage, low-skill, and low-prestige jobs with little opportunity for advancement or economic stability (Brown and Schafft 2011).

HISPANICS AND LATINO IMMIGRANTS

The U.S. relationship with Latino immigrants is a contentious one, alternating between need and suspicion. As the longest and largest immigration flow into the United States, immigration from Central and South America has been fundamental to the economic success of several industries and regions in the United States (Durand, Massey, and Capoferro 2005; Zúñiga and Hernández-León 2005). Encouraged by federal and state governments to work in the agricultural and manufacturing sectors, Latino immigrants occupy jobs in the "second tier" economy, which is characterized by seasonal, low-wage, and low-prestige employment (Portes and Sensenbrenner 1993). Wages and employment conditions are dictated by large agro-business and manufacturing firms, which make large profits off the poorly paid labor of migrants. Latino immigrants—in the country legally or not—have little recourse for unfair and inhumane working conditions and compensation. Latino immigrants and native-born Hispanics alike also experience regular discrimination that limits educational attainment, political participation, housing equity, and health care access (Light 2006; Holmes 2013). Moreover, economic restructuring and discriminatory policies in states where Latino immigrants have traditionally settled have begun to shift immigration into new states and communities—many of them rural—that may have had little or no experience with immigration in the past (Durand et al. 2005; Zúñiga and Hernández-León 2005; Massey 2008; Parrado and Kandel 2008). In these "new destinations," immigrants often find themselves in communities with few and difficult-to-access resources, school systems with little ability to support and teach English-language learners, and neighbors already concerned with limited economic opportunities in their communities. All of these factors create additional barriers for Latinos in rural America, immigrants and nonimmigrants alike, which is reflected in their high rural poverty rate.

NATIVE AMERICANS

Discussing Native Americans as a single, unified group is misleading. With more than 550 federally recognized tribal governments and communities, all with different histories, distinct cultural traditions, and varied spatial locations, "Native Americans" as a group identifier is largely one of convenience rather than substance, and it remains a controversial term (Dewees 2014). Regardless of their distinct identities and tribal differences, however, Native Americans do share some important historical and social experiences that have had a direct and significant effect on their social location and economic well-being. As colonized people, Native Americans have experienced centuries of state-endorsed violence and marginalization. Although individual tribes have had treaties with both the pre-Revolutionary War government and the post-Revolution United States, they have endured near extermination; forced removal from their land; the forced removal of their children; subpar access to social welfare, education, and health services; and a corrupt and mismanaged federal bureau that historically failed to ensure their interests and rights (Rural Sociological Society Task Force 1993; Dewees 2014).

Today many Native Americans live on or near the more than 300 federally recognized reservations, many of which are not near their traditional spaces and occupy remote rural and unproductive land (Dewees 2014). When originally established, however, these "trusts" constituted near concentration camp conditions in which Native Americans had little authority or power and had to rely almost entirely on rations from the military (Rural Sociological Society Task Force 1993). Today tribes have more authority over their internal and administrative affairs on reservations, but these "domestic dependent nations" are still reliant on the federal government for many social services, which tend to be underfunded and difficult to access (Dewees 2014). As a result of generations of violent colonialism and poorly funded services, reservations often lack basic infrastructure, and Native Americans generally have low educational attainment, poor health outcomes, shorter life expectancies, and high poverty rates.

CHILDREN

Although children do not necessarily experience the same racial and ethnic discrimination faced by minorities in rural America based on their age alone, they continue to have disproportionately high rates of poverty in general, and in rural areas specifically. It should be noted, of course, that poor children overwhelmingly come from poor families, and the high rural child poverty rate is directly related to elevated rates of poverty in rural communities more generally (Lichter and Graefe 2011). Childhood poverty is often considered a separate issue for several reasons. First, the lifelong effects of poverty during childhood are well documented and numerous. These effects include slower cognitive development, mental health challenges, poor health outcomes, higher obesity rates, poor school performance, and lower educational attainment (Iceland 2013; O'Hare 2009; Singh et al. 2010; Lichter and Graefe 2011; McLaughlin and Shoff 2014). Second, childhood poverty is a major concern for scholars and policy makers: poor children often grow up to be poor adults (O'Hare 2009; Sherman 2014). This connection is heightened in rural areas, where low educational attainment and poor health outcomes of poor children combine with very limited economic opportunities for adults, and where services to support poor families and children are more difficult to access (Iceland 2013; McLaughlin and Shoff 2014). In fact, the rurality of place is directly correlated with the rate of childhood poverty, and "poverty rates tend to be high in the most rural places" (McLaughlin and Shoff 2014, 367).

Family structure also has a significant and direct impact on childhood poverty (Snyder, McLaughlin, and Findeis 2006). Children in single-parent households are more likely to be poor than children in two-parent households, a fact that is intensified for children in single female-headed households (McLaughlin and Shoff 2014). It is in this statistic—that children in single female-headed households have significantly higher rates of poverty than in single male-headed households or two-parent households—that we begin to see the concept of intersectionality form.

THE INTERSECTION OF PEOPLE AND PLACES

Up to this point, individual and structural explanations, and poverty of people and poverty of place, have been treated as if they are completely separate, but in fact they are different perspectives on the same phenomenon and intersect in ways that are helpful for deepening our understanding of poverty. Several theories strive to elaborate this intersection and help advance the understanding of poverty and assist in balancing both agency and structure. These include theories of intersectionality, social exclusion, social isolation, social networks, and capital.

INTERSECTIONALITY

Various drivers make it more likely for certain groups in rural America to have higher rates of poverty than others, but it is equally important to recognize that one person can experience the marginalization of multiple group locations at the same time, all of which makes him or her more likely to be poor. But what does that mean for that individual? Consider the situation of an African American woman living in the rural southern Black Belt. People living in this region are more likely to be poor than people in most other places in the country, and the poverty they experience is typically deeper and longer lasting than in other regions. In addition, women are more likely to experience poverty than men, and African Americans have higher poverty rates than their non-Hispanic white neighbors. Because of an unequal and inequitable social structure that locates ruralness, femaleness, and blackness at or near the bottom of the hierarchy, this woman would experience the challenges and barriers of three separate social locations. This is the concept of intersectionality.

Perhaps the most important aspect of intersectionality is its compounding nature. Intersectionality theorists and scholars have posited that a person with multiple points of inequality and oppression will experience *more* marginalization than if he or she experienced any one of those locations individually (Crenshaw 1989; Dill and Zambrana 2009). This means that the level of marginalization a person experiences, and the related likelihood of experiencing poverty, do not depend on the social location of any one group. Rather, people with multiple points of marginalization inhabit a social location composed of that intersection, which is ultimately different from any of the individual components. "African American, female, in the rural South" is a social position that comes with more oppression and discrimination than that of a person in any one of those three categories alone (Crenshaw 1989). This person would be expected to experience more discrimination and oppression and more frequent and deeper poverty than would African American men, white women, or an African American woman in the urban Northeast.

This theory is borne out in the statistics throughout this book. Minority children, for example, are more likely to experience poverty than white children, and minority children living in rural areas are even more likely to experience poverty than minority children in urban areas. Nearly 46 percent of African American children in rural areas live in poverty (Brown and Schafft 2011). It is a similar situation for children living in same-sex households, who are particularly vulnerable to poverty, which is compounded yet again if those children have a minority status. African American children in same-sex households are more likely to be poor than children living in any other kind of household, with over 52 percent living in poverty (Badgett et al. 2013). Hard numbers on minority children living in same-sex households in rural communities are not available, but due to the social location of ruralness, one might hazard a guess that their poverty rates are even higher.

There are problems with intersectionality. For example, what happens with seemingly contradictory social locations (such as poor, rural, white, Appalachians)? Does one status dominate others, or do they mitigate each other? Another issue is how to test and measure this theory (Henderson and Tickamyer 2009). The value of intersectionality comes from explicitly linking the fortunes of individuals with the effects of complex social locations, thus emphasizing the interplay of multiple influences and forces.

SOCIAL EXCLUSION AND SOCIAL ISOLATION

As described in chapter 3, poverty in the United States is primarily viewed as a condition of absolute deprivation rather than a relational status. In other advanced industrial and postindustrial societies, especially in the European Union (EU), poverty is defined in relative terms that emphasize its relationship to inequality. The official U.S. government-determined poverty line defines who is poor by income below an absolute amount based on the cost of basic needs such as food and shelter,[7] whereas relational measures assess poverty relative to median income. In principle, these relative measures are set regardless of degree or amount of hardship experienced at or below either 50 or 60 percent of median income (Shucksmith 2016). The driving rationale is to define poverty as the inability to participate in the lifestyle or standard of living enjoyed by the majority of the population in a society. Poverty then becomes a form of inequality in a stratification system. Issues of inequality and relative position in class and status hierarchies lie behind many explanations for poverty, although these are less frequently stated explicitly in U.S. poverty research. In practice, there is probably less difference in who gets classified as poor using alternative measures, but there is a big difference in how poverty is conceptualized and explained. One of the biggest differences in the explanation of poverty can be seen in the application of theories of social exclusion.

Social exclusion has been used in multiple ways, shifting over time and varying by analysis. Shucksmith (2016) cites Burchardt, Le Grand, and Piachaud (2002) to locate its original use in France, where it referred to people not covered by the social insurance system. Later it came to refer to those who were unemployed or "excluded" from the labor market, especially as the result of the trends described previously: globalization, neoliberalism, and the world capitalist system. Other forms of exclusion have been defined, both theoretically and practically, to show that social exclusion has multiple dimensions. Thus, individuals and groups can experience exclusion in terms of education, housing, health care, political participation, and so forth, with poverty as the outcome of their inability to access these and other social goods (Shucksmith 2012, 2016). *Why* exclusion occurs, however, is not always obvious. Is it the result of underlying processes of class formation and reproduction? Other stratification hierarchies? Alternatively, do individuals exclude themselves from social interaction and institutions?

Its critics contend that social exclusion is primarily a different term for poverty, a way to diminish the importance of social class and theories of class stratification, and even a disguised version of the culture of poverty "blame the victim" discourse (Shucksmith 2012). According to its proponents, social exclusion's strengths are its multidimensionality, fluidity, emphasis on local context, and explicit connection to systems of inequality (Milbourne 2004; Reimer 2004; Shucksmith 2012). Shucksmith (2012) argues that social exclusion can be understood as the ability of individuals and groups to access valued social resources, whether a job, social insurance, voting rights, or social services. In doing so, he highlights parallels with a theory of social class and inequality based on Bourdieu's (1986) concept of symbolic capital.

The concept of social exclusion is strongly associated with relative measures and perspectives on poverty, but in many ways social exclusion theories share similarities with homegrown social isolation theories. Primarily associated with urban poverty studies, this explanation highlights the physical and social isolation of poor urban ghetto dwellers, typically African American and other racial and ethnic minorities, whose neighborhoods lack the resources, role models, and stability that create opportunity for avoiding or overcoming poverty (Wilson 1996, 2012). Parallels have been found in isolated, class polarized rural communities in the Mississippi Delta and rural Appalachia (Duncan 2014) and presumably exist in other locations that share the lack of jobs, services, and civic engagement that characterize the deprivations of social isolation. As is the case with social exclusion, forms of symbolic capital feature prominently in social isolation explanations for poverty, both rural and elsewhere.

FORMS OF CAPITAL

The roles of human and financial capital are standard categories of economic analysis that have obvious meaning for poverty studies, and there is substantial evidence that rural areas suffer deficits in both types of capital. Other forms of capital, lumped under the general term of *symbolic capital*, also should be considered when attempting to explain rural poverty (Bourdieu 1986). Symbolic capital includes nonmaterial types of resources accessed by individuals and groups and often is reflective of relationships between them. These include social, cultural, and moral capital (Sherman 2009b; and chapter 8 this volume). Social capital consists of social networks and connections that can be used or exchanged for other resources, such as friends and acquaintances supplying information about jobs or other opportunities. Cultural capital refers to the acquired tastes, beliefs, and values that reflect and determine one's place in society. It has echoes of the culture of poverty theory discussed earlier but avoids normative or value judgments. Do you prefer opera or country music? Sushi or burgers? Budweiser or craft beer? Although these examples appear trivial, they illustrate that cultural capital serves as a marker and maker of class position. Cultural capital has been compared to a toolkit, acquired through socialization and association, that determines opportunity and access to other resources (Swidler 1986; Duncan 2014). Moral capital is similar but reflects value judgments of worthiness within a particular context or social setting. Are you viewed as having a strong work ethic, devout religious adherence, or solid family values? Although these signs of virtue do not directly put food on the table, they can influence access to opportunities that may provide material support. Chapter 8 explores the relationship between forms of capital and rural poverty at length. The important point for understanding rural poverty is that all forms of capital serve as valued resources that influence poverty risk and the ability to overcome it within its context.

These capitals are associated with both individuals and groups, although they specifically mark social relationships. At least one form of social capital—social networks—also has been conceptualized collectively and spatially, most often at community and societal levels. The kinds of networks and connections found in a community can act either as stimulants or impediments to economic development, mobility, and poverty reduction. Social networks that are "horizontal" connect individuals across similar social strata and promote democratic participation conducive to economic growth and well-being, whereas "vertical" networks represent hierarchical connections that concentrate power at the top, are subject to corruption, and are obstacles to development (Putnam 2000; Duncan 2014). A slightly different conceptualization distinguishes between "bridging" and "bonding" social capital, with the former making connections across different groups—tying disparate parts of society together—and the latter reinforcing tight-knit bonds among people with similar characteristics—creating more homogeneous connections. The implication is that the broader links of bridging social capital promote democracy, participation, and economic development, whereas the latter are subject to fostering social exclusion (Putnam 2000). In both formulations, the types of networks that characterize a community or society are linked to its economic fortunes.

These ideas have been applied to understanding differential rates, effects, and outcomes of poverty in rural communities, and there is some support for associating horizontal and bridging social capital with better poverty outcomes. For example, qualitative research that compared three poor rural communities in different regions of the country, all with different demographic profiles and histories of social provision and class structures, found that the community most able to draw on broad horizontal networks and bridging social capital was also the community most able to assist people in poverty and enable them to overcome it (Duncan 2014).

CONCLUSION

Forms of capital, social exclusion, social isolation, and intersectionality can be coherently linked together to better understand poverty. They demonstrate the multidimensionality of the causes and consequences of poverty, the connections across different scales and levels of analysis, the benefit of thinking of poverty as a form of inequality and position in sets of hierarchies rather than a static condition, and the importance of access to resources whether at the individual, group, or spatial level. Most important, these theories bridge the micro–macro and individual–structural divides that characterize many other efforts to explain poverty. They demonstrate the value of avoiding dualistic, either-or arguments and instead seek ways to integrate the individual with the society and human agency with social structure.

Individual behavior and action is important and cannot be predicted in a deterministic way, but it is influenced by powerful economic and social forces that make some outcomes much more likely than others. Whether an individual, structural, or integrative model, our theories are used to discover trends and associations and to explain phenomena in the aggregate rather than the experiences of specific individuals. There always will be exceptions, sometimes many, but the key to understanding a social phenomenon such as poverty is found in the larger patterns. The complexity of all these systems and forces operating together make social life predictable but not inevitable.

Social scientists are often criticized for failing to have satisfactory and direct causal explanations for social phenomena, or for making everything too complicated by considering the effects of multiple variables and factors. Unlike in the physical sciences, it is difficult to run experiments on our research subjects—societies and human beings. We are unable to hold all of the possible factors that might influence an outcome constant while subjecting a person to an experimental treatment that will demonstrate causality. Some experiments are feasible, but the ones most likely to determine influence and causality typically are not. Certainly, rural poverty is one of those highly complex conditions that is influenced by several factors under innumerable contexts. In other words, it is complex.

This does not mean that it is not important to attempt to disentangle the complexities, particularly for policy purposes. Policy fails most spectacularly when the diagnosis of a social problem is oversimplified, without recognition of all the intricacies, multiple dimensions, contextual influences, and conditional relationships. Policy is supposed to provide the cure for a social ill or problem, but if the problem itself is not properly understood, it is unlikely to respond as predicted or desired. Understanding and explaining rural poverty in the United States requires a willingness to engage in the complexities of social life.

NOTES

1. How rurality is measured is a topic of much debate. Competing definitions and classifications are described in chapters 1 through 3.

2. Alternatively, the rural brain drain depletes rural communities of the most promising youth who are unlikely to find opportunities in impoverished places (Carr and Kefalas 2009; Sherman and Sage 2011; Petrin, Schafft, and Meece 2014).

3. Critics of the culture of poverty point out that it is more accurately described as a subculture existing within the larger culture and society, and one to which people from any socioeconomic background can belong.

4. Chapter 9 has more information on jobs and the rural economy.

5. The majority of LGBTQ research in rural America has focused on identity, religion, and culture. For more on these issues, see work by Emily Kazyak, Mary L. Grey, Arlene Stein, and Colin R. Johnson.

6. There is much debate regarding the use of the terms Native American and American Indian. Native American will be used to identify this group throughout this book.

7. The determination of the poverty line was originally devised in the 1960s to reflect the cost of a minimally nutritious diet and its relationship to other basic needs. How well it captures under- or overestimates of real poverty is quite controversial today. Review chapter 3 for the details of its source and adequacy.

REFERENCES

AAUW. 2016. "The Simple Truth About the Gender Pay Gap." http://www.aauw.org/files/2016/02/SimpleTruth_Spring2016.pdf.

Badgett, M. V. Lee, Laura E. Durso, and Alyssa Schneebaum. 2013. "New Patterns of Poverty in the Lesbian, Gay, and Bisexual Community." Report for the Williams Institute, UCLA School of Law. http://williamsinstitute.law.ucla.edu/wpcontent/uploads/LGB-Poverty-Update-Jun-2013.pdf.

Betz, Michael, Mark Partridge, Michael Ferran, and Linda Lobao. 2015. "Coal Mining, Economic Development, and the Natural Resources Curse." *Energy Economics* 50 (July):105–16.

Billings, Dwight B., and Kathleen M. Blee. 2000. *The Road to Poverty: The Making of Wealth and Hardship in Appalachia.* New York: Cambridge University Press.

Billings, Dwight, and Ann R. Tickamyer. 1993. "Uneven Development in Appalachia." In *Forgotten Places: Uneven Development in Rural America*, ed. Thomas A. Lyson and William W. Falk, 7–29. Lawrence: Kansas University Press.

Bourdieu, Pierre. 1986. "The Forms of Capital." In *Handbook of the Theory and Research for the Sociology of Education*, ed. John G. Richards, 241–58. New York: Greenwood Press.

Breathitt, Edward T. 1967. "The People Left Behind." Report by the President's National Advisory Commission on Rural Poverty. http://files.eric.ed.gov/fulltext/ED016543.pdf.

Brown, David L., and Kai A. Schafft. 2011. *Rural People and Communities in the 21st Century: Resilience and Transformation*. Malden, MA: Polity.

Burchardt, Tania, Julian Le Grand, and David Piachaud. 2002. "Introduction." In *Understanding Social Exclusion*, ed. John Hills, Julian Le Grand, and David Piachaud, 1–12. Oxford: Oxford University Press.

Carr, Patrick J., and Maria J. Kefalas. 2009. *Hollowing Out the Middle: The Rural Brain Drain and What It Means for America*. Boston: Beacon.

Council of Economic Advisors. 2015. "Gender Pay Gap: Recent Trends and Explanations." Issue Brief. https://www.whitehouse.gov/sites/default/files/docs/equal_pay_issue_brief_final.pdf.

Crenshaw, Kimberle. 1989. "Demarginalizing the Intersection of Race and Sex: A Black Feminist Critique of Antidiscrimination Doctrine, Feminist Theory and Antiracist Politics." *The University of Chicago Legal Forum* 140:139–67.

Dewees, Sarah. 2014. "Native Nations in a Changing Global Economy." In *Rural America in a Globalizing World: Problems and Prospects for the 2010s,* ed. Conner Baily, Leif Jensen, and Elizabeth Ransom, chap. 24. Morgantown: West Virginia University Press.

Dill, Bonnie Thornton, and Ruth Zambrana, eds. 2009. *Emerging Intersections*. New Brunswick, NJ: Rutgers University Press.

Duncan, Cynthia M. 2014. *World's Apart: Poverty and Politics in Rural America,* 2nd ed. New Haven, CT: Yale University Press.

Durand, Jorge, Douglas S. Massey, and Chiara Capoferro. 2005. "The New Geography of Mexican Immigration." In *New Destinations: Mexican Immigration in the United States*, ed. Victor Zúñiga and Ruben Hernández-León, 1–22. New York: Russell Sage Foundation.

Economic Research Service. 2016. "Rural Education." http://www.ers.usda.gov/topics/rural-economy-population/employment-education/rural-education.aspx.

Falk, William W., and Linda M. Lobao. 2003. "Who Benefits from Economic Restructuring? Lessons from the Past, Challenges for the Future." In *Challenges for Rural America in the Twenty-First Century*, ed. D. Brown and L. Swanson, 152–67. University Park: Pennsylvania State University Press.

Falk, William W., and Thomas A. Lyson. 1988. *High Tech, Low Tech, No Tech: Recent Industrial and Occupational Change in the South*. Albany, NY: State University of New York.

Falk, William W., Michael D. Schulman, and Ann R. Tickamyer. 2003. *Communities of Work: Rural Restructuring in Local and Global Contexts*. Athens: Ohio University Press.

Frank, Andre Gunder. 1989. "The Development of Underdevelopment." *Monthly Review* 41(2):27–37.

Gates, Gary J. 2014. "Food Insecurity and SNAP (Food Stamps) Participation in LGBT Communities." Report for the Williams Institute, UCLA School of Law. http://williamsinstitute.law.ucla.edu/wp-content/uploads/Food-Insecurity-in-LGBT-Communities.pdf.

Green, John J. 2014. "The Status of African Americans in the Rural United States." In *Rural American in a Globalizing World: Problems and Prospects for the 2010s,* ed. Conner Baily, Leif Jensen, and Elizabeth Ransom, chap. 22. Morgantown: West Virginia University Press.

Handler, Joel F. 1995. *The Poverty of Welfare Reform*. New Haven, CT: Yale University Press.

Harris, Rosalind P., and Dreamal Worthen. 2003. "African Americans in Rural America." In *Challenges for Rural America in the Twenty-First Century*, ed. David L. Brown and Louis E. Swanson, chap. 2. State College, PA: Pennsylvania State University Press.

Henderson, Debra, and Ann R. Tickamyer. 2009. "The Intersection of Poverty Discourses: Race, Class, Culture, and Gender." In *Emerging Intersections*, ed. Bonnie Thorton Dill and Ruth Enid Zambrana, 50–72. New Brunswick, NJ: Rutgers University Press.

Hochschild, Arlie, with Anne Machung. 2003 (original ed. 1987). *The Second Shift: Working Parents and the Revolution at Home*. New York: Viking Penguin.

Holmes, Seth. 2013. *Fresh Fruit, Broken Bodies: Migrant Farmworkers in the United States*. Berkeley: University of California Press.

Housing Assistance Council. 2012. "Poverty in Rural America: Rural Research Brief." http://www.ruralhome.org/storage/research_notes/ rrn_poverty.pdf.

Iccland, John. 2013. *Poverty in America: A Handbook,* 3rd ed. Berkeley: University of California Press.

Irwin, Elena G., and Jill Clark. 2006. "Wall Street vs. Main Street: What Are the Benefits and Costs of Wal-Mart to Local Communities?" *Choices* 21(2):117–22. http://www.choicesmagazine.org/2006-2/grabbag/2006-2-14.htm.

Jensen, Leif, and Eric B. Jensen. 2011. "Employment Hardship Among Rural Men." In *Economic Restructuring and Family Well-Being in Rural America*, ed. Kristin E. Smith and Ann R. Tickamyer, 40–59. State College, PA: Pennsylvania State University Press.

Katz, Michael. 1989. *The Undeserving Poor: From the War on Poverty to the War on Welfare*. New York: Pantheon.

Lewis, Oscar. 1959. *Five Families: Mexican Case Studies in the Culture of Poverty*. New York: Basic.

Lichter, Daniel, and Leif Jensen. 2001. "Rural Poverty and Welfare Before and After PRWORA." *Rural America* 16(3):28–35.

Lichter, Daniel T., and Deborah Roempke Graefe. 2011. "Rural Economic Restructuring: Implications for Children, Youth, and Families." In *Economic Restructuring and Family Well-Being in Rural America*, ed. Kristin E. Smith and Ann R. Tickamyer, chap. 1. State College: Pennsylvania State University Press.

Light, I. 2006. *Deflecting Immigration: Networks, Markets, and Regulation in Los Angeles*. New York: Russell Sage Foundation.

Lobao, Linda M., Lazarus Adua, and Gregory Hooks. 2014. "Privatization, Business Attraction and Social Services Across the United States: Local Governments' Use of Market-Oriented Neoliberal Policies in the Post-2000 Period." *Social Problems* 61(4):644–72.

Lobao, Linda M., Gregory Hooks, and Ann R. Tickamyer, eds. 2007. *The Sociology of Spatial Inequality*. New York: SUNY Press.

——. 2008. "Poverty and Inequality Across Space: Sociological Reflections on the Missing-Middle Subnational Scale." *Cambridge Journal of Regions, Economy & Society* 1(April):89–113.

Massey, Douglas. 2008. *New Faces in New Places: The Changing Geography of American Immigration.* New York: Russell Sage Foundation.

McLaughlin, Diane K., and Carla Shoff. 2014. "Children and Youth in Rural America." In *Rural America in a Globalizing World: Problems and Prospects for the 2010s*, ed. Conner Baily, Leif Jensen, and Elizabeth Ransom, chap. 19. Morgantown: West Virginia University Press.

Milbourne, Paul. 2004. *Rural Poverty: Marginalization and Exclusion in Britain and the United States.* London, UK: Routledge.

O'Hare, William P. 2009. "The Forgotten Fifth: Child Poverty in Rural America." Durham, NH: Report for the Carsey Institute, University of New Hampshire. http://scholars.unh.edu/cgi/viewcontent.cgi?article=1075&context=carsey.

Parrado, Emilio A., and William Kandel. 2008. "New Hispanic Immigrant Destinations: A Tale of Two Industries." In *New Faces in New Places: The Changing Geography of American Immigration*, ed. Douglas S. Massey, 99–123. New York: Russell Sage Foundation.

Partridge, Mark, Michael Betz, and Linda Lobao. 2013. "The Natural Resource Curse and Poverty in Appalachian America." *American Journal of Agricultural Economics* 95:449–56. http://ajae.oxfordjournals.org/cgi/reprint/aas086?ijkey=EMmvu4bLJz Udwa9&keytype=ref

Petrin, Robert A., Kai Schafft, and Judith L. Meece. 2014. "Educational Sorting and Residential Aspirations Among Rural High School Students: What Are the Contributions of Schools and Educators to Rural Brain Drain?" *American Educational Research Journal* 51(2):294–326.

Portes, Alejandro, and Julia Sensenbrenner. 1993. "Embeddedness and Immigration: Notes on the Social Determinants of Economic Action." *American Journal of Sociology* 98:1320–50.

Preston, Deborah B., and Anthony R. D'Augelli. 2013. *The Challenges of Being a Rural Gay Man: Coping with Stigma.* New York: Taylor and Francis.

Putnam, Robert D. 2000. *Bowling Alone: The Collapse and Revival of American Community.* New York: Simon & Schuster.

Rank, Mark. 2004. *One Nation, Underprivileged: Why American Poverty Affects Us All.* New York: Oxford University Press.

Reimer, William. 2004. "Social Exclusion in a Comparative Context." *Sociologia Ruralis* 44(1):76–94.

Rostow, Walt W. 1960. *The Stages of Economic Growth: A Non-Communist Manifesto.* Cambridge, UK: Cambridge University Press.

Rural Sociological Society Task Force on Persistent Rural Poverty. 1993. *Persistent Poverty in Rural America.* Boulder, CO: Westview Press.

Sachs, Carolyn. 2014. "Gender, Race, Ethnicity, Class and Sexuality in Rural America." In *Rural America in a Globalizing World: Problems and Prospects for the 2010s*, ed. Conner Baily, Leif Jensen, and Elizabeth Ransom, part 4. Morgantown: West Virginia University Press.

Schram, Sanford. 1995. *Words of Welfare: The Poverty of Social Science and the Social Science of Poverty.* Minneapolis: University of Minnesota Press.

Shapiro, Henry David. 1966. *A Strange Land and Peculiar People: The Discovery of Appalachia, 1870–1920.* New Brunswick, NJ: Rutgers University Dissertation.

Sherman, Jennifer. 2009a. "Bend to Avoid Breaking: Job Loss, Gender Norms, and Family Stability in Rural America." *Social Problems* 56(4):599–620.

——. 2009b. *Those Who Work, Those Who Don't: Poverty, Morality, and Family in Rural America*. Minneapolis: University of Minnesota Press.

——. 2014. "Rural Poverty: The Great Recession, Rising Unemployment, and the Under-Utilized Safety Net." In *Rural America in a Globalizing World: Problems and Prospects for the 2010s*, ed. Conner Baily, Leif Jensen, and Elizabeth Ransom, chap. 27. Morgantown: West Virginia University Press.

Sherman, Jennifer, and Rayna Sage. 2011. "Sending Off All Your Good Treasures: Rural Schools, Brain-Drain, and Community Survival in the Wake of Economic Collapse." *Journal of Research in Rural Education* 26(11):1–14.

Shucksmith, Mark. 2012. "Class, Power and Inequality in Rural Areas: Beyond Social Exclusion?" *Sociologia Ruralis* 52(4):377–97.

——. 2016. "Social Exclusion in Rural Places." In *International Handbook of Rural Studies*, ed. Mark Shucksmith and David L. Brown, 433–49. London, UK: Routledge.

Singh, Gopal K., Mohammad Siahpush, and Michael D. Kogan. 2010. "Rising Social Incqualities in U.S. Childhood Obesity, 2003–2007." *Annals of Epidemiology* 20(1): 40–52.

Smith, Kristin E. 2011. "Changing Roles: Women and Work in Rural America." In *Economic Restructuring and Family Well-Being in Rural America*, ed. Kristin E. Smith and Ann R. Tickamyer, chap. 3. State College: Pennsylvania State University Press.

Smith, Kristin E., and Ann R. Tickamyer, eds. 2011. *Economic Restructuring and Family Well-Being in Rural America*. State College: Pennsylvania State University Press.

Snyder, Anastasia R., Diane K. McLaughlin, and Jill Findeis. 2006. "Household Composition and Poverty Among Female-Headed Households with Children: Difference by Race and Residence." *Rural Sociology* 71(4):597–624.

Stein, Arlene. 2001. *The Stranger Next Door: The Story of a Small Community's Battle over Sex, Faith, and Civil Rights*. Boston: Beacon.

Struthers, Cynthia B. 2014. "The Past Is the Present: Gender and the Status of Rural Women." In *Rural America in a Globalizing World: Problems and Prospects for the 2010s*, ed. Conner Baily, Leif Jensen, and Elizabeth Ransom, chap. 25. Morgantown: West Virginia University Press.

Swidler, Ann. 1986. "Culture in Action: Symbols and Strategies." *American Sociological Review* 51(2):273–86.

Tickamyer, Ann R. 2006. "Rural Poverty." In *Handbook of Rural Studies*, ed. Paul Cloke, Terry Marsden, and Patrick Mooney, 411–26. London, UK: Sage.

Tickamyer, Ann R., and Cynthia M. Duncan. 1990. "Poverty in Rural America." *Annual Review of Sociology* 16:67–86.

Tickamyer, Ann R., and Debra A. Henderson. 2011. "Livelihood Practices in the Shadow of Welfare Reform." In *Economic Restructuring and Family Well-Being in Rural America*, ed. Kristin Smith and Ann R. Tickamyer, 294–319. State College: Pennsylvania State University Press.

Tickamyer, Ann R., Debra A. Henderson, Julie A. White, and Barry Tadlock. 2000. "Voices of Welfare Reform: Bureaucratic Rationality vs. Participant Perceptions." *Affilia* 15(2):173–92.

Tickamyer, Ann R., and Anouk Patel-Campillo. 2016. "Sociological Perspectives on Uneven Development." In *Sociology of Development Handbook*, ed. Gregory Hooks, chap. 12. Berkeley: University of California Press.

Tickamyer, Ann R., and Teresea Wood. 2003. "The Social and Economic Context of Informal Work." In *Communities of Work: Rural Restructuring in Local and Global Context*, ed. William W. Falk, Michael Shulman, and Ann R. Tickamyer, chap. 17. Athens: Ohio University Press.

Weber, Max. 1930. *The Protestant Ethic and the Spirit of Capitalism.* New York: Allen and Unwin. Translated by Talcott Parsons. Available on line at http://www.d.umn.edu/cla/faculty/jhamlin/1095/The%20Protestant%20Ethic%20and%20the%20Spirit%20of%20Capitalism.pdf

Wray, Matt. 2006. *Not Quite White: White Trash and the Boundaries of Whiteness.* Durham, NC: Duke University Press.

Wilson, William J. 1996. *When Work Disappears: The World of the New Urban Poor.* New York: Alfred A. Knopf.

——. 2012. *The Truly Disadvantaged: The Inner City, the Underclass, and Public Policy,* 2nd ed. Chicago: University of Chicago Press.

Zúñiga, Victor, and Ruben Hernández-León, eds. 2005. *New Destinations: Mexican Immigration in the United States.* New York: Russell Sage Foundation.

PART III

Vulnerable Populations in Rural Places

Part III describes the unique challenges faced by women, racial minorities, and immigrants, the most vulnerable populations in rural America. These groups experience disproportionately high rates of poverty even after accounting for government assistance. Together the chapters underscore how crucial it is that public policies and programs recognize the special circumstances and needs of these vulnerable groups if poverty and social inequities in rural areas are to be reduced.

Chapter 5, "Changing Gender Roles and Rural Poverty," paves the way by examining changing gender roles and relations in rural America and how these roles are linked to rural poverty. We learn that declining marriage and fertility rates have challenged the traditional roles of women primarily as caretaker and men as breadwinners since the 1950s. The force of the Great Recession of the late 2000s and subsequent loss of stable male employment turned this model on its head for many rural families as women found employment to help make ends meet (mostly low-skill and low-wage) and the unemployed fathers of their children became caretakers.

Chapter 6, "Racial Inequalities and Poverty in Rural America," explores the role that "racialized" social systems may have had in generating the disproportionately high rates of poverty and the concentrated persistence of poverty among rural racial minority groups. After reviewing the disturbing facts that rates of poverty are higher in general for rural minorities versus rural whites, and that rural minorities also face significantly higher degrees of spatially concentrated poverty, the chapter examines the history of racism and racist rhetoric (e.g., "welfare dependency" for African Americans) that has produced racist institutions (school systems, health care systems, government agencies, etc.) and, consequently, race-bound antipoverty policies. The author underscores the need for "race conscious" research and government intervention in addressing rural poverty.

Chapter 7, "Immigration Trends and Immigrant Poverty in Rural America," reviews historical trends in immigration to rural America and factors that account for changes in the size and ethnic composition of the rural immigrant population over time. The authors also describe differences in poverty rates between rural counties of varying levels of immigrant populations. We learn that recent immigrants to rural America are at higher risk of poverty than their urban counterparts, largely due to low employment prospects and social and economic isolation in rural communities characterized by "small ethnic populations and residential segregation." Because current safety net policies largely bar immigrants from participating, their needs are unmet, and the consequences of poverty, especially for their children, are severe.

CHAPTER 5

Changing Gender Roles and Rural Poverty

Kristin Smith

INTRODUCTION

A bumper sticker on a vehicle in a rural town in New Hampshire read: "NO FARMS, NO FARM GIRLS." The image of a rugged, no nonsense, and independent girl confidently driving a tractor in the hot sun comes to mind. In rural families, even girls must be self-sufficient and capable, given shrinking family size and the amount of farm work to be done. This image is consistent with the common perception of hard-working, self-sufficient, and virtuous rural people living in a peaceful countryside.

The common perception of rural family life typically does not include an image of gender equality or blurred gender lines. Rather, the conventional view of the rural family is of a small-scale independent farmer eking out a living by farming a small piece of land, with his stay-at-home wife caring for the home and numerous children (Fink 1992; Coontz 1992). This portrays a gendered division of labor within the context of poverty or near poverty predicated on traditional gender ideologies of appropriate roles for men and women (Tigges and Choo 2011), whereby a system of separate spheres is maintained. Children in this picture are reared in intact, two-parent families surrounded by supportive kin and community networks, consistent with the agrarian ideology of individualism and self-sufficiency combined with strong community networks and mutual help (Naples 1994). Although these are somewhat contradictory tendencies, both are necessary for survival in rural areas where jobs are scarce and low paying, resources are limited, and families must be self-sufficient but also reliant on neighbors and family to get by.

Many rural families are struggling to get by, and poverty is a persistent problem in rural America, with overall poverty rates higher in rural than urban areas. In 2014, the nonmetropolitan poverty rate was 18 percent compared with the metropolitan rate of 15 percent (USDA 2015). The Great Recession and continued declines in manufacturing and resource-based industries have resulted in fewer jobs and increased unemployment in rural areas (Jensen, Mattingly, and Bean 2011). At the height of the Great Recession, nonmetropolitan unemployment rates rose to levels unseen in more than twenty-five years—9.8 percent in 2009, which was higher than the 8.7 percent in metropolitan areas (McBride and Kemper 2009). Poverty is particularly high in the rural South, at 22 percent, and in the West, at 18 percent (USDA 2015). Rural minority populations have the highest poverty rates in the United States; 30 percent or more of rural African Americans, Native Americans, or Hispanics live in poverty, compared with 13 percent of rural whites (Anderson and Weng 2011; Lichter and Graefe 2011).

This chapter presents a picture of contemporary rural family life and gender roles and relations within the context of rural poverty. Tickamyer (1996) calls for scholars to demythologize rural life and gender roles and relations; by so doing we will improve our understanding of rural areas and families and create effective policies. Despite the stereotype of a more traditional division of labor in rural families, rural women have histori-cally engaged in productive activity (Sachs 1983), and a large share of rural women are employed today. Likewise, a growing proportion of rural men provide care for their children and are engaged in child rearing. The growth of single mothers in rural areas has contributed to a gendered pov-erty, as one in three rural single mothers was in poverty in 2013 (Carson and Mattingly 2014). Family life and gender roles among families living in poverty vary in rural areas and regions by race and ethnic group, one reality that the rural idyll fails to recognize. Rural families at the edge of poverty may be challenged by rigid gender norms, domestic violence, disabilities, the lack of access to services or public transportation, and the work requirements associated with work-first welfare programs, all of which can prove detrimental to economic and marital stability. Although many of these factors are related to changing gender roles and rural pov-erty, the focus of this chapter is on employment-related factors.

The analysis is focused on heterosexual rural families due to data con-straints. Although heterosexual, two-parent families are the norm in rural areas, LGBTQ people live and raise families in rural areas, and scholars show that the study of sexuality requires a place-based lens (Keller and Bell 2014). In particular, the study of sexualities in urban-based research has been shown not to be applicable in the rural context.

This chapter examines the extent to which gender roles and relations have changed in rural America and explores how these changes are related to rural poverty. First, the societal and structural shifts influencing changing gender roles are presented. Next, recent data are examined demonstrating the acceleration of shifting gender roles during the Great Recession. Finally, the implications of changing gender roles and relations for rural poverty are discussed.

SHIFTING GENDER ROLES

Despite the conception that rural places remain idyllic and are immune to change, several societal shifts have contributed to a transformation of rural family life and gender roles since the 1950s. Shifting family structure is one of the most important changes in the American family. Increasingly, children in rural areas are being reared in one-parent families, typically single-mother families. Due in part to delayed marriage, increasing nonmarital fertility, rising divorce rates, and increased cohabitation, rural families increasingly resemble urban families (Glasgow 2003; O'Hare, Manning, Porter, and Lyons 2009). Rural fertility has decreased such that fertility rates by place have nearly converged (Jones and Tertilt 2006), and rural households are now smaller than urban households, reflecting the aging population and lower birthrates. Despite these areas of convergence, rural places still have higher rates of marriage, and rural women marry at younger ages and are more likely to have their first birth within marriage (Snyder, Brown, and Condo 2004). Rural women are also more likely than urban women to marry following a nonmarital birth (Albrecht and Albrecht 2004).

Economic restructuring and globalization have produced structural shifts in the rural economy, negatively affecting the rural labor market and families' financial well-being (Smith and Tickamyer 2011). Across the United States, higher paying, typically male jobs in manufacturing, farming, or resource extraction have disappeared, replaced by low-paying, typically female jobs in the service sector. For example, in 1979, the share of jobs that were in manufacturing constituted 29.3% of the rural economy; by 2007, the share had declined to 17.4%, a decline of 11.9 percentage points (Smith and Tickamyer 2011). Manufacturing jobs provided a family wage with benefits (such as health insurance and job flexibility) and maintained a standard of living that enabled stable and secure employment. In addition, these jobs offered paid vacations and sick leave, and provided pensions. Service sector jobs, on the other hand, are low paying, do not provide full-time employment, and lack benefits such as health insurance, job flexibility, or paid sick leave. Rural labor markets lack diversity, and when a local industry declines or goes away, the effect on the local community and families is felt immediately because there are few other sources of good employment. These displaced workers are often forced to travel long distances to secure a new job, or to work in the growing service industry at a lower income. A ripple effect travels throughout the community as the town struggles to maintain the remaining businesses with fewer residents employed, lowered median incomes, and depressed morale.

Economic restructuring has hit rural men particularly hard, resulting in high levels of unemployment, chronic underemployment, and declining wages (Jensen and Jensen 2011). The loss of stable male employment also has tested the fortitude of the masculine ideal (i.e., the notion that men's identity and success is linked to their ability to provide economically for their family). Sherman (2011) chronicles the challenges facing rural men after the closure of a logging mill and related industries in a small California town. Following male job loss, family economic stability and marital success relied on how men coped with their perceived failed masculinity as they no longer could fulfill the economic provider role. Some men had flexible gender ideologies and were able to redefine masculinity to encompass nurturing children and downplayed the link between masculinity and successful breadwinning as their wives gained employment and took on the economic provider role. These families shifted gender roles and recast gender role ideologies to avoid falling into poverty. In contrast, families with men who clung to an unattainable masculinity predicated on successful breadwinning often experienced new tensions and increased familial stress. Traditional gender ideologies maintained a gendered division of labor, and the stress of continued male joblessness led to poverty and marital instability.

Another implication of the loss of stable male employment is the rising need for women's paid employment. The rise of the service sector created job opportunities for women as families increasingly needed women's paid employment (Falk and Lobao 2003; Levy 1998). The rise in rural women's employment has provided needed family income and helped families that struggle to remain above the poverty line. Fifty-seven percent of rural women were employed in 1970. Rural women's employment peaked at 74 percent in 2001, before declining to 71 percent by 2007

(Smith 2011). Since 2007, rural women's employment has declined over the Great Recession to 68 percent in 2013.

After decades of slightly lower employment rates among rural women compared with urban women, employment rates converged in 2003, owing to a larger decline in employment among urban women after 2000. Employment rates have since reverted once again to slightly lower rates among rural women. Surely, some rural women entered employment in response to declining men's labor market prospects; however, the rise in single-mother families, increased educational attainment among women, more acceptance of women's roles outside the home, and a change in women's attitudes toward work and economic independence invariably also played a role.

Nelson (2011) studied employment strategies among predominantly white, rural, low-income families in Vermont. Economic restructuring and global outsourcing reduced the number of what Nelson labels "good jobs households" in rural America, resulting in a bifurcated labor market, increased economic inequality between the classes, and lower overall social cohesion. Low-income families that fell into the good jobs households had at least one earner with a full-time, year-round job with a stable work schedule, benefits, paid vacations, and access to job flexibility. Good jobs households also relied on a dual-earner strategy, and typically at least one earner worked an additional part-time job to bolster financial resources. The key to the success of good job households was the stability of one earner's work schedule (typically a day shift) and access to paid time off, which allowed the other spouse to plan child care and his or her own work schedule. "Bad jobs households" were those in which the primary earner had a job with a varying or unpredictable work schedule and no job flexibility. Because many of these families only owned one car, this unpredictable nature of work posed difficulties in arranging child care and often prohibited the other spouse from entering the formal paid employment sector. Therefore, the bad jobs households typically relied on the sole male breadwinner model. The changing rural labor market and the decline in male jobs that pay a family wage (i.e., a wage that can support a family) has eroded the effectiveness of the sole male breadwinner model, particularly among low-wage families, often resulting in the need for a second income to remain above poverty.

Tigges and Choo (2012) built upon Nelson's work by considering the gendered nature of those employed in good versus bad jobs. In rural areas, women increasingly work in service occupations with these bad jobs' characteristics: low wages, no benefits, no paid sick time or vacation leave, and inflexible work schedules. They found that half of married women in their rural Wisconsin sample have standard work, defined as a full-time, year-round job, and nearly three-quarters of their husbands do. They argue that the construction of standard work around "the ideal worker" norm (Williams 2000), which is predicated on a system in which men are breadwinners and are devoted to their work without any outside responsibilities because they have a full-time homemaker spouse, relegates women to nonstandard work because women typically are responsible for family care and do not fit the ideal worker norm. In essence, the gendered division of labor in the home, with women having primary responsibility for the care of children and maintaining the home, coupled with difficult access to affordable child care, precludes women from accessing the types of jobs that offer stable work schedules, paid sick days, and health insurance—the very benefits workers with family responsibilities need.

In 2010, 33 percent of rural single-parent households were poor, up 2 percentage points from 2000. There was a rise in single-parent households in rural areas in the 1980s and 1990s, but it has remained stable since 2000, consistent with trends in the nation overall. However, Hispanics and those with less than a high school degree experienced increases in single-parent households over the decade (Carson and Mattingly 2014). The majority of single parents in rural America are women, and the pathway to being a single mother in rural areas is frequently through divorce. Upon divorce, rural single mothers often fall into poverty, which represents a real struggle for these families who are often reliant on the low-wage service sector to make ends meet.

Rural jobs are less "family friendly" than urban jobs. Glauber and Young (2015) find that rural mothers are less likely to have paid sick days, paid vacation days, health insurance, parental leave, and flextime than urban mothers. Rural women also have reduced diversity in job opportunities (Smith 2008), with many working in low-wage jobs, often in poverty. The low-wage sector of the workforce is characterized as having unstable work hours, limited time or no time off for family care, limited health insurance benefits, and rarely any child care assistance or benefits (Odle-Dusseau, McFaddan, and Britt 2015). This lack of resources associated with low-wage jobs (such as wages, flexibility, and autonomy) leaves women with family care responsibilities, who often are employed yet in poverty, without a means of negotiating their work–family conflict.

Smith and Glauber (2013) found that the spatial wage gap—the difference in wages between rural and urban places—among women has increased, particularly by education level. Highly educated women have increased their employment and wages, but the gains to education are lower in rural than urban areas. The spatial wage gap was only 5 percent for women without a high school diploma, but it was 15 percent for women with a college degree and 26 percent for women with advanced degrees. They argue that the rural–urban gap in wages, particularly among college-educated women, is due primarily to the overrepresentation of women in lower-paying, female-dominated occupations and industries. This oversupply of workers, or crowding, depresses wages and leads to economic inequality between rural and urban women. Even in the low-wage labor market, wages in rural areas are depressed to a greater extent than in urban areas, likely resulting in increased incidence of the working poor among rural families.

These societal changes have ushered in shifts in gender roles and increased gender equality. Overall, rural women are working outside the home and contributing to family income. Likewise, rural men are engaging in the care of children and the home. Traditional gender ideology, however, continues to guide the division of labor within the home and has implications for family breadwinning patterns, wives' earnings relative to their husbands', and poverty in rural areas.

CHANGING GENDER ROLES DURING THE GREAT RECESSION

Times of economic decline and uncertainty often push families to reconsider how they organize their work and family lives and allocate men's and women's time. Some families cling to traditional gender roles despite the difficulty in fulfilling those roles, and other families redefine what they consider appropriate female or male roles (Sherman 2011; Gerson 2010). The negative outcomes of the Great Recession have been multifaceted, affecting many areas of family economic well-being. The U.S. economy lost 8.7 million jobs between December 2007 and January 2010 (Bureau of Labor Statistics [BLS] 2012), with 1.2 million jobs lost in rural areas between July 2007 and July 2010 (Gallardo and Bishop 2010). Although the recession officially ended in June 2009, the national unemployment rate remained high well into 2012. The recession affected men's employment more than women's, with 69 percent of the jobs lost being held by men (Smith 2012). Overall unemployment reached a high of 10.0 percent in October 2009, with men's unemployment at 11.2 percent and women's at 8.7 percent (BLS 2012). In rural areas, men's unemployment was 12.8 percent in 2010, a rise of 6.2 percentage points from 2007, and women's unemployment was 8.1 percent, a rise of 3.1 percentage points (Mattingly, Smith, and Bean 2011). Given these very high unemployment rates, particularly for men, it is not surprising that during the Great Recession rural poverty increased (Jensen, Mattingly, and Bean 2011). This section reviews research on women's and wives' increased breadwinning role and fathers' increased role in care provision.

INCREASED BREADWINNING AMONG RURAL WOMEN DURING THE GREAT RECESSION

Many rural families today are turning to women as economic providers for several reasons. There is an increased need for women's income for married couples because rural men's wages have declined since 1980, and rural men are less likely to be working and earn less than their urban peers (Smith 2011). Unemployment and chronic underemployment are higher in the rural United States for both men and women (Jensen and Jensen 2011). Furthermore, increased divorce rates and the rise of nonmarital childbearing present an obvious need for female income.

Job loss during the Great Recession hit male-dominated occupations harder than female-dominated ones, leaving families who relied primarily on men's employment without their primary breadwinner and with reduced family income. Wives responded to male job loss by increasing their labor force activity either by looking for work, gaining employment, or increasing their work hours. Wives with lower education levels, however, were less likely to get jobs than wives with higher education levels, as were rural wives compared with urban wives. Mattingly and Smith (2010) find evidence of an added worker effect among wives during the 1982–1983, 1990–1991, and the 2007–2009 recessions, with wives entering the labor force and increasing their work hours when their husbands stopped working during the recessions. The effect was strongest during the 2007–2009 recession. Despite increased employment among wives with husbands who experienced job loss, overall wives' employment decreased during the Great Recession from 72 percent in 2007 to 71 percent in 2009, and then decreased to 69 percent in 2012 due to the contraction of jobs across all sectors of the economy except health and education.

These patterns occurred to a large extent in rural areas. Men's job loss in rural areas was higher than women's, and rural unemployment reached record levels, higher than those seen in urban areas. Rural families in economic decline turned to wives' economic provisioning, evidenced by the rise in employed wives' economic contribution to family earnings (Smith 2009, 2010). Smith and Schaefer (2014) report that between 2004 and 2007, employed wives in urban areas contributed less to family earnings than their rural counterparts (43 percent compared with 45 percent), as shown in figure 5.1. Contributions converged in 2008 and again in 2011 and 2012 when employed wives' contribution to family earnings in urban and rural became more similar. Although the gaps between employed wives in urban and rural areas converged during the recession, in both rural and urban places, employed wives' share increased. Furthermore, these increases in employed wives' contributions to family earnings corresponded to decreases in husbands' employment rates.

Mattingly and Smith (2010) show trends in family breadwinning patterns from 1970 to 2009. Overall, rural married couples have shifted away from the husband-as-sole-provider model, which decreased from 42 percent in 1970 to 20 percent in 2009. As rural married women's employment rates rose, the proportion of married couples with spouses who both provide about equal earnings rose, as well as families where the wife was the primary or sole provider. In both time periods, the most common family breadwinning type was one in which both spouses were employed, but the husband

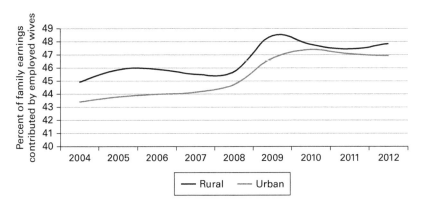

Figure 5.1 Employed wives' contribution to family earnings by metropolitan status, 2004–2012.

Source: Current population survey, Annual Social and Economic Supplement (ASEC), 2005–2013.

was the primary provider (just under 40 percent of rural married couples in both time periods). By 2013, rural women were more likely than urban women to be married, and the proportion of husband primary-earner families was higher in rural areas (Smith 2015a).

These changes in family breadwinning patterns imply that rural wives are playing an increased role in the economic security of families. As rural men's wages have declined from 1969 to 2006, rural women's inflation-adjusted earnings rose from $23,000 to $27,000—an increase of 15 percent (Smith 2008). This rise in women's earnings, in turn, has been a major driver in the rise in family income among married couples with an employed wife (Smith, 2015b). More recently, however, wage growth has expanded more rapidly for educated and higher-earning women, somewhat similar to the pattern for men, resulting in a rise in wage inequality among women. The Great Recession exacerbated this trend as women with lower education levels were more likely to lose jobs (Mattingly, Smith, and Bean 2011).

These trends have implications for income inequality and family poverty because there are vast differences in family income by family breadwinning type in rural areas. Rural married-couple families had more than double the median family income of single women in 2013 ($72,000 compared with $28,000), due in part to a greater likelihood of marriage among individuals with higher education and earnings and to the fact that most married-couple families have two earners (figure 5.2). Rural married couples in which the husband was the primary provider or spouses with equal earners had the highest median family income in 2013, at $85,000 and $83,000, respectively. In contrast, rural couples in which the wife or the husband was the sole provider had that lowest median family income at $49,000 and $50,000, respectively. Yet wives' contribution to family income varied greatly depending on family breadwinning type, with the highest contribution among wife primary- and wife sole-provider families (67 percent and 64 percent, respectively) and the lowest contribution among husband primary provider families (24 percent), which excludes husband sole-provider families, which by definition means that wives did not contribute financially to the family. In single women families, rural women without children had higher family income than single women with children ($30,000 and $22,000, respectively).

Single-women families are particularly vulnerable to poverty, especially in rural areas (table 5.1). In 2013, 28.3 percent of rural single women were in poverty, higher than their urban counterparts (23.2 percent), and more than five times higher than rural and urban married women

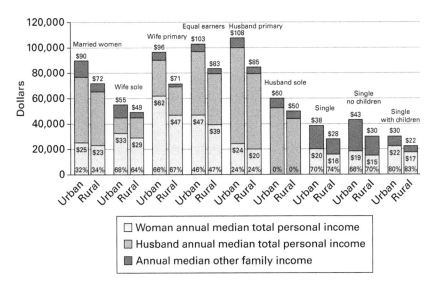

Figure 5.2 Women's contribution to total family income and total income by income types, by marital status, and by family type, urban and rural, 2013.

Source: Smith 2015a.

Table 5.1 Percent of Families in Poverty, by Marital Status and Family Type, Urban and Rural, 2013

	Percent in poverty	
	Rural	Urban
Married couples	5.3	4.8
• Wife sole earner	12.0	11.3
• Wife primary earner	4.2	2.4
• Equal earners	1.1	1.2
• Husband primary earner	1.6	1.4
• Husband sole earner	10.6	9.9
Single women	28.3	23.2
• Single, no children	25.1	19.6
• Single, with children	36.3	31.4

Note: Excludes couples where neither spouse is employed; women are between eighteen and sixty-four years old. Data from Current Population Survey, ASEC, 2014.

(approximately 5 percent for both). More than one in three rural single women with children were in poverty (36.3 percent). Poverty differs depending on married-couple family type. Higher rates of poverty were apparent among rural married couples in which the wife or husband was the sole provider (12 and 10.6 percent, respectively). Married-couple families with two earners were rarely in poverty.

Family income is much higher in urban than in rural areas across all family types, due in part to higher personal income among women living in urban areas compared with corresponding women in rural areas (figure 5.2). However, the *share* of married women's income (i.e., women's income as a proportion of total family income) by place is similar across marital and breadwinner status. One exception is that rural women in married couples in which the wife was the sole earner contributed a lower proportion of family income than similar urban married women (64 percent and 68 percent, respectively). Another variation by place is that rural women in married couples in which the husband was either the primary or an equal earner had similar family income levels ($85,000 and $83,000, respectively), whereas in urban areas husband primary-earner families had higher family incomes. Finally, single women in rural areas contributed a higher share of median family income than single urban women (74 percent and 70 percent, respectively). These analyses do not account for any cost of living differences between urban and rural families.

INCREASED CARE PROVISION AMONG MEN

Men's roles shifted during the Great Recession. As men experience job loss and reduced work obligations during economic decline, the question arises as to whether these men will spend more time caring for children or doing housework. Research using the American Time Use Survey show that overall men's time spent working declined during the recession, but there was not a concurrent rise in time men spent doing housework (Aguiar, Hurst, and Karabarbounis 2011). Rather, men's time in leisure increased during the Great Recession. More nuanced analysis of fathers' time allocation reveals an uptick in fathers' time spent caring for children, but not in housework (Berik and Kongar 2013; Sayer, Smith, and Gupta 2013).

Using the Survey of Income and Program Participation child care topical module data, scholars show an uptick in the proportion of all fathers providing care for their children during the Great Recession between 2005 and 2011 (Smith 2015c; Laughlin and Smith 2015). In 2005, before

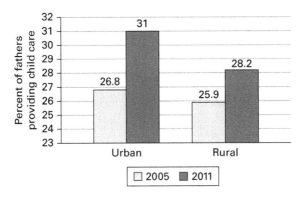

Figure 5.3   Fathers providing care for children under 15 with employed mothers, by urban and rural location, 2005 and 2011.

the Great Recession, 27 percent of married fathers provided child care to their children under fifteen years old while the mother worked. This proportion rose to 31 percent by 2011 in the aftermath of the Great Recession. This rise in father-provided child care is linked to declines in married fathers' employment over the Great Recession, as declining employment among married fathers suggests that fathers in 2011 had more time available to care for children than fathers did in 2005.

Married fathers' employment declined over the recession in both rural and urban areas by the same amount (4 percentage points), from 92 percent in 2005 to 88 percent in 2011. In 2005, rural and urban married fathers provided child care in statistically similar proportions while their wives worked for pay. Over the Great Recession, a spatial gap in father care emerged; by 2011, 31 percent of fathers in urban areas but only 28.2 percent of fathers in rural areas provided care (figure 5.3). Given the similar employment rates among rural and urban married fathers in 2005 and 2011, and the similar levels of father care in 2005, the larger proportion of care provision among urban fathers compared to rural fathers in 2011 may be indicative of rural fathers' more rigid view of appropriate gender roles and masculinity, similar to the results found by Sherman (2011).

Typically fathers who are in poverty do not have full-time work and thus may have more time to care for their children while the mother is employed. Figure 5.4 shows the percentage of fathers who had an employed wife and who cared for their children under age fifteen by family poverty status. Across place and time, married fathers in poverty were more likely to

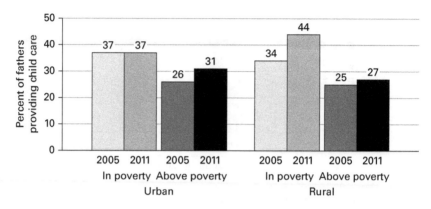

Figure 5.4   Percentage of fathers who have an employed wife and who care for children under 15, by poverty status, urban and rural, 2005 and 2011.

provide child care while the mother was working than fathers living above the poverty level. The proportion of rural fathers who were in poverty and who provided care to their children under age fifteen increased from 34 percent in 2005 to 44 percent in 2011. There was no change in the provision of father care among urban married fathers who were in poverty, but a larger proportion of urban married fathers who were not in poverty provided care for their children in 2011 compared with 2005.

EFFECTS OF CHANGING GENDER ROLES ON RURAL POVERTY

Research shows that rural families that embrace flexible gender roles are better able to adapt to family economic downturns and are better able to avoid falling into poverty (Nelson 2011; Sherman 2014). When male jobs disappear in rural areas, rural families can retain a traditional division of labor and struggle financially as men seek employment in the decreasing number of traditionally male-dominated jobs. Or families can redefine masculinity and embrace a shift in gender roles, and potentially avoid poverty as women gain employment in the service sector (Sherman 2014). In communities with traditional views on the roles of men as economic providers and women as homemakers, women often enter employment in the service sector because men will forgo employment in feminized positions (Nelson and Smith 1999; Sherman 2009). The cultural norms and gender ideology of these men make it difficult for them to accept jobs in service or care-work industries (Sherman 2009). Sherman found that it is the men's gender ideology that directs the family's gender strategy and division of labor; thus, men who struggle with accepting nontraditional gender norms also struggle with marital and emotional well-being. Unemployment for men can add to marital problems when men's identity as the economic provider is questioned, leading in some cases to marital instability and increased single parenting, which are associated with rural poverty.

Women's contributions to the family have grown over the recession due in part to declining men's employment and earnings, but also due to women's increased labor market participation. Families typically have higher earnings if both spouses are employed (due in part to the fact that women and men with high education levels and high earnings typically marry each other), and family income rose due to increased women's earnings, as men's earnings decreased over the recession (Smith 2015a). Even with rural women's increased employment and earnings, rural women earn less than urban women (Smith and Glauber 2013), receive lower returns to their human capital (McLaughlin and Perman 1991), and are in more sex-segregated occupations (Cotter et al. 1996).

Women's jobs typically are poorly paid relative to men's, so the rise in women's employment has not made up for the losses in male income, particularly among families at the poverty line, as male earnings at the lowest income quintile have decreased (Autor, Katz, and Kearney 2008). Families are more likely to experience poverty when women are the primary or sole breadwinner (Anderson and Weng 2011; Lichter and Graefe 2011). Wives' increased earnings power can push couples toward greater gender equality or challenge traditional power structures within the family and cause discord (Chelsey 2011), calling attention to how families respond to changing economic circumstances. Given the lack of job growth in rural areas since the Great Recession and continued economic restructuring, it is likely that rural families will continue to rely on women as primary breadwinners, which will put more families at risk of being working poor.

CONCLUSION

Changes in the gendered nature of work, the gendered division of labor in the home, and the interplay with gender identities will continue to influence rural families in the future. This requires understanding how impoverished families cope with the changes in the workforce, the continued loss of male jobs in manufacturing and resource-based industries that paid a family wage, and the rise in female-dominated jobs primarily in the service sector that do not offer wages that allow one to support a family. Job recovery after the Great Recession has been lackluster, and wages have remained stagnant primarily for workers in the low-wage job market. Gender roles for rural women and men have been shifting for several decades, but during the Great Recession the changes were more pronounced. Rural men in poverty increased their care of children, and rural employed women's contributions to family earnings rose significantly.

Will rural women and men maintain their expanded gender roles as male jobs return, family incomes rise, and poverty levels decrease? Or will we see a return to prerecession levels of father involvement in child care and job exits among women? And what of single-women families that continue to struggle in rural areas, being dependent on the limited number of low-wage jobs and lacking support to manage the demands of their jobs while maintaining their family responsibilities?

Rural families in poverty face challenges in balancing work and family that differ from those of the more researched middle and upper classes, or professional workers. Families in poverty live in constant stress, pinching each penny and stretching each dollar. The high cost of high-quality, center-based child care is usually out of reach for rural families, but this is one of the factors that rural families in poverty need to enable them to hold a steady, full-time job. Unreliable transportation often makes commuting to jobs difficult or impossible. The lack of jobs in combination with unreliable transportation and inadequate child care make it difficult for rural families to be in compliance with the mandated work requirements of work-first welfare programs (Brown and Lichter 2004). Poor rural women and their families also face additional challenges from lack of services for domestic violence to a legal system that is unaware and unforgiving of the problems they encounter in trying to earn a living, leading to further family disruption and creating yet more obstacles to escaping poverty (Pruitt 2008a, 2008b; Pruitt and Wallace 2011).

Although single mothers have the highest risk of poverty and the greatest barriers to employment, married couples reliant on one earner have elevated risks of poverty as well. More research is needed to fully understand the long-term implications of the survival strategies of rural families in poverty, focusing specifically on variations by family type.

Case Study: *In re Bow*, Nevada Supreme Court (1997)

Lisa R. Pruitt

One-third of rural single mothers were living in poverty in 2013, a rate more than 5 times that of married women, whatever their place of residence.[1] This high rate of poverty is attributable, at least in part, to obstacles to rural women's employment and the unfavorable conditions in which nonmetropolitan women often work: unpredictable hours, for low pay, often in temporary or otherwise contingent employment.[2] Additionally, single rural mothers face the tremendous obstacle of finding good, affordable childcare. Single parents historically relied on networks of kith and kin—mostly female—for childcare, but extended family members increasingly have also joined the labor force and are thus no longer available.[3] To get access to better-paying jobs, rural workers typically must travel great distances.[4] The dearth of public transportation in nonmetropolitan areas has made this feat more challenging,[5] a reality that leaves many depending on unreliable automobiles with poor gas mileage.[6]

Rural single mothers, however, face more than the day-to-day challenges of poverty; the welfare of their children often rests solely upon their shoulders. High levels of child poverty are characteristic of rural areas,[7] and the increased rates of child poverty that resulted from the Great Recession have not yet fully receded in rural places, though it is now fully abated in urban locales.[8] Children in poor families face increased risks of poor health, slower cognitive development, poorer performance in school, and lower educational prospects.[9] Many effects of poverty, such as a lack of supervision of children, a lower standard of hygiene, and food insecurity, are also signs of "neglect," the legal term for a parent's failure to provide for a child's basic needs.[10] Neglect, in turn, is most often cited as the primary reason for child removal and subsequent termination of parental rights.[11] What follows is a real-world illustration of the consequences of rural poverty for one single mother.

In 1997, the Supreme Court of Nevada upheld a trial court finding that Adrina Recodo, a Native American mother of three-year-old Michael, was an unfit parent.[12] The court, therefore, terminated Adrina's parental rights. Adrina grew up on a "very rural" Native American reservation in southern Nevada, living with her grandmother. In 1992, Adrina gave birth to a son, Michael; she already had four children, three of whom lived with her former husband, who had physically abused her. Adrina struggled financially following her divorce, and she eventually placed Michael in foster care with Native American foster parents in April 1993. Adrina and her social worker understood that the foster placement would last six months, with the goals during that time being for Adrina to get her GED, find a job in Las Vegas during the week, and care for Michael on the weekends.

The reservation where Adrina lived was about fifty miles from Las Vegas, the nearest place where Adrina could finish her GED and find better job prospects. Without her own vehicle, Adrina initially borrowed her grandfather's car; eventually, she could not afford gas for daily trips. Adrina thus began either staying with friends in Las Vegas or studying and sleeping in the car. Adrina sometimes had to forgo eating so that she could pay for gas to travel between Las Vegas and Michael, who remained on the reservation. Things became more difficult in May 1993 when the car broke down and Adrina's grandparents sold it. With no other means of transportation, Adrina tried to cycle or get rides to and from Las Vegas.

In June, Michael was moved to state care in Las Vegas. Adrina was by then living with a male friend there, but she did not have the ability to take care of Michael. Unable to maintain steady employment (Adrina had three jobs between 1993 and 1995) or to get appropriate housing—two conditions among others imposed by the state as requirements of reunification with Michael—Adrina faced a petition to terminate parental rights in November 1994. Adrina's reunification attempts had shown notable improvements over time: she was able to buy a car (with assistance), began seeing a psychologist, made a greater effort to maintain employment, and lost contact with the Department of Child and Family Services only once or twice. Nevertheless, the trial court found Adrina an unfit parent and terminated her parental rights to Michael.

Adrina appealed, but a majority of the Nevada Supreme Court concluded that she "did nothing to establish stability in her life," and that one and a half years was sufficient to determine whether Adrina would be able to provide a stable environment for her child. Dissenting Justice Springer took issue with the majority's reasoning, pointing out that poor parents are more likely to have their parental rights terminated—and that they typically lose their children to more affluent foster parents. Rather than reading Adrina's persistent struggles as a reflection of her "instability" or unwillingness to care for Michael, Justice Springer highlighted her situation as that of a poor, rural, single parent unable to break the cycle of poverty. He noted that Adrina had received no state assistance with her requirement to get adequate housing, nor was she able to rely on public transportation to take her the fifty miles between Las Vegas and the reservation. Justice Springer wrote: "Ms. Recodo's children were taken away from her just because she was poor."[13] He described Ms. Recodo as "destitute," observing that "on many occasions she was faced with the choice of eating or spending the money on transportation that would take her to school or to try and find a job."[14] He concluded that "the record is replete with descriptions of the almost insurmountable obstacles put in the way of Ms. Recodo by the State."[15] Though she tried to improve her situation, she was unable to avoid termination.

Adrina Recodo's story illustrates a life-changing consequence of rural poverty and the enormous hurdles (e.g., lack of childcare, limited transportation options) that poor rural residents often face in their quest for economic stability. In the case of Adrina, these obstacles resulted in the permanent loss of her child. The case also illustrates varying judicial perspectives on rural poverty, as well as on the degree of state responsibility for this phenomenon and its consequences.

NOTES

1. See Marybeth J. Mattingly, Kristin E. Smith, and Jessica A. Bean, "Unemployment in the Great Recession: Single Parents and Men Hit Hard," *Carsey Institute Issue Brief*, no. 35 (Summer 2011): http://scholars.unh.edu/cgi/viewcontent.cgi?article=1143&context=carsey.

2. Carolyn Sachs, "Gender, Race, Ethnicity, Class, and Sexuality in Rural America," in *Rural America in a Globalizing World: Problems and Prospects for the 2010s*, ed. Conner Bailey, Leif Jensen, and Elizabeth Ransom (Morgantown: West Virginia University Press, 2014): 421, 423.

3. *Rural Communities: Legacy and Change*, ed. Cornelia Butler Flora, Jan L. Flora, and Stephan P. Gasteyer (Boulder, CO: Westview, 2014): 127.

4. Ibid.

5. See U.S. Department of Agriculture, *Rural Transportation at a Glance* 3 (2005), available at http://www.ers.usda.gov/publications/aib-agricultural-information-bulletin/aib795.aspx.

6. Flora et al., *Rural Communities*, 127 note 3.

7. Diane K. McLaughlin and Carla Shoff, "Children and Youth in Rural America," in *Rural America in a Globalizing World*, ed. Conner Bailey, Leif Jensen, and Elizabeth Ransom (Morgantown, WV: West Virginia University Press, 2014), 365, 367.

8. Thomas Hertz and Tracey Farrigan, "Understanding the Rise in Rural Child Poverty, 2003–2014," USDA (May 2016), http://www.ers.usda.gov/media/2088379/err208a.pdf.

9. Ibid.

10. See Lisa R. Pruitt and Janet L. Wallace, "Judging Parents, Judging Place: Poverty, Rurality and Termination of Parental Rights," *Missouri Law Review*, 77 (2011): 112–113.

11. Mary Keegan Eamon and Sandra Kopels, "'For Reasons of Poverty': Court Challenges to Child Welfare Practices and Mandated Programs," *Children and Youth Services Review* 26 (2004): 821, 823.

12. *Matter of Parental Rights Bow*, 113 Nev. 141, 143 (1997) overruled by *In re Termination of Parental Rights as to N.J.*, 116 Nev. 790 (2000) abrogated by *In re Parental Rights as to N.D.O.*, 121 Nev. 379 (2005); Recodo v. State (*In re* Bow), 930 P.2d 1128 (Nev. 1997) (upholding termination of mother's parental rights), overruled on other grounds by *In re N.J.*, 8 P.3d 126 (Nev. 2000).

13. *Matter of Parental Rights Bow*, 113 Nev., 153.

14. *Ibid.*, 156.

15. *Ibid.*

REFERENCES

Aguiar, Mark, Erik Hurst, and Loukas Karabarbounis. 2011. "Time Use During Recessions." NBER Working Paper No. 17259. National Bureau of Economic Research.

Albrecht, Don, and Carol Albrecht. 2004. "Metro/Nonmetro Residence, Nonmarital Conception, and Conception Outcomes." *Rural Sociology* 69(3):430–52.

Anderson, Cynthia D., and Chih-Yuan Weng. 2011. "Regional Variation in Low-Wage Work Across Rural Communities." In *Economic Restructuring and Family Well-Being in Rural America,* ed. K. Smith and A. Tickamyer, 215–30. University Park: Pennsylvania State University Press.

Autor, David, Lawrence Katz, and Melissa S. Kearney. 2008. "Trends in U.S. Wage Inequality: Revising the Revisionists." *The Review of Economics and Statistics* 90(2):300–23.

Berik, Gunseli, and Ebru Kongar. 2013. "Time Allocation of Married Mothers and Fathers in Hard Times: The 2007–09 US Recession." *Feminist Economics* 19:208–37.

Bokemeier, Janet, and Ann R. Tickamyer. 1985. "Labor Force Experiences of Nonmetropolitan Women." *Rural Sociology* 50:51–73.

Brown, J. Brian, and Daniel Lichter. 2004. "Poverty, Welfare and the Livelihood Strategies of Nonmetropolitan Single Mothers." *Rural Sociology* 69(2):282–301.

Bureau of Labor Statistics. 2012. "Economic and Employment Data." Washington, DC: Bureau of Labor Statistics. www.bls.gov/data/#unemployment.

Carson, Jessica, and Marybeth Mattingly. 2014. "Rural Families and Households and the Decline of Traditional Structure." In *Rural America in a Globalizing World*, ed. Conner Bailey, Elizabeth Ransom, and Leif Jensen, 347–64. Morgantown: West Virginia University Press.

Chelsey, Noelle. 2011. "Stay-at-Home Fathers and Breadwinning Mothers: Gender, Couple Dynamics, and Social Change." *Gender & Society* 25(5):642–64.

Coontz, Stephanie. 1992. *The Way We Never Were: American Families and the Nostalgia Trap.* New York: Basic.

Cotter, David A., JoAnn DeFiore, Joan M. Hermsen, Brenda Marsteller Kowalewski, and Reeve Vanneman. 1996. "Gender Inequality in Nonmetropolitan and Metropolitan Areas." *Rural Sociology* 61:272–88.

Falk, William, and Linda Lobao. 2003. "Who Benefits from Economic Restructuring? Lessons from the Past, Challenges for the Future?" In *Challenges for Rural America in the Twenty-First Century*, ed. David Brown and Louis Swanson, 152–65. University Park: Pennsylvania State University Press.

Fink, Deborah. 1992. *Agrarian Women: Wives and Mothers in Rural Nebraska 1880–1940.* Chapel Hill: University of North Carolina Press.

Gallardo, Roberto, and Bill Bishop. 2010. "Cost of Recession: 1.2 Million Rural Jobs." *The Daily Yonder*, September 15. http://www.dailyyonder.com/job-loss/2010/09/15/2935/.

Gerson, Kathleen. 2010. *Unfinished Revolution: How a New Generation Is Shaping Family, Work and Gender in America.* Oxford: Oxford University Press.

Glasgow, Nina. 2003. "Older Rural Families." In *Challenges for Rural America in the Twenty-First Century*, ed. David Brown and Louis E. Swanson, 86–96. University Park: Pennsylvania State University Press.

Glauber, Rebecca, and Justin Robert Young. 2015. "On the Fringe: Family-Friendly Benefits and the Rural-Urban Gap Among Working Women." *Journal of Family Economic Issues* 36:97–113.

Jensen, Leif, and Eric Jensen. 2011. "Employment Hardship Among Rural Men." In *Economic Restructuring and Family Well Being in Rural America*, ed. Kristin Smith and Ann R. Tickamyer, 40–59. University Park: Pennsylvania State University Press.

Jensen, Leif, Marybeth J. Mattingly, and Jessica A. Bean. 2011. "TANF in Rural America: Informing Re-Authorization." Policy Brief No. 19. Durham, NH: Carsey Institute.

Jones, Larry E., and Michele Tertilt. 2006. "An Economic History of Fertility in the U.S.: 1826–1960." Working Paper 12796. Cambridge, MA: National Bureau of Economic Research.

Keller, Julie, and Michael Bell. 2014. "Rolling in the Hay: The Rural as Sexual Space." In *Rural America in a Globalizing World*, ed. Conner Bailey, Elizabeth Ransom, and Leif Jensen, 506–22. Morgantown: West Virginia University Press.

Laughlin, Lynda. 2013. "Who's Minding the Kids? Child Care Arrangements: Spring 2011." Washington, DC: U.S. Census Bureau.

Laughlin, Lynda, and Kristin Smith. 2015. "Father-Provided Child Care Among Married Couples in a Recessionary Context." SEHSH Working Paper No. 2015-16. Washington, DC: U.S. Census Bureau.

Levy, Frank. 1998. *The New Dollars and Dreams: American Incomes and Economic Changes.* New York: Russell Sage Foundation.

Lichter, Daniel T., and Deborah Roempke Graefe. 2011. "Rural Economic Restructuring: Implications for Children, Youth, and Families." In *Economic Restructuring and Family Wellbeing in Rural America*, ed. Kristin Smith and Ann R. Tickamyer, chap. 1. University Park: Pennsylvania State University Press.

Mattingly, Marybeth, and Kristin Smith. 2010. "Changes in Wives Employment When Husbands Stop Working? A Recession-Prosperity Comparison." *Family Relations* 59:343–57.

Mattingly, Marybeth, Kristin Smith, and Jessica A. Bean. 2011. "Unemployment in the Great Recession: Single Parents and Men Hit Hard." Issue Brief No. 35. Durham, NH: Carsey Institute, University of New Hampshire.

McBride, Timothy, and Leah Kemper. 2009. "Impact of the Recession on Rural America: Rising Unemployment Leading to More Uninsured in 2009." Brief No. 2009-6. Omaha, NE: Rupri, Center for Rural Health Policy Analysis, www.unmc .edu/ruprihealth.

McLaughlin, Diane K., and Laurie Perman. 1991. "Returns vs. Endowments in the Earnings Attainment Process for Metropolitan and Nonmetropolitan Men and Women." *Rural Sociology* 56:339–65.

Naples, Nancy A. 1994. "Contradictions in Agrarian Ideology: Restructuring Gender, Race-Ethnicity, and Class." *Rural Sociology* 59(1):110–35.

Nelson, Margaret K. 2011. "Between Family and Friendship: The Right to Care for Anna." *Journal of Family Theory & Review* 3(4):241–55.

Nelson, Margaret K., and Joan Smith. 1999. *Working Hard and Making Do: Surviving in Small Town America.* Los Angeles: University of California Press.

Odle-Dusseau, Heather, Anna McFadden, and Thomas Britt. 2015. "Gender, Poverty, and the Work-Family Interface." In *Gender and the Work-Family Experience: An Intersection of Two Domains*, ed. Maura J. Mills, 39–55. New York: Springer.

O'Hare, William P., Wendy Manning, Meredith Porter, and Heidi Lyons. 2009. "Rural Children Are More Likely to Live in Cohabiting-Couple Households." Policy Brief No. 14. Durham, NH: Carsey Institute, University of New Hampshire.

Pruitt, Lisa R. 2008a. "Gender Geography, and Rural Justice." *Berkeley Journal of Gender, Law & Justice* 23:338–89. http://papers.ssrn.com/sol3/papers.cfm?abstract _id=1103559, accessed April 12, 2016.

——. 2008b. "Place Matters: Domestic Violence and Rural Difference." *Wisconsin Journal of Law, Gender & Society* 23:347–415. http://papers.ssrn.com/sol3/papers .cfm?abstract_id=1276045, April 12, 2016.

Pruitt, Lisa, and Janet L. Wallace. 2012. "Judging Parents, Judging Place: Poverty, Rurality and Termination of Parental Rights." *Missouri Law Review* 77, no. 1.

Raley, Sara B., Suzanne M. Bianchi, and Rong (Wendy) Wang. 2012. "When Do Fathers Care? Mothers' Economic Contribution and Fathers' Involvement in Childcare." *American Journal of Sociology* 117(5):1422–59.

Sachs, Jacqueline. 1983. "Talking About the There and Then: The Emergence of Displaced Reference in Parent-Child Discourse." *Children's Language* 4:1–28.

Sayer, Liana, Kristin Smith, and Sanjiv Gupta. 2013. "Gender, Class and Time Use During the Great Recession." Paper presented at the 2012 American Sociological Association meetings.

Sherman, Jennifer. 2009. *Those Who Work, Those Who Don't: Poverty, Morality, and Family in Rural America.* Minneapolis: University of Minnesota Press.

——. 2011. "Men Without Sawmills: Job Loss and Gender Identity in Rural America." In *Economic Restructuring and Family Well-Being in Rural America*, ed. Kristin Smith and Ann R. Tickamyer, 82–102. University Park: Pennsylvania State University Press.

———. 2014. "Rural Poverty: The Great Recession, Rising Unemployment, and the Under-Utilized Safety Net." In *Rural America in a Globalizing World*, ed. Conner Bailey, Elizabeth Ransom, and Leif Jensen, 523–39. Morgantown: West Virginia University Press.

Smith, Kristin. 2008. "Working Hard for the Money: Trends in Women's Employment, 1970–2007." Report on Rural America No. 5. Durham, NH: Carsey Institute, University of New Hampshire.

———. 2009. "Increased Reliance on Wives as Breadwinners During the First Year of the Recession." Issue Brief 9. Durham, NH: Carsey Institute, University of New Hampshire.

———. 2010. "Wives as Breadwinners: Wives' Share of Family Earnings Hits Historic High During the Second Year of the Great Recession." Factsheet 20. Durham, NH: Carsey Institute, University of New Hampshire.

———. 2011. "Changing Roles: Women and Work in Rural America." In *Economic Restructuring and Family Well-Being in Rural America*, ed. Kristin E. Smith and Ann R. Tickamyer, 60–81. University Park: Pennsylvania State University Press.

———. 2012. "Recessions Accelerate Trend of Wives as Breadwinners." Issue Brief 56. Durham, NH: Carsey School of Public Policy, University of New Hampshire.

———. 2015a. "After Great Recession, More Married Fathers Providing Child Care." Issue Brief 79. Durham, NH: Carsey School of Public Policy, University of New Hampshire.

———. 2015b. "Family Income Composition." In *Emerging Trends in the Social and Behavioral Sciences*, ed. Robert Scott and Stephen Kosslyn. Hoboken, NJ: Wiley.

———. 2015c. "Women as Economic Providers: Dual-Earner Families Thrive as Women's Earnings Rise." Issue Brief 84. Durham, NH: Carsey School of Public Policy, University of New Hampshire.

Smith, Kristin, and Rebecca Glauber. 2013. "Exploring the Spatial Wage Penalty for Women: Does It Matter Where You Live?" *Social Science Research* 42(5):1390–1401.

Smith, Kristin, and Marybeth Mattingly. 2012. "Rural Families in Transition." In *International Handbook of Rural Demography*, ed. Laszlo Kulcsar and Katherine Curtis, 239–53. New York: Springer.

Smith, Kristin, and Andrew Schaefer. 2014. "Families Continue to Rely on Wives as Breadwinners Post Recession: An Analysis by State and Place Type." Issue Brief 75. Durham, NH: Carsey Institute, University of New Hampshire.

Smith, Kristin, and Ann R. Tickamyer, eds. 2011. *Economic Restructuring and Family Well-Being in Rural America*. University Park: Pennsylvania State University Press.

Snyder, Anastasia R., Susan L. Brown, and Erin P. Condo. 2004. "Residential Differences in Family Formation: The Significance of Cohabitation." *Rural Sociology* 69:235–60.

Struthers, Cynthia. 2014. "The Past Is the Present: Gender and the Status of Rural Women." In *Rural America in a Globalizing World*, ed. Conner Bailey, Elizabeth Ransom, and Leif Jensen, 489–505. Morgantown: West Virginia University Press.

Tickamyer, Ann R. 1996. "Rural Myth, Rural Reality: Diversity and Change in Rural America for the 21st Century." Keynote address at the NEC*TAS Rural Conference, Santa Fe, NM.

Tickamyer, Ann R., and Debra Henderson. 2003. "Rural Women: New Roles for the New Century?" In *Challenges for Rural America in the Twenty-First Century*, ed. David Brown and Louis Swanson, 109–17. University Park: Pennsylvania State University Press.

Tigges, Leann M., and Hae Yeon Choo. 2012. "Family Matters: Gendered Employment and the Rural Myth." In *International Handbook of Rural Demography*, ed. László and Katherine J. Curtis, chap. 16. New York: Springer.

USDA, 2015. "Rural Poverty and Well-Being." http://www.ers.usda.gov/topics/rural-economy-population/rural-poverty-well-being/poverty-overview.aspx.

Willams, Joan. 2000. *Unbending Gender: Why Family and Work Conflict and What to Do About It*. New York: Oxford University Press.

CHAPTER 6

Racial Inequalities and Poverty in Rural America

Mark H. Harvey

"It should be very clear that we are dealing with a problem of social structure, not a problem of social misfits."

—Gene F. Summers, "Minorities
in Rural Society," 1991

"Clearly, discussions and analyses of poverty concentration in rural America cannot be separated from the issue of race."

—Daniel T. Lichter and
Kenneth M. Johnson,
"The Changing Spatial Con-
centration of America's Rural
Poor Population," 2007

INTRODUCTION

Rates of poverty among rural racial minorities are two to three times higher than that for rural whites (USDA Economic Research Service 2015b). Such disparities in social outcomes were long held to be caused by racial differences conceptualized as biological differences: the fact that people of European origin were less likely to be poor was explained as an outcome of their more highly developed brains and greater intelligence. There is, however, no biological basis for categorizing humans into racial groups; race is a *social* fact, not a natural one (Emirbayer and Desmond 2015). As social facts, racial groups are outcomes of social processes of racialization, the origins of which trace to the beginning of the modern era in the sixteenth century and whose causes include the development of the global capitalist economic system, the nation-state-based political system, and the human sciences. Racialization also exerted effects on the construction of each of these systems and linked them together to constitute comprehensively racialized social systems at the national level (Fredrickson 2002), or what Winant (2001) calls the "world racial system." As the quintessential modern nation, the United States developed with racism playing a particularly determinant role. Despite the progress toward racial justice made in recent decades, racism continues to fundamentally shape the U.S. economy, politics, and culture (Alexander 2010).

Over twenty years ago, the Taskforce on Persistent Rural Poverty (1993) noted that questions of race and racism never received much attention from rural sociologists. This remains true today. In the past two decades, only a handful of studies have examined how extreme rates of poverty among minorities are reproduced in rural America. Moreover, the few studies that have been done are marked by a number of shortcomings. First, most focus on African Americans concentrated in the region of the South known as the Black Belt (see the case study/appendix to this chapter; Duncan 2014; Harris 2013; Harvey 2013a; Harris and Worthen 2003; Green 2002). Although the increasing settlement of new immigrants in rural areas has sparked some recent research on rural Latinos (Lichter 2012; Chavez 2005), scant attention has been given to the Borderlands region of the Southwest where poverty among rural Latinos is most concentrated and persistent (Harvey 2011, 2013b; Harvey and Pickering 2010; Pickering et al. 2006; Fontenot et al. 2010; Saenz and Torres 2003). Finally, even less attention has been paid to rural Native Americans living on and around reservation lands (Harvey and Pickering 2010; Pickering and Jewel 2008; Gonzales, Lyson, and Mauer 2007; Pickering et al. 2006; Gonzales 2003; Pickering 2000, 2001).

Perhaps more problematic than the lack of literature is the fact that studies of rural minority poverty do not analyze the specific role of institutionalized systems of racial domination as factors in its production. Rather, attention is focused on other factors such as political and economic structures, levels of human capital, and social capital or network ties. To the extent that racism is considered, it is inadequately conceptualized in two basic respects: (1) it is treated as an epiphenomenon of economic and political arrangements, and (2) it is reduced to the legacies of white supremacist systems of slavery, segregation/debt peonage, and forced removal. As such, there is no research that examines how rural minority poverty is generated today by contemporary structures of racial domination, that is, by a racism not reducible to the fading echoes of historical systems of domination (see Albrecht, Albrecht, and Murguia 2005 for a partial exception). The failure to theorize racial domination in rural America reduces racism to something that existed mainly in the past, confuses systems of racial domination with softer forms of ethnic discrimination, and leads to the view that the legacy effects of historical racism are fading with the mere passage of time. The policy implication of these misconceptions is that nothing needs to be done by the government to confront the specifically racial dimensions of minority poverty.

Other chapters in this book focus on the economic, political, human capital, and civic factors involved in rural poverty. This chapter focuses on the systems of racial domination found in America's rural minority regions and examines the specific ways racism is woven into the institutional structure (economic, political, and civic) of minority communities and how it functions to systematically trap huge segments of these populations in poverty. The scholarly silence on this question makes it the proverbial elephant in the room in our understanding of rural poverty more generally.

The chapter begins with a brief overview of how specialists in racial and ethnic relations conceptualize race and racism. Next, the empirical pattern of poverty found across America's three major rural minority groups is presented with attention to how it compares to that of poor rural whites. To understand how race interacts with place to generate minority poverty, the rural regions and communities in which rural minority poverty is most concentrated are analyzed with attention to the role of systems of racial domination or white supremacy in the construction and operation of their economic, political, and civic spheres. A common set of racialized institutional conditions found across all three regions is described. In each case, these poverty-generating institutional arrangements are not merely legacies of historical systems of white supremacy but outcomes of the *interaction* of those systems with the race-based civil rights movement, the race-conscious federal government programs of the 1960s, and white resistance to racial progress. Finally, data from recent case studies of poor rural minority communities are drawn on to illustrate some specific ways in which racialized institutional structures generate extreme rates of rural minority poverty. The chapter concludes with a brief discussion of policy recommendations that would likely reduce minority poverty but are routinely rejected or unfunded by policy makers, many of whom subscribe to the new racial ideology of "color-blind universalism"—the belief that racism no longer plays any role in the production of racial inequalities and thus race should play no role in the construction of antipoverty policy (Emirbayer and Desmond 2015).

RACIALIZATION PROCESSES AND RACIALIZED SOCIAL STRUCTURES

The failure of scholars to deal adequately with the role of race in rural minority poverty is related to the difficulties scholars of all stripes continue to have conceptualizing it. Those who specialize in race and ethnicity continue to debate basic questions: What is race? What is racism? And how do these phenomena differ, if at all, from ethnicity and ethnic discrimination? Engaging these debates is far beyond the scope of this chapter, but some basic points about race and racism on which there is broad scholarly agreement are briefly reviewed.

First, racial groups and racism are attributes of a particular type of social structure, not human biology. Not all societies categorize people by race, and those that do have only done so for a few hundred years. The existence of racial minorities is a feature or outcome of a *racialized social system*; that is, a society in which one social group secures economic, political, and cultural domination over others in part through the construction of an ideology of "racial" difference. What is specific about systems of racial domination in contrast to ethnic domination is that racial ideologies define subordinated groups as permanently incapable of assimilating to the dominant group's culture, i.e., the "mainstream." Moreover, the alleged inability to assimilate is held to be grounded in factors that are innate or essential to the subordinated groups. Initially, the essence of racial difference was conceptualized as biological; as noted, Europeans were believed to be intellectually superior to other races due to their superior brains. Today, social exclusion and domination on the basis of race operate more through cultural racism, i.e., the essentialization of alleged *cultural* differences held to obtain between racial groups. For example, many Americans believe that the high rate of poverty among African Americans is due to the prevalence of a "culture of poverty" that does not value education and hard work. Whereas biological racism located the cause of African American poverty in the black body (i.e., its physical essence), the new cultural racism locates it in these alleged cultural beliefs and practices (Fredrickson 2002).

Another point on which there is broad agreement is that the process of racialization, or the invention of the social category of race, was crucial to the development of the modern global capitalist economy and nation-state system (Winant 2001). The idea of race provided the moral justification and legal basis for the conquest, extermination, and enslavement of non-European peoples by Europeans who were, at the very same time, attacking their aristocratic regimes because they were an affront to the universal and natural rights of man. By defining non-Europeans as something less than men, race made the crimes committed against them morally acceptable. For example, although slavery had existed in various forms since the dawn of history, the uniquely dehumanizing and commoditized form of *chattel* slavery practiced in the U.S. South only emerged in the late seventeenth century through the combination of a rise in demand for field labor with the emerging practice of ascribing essential meaning to human bodies based on color and geographic origin. The ascription of racial meaning did not reflect any real differences between people assigned to what eventually came to be seen as the "black" and "white" races. Rather, the practice of ascription itself, *combined* with the practice of chattel slavery, functioned to *racialize* the social relation between people of European origin and those of African origin, transforming them into permanently different and unequal "races" (Emirbayer and Desmond 2015; Frederickson 2002).

Understanding racial groups as outcomes of racialization processes offers some analytical advantages for thinking about racial inequality and poverty. First, it allows us to see the objects of analysis—racial groups—in a relational sense, that is, as situated in structured positions of racial dominance (white) and subordination (nonwhite) and thus in constant tension (Emirbayer and Desmond 2015). Second, it allows us to see how structures of racial domination—and the always present practices of resistance and accommodation to them—vary across space and change over time in relation to variation in other types of social relations including economic, political, and religious/ideological relations (Fredrickson 2002). Finally, racialization illuminates how different empirical manifestations of racial domination—e.g., slavery, Jim Crow, and mass incarceration (Alexander 2010)—are comprised of analytically distinct dimensions including, for example, a "horizontal" dimension (how individuals see and treat racialized others) and a "vertical" dimension (how access to power, status, and resources is structured between racialized groups) (Telles 2004).

THE RACIAL AND SPATIAL PATTERNING OF POVERTY IN RURAL AMERICA

According to 2010 U.S. census data, 22 percent of America's rural population belongs to a racial or ethnic minority group. (Please note, "rural" is defined here using the Housing Assistance Council's "rural and small town" designation.) Although African Americans long constituted the nation's largest rural minority, their 8.3 percent share of the rural population was eclipsed in 2010 by Hispanics, whose rapid growth propelled them to 9.3 percent. Native Americans make up about 2 percent of the rural population, Asian Americans equal about 1 percent, and those identifying as "more than one race" constitute about 2 percent. Thus, African Americans and Hispanics together constitute nearly 80 percent of the rural minority population (Housing Assistance Council 2012).

Compared to rural whites (as well as to urban minorities), rural minorities are much more likely to be poor. In 2014, 15 percent of non-Hispanic rural whites were in poverty, whereas 37 percent of rural African Americans, 33 percent of rural Native Americans, and 28 percent of rural Hispanics lived below the poverty line (USDA Economic Research Service 2015b). Rural minorities are also much more likely than whites to experience correlates of poverty. For example, in the wake of the 2007 financial collapse, unemployment among rural African Americans leaped 9 percentage points to about 19 percent in 2011 and among Hispanics it jumped 5.5 points to about 11 percent. In contrast, unemployment among rural whites increased only 3.2 percentage points to about 8 percent (USDA Economic Research Service 2011). Higher rates of unemployment and joblessness mean that minority families are also more likely than whites to rely on welfare programs (Pickering et al. 2006), experience problems with housing (Housing Assistance Council 2012), and suffer health problems (Burton et al. 2013); they also are less likely to achieve levels of education needed to obtain a decent job (Brown and Schafft 2011).

The extreme inequality in rates of poverty between rural whites and minorities is accompanied by a similarly extreme difference in the degree to which group members experience *spatially concentrated poverty*, that is, live among large numbers of other poor people in what are effectively rural ghettos (Lichter, Parisi, and Taquino 2012). The minority poor are heavily concentrated in rural regions, counties, towns, and neighborhoods lacking employment opportunities, effective public services, and networks of social capital. These community conditions compound the individual-level disadvantages of living in a poor family and reduce the likelihood that any particular individual will have access to the resources needed to escape poverty. Thus, for residents of such communities, moving out of poverty often requires moving to a more economically vibrant place.

The spatial concentration of rural minorities and the rural minority poor exists at two different geographic scales, the regional and the local. Figure 6.1 shows the places in which the poorest rural counties in the United States are clustered. As such, it highlights the three rural regions

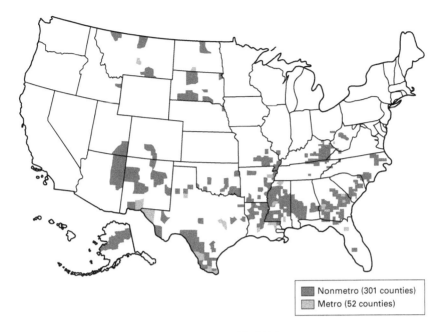

Figure 6.1   Persistent-poverty counties, 1980–2011.

Source: USDA, Economic Research Service, using data from the U.S. Census Bureau.

in which the minority poor are concentrated: the Black Belt of the Deep South, the Borderlands of the Southwest, and the Native American reservation lands concentrated in the Southwest and Upper Midwest. (Note, it also highlights the Appalachian region in which white rural poverty is most concentrated.) African Americans are by far the most regionally concentrated minority group with 83 percent of all rural African Americans residing in the Black Belt region. Less concentrated, but still heavily so, are rural Hispanics, slightly more than half of whom reside in the Borderlands region of Texas, New Mexico, Arizona, and California, with 25 percent in Texas alone. Similarly, slightly more than half of all Native Americans live in only five states (Oklahoma, Arizona, New Mexico, Alaska, and North Carolina), with about one-third residing on reservation or tribal lands (Housing Assistance Council 2012; Brown and Schafft 2011).

Each rural minority region exhibits a rate of poverty well above the national average (Fontenot et al. 2010), but poverty rates within them vary widely across counties, cities, and neighborhoods. At these levels, the minority poor tend to be concentrated in "high-poverty" places, that is, places with poverty rates of 20 percent or higher. According to Burton et al. (2013), the degree to which poor rural minorities are concentrated in such places is "often staggering" as 67 percent of poor rural African Americans live in such counties. The proportion of poor rural Hispanics in high-poverty counties is significantly lower at 39 percent and is trending downward due to the diasporic pattern of new immigrant settlement. That said, it remains 50 percent higher than the 27 percent of rural whites who live in such counties (comparable data on Native Americans are not available) (Lichter et al. 2012). In addition, these places tend to exhibit *persistent high poverty*; that is, they have had poverty rates of 20 percent or higher since at least 1980 (Burton et al. 2013). Finally, rates of minority poverty in the poorest counties in these regions often exceed 40 percent (Pickering et al. 2006; Harvey 2013a).

During the 1990s, the strong growth of the U.S. economy contributed to significant declines in poverty among rural minorities in the Black Belt and Borderlands regions. Moreover, overall declines in poverty were accompanied by declines in the spatial concentration of minority poverty across both regions at the county level, suggesting that broad economic growth alone may contribute to the reduction of concentrated poverty (Fontenot et al. 2010). Rural counties, however, cover vast geographic territories containing many local places that often vary widely in economic resources; government services; influence on regional, state, and federal policy decisions; and civic conditions. Lichter et al. (2012) analyzed patterns and trends in minority poverty at the *subcounty* levels of cities, towns, and "census-designated places." They found that from 2000 to 2009 rural minority poverty actually became *more* concentrated at these spatial scales, suggesting a trend toward the further ghettoization of poor rural minorities, not only away from whites but also from more affluent members of their own minority groups. In their words, "the poor are increasingly sorted into high-poverty cities, small towns and rural places while the non-poor are being redistributed into non-poor communities" (378).

In sum, rates of rural minority poverty and the degree to which it is spatially concentrated mark it as qualitatively different from that experienced by rural whites. The extremely high rates of minority poverty are no doubt related to the degree to which these groups are concentrated in uniquely disadvantaged places. Understanding rural minority poverty thus requires understanding the particular characteristics of the regions and communities that generate it, including the structure of their economic, political, and civic spheres (Lichter et al. 2012, 367–68). This, in turn, requires examining the historical development, transformation, and reorganization of these institutions under different racial regimes (Alexander 2010).

RACIALIZED SOCIAL STRUCTURES AND MINORITY POVERTY IN THE BLACK BELT, BORDERLANDS, AND RESERVATION LANDS

Harris (2013) is among the few rural sociologists who treat contemporary racism as a key causal factor in rural minority poverty. In reference to the Black Belt region, she writes: "Racism has in effect been the impetus for and has deepened and intensified the impacts of historically weak investments in economic diversification, basic education and skills training rendering the region much weaker economically than any other in the country" (3). Echoing Winant's (2001) argument that racism becomes a factor in its own reproduction over time through a process of "circular and cumulative causation," she also notes: "It can be argued in fact that the *interrelationship* between racism, diminished African American economic power, low social mobility, constricted civic culture and the sustained underdevelopment of the Black Belt plantation south economy form *mutually reinforcing feedback* loops" (Harris 2013, 3, emphasis added).

Understanding how these feedback loops operate is key to explaining the extreme rates of rural minority poverty we see today. This requires an ethnographic and historical-institutional approach that examines the role of race in determining the social contexts in which residents of these communities interact with each other in the conduct of commerce, governance, education, recreation, worship, and civic engagement, among many other things. Of course, these contemporary contexts must be understood with reference to their broader historical-institutional determinants (Duncan 2014).

As noted previously, case studies of America's rural minority communities are few, focus mainly on the Black Belt, and pay insufficient attention to the role of race and racism. Thus, what follows draws heavily on my own research on persistent high-poverty minority places (Harvey 2011, 2013a, 2013b; Harvey and Pickering 2010; Pickering et al. 2006) and the limited literature (Duncan 2014; Pickering and Jewell 2008; Pickering 2000, 2001; Hyland 2008; Wright Austin 2006; Schultz 2006; Gonzales 2003; Gonzales et al. 2007; Gutiérrez 1998; Maril 1989) to (1) describe the basic institutional structures common to communities across the

Black Belt, Borderlands, and reservation regions today and (2) explain the role of racialization in the production and maintenance of these structures. The common pattern can be briefly summarized as follows:

1. Extremely weak and undiversified private sector labor markets.
2. Heavy reliance on federal government transfer programs. This reliance is not limited to that of the poor on welfare programs. Rather, it includes the broad reliance of the middle class, e.g., teachers, health care workers, and nonprofit administrators, among others, on government-funded employment.
3. Ineffective and unaccountable political institutions (e.g., county boards, city councils, school boards) marked by elite rule and patronage practices.
4. Fractured and highly fractious civil societies divided by complex lines of race, class, politics, and family and that lack the basic hallmarks of civil society, i.e., an orientation toward a common good and independence from elite control.

In each region, each of these institutional shortcomings intersects with the others to form thoroughly racialized social structures or regimes (Wright Austin 2006) that systematically generate extreme rates of poverty among minority residents. In what follows, I highlight the ways in which processes of racialization played—and continue to play—a determinant role in the organization of these regimes. I show how the contemporary regimes are outcomes of three stages of conflict between forces of racial domination and racial progress. These stages include (1) the establishment of white supremacist political and economic regimes in the nineteenth century, (2) the civil rights era movement to dismantle them during the 1950s and 1960s, and (3) white resistance to racial integration, specifically the race-conscious federal government policies and programs necessary to achieve it, that emerged in the 1970s and gained momentum in the 1980s and 1990s. Analysis of these stages and the interactions between them illustrates how the significant achievements of the civil rights era were but a partial victory in the struggle against racism. It also explains how social institutions and practices in these places remain racialized today in ways that are inherently linked to yet clearly distinct from past arrangements. One key difference is that the role of racism in the operations of contemporary institutions is more difficult to confront today precisely because the processes that reproduce racial inequality are less overtly racial than they formerly were. Indeed, the dominant racial ideology of color blindness—which argues that the fact that race *should not* matter requires that we, especially our federal government, act as if it *does not* matter—encourages active ignorance of racism (Emirbayer and Desmond 2015; Omi and Winant 1994).

THE ERA OF OVERT WHITE SUPREMACY AND THE FOUNDATIONS OF RURAL MINORITY POVERTY

The foundations of the four institutional conditions that mark America's regions of rural minority poverty were laid during the era of overt white supremacy. For roughly 300 years (1667–1965) white supremacy was a pillar in the social structure of what became the United States of America. A brief look at that history suggests that rates of poverty among rural racial minorities remain astronomically high today because the very development of the nation's political and economic systems were predicated on the treatment of people of non-European descent as fit only for servitude or extinction (Snipp 1996). As argued by Omi and Winant (1994), government, from the federal to the state and local levels, played a central role in constructing regional racial regimes tailored to meet the specific demands of white elites. Although there is much variation between the experiences of African Americans, Hispanic Americans, and Native Americans, the incorporation of each group into American society by state violence and their categorization by the state as people ineligible for citizenship on the basis of race was key to their economic hyperexploitation, political marginalization, and social denigration.

The first African Americans were essentially prisoners of war subjected to forced migration, lifelong servitude, and myriad forms of violence. Concentrated in slavery in the Black Belt region, African Americans experienced the cruel irony of being the main engine of global capitalist development while lacking the right to own even their own bodies. Following the end of slavery in 1865, the federal government's refusal to grant land to the "freedmen" left most African Americans economically dependent on whites. This allowed white elites to establish a new regime of racial domination in the South based on segregation. Sanctioned by the U.S. Supreme Court's decision in *Plessey v. Ferguson* (1896), state- and local-level "Jim Crow" laws functioned to hold rural African Americans in the Black Belt in a condition of quasi-slavery for another hundred years (Alexander 2010).

The largest subgroup of Hispanics, Mexican Americans, became "Americans" through the conquest of Mexico in 1848 and the incorporation of roughly half its territory including more than 100,000 of its residents. Wide variation in the class, culture, and phenotypical characteristics of the conquered population made their initial racial status, and thus eligibility for citizenship, ambiguous. Ultimately, the flood of Anglo settlers into the Borderlands and their appropriation of Mexican-owned land contributed to the consolidation of the identity of people of Mexican descent as "nonwhite" (Nakano Glenn 2002). As such, U.S.-born Mexican Americans were deemed ineligible for citizenship until 1898, and the right of Mexican immigrants to naturalize as citizens was withheld until 1940 (Emirbayer and Desmond 2015). Lacking rights, the economic, political, and social status of Mexican Americans collapsed relative to that of the Anglos. By 1900, a thoroughly racialized social structure akin in many ways to that of the Black Belt placed most land and political power in the hands of whites and reduced Mexican Americans to politically disenfranchised laborers (Bender 2010). The downward spiral experienced by Mexican Americans occurred during the era (1880–1924) in which the U.S. government eventually barred all immigration from Asia, making people of Mexican descent—on both sides of the border—the primary source of cheap and seasonal labor in the West. The binational system of migrant labor established at that time remains central to the U.S. economy today and a driving force behind the concentration of poverty in the region (Pickering et al. 2006). (See chapter 7 for an analysis of immigration in rural America today.)

Finally, U.S. military aggression caused the mass loss of life and land among Native Americans and their forced removal to geographically isolated reservation lands. The varied experiences of the more than 500 Native American tribes recognized by the federal government defy easy generalization, but conquest followed by removal and isolation from the mainstream economy and polity was the general pattern (Pickering 2000). Like rural African Americans and Mexican Americans, Native Americans living on and around reservations were formally denied citizenship, in their case until 1924, with certain states prohibiting them from voting until 1957. In contrast to the other groups, white domination of Native Americans was imposed more directly by the federal government through its Bureau of Indian Affairs (BIA). In some cases, federal overseers encouraged tribes to assimilate to white culture and society by privatizing their lands and training them to be small farmers. Such policies however, for example, the Dawes Act (1877), also resulted in the transfer of tribal land to white settlers and the spatial and social fragmentation of tribal communities. Akin to Mexican Americans, the denial of citizenship rights and loss of land reduced many Native Americans to a source of cheap seasonal labor for white farmers, particularly in the Upper Midwest (Gonzales 2003; Pickering 2000, 2001).

In the Black Belt and Borderlands, the white elites' demand for cheap and readily available labor led them not only to deny rights to racial minorities but to actively block the development of diversified local economies and labor markets, good governance, and open civil societies. These practices produced racially polarized class and civic structures in which white elites held monopolies on resources and power (Duncan 2014; Quadagno 1994; Maril 1989). As such, investments in basic infrastructure that would have facilitated economic development, but also would have created new competition for labor, were minimized. So, too, were investments in public education that might have given minority children a pathway out of agricultural, extractive, and domestic labor. Federal welfare benefits were also kept pitifully low and largely out of the reach of minority families. Finally, those who challenged these arrangements faced legal barriers as well as extra-legal obstacles in the form of white supremacist civic organizations such as the Ku Klux Klan. The process of racial domination played out somewhat differently on the reservation lands. In the end, however, direct domination via the BIA, assisted by select tribal collaborators (see below), also produced racially fractured economic, government, and civic structures (Pickering 2000).

Finally, in each case elites used race to garner the support of the white working class by offering them material, political, and psychological benefits of whiteness. Poor whites enjoyed relatively better jobs and higher wages than minorities, the right to vote, and the positive feeling or "psychological wage" associated with membership in the "superior" race (Nakano Glenn 2002).

THE CIVIL RIGHTS ERA: RACIAL PROGRESS AND THE PARTIAL TRANSFORMATION OF RACIAL DOMINATION IN RURAL MINORITY COMMUNITIES

During the 1960s, resistance to racism in the United States reached its apex. The combination of the civil rights movement with new, racially progressive federal government policies finally relegated America's *overtly* white supremacist system to an artifact of history. At the same time, however, the success of the movement and the new policies created new forms of racialized institutions and practices that not only continued to pit minority groups against whites but also created or exacerbated fissures, factions, and conflicts within the minority groups themselves over access to power and resources.

As was the case in the construction of white supremacy, government played a central role in its dismantlement. Rather than acting to exclude minorities on the basis of race, the federal government reversed course, actively striking down state and local race laws and taking affirmative steps to ameliorate racial inequality and injustice. These steps included the *de facto* extension of the rights of citizenship to rural minorities through the passage of the Civil Rights Act of 1964, the Voting Rights Act of 1965, and the Indian Education and Self-Determination Act of 1975. At the same time, new federal government programs and policies targeting high-poverty areas and racial minorities granted minority communities access to and control over substantive resources including government jobs and contracts (Quadagno 1994; Pickering 2000).

Across each region examined here, these *overtly racially progressive* policies and programs resulted in the elevation of rural minorities to positions of political power at the local level and the development of a minority middle class employed in the administration and delivery of social programs. Key to these achievements was the fact that the right to vote was accompanied by access to substantive resources made available through the new federal antipoverty, education, and economic development programs delivered through the Office of Economic Opportunity (OEO). The OEO was created specifically to bypass white power structures at the state and local levels and grant control over federal program administration directly to minority leaders. This gave minorities control, for the first time, over the distribution of government-funded jobs, contracts, and services. This, in turn, allowed minority leaders to win election to local government offices and maintain office through the practice of distributing these resources as patronage—a practice that white ethnic groups in urban areas employed to secure political power and make economic gains a century earlier (Quadagno 1994). As Gutiérrez (1998) writes in reference to the Borderlands city of which he became the first Chicano mayor, as Mexican Americans took control, "grants from Washington DC began to pour in" and "we nearly tripled the size of the . . . school operating budget" (212). Indeed, Bureau of Labor Statistics data show massive growth in public sector employment in these areas between 1970 and 1990, with "government" accounting for 40 to 50 percent of *total earnings* in the poorest counties in each region—roughly three times the national average (Pickering et al. 2006). Given the decrepit state of private sector labor markets, achievement of middle-class status effectively depended upon obtaining a job in expanding school systems, health care systems, community action agencies, and other government and government-funded nonprofits.

The dismantlement of overtly white racial regimes in these regions required no less than the creation of a new arm of the federal welfare state that targeted assistance directly to racial minorities, i.e., the "minority welfare state" (Quadagno 1994). The benefits these programs delivered to minority communities were extremely significant; however, they were far from a panacea. The transfer of some local-level political power to minority leaders operating within the corrupt and racialized systems of government established under white supremacy could not but produce new forms of minority patronage or machine politics under which the economic well-being of residents became linked to the support they exhibited for the new minority political elites. Thus, as under the white regimes, residents remained in a structural position of weakness relative to political elites, making it difficult for them to hold officials accountable. Lack of accountability, in turn, allowed incompetence, nepotism, and corruption to continue to flourish as it did under the old white regimes. These issues, in turn, continued to deter private sector actors from making investments in the regions as well as fueled residents' lack of trust in government (Harvey 2013a, 2013b; Gonzalez et al. 2007).

Today, white leaders as well as many minority leaders cite corrupt and incompetent local government for the lack of economic development and persistence of poverty in the these regions. Minority officials, especially those who emphasize racial inequality, are typically the main targets of this critique. However, it must be emphasized that minority leaders did not invent systems of rural machine politics—they inherited them. What is more, while machine politics are clearly problematic, the fact that they have facilitated racial progress in these areas—as they did for the urban Irish of the nineteenth century—means that they should not be universally condemned (Gutiérrez 1998). For it must also be noted that the white political elite in these regions did not quietly accept minority equality, never mind leadership. While minorities took control of some local-level offices, whites generally retained office at the more powerful county and state levels as well as control over most private sector resources.

RACISM AND MINORITY POVERTY IN THE POST–CIVIL
RIGHTS ERA OF "COLOR BLINDNESS"

The overt racial conflicts of the civil rights era resulted not in the destruc-
tion of rural white supremacy but in the establishment of new states of
racial equilibrium between white supremacy and movements for racial
progress (Omi and Winant 1994; Emirbayer and Desmond 2015). In the
end, both sides made adjustments and accommodations that are reflected
today in racial playing fields that are more complex, multidimensional,
and opaque than those of the 1960s. The character of these fields stems
from the fact that significant numbers of minorities have moved up
into the middle class in tandem with the rise of the racial ideology of
color-blind universalism. As a racial ideology, color-blind universalism
perpetuates racial inequality by reducing "racism" to erstwhile overt systems of legal domination such as Jim Crow and thus relegating it to the
past (Thernstrom and Thernstrom 1997). As such, color-blind ideology
functions to obscure the role of racism in three basic forms of racialized
conflict observed in each region today: (1) between white political and
economic elites and minority political elites, (2) among different factions
of minority political elites, and (3) between the minority middle class
and the minority poor. Each region illustrates one of these dimensions of
conflict, but each type of conflict exists in every region.

1. WHITE POLITICAL AND ECONOMIC ELITES VS. MINORITY POLITICAL ELITES IN THE BLACK BELT

Nowhere does the white-versus-minority aspect of racial conflict remain
more visible than in the Black Belt where the acquisition of political power
by African Americans at the local level was not accompanied by comparable
gains in the private sector, which remain thoroughly dominated by whites.
Thus, the institutional structure of the Black Belt is defined by what might
be called racially bifurcated elite rule. This is a type of elite rule in which
(1) those who hold political power are separate from, and hold interests that
are opposed to, those who hold private economic power along a racial line;
and (2) the economic and bureaucratic interests of both groups have little
connection to the interests of the residents of the region, especially the poor
(Duncan 2014; Harvey 2013a; Schultz 2006; Wright Austin 2006).

Across the Black Belt, African American elected officials oversee the
administration of city governments, school districts, and other core public

institutions. In some cases, these officials are merely the "black faces" of white elites who believe that they cannot win elections themselves due to their race. In other cases, however, these officials represent authentic alternatives to white elite rule. In either case, elected officials in the region often secure long tenure in office though practicing a post–civil rights era version of racialized machine politics comprised of two main elements: the allocation of public resources to supporters as political patronage, and the use of racialized discourse to portray their competition as categorically unworthy of public trust.

Regarding the former tactic, nearly every community study conducted in the region over the past twenty-five years has found that patronage remains a significant problem and is practiced by both white and black elected officials. Regarding the latter, studies also suggest that both black and white political elites use racialized discourse in their election campaigns. For example, African American leaders who emerged from the civil rights movement often seek to secure the black vote by fostering a sense of racial solidarity against white candidates whom they portray as not caring about blacks and seeking to reestablish total white control over the region. The effectiveness of this tactic is likely enhanced by the stark juxtaposition of nearly all-white elite neighborhoods, dinner clubs, churches, and private schools on one side versus all-black shanty towns, community centers, and public schools on the other (Duncan 2014; Harvey 2013a).

In contrast, white candidates—or their black stand-ins—use more subtle and nuanced racial discourse, in other words, color-blind discourse, to indict their opponents as unworthy. For example, African American leaders who emphasize the need to remedy racial inequalities are characterized as "dinosaurs" who cannot get past the pain of a bygone era; as "reverse racists" who only care about blacks; or as cynical opportunists who "cry racism" to keep the white and black communities divided and thereby keep themselves ensconced in office. Additionally, racial code words or dog whistles developed during the late 1960s are also employed, such as charging African American leaders with encouraging welfare dependency and tolerating criminality (Harvey 2013a; Duncan 2014).

2. MINORITY POLITICAL ELITES VS. MINORITY POLITICAL ELITES ON THE RESERVATIONS

In each region, systems of overt white supremacy operated in part through garnering some degree of collaboration from select factions of minority groups. Dividing the dominated groups internally and granting responsibilities and privileges to preferred factions produced more effective and efficient systems of racial control. It also established deep fissures within minority communities that remain salient today and constrain the ability of minority leaders to create community and economic development.

The intragroup dimension of racialized conflict and its effects on local institutional conditions is particularly evident in the Native American reservation lands where the federal government began selecting particular tribal clans as collaborators in the mid-to late-nineteenth century (Pickering 2000). Often the selection of one clan to oversee others tracked preexisting lines of familial and cultural distinction. Moreover, the factions selected for leadership tended to be those that were more assimilated to white culture or viewed as more amenable to it. This practice of divide and rule on the part of the federal government racialized what had previously been mere cultural differences within tribes by making access to material resources and political power contingent upon assimilation to whiteness and subservience to white interests. Among some tribes, clans selected for collaboration became known as "mixed-bloods" (Pickering 2000; Gonzales 2003).

A key factor in the racial progress achieved during the civil rights era was the cultivation of race consciousness and racial pride among minority groups. In some tribal areas—for example, among the Lakota Sioux of the Great Plains—this led to the emergence of a new group of leaders who became known as "full-bloods" and who were committed to the restoration and maintenance of traditional cultural practices. (Note, the reference to blood marks a social-political distinction, not a biological one.) The emergence of the full-blood faction occurred during the early 1970s as the federal government was granting tribes greater authority over administrative processes. Since that time, struggles for control over tribal government and federal resources have been organized along the mixed-blood versus full-blood distinction. This, in turn, has undermined the ability of tribes to unite behind development projects. For example, mixed-blood factions tend to pursue economic development strategies oriented toward the assimilation of the tribes to the mainstream. Lacking marketable resources, one strategy these leaders pursue is the commoditization of tribal culture to create a "cultural tourism" industry. Full-bloods are offended by the idea of exploiting their tribal cultures for economic purposes and thus tend to oppose such plans (Pickering and Jewell 2008).

The intersection of tribal factionalization with patronage practices has curbed the ability of tribes to parlay the financial windfalls garnered through Indian gaming into development projects. Gonzales (2003) notes that during the 1990s tribes that opened casinos witnessed an average drop in unemployment from 38 percent to 13 percent, and in the year 2001 alone they accrued $12.7 billion in revenue from gaming. These windfalls, however, often "created or exacerbated existing cleavages between tribal members over power and control of tribal resources" (Gonzales 2003, 52). On one side, some argued that tribal governments should control gaming revenues to make investments that would contribute to long-term development. Others maintained that the problem of accountability among tribal governments warranted that gaming revenues be distributed directly to tribal members on a per capita basis. Regardless of which argument prevailed, economic development on many reservations has been significantly constrained by racially instituted factional struggles not only for control over tribal resources but also over what it means to be Native American.

3. THE MINORITY ADMINISTRATIVE MIDDLE CLASS VS. THE MINORITY POOR IN THE BORDERLANDS

The issue of race is perhaps most complex and subtle in the Borderlands where centuries of Spanish control (1600s–1820), extensive intermarriage between Anglos and people of Mexican descent, and the ongoing influx of new immigrants from Mexico has produced a racialized social structure that is more ambiguous, fluid, and linked to class, culture, nationality, and legal status than in the other regions.

In the Borderlands, the effects of the changes wrought by the policies and programs of the civil rights era were significantly leveraged by concurrent changes to U.S. immigration, labor, and development policies toward Mexico. These major changes included passage of the Hart-Cellar Immigration Act of 1964, which reduced the number of Mexican immigrants who could enter the country legally; the termination of the the *Bracero* guest-worker program, which effectively criminalized thousands migrant workers upon whom U.S. growers continue to depend for labor; and the initiation of the Borderlands Industrialization Program, which established the "twin-plant" manufacturing zone that now straddles the U.S.-Mexico border. These policies, in combination with the civil rights era extension of rights and government resources to minority communities, fueled a massive increase in the settlement of poor immigrants in the region, fueled massive growth of local government, laid the grounds for the problem of undocumented immigration (Harvey and Pickering 2010; Pickering et al. 2006), and fueled the rise of racist discourse about Mexican immigrants that constructs them as "illegals," criminals, and welfare recipients (Huntington 2004).

As noted by Maril (1989), the rise of many Mexican Americans in the region out of migrant labor and into the middle class was predicated upon the growth of the immigrant population and the explosion it fueled in the number of welfare state service workers. Despite the fact that the Mexican American middle class and the immigrant poor belong to the same racial group, many take care to distance themselves from them socially by employing racialized anti-Mexican immigrant discourse. For example, a South Texas small business owner complained that, "Mexicans come in with nothing but sandals. By the time their kid is four, they have gold chains, new clothes, and new trucks while I'm still sitting here in the same place." He added, "Mexican immigrants have no interest in becoming acculturated to U.S. norms" (Harvey and Pickering 2010, 73). These comments reflect the adoption by many middle-class Mexican Americans of the discourse that has been applied to Mexican immigrants in recent decades and which portrays them as a grave threat to what many see as America's essentially Anglo-Saxon core culture (Huntington 2004).

The general extent to which the Mexican American administrative class in the Borderlands holds these views of poor immigrants and how they affect their behavior toward them remain open questions. However, case study research indicates that administrator views of the poor are not static but vary in accordance with the nature of social programs they deliver. For example, research on the implementation of a punitive "workfare" program in South Texas suggests that it was associated with caseworkers holding more negative views of clients (Harvey and Pickering 2010). Prior to the implementation of workfare, the primary mandate given to caseworkers was to minimize client complaints by avoiding administrative errors that would deny families access to assistance. Thus, caseworker–client interactions were cooperatively geared toward meeting client needs. Under the new system, caseworkers' primary role became the denial of services to as many families as possible, even those who qualified for them (Harvey 2011, 2013b). That change in bureaucratic imperative changed the nature of caseworker–client interactions from cooperative to conflictual, making it less likely that caseworkers would see clients as sympathetic and more likely that they would see them as undeserving and perhaps racialized others. That hypothesis remains to be tested; however, the broader point is that officially color-blind social policies like workfare may exacerbate racial inequality by creating interaction contexts that increase the likelihood that racial stereotypes will become salient to caseworkers (Harvey and Pickering 2010; Watkins-Hayes 2009).

CONCLUSION

Many scholars have shown how the breadth, depth, and spatial concentration of the poverty found among rural minorities today is an outcome of the legacies of historical white supremacy (e.g., Duncan 2014; Brown and Schafft 2011). What is needed now is an understanding of how contemporary structures of racial domination are organized, legitimated, and implicated in regimes that continue to produce extreme rates of rural minority poverty. This requires the application of a contemporary theory of race and racism that accounts for variation in the multiple dimensions of systems of racial domination (i.e., individual/psychological, interactional, and institutional/structural) to illuminate the ways in which America's rural regimes of white supremacy both *were* and *were not* transformed by the civil rights revolution (Emirbayer and Desmond 2015; Omi and Winant 1994).

This chapter has shown how extremely high rates of poverty among rural minorities are accompanied by extreme levels of spatially concentrated poverty and distorted local institutional structures marked extremely weak private sector labor markets, over-reliance on government employment, political factionalization and corruption, and civil societies divided by race, clan, faction, and even immigration status. This broad pattern suggests that the character and causes of rural minority poverty are qualitatively different from those of rural white poverty. It has also explained the pattern by reference to a common set of racial factors that includes historical systems of white supremacy and their legacies, yet is not reducible to them. Other key factors include the partial victory of the civil rights movement, which functioned not to deracialize these communities (an impossible task) but re-racialize them in more complex and subtle ways, thereby establishing new forms of accommodation to racial domination as well as new forms of resistance (Omi and Winant 1994). Like reflections in a fun-house mirror, the new racialized structures and practices that generate rural minority poverty today appear quite different from the originals, yet at the same time remain clearly recognizable.

What steps can be taken to confront the unconscionable rates of minority poverty in rural America? The analysis presented here has focused on the role of government in both constructing and confronting the systems of racial domination that produce racialized poverty. Nearly every scholar who has addressed this question has noted the need for major new federal government interventions that would provide resources and coordinate regionally oriented investments in physical infrastructure, public education, workforce development training, and governance, among other things (see Duncan 2014; Harris 2013; Wimberly 2002). To date, these recommendations have gone largely unheeded or unfunded. While the lack of federal government action is due to many factors, one of the most consequential is the influence of the racial ideology of color-blind universalism. By denying and obscuring the role of racialization in the creation of social inequalities between groups constituted as "races," color blindness presents the character and causes of minority poverty as no different from those driving white poverty. As such, the remedies are also held to be the same. Thus, whereas the evidence indicates the need for significant federal government intervention in these areas that takes account of the the role or race, i.e., a second "Great Society" or renewed "war on poverty," color blindness maintains that only the same types of minor human capital development programs that may achieve some success in more economically vibrant, institutionally strong, and whiter areas are warranted.

Scholars have hardly begun to analyze the role of contemporary racism as a factor in rural minority poverty. This failure has allowed the ideology of color blindness to maintain its hegemonic status in the realm of public discourse about minority poverty and policy. If the kinds of federal interventions advocated by scholars are to ever occur in these regions—as they should—a new public discourse about the relation between race and poverty in rural America will be necessary. This will require new sociological work on minority poverty informed by new theoretical paradigms that conceptualize racial inequalities as outcomes of ever ongoing interactions between forces of racial domination and racial progress.

Case Study: Engaging Black Geographies—How Racism Continues to Produce Poverty within the Black Belt South

Rosalind P. Harris

The roots of protest and activism historically, as well as current mobilizations within the Black Belt South (the historic slave-plantation belt highlighted in figure 6.1), have been eclipsed by representations that emphasize deficits and powerlessness within the region that "naturalize . . . poor and black agony and distress" (McKittrick and Woods 2007). As recently as 2001, a mobilization—called the Black Belt Initiative (BBI)—challenged these representations by demonstrating that community people could directly influence the development of policies that make a difference in their lives.

The story of the BBI begins in 2001 when then Senator Zell Miller of Georgia secured $250,000 for the University of Georgia (UGA), through the Energy and Water Appropriations Act, to study the feasibility of establishing a Black Belt Regional Commission to address economic problems in the region. Miller's funds were matched by Macon, Georgia timberman Ben Griffith. In providing the funds to UGA, Miller requested that "poverty not race . . . be the guiding principle . . . and . . . those doing the study will take that into consideration." Revisiting the demographic profile of the region discussed in this chapter, it is clear that approaching the study in the manner that Miller requested "reflected a long-established way of constructing the region by subverting history and decontextualizing the intersecting dynamic forces—gender, race, class, racism, sexism, spatial exploitation/dislocation, and so forth that play ongoing roles in shaping and reshaping the region" (Harris 2013, 8).

Initially, members of the UGA research team developed a methodology that focused on gathering information from members of the business community, academia, government, and nongovernmental organizations. It was noted early in the project that members of the 1890 historically black land-grant community were not involved. As a result, faculty from Tuskegee University, an institution with a long history of involvement within Black Belt communities, joined the conversation. They noted right away that there was one very important voice missing from the conversation about the form that a Black

Belt regional commission should take. This voice was the community voice. Members of the Tuskegee team proposed a methodology that would support community-based organizations, community people, and 1890 land-grant institutions in working collaboratively to gather information from community people about their primary areas of concern and the type of governance structure that a regional commission should have.

It was clear from the initial discussion that UGA and Tuskegee had very different ideas about who should be involved in shaping policy for the region. UGA continued with its plans to poll members of the business community, academia, government, and nongovernmental institutions. It conceded that Tuskegee could move forward in gathering information from community people, but there were tensions and conflicts around this issue throughout the two-year project period.

Data collected and analyzed by Tuskegee reflected that the primary issues that a regional commission needed to focus on were education, health care, housing, job training, and local leadership development. In contrast, the data from UGA reflected concerns with infrastructure development and macroeconomic development. Tuskegee's data also reflected that it was important for the governance structure of the regional commission to include a community constituency board with funding allocated for the issues community people determined to be of primary importance and allocations for infrastructure capped at 25 percent. Again, in contrast, UGA's model for governance was top-heavy with business people, academics, and government officials as decision makers.

There were no provisions made for the inclusion of community people in decision-making roles, nor mechanisms for allocating funds for human and community resource development. In 2003, House bills were introduced for creating regional commissions based on the respective models. Ultimately, the Southeast Crescent Commission, based on the UGA model, was authorized in the 2008 Farm Bill (Wimberley, Morris, and Harris 2014).

Redlining, legally sanctioned voter suppression, and, as in the case of the BBI, the marginalizing practices of universities, modernize the dynamics of historical racism, critical to the arrested power within black geographic spaces. Towns and hamlets within the Black Belt South offer powerful cases in this regard.

REFERENCES

Albrecht, Don E., Carol Mulford Albrecht, and Edward Murguia. 2005. "Minority Concentration, Disadvantage, and Inequality in the Nonmetropolitan United States." *The Sociological Quarterly* 46:503–23.

Alexander, Michelle. 2010. *The New Jim Crow: Mass Incarceration in the Age of Colorblindness.* New York: New Press.

Bender, Steven W. 2010. *Tierra y Libertad: Land, Liberty and Latino Housing.* New York: New York University Press.

Brown, David L., and Kai A. Schafft. 2011. *Rural People and Communities in the 21st Century: Resilience & Transformation.* Cambridge, UK: Polity Press.

Burton, Linda M., Daniel T. Lichter, Regina S. Baker, and John M. Eason. 2013. "Inequality, Family Processes, and Health in the 'New' Rural America." *American Behavioral Scientist* 57(8):1128–51.

Chavez, Sergio. 2005. "Community, Ethnicity, and Class in a Changing Rural California Town." *Rural Sociology* 70(3):314–35.

Duncan, Cynthia M. 2014. *Worlds Apart: Poverty and Politics in Rural America,* 2nd ed. New Haven, CT: Yale University Press.

Emirbayer, Mustafa, and Mathew Desmond. 2015. *The Racial Order.* Chicago: University of Chicago Press.

Fontenot, Kayla, Joachim Singelmann, Tim Slack, Carlos Siordia, Dudley L. Poston Jr., and Rogelio Saenz. 2010. "Understanding Falling Poverty in the Poorest Places: An Examination of the Experience of the Texas Borderland and Lower Mississippi Delta, 1990–2000." *Journal of Poverty* 14:216–36.

Fredrickson, George M. 2002. *Racism: A Short History.* Princeton, NJ: Princeton University Press.

Gonzales, Angela A. 2003. "American Indians: Their Contemporary Reality and Future Trajectory." In *Challenges for Rural America in the 21st Century,* ed. David L. Brown and Louis E. Swanson, 43–56. University Park: Pennsylvania State University Press.

Gonzales, Angela A., Thomas A. Lyson, and K. Whitney Mauer. 2007. "What Does a Casino Mean to a Tribe? Assessing the Impact of Casino Development on Indian Reservations in Arizona and New Mexico." *Social Sciences Journal* 44(3):405–419.

Green, Gary P. 2002. "Community Change in Harmony, Georgia: 1943–1993." In *Persistence and Change in Rural Communities: A 50-Year Follow-Up to Six Classic Studies,* ed. Albert E. Luloff and Richard S. Krannich, 71–94. New York: CABI.

Gutiérrez, José A. 1998. *The Making of a Chicano Militant: Lessons from Cristal.* Madison: University of Wisconsin Press.

Harris, Rosalind P. 2013. "Community-University Partnerships for Change in the Black Belt South." *Professional Agricultural Workers Journal* 1(1):1–14.

Harris, Rosalind P., and Dreamal Worthen. 2003. "African Americans in Rural America." In *Challenges for Rural America in the 21st Century,* ed. David L. Brown and Louis E. Swanson, 32–42. University Park: Pennsylvania State University Press.

Harvey, Mark H. 2011. "Welfare Reform and Household Survival: The Interaction of Structure and Network Strength in the Rio Grande Valley, Texas." *Journal of Poverty* 15(1):43–64.

Harvey, Mark H. 2013a. "Consensus-Based Community Development, Concentrated Rural Poverty, and Local Institutional Structures: The Obstacle of Race in the Lower Mississippi Delta." *Community Development* 44(2):257–73.

———. 2013b. "Inside the 'Smoke-Filled Room': Neoliberal Devolution and the Politics of Workfare in the Rio Grande Valley of Texas." *International Journal of Urban and Regional Research* 37(2):641–62.

Harvey, Mark H., and Kathleen Pickering. 2010. "Color-Blind Welfare Reform or New Cultural Racism? Evidence from Rural Mexican- and Native-American Communities." In *Welfare Reform in Rural Places: Comparative Perspectives*, ed. Paul Milbourne, 61–79. Bingley, UK: Emerald.

Housing Assistance Council. 2012. "Race and Ethnicity in Rural America." Rural Research Brief. April. http://www.ruralhome.org/storage/research_notes/rrn-race-and-ethnicity-web.pdf.

Huntington, Samuel P. 2004. "The Hispanic Challenge." *Foreign Policy* (March /April):30–45.

Hyland, Stanley. 2008. "Commentary: Reflections on the Culture of the Lower Mississippi Delta: Challenges and Opportunities." *Journal of Health and Human Services Administration* 31(1):156–67.

Lichter, Daniel T. 2012. "Immigration and the New Racial Diversity in Rural America." *Rural Sociology* 77:3–35.

Lichter, Daniel T., and Kenneth M. Johnson. 2007. "The Changing Spatial Concentration of America's Rural Poor Population." *Rural Sociology* 72:331–58.

Lichter, Daniel T., Domenico Parisi, and Michael C. Taquino. 2012. "The Geography of Exclusion: Race, Segregation, and Concentrated Poverty." *Social Problems* 59(3):364–88.

Maril, Robert L. 1989. *Poorest of Americans: The Mexican-Americans of the Lower Rio Grande Valley of Texas*. Notre Dame, IN: University of Notre Dame Press.

Nakano Glenn, E. 2002. *Unequal Freedom: How Race and Gender Shaped American Citizenship and Labor*. Cambridge, MA: Harvard University Press.

Omi, Michael, and Howard Winant. 1994. *Racial Formation in the United States: From the 1960s to the 1990s*. New York: Routledge.

Pickering, Kathleen. 2000. "Alternative Economic Strategies in Low-Income Rural Communities: TANF, Labor Migration, and the Case of the Pine Ridge Indian Reservation." *Rural Sociology* 65(1):148–67.

———. 2001. "Legislating Development Through Welfare Reform: Indiscernible Jobs, Insurmountable Barriers, and Invisible Agendas on the Pine Ridge and Rosebud Indian Reservations." *Political and Legal Anthropology Review* 24:38–52.

Pickering, Kathleen, and Benjamin Jewell. 2008. "Nature Is Relative: Religious Affiliation, Environmental Attitudes, and Political Constraints on the Pine Ridge Indian Reservation." *Journal of the Study of Religion, Nature and Culture* 2(1):135–58.

Pickering, Kathleen, Mark H. Harvey, Gene F. Summers, and David Mushinski. 2006. *Welfare Reform in Persistent Rural Poverty: Dreams, Disenchantments and Diversity*. University Park: Pennsylvania State University Press.

Quadagno, Jill. 1994. *The Color of Welfare: How Racism Undermined the War on Poverty*. New York: Oxford University Press.

Saenz, Rogelio, and Cruz C. Torres. 2003. "Latinos in Rural America." In *Challenges for Rural America in the Twenty-First Century*, ed. David L. Brown and Louis E. Swanson, 57–70. University Park: Pennsylvania State University Press.

Schultz, Mark. 2006. *The Rural Face of White Supremacy*. Urbana: University of Illinois Press.

Snipp, C. Mathew. 1996. "Understanding Race and Ethnicity in Rural America." *Rural Sociology* 61(1):125–42.

Summers, Gene F. 1991. "Minorities in Rural Society." *Rural Sociology* 56(2):177–88.

Task Force on Persistent Rural Poverty. 1993. *Persistent Poverty in Rural America*. Boulder, CO: Westview Press.

Telles, Edward E. 2004. *Race in Another America: The Significance of Skin Color in Brazil*. Princeton, NJ: Princeton University Press.

Thernstrom, Stephen, and Abigail Thernstrom. 1997. *America in Black and White: One Nation, Indivisible*. New York: Touchstone.

USDA Economic Research Service. 2011. "Rural America at a Glance." Economic Information Bulletin No. 85.

———. 2015a. "Persistent Poverty" (map). https://www.ers.usda.gov/data-products/county-typology-codes/descriptions-and-maps.aspx#ppov.

———. 2015b. "Rural Poverty and Well-Being: Poverty Demographics." http://www.ers.usda.gov/topics/rural-economy-population/rural-poverty-well-being/poverty-demographics.aspx.

Watkins-Hayes, Celeste. 2009. "Race-ing the Bootstrap Climb: Black and Latino Bureaucrats in Post-Welfare Reform Offices." *Social Problems* 56(2):285–310.

Wimberley, Ronald C., Libby V. Morris, and Rosalind P. Harris. 2014. "A Federal Commission for the Black Belt South." *Professional Agricultural Workers Journal* 2(1):1–9.

Wimberly, Ronald C. 2002. "The Regionalization of Poverty: Assistance for the Black Belt South?" *Southern Rural Sociology* 18(1):294–306.

Winant, Howard. 2001. *The World Is a Ghetto: Race and Democracy Since World War II*. New York: Basic.

Wright Austin, S. D. 2006. *The Transformation of Plantation Politics: Black Politics, Concentrated Poverty, and Social Capital in the Mississippi Delta*. Albany: State University of New York Press.

CHAPTER 7

Immigration Trends and Immigrant Poverty in Rural America

Shannon M. Monnat and Raeven Faye Chandler

Demographic data confirm that the United States is, indeed, a nation of immigrants. As early as 1850, immigrants[1] represented nearly 10 percent of the U.S. population. More than 41 million immigrants now live in the United States, representing 13.1 percent of the total population. Immigrants remain geographically concentrated in traditional gateway cities such as Los Angeles, Miami, New York, Houston, and Chicago (Migration Policy Institute 2015). However, recent geographic dispersion of immigrants from these traditional gateways, and directly from other countries, to southeastern and midwestern suburban and rural communities with little recent experience with nonwhite immigrants has generated hundreds of scholarly works on new rural immigrant destinations over the past fifteen years. Despite these changes in the distribution of immigrant origin countries and settlement patterns, newcomers today struggle no less than their nineteenth-century predecessors with social, residential, and economic integration. Moreover, recent immigrants to the rural United States may face even greater economic difficulties, including higher poverty rates, than their peers in metropolitan areas. There are several reasons for this, including that most new rural immigrant destinations lack significant native-born exposure to immigrants, employment prospects are more limited in some new destinations, and newcomers are at risk of social and economic isolation due to small co-ethnic populations and residential segregation (Crowley and Ebert 2014; Lichter 2012; Lichter, Sanders, and Johnson 2015; Marrow 2011).

This chapter summarizes the history of immigration to rural America and describes rural immigrant population change over time. County-level census data are used to describe the distribution of immigrant poverty across rural America, highlighting differences in immigrant poverty rates between rural counties with historically large immigrant populations ("established immigrant destinations"), counties without historically large immigrant populations but substantial immigrant population growth since 1990 ("new immigrant destinations"), and rural counties without large or high-growth immigrant populations ("nonimmigrant destinations"). Comparisons are made of the human capital characteristics of immigrants and labor market factors that may be associated with variation in immigrant poverty across these different types of rural destinations.

HISTORY OF IMMIGRATION TO RURAL AMERICA

U.S. immigration policy has been a touchstone of political debate for decades and remains a hot-button issue in current politics. Contemporary immigration controversies mostly surround Mexican immigrants. This was vividly highlighted in this statement made by Donald Trump in his 2016 presidential campaign announcement speech: "When Mexico sends its people, they're not sending their best. They're sending people that have lots of problems, and they're bringing those problems. They're bringing drugs. They're bringing crime. They're rapists. And some, I assume, are good people" (Trump 2015), as well as this statement Trump made during the final Presidential debate: "We have some bad hombres and we're going to get them out." Trump's campaign promises to build a wall between the United States and Mexico and to deport the millions of undocumented immigrants living in the United States have continued since he took office.

Though denounced by many, Trump's sentiments about Mexican immigrants and his proposed deportation policies struck a chord with a non-negligible share of U.S. citizens concerned with the economic implications of recent Mexican immigration, particularly in the aftermath of the Great Recession from which many parts of the United States are still recovering. However, hostility toward immigrants has not always been targeted at Mexican immigrants. Before the 1960s, most immigrants came from Europe, and they too stirred controversy. This section describes historical trends in rural immigration, factors contributing to those trends, and controversies surrounding U.S. immigration policy. Data are from the Migration Policy Institute (2015) Data Hub, the U.S. Census Bureau historical census statistics on the foreign-born population of the United States, 1850–1990 (Gibson and Lennon 1999), the Decennial Census 2000 (U.S. Census Bureau 2000), and American Community Survey 2009–2013 (U.S. Census Bureau 2015).

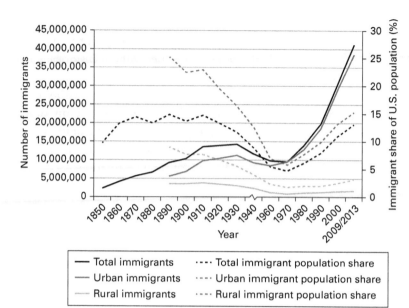

Figure 7.1   U.S. immigrant total, urban, and rural population and share, 1850–2009/2013.

Sources: Migration Policy Institute (MPI) Data Hub, 2015 and U.S. Census Bureau, Historical Census Statistics on the Foreign-Born Population of the United States: 1850–1990, Table 18; Decennial Census 2000; American Community Survey 2009/2013.

Note: U.S. Census Bureau did not report the immigrant urban and rural population shares until 1890 and did not provide data on the urban and rural population for 1950.

Migration to the United States has fluctuated significantly over the past 120 years (figure 7.1). After peaking at 14.8 percent in 1890, the immigrant population declined to a low of 4.7 percent in 1970 but has increased rapidly since the 1970s. As of 2013, 41.3 million immigrants (13.1 percent of the U.S. population) were estimated to be living in the United States. Immigrants to the United States have historically been drawn to large metropolitan gateways that house large populations of co-ethnic nationals. In the late 1800s, about a quarter of the urban population was foreign born compared to 9 percent of the rural population. Immigrants still comprise a larger share of the urban population (15.3 percent) than the rural population (3.2 percent), but the absolute number and share of immigrants in rural areas is larger now than at any time since 1940.

Immigrants of the late nineteenth and early twentieth centuries were almost entirely of European origin. Between 1880 and 1970, however, the European share of immigrants declined from 86.2 percent to 61.7 percent,

Table 7.1   Nonmetropolitan Immigrants by World Region of Birth, 2009–2013

Region	Total	Percent of total nonmetropolitan immigrant population
Africa	37,760	2.20%
Asia	283,705	16.50
Europe	216,992	12.62
North America	72,077	4.19
Oceania	16,513	0.96
Latin America	1,092,168	63.53
Mexico	881,177	80.68
Other Central America	113,792	10.42
South America	46,489	4.26
Caribbean	50,710	4.64
Total	1,719,215	

Source: American Community Survey, 2009/2013.

Note: Percentages for Mexico, other Central America, South America, and Caribbean use Latin America total as base.

and European immigrants now represent just 11.9 percent of the total immigrant population. The share of immigrants from Latin America, on the other hand, increased from just 1.3 percent in 1880 to 19.4 percent by 1970, and Latin American immigrants now comprise over half (52.5 percent) of all immigrants in the United States. Latin American immigrants (particularly those from Mexico) make up an even larger share (two-thirds) of all nonmetropolitan[2] immigrants (table 7.1). However, immigration from Latin America, especially Mexico, has leveled off over the past decade, attributable in part to the economic recession and improving economic conditions in Latin American countries. Asians are now the fastest-growing U.S. immigrant group. There is little research on nonmetropolitan Asians, but they comprise a non-negligible 16.5 percent of nonmetropolitan immigrants. They are concentrated almost entirely in Hawaii, university towns, and refugee resettlement communities.

FACTORS CONTRIBUTING TO RURAL IMMIGRATION TRENDS

Immigration reflects interrelated economic, political, and social shifts occurring at global, regional, and local levels (Durand, Massey, and Charvet 2000; Massey and Capoferro 2008). Although the specific reasons for migrating to rural areas of the United States vary across groups over time,

U.S. migration has historically been economically driven. The first large group of migrant farmworkers in rural California was the Chinese, who were imported to build the transcontinental railroad and subsequently recruited by large farms as cheap labor. By the early 1880s, the Chinese represented 75 percent of seasonal farmworkers in California (Martin et al. 2006). The great wave of European immigration to the U.S. Northeast and Midwest in the late 1800s, which included the Polish, Germans, Scandinavians, Italians, Greeks, Slavs, Scottish, and Irish, was driven largely by the desire to escape poverty and overpopulation in Europe and the promise of economic prosperity in the United States, including opportunities in farming, timber harvesting, and coal mining (Cance 1912; Glazer and Moynihan 1963; Lichter 2012; Zeitlin 1980). The motivation to earn a living and provide for one's family that drove European migration in the 1800s and early 1900s is mirrored today among immigrants from Mexico and other Latin American countries who wish to do the same.

Although early European immigrants, especially non-Protestant Jews, Irish, Poles, and Italians, were not considered white and often suffered xenophobic exclusion and ethnically based discrimination, restrictions barring immigrant entry to the United States during its first 100 years were minimal. Restrictions focused instead on limiting the entry of "undesirable" immigrants, including prostitutes, low-skilled contract workers, and the Chinese, especially during the late 1800s and 1920s. Moreover, the U.S. government has traditionally made exceptions to its immigration laws to increase the supply of immigrant labor for agriculture and related industries such as meat packing and food processing (Martin et al. 2006). Several such immigration policies since the 1940s contributed to contemporary rural immigration flows, particularly immigration from Mexico. Chief among these was the Bracero Agreement (1942–1964) between the United States and Mexico that permitted Mexican nationals entry to the United States as temporary agricultural workers during WWII labor shortages in exchange for stricter border security and the return of undocumented Mexican immigrants to Mexico. The program also called for wage guarantees, housing, and food, but these terms were often disregarded by U.S. farm operators. Under the program's terms, Mexican workers were allowed to stay in the United States for up to six months, and the program placed caps on the number of migrants who could enter the United States. However, illegal recruitment practices among U.S. farm operators, and food shortages, labor conflicts, and population growth in Mexico, resulted in longer stays and continued illegal border crossings, including the migration of laborers' family members to the United States (Martin et al. 2006; Massey and Liang 1989). Rapid growth in undocumented, predominantly low-income, and poorly educated Mexican migrants prompted the U.S. government to implement "Operation Wetback"[3]—rapid-response tactics to quickly deport laborers and their families and keep Mexicans from entering the United States. The program was short-lived, as U.S. farm owners continued to illegally recruit low-wage undocumented workers.

Following the Bracero program, Congress passed the landmark Immigration and Nationality Act (1965), which favored family reunification and skilled immigrants and imposed the first limits on immigration from the Western Hemisphere. In 1986, Congress enacted another major law, the Immigration Reform and Control Act (IRCA), which focused on penalizing employers of undocumented migrants and increasing border patrol. IRCA's stepped-up border controls did make illegal entry into the United States more expensive and dangerous, but it failed to deter young Mexican men from entering, and it kept those who succeeded in crossing in the United States longer.

In addition, approximately 2.8 million undocumented immigrants were legalized under IRCA through two programs. The general legalization program legalized 1.7 million undocumented immigrants who had been in the United States since January 1, 1982. The Special Agricultural Worker (SAW) program provided a pathway to citizenship for farmworkers who completed at least ninety days of farm work from 1985 to 1986 and resulted in the legalization of 1.2 million farmworkers, 90 percent of whom were Mexican (Martin et al. 2006). With the desire to escape highly populated cities, rising housing costs, and crime, and with the pull of new low-skill employment in low cost-of-living areas, some of these newly legal residents traveled beyond the West to cities and small towns with previously small or nonexistent Latin American immigrant populations. Many undocumented residents, who were family members, friends, or coworkers of the newly legalized residents, followed (Martin et al. 2006).

Increasing U.S. and international demand for processed and prepackaged foods drove new employment opportunities for immigrants. To meet growing demand and cut costs, factory operators found ways to deskill and routinize production. Many relocated their plants from the heavily unionized Northeast and North-Central United States to the rural Southeast and Midwest where agricultural inputs were closer and land and labor was cheaper (Kandel and Parrado 2005), thanks to successful union-busting by major players such as Hormel and Oscar Meyer decades earlier. This restructuring of the food processing industry led to widespread recruiting of nonunionized, low-skill immigrants from California and Texas and directly from Mexico and Central America (Gozdziak and Martin 2005).

These economic drivers, along with increasing hostility toward immigrants in southwestern states, the now greater danger associated with crossing back and forth over the border, and restrictive local and state policies (e.g., California's Proportion 187 in 1994), contributed to unprecedented Hispanic (mostly Mexican) migration from urban settlements in the West to rural destinations in the Midwest and Southeast throughout the 1980s and 1990s (Johnson and Lichter 2008; Kandel and Cromartie 2004; Lichter and Johnson 2006; Massey 2008; Parrado and Kandel 2008; Singer 2004). Many immigrants bypassed traditional destinations altogether and migrated directly from their sending countries to the rural United States (Lichter and Johnson 2006). To be sure, large cities, especially Chicago, New York, and Los Angeles, retain the bulk of the U.S. immigrant population and continue to experience the majority of immigrant population growth (Lichter and Johnson 2006). However, at 3.2 percent, immigrants currently comprise a larger proportion of the rural population than at any time since the 1940s. Although the rural immigrant population is small relative to the urban immigrant population, the geographic diversification of immigrants has transformed the face of the rural United States and raised questions about the economic and social incorporation of newcomers into rural communities and in U.S. society more broadly.

RECENT RURAL IMMIGRATION

In this section, recent trends in rural immigration are presented using data from the 1990 and 2000 Decennial Censuses of Population and the 2009/2013 American Community Survey (ACS) five-year estimates.[4] The county is the unit of analysis. Counties are designated as metropolitan or nonmetropolitan using the 2013 United States Department of Agriculture's Economic Research Service (USDA, ERS) Rural-Urban Continuum Codes. Using the 2013 classifications ensures that the analyses are restricted to *current* nonmetropolitan counties. Counties that were once nonmetropolitan but had enough population growth by 2010 to be classified as metropolitan are therefore excluded.

The distribution of nonmetropolitan immigrant population growth varies significantly by region. These trends are illustrated in table 7.2

Table 7.2 Nonmetropolitan Foreign-Born Population by Region, 1990, 2000, and 2009/2013

| | 1990 | | | 2000 | | | 2009/2013 | | | % Change FB pop. 1990–2009/2013 | % Change noncitizen pop. 1990–2009/2013 |
	FB pop.	% FB	% Noncitizens	FB pop.	% FB	% Noncitizens	FB pop.	% FB	% Noncitizens		
Northeast	106,433	2.4	37.7	114,386	2.5	43.9	135,457	2.9	46.5	27.3	57.0
Midwest	157,250	1.1	43.0	280,467	1.9	60.4	371,562	2.4	62.8	136.3	244.8
South	258,639	1.5	59.8	534,861	2.8	68.4	768,102	3.9	71.7	197.0	256.2
West	191,837	3.9	56.9	325,035	5.6	63.6	444,094	6.8	64.7	131.5	155.1
Total	714,159	1.8	51.7	1,254,749	2.9	62.1	1,719,215	3.8	64.0	140.7	198.3

Source: U.S. Census Bureau, Decennial Census 1990 and 2000 and American Community Survey, 2009/2013.

Notes: % FB = percentage of total population that is foreign born.

% noncitizens = percentage of total foreign-born population that are not naturalized U.S. citizens.

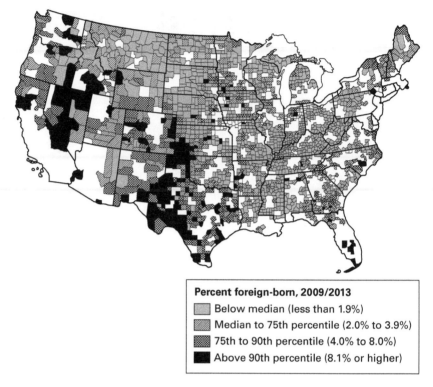

Percent foreign-born, 2009/2013

- Below median (less than 1.9%)
- Median to 75th percentile (2.0% to 3.9%)
- 75th to 90th percentile (4.0% to 8.0%)
- Above 90th percentile (8.1% or higher)

Figure 7.2 Percent foreign-born in nonmetropolitan counties, 2009/2013.

Source: American Community Survey, 2009/2013.

and figures 7.2 and 7.3. Whereas the nonmetropolitan Northeast experienced a foreign-born population increase of just 27 percent between 1990 and 2009/2013, the foreign-born population more than doubled in the Midwest, South, and West. The percentage of immigrants who are not naturalized citizens[5] also increased in all four regions between 1990 and 2009/2013, with the largest increases in the Midwest and South. Increases in noncitizen immigrants are important because noncitizens are at higher risk of poverty, which is discussed in more detail later.

Nearly half of nonmetropolitan immigrants live in the South, and over three-quarters are Latin American (mostly Mexican). Over half (51 percent) of immigrants in the South reside in Texas, and 74 of the 198 counties with foreign-born populations above the ninetieth percentile are in Texas (figure 7.2). Counties in other southern states, particularly

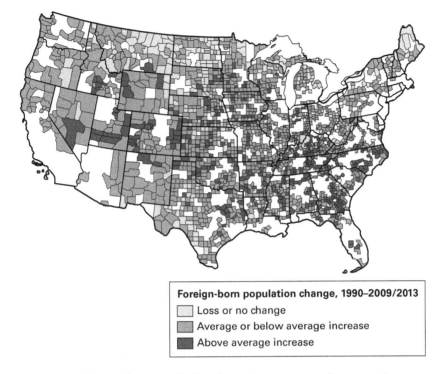

Figure 7.3 **Foreign-born population change in nonmetropolitan counties, 1990–2009/2013.**

Source: Author calculations using data from Decennial Census 1990; American Community Survey, 2009/2013.

Alabama, Georgia, and Mississippi, however, experienced the most foreign-born population growth between 1990 and 2009/2013 (figure 7.3). This is largely the result of the movement of processed food and textile production facilities from the Northeast to the South throughout the 1980s and 1990s, which drew low-skill immigrant workers seeking escape from low-wage seasonal farm work in the West. For example, in the late 1980s, Mohawk Industries, which specializes in flooring manufacturing, moved its production from central New York to Gordon County, Georgia. Shaw Industries, the largest carpet manufacturer in the world, is also a large employer of immigrants in Gordon County. As a result, 5,140 immigrants resided in Gordon County by 2009/2013, whereas the county was home to just 225 immigrants in 1990.

    In the nonmetropolitan West, the foreign-born population is most pronounced in Washington, Oregon, northern and east-central California,

New Mexico, Nevada, Colorado, and Idaho. Although immigrants have dispersed from the West to other parts of the country, the nonmetropolitan West experienced immigrant population growth of 131.5 percent between 1990 and 2009/2013, and immigrants remain most concentrated in the West. Wasatch County, Utah, is an example of a county with rapid immigrant population growth driven by economic factors. Whereas only 69 immigrants lived in Wasatch in 1990, more than 2,500 immigrants lived there in 2009/2013. Tourism, a major employment industry for immigrants, comprises much of the economy in Salt Lake and Summit counties, which border Wasatch. Also, some of the 2002 Winter Olympic events were held in Wasatch, increasing the demand for low-skill labor in the tourism and recreation industry.

A number of midwestern nonmetropolitan counties also experienced above average foreign-born population growth between 1990 and 2009/2013 (figure 7.3), especially in Kansas, Missouri, Iowa, Nebraska, mid-southern Minnesota, and eastern South Dakota. In all midwestern states, however, there were nonmetropolitan counties that experienced immigrant population loss, perhaps because earlier migrants to those midwestern counties relocated to other midwestern counties for new employment opportunities. Dawson County, Nebraska, which experienced an increase from just 138 immigrants in 1990 to 4,391 immigrants in 2009/2013, is a good example of midwestern immigrant population growth. Tyson Fresh Meats, which began operations in Dawson County in the early 1990s, along with Frito-Lay and Monsanto, employ large numbers of low-skilled immigrant workers in Dawson.

Finally, the Northeast contains the smallest share of nonmetropolitan immigrants. Just 7.8 percent of all nonmetropolitan immigrants live in the Northeast. Immigrants in the Northeast are the most likely to be naturalized citizens and the least likely to be from Latin America. In 1990, several nonmetropolitan counties in New England were home to comparatively larger foreign-born populations than in 2009/2013, attributable almost entirely to migration from Canada. By 2009/2013, only a handful of New England counties remained home to significant immigrant populations (figure 7.2). These include Aroostook County in northern Maine; Clinton, Essex, and Franklin counties in northern New York; Caledonia County in northern Vermont; Coos and Grafton (home of Dartmouth University) counties in New Hampshire; and Franklin County in Massachusetts.

RURAL IMMIGRANT POVERTY IN THE
CONTEMPORARY UNITED STATES

Poverty has historically been and remains a fact of life for a large share of U.S. immigrants. Between 1960 and 2000, the poverty rate among immigrant-headed households increased from 14.1 percent to 17.4 percent, whereas the poverty rate among native-born households declined from 20.9 percent to 11.8 percent (Hoynes, Page, and Stevens 2006), but this trend may be changing. Between 1994 and 2000, poverty rates fell more quickly for immigrants than for native-born households (although immigrants maintained higher rates of poverty), and immigrants experienced greater increases than native-born households in real median family income (Chapman and Bernstein 2002). However, this was a period of strong U.S. economic growth (after the early 1990s recession and before the early 2000s recession). Moreover, these national poverty estimates are driven by metropolitan poverty because most of the population lives in metropolitan areas. Data constraints such as these often make understanding rural immigrant poverty more challenging.

In this section, the current distribution of immigrant poverty across the nonmetropolitan United States is described. Although the presentation is limited to nonmetropolitan counties, it is important to note that a large proportion of immigrants living in metropolitan counties cross county boundaries to work in nonmetropolitan counties (Martin et al. 2006). Therefore, employment opportunities and conditions in nonmetropolitan areas affect metropolitan immigrant poverty rates as well.

There is substantial spatial variation in nonmetropolitan immigrant poverty (figure 7.4). There are clusters of especially high immigrant poverty in the eastern and southern gulf areas of Texas, southern North Carolina, New Mexico, eastern West Virginia, southwestern Arkansas, and northern Montana. Conversely, there are clusters of especially low immigrant poverty in Vermont, central Maine, southern North Dakota, and southern South Dakota. Of note, no counties in New England are in the highest quartile of immigrant poverty, which likely reflects both the low representation of Latin American immigrants (especially Mexicans) in New England and the stronger economy in some New England states (Vermont, Connecticut, Massachusetts) relative to the rest of the country.

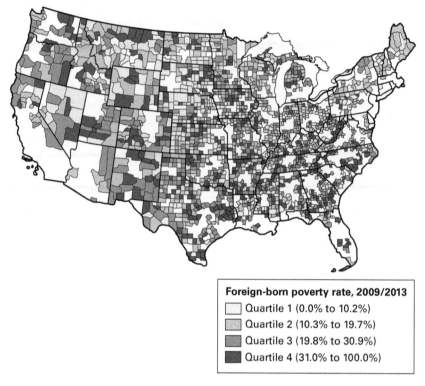

Foreign-born poverty rate, 2009/2013
- Quartile 1 (0.0% to 10.2%)
- Quartile 2 (10.3% to 19.7%)
- Quartile 3 (19.8% to 30.9%)
- Quartile 4 (31.0% to 100.0%)

Figure 7.4   Foreign-born poverty rates in nonmetropolitan counties, 2009/2013.

Source: American Community Survey 2009/2013.

Figure 7.5 presents average county-level poverty rates overall and by region for nonmetropolitan counties with at least 100 foreign-born residents[6] (all racial/ethnic groups) for native-born, foreign-born, foreign-born naturalized citizens, and foreign-born noncitizens.[7] The average foreign-born poverty rate for nonmetropolitan counties is 23.2 percent compared to 17.5 percent for native-born residents, but the foreign-born disadvantage is driven entirely by high poverty rates among noncitizens. Whereas the average poverty rate among naturalized citizens is only 14.4 percent, it is 28.9 percent among noncitizens.

Citizenship affects poverty risk in at least two ways. First, most immigrants who are not naturalized are not eligible for federal poverty relief programs, including Temporary Assistance for Needy Families (TANF), the Supplemental Nutrition Assistance Program (SNAP), Medicaid, and the Children's Health Insurance Program (CHIP).[8] Under current safety

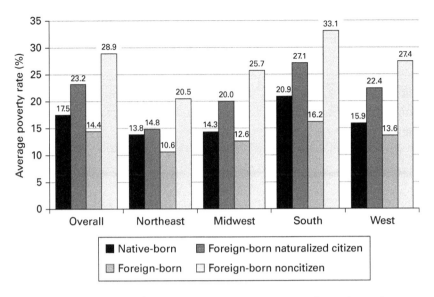

Figure 7.5   Nonmetropolitan county average poverty rates for native and foreign-born residents by region, 2009/2013.

Source: American Community Survey 2009/2013.

Note: Among counties with at least 100 foreign-born residents (N=1,477).

net program policies, most immigrants must be *lawful permanent residents* (LPRs) for at least five years to qualify. States may choose to provide safety net services to immigrants who are ineligible for federal programs by fully funding those services themselves, but most states currently do not have these programs (Pew Charitable Trusts 2014). Even when programs are available, immigrants may be reluctant to apply for fear it will jeopardize future citizenship, they will be required to repay costs, or they will be deported. Lichter et al. (2015) provide evidence of these deterrents, showing that only 9.9 percent of poor rural Latino infants who are born in the United States (and are therefore U.S. citizens and eligible for safety net programs) reside in families accessing government cash assistance. These current policies both increase poverty risk during periods of job loss and medical emergency and increase the likelihood that immigrants will be subject to involuntary part-time work and marginal jobs, which predominate in rural areas (Findeis and Jensen 1998; Lichter and Crowley 2002). Indeed, although labor force participation is higher among immigrants than among the native born (Grieco et al. 2012), immigrants—particularly noncitizen immigrants—are at higher risk of involuntary part-time and short-term work than native-born workers (Slack and Jensen 2007). The second related way that citizenship status can affect poverty is through employer treatment of immigrant workers. Undocumented immigrants currently have few legal protections against employer abuses, including wage theft, and they may fear that reporting employer abuses could lead to deportation.

The South has the largest share of noncitizen immigrants, particularly from Mexico. These factors may partly explain why the South has the highest average nonmetropolitan immigrant poverty rates among the four regions (figure 7.5). Mexican immigrants are at especially high risk of poverty in rural areas because they are typically young, are uneducated, have limited English proficiency, are often undocumented, and often work in low-wage and seasonal jobs, particularly in the South (Effland and Butler 1997; Martin et al. 2006). High poverty rates in the rural South, in general, reflect the lack of union presence, much lower wages, and less industrial diversification relative to southern urban labor markets and rural labor markets in other parts of the country (Lichter and Jensen 2002).

In all four regions, high noncitizen poverty rates drive average foreign-born poverty rates higher than average native-born poverty rates. The gap between the average naturalized citizen poverty rate and noncitizen poverty rate is smallest in the Northeast at 10 percentage points and largest in the South at 16.9 percentage points. It is noteworthy that, in all four regions, the naturalized citizen poverty rate is lower than the native-born poverty rate because the native-born rate includes groups with historically high rates of poverty, including African Americans in the South and Native Americans in the West.

COMPARISONS OF RURAL IMMIGRANT POVERTY IN ESTABLISHED, NEW HIGH-GROWTH, AND NONIMMIGRANT DESTINATIONS

Beyond regional differences, it is important to consider how poverty varies between immigrants residing in rural areas with long histories of immigration compared to places with little previous experience with immigrants but recent rapid immigrant population growth. Both destination types are present in all four regions of the United States. New destinations differ from established gateways in many ways that create challenges for immigrants to new rural destinations. New destinations have less access to support networks; limited, crowded, and poor-quality housing; limited access to reliable transportation needed for traveling to work and services; residential isolation; and linguistic challenges associated with living in communities where most residents have never interacted with non-English speakers and are sometimes hostile to foreign-born, especially nonwhite, newcomers (Atiles and Bohon 2003; Burton et al. 2013; Gouveia and Saenz 2000; Gozdziak and Martin 2005; Kandel and Parrado 2005; Leclere, Jensen, and Biddlecom 1994; Lichter et al. 2010, 2015; Lichter 2012; Marrow 2011; Parrado and Kandel 2008).

Rural communities also face challenges from rapid immigrant population growth, including racial tensions between newcomers and native-born whites and African Americans who may perceive immigrants, especially Latino immigrants, as economic threats (McClain et al. 2007). Also, rural new destination communities may face increased demand on local infrastructure and resources from rapid population growth (Crowley and Lichter 2009; Dondero and Muller 2012; Singer 2004). Many rural communities have, however, benefited from immigrant population growth because newcomers offset population loss and stave off economic stagnation or decline (Brown 2014; Donato et al. 2007; Johnson 2011, 2014; Lichter and Johnson 2006).

Comparisons of average county-level immigrant poverty rates for rural established immigrant destinations (i.e., those with a history of substantial immigrant populations), new immigrant destinations (i.e., recent high-growth immigrant populations), and nonimmigrant destinations (all other counties) are presented next. In 1990, there were 714,159 immigrants residing in nonmetropolitan counties in the United States, representing 1.8 percent of the total nonmetropolitan population. "Established immigrant destination counties" are those that were home to at least twice this overall nonmetropolitan percentage of immigrants in 1990 (3.6 percent). "New immigrant destination counties" were classified using two steps. First, all nonmetropolitan counties that grew by at least 200 immigrants between 1990 and 2009/2013 (N=903) were selected, which eliminated fast-growing counties that added only small numbers of immigrants. Second, counties that experienced above average nonmetropolitan immigrant population growth (greater than 285 percent) between 1990 and 2009/2013 were identified. This approach yielded 214 nonmetropolitan established destination counties, 361 nonmetropolitan new

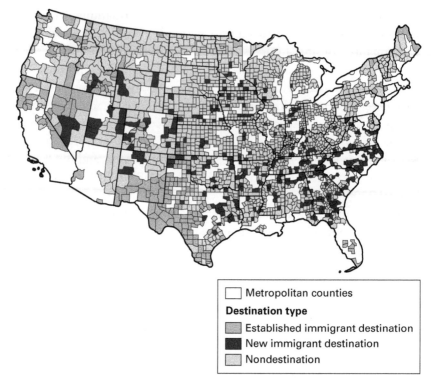

Figure 7.6   Nonmetropolitan established and new immigrant destinations.

Source: Author classification based on Census 1990 and American Community Survey 2009/2013.

destination counties, and 1,401 other nonmetropolitan counties ("nonimmigrant destination counties") (figure 7.6).

Established destinations are home to about 35 percent of nonmetropolitan immigrants. The majority of the 214 nonmetropolitan established destinations are in Texas (86), California (14), New Mexico (14), Idaho (13), Washington (11), and Nevada (9). These are areas of long-term residence among mostly Mexican immigrants. Established destinations in Florida represent long-term Cuban populations, and established destinations in New England and northern New York represent mostly Canadian immigrants. With the exceptions of Texas and Florida and a handful of counties in Oklahoma, Louisiana, and Arkansas, the nonmetropolitan South had little experience with immigration before 1990. New destinations (N=361) are home to about 29 percent of nonmetropolitan immigrants and are disproportionately located in the South (figure 7.6).

Many of these are in North Carolina (45), Georgia (43), Kentucky (21), Tennessee (19), Arkansas (17), Mississippi (16), and Virginia (16), but 25 Texas counties are also new destinations. Just 2 percent of nonmetropolitan midwestern counties are classified as established immigrant destinations (and nearly all are in Kansas), but 10 percent of nonmetropolitan midwestern counties are new immigrant destinations, mostly in Nebraska (12), Iowa (14), and Indiana (14).

The majority of nonmetropolitan counties in all regions are nonimmigrant destinations (N=1,401), including all nonmetropolitan counties in North Dakota, and nearly all in Michigan, Ohio, and Pennsylvania. Many of these counties *do* have immigrant populations, but the populations are very small. Nevertheless, a substantial number of immigrants (612,880), representing 36 percent of nonmetropolitan immigrants, live in the 1,401 nonimmigrant destination counties—more than the number of immigrants in either nonmetropolitan established destinations (600,291) or new destinations (506,044).

Average immigrant poverty rates and the gap in poverty rates between immigrants and native-born residents vary significantly between nonmetropolitan established, new, and nonimmigrant destinations (table 7.3). Average poverty rates for both native- and foreign-born residents are lowest in nonimmigrant destinations and highest in new destinations. Nonmetropolitan established destinations have an average foreign-born poverty rate of 23.3 percent, compared to 29.0 percent in new destinations, and 21.0 percent in nonimmigrant destinations. The gap between the average native- and foreign-born poverty rates is also the largest in new destinations (10.3 percentage points). As explained earlier, poverty rates are higher among noncitizens. New destinations have a significantly higher average noncitizen poverty rate (33.9 percent) than both established (28.2 percent) and nonimmigrant (27.2 percent) destinations. However, large standard deviations for these poverty rates indicate that there is substantial variability in poverty rates among counties *within* each type of destination, with some counties having very low and other counties having very high poverty rates. This confirms that immigrant economic mobility has been highly segmented across the United States (Martin et al. 2006).

Table 7.3 also displays average county-level poverty rates for children living in the United States with native-born versus foreign-born parents.[9] In 2009/2013, 840,078 nonmetropolitan children (8.5 percent) lived with at least one immigrant parent. Of those, 286,977 (34.2 percent)

Table 7.3 Average Nonmetropolitan County Poverty Rates by Destination Type, 2009/2013

	Nonmetropolitan counties (N=1,477) (%)	Established destinations (N=205) (%)	New destinations (N=357) (%)	Nonimmigrant destinations (N=915) (%)
Native-born	17.5 (6.1)	17.3 (6.4)[b]	18.7 (6.2)[a,c]	16.9 (5.9)[b]
Foreign-born	23.2 (14.2)	23.3 (11.2)[b,c]	29.0 (14.4)[a,c]	21.0 (14.0)[a,b]
Naturalized citizens	14.4 (14.8)	14.1 (10.3)	16.1 (16.2)[c]	13.6 (15.1)[b]
Noncitizens	28.9 (19.5)	28.2 (14.1)[b]	33.9 (17.6)[a,c]	27.2 (20.9)[b]
	Nonmetropolitan counties (N=1,132)	Established destinations (N=194)	New destinations (N=331)	Nonimmigrant destinations (N=607)
Children with native-born parents	23.1 (9.6)	22.3 (10.2)[b]	24.7 (10.0)[a,c]	22.5 (9.1)[b]
Children with at least one foreign-born parent	31.4 (21.4)	29.1 (16.6)[b]	40.0 (20.6)[a,c]	27.4 (21.8)[b]

Source: American Community Survey 2009/2013.

Notes: Poverty rates represent the percentage of the population below 100 percent of the federal poverty level. Overall poverty rates (top section of the table) are calculated among counties with at least one hundred immigrants and not missing on poverty rates; child poverty rates (bottom section of the table) are calculated among counties with at least one hundred children living with immigrant parent(s).

[a] Denotes significant difference from established destinations at $p<0.05$.

[b] Denotes significant difference from new destinations at $p<0.05$.

[c] Denotes significant difference from nonimmigrant destinations at $p<0.05$.

were in poverty. The percentage of children living with immigrant parents and their poverty rates vary considerably across destination types. Nearly one-quarter of children in established destinations live with at least one foreign-born parent compared to 12.5 percent in new destinations and 6.1 percent in nonimmigrant destinations.

Average county poverty rates are higher among children of immigrants (the second generation) than among children of native-born parents in all three destination categories, but children of immigrants in new destinations are the most disadvantaged by far. In the average nonmetropolitan new destination, 40 percent of children of immigrants are in poverty. The poverty gap between children with native-born versus immigrant parents is also the largest in new destinations (15 percentage points). Nearly all of the highest poverty rates among children of immigrants in new destinations are in the South. In Greene County, Tennessee, for example,

86 percent of the 773 children with at least one immigrant parent are in poverty. In Coffee County, Georgia, of the 1,532 children of immigrants, 78 percent are in poverty, and *all* of the 134 children of immigrants in Clay County, North Carolina, are in poverty.

Child poverty is especially problematic because it places children on a disadvantaged path from the starting gate (Lichter et al. 2015) and influences later health outcomes, educational attainment, and transitions to productivity in adulthood (Clotfelter, Ladd, and Vigdor 2012; Duncan, Ziol-Guest, and Kalil 2010). Given now long-term declines in intergenerational socioeconomic mobility in the United States, the emergence of a more rigid class structure, and changing employment conditions that make it more difficult to lift a family out of poverty (McCall and Percheski 2010; Van Hook, Brown, and Kwenda 2004), the odds that poor children will also be poor adults are increasingly high (Borjas 2011). This is especially the case among children of Mexican immigrants. Although children of Mexican immigrants are more likely to live in two-parent families with a working male head than children of native-born parents, and living in a two-parent family is protective against poverty (Lichter and Landale 1995), children of Mexican immigrants still experience disproportionately high poverty rates (Lichter, Qian, and Crowley 2005).

There is some room for optimism as recent research provides evidence of intergenerational upward mobility (improvements in income and reductions in poverty) from the first to second generation (Alba, Kasinitz, and Waters 2011; Borjas 2006; Park and Myers 2010; Park, Myers, and Jimenez 2014). Research, however, also notes third-generation stagnation or decline (Tran and Valdez 2015), and progress appears to be proceeding unevenly, with some immigrants and their children achieving a version of the American dream in certain places as others face persistent poverty elsewhere (Martin et al. 2006). Unfortunately, no existing research disaggregates intergenerational mobility between metropolitan and nonmetropolitan immigrants, leaving questions about whether the new second generation born in rural areas will be able to merge into the economic mainstream similar to generations of past immigrants.

The human and social capital immigrants bring with them from their native countries heavily influenced economic well-being. It is important to understand whether immigrant poverty rates are higher in rural new destinations simply because of this negative selection. That is, is immigrant poverty higher in new destinations simply because immigrants in new destinations lack the education and English proficiency necessary to secure jobs with high enough wages to keep them out of poverty? Also, year of entry can influence poverty risk because employment is easier to maintain during strong economic periods than during recessions. Moreover, those with more time in the United States have had longer to adjust and adapt to U.S. customs and practices and may have less difficulty navigating employment and safety net systems than those who arrived more recently. Finally, as previously emphasized, rural immigration has historically been economically driven. Labor force demand, wages, and the need for low-skill versus high-skill workers vary across industries, and industry composition varies across destinations. Labor market differences across destination types may help us better understand differences in poverty rates.

In the average nonmetropolitan county, immigrant median income is $20,482, but immigrant median income is lower in new destinations ($19,566) than in established ($20,280) and nonimmigrant destinations ($20,884) (table 7.4). Yet, on average, immigrants to new destinations bring with them better human capital than those in established destinations. In the average established destination, 52.8 percent of immigrants lack a high school diploma (compared to 47.1 percent in the average new destination), and only 12 percent have a four-year college degree or more (compared to 13.4 percent in the average new destination). English speaking is also more prevalent in new versus established destinations. Immigrants in nonimmigrant destinations are much more educated and more likely to speak English than those in either established or new destinations. The number of immigrants with stronger human capital moving to nonimmigrant destinations may partly explain their lower poverty rates relative to their peers in new and established destinations. However, higher immigrant poverty rates in new compared to established destinations cannot be explained simply by lower educational attainment and difficulty speaking English among immigrants in new destinations, given that immigrants in new destinations are stronger on those markers than immigrants in established destinations.

Immigrants in new destinations do have a comparative disadvantage when it comes to period of entry. Immigrants in established and nonimmigrant destinations have been in the United States longer than those in new destinations, and a much larger percentage of immigrants in the average new destination (41.5 percent) entered the United States during the economically volatile 2000s. Moreover, the average percentage of immigrants who are not U.S. citizens is lower in both established destinations (66.7 percent) and nonimmigrant destinations (57.2 percent) than in new destinations (72.7 percent). As noted earlier, lack of citizenship reduces access to the critical safety net resources needed to help pull families out of poverty.

Table 7.4 Average Characteristics of the Foreign-Born Population in Nonmetropolitan Counties by Destination Type, 2009/2013

	Nonmetropolitan counties (N=1,477)	Established destinations (N=205)	New destinations (N=357)	Nonimmigrant destinations (N=915)
Median income (2013 constant dollars)	20,482 (7,890)	20,280 (6,685)	19,566 (5,751)	20,884 (8.783)
Percent age 25+ without high school diploma	38.6 (20.8)	52.8 (20.8)	47.1 (17.8)	32.1 (19.0)
Percent age 25+ with 4-year college degree or higher	18.1 (14.6)	12.0 (13.6)	13.4 (10.4)	21.4 (15.3)
Percent who speak language other than English at home	74.4 (18.0)	85.3 (15.1)	83.3 (12.0)	68.5 (17.9)
Percent age 5+ who speak English well or very well	48.3 (13.8)	47.4 (11.6)	48.0 (12.5)	48.6 (14.8)
Percent noncitizens	62.3 (17.4)	66.7 (15.0)	72.7 (12.9)	57.2 (17.3)
Year of entry to United States				
Entered before 1990 (%)	36.1 (16.6)	42.2 (15.1)	25.2 (11.2)	39.1 (16.8)
Entered 1990–1999 (%)	24.2 (12.4)	25.2 (8.8)	28.0 (11.5)	22.5 (13.1)
Entered 2000–2009 (%)	34.0 (15.2)	28.3 (11.3)	41.5 (13.9)	32.3 (15.4)
Entered in 2010 or later (%)	5.7 (7.8)	4.4 (5.2)	5.4 (7.2)	6.1 (8.5)
Labor market characteristics				
Percent unemployment rate (civilian population, age 16+)	5.2 (1.9)	5.0 (2.0)	5.5 (1.9)	5.2 (1.9)
County economic dependency				
Farming (%)	12.1	28.8	12.9	8.1
Mining (%)	5.8	11.7	2.5	5.8
Manufacturing (%)	33.0	8.8	44.8	33.8
Federal/state government (%)	12.3	20.0	7.8	12.3
Services (%)	6.2	7.8	5.9	6.0
Nonspecialized (%)	30.6	22.9	26.1	34.0

Source: American Community Survey 2009/2013.

Note: Among counties with at least one hundred foreign-born residents with no missing data on variables of interest.

Finally, there are important labor market differences across the three types of destinations. The ACS does not provide detailed county-level employment information for immigrants, so table 7.4 presents the average county unemployment rates for the whole civilian population as well as the percentage of nonmetropolitan counties falling into each of the USDA Economic Research Service's economic dependency types by destination.[10] The average unemployment rate is higher in new destinations than in either established or nonimmigrant destinations. Agriculture, mining, manufacturing, and services are industries that employ large percentages of nonmetropolitan immigrants. However, wages, employment conditions, and job security vary tremendously across these industries and are not evenly distributed across the country. Table 7.4 also presents the percentage of nonmetropolitan counties falling into each of the USDA Economic Research Service's economic dependency types by destination. Established destinations are the most dependent on farming; 28.8 percent of nonmetropolitan established destination counties are farming dependent. Immigrants employed in farming are at high risk of poverty due to low wages and mostly seasonal and unpredictable work schedules (Martin et al. 2006). However, a fifth of established destinations are dependent on state or federal government employment, somewhat buffering them from the risk of unemployment and poverty that often occur during economic downturns. New destinations are the most dependent on manufacturing; 44.8 percent of nonmetropolitan new destinations depend on manufacturing as their major source of employment, and fewer than 8 percent are reliant on federal or state government employment. Rural manufacturing was hit hard during the Great Recession (2007–2009), and low-skill immigrants experienced greater job loss and underemployment during the recession than the native born, which may have partially contributed to higher immigrant poverty rates in new destinations. There is some evidence, however, that among those with a high school diploma or more, immigrants experienced a stronger post-recession job recovery than did the native-born population (Enchautegui 2012), leaving room for optimism that rural immigrant poverty may decline as the economy strengthens.

CONCLUSION

The 1990s and 2000s were characterized by considerable immigrant population growth in rural United States. Although immigrants have traditionally been drawn to urban gateways, parts of rural U.S. have been home to a non-negligible share of immigrants throughout the past 170 years. Despite changes in the composition and distribution of the U.S. immigrant population, today's immigrants face just as many, and perhaps more, challenges to successful incorporation into U.S. society as did prior immigrant generations. A combination of several political and economic forces contributed to the increase in rural immigration over the past twenty years, including immigration policy exemptions allowing farm operators to recruit foreign workers, U.S.–Mexico border militarization and increasing hostility toward immigrants in the U.S. Southwest, increased U.S. and global demand for processed foods and disposable products, and the restructuring of U.S. manufacturing.

The rural United States is now home to 1.7 million immigrants, and immigrants currently comprise a larger share of the rural population than at any time in the previous sixty years. Immigrants remain geographically concentrated in large cities, but the dispersion of Latin American–origin immigrants to rural areas with little or no previous experience with nonwhite immigrants has changed the face of the rural U.S. and prompted questions about the ability of these communities to absorb this new population and about the ability of the immigrants themselves to incorporate. Despite being more highly educated and English-proficient, immigrants in rural new destinations have lower average incomes and higher average poverty rates than those in rural established destinations. This is at least partly due to a greater presence of noncitizens and more recently arrived immigrants in new compared to established destinations, but it is also related to the mix of industries in different destinations and the resilience of those industries to economic downturns. Much of the progress rural immigrants made toward closing the poverty gap in the late 1990s and early 2000s halted or reversed during the Great Recession of the late 2000s (Crowley, Lichter, and Turner 2015). Current safety net policies restrict immigrant eligibility for programs that could help pull them out of poverty. These findings are consistent with those of Lichter et al. (2015), who note that even when they "play by the rules" (i.e., obtain education, learn English), structural conditions, including lower wages in rural new destinations and restrictions on safety nets, place immigrants in rural new destinations at especially high risk of poverty.

High poverty rates among children of immigrants are especially concerning because childhood poverty is likely to be a greater barrier to upward mobility now than in past generations (McCall and Percheski 2010; Van Hook et al. 2004). Rural immigrant poverty is often exacerbated by native-born youth out-migration, poor access to health services, and underfunded and poor-quality schools, all of which limit opportunities for upward mobility (Dondero and Muller 2012). Although children of immigrants represent just 8.5 percent of all nonmetropolitan children, they represent nearly 12 percent of those living in poverty. A staggering one-third of nonmetropolitan children of immigrants are in poverty, and in new destinations, the average poverty rate among children of immigrants is 40 percent, characterizing what Lichter et al. (2015) refer to as the "ghettoization of rural immigrants." Yes, rural areas contain comparatively small numbers of immigrants today, but if current fertility trends continue, children of immigrants (especially Latinos) will represent a much larger percentage of rural residents in the decades to come. Therefore, high poverty rates among rural children of immigrants have important implications for the future of many rural areas, especially those in the South and West, where 70 percent of nonmetropolitan immigrants now live. Nearly one-quarter of all U.S. births today are to Latinos (J. Martin et al. 2013), and Latino childbearing is highest among the poorest and most disadvantaged immigrants (Lichter et al. 2012). Growth in the rural Latino population is now driven by fertility rather than continued immigration, which has leveled off (Lichter et al. 2012). Therefore, the effects of current immigration policies are most salient for the children and grandchildren of immigrants (i.e., the second and third generations), who will play a growing role in the future economies of many rural areas and in the United States at large.

The challenges of reducing rural immigrant poverty are considerable, but not insurmountable. Marriage and employment promotion, often cited as major antidotes to poverty, are likely to be less effective in reducing poverty among immigrants because most immigrants with children are already married and employed. Rather than unemployment, low wages and underemployment (part-time, seasonal work) seem to be the major drivers of immigrant poverty (Slack and Jensen 2007). Wages among immigrant farmworkers are especially low (Martin and Jackson-Smith 2013), despite evidence debunking large farm operators' claims that low wages are necessary to maintain low food costs (Martin et al. 2006). Moreover, agricultural workers are largely excluded from laws that protect other workers, including the right to overtime pay. Most immigrants who are farmworkers work for large farm corporations rather than small family farms. Modifications to current U.S. guest worker programs to allow migrant workers to move freely between employers might be one way to diminish seasonal unemployment and favor employers who provide the best working conditions and compensation (Martin et al. 2006).

Of course, most rural immigrants are not farmworkers, and more diversified strategies are needed to reduce poverty among immigrants working in manufacturing and services. Some rural areas with large immigrant populations may benefit from investing in training and apprenticeship programs in industries and occupations primed for growth in rural areas, including green energy, telecommunications, and health care for the aging baby boomer population. These training programs are likely to be especially appealing to immigrants if they include concomitant training in English. Apprenticeship programs such as these would also benefit native-born rural residents who may not be interested in or have the resources to attend college.

It is clear that noncitizen immigrants drive high immigrant poverty rates, so the key to reducing immigrant poverty rates is reducing poverty rates among noncitizens. Policy proposals from divergent sides of the political spectrum range from rounding up and deporting all undocumented immigrants and their children, which has been shown to be a largely ineffective strategy (Martin et al. 2006), to providing a pathway to citizenship for undocumented immigrants who are currently in the United States and can document employment. The path we go down will have major implications for whether the children of today's rural immigrants— most of whom are native-born American citizens—will escape poverty and achieve upward mobility as previous generations of immigrants have done.

Case Study: Immigration and New Rural Residents

J. Celeste Lay

Until the early 1990s, Perry was similar in most ways to other small, Iowa towns. Founded in 1869 by Harvey Willis, Perry was a railroad and manufacturing town for most of its history. Its first meatpacking plant opened in 1920; in the 1960s and 1970s, jobs at the local Oscar Mayer plant were some of the most coveted in the community. Residents in Perry were long-timers; many had roots going back several generations, and in 1990, nearly everyone (99.2 percent) was white.[1]

Things began to change when Oscar Mayer sold the plant to Iowa Beef Packers in 1988. The "new breed" of meatpacking companies, taking advantage of right-to-work laws and new technology that made skilled butchers unnecessary, moved their operations to small towns across the Midwest and South. Predictably, they slashed wages and benefits and increased line speeds. When there were inevitable labor shortages, the plants began to recruit Latinos, first from U.S. cities and then from Mexico and parts of Central America (Warren 2007; Johnson-Webb 2002; Krissman 2000).

Between 1988 and 2000, Perry was transformed. In the 2000 Census, nearly one-quarter of Perry residents identified as Hispanic. The rate of immigration slowed slightly over the next decade; by 2010, Latinos made up 35 percent of Perry residents (see table 7.5).

Getting Settled

Such substantial demographic change, called "rapid ethnic diversification," had enormous effects on the community (Grey 2006; Grey, Devlin, and Goldsmith 2009). As one would expect with any sudden increase in

Table 7.5 Population Characteristics of Perry, Iowa, 1990 and 2010

	1990	2010
Population[a]	6,652	7,702
Ethnic composition		
% Non-Hispanic white[a]	99.2	61.1
% Latino[a]	0.7	35.0
% Foreign-born	1.2	21.8[b]
Socioeconomic status		
% Bachelor's degree or higher	13.4	10.8[b]
% Below poverty line	11.5	15.1[b]
Median household income	$21,999	$35,881[b] ($21,506 in 1990 dollars)
Per capita income	$12,653	$16,885[b] ($10,120 in 1990 dollars)

[a] *Source*: U.S. Census Bureau, Census 1990 and 2010.

[b] *Source*: American Community Survey Estimates, 2005–2009, U.S. Census Bureau.

population, Perry experienced a housing shortage in the first several years after immigrants began to arrive. Male migrants came and went in Perry with regularity, as some would work only a short time and leave. Because the plant did not offer health insurance until one had worked for several weeks, and meatpacking is one of the most dangerous jobs in the country, the local hospital saw its uninsured costs rise exponentially.

By the mid- to late-1990s, turnover rates at the plant slowed, men brought their wives and children, and families began to put down roots in the community. Public schools had to increase their resources for the rapidly growing number of students who did not speak English. The strain on public services, however, was a short-term crisis (Congressional Budget Office 2007). Today, excepting first-generation immigrants, Latino residents in Perry were born in the United States and most speak English as their first (and often only) language.

Social and Economic Incorporation

Perry is somewhat poorer today than in 1990. The poverty rate was higher in Perry in 2010 than in 1990, but this was also true nationally. Perry's 2010 poverty rate was identical to the U.S. rate. The median income stayed the same between 1990 and 2010 (as it did nationally), but Perry's per capita income declined, indicating that a large portion of the population had extremely low incomes.

Even with low incomes, a job in the meatpacking plant offered immigrants several benefits. Not only were the jobs year-round and relatively stable, but many families appreciated small town life. They preferred the relatively quiet and peaceful communities to cities because of lower crime, better schools, and opportunities for social and economic mobility "precisely when similar opportunity [had] begun to stagnate, become saturated, or even decline in the traditional immigrant gateways" (Marrow 2011, 241; Donato et al. 2007).

Social stratification did not begin with immigration in Perry and other small towns. There had always been divisions along social, economic, and ethnic lines (Duncan 1999). Perry has always been a working class community, however, and Latino migrants do not hold a significantly lower status than the majority of white residents.

Still, interethnic relations were not always easy. In the early years, many Perry residents resented the changes at the plant and did not welcome the newcomers, but most residents no longer see Perry's immigrants as "outsiders." In most ways, immigrants have been incorporated into the community. Latino immigrants have opened businesses along the town's main streets and have become more active in civic life through organizations such as Hispanics United for Perry. Interethnic dating is no longer an oddity at the local high school, and Latino and white residents come together not only in support of the local football team but also to grieve the loss of local men killed in the line of duty in Iraq and Afghanistan. Although most small towns watch their best and brightest move away for college and jobs, towns like Perry have a burgeoning number of hard-working young people who want to stay in or return to small towns to raise their families.

This pattern of initial suspicion followed by acceptance and incorporation is not unique to Perry, but it is certainly not the case that interethnic relations always go smoothly. Larger towns and cities often have higher levels of residential segregation and more economic stratification. As such, there is less interaction between existing residents and newcomers, and it is more difficult for low-wage immigrant workers to join the local economic mainstream. In these communities, immigrants remain on the outside, and incorporation is a longer, more difficult process. Larger cities may want to look at these small, insular communities as a model for successful transition.

---

[1] More on Perry and the effects of immigration can be found in J. Celeste Lay, *A Midwestern Mosaic: Immigration and Political Socialization in Rural America* (Philadelphia, PA: Temple University Press, 2012).

NOTES

1. We use the terms *immigrant* and *foreign-born* interchangeably. The U.S. Census Bureau uses "foreign-born" to refer to anyone who is not a U.S. citizen at birth, including naturalized citizens, lawful permanent residents, temporary migrants (e.g., foreign students, workers on visas), humanitarian migrants (e.g., refugees), and undocumented migrants. Individuals born in Puerto Rico or a U.S. Island Area, as well as those born abroad of at least one U.S. citizen parent, are native born.

2. We use the term *nonmetropolitan* rather than *rural* because the trends described throughout the chapter are for counties outside the bounds of metropolitan areas, as defined by the Office of Management and Budget (OMB), but include some urban populations. Metropolitan areas include counties containing an urban core of 50,000

or more population (or a central city) as well as neighboring counties that are highly integrated with the core county as measured by commuting patterns.

3. "Wetback" is a pejorative term originally applied to Mexicans who crossed the Rio Grande and then was extended to all Mexican laborers, including those who are legal residents.

4. The American Community Survey (ACS) took the place of the decennial census long-form, which was discontinued in 2010. The Census releases annual county population estimates from the ACS for counties with a population of 65,000+, three-year estimates for counties with a population of 20,000+, and five-year estimates for all counties. To be inclusive of all counties, the 2009/2013 five-year estimates were used, the most recently available estimates at the time of writing. The five-year estimates are the most reliable, especially for geographic areas with small populations. The trade-off of inclusivity and reliability is the inability to describe annual change.

5. Noncitizen does not necessarily imply undocumented status. In addition to undocumented residents, noncitizens may be lawful permanent residents, temporary migrants (such as foreign students or workers on visas), or humanitarian migrants (such as refugees).

6. County-level estimates for foreign-born poverty rates are unstable for counties with small foreign-born populations, so estimates were limited to those with at least 100 foreign-born residents.

7. Separate poverty rates are not available for undocumented immigrants. Undocumented immigrants are included in the calculations for noncitizen poverty rates, but there is no way to know what percentage of them is represented in these calculations. Given that undocumented immigrants have higher poverty rates than other immigrants, the poverty estimates for noncitizen immigrants are likely conservative (i.e., the rates would be higher if the Census had data on all undocumented immigrants).

8. There are some exceptions to this rule, including for refugees, asylees, battered spouses and children, and victims of severe human trafficking.

9. Children in two-parent households where both parents are native born and children living in one-parent households where that parent is native born are classified as living with native-born parents. Children in households where at least one parent is foreign born are classified as living in an immigrant-parent household.

10. True unemployment rates are much higher because discouraged workers who are no longer in the labor market are not included in unemployment counts. These data provide especially conservative estimates for counties with large shares of undocumented immigrants. Many undocumented immigrants are not included in unemployment counts because they do not qualify or are fearful of applying for unemployment insurance.

REFERENCES

Alba, Richard D., Philip Kasinitz, and Mary C. Waters. 2011. "The Kids Are (Mostly) Alright: Second-Generation Assimilation: Comments on Haller, Portes and Lynch." *Social Forces* 89(3):763–73.

Atiles, Jorge H., and Stephanie A. Bohon. 2003. "Camas Calientes: Housing Adjustments and Barriers to Social and Economic Adaptation Among Georgia's Rural Latinos." *Southern Rural Sociology* 19(1):97–122.

Borjas, George J. 2006. "Making It in America: Social Mobility in the Immigrant Population." *Future of Children* 16(2):55–71.

———. 2011. "Poverty and Program Participation Among Immigrant Children." *The Future of Children* 21:247–66.

Brown, David L. 2014. "Rural Population Change in Social Context." In *Rural America in a Globalizing World: Problems and Prospects for the 2010s*, ed. Conner Bailey, Leif Jensen, and Elizabeth Ransom, 299–310. Morgantown, WV: West Virginia University Press.

Burton, Linda M., Daniel T. Lichter, Regina S. Baker, and John M. Eason. 2013. "Inequality, Family Processes and Health in the 'New' Rural America." *American Behavioral Scientist* 57(8):1128–51.

Cance, Alexander E. 1912. "Immigrant Rural Communities." *Annals of the American Academy of Political and Social Science* 4:69–80.

Chapman, Jeff, and Jared Bernstein. 2002. "Immigration and Poverty." Economic Policy Institute Briefing Paper. Washington, DC. http://www.epi.org/publication /briefingpapers_bp130/.

Clotfelter, Charles T., Helen F. Ladd, and Jacob L. Vigdor. 2012. "New Destinations, New Trajectories? The Educational Progress of Hispanic Youth in North Carolina." *Child Development* 83:1608–22.

Congressional Budget Office. 2007. "The Impact of Unauthorized Immigrants on the Budgets of State and Local Governments." http://www.cbo.gov/ftpdocs/87xx /doc8711/12-6-Immigration.pdf.

Crowley, Martha, and Kim Ebert. 2014. "New Rural Immigrant Destinations: Research for the 2010s." In *Rural America in a Globalizing World: Problems and Prospects for the 2010s*, ed. Conner Bailey, Leif Jensen, and Elizabeth Ransom, 401–18. Morgantown, WV: West Virginia University Press.

Crowley, Martha, and Daniel T. Lichter. 2009. "Social Disorganization in New Latino Destinations?" *Rural Sociology* 74(4):573–604.

Crowley, Martha, Daniel T. Lichter, and Richard N. Turner. 2015. "Diverging Fortunes? Economic Well-Being of Latinos and African Americans in New Rural Destinations." *Social Science Research* 51:77–92.

Dondero, Molly, and Chandra Muller. 2012. "School Stratification in New and Established Latino Destinations." *Social Forces* 2:477–502.

Donato, Katherine M., Charles M. Tolbert II, Alfred Nucci, and Yukio Kawano. 2007. "Recent Immigrant Settlement in the Nonmetropolitan United States: Evidence from Internal Census Data." *Rural Sociology* 72(4):537–59.

Duncan, Cynthia M. 1999. *Worlds Apart: Why Poverty Persists in Rural America*. New Haven, CT: Yale University Press.

Duncan, Greg J., Kathleen M. Ziol-Guest, and Ariel Kalil. 2010. "Early-Childhood Poverty and Adult Attainment, Behavior, and Health." *Child Development* 81:306–25.

Durand, Jorge, Douglas S. Massey, and Fernando Charvet. 2000. "The Changing Geography of Mexican Immigration to the United States: 1910–1996." *Social Science Quarterly* 81(1):1–15.

Effland, Anna B., and Marguerite A. Butler. 1997. "Fewer Immigrants Settle in Non-Metro Areas and Most Fare Less Well Than Metro Immigrants." *Rural Conditions and Trends* 8(2):60–65.

Enchautegui, Maria E. 2012. *Hit Hard but Bouncing Back: The Employment of Immigrants During the Great Recession and the Recovery.* Washington, DC: Urban Institute.

Findeis, Jill L., and Leif Jensen. 1998. "Employment Opportunities in Rural Areas: Implications for Poverty in a Changing Policy Environment." *American Journal of Agricultural Economics* 80(5):1001–8.

Gibson, Campbell J., and Emily Lennon. 1999. Historical Census Statistics on the Foreign-born Population of the United States: 1950–1990. Washington, DC: U.S. Census Bureau. https://www.census.gov/population/www/documentation/twps0029 /twps0029.html.

Glazer, Nathan, and Daniel Patrick Moynihan. 1963. *Beyond the Melting Pot.* Cambridge, MA: MIT Press.

Gouveia, Lourdes, and Rogelio Saenz. 2000. "Global Forces and Latino Population Growth in the Midwest: A Regional and Subregional Analysis." *Great Plains Research* 10:305–28.

Gozdziak, Elzbieta M., and Susan F. Martin, eds. 2005. *Beyond the Gateway: Immigrants in a Changing America.* New York, NY: Lexington Books.

Grey, Mark A. 2006. "State and Local Immigration Policy in Iowa." In *Immigration's New Frontiers: Experiences from the Emerging Gateway States,* ed. Greg Anrig Jr. and Tova Andrea Wang, 33–66. New York, NY: Century Foundation Press.

Grey, Mark A., Michele Devlin, and Aaron Goldsmith. 2009. *Postville, U.S.A.: Surviving Diversity in Small-Town America.* Boston, MA: GemmaMedia.

Grieco, Elizabeth M., Yesenia D. Acosta, G. Patricia de la Cruz, et al. 2012. *The Foreign Born Population in the United States: 2010.* Washington, DC: U.S. Census Bureau. https://www.census.gov/prod/2012pubs/acs-19.pdf.

Hoynes, Hilary, Marianne Page, and Ann Huff Stevens. 2006. "Poverty in America: Trends and Explanations." *Journal of Economic Perspectives* 20(1):47–68.

Johnson, Kenneth. 2011. "The Continuing Incidence of Natural Decrease in American Counties." *Rural Sociology* 76(1):74–100.

———. 2014. "Demographic Trends in Nonmetropolitan America: 2000–2010." In *Rural America in a Globalizing World: Problems and Prospects for the 2010s,* ed. Conner Bailey, Leif Jensen, and Elizabeth Ransom, 311–29. Morgantown, WV: West Virginia University Press.

Johnson, Kenneth, and Daniel T. Lichter. 2008. *Population Growth in New Hispanic Destinations.* Policy Brief No. 8. Durham, NH: Carsey Institute.

Johnson-Webb, Karen D. 2002. "Employer Recruitment and Hispanic Labor Migration: North Carolina Urban Areas at the End of the Millennium." *The Professional Geographer* 54:406–21.

Kandel, William, and John Cromartie. 2004. "New Patterns of Hispanic Settlement in Rural America." USDA ERS Rural Development Research Report (RDRR-49). Washington, DC.

Kandel, William, and Emilio Parrado. 2005. "Restructuring of the U.S. Meat Processing Industry and New Hispanic Migrant Destinations." *Population and Development Review* 31:447–71.

Krissman, Fred. 2000. "Immigrant Labor Recruitment: U.S. Agribusiness and Undocumented Migration from Mexico." In *Immigration Research for a New Century,* ed. Nancy Foner, Ruben G. Rumbaut, and Steven J. Gold, 277–321. New York, NY: Russell Sage.

Leclere, Felicia, Leif Jensen, and Ann E. Biddlecom. 1994. "Health Care Utilization, Family Context, and Adaptation Among Immigrants to the United States." *Journal of Health and Social Behavior* 35(4):370–84.

Lichter, Daniel T. 2012. "Immigration and the New Racial Diversity in Rural America." *Rural Sociology* 77(1):3–35.

Lichter, Daniel T., and Martha Crowley. 2002. "Poverty in America: Beyond Welfare Reform." *Population Bulletin* 57(2):3–36.

Lichter, Daniel T., and Leif Jensen. 2002. "Rural America in Transition: Poverty and Welfare at the Turn of the 21st Century." In *Rural Dimensions of Welfare Reform*, ed. Bruce A. Weber, Greg J. Duncan, and Leslie E. Whitener, 77–110. Kalamazoo, MI: Upjohn Institute.

Lichter, Daniel T., and Kenneth M. Johnson. 2006. "Emerging Rural Settlement Patterns and the Geographic Redistribution of America's New Immigrants." *Rural Sociology* 71:109–31.

Lichter, Daniel T., Kenneth M. Johnson, Richard N. Turner, and Allison Churilla. 2012. "Hispanic Assimilation and Fertility in New U.S. Destinations." *International Migration Review* 46:767–91.

Lichter, Daniel T., and Nancy S. Landale. 1995. "Parental Work, Family Structure, and Poverty Among Latino Children." *Journal of Marriage and the Family* 57:346–54.

Lichter, Daniel T., Domenico Parisi, Michael C. Taquino, and Steven Michael Grice. 2010. "Residential Segregation in New Hispanic Destinations: Cities, Suburbs, and Rural Communities Compared." *Social Science Research* 39:215–30.

Lichter, Daniel T., Zhenchao Qian, and Martha Crowley. 2005. "Child Poverty Among Racial Minorities and Immigrants: Explaining Trends and Differentials." *Social Science Quarterly* 86(5):1037–59.

Lichter, Daniel T., Scott R. Sanders, and Kenneth M. Johnson. 2015. "Hispanics at the Starting Line: Poverty Among Newborn Infants in Established Gateways and New Destinations." *Social Forces* 94(1):209–35.

Marrow, Helen. 2011. *New Destination Dreaming: Immigration, Race, and Legal Status in the Rural American South*. Palo Alto, CA: Stanford University Press.

Martin, Philip, Michael Fix, and J. Edward Taylor. 2006. *The New Rural Poverty: Agriculture and Immigration in California*. Washington, DC: The Urban Institute.

Martin, Philip, and Douglas Jackson-Smith. 2013. "Immigration and Farm Labor in the U.S." Policy Brief 4. National Agricultural & Rural Development Policy Center. http://www.nardep.info/uploads/Brief_FarmWorker.pdf.

Massey, Douglas S. 2008. *New Faces in New Places: The Changing Geography of American Immigration*. New York, NY: Russell Sage Foundation.

Massey, Douglas S., and Chiara Capoferro. 2008. "The Geographic Diversification of American Immigration." In *New Faces in New Places: The Changing Geography of American Immigration*, ed. Douglas S. Massey, 25–50. New York, NY: Russell Sage Foundation.

Massey, Douglas S., and Zai Liang. 1989. "The Long-Term Consequences of a Temporary Worker Program: The U.S. Bracero Experience." *Population Research and Policy Review* 8(3):199–226.

McCall, Leslie, and Christine Percheski. 2010. "Income Inequality: New Trends and Research Directions." *Annual Review of Sociology* 36:329–47.

McClain, Paula D., Monique L. Lyle, Niambi M. Carter, et al. 2007. "Black Americans and Latino Immigrants in a Southern City." *DuBois Review* 4(1):97–117.

Migration Policy Institute. 2015. "U.S. Immigrant Population by State and County, 2009–2013." http://www.migrationpolicy.org/programs/data-hub/charts/us-immigrant-population-state-and-county.

Park, Julie, and Dowell Myers. 2010. "Intergenerational Mobility in the Post-1965 Immigration Era: Estimates by an Immigrant Generation Cohort Method." *Demography* 47(2):369–92.

Park, Julie, Dowell Myers, and Tomas R. Jimenez. 2014. "Intergenerational Mobility of the Mexican-Origin Population in California and Texas Relative to a Changing Regional Mainstream." *International Migration Review* 48(2):442–81.

Parrado, Emilio A., and William Kandel. 2008. "New Hispanic Migrant Destinations: A Tale of Two Industries." In *New Faces in New Places: The Changing Geography of American Immigration*, ed. Douglas S. Massey, 99–123. New York, NY: Russell Sage Foundation.

Singer, Audrey. 2004. *The Rise of New Immigrant Gateways*. Washington, DC: Brookings Institution, Center for Urban and Metropolitan Policy.

Slack, Tim, and Leif Jensen. 2007. "Underemployment Across Immigrant Generations." *Social Science Research* 36(4):1415–30.

The Pew Charitable Trusts. 2014. "Mapping Public Benefits for Immigrants in the States." http://www.pewtrusts.org/~/media/assets/2014/09/mappingpublicbenefitsforimmigrantsinthestatesfinal.pdf.

Tran, Van C., and Nicol M. Valdez. 2015. "Second-Generation Decline or Advantage? Latino Assimilation in the Aftermath of the Great Recession." *International Migration Review* (Fall):1–36.

Trump, Donald. 2015. "Presidential Campaign Announcement Speech." New York, NY, June 15.

U.S. Census Bureau. 1990. 1990 Census of the Population and Housing, Summary File 3. Washington, DC. Accessed March 3, 2017.

——. 2000. 2000 Census of the Population and Housing, Summary File 3. Washington, DC. Accessed March 3, 2017.

——. 2015. American Community Survey, 2009–2013. Washington, DC. Accessed March 3, 2017.

Van Hook, Jennifer, Susan I. Brown, and Maxwell Ndigume Kwenda. 2004. "A Decomposition of Trends in Poverty Among Children of Immigrants." *Demography* 41:649–70.

Warren, Wilson J. 2007. *Tied to the Great Packing Machine: The Midwest and Meatpacking*. Iowa City: University of Iowa Press.

Zeitlin, Richard H. 1980. "White Eagles in the Woods: Polish Immigration to Rural Wisconsin, 1857–1900." *Polish Review* 25(1):69–92.

PART IV

Community and Societal Institutions

Part IV considers institutional barriers that should be recognized and addressed by antipoverty policies targeting rural poverty. The first of these is symbolic forms of capital: social capital, cultural capital, human capital, moral capital. We learn in Chapter 8, "Rural Poverty and Symbolic Capital: A Tale of Two Valleys," that social capital can help rural families survive through tough times by providing economic support such as access to jobs and noneconomic support such as child care, housing, education, aid, and social support. Symbolic support should not be taken for granted, however, because it is not present in all rural areas, and its absence exacerbates the consequences of poverty for residents of rural communities *relative to* urban areas where formal food banks and shelters assist those with similar needs.

Chapter 9, "The *Old* Versus the *New* Economies and Their Impacts," reviews the effects of two economic trends that have reshaped income earning opportunities in rural communities: globalization and the restructuring of the U.S. economy. Underemployment and unemployment, in particular, are studied over time in accordance with the rise and fall of certain industries and occupations. The replacement of good jobs in manufacturing supporting a foothold in the middle class with low-wage, low-skill jobs has decreased the ability of rural residents to support their families through employment alone. Because work no longer keeps families out of poverty, antipoverty policies that go beyond traditional "work support" programs are needed.

Chapter 10, "Food Insecurity and Housing Insecurity," explains how the geography of rural areas limits access to affordable rental housing units, to affordable healthy food, and to the social service institutions that address these needs, particularly when compared to resources available in urban areas.

Chapter 11, "The Environment and Health," examines environmental hazards facing rural areas of the United States and describes their impacts on the health status of rural communities and residents. The authors underscore that negative health impacts are accentuated by financial and geographic barriers in accessing primary and emergency care due to lower levels of medical professionals, accelerated rates of hospital closures and consolidations, and lower rates of health insurance coverage. Low-income rural communities bear a disproportionally large share of environmental burdens, which raises issues of distributive injustice and a call for research that will conclusively link health status and environmental hazards.

Chapter 12, "Education and Information," examines institutional differences between rural and urban schools that disadvantage rural children and reduce the probability that education will be their route out of poverty. We learn that rural schools are more likely than urban schools to be linked to their communities and thus to reflect local, and often disparate, ideas about the purpose of education that are sometimes at loggerheads with education policies. Recent federal policies that allocate education grants on the basis of the number of students and require submission of complex applications have placed rural school districts at a disadvantage. Consequently, rural schools fall short of their role as "engines" for social equality. The failure to locate postsecondary training and colleges in rural areas forces the brightest of rural students to migrate to urban areas, draining their communities of human capital.

———

CHAPTER 8

Rural Poverty and Symbolic Capital

A TALE OF TWO VALLEYS

Jennifer Sherman

A lot of people leave and come back. There's something about staying in a safe community, even in poverty, that's easier for them than it is elsewhere. . . . It's easier to live poor
here than it is in the big cities. It's safer.

—Cathy Graham, fifty-year-
old married schoolteacher,
Golden Valley, California

It's not—I call it the rat race, but it's not wake up, go to work, it's not that routine of,
every day you are surviving to make more money. That's what—being a parent now, that's
what I really enjoy. It's not live every day to make more money.

—Chad Lloyd, twenty-eight-
year-old married sawmill
worker and father of three,
Paradise Valley, Washington

INTRODUCTION

What motivates people to live in rural communities, particularly in places
where jobs are scarce, and survival is a struggle? Often rural residents will
remark that a particular rural community is "a good place to raise a family." When prodded for more detail on what this means to an individual,
many talk about beauty, safety, a slow pace of life, and being "out of the
rat race." These idealized understandings of what it means to live in a
rural community both capture and leave out much of what is vital to
understanding the challenges and rewards faced by rural families. This
chapter explores the types of resources rural families rely on for survival,
social status, and meaning. In particular, it looks at the roles of symbolic
forms of capital in rural communities, which both aid and impede families in their various struggles to get by in remote places when jobs and
economic capital are scarce.

Many rural communities lack the benefits that draw people to urban and suburban settings, such as retail services, economic opportunities, and racial or ethnic diversity. However, rural life often comes with numerous advantages that residents who are well integrated into a community can draw upon to aid in survival. This chapter investigates and illustrates some of the less tangible forms of rural advantage as well as the types of challenges poor rural families face. The ways in which symbolic capital affects the experiences of poverty, unemployment, and underemployment in rural communities is examined in depth. Two case studies are woven into the chapter that draw on the author's in-depth qualitative work in two towns in the Pacific Northwest: "Golden Valley," California, from 2003 to 2004, and "Paradise Valley," Washington, from 2014 to 2015.[1] Both are small, remote, mostly white rural communities that have economic roots in logging, mining, and ranching. Golden Valley's forest-dependent economy was in collapse during this time, resulting in widespread poverty for its population. Paradise Valley's economy, on the other hand, had transitioned decades earlier to a heavy reliance on tourism and second-home ownership, resulting in more jobs and economic opportunities but also in deep inequality and persistent poverty at the bottom of the income ladder. The similarities and differences of these communities illustrate the ways in which different types of real and symbolic capital organize social life and influence poor families' chances of survival in rural American communities.

THE FORMS OF CAPITAL, REAL AND SYMBOLIC

The concept of "symbolic capital" is based on the work of Pierre Bourdieu, who argued that the categories and hierarchies upon which social life is organized are based not solely in differences in income and wealth ("real" or economic capital) but also in differences of other types of resources that are not strictly economic in nature but act in similar ways. He referred to these types of resources as *symbolic capital* (Bourdieu 1986). Symbolic capital consists of noneconomic boundary markers between people that may be traded for one another, and for economic capital, depending on the social setting. Some of the types of symbolic capital commonly studied by sociologists include social capital, cultural capital, human capital, and moral capital. *Social capital* consists of one's social connections and the network-based resources that can be accessed by those within the social network to procure benefits (Bourdieu 1986;

Coleman 1988; Putnam 2001). A person's social network may have resources of time, money, or other goods and services such as food, labor, and access to potential job opportunities, which they share with others in the network. *Cultural capital* consists of tastes, manners, and preferences that help to distinguish groups of people from each other, such as knowledge of, interest in, and preferences for such things as art, music, and entertainment. In certain circles and social settings, cultural capital may be traded for social connections, as well as potential job opportunities, as in the case of manners and self-presentation, which can help or hurt a job candidate (Bourdieu 1986; Woodward 2013). *Human capital* consists of investments in individual education, training, and job experience, with higher levels being converted into higher salaries, labor market opportunities, and job benefits (Becker 2009). Finally, *moral capital,* which has been documented in rural American settings, consists of external exhibitions of one's morality according to locally constructed norms and understandings. It may be such things as outwardly manifesting one's work ethic and family values within a community where these values are considered important. Like other forms of symbolic capital, moral capital can be traded for advantages in social settings as well as in school (where human capital is obtained) and in the labor market (Sherman 2006, 2009; Sherman and Sage 2011). Together, the various forms of real and symbolic capital contribute to a person's social class status within a society and to the person's life chances, opportunities, and choices.

The relative value and importance of different types of symbolic capital depend heavily on the social setting in which a person or family resides. In many U.S. settings, economic capital, in the forms of income and wealth, dominates social hierarchies and is the strongest indicator and predictor of advantage. Although economic capital is rarely unimportant in a capitalist society, in different settings other types of symbolic capital may be of greater or lesser importance, particularly when economic capital is scarce (Flora and Flora 2013; Sherman 2009). In settings such as remote, high-poverty rural communities, the lack of available economic capital can lead to a heavy reliance on symbolic forms of capital, which enable residents to create and sustain social boundaries and maintain social hierarchies in the absence of significant economic divisions and opportunities. The availability and usefulness of different types of real and symbolic capital constrain opportunities and create relative advantages for people within their unique social settings, depending on the social and economic organization of a community. Particularly when poverty is endemic and economic capital scarce, symbolic forms of capital can play vital roles in structuring social and economic life. Symbolic and real capital, however, are just one way in which social boundaries are built and maintained. In more heterogeneous societies and communities, the effects of symbolic capital are influenced by and intertwined with other social divisions, including those based in race and ethnicity, gender, age, and sexuality. These two case studies describe relatively homogenous communities in which social class plays a pivotal role in structuring social life and in which other axes of division are less central to social organization.

RURAL POVERTY AND THE IMPORTANCE OF SYMBOLIC CAPITAL

In much of rural America, deindustrialization and economic decline have dominated the last half-century, a trend that accelerated during the Great Recession of 2007–2009 (Grusky, Western, and Wimer 2011; Hamilton et al. 2008; Smith and Tickamyer 2011; see also chapter 9 in this book). Across rural America, declines in land-based industries, extractive industries, and manufacturing left many places without strong economies and living-wage jobs, particularly for men. Some rural communities have seen growth in other sectors, such as service and tourism, or growth in new extractive industries, such as hydraulic fracturing. Other communities struggle to reinvent themselves with limited prospects for building healthy postindustrial economies (Hamilton et al. 2008). Lack of jobs and incomes affects rural communities in multiple ways, often resulting in loss of local businesses and decreasing services as well as the destabilization of social life and the out-migration of young adults.

For those who remain in rural communities without economic opportunities, survival options are often constrained by cultural understandings and social structures, which provide the cultural "tool kit" (Swidler 1986) residents have at their disposal for making sense of their lives and defining success and failure. Many rural communities are characterized by cultural conservatism (Bageant 2008; Frank 2004), which often includes understandings that stigmatize poverty, unemployment, and underemployment as individual failures rather than as outcomes of larger structural conditions (Fitchen 1991; Sherman 2009). Such stigma can heavily influence social life and available survival strategies for rural families experiencing economic strain, often limiting access to real and symbolic forms of capital (Sage and Sherman 2014; Sherman 2009; Whitley 2013). Symbolic capital such as social, cultural, and moral capital may help to mitigate conditions of poverty, but symbolic capital also presents challenges for low-income and poor rural families who lack access to this noneconomic resource. The following sections explore ways in which symbolic capital both helps and hinders rural poor families' survival.

SOCIAL CAPITAL AND RURAL POVERTY

In rural settings in which income and wealth are scarce, the different forms of symbolic capital take on increased importance and have serious positive and negative effects on families struggling to survive. Generations of rural sociologists have documented the importance of social capital in high-poverty rural communities and have studied its benefits for families as well as the challenges faced by those families and communities that lack it. Duncan (1999) documents the stark differences in community outcomes for rural communities that experience high versus low levels of social capital due to social structures and legacies of inequality. Flora and Flora (2013) similarly describe the importance of social capital in rural communities and raise concerns about the ability of communities to defend themselves against economic and social challenges in its absence (Flora and Flora 2014). For families in poor rural communities, social capital can often mean the difference between aid through difficult times and facing difficulties alone (Whitley 2013). Social capital can substitute for economic capital in multiple ways for individuals and families, providing access to job opportunities through social networks and other types of informal support. The following quotes, from interviews conducted in Golden Valley and Paradise Valley, illustrate several different ways in which social capital operates to substitute for economic capital in rural communities.

Grace Prader, a forty-five-year-old secretary and married mother of two in Golden Valley, discusses her inability to find affordable housing due to her family's low income and the community's lack of low-cost housing:

> We were caretaking a place for seven, eight years. And the guy calls and says, "By the way, I've just sold the place." And I said, "Oh, OK." And we'd lived there for seven, eight years, we'd accumulated a lot of stuff and a lot of garbage. And so my mother-in-law let us have her camp trailer, and at that point we moved, me and [my husband], and him working, making

$7.50 an hour at that time. There's no way that we could get the down payment to either buy a house or rent. I mean, we just, so my thought was, "Well, we'll just park a camp trailer down at the fairgrounds." It was fine. And then we ended up moving into another spot, caretaking it, and she said, "How long are you gonna be here?" I said, "I don't see us here for more than three years." She said, "Fine. Then you can have it rent-free." That was really the only way we could do it on that paycheck.

Shawn Murphy, forty-three-year-old restaurant manager and single father of one in Paradise Valley, describes a lack of child-care options, a constraint that would otherwise affect families not only in their amount of leisure time but in their ability to work at service sector jobs like his, which requires him to be available at night and on weekends:

When it comes to my child-care challenge, it's like, yeah, on a large scale, there's a need and a challenge in child care still. But on a small scale, there's a network of friends that you can always pretty much say, "Hey, you know, can you step in for two hours or whatever? And I'll help you out." There's this whole informal network of tangible support when it comes to some of those—being in a big city, what are you gonna do? Something comes up, and there's no daycare option, and you may not have that community support network. Everyone's busy. Everyone else's kids are in child care, too. And here there's this flexibility.

Nicole Goodman, a twenty-five-year-old care worker and married mother of two in Golden Valley, discusses community-level charity provided on an informal level for families in need:

If your house burns down, like somebody's did recently, everybody's like, "What can we do, what can we do?" They come right over and start donating and helping. There's not money here, but everybody teams together to take care of everybody.

In all of these examples, social capital provides noneconomic benefits that help families survive in the absence of sufficient economic capital, allowing them to mobilize informal networks to fill in the gaps in economic capacity and formal infrastructure. Grace's social networks help her through what could otherwise be a serious crisis, providing her with low-cost housing through the community's informal tradition of having less-privileged families "caretake" property for owners who have moved away in search of better jobs and economic prospects. Caretakers like Grace pay little to no rent in return for taking care of the property for someone who knows and trusts them. For Grace, her social integration provides what neither the labor market nor the community's infrastructure can, allowing her to substitute social capital for economic capital in the local housing market. Shawn illustrates a similar scenario. Like Grace, Shawn can draw on his social networks to help provide what his income and Paradise Valley's infrastructure cannot: in his case, after-hours, trustworthy child care.

Nicole's story illustrates an aspect of social capital that plays a vital role in many cohesive rural communities. It is not uncommon to hear stories like this one in rural communities. Well-known families who experience disasters or illness are helped by the larger community in informal ways, such as throwing spaghetti-feed fund-raisers to help pay for hospital bills, or providing hands-on help with necessary home repairs after a natural disaster. This practice is certainly not unheard of in urban areas, where churches and other civic and social groups may engage in similar acts of collective, informal charity. But it is particularly common in rural communities such as Golden Valley, where formal infrastructure for handling emergencies, disasters, and medical crises is lacking or nonexistent and poor families frequently are un- or underinsured. In the case Nicole described, as in many similar stories from rural residents, social capital compensates for economic capital and aids in survival for socially integrated families who lack significant income or wealth.

In all of these cases, and in many other scenarios throughout rural America, social capital plays an important role in allowing families to share resources with others in their networks to get through difficult times. In places without healthy economies, social capital can become extremely important to survival.

The importance of social capital for rural families does not make it universally available to all, however. It is important to note that families who are not well integrated into their communities will likely lack the social capital they need to get them through difficult times. Lack of integration can occur for multiple reasons, including recent in-migration, prejudices along race or ethnic boundary lines, remote living, or lack of other types of symbolic capital, such as cultural or moral capital. For Paradise Valley resident Allison Lloyd, a twenty-eight-year-old, married, stay-at-home mother of three who moved there eight years earlier, her short tenure in the community, the remoteness of the family's rented home, and her lack of cultural capital contribute to her isolation from the community's social networks. She describes a very different experience from that of Shawn Murphy within the same setting. Unlike Shawn, Allison's inability to find reliable child care prohibits her from taking on paid work, and instead she cares for her children full-time. I asked if she felt that she had enough support for her family, and she responded:

> Allison: We have nothing, which has been really hard on my husband and I just for a long while, actually, but the only support we really had in the past was my husband's dad and his wife, and that was only like once every two months, if that. You know, we could have them watch the kids if we needed to, but we're pretty much on our own. You know, and that's really hard to know that we don't have anybody to turn to if we need something or if we need help with something.
>
> Q: *You really feel that way?*
>
> Allison: Yeah. I mean, we know people. We have acquaintances. We don't have a lot of really close friends.

Allison's discussion illustrates the opposite end of the social spectrum: a low-income family that lacks the kinds of developed social networks that might provide them with social capital. Instead of feeling that her needs are met informally, Allison describes lacking the type of child care support that Shawn has in the same community. As this example suggests, social capital can provide poor rural families with resources, but its lack can create additional challenges in communities that do not have an adequate formal infrastructure to provide for low-income and poor families' needs. Like other forms of capital, social capital works as a source of social division as well as a resource for those families lucky enough to have access to it. For Allison, it helps to reinforce social exclusion and isolation by further impeding her ability to engage in adult social activities that might require her to have child care. Her isolation then contributes to her lack of social networks, impeding her ability to forge social capital, and creating a feedback loop that is difficult to interrupt.

CULTURAL CAPITAL AND RURAL POVERTY

The importance of cultural capital is often discussed in urban settings where cultural differences can be stark and visible and culture easily

categorized as high or low (Bourdieu 1984; Lamont 1992). It is less frequently documented in rural settings where communities are less likely to
contain the same level of cultural diversity, and often residents share cultural norms and understandings with little variation. Such is the case in
Golden Valley where homogenous cultural understandings provide little
space for cultural capital to come into play; rarely did cultural capital
play an important role in dividing or structuring social life there. For
rural communities with greater diversity, however, culture can become
another axis on which social divisions rest and resources are divided and
allocated. Particularly in rural communities that have experienced in-
migration by newcomers with cultural backgrounds that are distinct from
those of long-time residents, cultural distinctions can play an important
role in structuring daily life and social and economic opportunities. As
with social capital, in these situations, cultural capital may help form and
maintain social hierarchies, providing resources and access to some families while simultaneously denying these advantages to others whose cultural norms, beliefs, and expectations mark them as different. Researchers
have documented rural community divisions grounded in cultural differences of ethnicity, religion, and sexuality (Crowley and Lichter 2009;
Devine 2006; Stein 2001). In these cases, deep cultural divisions allow for
judgment and exclusion of one social group by another, resulting in the
systematic denial of resources.

Cultural differences do not have to be gaping divides in worldviews
and belief systems to provide the basis for social divisions, however. In
the case of Paradise Valley, cultural differences are extremely important,
but not necessarily grounded in deeply held religious or moral beliefs.
In this community, cultural capital is not built on differences in ethnic backgrounds (most residents are white and of European descent) or
religious belief systems. Rather, cultural capital is built on differences in
tastes and preferences for things such as art, music, food and drink, and
leisure activities, as well as differences in aspirations for children's outcomes. The bulk of affluent newcomers to the area share similar interests in "high culture" forms of art, music, and food and drink (Bourdieu
1984) and strongly prefer outdoor sports activities such as hiking and
skiing over leisure pursuits such as television, motorized vehicle use,
or video games. These kinds of cultural differences can serve to structure social life, including influencing who is in one's social networks.
Families in Paradise Valley choose different venues for eating, shopping,
and recreating, effectively segregating themselves in ways that result in

different levels of exposure to cultural capital for children as well as the formation of social networks with vastly different access to economic, social, and human capital. Choosing to go to an upscale coffee shop versus drinking coffee at the grocery store deli affects whom one interacts with socially, as does choosing to drink Budweiser at a modest bar versus craft beer at an upscale pub. For children, going to dance, ski, and music lessons after school results in very different experiences and exposure than does watching television or playing video games at home. Thus, not only can cultural capital be traded for other forms of real and symbolic capital in this setting, but it also serves to maintain and reinforce social divisions.

Hannah Lowry, a well-integrated, middle-class, forty-five-year-old married mother of two, has a college education and an extensive background in art and literature. She explained how she perceives social divisions within the community, which she describes as being based on different interests that belie different cultural norms:

> On weekends . . . we're out backpacking with a group of friends or doing a day hike with a bunch of ladies. And then I have a book club once a month. . . . I get to go to book club . . . and not everybody has that luxury. The people I end up spending time with are the people who have that luxury. But there's also a lot of families that go hunting together. I don't want to go hunting, so I'm not friends with those families, because they're going ATVing and hunting, and they're having a great time outdoors together with other families who do that. But we're not. We're friends to, like, say hi on the street.

Although her description of variations in cultural interests makes them sound benign, for those on the "low culture" side of the divide such as Allison Lloyd (introduced previously), these differences clearly have a hierarchical quality that affects where they stand on the social ladder in Paradise Valley. Here is how Allison described it:

> I think that people think that I'm a—that's why I call myself a redneck. 'Cause, like my brother came up here and he was like, "God, I can't believe that you do that. You go hunting? You let your kids ride a 4-wheeler in your front yard?" You know, I think a lot of people, um, there's a lot of people that have assumptions about me, and that's fine. They can assume all they want, but I think I'm a good person.

For residents of Paradise Valley, cultural capital opens doors to social capital in important ways. It helps form the basis of the social networks that Shawn Murphy and Hannah Lowry build, which include other educated adults with similar cultural norms as well as resources often of financial and human capital. In this way, social and cultural capital are mutually reinforcing in Paradise Valley. Families with interests in high culture activities take advantage of the community's opportunities to enjoy art, theater, music, dance, and outdoor recreation and are exposed to others with similar interests—and similar resources—through these pursuits. This contrasts with families with lower culture interests, who often find themselves more isolated from the community and lacking access to formal social opportunities and activities. Cultural capital structures who interacts with whom, and where. For example, when asked about her local activities, Maria Setzer, a forty-year-old artist and married mother of two explained:

> I used to play in the orchestra. I did a lot of volunteer stuff for the art gallery . . . and I used to help facilitate a dance class, we called it freestyle dance, at the studio. I used to do that once a week. So things here and there.

Although Maria's family lives on less than 200 percent of the poverty line, she feels well integrated in Paradise Valley and has strong social connections there. Her description of social activities differs clearly from that of Wendy Harris, a thirty-seven-year-old, married, stay-at-home mother of one who also survives on the low income provided by her husband's job as a long-haul truck driver. She explained her community pursuits:

> Wendy: I will not go to the theater thingy. . . . The Easter thing every year that they do, I usually go down and hang out for that. Just that kind of thing . . .
>
> Q: *Do these things cost money?*
>
> Wendy: They have to be free. They can't cost me money, especially comin' off two years of not havin' any money. It's gotta be somethin' that's—or very minimal cost. . . . Every weekend my aunt and I make a point of going yard-saling. I know that's not community, but you know how many people you see at yard sales? [laughs] We see a lot of people at yard sales, so I get most of my social gathering that way. Almost every other day, now that [my husband]'s working and I can afford a cup of coffee, we go to coffee down at [the grocery store].

Maria's cultural pursuits put her family into contact with many of Paradise Valley's elite residents, but Wendy's activities ensure that she only interacts with other low-income families who also lack significant cultural capital.

Like social capital, cultural capital in Paradise Valley serves to help some families gain access to social and human capital while effectively barring others. Those with high amounts of cultural capital can maintain their social status whether or not they have significant income or wealth, which increases their ability to build and utilize social capital. Those lacking cultural capital encounter boundary lines that effectively exclude them from many of the community's other resources, exacerbating both financial strain and social isolation. In these ways, cultural capital, similar to social capital itself, can either ease the strain of poverty and low income or further disadvantage individuals and families.

HUMAN CAPITAL AND RURAL POVERTY

In most parts of the United States, it is taken for granted that education and training are required to succeed in the labor market. In rural communities, however, human capital can operate differently than it does in places with more diverse economies and opportunities. In communities where jobs for more educated adults are scarce, the outcome of advanced education can be more complicated. As in urban communities, in rural communities human capital is often vital in securing better jobs, incomes, and benefits, but returns to human capital are often lower in rural areas, particularly when highly skilled and high-paid jobs for more educated adults are scarce. Rural scholars have long expressed concern over the problem of "brain drain" in rural communities as young adults, often the community's "best and brightest," out-migrate to pursue education and work opportunities elsewhere (Carr and Kefalas 2009; Corbett 2007; Petrin, Schafft, and Meece 2014; Sherman and Sage 2011). Advanced education often offers the promise of better lives for young adults, but without significant job opportunities or amenities to lure them back home, education can become the vehicle that strips rural communities of talented and energetic individuals who leave to pursue better opportunities elsewhere. Some may return with increased human capital to invest in their home communities, but many do not. The brain drain process decreases human capital at the community level, and it often results in demographics skewed toward older adults. In such places, local schools are the channel through which the brain drain process often begins.

Despite its contribution to brain drain, human capital is important for finding and securing employment in most labor markets, including rural ones. For Angelica Finch of Golden Valley, a thirty-eight-year-old grade school secretary and married mother of three, lacking a high school diploma meant more than a decade of low-wage and insecure jobs that didn't lift her family above the poverty line. For Angelica, it took years of going to school hours away while working full time to secure an AA-degree. But as she explained, the degree opened doors to a better job for her, allowing her to pull her family out of poverty: "The education paid off, but it took a long time. . . . [Without my education] I don't think we would've made it."

For twenty-eight-year-old Chad Lloyd of Paradise Valley, who dropped out of high school and later earned his GED, lacking a high school diploma meant having to work his way up from sweeping floors to prove himself to his employer.

> Chad: I strongly believe that if an employer sees that you got your GED, either he thinks that a) you're a quitter, you decided you didn't want to do it, or b) you had something major come up in your life, and you weren't able to finish school. And I think that a) is a big part of it. "You didn't even finish high school. Why should I hire you?"
>
> Q: *So you think it's been a stigma?*
>
> Chad: I think so, a big one.

In Chad's case, he was able to slowly gain skills on the job and rise through the ranks, investing in human capital through experience. But the years he spent working for poverty-level wages put his family at a financial disadvantage, and he still struggles to support his wife Allison and their three children. Owning a house, a dream for the couple, is perpetually out of reach. As these examples suggest, human capital investment can make an important difference between poverty and the hopes of a middle-class existence for rural families, just as it does in urban settings.

Human capital can be very important in rural labor markets, but it doesn't always provide the expected payoffs. Before Golden Valley's economic collapse and Paradise Valley's shift to a tourism-focused economy, the mainstays of both communities were forest-based jobs, many of which didn't require or demand a college degree, or even a high school diploma. In many rural communities, there are insufficient jobs for those with higher training and education, making the rewards of human capital less certain. For thirty-three-year-old Sabena Griffin, a cohabiting mother of two, college was always a goal: "I was like, I got to support myself. I'm going to college because I am not going to depend on anybody."

The Paradise Valley native put herself through college with summer jobs and student loans to gain a specialized nursing degree. However, jobs in her field are not available in Paradise Valley, and Sabena has to commute nearly an hour over a mountain pass for work. Since having her second child, she wonders whether the commute is worth it, and considers leaving the area:

> I think the only thing that would keep me from staying here is if I couldn't support my family, and that's hard when my job is so specialized. And so I commute to Grass Flats, and that is daunting with a three-month-old. You know, I look at that, and I am like, oh my gosh, I don't know how I am going to do it. And so I am thinking about cutting back my hours to not be full time and just kind of fill in. But I don't know if I can afford it. . . . [But] it is a very dangerous road. There has been some days where I am like, oh my goodness, I shouldn't have drove today.

These types of challenges make the acquisition of human capital a complicated issue in many rural communities, and often the brain drain dilemma contributes to ambivalence regarding the purpose and value of education.

The following quotations illustrate this range of perspectives on the importance of education, as well as the correlation between human capital and employment.

April Layton, thirty-two-year-old secretary and married mother of two, Golden Valley:

> I want [my children] to leave Golden Valley, and go to college, and then if after they do something with their lives that way, if they choose to come back and can make a living, then they're welcome to come back. I really want them to leave.

Tilda Conner, thirty-six-year-old care worker and cohabiting mother of one, Paradise Valley:

> I hope that she goes to college. She's got so many great ideas. And I want her to be—every parent wants their kid to be better than they were, and I do.

Greg Smith, forty-two-year-old unemployed married father of two, Golden Valley:

> In all my life, a high school diploma wasn't something that was necessary to do anything but go on to the next school. I mean, a job resume, who wants to know if you've got a high school diploma? You know, and then everybody I've seen go to college, including myself, it didn't affect their life at all hardly.

Caleb Graham, twenty-six-year-old unemployed, single, Paradise Valley:

> I wasn't the best student. Actually, I was a horrible student. I kind of kick myself in the butt now, 'cause I know I could have done better, but I was angry at everyone and just figured it was a waste of my time.

Payoffs to human capital in cohesive rural communities are often further complicated by local perceptions of individuals such as Caleb, who don't leave, and the assumption that out-migration is the only worthwhile path. Young adults who leave to pursue education are often welcomed back to their communities (Carr and Kefalas 2009; Fitchen 1991), and those who don't leave are often judged as unworthy on multiple levels. The following quotes illustrate negative impressions of local kids who fail to out-migrate in pursuit of higher education.

Hannah Lowry, forty-five-year-old nonprofit employee and married mother of two, Paradise Valley:

> Nothing good happens to kids who stay here without going somewhere else. It's a very small community there are a lot of small—"small-minded" is too harsh—conservative values. There's nothing a kid can do here work-wise after high school that's at all challenging or rewarding.

Jeff Taylor, thirty-three-year-old mechanic and married father of two, Golden Valley:

> The ones we get to keep are the ones that you didn't want. You want 'em to leave. Seems like that's what happens a lot. And that happens with a lot of the drugs I think around here. You know, the ones that have no future, I mean just didn't get an education, or they're stuck here, they turn to drugs.

Human capital plays a complex role for adults and children in many rural communities. Although education has the potential to allow low-income and poor children to improve upon their parents' social and economic trajectories as adults, when rural communities lack job opportunities, out-migration may be necessary for returns on human capital investment (Carr and Kefalas 2009; Corbett 2007). Furthermore, human capital is often more accessible to those with more real and symbolic capital resources, and those who lack such advantages frequently encounter greater struggles in school and in acquiring education, leaving them even more disadvantaged in their communities' social settings and labor markets (Calarco 2014; Fan and Chen 2001; Lareau 2003; Sage and Sherman 2014; Sherman and Sage 2011; Smith, Brooks-Gunn, and Klebanov 1997). Human capital can be an advantage, but it also can help to reproduce disadvantage by funneling communities' best resources—their most talented and promising young adults—away into more urban settings. This process cuts these young adults off from their families and communities and leaves rural places with fewer educated and energetic leaders to help shape their futures.

MORAL CAPITAL AND RURAL POVERTY

In Golden Valley, outwardly exhibiting one's moral worth resulted in opportunities that were denied to those who appeared to lack it. Similar to other forms of symbolic capital, in this setting, morality worked to create boundaries between people and could be traded for other resources such as job opportunities and social capital. Why did morality come to be so important that it evolved into a form of capital that could be traded? Research suggests that for people living on the margins of U.S. society, struggling with both poverty and job loss, conceptions of morality can help create new understandings of what it means to be successful (Bourgois 1995; Gowan 2010; Purser 2009; Sherman 2009). In Golden Valley, notions of proper work ethic and morally acceptable activities help create those definitions of success. At the same time, these moral understandings influence the choices people make about how to best survive unemployment and poverty, dictating proper behaviors and coping strategies. In this community, being able to illustrate your moral fortitude in the face of struggle is as important as having a high income (Sherman 2006, 2009). Subsequent work has documented the ways in which moral capital comes into play in the pursuit of multiple types of resources, including access to education (Sage and Sherman 2014; Sherman and Sage 2011) and healthy food (Whitley 2013).

In small, homogenous rural communities, qualities such as independence and hard work often form the basis of moral capital, which can be traded for both economic benefits and social status. In many such communities, people's activities are visible and known. For those who manifest their work ethic and moral values through culturally acceptable work activities—paid jobs, subsistence work, and even through the receipt of "earned" government aid such as Unemployment Insurance—there can be payoffs in both social support and economic opportunities. For those who fail to illustrate their moral worth— either through receipt of means-tested government aid or involvement in illicit activities such as drug dealing—both labor market opportunities and informal charity are frequently limited. Figure 8.1 illustrates the range of morally acceptable and unacceptable coping activities in Golden Valley. In this community, the importance of moral capital means that the majority of residents do their best to avoid stigmatized coping strategies, regardless of how badly they might need them. Thus, morality is both a positive force, helping people to access social and economic capital, and a negative control that discourages behaviors seen as damaging to the community and its families, whether or not they might aid in survival.

For many Golden Valley residents, the community's moral norms, which include a strong stigma around means-tested programs such as Temporary Aid to Needy Families (TANF, also known colloquially as "welfare"), convince them to find other ways to survive. For example, George Woodhouse, who worked at the sawmill for thirty years before losing his job, explained why he and his wife choose subsistence activities

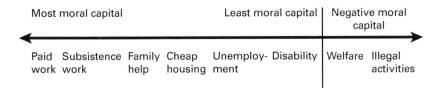

Figure 8.1   Moral value of coping strategies in Golden Valley.

Source: Sherman (2009, 68).

such as hunting and fishing to supplement their diet rather than utilizing means-tested government aid programs:

> We don't try to get food stamps or welfare or anything like that. I mean, basically, we probably could. But I don't know—we were always brought up that you worked for what you got, you didn't have welfare and stuff like that. If you didn't work, then you cut back on what you was eatin' until you got a better job.

Rather than relying on the government to provide for them, Golden Valley residents often rely heavily on the local environment and their physical labor. Although men like George might no longer have jobs, they can still manifest work ethic in other ways, often through informal work. Continuing to manifest one's work ethic through these sorts of activities, even when lacking a paying job, signals to others in the community that you are still an upstanding, moral citizen rather than a lazy, immoral "freeloader." Emily Richards, a married mother of two, explained that "you want people to think you're a hard worker" whether or not you can find paid work. For those who choose survival strategies that display moral capital to the community, the result is frequently better access to social support and social capital as well as to job opportunities.

Although it does not play as large a role in structuring daily life and behavioral choices in Paradise Valley, the importance of moral capital is visible there too. Sporadically employed and often homeless, Caleb Graham (introduced in the previous section) spoke about the difficulties he'd had in school, including a learning disability and a reputation as a troublemaker. His struggles dampened his interest in education, and he barely graduated from high school and did not pursue advanced education. His lack of human capital consigns Caleb to the bottom of Paradise Valley's labor market, but his lack of moral capital damages him more deeply, making finding and keeping even low-wage jobs difficult for him:

> Caleb: I'd work for however long they needed me and then I'd go some-
> place else. They either wouldn't want to hire me or the only way
> I'd get paid is if I worked under the table.
> Q: Why would that be?
> Caleb: Mostly I don't know, but it's also because apparently I've gotten
> a reputation around the valley, I'm not sure how, as a drug dealer,

a troublemaker. I look at 'em, and I'm like, "Really? I'll take a drug test right now. I don't do drugs."

Q: *A drug dealer?*

Caleb: Yeah, 'cause it's like, my dad was friends with a couple of drug dealers, and apparently they connected dots. I'm like, "You can connect all the dots you want. It's not gonna add up." Some of my friends are partiers, and just because I'm friends with them; they think that I'm like that, too. It's hard to change what people think on first glance.

As Caleb illustrates, moral capital often operates at the family level. Moral stigma, or negative moral capital (Sherman 2006), can brand entire extended families as unworthy of jobs, education, or community help throughout the life course. In both Golden Valley and Paradise Valley, multiple families complained about difficulties that occur in local schools when children are believed to come from families who lack moral capital. Schools and teachers heavily invest in the children of families with high moral capital, treating them as if destined for greatness, but children whose families lack moral capital frequently receive little investment from schools and teachers. Derek Lloyd, a thirty-eight-year-old married public employee and father of two in Golden Valley, explains it this way:

Now there's a percentage of kids in school that it wouldn't even dawn on 'em to go work for it, and [they think] somebody's gotta give that to me. And I see that a lot here. We have in some cases third and fourth generation of welfare families that that's almost their legacy. I mean, they wouldn't even think about college, or think about what their career is. You know, why would you? And you know, that scares me.

Wendy Harris, a thirty-seven-year-old married, stay-at-home mother of one in Paradise Valley, has another outlook:

Well, I was a straight-A student up until high school, and then from there, that's when—I don't know, things changed. I don't know why. . . . Well, the principal at the time, the system up here at the time, if you got in trouble, you had to go to an in-house, which is, you're stuck in this tiny little room all day doin' your work. Sometimes it didn't have windows, you didn't even have a window. But if you proceeded to get caught again or anything, you got suspension. He never gave me suspension. He kept me in that room. And I would get in trouble for the stupidest things at times. It got to the point where—and this was because my cousins were ahead of me. And I'm the spittin' image of my cousin. So he figured I'd be just as much trouble. So the slightest thing I did, I got in trouble. And that's when I gave up. I gave up trying to pull the straight A's and stuff like that. I gave up. If I'm gonna be in trouble for stupid things, you know, forget it.

Jeff and Rosemary Taylor, thirty-three-year-old mechanic, thirty-six-year-old school secretary, and married parents of two in Golden Valley, explain:

Jeff: You can almost pick, he's not gonna make it, he's gonna make it. Not necessarily exactly, 'cause you know, some can turn it around, do some good things. But then there are those other ones that, just their history and what their family's done and what they're doing, you just see the same pattern of going the wrong way. It's kind of hard, especially since you know the families so well. . . .
Rosemary: It's like they don't have a chance. You know, they're labeled . . . [by] the teachers and stuff. I mean, a lot of 'em are you know, really smart. And I've heard people say, "Well, look at his dad. He's gonna wind up just like his dad." You know, that's not good.

As with other forms of symbolic capital, moral capital can work in both positive and negative ways in rural communities. For those who have large amounts of moral capital, manifesting one's morality can mean access to other forms of symbolic capital, including economic capital in the form of job opportunities; social capital in the form of strong, supportive networks willing to provide both economic and informal help; and human capital in the form of encouragement, teacher attention, and positive reinforcement in school. But for those families who lack moral capital, these forms of advantage can be difficult to access, leaving them without significant resources and exacerbating the struggles that poor families face. Particularly difficult for poor rural residents is the cultural notion that paid work is the most moral activity and that aid is seen as lacking moral value. For those who are unable to find paid work, they must choose between survival strategies that often bring in little economic capital, but help garner moral capital, and those that bring in more income (e.g., TANF or illegal activities), but lack moral capital. In either case, survival options are limited and come with repercussions.

CONCLUSION

For poor and low-income rural families, the various types of symbolic capital provide important means for gathering resources and meeting basic needs in the absence of sufficient income or wealth. As this chapter has illustrated, symbolic capital can be traded for both monetary and nonmonetary resources including child care, housing, jobs, education, aid, and social support. For poor individuals and families who have high amounts of symbolic capital, surviving on lower incomes can be somewhat more manageable, enabling people to live more comfortably and enjoy the quiet, safety, and escape from the "rat race" that rural communities can provide. For many such families, symbolic capital is at the base of the seemingly intangible benefits that they feel come with living in small, cohesive, rural communities.

For poor individuals and families who lack symbolic capital, this lack becomes another means of exclusion, exacerbating and deepening poverty, marginalization, lack of opportunities, and lack of power. This chapter focused on communities in which real and symbolic capital form the main sources of division and inclusion, but in more complex and diverse rural communities, such forms of capital can be just one part of a larger system of boundaries and exclusions based on attributes such as race and ethnicity, which are discussed in depth elsewhere in this book. As the stories in this chapter have illustrated, symbolic capital can provide access to resources, but it also can provide sources of division within communities—whether communities are more homogenous or more diverse. For those whose experiences, understandings, cultural norms, or behaviors cause them to lack access to significant amounts of symbolic or real capital, the social divides that symbolic capital creates, exacerbates, and reproduces can mean even greater challenges and struggles. Particularly in communities where formal structures for combating or easing poverty such as shelters, charitable organizations, and food banks are lacking, those families who are unable to access informal support through trading symbolic capital often find themselves worse off than they might be in larger cities with more formal infrastructure for these types of support. Symbolic capital provides many of the benefits that are often associated with rural life, but it also creates and sustains many forms of exclusion that further disenfranchise the most marginal and struggling individuals and families.

Case Study: Symbolic Capital and Sources of Division in "Golden Valley," California, and "Paradise Valley," Washington

Jennifer Sherman

The two field sites that inform this chapter were chosen specifically for their similarities to and their differences from one another. In many ways, they represent the extremes on the spectrum of possibility for rural communities with declining natural resource bases. Hamilton et al. (2008) argue that there are four types of rural American communities: chronically poor communities, declining resource-dependent communities, amenity-declining communities, and amenity-rich communities. Chronically poor communities tend to have the fewest resources and the worst prospects, whereas amenity-rich communities tend to be doing the best in both economic and population growth. According to this scheme, Golden Valley would be a declining resource-dependent community, and Paradise Valley would be an amenity-rich community.

This typology hides much of what is similar about these two communities. Both are located in steep mountain ranges in the Pacific Northwest and have economic roots in mining, logging, ranching, and farming. These once-bustling industries declined precipitously throughout the region in the latter half of the twentieth century. For Golden Valley, the collapse of the forest industry decimated the local economy, resulting in a rapid loss of men's jobs that were not replaced. These changes left families without male earners and meant widespread poverty and economic struggle around the valley. Paradise Valley might have been on a similar trajectory but for its transition into a tourism-based economy built around its outdoor amenities. As extractive industries dried up and the Forest Service down sized, increasing numbers of weekend visitors, second-home owners, and amenity migrants entered the valley, changing it forever. Recent waves of in-migrants have included counterculture hippies, back-to-the-landers, wealthy retirees, and young families hoping to get away from the fast-paced lifestyle of Seattle and other western cities. For many in-migrants, moving to Paradise Valley means significantly lower incomes than they had elsewhere, but often the wealth they bring with them allows them access to homes and financial security that their current incomes would have been insufficient to provide.

Golden Valley has remained a mostly small and homogenous community. Paradise Valley grew and experienced housing and population booms and now is a much more diverse community where residents differ in income, wealth, education, cultural norms, and experiences. These differences translate into very different social systems and systems of social boundaries.

In Golden Valley, the community's lack of meaningful distinctions meant that most real and symbolic forms of capital played insignificant roles in structuring social life there. Few residents had significant wealth or income, so economic capital did not provide a common source of social class status. Similarly, the community shared a long history and had experienced little in-migration, so culture remained mostly shared by residents and provided little basis for distinction or social boundaries. Although human capital mattered to a degree, the lack of jobs also muted rewards for education in Golden Valley. Social capital did play an important role in residents' lives, however, and was traded mostly for the types of in-kind help described in this chapter. The form of symbolic capital that became most salient in this setting was moral capital, which provided the strongest axis along which the community could divide itself, allowing people with little access to money or education to prove themselves successful in work ethic and family values. In Golden Valley, notions of proper work ethic and morally acceptable activities helped create those definitions of success. At the same time, these moral understandings influenced the choices people made about how to best survive unemployment and poverty, dictating proper behaviors and coping strategies. For residents of Golden Valley, this form of symbolic capital heavily influenced both their life choices and their social standing in the community.

Paradise Valley, with its diversity, provided access to multiple forms of real and symbolic capital, which resulted in a much more complex system of social boundaries and social divisions. Although incomes were constrained by the labor market and its dearth of higher-paying jobs, wealth was not similarly absent. Many residents brought significant wealth to the valley from their previous jobs and homes, invested in real estate that provided more wealth, and the processes of gentrification raised land values around the area. For those long-time residents who had inherited land, this process also increased their wealth. Thus, access to wealth and land provided a significant source of social division in Paradise Valley. In this community, other sources of symbolic capital were abundant as well. Many new residents brought high levels of human capital with them, allowing them to out-compete less-educated residents in the local labor market. Higher levels of education and job experience were necessary for most year-round, better-paid, and flexible jobs there, including those in schools, medical care, nonprofit organizations, environmental research, and even higher-end construction and carpentry. Thus, human capital provided another important axis of distinction and division. The same was true of cultural capital, which as this chapter illustrates, differed greatly between newcomers and valley natives. Moral capital also came into play in Paradise Valley in ways similar to Golden Valley, and a family's moral status could affect children's chances in school or adults' chances of finding employment. Finally, social capital differed greatly between those who did and those who did not have multiple forms of symbolic and real capital to trade, resulting in social networks with very high amounts of resources, networks with very few resources, and the exclusion of families who were from both advantaged and disadvantaged networks.

As these two communities illustrate, the social, economic, and labor market structure of a rural community heavily affects both the ways in which it divides itself and the chances residents have for success within it.

NOTE

1. To protect the confidentiality of participants, all names of people and places in this chapter are pseudonyms.

REFERENCES

Bageant, Joe. 2008. *Deer Hunting with Jesus: Dispatches from America's Class War*. New York: Crown.

Becker, Gary S. 2009. *Human Capital: A Theoretical and Empirical Analysis, with Special Reference to Education*. Chicago: University of Chicago Press.

Bourdieu, Pierre. 1984. *Distinction: A Social Critique of the Judgement of Taste*. Cambridge, MA: Harvard University Press.

——. 1986. "The Forms of Capital." In *Handbook of Theory and Research for the Sociology of Education*, ed. John G. Richardson, 241–58. New York, NY: Greenwood.

Bourgois, Philippe. 1995. *In Search of Respect: Selling Crack in El Barrio*. Cambridge, MA: Cambridge University Press.

Calarco, Jessica McCrory. 2014. "Coached for the Classroom: Parents' Cultural Transmission and Children's Reproduction of Educational Inequalities." *American Sociological Review* 79(5):1015–37.

Carr, Patrick J., and Maria J. Kefalas. 2009. *Hollowing Out the Middle: The Rural Brain Drain and What It Means for America*. Boston: Beacon.

Coleman, James Samuel. 1988. "Social Capital in the Creation of Human Capital." *American Journal of Sociology* 94(supp.):S95–120.

Corbett, Michael. 2007. *Learning to Leave: The Irony of Schooling in a Coastal Community*. Nova Scotia, Canada: Fernwood Publishing.

Crowley, Martha, and Daniel T. Lichter. 2009. "Social Disorganization in New Latino Destinations?" *Rural Sociology* 74(4):573–604.

Devine, Jennifer. 2006. "Hardworking Newcomers and Generations of Poverty: Poverty Discourse in Central Washington State." *Antipode* 38(5):953–76.

Duncan, Cynthia M. 1999. *Worlds Apart: Why Poverty Persists in Rural America*. New Haven, CT: Yale University Press.

Fan, Xitao, and Michael Chen. 2001. "Parental Involvement and Students' Academic Achievement: A Meta-Analysis." *Educational Psychology Review* 13:1–23.

Fitchen, Janet M. 1991. *Endangered Spaces, Enduring Places: Change, Identity, and Survival in Rural America*. Boulder, CO: Westview.

Flora, Cornelia Butler, and Jan L. Flora. 2013. *Rural Communities: Legacy and Change*, 4th ed. Boulder, CO: Westview.

———. 2014. "Community Organization and Mobilization in Rural America." In *Rural America in a Globalizing World: Problems and Prospects for the 2010's*, ed. Elizabeth Ransom, Conner Bailey, and Leif Jensen. Morgantown: West Virginia University Press.

Frank, Thomas. 2004. *What's the Matter with Kansas? How Conservatives Won the Heart of America*. New York: Metropolitan.

Gowan, Teresa. 2010. *Hobos, Hustlers, and Backsliders: Homeless in San Francisco*. Minneapolis, MN: University of Minnesota Press.

Grusky, David B., Bruce Western, and Christopher Wimer. 2011. "The Consequences of the Great Recession." In *The Great Recession*, ed. David B. Grusky, Bruce Western, and Christopher Wimer, 3–20. New York: Russell Sage Foundation.

Hamilton, Lawrence C., Leslie R. Hamilton, Cynthia M. Duncan, and Chris R. Colocousis. 2008. "Place Matters: Challenges and Opportunities in Four Rural Americas." *Carsey Institute Reports on Rural America* 1(4):2–32.

Lamont, Michèle. 1992. *Money, Morals, and Manners: The Culture of the French and American Upper-Middle Class*. Chicago: University of Chicago Press.

Lareau, Annette. 2003. *Unequal Childhoods: Class, Race, and Family Life*. Berkeley: University of California Press.

Petrin, Robert A., Kai A. Schafft, and Judith L. Meece. 2014. "Educational Sorting and Residential Aspirations Among Rural High School Students: What Are the Contributions of Schools and Educators to Rural Brain Drain?" *American Educational Research Journal* 51(2):294–326.

Purser, Gretchen. 2009. "The Dignity of Job-Seeking Men." *Journal of Contemporary Ethnography* 38(1):117–39.

Putnam, Robert D. 2001. *Bowling Alone: The Collapse and Revival of American Community*. New York: Simon & Schuster.

Sage, Rayna, and Jennifer Sherman. 2014. "'There Are No Jobs Here': Opportunity Structures, Moral Judgment, and Educational Trajectories in the Rural Northwest." In *Dynamics of Social Class, Race, and Place in Rural Education*, ed. Craig B. Howley, Aimee Howley, and Jerry J. Johnson, 67–94. Charlotte, NC: Information Age.

Sherman, Jennifer. 2006. "Coping with Rural Poverty: Economic Survival and Moral Capital in Rural America." *Social Forces* 85(2):891–913.

——. 2009. *Those Who Work, Those Who Don't: Poverty, Morality, and Family in Rural America*. Minneapolis: University of Minnesota Press.

Sherman, Jennifer, and Rayna Sage. 2011. "'Sending Off All Your Good Treasures': Rural Schools, Brain-Drain, and Community Survival in the Wake of Economic Collapse." *Journal of Research in Rural Education* 26(11):1–14.

Smith, Judith R., Jeanne Brooks-Gunn, and Pamela K. Klebanov. 1997. "Consequences of Living in Poverty for Young Children's Cognitive and Verbal Ability and Early School Achievement." In *Consequences of Growing Up Poor*, ed. Greg J. Duncan and Jeanne Brooks-Gunn, 132–67. New York: Russell Sage Foundation.

Smith, Kristin E., and Ann R. Tickamyer, eds. 2011. *Economic Restructuring and Family Well-Being in Rural America*. University Park: Pennsylvania State University Press.

Stein, Arlene. 2001. *The Stranger Next Door: The Story of a Small Community's Battle Over Sex, Faith, and Civil Rights*. Boston: Beacon Press.

Swidler, Ann. 1986. "Culture in Action: Symbols and Strategies." *American Sociological Review* 51(2):273–86.

Whitley, Sarah. 2013. "Changing Times in Rural America: Food Assistance and Food Insecurity in Food Deserts." *Journal of Family Social Work* 16(1):36–52.

Woodward, Kerry C. 2013. *Pimping the Welfare System: Empowering Participants with Economic, Social, and Cultural Capital*. Lanham, MD: Lexington.

CHAPTER 9

The *Old* Versus the *New* Economies and Their Impacts

Brian Thiede and Tim Slack

INTRODUCTION

Economic hardship is linked to changes in the availability and quality of jobs (Grusky, Western, and Wimer 2011). Most scholars agree that work does not offer oft-assumed promises of an above-poverty standard of living and upward mobility in the labor market, important tenets of the American Dream. Although the Great Recession has encouraged reflection about the plight of workers and the unemployed, empirical evidence shows that a large share of workers faced volatile labor market conditions long before this most recent economic crisis (Hacker 2008). Decades of economic restructuring have produced a new economy in which the odds of employment—particularly stable, well-paid employment with insurance and other benefits—are worse for rural workers (Kusmin 2014). Conditions in the postrecession era should be put into a broader context of social change. How and to what extent does this "new" economy represent a rupture from the past? What are the possible and probable paths forward?

This chapter provides general insights into the new rural economy and its historical antecedents. The chapter begins by tracing changes in the U.S. labor market over the last fifty years, with a special focus on the implications for poverty and economic well-being in rural areas. An original descriptive analysis is provided that moves beyond the question of poverty as officially defined by the U.S. government to assess the issue of underemployment in rural areas from 2002 to 2012. The chapter concludes with a discussion of the challenges and opportunities of this new economy for rural people and places moving forward.

SEPARATING THE OLD AND THE NEW

Discussions of things old and new must begin by marking the point of transition. In doing so, scholars often mistakenly imply that the "new" represents a break from a static, unchanging past. In fact, this is rarely the case, and the rural labor market dynamics discussed here are no exception. Rural economies and the work rural people pursue to make a living are never static; rather, they are subject to ongoing forces of social change. During the early years of the United States (as an independent nation-state), the vast majority of the population was rural, and most people found employment in agriculture and extractive activities. At the beginning of the nineteenth century, nearly 95 percent of the U.S. population resided in rural areas (Iceland 2014). In the late nineteenth and early twentieth centuries, however, the nation was transformed by the Industrial Revolution and urbanization. By the 1920 census, the U.S. population crossed the threshold from majority-rural to majority-urban for the first time (U.S. Census Bureau 2015). From this longer-term perspective, what now might be considered the "old" economy of the 1920s represented a dramatic departure from the century that preceded it.

Throughout the early twentieth century, industrialization fueled the migration of rural workers off of farms and into urban factories, a process facilitated by the increasing mechanization of agriculture. By 1950, nearly one out of three American workers was employed in manufacturing (Lee and Mather 2008). This rapid change, spanning from the end of World War II to the early 1970s, is often referred to as the Fordist period because of the prominent role of large-scale, standardized manufacturing. As the name suggests, many features of the economic structure during this period (e.g., assembly-line work in large factories or plants) were rooted in industrial innovations similar to Henry Ford's automobile production systems. Many view this period as a golden age for working- and middle-class Americans. It was a time when U.S. manufacturing attained global dominance, the welfare state expanded to promote economic growth and the social safety net, organized labor held considerable sway over industry and politics, and declines in inequality and poverty corresponded with improving standards of living for common people.

In contrast, the years since the 1970s are cast as the post-Fordist era. Since then, new forces of social and economic changes—chief among them globalization—have taken hold and changed the number, type, and quality of jobs available to American workers. It is the economic circumstances of this final era that is characterized in this chapter as the "new" economy, and which is placed in comparative perspective with the "old" postwar Fordist period before it.

ECONOMIC CHANGE AND THE NEW ECONOMY

In the 1970s, the foundations of the postwar industrial economy began to shift, ushering in the age of globalization (Robinson 2001). In broad terms, shifts from nationally to globally oriented systems of production, and the entrance of new international competitors with very low production costs, brought changes in the composition of the U.S. labor market. Three interrelated trends are emblematic: (1) declining labor union membership and coverage, (2) deindustrialization and a corresponding increase in the size of the service sector, and (3) shifts toward nonstandard employment arrangements, such as subcontracting and franchising (Brady, Baker, and Finnigan 2013; Kalleberg, Reskin, and Hudson 2000; Morris and Western 1999; Weil 2014). In various ways, each of these changes eroded the power of labor versus corporate managers and investors, and undermined the quality of most workers' jobs (Western and Rosenfeld 2011). Some scholars have suggested that the implication of these changes was a "great U-turn," whereby prior trends of income equalization and broadly shared economic prosperity were reversed and replaced with growing income inequality and wealth concentration (Harrison and Bluestone 1988). Indeed, by some measures, inequality today is at its highest levels since before World War II (Saez 2013). However, it is important to emphasize that the process of economic restructuring was, and continues to be, an inherently spatial process. As the term *globalization* would suggest, changes have occurred in the distribution of sites of production and in the flows of labor and capital across countries around the world. Restructuring also has involved unevenly distributed changes across local labor markets and changing relations between rural and urban areas within the United States (Falk, Schulman, and Tickamyer 2003).

CHANGING INDUSTRIAL-OCCUPATIONAL COMPOSITION

Substantial changes in the composition of rural labor markets reflect the changing U.S. economy. The locus of rural employment first shifted out of agriculture and into manufacturing, then increasingly into the service sector. These changes reflect the restructuring of the agricultural sector and processes of globalization. They also underscore the relational nature of rural and urban labor markets within the United States, and between rural America and global markets (Lichter and Brown 2011). This period of globalization corresponded with changes in rural–urban dynamics, including rural-to-urban migration, urban-to-rural shifts in production activities, and reduced spatial and temporal barriers between remote rural areas and urban centers. Changes in the structure of rural labor markets also have had significant implications for the economic status of households (e.g., poverty) by affecting the likelihood of employment and the wages of those employed (Cotter 2002).

Discussions of economic restructuring during the twentieth century often focus on the globalization of capital and supply chains associated with the deindustrialization of high-income economies. These are critical processes to be sure. In rural America, however, long-term changes in the structure of the economy and labor markets should also be put in the context of a dramatic agricultural transition that played out across the entire twentieth century. Although U.S. agriculture is deeply embedded in world markets and was therefore shaped by the forces of post-1970s globalization as well, significant restructuring in this sector can be traced back decades before that. The net result is that the share of rural workers employed on farms or working as unpaid laborers on family farms has declined to just slightly more than a rounding error over the past five to six decades.

Lobao and Meyer (2001) show that the agricultural sector has become increasingly consolidated, as indicated by declining shares of workers in the agricultural sector, reductions in the number of farms, and increasing acreage per farm. For example, from 1940 to 1995, the farm population (as a percentage of the total population) declined from 23.1 percent to 1.8 percent (Lobao and Meyer 2001). As well, on-farm work was decreasingly likely to fully support households: by the end of the 1990s, upwards of 90 percent of household income among farmers came from nonfarm sources (Lobao and Meyer 2001; Sommer et al. 1998). Shifts away from an agricultural labor market also adversely affected the many businesses that supported the agricultural economy (Lobao and Meyer 2001).

The shift in rural labor away from farms initially corresponded with an increase in rural manufacturing (Albrecht and Albrecht 2000). Contrary to popular belief, manufacturing employed a larger share of workers in rural than urban areas as early as 1970 (Barkley and Hinschberger 1992). Rural manufacturing has been disproportionately, but not exclusively, centered on natural resources and agriculture. For instance, traditional types of rural manufacturing include those focused on food and fuel; textiles and leather; and furniture, lumber, and wood (Fuguitt, Brown, and Beale 1989; Henderson 2012). In 1980, 18 percent of rural workers employed in manufacturing were in the textile and apparel sector, compared to 7.9 percent of urban workers; likewise, 11.9 percent of rural manufacturing workers had positions in the furniture, lumber, and wood sector, versus 3.7 percent in urban areas. The shift toward rural manufacturing continued through the next two decades (Fuguitt et al. 1989). By the 2000 census, 17 percent of rural workers were employed in manufacturing, 3 percentage points higher than the 14 percent among urban workers (Vias 2012).

Shifts toward manufacturing were in part driven by technological changes. New production, communications, and transportation technologies facilitated shifts in manufacturing away from traditional urban industrial centers and into rural (and suburban) areas. In many cases, the driver of industrial decentralization was not the technology itself but labor costs, which were the most variable input due to growing global competition. The places that saw such increases in manufacturing were often both rural and located away from the urban cores of the Northeast and Midwest (Fuguitt, Brown, and Beale 1989). These emerging manufacturing sites were often in regions (e.g., the South) where antagonism toward labor unions and labor protections, low wages, and other factors associated with low labor costs made these places attractive (Eckes 2005).

The implications of the changing nature of U.S. manufacturing for labor were ambiguous. The increase in manufacturing jobs arguably mollified the adverse effects of the agricultural transition in many rural labor markets. The shift toward rural (and southern) manufacturing, however, can also be viewed as an integral step toward the declining power of workers' unions and labor in the United States more generally. Relocation to these areas was part of a broader trend toward low-cost (i.e., low-wage) and nonunionized manufacturing (Eckes 2005; Falk and Lyson 1988; Holmes 2013). A considerable share of the manufacturing that emerged in rural areas in the 1970s involved low-skilled production such as textile and apparel production, which was (and still is) more vulnerable to global competition than high-skilled processes such as fuel and chemical production (Henderson 2012; Lyson and Tolbert 1996). As a result, the initial benefits of rural manufacturing were somewhat eroded over time (Bascom 2000). Indeed, Vias (2000, 278) argues that the relatively cheap, low-skilled labor that provided rural areas with their initial advantage relative to urban areas in the early stages of industrial decentralization eventually constituted a source of disadvantage. That is, as a more global market emerged, low-skilled manufacturing eventually shifted to sites with even lower production costs, undercutting low-cost rural workers in the United States in what some have characterized as a "race to the bottom" (Tonelson 2002).

From the 1970s, when the share of rural workers in manufacturing surpassed that of urban workers, to the year 2000, service sector employment in rural areas increased dramatically. By 2000, the service sector was home to at least two-thirds of all jobs in rural labor markets (Gibbs, Kusmin, and Cromartie 2005). In many cases, these shifts corresponded with more women participating in the labor force and declining employment among men (Burton, Lichter, Baker, and Eason 2013). Evidence suggests that rural service jobs are disproportionately low-skilled and low-quality positions. In 2000, 42.2 percent of the nonmetropolitan workforce was employed in a low-skill job, more than 8 percentage points higher than the 34 percent in metropolitan labor markets (Gibbs et al. 2005).

This figure is but one indicator that the debate about shifts from "good jobs" to "bad jobs"—which has largely been an aspatial conversation—is particularly relevant to rural labor markets. Prior research shows that rural workers are more likely to find employment in nonstandard positions than are their urban counterparts (McLaughlin and Coleman-Jensen 2008). Kalleberg and colleagues (2000) define such positions as those meeting at least one of four criteria: (1) a lack of a clearly defined (or any) employer; (2) a weak attachment between workers and their de jure employer; (3) an employer who does not control how workers do their job; and (4) workers who cannot assume continuity of employment. Although their research documents some exceptions to the link between nonstandard work and bad jobs, defined according to low pay and absent benefits, it largely supports the conclusion that increases in nonstandard work have a negative effect on workers' economic status. Therefore, the disproportionate share of the rural workforce in nonstandard employment is another marker of the relative disadvantages that rural workers face in the new economy.

Arguably the most salient characteristic of the new, post-Fordist economy is the declining likelihood that families can attain a stable, above-poverty standard of living through the work of a single member (Slack 2010). Insecure, low-paying work and related spells of unemployment are increasingly common for rural workers. Although a nontrivial share of rural families is in poverty despite having one or more members employed (Slack 2010), such job disruptions also put those who are above the poverty line at risk of falling below it and increase the degree of hardship faced by already-poor families. In contrast, a small and perhaps shrinking group of well-educated workers maintain access to the remaining good jobs, and such bifurcation represents one of the central drivers of the growing inequality after the U-turn.

DIVERSITY IN THE NEW ECONOMY

A clear *periodization* of rural labor markets in the United States can be seen over the past half-century or more. That is, a transition out of agriculture and into manufacturing during the early phases of globalization was followed by a subsequent shift toward the service sector along with increases in nonstandard employment within industrial groups. Rural America is also characterized by diversity across space, reflecting patterns of uneven development over time. Rural America includes some of the most socially and economically marginal regions of the country (McGranahan 2003). To underline the challenges of constructing a single narrative of change in rural America over time, some examples of exceptions to the periodization just described are provided. Even these exceptional cases, however, support many common claims about rural disadvantage.

For one, changes in the global food system have been associated with the emergence of new economic centers in rural areas centered on food processing and meatpacking facilities (Broadway 2007; Kandel and Parrado 2005). In contrast to the decline in agricultural labor across rural America as a whole, the places where such food processing facilities have emerged have seen renewed links between labor markets and agricultural activities, and growth in food-related manufacturing. A substantial number of these facilities are located in small towns in the Midwest and Southeast where the construction of a single processing plant can represent a huge boon to the local economy (Broadway 2007). Workers in these plants are disproportionately of Hispanic origin, and thus they also represent major drivers of demographic change (Kandel and Parrado 2005). These boomtowns are unique economically and in terms of their rapidly increasing racial and ethnic diversity. Of course, many characteristics of rural food processing jobs are consistent with the larger narrative of work in the new economy: limited or nonexistent collective bargaining, weak worker protections (e.g., against occupational hazards), low pay, and variable hours. Some suggest that rural food processing constitutes the quintessential bad job (Broadway 2007).

Another example of diversity in the new economy is the oil and natural gas industry. This sector was transformed in the past decade through technological advances, namely hydraulic fracturing ("fracking") processes, which facilitate extraction of previously inaccessible resources. Rural labor markets located near these resource deposits have seen a large uptick in employment, both in oil and gas services directly and in the many goods- and service-providing establishments that support these activities. Between 2001 and 2010, employment in rural counties with significant oil and gas extraction activity increased by more than 5 percent, which stands in sharp contrast to the 2 percent decline in employment across other rural counties (Kusmin 2014). Similar trends persisted through 2013, with employment growth in extraction-oriented rural counties outpacing other rural counties by 2 percent (Kusmin 2014). Of course, rapid increases in employment driven by the growth of a single sector also create vulnerabilities. Recent data do not yet capture the full implications of a subsequent bust of the U.S. natural gas market, but good news is unlikely. As such, this case also underlines the boom-and-bust nature of resource-dependent economies—a salient problem in many rural areas (Freudenburg 1992).

Although the changes in oil- and gas-producing rural counties are unique vis-à-vis other places, this example also points to an important source of continuity within many rural labor markets: homogeneity and dependence. Although considerable diversity exists in labor markets and economic structures across rural America as a whole, many rural places are characterized by dependence on a limited set of, or even single, industries. Rural counties represent very large majorities of U.S. counties classified as farming-dependent (92 percent), mining-dependent (88 percent), manufacturing-dependent (65 percent), and federal and state government-dependent (55 percent) (U.S. Economic Research Service as cited in Slack 2014). The lack of industrial diversity reflects several disincentives for firms considering locating in rural areas, including geographic (e.g., spatial isolation), demographic (e.g., low population density), and social (e.g., low educational attainment) issues. Rural markets are more vulnerable to booms and busts (e.g., commodity and food price changes), provide few opportunities for laid-off workers or workers with skills mismatched with the dominant industry, and may be skewed by narrowly defined community development policies (Freudenberg 1992; Hamrick 2001; Joshi et al. 2000; Markhusen 1980). Rural residents often are motivated to turn to the informal sector as a livelihood strategy due to the lack of industrial diversity (Slack and Jensen 2010).

ECONOMIC RESTRUCTURING AND DEMOGRAPHIC CHANGE

Discussions of work and poverty in rural areas face an underlying question of whether rural economic disadvantages reflect the unique structural conditions of rural economies and labor markets or systematic differences in population characteristics (Weber et al. 2005). This debate cannot be resolved here. The interaction between structural and demographic change arguably makes it unresolvable. However, three demographic conditions are integrally linked to the emergence and future trajectory of the new rural economy.

INCREASING RACIAL AND ETHNIC DIVERSITY

The racial and ethnic composition of the rural labor force has always been more diverse than commonly portrayed (Jensen and Tienda 1989), yet recent changes have ushered in a new era of diversity, and with it the potential for both tension and socioeconomic change (Lichter 2012). Here, the most salient trend is the increasing Hispanic share of the rural population, which has coincided with the emergence of new immigrant destinations across the country (Lichter and Johnson 2009). In the rural economy, these changes in part reflect the new geography of low-skill, low-paying work where Hispanic-origin immigrant workers often find employment (Kandel and Parrado 2005). The relative youth and high fertility of many Hispanic populations means that they will constitute a larger and growing share of the labor force into the future (Johnson and Lichter 2008). In many cases, these changes will offset trends toward population loss and aging. The extent to which such effects translate into sustainable community development will hinge on whether and how new Hispanic populations integrate into rural communities socially and in terms of human capital characteristics (Stamps and Bohon 2006).

EDUCATIONAL ATTAINMENT

Questions about education are not limited to the emerging Hispanic population in rural America. Rural disadvantages in education and other dimensions of workers' skillsets have been characteristic of the old and new economies, but skills gaps are an increasingly salient axis of rural–urban inequality in the new economy (Jensen and McLaughlin 1995). Not only are the remaining good jobs skewed toward high-skilled workers, but these jobs are also disproportionately located in urban areas, albeit with some "rural spillover" (McGranahan 2003). This incentivizes continued, if not deepening, rural-to-urban migration among higher-skilled (often young) rural workers. This process, called "brain drain," has the potential to reinforce rural economic disadvantage into the future by, for example, shaping firms' location decisions (Carr and Kefalas 2009; Domina 2006).

AGING

In addition to the out-migration of high-skilled workers in particular, many rural areas have experienced substantial net out-migration of young adults in general. Given that many of these migrants are of reproductive age, this yields lower fertility rates, natural population decrease, and population aging in many rural areas (Johnson 2011). In such cases, population aging is typically associated with economic decline, presumably as a result of both declining demand for goods and services and declines in the size and skill of the labor force. The population aging of many rural communities will almost certainly continue into the future as a result of the demographic momentum inherent in their age structures, which poses unique and largely unprecedented challenges for rural employment and rural economies (Slack and Rizzuto 2013).

That said, many rural areas have also experienced population aging from disproportionate *in-migration* of older adults, driven by the emergence of rural retirement destinations (Brown and Glasgow 2008). In these cases, population aging often is associated with an uptick in employment opportunities, some of which may include relatively high-skill and high-quality health care jobs.

RURAL EMPLOYMENT HARDSHIP IN THE EARLY 2000S IN COMPARATIVE PERSPECTIVE

This section describes contemporary data that underscores the challenges faced by rural workers in the new economy. Given the strong links between employment and poverty in the United States, it follows that those who are out of work or living in a labor market where large shares of the working-age population are not employed will experience an increased likelihood of economic hardship. Data from the USDA's Economic Research Service show that "low employment" counties—places where more than one-third of the working-age population is not employed—are disproportionately located in rural areas.[1] The rural–urban comparison in

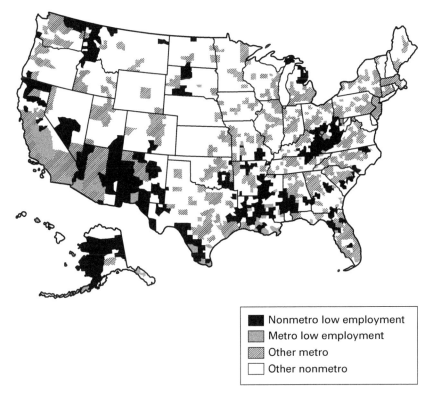

Figure 9.1   Low-employment counties, 2000.

Source: Economic Research Service, County Policy Types, USDA.

Note: Low-employment counties are those where less than 65 percent of residents 21 to 64 years old were employed in 2000.

this regard is stark: 86 percent of the counties that fit this definition are rural. Figure 9.1 provides a map of these places. Areas characterized by especially low employment are clustered in the Lower Mississippi Delta, the Black Belt, Central Appalachia, Native American reservations, and along the U.S.–Mexico border. Of course, the high level of economic distress in these regions is not solely a function of the new economy. In many cases, it is also the result of old and long-standing political economies of subordination and oppression in plantation agriculture, coal mining, and the federal reservation system—systems often undergirded by racist ideologies (Snipp 1996).

Employment typically represents a necessary condition for escaping economic hardship among the poor, but it should not be mistaken as a sufficient condition for doing so. In what follows, an original descriptive analysis is provided that compares employment hardship among rural and urban workers from 2002 to 2012, drawing on data from the country's most comprehensive annual national labor force survey, the March Current Population Survey (CPS). Linked annual data files from the March CPS were analyzed over this period to examine the employment circumstances of individuals aged eighteen to sixty-four years (i.e., those of working age).[2] This approach extends analysis presented in Slack (2014) by carrying the record forward through the Great Recession and the very slow economic recovery that followed.

The focus of this volume is on poverty, but the official poverty measure used by the U.S. federal government has well-documented limitations (Citro and Michel 1995). Due to this chapter's focus on labor markets, the analysis pivots from the consideration of economic hardship as measured by poverty (i.e., having a very low income) to examine underemployment, which captures broader forms of disadvantage. The concept of underemployment encourages us to think about different types of hardship that workers face as they endeavor to make a living in the labor market. Although measures of both poverty and underemployment capture ways people are struggling economically, they are not synonymous. Not only are different types of information used to develop each measure, but the populations of people assessed by each differs as well. Poverty is determined for nearly all members of the civilian population, whereas underemployment focuses on adults in the labor force (i.e., those of working-age who are either employed or actively looking for work).[3] Therefore, it is possible to be underemployed but not be a member of a poor family or to be a member of a poor family but not be underemployed. The measurement of underemployment is detailed further in the following discussion, but the larger point is simply that it is necessary to think about the multidimensional types of hardship workers face in the American labor market.

Using the Labor Utilization Framework (LUF) developed by Clogg and Sullivan (Clogg 1979; Clogg and Sullivan 1983; Sullivan 1978), the operational states of underemployment examined here are:

Discouraged workers: individuals who would like to be employed but are currently not working and did not look for work in the past four weeks due to discouragement with their job prospects (official measures do not count these workers as "in the labor force" because they are neither employed nor looking for work);

Unemployed workers: consistent with the official definition, individuals who are not employed but (a) have looked for work during the previous four weeks, or (b) are currently on layoff but expect to be called back to work;

Low-hour workers (or involuntary part-time): consistent with the official definition of those who are working "part-time for economic reasons" (i.e., those employed fewer than thirty-five hours per week only because they cannot find full-time employment); and

Low-income workers: includes full-time workers (i.e., those employed thirty-five or more hours per week) whose average weekly earnings in the previous year were less than 125 percent of the individual poverty threshold.

All other workers are defined as adequately employed, and those who are not employed and do not indicate a desire to be so are defined as not in the labor force. The latter group is not included in our analysis.

Figure 9.2 shows the percentage of workers who are underemployed (cumulatively by any type) from 2002 to 2012 in rural and urban areas, and the difference between the two (i.e., rural underemployment *minus*

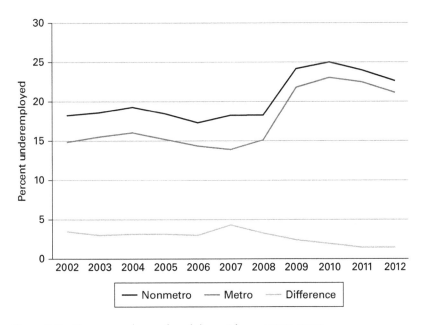

Figure 9.2   Percent underemployed, by residence, 2002–2012.

Source: U.S. Census Bureau, March Current Population Surveys, 2002–2012.

urban underemployment). Several important stories emerge from these data. The first is the markedly negative effect that the Great Recession, spanning December 2007 to June 2009, wrought on working people. In 2007, underemployment stood at 14.9 percent of the labor force nationally. In the subsequent three years, underemployment climbed to 15.5 percent in 2008, 21.9 percent in 2009, and ultimately topped out at 23.3 percent in 2010 before a degree of recovery began to take hold. In other words, by the end of the first decades of the 2000s, nearly one-quarter of U.S. workers found themselves underemployed, a truly staggering statistic.

The circumstances of U.S. workers continued to deteriorate after the official end of the Great Recession in 2009. Many economic indicators, including underemployment and poverty, are *lagging* in nature. That is, even after the economy starts growing again at an aggregate level following a downturn, the economic circumstances of average people continue to deteriorate for some time before they begin to realize the benefits of recovery.

The other story these data tell is of the persistent labor market disadvantages faced by rural workers relative to their urban counterparts. Even though trends in underemployment rates have run in parallel in rural and urban areas over the ten-year period, rural workers have been subject to higher levels of underemployment in every single year examined. More specifically, between 2002 and 2012 rural workers faced an average underemployment rate of 20.4 percent versus 17.6 percent in urban areas. And in 2010, in the wake of the Great Recession, rural and urban underemployment stood at 25.0 percent and 23.0 percent, respectively. Again, these are staggering statistics when one considers the links between the status of workers and the economic well-being of the families that depend on them. The rural disadvantage observed here is not new to the 2000s; it is a trend that dates back as long as data have been available for this type of analysis (Slack and Jensen 2002).

If underemployment by type is unpacked over this period, the data show that rural workers face higher rates of underemployment by low income (7.9 percent versus 5.9 percent in urban areas), and to a lesser degree by unemployment (7.0 percent versus 6.7 percent in urban areas) and low hours (4.5 percent versus 4.0 percent in urban areas). The only type of underemployment that remains at an equal level across residential areas over the ten-year period is discouragement (0.9 percent in both contexts). Examining trend data by year shows that unemployment and

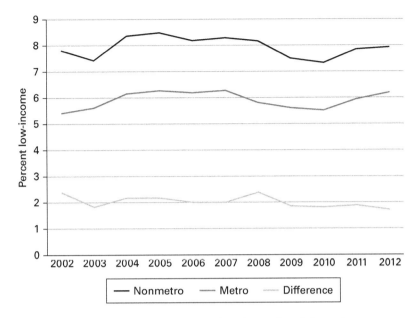

Figure 9.3   Percent of workers considered underemployed due to low income, by residence, 2002–2012.

Source: U.S. Census Bureau, March Current Population Surveys, 2002–2012.

low-hours work started the period higher in rural areas, but the Great Recession brought about convergence in these measures between rural and urban areas as unemployment and involuntary part-time work rose in urban contexts toward rural levels. However, as illustrated in figure 9.3, the economic crisis only led to convergence in unemployment and low-hours work: low-income work remained a defining feature of the rural labor market throughout the period. At a decade-long average of 7.9 percent, low income stood as the single largest contributor to underemployment in rural settings (unemployment was the primary culprit in urban areas), averaging 2.0 percent higher than was the case in urban contexts across the period. This is an especially notable point for the purposes of this volume because it suggests that a disproportionate share of rural workers face economic hardship despite substantial labor market attachment. The implication is that the new rural economy leaves many behind, even many of those fully participating in it.

Figure 9.4 presents data on underemployment across major industrial sectors pooled for the ten years spanning 2002 to 2012. These data tell an important story about employment hardship in old and

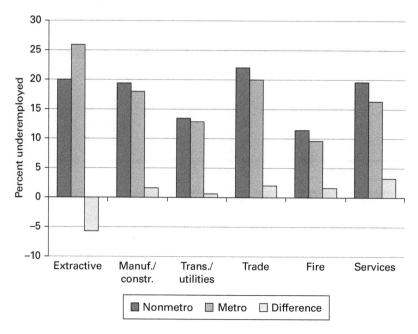

Figure 9.4   Percent underemployed by industrial sector, by residence, 2002–2012.

Source: U.S. Census Bureau, March Current Population Surveys, 2002–2012.

new economic sectors, and it is a story with significant implications for economic well-being across the rural–urban divide. Additional analysis from the CPS not shown here indicate that the two industrial sectors that claim a greater share of the labor force in rural as compared to urban areas are manufacturing/construction (24.2 percent rural versus 18.2 percent urban) and extraction (5.5 percent rural versus 1.2 percent urban). Extractive industries include mining, agriculture, forestry, and fishing, sectors well known for high and persistent underemployment (Slack and Jensen 2004). Moreover, given the earlier discussion about shifts away from agricultural and extractive employment and the subsequent process of deindustrialization, this labor force balance suggests a precarious position for many rural workers. That is, rural labor markets are arguably over-leveraged on the old economy. The dominance of services in the new economy is also readily evident in these data as the sector claims the largest total share of workers in both rural and urban contexts (43.8 percent and 49.3 percent, respectively). As noted earlier in the chapter, however, there are substantial differences in the quality of service jobs between rural and urban areas. As one example, Gibbs and colleagues (2005) show that between 1980 and 2000 the share of low-skilled service jobs was between 4.4 and 5.6 percentage points greater in rural than in urban areas. What figure 9.4 makes abundantly clear is that underemployment impacts rural workers to a greater degree than their urban counterparts across every major industrial sector except the extractive sector. Note that extraction represents a very small segment of the urban labor market (only about 1 percent), underscoring the magnitude of the rural disadvantage.

Finally, table 9.1 presents data pooled across the period spanning 2002 to 2012 showing underemployment by residence for select worker characteristics. The table reveals well-known disadvantages in the modern labor market for younger, female, nonwhite, noncitizen, nonmarried, less educated, and/or nonunion workers. But what is especially notable is that underemployment is more pronounced for rural residents across every single group characteristic. The lone exception to this is labor union membership, which provides significant protection against underemployment in both rural and urban contexts alike. This final point provides reason for concern for American workers given trends toward deunionization in the new labor market and renewed antiunion sentiment in the political sphere (i.e., more states instituting so-called Right to Work laws and engaging in legal efforts to curb the influence of public sector unions). It also offers a point of optimism. Organized labor provided a tried-and-true mechanism for advancing the collective interests of working people in the old industrial economy, and it is still clearly linked to economic well-being in the new economy as well.

CONCLUSION

This chapter has traced the broad contours of change in the rural economy since the mid-twentieth century. The emergence of today's new rural economy occurred within a longer-term process of agricultural restructuring that undermined the once-central role of agriculture in the rural labor market and supported the process of urbanization, processes which profoundly changed the size and composition of the rural labor force. In the wake of these changes, manufacturing and, later, service sector jobs have grown in importance throughout rural America, a trend consistent with the restructuring of the U.S. economy more broadly. Despite these and other similarities (e.g., growing racial and ethnic diversity), the new

Table 9.1 Percent Underemployed by Residence by Select Characteristics, 2002–2012

	Rural (%)	Urban (%)	Difference (%)
Total	20.2	17.5	2.7
Age			
18–24	38.7	34.6	4.1
25–34	21.0	17.8	3.2
35–44	16.8	14.1	2.7
45–54	15.4	13.4	2.0
55–64	16.3	13.6	2.7
Gender			
Male	18.8	17.0	1.8
Female	21.8	18.1	3.7
Race/ethnicity			
White	18.3	14.2	4.1
Black	32.0	24.8	7.2
Hispanic	27.4	25.9	1.5
Other	27.0	17.0	10.0
Nativity			
Native	20.0	16.2	3.8
Second generation	20.6	18.8	1.8
Foreign-born, citizen	19.9	15.6	4.3
Foreign-born, noncitizen	27.7	26.9	0.8
Marital status			
Married	14.1	12.0	2.1
Never married	34.1	27.1	7.0
Divorced/separated	23.8	18.5	5.3
Widowed	23.8	19.3	4.5
Education			
Less than high school	36.8	36.1	0.7
High school	22.7	22.0	0.7
Some college	20.5	18.5	2.0
College degree or more	10.7	9.4	1.3
Labor union			
Union	4.9	5.1	−0.2
Nonunion	20.5	17.8	2.7

Source: U.S. Census Bureau, March Current Population Surveys, 2002–2012.

rural economy continues to produce conditions that disadvantage rural workers relative to their urban counterparts. This is made evident by the higher rates of underemployment consistently faced by rural workers across time and sector of employment.

What does all of this suggest going forward in the twenty-first century? One implication is that employment—whether in rural or urban environs—should not be assumed to be a sufficient condition for escaping poverty. Indeed, the link between work and poverty has been uniquely weak in rural relative to urban areas. From a policy perspective, this underscores the need to invest in "work support" programs that help to subsidize and reward the work efforts of those whose labor is met with inadequate returns. Examples include expanding the federal and state Earned Income Tax Credit program, raising the federal minimum wage and pegging it to inflation, devising programs aimed at offsetting work opportunity costs (e.g., child care and transportation subsidies), and expanding health care access to those unable to gain access through their workplaces via efforts like the Affordable Care Act. Although a point of great political contention in America, poverty rates are higher in the United States than in other similarly developed nations around the world not because their workers have higher earnings but because the governments of other nations redistribute far more of their national income for social welfare programs aimed at ameliorating economic inequality (Smeeding 2006).

Although much of the discussion in this chapter has been comparative, things "rural" and "urban" are always inextricably linked and interdependent on one another, never isolated. As Lichter and Brown (2011, 584) noted in a review, "Boundaries may divide people, but they also bring people together in intense patterns of social and economic interaction. . . . It is more difficult than ever to discuss social change in rural (or urban) America without acknowledging the other." At a macro level, the implication moving forward is that the seeming challenges of work in the new rural economy cannot be addressed in isolation from broader dynamics in the urban and global economies. And at a micro level, this means that workers and their families are increasingly embedded in a rapidly changing, interconnected, and volatile economic reality that poses significant and growing challenges to escaping poverty, and achieving and sustaining a decent standard of living. In the end, these are fundamental challenges to the ideas that underlie the American Dream.

Case Study: Buoyancy on the Bayou—Louisiana Shrimpers Face the Rising Tide of Globalization

Jill Ann Harrison

Work provides the backdrop against which entire communities and the people within them thrive. Friedland and Robertson (1990, 25) eloquently captured the significance of work when they stated that "work provides identities as much as it provides bread for the table; participation in commodity and labor markets is as much an expression of who you are as what you want." Therefore, changes in economic structures have implications that go far beyond the pocketbook. Working with shrimp fishers in a rural southeastern Louisiana bayou town I call Bayou Crevette provided insight into the ways workers respond when traditional ways of life are disrupted by globalization and occupational decline.

Shrimp fishing is deeply rooted in both the culture and economy of Louisiana. In the earliest days, shrimp was caught by hand-pulled seines and eaten mainly by Cajun settlers in a dried or salted form. But by the 1920s, refrigeration technology permitted trawl boats to travel farther distances for longer periods of time, which both increased landings and shifted production toward fresh and frozen shrimp that were much more appealing to U.S. consumers. By midcentury, consumer demand for shrimp far outstripped the seasonally limited supply, and shrimp came to be considered a luxury food with a high price tag.

Throughout the rest of the twentieth century, dockside prices for shrimp were fair and relatively stable. Shrimp fishing offered a secure living. Moreover, fishers' identities are tightly bound up with the work they perform. Most commercial shrimp fishers are owner-operators of their vessels and value the independence that being their own boss provides. Shrimp fishing is also tightly linked to family structure. Most grew up on trawl boats and learned the trade from parents and grandparents. As such, many understand the pursuit as something they were born to do. As in other rural communities, their deep connection to the rich ecosystem of southern Louisiana has instilled a strong pride in their ability to "live off the land," as they put it many times.

But around 2001, the industry—and this way of life—became imperiled. Dockside prices for shrimp tumbled precipitously and remained on a downward trajectory due to changes in the global economy for shrimp. Around this time, farm-raised imported shrimp flooded the U.S. market in unprecedented numbers. Since then, the increased volume of imported shrimp has decreased prices. This is good for shrimp-loving consumers, but it has been detrimental to those dependent on shrimp to earn a living.

Unlike many other rural workers who have faced industrial decline—farmers, miners, and loggers—shrimp fishers in Bayou Crevette have the unique option of securing well-paying jobs in the nearby oil industry. Many of these jobs require skills transferable from trawling (welding, engine repair, sea captaining, etc.). The lack of jobs has been shown by social scientists to be a catalyst for decline, but the case of Louisiana shrimp fishers permits an exploration of the noneconomic costs of occupational decline and job loss. After in-depth interviews with more than fifty individuals with ties to shrimp fishing, three primary patterns were observed in how folks responded.

First, some fishers, deemed "persisters," acknowledged that they could earn a more secure living working in other jobs, but they chose to stay in the industry. They, therefore, have *willingly* opted to endure a host of financial and personal struggles to try to fulfill what they perceive as their cultural calling. The most common way shrimpers explained their reluctance to leave the industry is with the phrase "it's in my blood." With this simple expression, they demonstrated that trawling was not merely a job but represented a physical part of themselves and constituted the foundation of their family history and personal identity. Maintaining their identities as fishers was, for them, worth the very real economic struggles they endured. As a result of industrial decline, some fishers experienced struggles of poverty for the first time in their lives, particularly those who did not have working spouses.

Other fishers left the industry behind for better employment opportunities out of economic necessity. Many of these former shrimpers, the "exiters," were better off financially, but many others experienced the exit as a personal tragedy. One ex-fisher carried a tattered photo of the boat that he sold in his wallet, which he pulled out when he said, "Losing my boat is like losing a baby. It hurts, you know? Like losing a baby." Other fishers lamented having to sit behind a desk and take orders from higher-ups, a significant departure from life as a trawler and something they mourned. Most complained that their new work schedule prohibited them from spending the winter (the fishing off-season) hunting, an important part of rural culture. As one fisher put it, "We was born to hunt and trap in the winter and come back over here in the summer to shrimp." In all, these narratives about the process and consequences of exiting show what workers lose when they leave behind a livelihood many considered to be their life's calling.

Finally, a small but enterprising group of fishers, called "innovative adapters," have changed their practices to adapt to the newly globalized market. In doing so, they remained viable producers while simultaneously preserving the meaningful occupational and cultural activities associated with their way of life. Adaptation requires two primary changes: (1) installing on-board freezers that enable fresh shrimp to be frozen the instant it is caught (increasing its quality and value), and (2) bypassing dockside processors to sell directly to consumers via farmers' markets or through Internet businesses. Retrofitting boats to accommodate freezers is expensive, but as one fisher noted, "If we lose, we lose everything now, or we lose everything later. There's no difference. We might as well try it. So we did, and so far we've been successful with it." By using the Internet to find new and lucrative markets for their higher-quality catch, these local actors are not only fighting against global forces but are using globalization in a judolike fashion to advance their agenda.

From Louisiana shrimp fishers' varied experiences with the globalization of their industry, we can gain a greater understanding of the importance of work in shaping our social and economic lives and our understanding of the world around us.

NOTES

1. An important factor underlying this pattern is the high rate of disability among prime age workers in the United States. In 2009, for example, the rate was 80 percent higher in rural (7.5 percent) than in urban areas (4.2 percent) (Bishop and Gallardo 2011).

2. Because the CPS uses a stratified cluster sampling design (i.e., it makes a special effort to incorporate groups that are harder to reach with surveys), it is necessary to use weights to produce reliable population estimates. In this analysis, the CPS person weights were divided by their means to yield weighted case sizes that are approximately equal to the sample size.

3. One state of underemployment—discouragement—described here is typically defined as "not in the labor force" because such workers are neither employed nor actively engaged in a job search. Underemployment brings these workers back into consideration.

REFERENCES

Albrecht, Don E., and Stan L. Albrecht. 2000. "Poverty in Nonmetropolitan America: Impacts of Industrial, Employment, and Family Structure Variables." *Rural Sociology* 65(1):87–103.

Barkley, David L., and Sylvain Hinschberger. 1992. "Industrial Restructuring: Implications for the Decentralization of Manufacturing to Nonmetropolitan Areas." *Economic Development Quarterly* 6(1):64–79.

Bascom, Johnathan. 2000. "Revisiting the Rural Revolution in East Carolina." *Geographical Review* 90(3):432–45.

Bishop, Bill, and Robert Gallardo. 2011. "The Geography of Disability." *Daily Yonder*. http://www.dailyyonder.com/geography-disability/2011/11/30/3619/#.

Brady, David, Regina S. Baker, and Ryan Finnigan. 2013. "When Unionization Disappears: State-Level Unionization and Working Poverty in the United States." *American Sociological Review* 78(5):872–96.

Broadway, Michael. 2007. "Meatpacking and the Transformation of Rural Communities: A Comparison of Brooks, Alberta and Garden City, Kansas." *Rural Sociology* 72(4):560–82.

Brown, David L., and Nina Glasgow. 2008. *Rural Retirement Migration*. Dordrecht, Holland: Springer.

Burton, Linda M., Daniel T. Lichter, Regina S. Baker, and John M. Eason. 2013. "Inequality, Family Processes, and Health in the 'New' Rural America." *American Behavioral Scientist* 57(8):1128–51.

Carr, Patrick J., and Maria J. Kefalas. 2009. *Hollowing Out the Middle: The Rural Brain Drain and What It Means for America*. Boston, MA: Beacon Press.

Citro, Constance F., and Robert T. Michael. 1995. *Measuring Poverty: A New Approach*. Washington, DC: National Academy Press.

Clogg, Clifford C. 1979. *Measuring Underemployment: Demographic Indicators for the United States*. New York: Academic Press.

Clogg, Clifford C., and Teresa A. Sullivan. 1983. "Demographic Composition of Underemployment Trends, 1969–1980." *Social Indicators Research* 12:117–52.

Cotter, David A. 2002. "Poor People in Poor Places: Local Opportunity Structures and Household Poverty." *Rural Sociology* 67(4):534–55.

Domina, Thurston. 2006. "What Clean Break? Education and Nonmetropolitan Migration Patterns, 1989–2004." *Rural Sociology* 71:373–98.

Eckes, Alfred E. 2005. "The South and Economic Globalization: 1950 to the Future." In *Globalization and the American South*, ed. James Charles Cobb and William Whitney Stueck, 36–65. Athens, GA: University of Georgia Press.

Falk, William W., and Thomas A. Lyson. 1988. *High Tech, Low Tech, No Tech: Recent Industrial and Occupational Change in the South*. Albany: State University of New York Press.

Falk, William W., Michael D. Schulman, and Ann R. Tickamyer. 2003. *Communities of Work: Rural Restructuring in Local and Global Contexts*. Athens: Ohio University Press.

Freudenburg, William R. 1992. "Addictive Economies: Extractive Industries and Vulnerable Localities in a Changing World Economy." *Rural Sociology* 57(3):305–32.

Friedland, Roger, and A. F. Robinson. 1990. *Beyond the Marketplace: Rethinking Economy and Society.* New York: Aldine de Gruyter.

Fuguitt, Glenn V., David L. Brown, and Calvin L. Beale. 1989. *Rural and Small Town America.* New York: Russell Sage Foundation.

Gibbs, Robert, Lorin Kusmin, and John Cromartie. 2005. "Low-Skill Employment and the Changing Economy of Rural America." Economic Research Report No. 10. Washington, DC: U.S. Department of Agriculture.

Grusky, David B., Bruce Western, and Christopher Wimer. 2011. *The Great Recession.* New York: Russell Sage.

Hacker, Jacob S. 2008. *The Great Risk Shift: The New Economic Insecurity and the Decline of the American Dream,* rev. ed. New York: Oxford University Press.

Hamrick, Karen S. 2001. "Displaced Workers: Differences in Nonmetro and Metro Experiences in the Mid-1990s." Rural Development Research Report No. 92. Washington, DC: U.S. Department of Agriculture.

Harrison, Bennett, and Barry Bluestone. 1988. *The Great U-Turn: Corporate Restructuring and the Polarizing of America.* New York: Basic.

Henderson, Jason. 2012. "Rebuilding Rural Manufacturing." *Main Street Economist* 2:1–6. Kansas City, MO: Federal Reserve Bank of Kansas City.

Holmes, Thomas J. 2013. "New Manufacturing Investment and Unions." Economic Policy Paper 13–2. Minneapolis, MN: Federal Reserve Bank of Minneapolis.

Iceland, John. 2014. *A Portrait of America: The Demographic Perspective.* Oakland, CA: University of California Press.

Jensen, Leif, and Diane K. McLaughlin. 1995. "Human Capital and Nonmetropolitan Poverty." In *Investing in People: The Human Capital Needs of Rural America,* ed. Lionel J. Beaulieu and David Mulkey, 111–38. Boulder, CO: Westview Press.

Jensen, Leif, and Tienda, Marta. 1989. "Nonmetropolitan Minority Families in the United States: Trends in Racial and Ethnic Economic Stratification, 1959–1986." *Rural Sociology* 54(4):509–32.

Johnson, Kenneth M. 2011. "The Continuing Incidence of Natural Decrease in American Counties." *Rural Sociology* 76(1):74–100.

Johnson, Kenneth M., and Daniel T. Lichter. 2008. "Natural Increase: A New Source of Population Growth in Emerging Hispanic Destinations in the United States." *Population and Development Review* 34(2):327–46.

Joshi, Mahendra L., John C. Bliss, Conner Bailey, Lawrence J. Teeter, and Keith J. Ward. 2000. "Investing in Industry, Underinvesting in Human Capital: Forest-Based Rural Development in Alabama." *Society & Natural Resources* 13(4):291–319.

Kandel, William, and Emilio A. Parrado. 2005. "Restructuring of the US Meat Processing Industry and New Hispanic Migrant Destinations." *Population and Development Review* 31(2):447–71.

Kalleberg, Arne L., Barbara F. Reskin, and Ken Hudson. 2000. "Bad Jobs in America: Standard and Nonstandard Employment Relations and Job Quality in the United States." *American Sociological Review* 65(2):256–78.

Kusmin, Lorin. 2014. "Rural America at a Glance, 2014 Edition." Economic Brief No. EB-26. Washington, DC: United States Department of Agriculture.

Lee, Marlene A., and Mark Mather. 2008. "US Labor Force Trends." Population Reference Bureau Bulletin 63, No. 2.

Lichter, Daniel T. 2012. "Immigration and the New Racial Diversity in Rural America." *Rural Sociology* 77(1):3–35.

Lichter, Daniel T., and David L. Brown. 2011. "Rural America in an Urban Society: Changing Spatial and Social Boundaries." *Annual Review of Sociology* 37(1):565–92.

Lichter, Daniel T., and Kenneth M. Johnson. 2009. "Immigrant Gateways and Hispanic Migration to New Destinations." *International Migration Review* 43(3):496–518.

Lobao, Linda, and Katherine Meyer. 2001. "The Great Agricultural Transition: Crisis, Change and Social Consequences of Twentieth Century US Farming." *The Annual Review of Sociology* 27(1):103–24.

Lyson, Thomas A., and Charles M. Tolbert. 1996. "Small Manufacturing and Nonmetropolitan Socioeconomic Well-Being." *Environment and Planning A* 28:1779–94.

Markhusen, Ann. 1980. "The Political Economy of Rural Development: The Case of Western US Boomtowns." In *The Rural Sociology of the Advanced Societies: Critical Perspectives*, ed. Frederick H. Buttel and Howard Newby, 405–32. Montclair, NJ: Allenheld, Osmun.

McGranahan, David A. 2003. "How People Make a Living in Rural America." In *Challenges for Rural America in the Twenty-First Century*, ed. David L. Brown and Louis E. Swanson, 135–51. University Park: Pennsylvania State University Press.

McLaughlin, Diane K., and Alisha J. Coleman-Jensen. 2008. "Nonstandard Employment in the Nonmetropolitan United States." *Rural Sociology* 73(4):631–59.

Morris, Martina, and Bruce Western. 1999. "Inequality in Earnings at the Close of the Twentieth Century." *Annual Review of Sociology* 25(1):623–57.

Robinson, William I. 2001. "Social Theory and Globalization: The Rise of a Transnational State." *Theory and Society* 30(2):157–200.

Saez, Emmanuel. 2013. "Striking It Richer: The Evolution of Top Incomes in the United States." Unpublished manuscript. https://elsa.berkeley.edu/~saez/saez-UStopincomes-2012.pdf.

Slack, Tim. 2010. "Working Poverty Across the Metro–Nonmetro Divide: A Quarter Century in Perspective, 1979–2003." *Rural Sociology* 75(3):363–87.

———. 2014. "Work in Rural America in the Era of Globalization." In *Rural America in a Globalizing World: Problems and Prospects for the 2010s*, ed. Conner Bailey, Leif Jensen, and Elizabeth Ransom, 573–90. Morgantown: West Virginia University Press.

Slack, Tim, and Leif Jensen. 2002. "Race, Ethnicity, and Underemployment in Nonmetropolitan America: A 30-Year Profile." *Rural Sociology* 67:208–33.

———. 2004. "Employment Adequacy in Extractive Industries: An Analysis of Underemployment, 1974–1998." *Society and Natural Resources* 17:129–46.

———. 2010. "Informal Work in Rural America: Theory and Evidence." In *Informal Work in Developed Nations*, ed. Enrico A. Marcelli, Colin C. Williams, and Pascale Joassart, 175–91. New York, NY: Routledge.

Slack, Tim, and Tracey E. Rizzuto. 2013. "Aging and Economic Well-Being in Rural America: Exploring Income and Employment Challenges." In *Rural Aging in 21st Century America*, ed. Nina Glasgow and E. Helen Berry, 57–75. New York: Springer.

Smeeding, Tim. 2006. "Poor People in Rich Nations: The United States in Comparative Perspective." *Journal of Economic Perspectives* 20:69–90.

Snipp, C. Mathew. 1996. "Understanding Race and Ethnicity in Rural America." *Rural Sociology* 61:125–42.

Sommer, Judith E., et al. 1998. "Structural and Financial Characteristics of US Farms, 1995." Twentieth Annual Family Farm Report to Congress, No. 33620. Washington, DC: United States Department of Agriculture.

Stamps, Katherine, and Stephanie A. Bohon. 2006. "Educational Attainment in New and Established Latino Metropolitan Destinations." *Social Science Quarterly* 87(5):1225–40.

Sullivan, Teresa A. 1978. *Marginal Workers, Marginal Jobs: Underutilization of the US Work Force.* Austin: University of Texas Press.

Tonelson, Alan. 2002. *The Race to the Bottom: Why a Worldwide Worker Surplus and Uncontrolled Free Trade Are Sinking American Living Standards.* Boulder, CO: Westview Press.

U.S. Census Bureau. 2015. "Urban and Rural Populations: 1790–1990." Accessed July 30. http://www.census.gov/population/www/censusdata/files/table-4.pdf.

Vias, Alexander C. 2012. "Perspectives on US Rural Labor Markets in the First Decade of the Twenty-First Century." In *International Handbook of Rural Demography*, ed. Laszlo J. Kulcsar and Katherine J. Curtis, 273–91. Dordrecht, Holland: Springer.

Weber, Bruce, Leif Jensen, Kathleen Miller, Jane Mosley, and Monica Fisher. 2005. "A Critical Review of Rural Poverty Literature: Is There Truly a Rural Effect?" *International Regional Science Review* 28(4):381–414.

Weil, David. 2014. *The Fissured Workplace.* Cambridge, MA: Harvard University Press.

Western, Bruce, and Jake Rosenfeld. 2011. "Unions, Norms, and the Rise in US Wage Inequality." *American Sociological Review* 76(4):513–37.

CHAPTER 10

Food Insecurity and Housing Insecurity

Alisha Coleman-Jensen and Barry Steffen[1]

INTRODUCTION

Families living in or near poverty may struggle to meet their most basic needs for adequate food and shelter. In extreme cases, some families experience outright persistent hunger or homelessness. Although most Americans, even those in poverty, do not experience food and housing hardships that severe, they may face serious hardships referred to as "food insecurity" and "housing insecurity." Being unable to obtain adequate nutritious food and decent, affordable housing can have negative effects on families and individuals, as evidenced by poor physical and mental health of both adults and children and adverse developmental outcomes for children. An idyllic scene of rural America often depicts vegetable gardens, family farms, and welcoming porches. As is made clear throughout this book, however, such situations are not the reality for many rural poor. In rural areas across the United States, food is not always in abundance, and living arrangements are not always ideal. This chapter explores these issues further, examining what the federal government means by the terms *food insecurity* and *housing insecurity*, considering what experiencing these difficulties means for rural residents, and comparing how their experiences differ from similar households in other "residence areas"—suburban areas and principal cities.[2]

FOOD INSECURITY

Most U.S. households are able to obtain adequate food for all their members. Each year, however, a minority of American households experience food insecurity at times. In 2014, 14 percent of U.S. households struggled

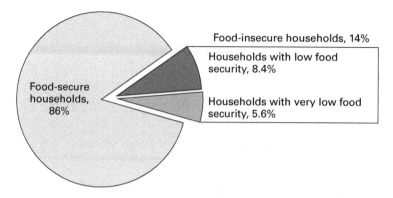

Figure 10.1 U.S. households sorted by food security status, 2014.

Source: Alisha Coleman-Jensen, Mathew P. Rabbitt, Christian Gregory, and Anita Singh. 2015. "Household Food Security in the United States in 2014." Economic Research Report No. 194. Washington, DC: U.S. Department of Agriculture, Economic Research Service. http://www.ers .usda.gov/publications/err-economic-research-report/err194.aspx.

to put enough food on the table (figure 10.1). In rural or nonmetropolitan counties, 17.1 percent of households were food insecure. The U.S. Department of Agriculture (USDA) defines food-insecure households as those that "were, at times, unable to acquire adequate food for one or more household members because they had insufficient money and other resources for food" (Coleman-Jensen, Rabbitt, Gregory, and Singh 2015, 8). During 2014, the severe range of food insecurity, described as very low food security, affected 5.6 percent of U.S. households overall and 7.3 percent of households in rural counties. Households with very low food security "were food insecure to the extent that eating patterns of one or more household members were disrupted and their food intake reduced, at least some time during the year, because they could not afford enough food" (Coleman-Jensen et al. 2015, 8). Households classified as experiencing very low food security report cutting the size of or skipping meals, being hungry because they could not afford enough food, and in some cases going a whole day without eating.

Research shows that food insecurity is related to poor health outcomes for adults. For example, it appears that food insecurity contributes to reduced nutrient intake, postponing medical care, inability to afford prescriptions, diabetes and other chronic conditions, and poor mental health (for a review, see Bread for the World Institute 2016, and Food Research and Action Center 2014). Food insecurity is a risk factor for problematic health, developmental, and educational outcomes for children as well. For example, household food insecurity has been linked to poorer health, anemia, more illnesses, behavioral problems, depression, chronic health conditions, and lower educational achievement among children (for a review, see Coleman-Jensen, McFall, and Nord 2013). Difficulty obtaining adequate food is problematic in its own right, and the associated consequences carry high costs for individuals, communities, and the nation.

HOW IS FOOD SECURITY MEASURED?

U.S. food security measurement began in 1995 (for a brief history, see Coleman-Jensen 2015). The prevalence and severity of food insecurity in U.S. households is monitored annually by the Economic Research Service of USDA (U.S. Department of Agriculture 2017). The questions used to assess food security are included in the Current Population Survey Food Security Supplement (CPS-FSS). The CPS is a federal survey that is the source for national unemployment and poverty statistics.[3] Food security status is determined by responses to a series of survey questions about conditions and behaviors that characterize households having difficulty meeting basic food needs (see "Questions Used to Assess the Food Security of Households in the CPS Food Security Survey" on p. 287 and figure 10.2). Each question asks about experiences in the past twelve months and specifies a lack of money and other resources to obtain food as the reason for the hardship, thus excluding voluntary fasting or dieting from the measure (Coleman-Jensen et al. 2015).[4]

RECENT TRENDS IN U.S. FOOD INSECURITY

Food insecurity increased substantially with the 2007–2009 recession and has remained at a relatively high level (figure 10.3). In 2007, 11.1 percent of U.S. households were food insecure, but by 2008, the prevalence had increased to 14.6 percent. Food insecurity reached a high of 14.9 percent of U.S. households in 2011 and declined to 14.0 percent in 2014, but remained above prerecession levels (Coleman-Jensen et al. 2015).

Trends in food insecurity rates across rural and urban residence areas (measured here as nonmetropolitan counties or metropolitan areas divided into principal cities and suburban areas) followed a similar pattern to that of the United States as a whole (figure 10.4).[5] Since the recession,

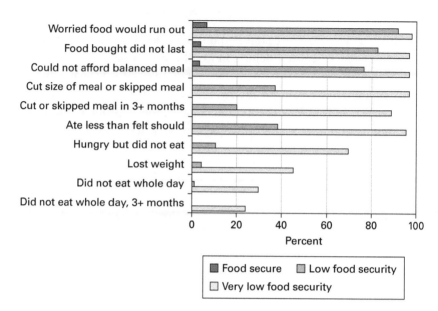

Figure 10.2   Percentage of households reporting each indicator of food insecurity, by food security status, 2014.

Source: Alisha Coleman-Jensen, Mathew P. Rabbitt, Christian Gregory, and Anita Singh. 2015. "Household Food Security in the United States in 2014." Economic Research Report No. 194. Washington, DC: U.S. Department of Agriculture, Economic Research Service. http://www.ers.usda.gov/publications/err-economic-research-report/err194.aspx.

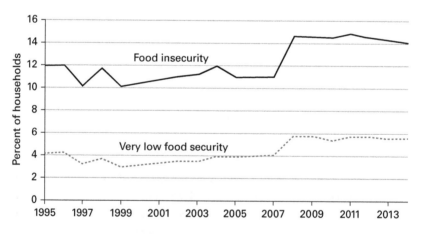

Figure 10.3   Trends in the prevalence of food insecurity and very low food security in U.S. households, 1995–2014.

Source: Alisha Coleman-Jensen, Mathew P. Rabbitt, Christian Gregory, and Anita Singh. 2015. "Household Food Security in the United States in 2014." Economic Research Report No. 194. Washington, DC: U.S. Department of Agriculture, Economic Research Service. http://www.ers.usda.gov/publications/err-economic-research-report/err194.aspx.

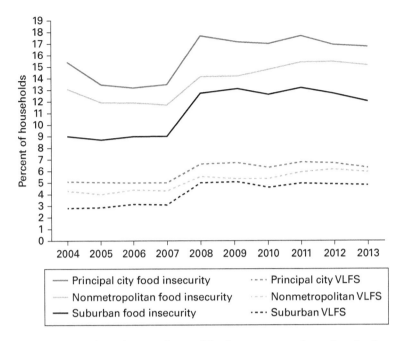

Figure 10.4 Trends in the prevalence of food insecurity and very low food security (VLFS) in U.S. households, 2004–2013.

Source: Calculated by USDA, Economic Research Service, using data from the Current Population Survey Food Security Supplement, 2004–2013.

however, food insecurity has continued to worsen in rural areas (nonmetropolitan counties) while improving somewhat in more urban areas (metropolitan areas divided into suburban areas and principal cities). The prevalence of food insecurity in principal cities had begun to decline, from 17.7 percent in 2008 to 16.7 percent in 2013. However, food insecurity in rural counties continued to increase after the recession officially ended, from 14.2 percent in 2008 to 15.1 percent in 2013. This increase in rural food insecurity is counter to the trend observed immediately after the recession when rural counties appeared less affected by rising food insecurity rates than urban areas (Coleman-Jensen 2012). It appears that the recession may have had a less immediate effect in rural areas, but food insecurity in rural areas continued to worsen after the official end of the recession. There is evidence that economic recovery in rural counties has lagged behind the recovery in urban areas. Rural employment gains since the recession have been lower than employment growth

Table 10.1 Prevalence of Food Insecurity and Very Low Food Security by Residence Area and Selected Household Characteristics (% of Households), 2014[1]

Category	Metropolitan, in principal cities		Metropolitan, not in principal cities		Nonmetropolitan	
	Food insecure	Very low food secure	Food insecure	Very low food secure	Food insecure	Very low food secure
All households	15.7 [S]	5.9 [S]	11.8	4.8	17.1 [C,S]	7.3 [C,S]
Household composition[2]						
With children <18 years	22.3 [S]	6.8 [S]	15.4	4.9	23.6 [S]	7.6 [S]
Married-couple families	14.3 [S]	2.9	10.0	2.8	17.9 [C,S]	4.3 [C,S]
Female head, no spouse	37.1 [S]	13.7	31.7	12.0	36.0	12.5
Male head, no spouse	23.00	7.3	18.7	4.6	24.0	14.4 [C,S]
With no children <18 years	12.8 [S]	5.5 [S]	9.9	4.8	14.4 [C,S]	7.1 [C,S]
More than one adult	11.1 [S]	4.6 [S]	8.1	3.7	11.5 [S]	5.1 [S]
Women living alone	15.3	6.5	13.9	7.0	19.9 [C,S]	9.8 [C,S]
Men living alone	14.2	6.7	12.3	6.6	17.2 [C,S]	10.4 [C,S]
With elderly	11.5 [S]	4.2 [S]	7.6	2.7	10.1 [S]	3.8 [S]
Elderly living alone	10.2	4.4	8.2	3.4	11.4 [S]	4.8
Race/ethnicity of households						
White non-Hispanic	9.2	3.8	8.7	3.9	14.9 [C,S]	6.8 [C,S]
Black non-Hispanic	28.4 [S]	11.9 [S]	22.0	9.0	29.1 [S]	8.7 [C]
Hispanic[3]	22.4	6.7	21.2	6.7	27.2 [C,S]	8.8 [C]
Other non-Hispanic	9.0	2.6 [S]	9.8	4.6	25.2 [C,S]	12.4 [C,S]
Household income-to-poverty ratio						
Under 1.00	39.0	16.6	38.3	18.0	41.1	19.8 [C]
Under 1.30	37.1	15.5	36.1	16.6	38.9	18.6 [C]
Under 1.85	33.9	14.0	32.6	14.4	34.3	15.4
1.85 and over	7.3 [S]	2.1	5.6	2.1	7.0 [S]	2.4
Income unknown	11.4 [S]	4.2	9.0	3.3	10.7	4.3
Census geographic region						
Northeast	17.6 [S]	6.1 [S]	10.7	4.4	14.4 [S]	6.1 [S]
Midwest	18.6 [S]	6.9 [S]	10.6	4.8	14.8 [C,S]	6.8 [S]
South	15.2 [S]	6.3	13.2	5.5	19.5 [C,S]	7.8 [C,S]
West	13.5 [S]	4.9 [S]	11.3	4.0	17.2 [C,S]	7.4 [C,S]

Source: Calculated by author using data from the USDA Economic Research Service, Current Population Survey Food Security Supplement, December 2014.

in urban areas, and in mid-2015 rural employment remained below the prerecession employment peak in 2007. Meanwhile, urban employment growth has been consistently rising and by mid-2015 had far surpassed the prerecession urban employment peak (Kusmin 2015). Nationally, trends in employment are closely linked to trends in food insecurity (Nord, Coleman-Jensen, and Gregory 2014). This important relationship is borne out in rural areas.

Food security statistics by area of residence for 2014 are not precisely comparable to those for 2013. Therefore, changes from 2013 in the prevalence of food insecurity by area of residence should be interpreted with caution (Coleman-Jensen et al. 2015). In 2014, 17.1 percent of households in rural counties were food insecure (table 10.1). Of these, 7.3 percent were in the severe range of food insecurity described as very low food security. Across the residence area classifications, food insecurity was highest in rural counties (labeled nonmetropolitan in table 10.1), intermediate in principal cities (15.7 percent), and lowest in suburbs and other urban areas outside principal cities (11.8 percent; labeled metropolitan, not in principal cities).

The prevalence of food insecurity varies substantially not only across place but also across population subgroups. The prevalence of food insecurity tends to be higher in single-parent families and low-income families than in married-couple families and higher-income families. Similar patterns in the incidence of food insecurity by household characteristic emerge within each of the three residence areas.

Comparing across residence areas by household characteristics, food insecurity rates tended to be highest among those in rural counties. In 2014, food insecurity was higher among married couples with children in rural counties than among married couples with children in suburban or

---

S = Prevalence estimate is significantly different from corresponding prevalence estimate for suburban areas, "Metropolitan, not in Principal Cities," at the 90-percent confidence level.

C = Prevalence estimate is significantly different from corresponding prevalence estimate for "Metropolitan, in Principal Cities," at the 90-percent confidence level.

[1] Metropolitan area residence is based on 2013 Office of Management and Budget Delineation. Sample sizes (N) by residence area are 10,443 households in principal cities; 15,288 metropolitan households not in principal cities; 9,667 households in nonmetropolitan areas. N's exclude households for which food security status is unknown (0.2 percent of all households).

[2] A residual category, "other household with child," is not shown due to small sample sizes.

[3] Hispanics may be of any race.

principal city areas. Single-mother households residing in rural areas and principal city areas were worst off, with food insecurity rates of 36 and 37 percent, respectively (table 10.1). Women and men living alone experienced the highest food insecurity rates when they lived in rural areas. The elderly face higher food insecurity rates in rural and principal city areas than in suburban areas.

Across all residence areas, minority groups had higher food insecurity rates than non-Hispanic whites in 2014. Non-Hispanic blacks had similar food insecurity rates in principal cities and rural counties (about 29 percent). Non-Hispanic whites, Hispanics, and other non-Hispanics all faced higher food insecurity rates in rural counties than in urban areas. Other non-Hispanics had particularly high food insecurity prevalence rates in rural areas. Fully one-quarter of other non-Hispanics face food insecurity. Other non-Hispanics in rural areas are primarily Native Americans or Alaskan Natives.[6] Other research has shown very high food insecurity rates on rural Native American reservations (Bauer et al. 2012). High food insecurity prevalence rates among Native Americans are likely related to high poverty rates.

Across all residence areas, households with incomes below or near the federal poverty line face higher food insecurity rates than higher-income households. Within each income category, there were not significant differences in the prevalence of food insecurity by residence area in 2014. Food insecurity was experienced by about four in ten households living with incomes below the poverty line. In 2014, the federal poverty line was $24,008 for a family of two adults and two children. Poverty is clearly an important risk factor for food insecurity given the high incidence of food insecurity among those with incomes below the poverty line.

In the South and the West, food insecurity was more prevalent in rural counties than in principal city or suburban areas. In the Midwest, food insecurity was most prevalent in principal cities.

FACTORS RELATED TO FOOD INSECURITY

Food insecurity, an indicator of economic hardship, is related to poverty and low-income, as is evident in the statistics discussed previously. A number of other factors also are correlated with food insecurity. A report by Gundersen and Ziliak (2014) reviewed the recent literature on correlates of food insecurity. Research has examined factors related to currently being food insecure, to transitioning into or out of food insecurity, and to persistence of food insecurity. Some factors that have been shown to be particularly important to food insecurity are disabilities, poor physical health, poor mental health and mental illness, unemployment and type of employment, exposure to violence and other negative life events, low education, immigrant status, marital status and family composition, and changes in income. Most individual and household correlates of food insecurity appear to affect food insecurity similarly across residence areas; for example, having an adult with disabilities increases the likelihood of food insecurity regardless of where a household is located.

To understand factors that cause or are associated with food insecurity we must look beyond individuals and families. Local, state, and national conditions also affect a family's chances that they will be food insecure. Economic conditions, such as the availability of jobs and their wages, and policies such as the availability of public assistance are important predictors of food insecurity. At the national level, unemployment, inflation, and the price of food relative to other goods and services are strong predictors of the national food insecurity rate (Nord et al. 2014). Following the recession that ended in 2009, food insecurity rates appear to have remained relatively high due to high inflation (prices) and high food costs, in particular. These factors offset declines in unemployment. Put another way, as unemployment declined, food insecurity would be expected to decline, but prices increased, forcing families to stretch their incomes further to cover all their expenses. At the state level, numerous factors are associated with increased rates of food insecurity, including low average wages, high unemployment rate, high cost of rental housing, low participation in food assistance programs, and a high tax burden on low-income families (Bartfeld, Dunifon, Nord, and Carlson 2006). At the state and local level, food prices are important to a household's likelihood of food insecurity (Gregory and Coleman-Jensen 2013). Those in high-food-cost areas have a higher likelihood of food insecurity than similar households in low-food-cost areas. Another local or community-level factor related to food insecurity is the availability of emergency food assistance and local groups working to end hunger in their community (Morton, Bitto, Oakland, and Sand 2005). When food assistance is available, families are less likely to experience food insecurity.

FOOD INSECURITY IN RURAL AREAS

Some factors are particularly relevant to understanding food insecurity in rural areas. By definition, rural areas are sparsely populated, and residents tend to travel greater distances to stores and service providers. Households in rural areas may then face substantial time and financial costs to access food and food assistance. Data on food prices in rural areas across the country are poor because price data tend to be urbancentric. Some research does suggest that rural households often pay higher prices in small local stores or face greater costs to travel to larger stores farther away (Blanchard and Lyson 2002; Hardin-Fanning and Rayens 2015; Zimmerman, Ham, and Frank 2008). Traveling longer distances to a grocery store is related to a greater likelihood of food insecurity, which has an even greater impact for households lacking a vehicle (Stracuzzi and Ward 2010) or facing high gasoline prices (Webber and Rojhani 2010). One characteristic of the rural food environment that limits food access is a lack of a transportation infrastructure for those without a personal vehicle (USDA 2009).

Rural households also may have to travel to access emergency food providers because rural food pantries may have larger service areas and tend to be less formalized than urban emergency food providers (Molnar, Duffy, Claxton, and Bailey 2001). Because emergency food providers are locally run, their characteristics, eligibility guidelines, service hours, and availability vary widely. Rural food pantries may provide a smaller variety of foods, provide less food overall, and may provide food on a less frequent basis than urban pantries because rural pantries are more often volunteer run and do not have dedicated space to store items (Whitley 2013). However, most rural households responding to the CPS-FSS in recent years have indicated that food pantries are available in their local communities and that use of food pantries is as prevalent, or more prevalent, in rural areas as in urban areas (Coleman-Jensen 2012).

An idyllic view of rural America includes gardens, farms, hunting, and fishing as ways for rural families to produce or obtain their own food supply without as much reliance on typical grocery stores. Some research has found that rural low-income households are more likely to garden or receive foods from family's and neighbors' gardens than are urban low-income households (Morton et al. 2008). Research indicates that some rural poor families view hunting and fishing as a preferred way to obtain food rather than relying on federal or charitable food assistance (Sherman 2006). However, there are no large-scale studies to show that a significant portion of rural households use these means to cover a significant portion of their dietary needs. Having a garden is not significantly related to household food insecurity when other social and demographic factors are taken into account (Morton et al. 2008; Olson, Rauschenbach, Frongillo, and Kendall 1997). In general, gardening, farming, hunting, and fishing are not likely to make major contributions to improving food security in rural areas. These activities are costly, time-intensive, and skill-intensive and despite financial inputs (purchasing seeds, fishing supplies, etc.) and time investments may not result in significant food production due to factors outside the family's control (drought, pests, etc.). Community and school gardens, farm-to-fork programs, and farmers' markets tend to be more urban focused; spreading these programs to rural areas may benefit rural households at risk for food insecurity (Piontak and Schulman 2014).

Rural America is characterized by diversity. Rural counties are spread across the United States, which means that rural counties vary by race/ethnicity of residents, the presence of immigrants and their country of origin, the dominant industry or economic drivers, weather, geography, inequality, food environment, levels of poverty and unemployment, availability of community food assistance, cost of living, and influence of local, state, and federal policies on residents. Given this level of diversity across rural America, the incidence and severity of food insecurity surely differs within and across these rural counties. Local efforts to improve household food security must take the local context into account.

POLICIES AND PROGRAMS TO IMPROVE FOOD SECURITY

The USDA is the primary federal agency responsible for administering programs aimed at improving American diets and reducing food insecurity. The USDA administers fifteen domestic food and nutrition assistance programs, and these programs constitute about three-quarters of USDA's entire budget. The three largest food and nutrition assistance programs are SNAP (Supplemental Nutrition Assistance Program, formerly food stamps), WIC (Special Supplemental Nutrition Program for Women, Infants, and Children), and the National School Lunch and Breakfast Programs (Oliveira 2015). SNAP provides monthly benefits to households that meet income cutoffs and other eligibility guidelines. SNAP benefits are distributed on electronic benefit transfer (EBT) cards that function as debit cards; households can use the benefits to purchase approved foods at authorized food stores for home preparation. SNAP benefits also can be used to purchase seeds and plants that will produce food for the household to consume. The WIC program enables families with infants, young children, or pregnant/lactating women who are low-income and at nutritional risk to acquire supplemental nutritious food packages at authorized food stores. The program also provides health care referrals and nutrition education to participants. The National School Lunch Program serves nutritious meals to students in both public and private schools. Free or reduced-price lunches are available to low-income students. A number of other food and nutrition assistance programs target specific populations. One such program that is particularly relevant to rural food insecurity is the Food Distribution Program on Indian Reservations (FDPIR). This program provides monthly food packages to income-eligible households. Households cannot participate in both SNAP and FDPIR. FDPIR can be particularly important on Indian reservations where households must travel long distances to reach a food retailer; the food packages are distributed directly without requiring participants to visit a food store.

Research has shown that SNAP ameliorates food insecurity. A variety of different methods and approaches have been used to examine the effect of SNAP participation on household food insecurity. Strong recent evidence finds that SNAP improves household food security (Mabli et al. 2013; Nord and Prell 2011; Ratcliffe and McKernan 2011). SNAP appears to be effective at ameliorating food insecurity in both urban and rural areas. The prevalence of food insecurity decreased among both rural and urban households participating in SNAP for six months. The magnitude of the decline was similar across residence areas (Mabli 2014). Estimated participation rates suggest that SNAP reaches most eligible rural residents. In fiscal year 2013, the SNAP participation rate was about 90 percent among eligible rural residents and 84 percent among eligible urban residents (USDA 2015). This finding is consistent over time (Bailey 2014; McConnell and Ohls 2002). The absolute number of SNAP participants is lower in rural areas than in urban areas, given the smaller rural population, but the participation rate is higher in rural areas.

In qualitative research, the rural poor indicate that they prefer to rely on their earnings rather than government welfare assistance to make ends meet. Making ends meet without assistance is hard to realize as families make trade-offs between equally vital goods, struggle to get enough paid hours at their jobs, or struggle to find a job that pays enough to support a family (Tickamyer and Henderson 2011). Some rural poor residents express reluctance to utilize food assistance because they worry about how they will be perceived by their community members and prefer to rely on other strategies to obtain food (Sherman 2006). As such, in some rural communities, stigma may be a barrier for accessing and using assistance.

Federal food and nutrition assistance are important pieces of the puzzle in combating U.S. food insecurity, but these programs do not function in isolation. Local food assistance programs also are important in reducing poverty and unemployment nationally and locally, increasing incomes, supporting those with disabilities and other health conditions, providing access to physical and mental health services, and ensuring that all communities have access to affordable, healthful food. Finally, the rural poor must be willing to accept assistance when it is needed without risking judgment from their neighbors and communities.

HOUSING INSECURITY

Housing insecurity is another type of economic hardship that can result from poverty or low income. For most U.S. households, shelter is the most costly item in the household budget. After paying for shelter costs, such as rent and utilities, many poor and near-poor households become "shelter poor," meaning they have little discretionary income left to pay for other crucial needs such as food, health care, transportation, and education (Deidda 2015; Stone 2004). They may not be able to obtain safe and decent housing units within their price range or to maintain suitable indoor environments, putting their families at physical risk. They may have little opportunity to build cash buffers against personal financial crises, increasing their housing insecurity by increasing risk of missed payments, eviction, and homelessness. Housing hardships thus range from spending a large share of income on housing (housing cost burden), to lacking an adequate, stable, and permanent residence (housing insecurity), to completely lacking housing (homelessness). Rural residents are not exempt from such challenges, but they experience them in somewhat different ways than do residents of U.S. metropolitan areas. The housing insecure and the homeless in rural areas face different combinations of challenges and resources than similar individuals in urban areas, and they may be more invisible in the absence of service centers or homeless shelters that draw them together.

Housing is best understood as a somewhat lumpy bundle of services (Mitchell 1985). Any given housing unit offers a package of basic shelter, neighborhood security and amenities, access to transportation and social networks, personal consumption, productivity potential,[7] and financial investment potential. Such complexity and the household's role in choosing units account for the difficulty researchers have had in understanding how the quantity, quality, affordability, and public assistance of housing affect its occupants.

In recent decades, 30 percent of household income has become a conventional rule-of-thumb standard for housing costs that remain "affordable" (Pelletiere 2008). Households paying more than 30 percent of their income are defined as having a housing cost burden. The U.S. Department of Housing and Urban Development (HUD) defines housing costs between 30 and 50 percent of income as a moderate cost burden, and housing costs exceeding 50 percent of income as a severe cost burden (Steffen et al. 2015).

Housing has been recognized as a strong social determinant of health (Cutts et al. 2011). Housing cost, housing problems, neighborhood disorder, residential instability, and homeownership interact in ways that affect child development and well-being (Coley, Kull, Leventhal, and Lynch 2014). Parents may choose to spend a greater fraction of income for housing that offers a better and safer environment for children, but such choices require the sacrifice of other life-enhancing economic goods, especially for poor families. Predicted child achievement scores provide some empirical support for the conventional standard of housing affordability because scores increase as housing expenditures approach 30 percent of income, then decrease as cost burdens worsen (Newman and Holupka 2014).

Elevated housing cost burdens can lead directly to housing insecurity, frequent moves, and forced trade-offs involving crowded or physically inadequate units and deteriorated and hazardous neighborhoods. Housing insecurity is associated with food insecurity, poor health, lower weight, and developmental risk among young children (Cutts et al. 2011; Meyers et al. 1995). By increasing maternal stress, housing insecurity is directly associated with risk of child neglect and abuse (Warren and Font 2015). For poor children, moving three or more times in a child's first five years is significantly associated with decreases in school readiness as measured by attention problems and internalizing and externalizing behavior (Ziol-Guest and McKenna 2014). Ortiz and Zimmerman (2013) found that, in California, the observed benefits of homeownership for health are insignificant for racial and ethnic minorities even after controlling for socioeconomic status and suggest that lower levels of housing security among these populations may account for such differences. Unexpected health costs are found to be associated with the likelihood of family homelessness, particularly in areas with high housing costs (Curtis, Corman, Noonan, and Reichman 2013). Furthermore, both housing instability and food insecurity are linked with poor access to ambulatory care and high rates of acute care, suggesting that such challenges may lead to delays in seeking health care and lead to more use of acute care (Kushel, Gupta, Gee, and Haas 2006). Families in poverty are particularly susceptible to housing cost burdens and such negative outcomes because, by definition, they have less income to spend on housing.

When families are unable to afford housing, homelessness may result. Homelessness is less common, but still significant, in rural areas. Rural areas had an estimated 14 homeless individuals per 10,000 people in 2007, compared with 29 per 10,000 in urban areas. About 4 percent of the U.S. homeless population was in rural areas in 2007 (Henry and Sermons 2010).[8]

UNIQUE FEATURES OF RURAL HOUSING MARKETS

Through 2010, rural regions as a whole were continuing to gain population, although diminishing in their share of the U.S. population. From 2010 to 2014, however, rural America experienced its first overall loss of population, posting a net loss of 116,000 people. The population loss occurred in 1,300 rural counties in regions dependent on farming, manufacturing, or resource extraction (Kusmin 2015).

Rural populations have been declining for a longer period in the rural Midwest, central Appalachia, the South, and the midwestern and northeastern Rust Belt (Housing Assistance Council [HAC] 2012). Although a shrinking population can help reduce the demand for affordable housing, the housing stock in such areas tends to be older, less well maintained, and sometimes hazardous or obsolete. Furthermore, population loss has important implications for housing markets because vacant units quickly fall into disrepair.

Homeownership has a robust presence in rural areas. During 2013, a greater proportion of rural households were homeowners (73 percent) than of the nation as a whole (65 percent). Rural homeowners are more likely to be free of mortgage debt (48 percent) than the nation as a whole (36 percent), and their median remaining mortgage principal is less at $80,000 than the $121,324 in the nation as a whole. Several factors contribute to more prevalent homeownership in rural areas. Home prices are lower, reflecting the lower land values. During 2013, the median estimated value of owner-occupied dwellings was $120,000 in rural areas, compared with $160,000 nationwide. This difference reflects greater affordability: although the median home value in rural areas was 75 percent of the national median, the median household income in rural areas was 85 percent of the national median. A greater proportion of housing units are single-family detached structures: 72 percent in rural areas versus 64 percent nationwide. Even renters in rural areas are twice as likely to live in single-family units (43 percent) than are urban renters (HAC 2012).[9]

Despite typically lower housing costs in rural areas, those living in poverty may be unable to afford to purchase homes. In 2014, the personal poverty rate in rural areas was 16.5 percent, compared with 14.8 percent nationwide (DeNavas-Walt and Proctor 2015). A greater proportion of rural renters are in poverty than rural homeowners. Poverty rates among rural renters, at one-third, are much greater than they are for rural homeowners, with only 7 percent poverty (HAC 2012, 37).

Manufactured housing accounts for part of the greater homeownership rate and the single-family dwelling share in rural areas. It is an important source of rural housing, especially for poor households. Manufactured housing represents 5 percent of the occupied U.S. housing stock, but almost 13 percent within rural areas. Of the nation's 5.9 million occupied manufactured housing units in 2013, the majority (53 percent) were in the South. Homeowners occupied 77 percent of such units and renters 23 percent. Manufactured homes struggled against a bad reputation for decades, but safety, durability, and energy efficiency of the stock has increased dramatically since HUD began regulating manufactured housing in 1976.[10] Of the nation's 5.9 million occupied manufactured housing units in 2013, only 1 percent were reported with severe physical problems and another 4 percent with moderate physical problems; these rates differ little from those of standard site-built housing stock.[11] Improved quality and designs have helped make manufactured housing an attractive low-cost alternative to renting, but manufactured homes nevertheless lose value and offer little inherent asset-building potential without ownership of the underlying land (Boehm and Schlottman 2004).

The Housing Assistance Council (2012) highlights unique housing challenges that pertain to certain distressed rural regions. Such areas include the "colonias" settlements along the Mexican border that lack basic infrastructure, the farmworker housing of California's Central Valley, the flood-prone areas of the Lower Mississippi Delta, and remote tribal areas that have inadequate and crowded conditions. Other rural areas involved in oil and gas fracking face shortages of affordable housing that reach critical levels, but this potentially could wane when the drilling boom ends. Scenic rural areas such as the Rocky Mountains or southern Appalachia also are experiencing population growth, as are Sunbelt areas that continue to experience retiree migration (Kusmin 2015). Such upper-income migration could increase housing insecurity among lower-income residents who face rising home costs or displacement.

DEFINING AND MEASURING WORST-CASE HOUSING NEEDS

For more than twenty years, HUD has regularly measured and reported to Congress on severe housing problems that occur among renter households with very low incomes (less than 50 percent of area median income [AMI]), which qualify them for admission to federal housing assistance programs. For perspective, there were 3.4 million very low income renters in rural areas in 2013, constituting 14.8 percent of rural households.

HUD defines "worst case housing needs" as very low income renters who do not receive housing assistance and who have either a severe cost burden or live in a severely deficient housing unit. Over time, worst case needs have been increasingly dominated by severe rent burdens, which are present in almost 97 percent of worst case needs cases. About 6 percent of worst case needs cases have severe physical housing deficiencies, but only 3 percent of worst case needs result from deficiencies alone (Steffen et al. 2015).

Worst case needs increased dramatically across the nation in the past decade. Following the recession of 2007–2009, home mortgage foreclosures, job losses, and shrinking household incomes combined to increase the number of very low income renters, straining the already inadequate supply of affordable units and driving up rental costs. As a result, the number of worst case needs hit 8.5 million in 2011 before decreasing to 7.7 million in 2013 (table 10.2). Yet worst case needs were increasing even before the recession. During the ten-year span between 2003 and 2013, the tally increased 49 percent—five times the 10 percent increase in the number of U.S. households.[12]

Table 10.2   Very Low Income Renters and Those with Worst Case Needs, Nationwide and in Nonmetropolitan Areas, 2003–2013

	2003	2005	2007	2009	2011	2013
All very low income renters (thousands)	15,658	16,072	15,940	17,118	19,266	18,501
All worst case needs (thousands)	5,175	5,992	5,905	7,095	8,475	7,721
Prevalence of worst case needs	33.1%	37.3%	37.0%	41.4%	44.0%	41.7%
Nonmetropolitan very low income renters (thousands)	2,686	3,149	5,239	6,119	3,358	3,416
Nonmetropolitan worst case needs (thousands)	657	991	2,052	2,632	1,323	1,261
Prevalence of worst case needs	24.5%	31.5%	39.2%	43.0%	39.4%	36.9%

Source: Calculated by author from HUD reports to Congress on worst case housing needs, tables A-1A, A-6A, A-7 (Steffen et al. 2015).

In rural areas, worst case needs have both increased and decreased more rapidly than in the nation overall. There were 1.3 million very low income renters with worst case needs in rural areas in 2013— almost double (92 percent more than) the 2003 estimate. The statistics in table 10.2 also suggest that the surge in the number of very low income renters during the recession both began sooner and ended sooner in rural areas than it did in the nation as a whole, probably reflecting differences in rural employment markets.

In rural areas during 2013, severe housing problems afflicted 36.9 percent of the 3.4 million very low income renters, 20.1 percent of the 6.2 million renters of all incomes, and 5.5 percent of the 23.1 million households.

HOUSEHOLD TYPES AND POVERTY STATUS

Among the 3.4 million rural very low income renter households in 2013, a plurality of 1.3 million were families with children. Those that had no children included 0.8 million elderly households, 0.3 million other family households, and 1 million other nonfamily households. A majority, 60.8 percent (2.1 million), of very low income renter households in rural areas have extremely low incomes (defined as income not exceeding 30 percent of AMI). This ratio is similar to the 60 percent proportion of all very low income renters in the extremely low income group.

In considering the impact of rural poverty on housing insecurity, it is useful to understand the extent to which households classified as "poor" using the federal poverty threshold overlap with households that HUD classifies as "very low income" or "extremely low income" using AMI-based definitions (which are adjusted for family size). The national median income for a family of four was $64,400 in fiscal year 2013, but only $52,400 in rural areas (HUD 2012). Accordingly, a very low income limit, based on 50 percent of the national rural median, would be $26,200 on average in rural areas. Such a very low income definition only slightly exceeds the four-person poverty threshold of $23,834 in 2013 (U.S. Census Bureau 2013). The extremely low income limit for a family of four, at 30 percent of median, would be $15,720 on average in rural areas, significantly below the poverty threshold, but in high-cost urban areas, the extremely low income limit can exceed the poverty threshold. An estimated 58 percent of very low income renters and 88 percent of extremely low income renters are poor, showing that extremely low income is a good proxy for poverty overall.[13]

PUBLIC HOUSING ASSISTANCE

Across the nation, most deeply subsidized rental housing is provided by HUD. The Housing Choice Voucher, public housing, and assisted multifamily housing programs assist about 5 million renter households. The subsidies provided through these programs generally reduce the tenant's rent obligation to 30 percent of household income. In addition to HUD-assisted housing, the USDA's Rural Housing Service provides about 400,000 units in rural areas through the Section 515 program (HAC 2012). Similar to some of HUD's assisted multifamily programs, the Section 515 program provides interest credit rate subsidies to support affordable rental housing developments in rural areas. Another 2.2 million units of affordable rental housing have been placed in service through the Low Income Housing Tax Credit (LIHTC) program, of which roughly one-half may receive monthly rental assistance, in some cases including the deep rental assistance of HUD's Housing Choice Vouchers.[14]

The availability of housing assistance for very low income renter households is greater in rural areas than in central city and suburban areas,[15]

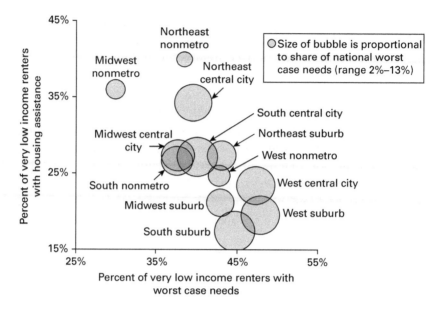

Figure 10.5 Geographic shares of worst case needs by prevalence of housing assistance and worst case needs, 2013.

and somewhat more prevalent in the Rust Belt regions—the Northeast and Midwest. The scatterplot (figure 10.5) illustrates that availability of housing assistance is inversely associated with the prevalence of worst case housing needs (Steffen et al. 2015). Although this reflects the definition that only *unassisted* very low income renters can have worst case needs, it also relates to the fact that rapid population growth within Sunbelt regions has occurred during an era of diminished federal resources for expanding housing assistance. Housing assistance has not kept up with growing need in many areas of the country.

In rural areas in 2015, 25.7 percent of renters with very low incomes received housing assistance, and 41.7 percent were unassisted and had worst case housing needs. The prevalence of housing assistance among rural very low income renters varies substantially across the country, from a low of 24.7 percent in the West to 26.6 percent in the South, 36.0 percent in the Midwest, and 40.0 percent in the Northeast. The prevalence of worst case needs in rural areas displays an inverse relationship, with a low of 30.0 percent in the Midwest, 37.5 percent in the South, 38.5 percent in the Northeast, and 42.7 percent in the West.

AFFORDABLE HOUSING SUPPLY

The principal cause of worst case needs is severe rent burdens that result from a shortage of affordable rental units. Nationwide in 2013, there were only 97.2 affordable units for every 100 very low income renters, and substantially fewer (65.3) affordable units per 100 extremely low income renters (table 10.3). Furthermore, because of suboptimal allocation, a substantial fraction of affordable units is not necessarily available to renters who need them the most. Higher-income renters often occupy less costly units than they can afford, and the most affordable vacant units of decent quality are quickly leased. Nationwide, there were only 65.2 affordable and available units per 100 very low income renters, and 39.0 affordable and available units per 100 extremely low income renters.

The affordable housing gap is somewhat less severe in rural areas. In 2013, there were 128.2 affordable units in rural areas per 100 very low income renters and 87.5 per 100 extremely low income renters. The ratios of affordable units that were actually available were also less

Table 10.3 Sufficiency of Affordable Rental Housing Stock, by Residence Area and Relative Income, 2013

Income	Income as percent of AMI	Housing units per 100 households		
		Affordable	Affordable and available	Affordable, available, and adequate
Central cities	0–30	56.6	38.2	33.0
	0–50	87.8	64.3	56.1
	0–80	132.5	101.5	90.0
Suburbs	0–30	64.4	35.3	32.5
	0–50	93.5	58.8	54.0
	0–80	138.4	98.1	91.1
Nonmetropolitan	0–30	87.5	45.3	40.7
	0–50	128.2	79.0	71.1
	0–80	142.0	105.9	95.9
Total	0–30	65.3	39.0	34.2
	0–50	97.2	65.2	58.1
	0–80	136.4	101.1	91.5

Source: HUD report to Congress on worst case housing needs, tables 2.6 and 2.8 (Steffen et al. 2015).

constrained than in the nation overall, with 79.0 units per 100 very low income renters and 45.3 per 100 extremely low income renters. The differences, however, are modest at best. Despite a looser housing market in rural areas than in the nation at large, a majority of the poorest renters in rural areas are forced to accept moderate or severe rent burdens to remain housed.

Severe housing cost burdens contribute greatly to housing insecurity or instability. When gross rent (contract rent plus utilities) consumes more than half of income, households become quite vulnerable to sudden expenses such as medical emergencies and to loss of income due to job layoffs. Such economic shocks can lead to nonpayment of rent and eviction, leaving poor options such as doubling-up with friends and family, which is often a crowded, stressful, and unstable housing situation, or becoming homeless.

EVIDENCE OF HOUSING INSECURITY

American Housing Survey (AHS) trend data suggest that renter evictions waxed and waned with the economic recession, but the changes are not statistically significant. Among renters in rural areas who moved within two years, eviction caused 1.4 percent of moves in 2007 and 2.1 percent in 2009, before declining to 1.1 percent in 2011 and 0.7 percent in 2013 (HUD 2015a).

Mortgage foreclosures also have produced new renter households. Homeownership rates in rural areas have decreased in most years since the 2005 record high of 76.3 percent, reaching 71.6 percent in 2015. The new renters helped absorb vacant rental units in rural areas, reducing the vacancy rate from 10.5 percent to 8.9 percent during the same period (HUD 2016). In 2013, an estimated 1.9 percent of recent-moving renters in rural areas were motivated by foreclosure, not significantly different from the rates of 1.7 percent in the suburbs and 0.8 percent in central cities.[16]

Among households experiencing severe housing problems, whether severe cost burdens or severe physical problems, housing insecurity is significantly higher. Table 10.4 presents estimates of the proportion of renters and owners that report various precursors and types of housing insecurity, such as missing one rent payment, missing two to three rent payments, having utilities shut off, or being threatened with eviction—as well as the self-reported prevalence of actual eviction or foreclosure. The

Table 10.4 Housing Insecurity Reported by Households with Severe Problems, by Residence Area, Tenure, and Relative Income, 2013

Income as percent of AMI	Missed 1 rent (or mortgage) payment	Missed 2–3 rent (or mortgage) payments	Utilities shut off	Threatened with eviction (renters)	Received eviction notice (renters)	Received foreclosure notice (owners)	In foreclosure (owners)
Central cities							
Renters							
All incomes	*5.1%*	*3.2%*	*2.6%*	*2.8%*	*0.8%*		
0–30% AMI	5.8%	5.7%	2.9%	3.2%	0.8%		
30–50%	5.8%	2.1%	2.6%	2.4%	—		
50%+	—	2.8%	—	1.8%	—		
Homeowners							
All incomes	*2.5%*	*5.7%*	*1.9%*			*1.3%*	*1.9%*
0–30% AMI	3.0%	6.4%	2.9%			2.0%	—
30–50%	—	7.5%	—			2.3%	1.4%
50%+	3.0%	3.7%	0.9%			1.5%	0.9%
Suburbs							
Renters							
All incomes	*4.4%*	*5.7%*	*2.3%*	*2.7%*	*0.8%*		
0–30% AMI	5.1%	6.4%	2.6%	3.3%	1.3%		
30–50%	4.1%	5.7%	2.1%	1.8%	—		
50%+	—	2.7%	—	1.8%	—		
Homeowners							
All incomes	*3.1%*	*6.4%*	*1.2%*			*2.0%*	*3.5%*
0–30% AMI	3.8%	6.6%	1.3%			3.5%	1.9%
30–50%	3.0%	7.2%	2.1%			3.4%	1.6%
50%+	2.7%	5.7%	—			3.7%	2.3%

(continued)

Table 10.4 (Continued)

Income as percent of AMI	Missed 1 rent (or mortgage) payment	Missed 2–3 rent (or mortgage) payments	Utilities shut off	Threatened with eviction (renters)	Received eviction notice (renters)	Received foreclosure notice (owners)	In foreclosure (owners)
Nonmetropolitan areas							
Renters							
All incomes	6.7%	5.8%	3.5%	3.4%	—		
0–30% AMI	8.2%	6.9%	4.2%	3.8%	—		
30–50%	4.5%	5.0%	—	—	—		
50%+	—	—	—	—	—		
Homeowners							
All incomes	5.2%	5.8%	1.4%			—	2.2%
0–30% AMI	4.4%	6.1%	0.9%			—	—
30–50%	8.2%	7.7%	—			—	—
50%+	3.7%	4.2%	1.5%			—	—

Source: HUD-PD&R tabulations of 2013 American Housing Survey data.

Note: Estimates based on fewer than five sampled cases are suppressed because they are unreliable. Foreclosure variables are percentages of owner-occupied homes with a loan secured by the property.

data include breaks by residence area and household income relative to area median income. The results suggest that the lower incomes associated with poverty generally exacerbate housing insecurity among renters, regardless of residence area, whereas housing insecurity among homeowners may have a different relationship with income. Because of limited sample sizes in rural areas, however, the differences between residence areas and income groups are not statistically significant, so no reliable conclusions can be drawn about such differences.

DOUBLING-UP IN RURAL AREAS

The American Housing Survey contains questions that shed light on households who may be doubled-up. According to 2013 AHS data (HUD 2015a), 916,000 households in rural areas (4 percent) had a household member who moved out during the previous twelve months. Some of those move-outs doubtless result from natural family dynamics and household formation, but in 27 percent of those cases the individual had been staying because he or she lacked money or financial support—which is not significantly different for central city or suburban households.[17] Among rural households with move-outs, 22 percent had more than one individual staying there. Most move-outs in rural areas, 58 percent, moved to a place of their own, similar to the 57 percent in central cities and 61 percent in the suburbs.

OPTIONS FOR THE HOUSING INSECURE

The 2013 AHS also provides insight into where renters think they would go if evicted, and where homeowners who have received a foreclosure notice would go if their loans were actually foreclosed (table 10.5). Homeowners who are facing foreclosure in central cities are significantly more likely than those in suburbs or rural areas to report that they will find a new home of their own (not necessarily an owned home).

Across all residence areas, renters with greater incomes are significantly more likely to think they would simply find a new home. Family, friends, and shelters are common resorts for the poorest families after eviction, but recent ethnographic research has shown that such alternatives do not necessarily increase housing stability (Desmond 2016). The prevalence of the "not reported" response to the AHS seen for extremely low income families suggests the possibility—consistent with Desmond's

Table 10.5 Perceived Housing Options If Households Should Be Evicted or Foreclosed, by Residence Area, Housing Tenure, and Relative Income

	Income as percent of AMI	New home (%)	Friends (%)	Family (%)	Different places (%)	Shelter (%)	Not reported (%)
Central cities							
Renters	*All incomes*	*59.6*	*9.4*	*20.4*	*1.3*	*2.1*	*7.2*
	0–30% AMI	44.9	11.0	27.6	1.6	4.7	10.3
	30–50%	57.9	10.1	22.5	0.8	3.0	5.7
	50%+	66.0	8.5	16.8	1.3	0.9	6.5
Homeowners	*All incomes*	62.8	—	24.4	—	—	—
Suburbs							
Renters	*All incomes*	*59.4*	*8.0*	*21.5*	*1.6*	*1.7*	*7.9*
	0–30% AMI	42.0	10.9	29.1	1.0	4.9	12.1
	30–50%	55.5	7.2	26.8	1.3	1.1	8.2
	50%+	65.8	7.3	17.6	1.9	0.9	6.6
Homeowners	*All incomes*	45.0	8.6	30.4	5.2	—	10.3
Nonmetropolitan areas							
Renters	*All incomes*	*56.2*	*6.5*	*27.4*	*1.2*	*1.7*	*7.0*
	0–30% AMI	41.9	5.5	38.5	2.1	3.9	8.2
	30–50%	54.1	7.9	28.8	1.1	1.8	6.4
	50%+	62.2	6.5	22.9	0.9	0.9	6.8
Homeowners	*All incomes*	42.8	—	30.8	—	—	—

Source: HUD-PD&R tabulations of 2013 American Housing Survey data.

Note: Estimates based on fewer than five sampled cases are suppressed because they are unreliable. Homeowners are included if they reported receiving a foreclosure notice.

findings—that for some of these vulnerable households, typical responses to eviction are not feasible or forethought has not occurred.

Overall, the distribution of perceived housing options for renters in case of an eviction does not differ greatly on the basis of residence area. In each residence area, evicted renters having extremely low incomes are significantly more likely than their higher-income counterparts to rely on their families.

Rural renters overall also express a significantly greater preference than central city or suburban renters for turning to family after eviction. City dwellers are more likely than rural renters to rely on friends.

RURAL HOMELESSNESS

Homelessness, defined as being forced to sleep in a place not intended for human habitation, is the most extreme variety of housing insecurity. Homelessness in rural areas is somewhat distinct from urban areas. Urban homeless individuals have greater access to shelters and transitional housing than do their rural counterparts. Rural homeless individuals and families may be living in cars, at campgrounds, "couch surfing" among friends or relatives, or doubling-up in the homes of family or friends (Trella and Hilton 2014). As such, rural homelessness tends to be somewhat hidden.

It is difficult to obtain reliable data on homelessness because federal surveys typically rely on address-based samples of respondents. HUD's Annual Homelessness Assessment Reports (AHAR) use different strategies to summarize the extent and nature of homelessness nationwide. The reports compile two types of data from state and local consortia of homeless service providers known as Continuums of Care (CoCs): annual point-in-time counts of sheltered and unsheltered homeless populations[18] and the administrative data that homeless service providers collect about sheltered populations through Homeless Management Information Systems. The 2014 AHAR thus represents the best available data about the state of homelessness, but it has limited information about rural areas because they are captured by CoCs covering the nonurban "balance of state" or entire states. The available data show a diverging trend between homelessness in urban areas and the rest of the country. The national point-in-time count during January 2014 found 578,000 homeless people, including 362,000 individuals and 216,000 people in families (HUD 2015b).

HOMELESS INDIVIDUALS IN THE 2014 POINT-IN-TIME COUNT

Forty-two percent of homeless individuals were unsheltered in 2014. CoCs in the fifty largest cities accounted for the largest share of homeless individuals: 46.1 percent of homeless individuals were found in major cities; 40.6 percent in smaller cities, suburbs, or regional CoCs; and 13.4 percent in the balance of state or statewide CoCs (Henry, Cortes, Shivji, and Buck 2014).

The count of homeless individuals in 2014 was 2 percent less than in 2013 and 13 percent less than in 2007. However, the change between 2013 and 2014 includes a slight increase of 0.4 percent in major cities, offset by decreases of 3.8 percent in the less populous smaller cities, suburbs, or regional CoCs, and of 4.7 percent in the balance of state and statewide CoCs.

HOMELESS FAMILIES IN THE 2014 POINT-IN-TIME COUNT

Homeless people in families were substantially less likely (11.3 percent) to be unsheltered during the count than the homeless individuals were. The distribution of the family homeless across CoC types was similar to homeless individuals: 45.3 percent in major city CoCs; 39.0 percent in smaller cities, suburbs, or regional CoCs; and 15.7 percent in the balance of state and statewide CoCs (Henry, Cortes, Shivji, and Buck 2014).

Like the trend for homeless individuals, the overall 2.7 percent decrease of homeless people in families conceals differences on the urban–rural dimension. Major city CoCs saw a slight increase of 1.2 percent; and the count decreased by 6.7 percent in smaller cities, suburbs, or regional CoCs and by 3.3 percent in the balance of state and statewide CoCs (Henry, Cortes, Shivji, and Buck 2014).

HOMELESS FAMILIES IN ADMINISTRATIVE DATA

Between 2007 and 2014, the number of people in families with children using shelters decreased by 5 percent in cities but increased 48.1 percent in suburban and rural areas. The number of poor families in such areas increased 29.5 percent over the same period. In the shorter period between 2013 and 2014, this sheltered family homelessness measure declined slightly (0.7 percent) in urban areas and increased 14.8 percent in suburban and rural areas (24,000 more individuals) (Solari et al. 2015, 3–12).

The sheltered families with children in suburban and rural areas during 2014 comprised 189,000 individuals, of whom 60.5 percent were children. Of the adults, more than three-fourths, 77.7 percent, were female, and 20.5 percent had a disability. The diversity on the basis of race and ethnicity reflects the economic cause of family homelessness: 38.1 percent white non-Hispanic, 15.9 percent white Hispanic, 34.6 percent black or African American, 3.9 percent other one-race, and 7.6 percent multiple races. Between 2013 and 2014, the black or African American sheltered individuals decreased in number and share, and white non-Hispanic individuals increased in number and share (Solari et al. 2015, 3–13).

As suggested by the AHS data, the homeless report shows that a substantial share of families with children who show up in shelters had been doubled-up: 27 percent of the adults nationwide had been staying with family and 15 percent had been staying with friends; 19 percent had been living in their own rented or owned home; 6 percent had been staying at a hotel or motel; and 24 percent came from an unsheltered situation (Solari et al. 2015, 3–14).

Follow-on research from a HUD-sponsored demonstration of policy options for homeless families with children suggests that those seeking shelter are as connected to the safety net as other deeply poor families and participate in SNAP at similar or higher rates. Among families in shelter in the sampled communities, 88 percent participated in SNAP, compared with 69 percent for families below 50 percent of the poverty line in the same counties. For homeless women with infants, however, families in shelter used WIC at lower rates than other families with eligible children (Burt, Khadduri, and Gubits 2016). Thus, homeless families with children seeking shelter are often connected to other elements of the public safety net such as food and nutrition assistance.

CONCLUSION

The twin forms of material deprivation discussed in this chapter, food insecurity and housing insecurity, share at least one important underlying cause: the insufficient level of household income known as poverty. The work of Ma, Gee, and Kushel (2008) demonstrates the high correlation between food insecurity and housing insecurity using the National Survey of America's Families. Their analysis of low-income[19] families with children finds that 61.9 percent of the severely food insecure have housing instability, and 66.9 percent of those with housing instability have food insecurity.

More empirical research is needed about the interrelationship between housing insecurity and food insecurity, and their causes, outcomes, and geographic distribution. The rapid increase in severe housing cost burdens since the turn of the twenty-first century has drawn awareness in the research and policy community to the need for better definition, standardization, validation, and measurement of housing insecurity in a way that better parallels successes in food insecurity research. Ma et al.

(2008) noted that there is no standard definition of housing instability at present; their working definition as "inability to pay mortgage, rent, or utility bills sometime in the prior year" is reasonable for a household with a home, but it does not capture doubling-up or homelessness, for example. This deficiency points to the inherent difficulty of measuring housing instability with a survey of households, or of housing units such as the AHS.

Despite such conceptual challenges, research about the intersection of food insecurity and housing insecurity is poised to advance in the near future. The Food Insecurity module included in the 2015 American Housing Survey should enable analysis of how severe housing cost burdens and other housing problems affect food insecurity, particularly in rural communities. Further, recent linkage of HUD administrative data with two surveys of the National Center for Health Statistics is opening new opportunities to explore the association of housing assistance programs with health and health care access, as well as food insecurity (Lloyd and Helms 2016).

Rural people and households are affected by food insecurity and housing insecurity, just as a notable portion of all American households are. In many ways, the solutions to these problems are the same for both rural and urban families. Federal nutrition and housing assistance certainly play important roles in ameliorating economic hardship for low-income families throughout the country and in rural communities. The nature of rural places creates unique challenges for the rural poor. In rural communities, limited geographic access can affect both housing and food insecurity. Housing insecurity is exacerbated by a lack of affordable rental housing units; food insecurity is exacerbated by a lack of affordable healthy food; and both problems relate to neighborhood characteristics and access. Rural poor families who face deprivation may also have limited access to local social service institutions such as food pantries or transitional housing that can provide immediate assistance to those in need.

Food insecurity and housing insecurity can be addressed by not only focusing on the symptoms of the problems—lack of adequate food and affordable housing for specific families—but also by addressing the underlying social and economic causes of the problems. Poverty and lack of economic opportunity in America's rural towns and countryside affect families in the most basic ways by limiting their ability to access the necessities of food and housing.

Questions Used to Assess the Food Security of Households in the CPS Food Security Survey

1. "We worried whether our food would run out before we got money to buy more." Was that often, sometimes, or never true for you in the last 12 months?
2. "The food that we bought just didn't last and we didn't have money to get more." Was that often, sometimes, or never true for you in the last 12 months?
3. "We couldn't afford to eat balanced meals." Was that often, sometimes, or never true for you in the last 12 months?
4. In the last 12 months, did you or other adults in the household ever cut the size of your meals or skip meals because there wasn't enough money for food? (Yes/No)
5. (If yes to question 4.) How often did this happen—almost every month, some months but not every month, or in only 1 or 2 months?
6. In the last 12 months, did you ever eat less than you felt you should because there wasn't enough money for food? (Yes/No)
7. In the last 12 months, were you ever hungry, but didn't eat, because there wasn't enough money for food? (Yes/No)
8. In the last 12 months, did you lose weight because there wasn't enough money for food? (Yes/No)
9. In the last 12 months did you or other adults in your household ever not eat for a whole day because there wasn't enough money for food? (Yes/No)
10. (If yes to question 9.) How often did this happen—almost every month, some months but not every month, or in only 1 or 2 months?

[Questions 11–18 were asked only if the household included children age 0–17.]

11. "We relied on only a few kinds of low-cost food to feed our children because we were running out of money to buy food." Was that often, sometimes, or never true for you in the last 12 months?
12. "We couldn't feed our children a balanced meal because we couldn't afford that." Was that often, sometimes, or never true for you in the last 12 months?
13. "The children were not eating enough because we just couldn't afford enough food." Was that often, sometimes, or never true for you in the last 12 months?
14. In the last 12 months, did you ever cut the size of any of the children's meals because there wasn't enough money for food? (Yes/No)
15. In the last 12 months, were the children ever hungry but you just couldn't afford more food? (Yes/No)
16. In the last 12 months, did any of the children ever skip a meal because there wasn't enough money for food? (Yes/No)
17. (If yes to question 16.) How often did this happen—almost every month, some months but not every month, or in only 1 or 2 months?
18. In the last 12 months did any of the children ever not eat for a whole day because there wasn't enough money for food? (Yes/No)

Source: Coleman-Jensen et al. (2015).

Case Study: Food Insecurity and Hunger in the Rural West

This case study is from 2011 in a rural county in Washington State with seventeen towns and a population of approximately 45,000 residents (U.S. Census Bureau 2010). The poverty level was twice the national average, and many of the towns were experiencing population and job opportunity declines, changes in grocery retailing to food deserts, and aging populations. As rural areas experience a lack of employment opportunities, increasing poverty, and declining population totals, communities also often experience local businesses closing, such as retail grocery stores (Blanchard and Lyson 2006; Kaufman 1998, 2000; Lyson and Raymer 2000). Researchers describe "food deserts" as places with no grocery or food retailing or only having a small grocer or convenience store that carries limited and expensive food items (Bitto, Morton, Oakland, and Sand 2003; Morton et al. 2005; Schafft, Jensen, and Hinrichs 2009).

Residents using community food pantries were interviewed. Charlie Wilson[1] is a 52-year-old lifelong single-male resident of Cloverdale, and his story illustrates the challenges rural low-income food-insecure individuals face with few community resources available to address hunger. Charlie discusses the changes in the area he has noticed:

> The county has changed a lot. Many of the smaller towns, like Cloverdale, had more businesses and more residents, but the area lost a lot of farming jobs. I remember as a kid driving through the different towns and the downtowns were full with different shops and cafes, most have hardly anything left anymore. It's also hard keeping the younger residents here.

For the majority of his adult life, Charlie farmed the family land passed down to him. Then, in early 2000, a major agricultural accident left him disabled. He reluctantly sold all but two acres of his land to a neighbor. He lives in the home in which he grew up and that his grandparents built, but the house is in need of major repairs. Charlie lives on limited resources and has found it very difficult to acquire enough food to last him through each month:

Things used to be easier when I was still farming, but after the accident I just couldn't do it anymore. To be honest, I would say that for a while I was depressed because my family had the land for so long and then *I lost it* [looks down at the floor]. I live on my savings and disability check, but I barely have enough to get me through each month.

Charlie answered some questions about how the issue of food deserts was affecting his food security in the changing rural landscape:

Q: *Do you shop in town for your groceries?*
A: When we had a grocery store I shopped in town, but the store closed about two years ago and so now I travel to Point View about 35 miles one-way to get groceries. Point View is the closest place I can get to that has a store with fairly good prices. Cloverdale has one convenient store left, but if you want a gallon of milk you will pay about twice as much as what you can get it for in Point View, and the expiration date is usually pretty close to being up.

The changing retail environment further challenges Charlie's ability to deal with his food insecurity. Charlie is living on a limited income, and now that he travels to purchase food the transportation expense cuts into his food budget. He shops once per month, and he has to be extremely strategic about what he buys. He eats more processed food than he would like because the shelf life of processed food is longer and his refrigerator and freezer space is limited.

Q: *Do you use any other resources to get food throughout the month?*
A: Yes, once a month Cloverdale has a food give-away at the local Grange community building. As a member of the Grange I used to provide resources [breaks eye contact and looks at the floor]; funny now I am receiving. The give-away is a blessing, but it would be nice if we got more food. Some of my friends told me I should apply for food stamps, but I just can't make myself do it. I know it might help, but I see and hear how people talk about other folks who use that assistance.
Q: *You've heard people talk negatively about residents who use food stamps?*
A: For sure, you go hungry or ask the community for support before accepting government hand-outs.

Charlie's reluctance to use food stamps speaks to the stigma this resource symbolizes in this rural setting. Charlie's views of using public assistance also mirror what other low-income individuals in the county expressed, that while going to a community pantry was embarrassing but necessary, applying for and using food stamps was out of the question.

Q: *How much food do you generally get at a give-away?*
A: One grocery bag, but if you have more people in your household then you get a little more food. One problem is [that the pantry] is only one time a month and it's not enough food to last someone for a week.
Q: *What types of items do you get at the food give-away?*
A: That's the other thing. It's a lot of food that is pretty bad for you, I mean nutritionally. You get a couple of cans of vegetables or fruit, which have high sodium or sugar, some cereal, pasta, pasta sauce, usually some sort of canned meat, and then snack items that are not very good for you. Sometimes we get fresh fruits and vegetables, but they are usually close to being rotten. I used to have a garden and would trade vegetables with my neighbors for meat. That all changed when I got hurt, I couldn't grow vegetables anymore, but my neighbors still gave me meat until they passed away.
Q: *Are there any other food resources you could use in the county?*
A: Other towns have food give-aways, but you are only supposed to go if you live in that town. I usually eat only once or twice a day; that way I have an easier time making it through the month.

Charlie's story mirrors many of the food-insecure residents in the county. The community assistance is limited by how often pantries take place and the items offered. Residents also are very reluctant to use food stamps as a strategy to address their hunger, and many participants discussed the challenges of food deserts and traveling farther to acquire food. The limited resources available in the rural setting left many residents in a perpetual cycle of food insecurity and a compromised diet.

[1] To ensure anonymity for the study area and participants, pseudonyms were used to alter the name of the county, communities, and community members, a common practice in qualitative research.

NOTES

1. The views expressed in this chapter are those of the authors and do not necessarily represent any views or policies of the U.S. Department of Housing and Urban Development, the U.S. Department of Agriculture, or the Economic Research Service.

2. In this chapter, residence area geographies supported by available government data are used. The food security and housing security estimates are for metropolitan and nonmetropolitan residence categories. Nonmetropolitan is not technically synonymous with "rural" but rural is used throughout the chapter for simplicity. Rural areas are defined as nonmetropolitan counties, in contrast to suburban areas and principal (or central) cities. Note, however, that metropolitan areas frequently include areas that are "rural" in the sense of being non-urbanized, and nonmetropolitan areas sometimes include micropolitan or other urbanized areas. Because the American Housing Survey used to describe housing characteristics is based on a panel of housing units tracked for several decades, the central city, suburb, and nonmetropolitan geographies presented follow the Metropolitan Statistical Areas defined in 1983 on the basis of the 1980 census. (The AHS for 2015 began a new sample of units.)

3. Each December the Food Security Supplement (FSS) is added to the basic monthly CPS. The monthly CPS includes about 54,000 households and is representative of the U.S. civilian, noninstitutionalized population. In 2014, 43,253 households completed the FSS. Statistics shown were calculated using CPS-FSS weights so the statistics are nationally representative. Standard errors were calculated using balanced repeated replication methods based on replicate weights computed for the CPS-FSS by the Census Bureau.

4. All households respond to ten questions about the household as a whole and adults in the household. Households with children respond to an additional eight questions about children's food conditions. The food security of each household is determined by the number of affirmative responses to the food security questions (affirmative responses to food-insecure conditions are "often," "sometimes," "almost every month," "some months but not every month," and "yes"). Households reporting no food-insecure conditions, or only one or two food-insecure conditions, are classified as food secure. Households are classified as food insecure if they report three or more food-insecure conditions. Food-insecure households without children are classified as having very low food security if they report six or more affirmative responses to food-insecure conditions. Food-insecure households with children are classified as very low food secure if they report eight or more conditions.

5. Figure 10.4 only shows food insecurity statistics by residence for the years 2004–2013. Food security prevalence statistics by area of residence are not precisely comparable with those from earlier or later years. Revised metropolitan statistical areas (MSAs) and principal cities within them were delineated by the Office of Management and Budget in 2013, based on revised standards developed by the U.S. Census Bureau in collaboration with other federal agencies. The revised delineations were implemented beginning with the 2014 Current Population Survey Food Security Supplement, so the 2014 food security statistics by area of residence are not precisely comparable with those from earlier years.

6. In these data, 73 percent of rural other non-Hispanics are Native Americans or Alaska Natives. In contrast, about 15 percent of other non-Hispanics in suburbs and 9 percent of principal city other non-Hispanics are Native Americans or Alaska Natives.

7. In 2013, 24 percent of owner-occupied dwellings overall, and 23 percent in rural areas, included one or more rooms used partially or totally for business. American Housing Survey, 2013 National Summary Tables (version 1.2), C-02-OO (HUD 2015a).

8. The most recent available data on homelessness are presented later in this chapter.

9. Homeowner statistics are drawn from the American Housing Survey, 2013 National Summary Tables (version 1.2), C-01-AO, C-01-OO, C-13-OO, and C-14A-OO (HUD 2015a). The median income statistics are from DeNavas-Walt and Proctor (2015), table 1.

10. Despite the improvements to newer manufactured housing stock, 22 percent of the occupied stock predates the 1976 HUD Code, and 66 percent predates the energy efficiency requirements of the 1996 HUD Code update (Talbot 2012).

11. Manufactured housing statistics are drawn from the American Housing Survey, 2013 National Summary Tables (version 1.2), C-01-AO and C-05-AO (HUD 2015a).

12. Estimates drawn from tables A-1a and A-1b of the corresponding Worst Case Needs reports, Steffen et al. (2015), and Hardiman et al. (2005).

13. Author's calculations from HUD report to Congress on worst case housing needs, tables A-6A, A-6B, A-7, A-8, based on tabulations of the American Housing Survey (Steffen et al. 2015).

14. Of 58.9 percent of LIHTC properties reported by state housing finance authorities in 2012, rental assistance status was reported for 68.5 percent of units, and 53 percent of those units had rental assistance. See tables 1 and 10 of Hollar (2014).

15. In HUD's classification of nonmetropolitan areas for worst case needs analysis, some rural areas within metropolitan regions are included as suburbs.

16. The authors gratefully acknowledge the assistance of George Carter of HUD's Office of Policy Development and Research for tabulating American Housing Survey data on recent movers and housing insecurity (tables 10.4 and 10.5). Statements about statistical significance related to tables 10.4 and 10.5 are based on formulas for 90 percent confidence intervals presented in HUD 2015b.

17. AHS 2013 National Summary Tables (version 1.2), S-07-AO (HUD 2015a).

18. The 2014 AHAR (Henry et al. 2014) states: "In 2014, the PIT estimates of both homeless people and beds were reported by 414 Continuums of Care (CoC) nationwide, covering virtually the entire United States. Sheltered counts are mandatory each year, and unsheltered counts are required every other year. Unsheltered counts were not required in 2014. Nonetheless, 323 CoCs (or 78 percent of all CoCs) reported unsheltered counts in 2014. For the CoCs that did not report unsheltered counts, the unsheltered counts from 2013 were rolled over into 2014."

19. Low-income for this work was defined as less than 200 percent of the federal poverty level.

REFERENCES

Bailey, Jon M. 2014. "Supplemental Nutrition Assistance Program and Rural Households." Center for Rural Affairs, Rural Family Economic Security Project. http:// files.cfra.org/pdf/snap-and-rural-households.pdf.

Bartfeld, Judi, Rachel Dunifon, Mark Nord, and Steven Carlson. 2006. "What Factors Account for State-to-State Differences in Food Security?" Economic Information Bulletin No. 20. Washington, DC: U.S. Department of Agriculture, Economic Research Service. http://www.ers.usda.gov/publications/eib-economic-information -bulletin/eib20.aspx.

Bauer, Katherine W., Rachel Widome, John H. Himes, Mary Smyth, Bonnie Holy Rock, Peter J. Hannan, and Mary Story. 2012. "High Food Insecurity and Its Correlates Among Families Living on a Rural American Indian Reservation." *American Journal of Public Health* 102(7):1346–52.

Bitto, Ella A., Lois Wright Morton, Mary Jan Oakland, and Mary Sand. 2003. "Grocery Store Access Patterns in Rural Food Deserts." *Journal for the Study of Food and Society* 6:35–48.

Blanchard, Troy, and Thomas Lyson. 2002. "Access to Low Cost Groceries in Nonmetropolitan Counties: Large Retailers and the Creation of Food Deserts." Rural Diversity Conference. http://srdc.msstate.edu/measuring/ruraldiversity.htm.

——. 2006. "Food Availability and Food Deserts in the Nonmetropolitan South." Southern Rural Development Center: Food Assistance Policy Brief Series, No. 12. Starkville, MS: Mississippi State University.

Boehm, Thomas P., and Alan Schlottmann. 2004. *Is Manufactured Housing a Good Alternative for Low-Income Families? Evidence from the American Housing Survey.* Washington, DC: U.S. Department of Housing and Urban Development, Office of Policy Development and Research.

Bread for the World Institute. 2015. "The Nourishing Effect: Ending Hunger, Improving Health, Reducing Inequality, 2016 Hunger Report." http://hungerreport.org/2016/.

Burt, Martha R., Jill Khadduri, and Daniel Gubits. 2016. "Are Homeless Families Connected to the Social Safety Net?" OPRE Report No. 2016–33. Washington, DC: U.S. Department of Health and Human Services, Administration for Children and Families, Office of Planning, Research and Evaluation. http://www.acf.hhs.gov /programs/opre/resource/are-homeless-families-connected-to-the-social-safety-net.

Coleman-Jensen, Alisha. 2012. "Predictors of U.S. Food Insecurity Across Nonmetropolitan, Suburban, and Principal City Residence During the Great Recession." *Journal of Poverty* 16(4):392–411.

——. 2015. "Commemorating 20 Years of U.S. Food Security Measurement." *Amber Waves* 13(9), 1–8. http://ers.usda.gov/amber-waves/2015-october/commemorating -20-years-of-us-food-security-measurement.aspx.

Coleman-Jensen, Alisha, William McFall, and Mark Nord. 2013. "Food Insecurity in Households with Children: Prevalence, Severity, and Household Characteristics, 2010–11." Economic Information Bulletin No. 113. Washington, DC: U.S. Department of Agriculture, Economic Research Service. http://www.ers.usda.gov/publications /eib-economic-information-bulletin/eib113.aspx.

Coleman-Jensen, Alisha, Mathew P. Rabbitt, Christian Gregory, and Anita Singh. 2015. "Household Food Security in the United States in 2014." Economic Research Report No. 194. Washington, DC: U.S. Department of Agriculture, Economic Research Service. http://www.ers.usda.gov/publications/err-economic-research-report/err194 .aspx.

Coley, Rebekah Levine, Melissa Kull, Tama Leventhal, and Alicia Doyle Lynch. 2014. "Profiles of Housing and Neighborhood Contexts Among Low-Income Families: Links with Children's Well-Being." *Cityscape: A Journal of Policy Development and Research* 16(1):37–60.

Curtis, Marah A., Hope Corman, Kelly Noonan, and Nancy E. Reichman. 2013. "Life Shocks and Homelessness." *Demography* 50:2227–53.

Cutts, Diana Becker, Alan F. Meyers, Maureen M. Black, Patrick H. Casey, Mariana Chilton, John T. Cook, Joni Geppert, Stephanie Ettinger de Cuba, Timothy Heeren, Sharon Coleman, Ruth Rose-Jacobs, and Deborah A. Frank. 2011. "U.S. Housing Insecurity and the Health of Very Young Children." *American Journal of Public Health* 101(8):1508–14.

Deidda, Manuela. 2015. "Economic Hardship, Housing Cost Burden and Tenure Status: Evidence from EU-SILC." *Journal of Family and Economic Issues* 36(4):531–56.

DeNavas-Walt, Carmen, and Bernadette D. Proctor. 2015. "Income and Poverty in the United States: 2014." Current Population Reports. P60–252. Washington, DC: U.S. Census Bureau.

Desmond, Matthew. 2016. *Evicted: Poverty and Profit in the American City.* New York, NY: Crown Publishers.

Food Research and Action Center. 2014. "Food Security, Health, and Well-Being." FRAC E-pub, Food Insecurity and Hunger in the United States: New Research, April. http://frac.org/pdf/frac-chw_food_insecurity_hunger_research_april2014.pdf.

Gregory, Christian A., and Alisha Coleman-Jensen. 2013. "Do High Food Prices Increase Food Insecurity in the United States?" *Applied Economic Perspectives and Policy* 35(4):679–707.

Gundersen, Craig, and James P. Ziliak. 2014. "Childhood Food Insecurity in the U.S.: Trends, Causes, and Policy Options." Future of Children, Fall Research Report. http://www.princeton.edu/futureofchildren/publications/journals/journal_details/index.xml?journalid=82.

Hardiman, David, Marge Martin, Mark Shroder, Barry Steffen, Scott Susin, David Vandenbroucke, and David Yao. 2005. *Affordable Housing Needs 2003: A Report to Congress on the Significant Need for Housing.* Washington, DC: Office of Policy Development and Research, U.S. Department of Housing and Urban Development.

Hardin-Fanning, Frances, and Mary Kay Rayens. 2015. "Food Cost Disparities in Rural Communities." *Health Promotion Practice* 16(3):383–91.

Henry, Meghan, Alvaro Cortes, Azim Shivji, and Katherine Buck. 2014. *The 2014 Annual Homeless Assessment Report (AHAR) to Congress: Part 1—Annual Point-in-Time Counts.* Washington, DC: Office of Community Planning and Development, U.S. Department of Housing and Urban Development.

Henry, Meghan, and William M. Sermons. 2010. "Geography of Homelessness." Research Reports on Homelessness. http://www.endhomelessness.org/library/entry/geography-of-homelessness.

Hollar, Michael K. 2014. *Understanding Whom the LIHTC Program Serves: Tenants in LIHTC Units as of December 31, 2012.* Washington, DC: Office of Policy Development and Research, U.S. Department of Housing and Urban Development. www.huduser.gov.

Housing Assistance Council. 2012. *Taking Stock: Rural People, Poverty, and Housing in the 21st Century.* Washington, DC: Housing Assistance Council. http://www.ruraldataportal.org/docs/HAC_Taking-Stock-Full.pdf.

Kaufman, Phil R. 1998. "Rural Poor Have Less Access to Supermarkets, Large Grocery Stores." *Rural Development Perspectives* 13:19–26.

———. 2000. "Consolidation in Food Retailing: Prospects for Consumers & Grocery Suppliers." *Agricultural Outlook* 273:18–22.

Kushel, Margot B., Reena Gupta, Lauren Gee, and Jennifer S. Haas. 2006. "Housing Instability and Food Insecurity as Barriers to Health Care Among Low-Income Americans." *Journal of General Internal Medicine* 21(1):71–77.

Kusmin, Lorin D. 2015. "Rural America at a Glance: 2015 Edition." Economic Information Bulletin No. 145. Washington, DC: U.S. Department of Agriculture, Economic Research Service. http://www.ers.usda.gov/publications/eib-economic-information-bulletin/eib-145.aspx.

Lloyd, Patricia C., and Veronica E. Helms. 2016. "NCHS-HUD Linked Data: Analytic Considerations and Guidelines." Hyattsville, MD: National Center for Health Statistics, Office of Analysis and Epidemiology. https://www.cdc.gov/nchs/data-linkage/hud-methods.htm.

Lyson, Thomas, and Annalisa Raymer. 2000. "Stalking the Wily Multinational: Power and Control in the U.S. Food System." *Agriculture and Human Values* 17(2):199–208.

Ma, Christine T., Lauren Gee, and Margot B. Kushel. 2008. "Associations Between Housing Instability and Food Insecurity with Health Care Access in Low-Income Children." *Ambulatory Pediatrics* 8(1):50–57.

Mabli, James. 2014. "SNAP Participation and Urban and Rural Food Security." Mathematica Policy Research, U.S. Department of Agriculture, Food and Nutrition Service. http://www.fns.usda.gov/measuring-effect-snap-participation-food-security-0.

Mabli, James, Jim Ohls, Lisa Dragoset, Laura Castner, and Betsy Santos. 2013. "Measuring the Effect of Supplemental Nutrition Assistance Program (SNAP) Participation on Food Security." USDA, Food and Nutrition Service. http://www.fns.usda.gov/sites/default/files/Measuring2013.pdf.

McConnell, Sheena, and James Ohls. 2002. "Food Stamps in Rural America: Special Issues and Common Themes." In *Rural Dimensions of Welfare Reform*, ed. Bruce A. Weber, Greg J. Duncan, and Leslie A. Whitener, chap. 14. Kalamazoo, MI: Upjohn Institute.

Meyers, Alan, Deborah A. Frank, Nicole Roos, Karen E. Peterson, Virginia A. Casey, L. Adrienne Cupples, and Suzette M. Levenson. 1995. "Housing Subsidies and Pediatric Undernutrition." *Archives of Pediatric Adolescent Medicine* 149(10):1079–84.

Mitchell, J. Paul. 1985. *Federal Housing Policy and Programs: Past and Present.* New Brunswick, NJ: Center for Urban Policy Research.

Molnar, Joseph J., Patricia A. Duffy, Latoya Claxton, and Conner Bailey. 2001. "Private Food Assistance in a Small Metropolitan Area: Urban Resources and Rural Needs." *Journal of Sociology and Social Welfare* 28:187–209.

Morton, Louis Wright, Ella A. Bitto, Mary Jane Oakland, and Mary Sand. 2005. "Solving the Problems of Iowa Food Deserts: Food Insecurity and Civic Structure." *Rural Sociology* 70:94–112.

———. 2008. "Accessing Food Resources: Rural and Urban Patterns of Giving and Getting Food." *Agriculture and Human Values* 25:107–19.

Newman, Sandra J., and C. Scott Holupka. 2014. "Housing Affordability and Child Well-Being." *Housing Policy Debate*. doi: 10.1080/10511482.2014.899261.

Nord, Mark, Alisha Coleman-Jensen, and Christian Gregory. 2014. "Prevalence of U.S. Food Insecurity Is Related to Changes in Unemployment, Inflation, and the Price of Food." Economic Research Report No. 167. Washington, DC: U.S. Department of Agriculture, Economic Research Service. http://www.ers.usda.gov/publications/err-economic-research-report/err167.aspx.

Nord, Mark, and Mark Prell. 2011. "Food Security Improved Following the 2009 Increase in SNAP Benefits." Economic Research Report No. 116. Washington, DC: U.S. Department of Agriculture, Economic Research Service. http://ers.usda.gov/publications/err-economic-research-report/err116.aspx.

Oliveira, Victor. 2015. "The Food Assistance Landscape: Fiscal Year 2014 Annual Report." Economic Information Bulletin No. 137. Washington, DC: U.S. Department of Agriculture, Economic Research Service. http://www.ers.usda.gov/publications/eib-economic-information-bulletin/eib137.aspx.

Olson, Christine M., Barbara S. Rauschenbach, Edward A. Frongillo Jr., and Anne Kendall. 1997. "Factors Contributing to Household Food Insecurity in a Rural Upstate New York County." *Family Economics and Nutrition Review* 10:2–17.

Ortiz, Selena E., and Frederick J. Zimmerman. 2013. "Race/Ethnicity and the Relationship Between Homeownership and Health." *American Journal of Public Health* 103(4):122–29.

Pelletiere, Danilo. 2008. "Getting to the Heart of Housing's Fundamental Question: How Much Can a Family Afford?" Washington, DC: National Low Income Housing Coalition.

Piontak, Joy Rayanne, and Michael D. Schulman. 2014. "Food Insecurity in Rural America." *Contexts* 13(3):75–77.

Ratcliffe, Caroline, and Signe-Mary McKernan. 2011. "How Much Does the Supplemental Nutrition Assistance Program Reduce Food Insecurity?" *American Journal of Agricultural Economics* 93(4):1082–98.

Schafft, Kai A., Eric B. Jensen, and Clare Hinrichs. 2009. "Food Deserts and Overweight Schoolchildren: Evidence from Pennsylvania." *Rural Sociology* 74:153–77.

Sherman, Jennifer. 2006. "Coping with Rural Poverty: Economic Survival and Moral Capital in Rural America." *Social Forces,* 85(2):891–913.

Solari, Claudia D., Stephanie Althoff, Korrin Bishop, Zachery Epstein, Sean Morris, and Azim Shivji. 2015. *The 2014 Annual Homeless Assessment Report (AHAR) to Congress: Part 2—Estimates of Homelessness in the United States.* Washington, DC: Office of Community Planning and Development, U.S. Department of Housing and Urban Development. https://www.hudexchange.info/hdx/guides/ahar/.

Steffen, Barry L., George R. Carter, Marge Martin, Danilo Pelletiere, David A. Vandenbroucke, Yunn-Gan David Yao. 2015. *Worst Case Housing Needs: 2015 Report to Congress.* Washington, DC: Office of Policy Development and Research, U.S. Department of Housing and Urban Development.

Stone, Michael E. 2004. "Shelter Poverty: The Chronic Crisis of Housing Affordability." *New England Journal of Public Policy.* 20(1):Article 16. http://scholarworks.umb.edu /nejpp/vol20/iss1/16.

Stracuzzi, Nena, and Sally Ward. 2010. "What's for Dinner? Finding and Affording Healthy Foods in New Hampshire Communities." New England Issue Brief No. 21. Durham, NH: University of New Hampshire, Carsey Institute.

Talbot, Jacob. 2012. "Mobilizing Energy Efficiency in the Manufactured Housing Sector." American Council for an Energy Efficient Economy Report No. A124. http://aceee .org/research-report/a124.

Tickamyer, Ann R., and Debra A. Henderson. 2011. "Livelihood Practices in the Shadow of Welfare Reform." In *Economic Restructuring and Family Well-Being in Rural America,* ed. Kristin E. Smith and Ann R. Tickamyer, chap. 16. University Park: Pennsylvania State University Press.

Trella, Deanna L., and Timothy P. Hilton. 2014. "'They Can Only Do So Much': Use of Family While Coping with Rural Homelessness." *Contemporary Rural Social Work* 6:16–39.

U.S. Census Bureau. 2010. "Summary of Files and American FactFinder." http://fact-finder2.census.gov.

———. 2013. "Poverty Thresholds for 2013 by Size of Family and Number of Related Children Under 18 Years." https://www2.census.gov/programs-surveys/cps/tables /time-series/historical-poverty-thresholds/thresh13.xls.

U.S. Department of Agriculture. 2009. "Access to Affordable and Nutritious Food: Measuring and Understanding Food Deserts and Their Consequences." Administrative Publication No. AP-036. Washington, DC: U.S. Department of Agriculture, Economic Research Service. http://www.ers.usda.gov/Publications/AP/AP036 /AP036.pdf.

———. 2015. "Trends in Supplemental Nutrition Assistance Program Participation Rates: Fiscal Year 2010 to Fiscal Year 2013." Nutrition Assistance Program Report Series, Office of Policy Support. Washington, DC: U.S. Department of Agriculture, Food and Nutrition Service. http://www.fns.usda.gov/sites/default/files/ops /Trends2010-2013.pdf.

U.S. Department of Housing and Urban Development. 2016. "U.S. Housing Market Conditions: Ownership and Vacancy Data." Washington, DC: U.S. Department of Housing and Urban Development, Office of Policy Development and Research. https://www.huduser.gov/portal/ushmc/hi_HOR.html.

———. 2012. "FY 2013 HUD Income Limits Briefing Material," Attachment 6. https:// www.huduser.gov/portal/datasets/il/il13/index.html.

U.S. Department of Housing and Urban Development and U.S. Census Bureau. 2015a. *American Housing Survey for the United States: 2013 National Summary Tables (version 1.2).* https://www.census.gov/programs-surveys/ahs/data/2013/ahs-2013-summary -tables/national-summary-report-and-tables---ahs-2013.html.

———. 2015b. "Appendix D. Nonsampling and Sampling Errors." *Codebook for the American Housing Survey, Public Use File: 1997 and later.* https://www.census.gov/content /dam/Census/programs-surveys/ahs/tech-documentation/AHS%20Codebook%20 2013.pdf; http://www2.census.gov/programs-surveys/ahs/2013/2013%20AHS%20 National%20Errors.pdf.

———. 2017. "Overview." Last modified February 21. https://www.ers.usda.gov/topics/food-nutrition-assistance/food-security-in-the-us.aspx.

Warren, Emily J., and Sarah A. Font. 2015. "Housing Insecurity, Maternal Stress, and Child Maltreatment: An Application of the Family Stress Model." *Social Service Review* 89(1):9–39.

Webber, Caroline B., and Arezoo Rojhani. 2010. "Food or Fuel: Rising Gasoline Prices and Food Access Among WIC Families in Nonmetropolitan Southwest Michigan." *Journal of Hunger and Environmental Nutrition* 5(4):484–97.

Whitley, Sarah. 2013. "Changing Times in Rural America: Food Assistance and Food Insecurity in Food Deserts." *Journal of Family Social Work* 16(1):36–52.

Zimmerman, Julie N., Sunny Ham, and Sarah M. Frank. 2008. "Does It or Doesn't It? Geographic Differences and the Costs of Living." *Rural Sociology* 73(3):463–86.

Ziol-Guest, Kathleen M., and Claire C. McKenna. 2014. "Early Childhood Housing Instability and School Readiness." *Child Development* 85(1):103–13.

CHAPTER 11

The Environment and Health

Danielle Christine Rhubart and Elyzabeth W. Engle

In the early 1980s, the people of Warren County, a rural, low-income area of North Carolina, learned that the state planned to put a hazardous waste landfill in their community. The landfill would become home to six thousand truckloads of toxic soil. In protest against the expected landfill and the health implications it would pose for the community, residents organized nonviolent protests against the state that garnered national media attention. In the end, approximately five hundred protesters were arrested, and the state moved forward with plans for the landfill. Although residents lost this battle, the grassroots organizing that occurred in Warren County to oppose an environmental hazard and its effects on human health is considered one of the first battles of what has become known as the environmental justice movement (Bullard 2000; Taylor 2014).

This chapter examines some of the environmental hazards facing rural areas of the United States and considers their impacts on the health status of rural communities and residents. The primary focus is on low-income rural communities that have borne a disproportionally large share of environmental burdens. These issues are linked to environmental justice literature, which helps to explain the historical, cultural, and socioeconomic processes that led to environmental and, subsequently, health inequities. This chapter draws on a concept developed by Michael Bell (2012) that he called *invironment*, which refers to the interconnectedness of the environment and individual health. Our bodies are, in fact, part of the invironment. This concept is a central tenant of the chapter because of its inherent acknowledgment of the interconnected relationship between our bodies and the environment. In this chapter, the word *environment* refers to the ecological, social, and economic processes that are removed

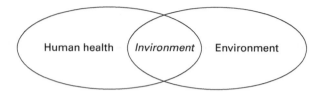

Figure 11.1   The distinction between the environment and the invironment.

from our individual lives. Figure 11.1 illustrates the distinction between the environment and the invironment.

The chapter begins with a background on environmental justice and then explores the invironmental impacts of environmental hazards on the health and well-being of low-income rural communities across multiple issues, including energy resource development, agriculture, climate change, and waste facility siting. Then the context of health care and disparities in health outcomes in rural America are examined to explicate the dynamic relationship between environmental hazards and the health of low-income rural communities.

BACKGROUND

Since the late 1970s and early 1980s, the environmental justice movement has grown as a tool for grassroots advocacy as well as an area of study (Bullard 2000; Brulle and Pellow 2006). In the years that followed, hundreds of organized efforts against environmental hazards occurred across both rural and urban communities in the United States. What unites all of these efforts is the desire (1) to ensure that all voices are included in the decision-making processes about environmental hazards *and* benefits, (2) to reduce the incidence of environmental hazards, and (3) to ensure environmental hazards are not disproportionately experienced by low-income and vulnerable populations. More recently, the Environmental Protection Agency (EPA) has institutionalized the values of environmental justice in its policy and regulatory processes. The EPA (2016a) defines environmental justice as "the fair treatment and meaningful involvement of all people regardless of race, color, national origin, or income, with respect to the development, implementation, and enforcement of environmental laws, regulations, and policies." This definition demonstrates the regulatory agency's commitment to increasing inclusivity of all voices in the policy process, emphasizing two different dimensions of justice: *distributive justice*, or who receives or is exposed to environmental "goods" and "bads"; and *procedural justice*, or fair access to information, participation in decision-making processes, and access to legal procedures (Walker 2012). Gordon Walker (2012) recognizes a third dimension of justice, *justice as recognition*, which considers who is (or who is not) given respect or valued within environmental or social issues. Because this chapter focuses on the health dimensions of environmental justice among impoverished rural populations driven by exposure and proximity to environmental hazards, it primarily considers the first dimension of justice—distributive justice.

More than two decades of environmental justice studies in the United States have overwhelmingly shown that, in general, ethnic minorities, indigenous people, people of color, and low-income communities experience a larger burden of harmful environmental exposure from air, water, and soil pollution from industrialization, militarization, and consumer practices than other citizens do (Mohai, Pellow, and Roberts 2009). These vulnerable populations are overrepresented among the rural poor (see chapters 1 and 6), making environmental justice a pressing concern for rural scholars, practitioners, and policy makers. In many ways, rural America may be considered a "dumping ground" for locally undesirable land uses (LULUs) that have important implications for environmental and human health (Lichter and Brown 2011, 582). The siting of LULUs often takes advantage of low-income rural people and places that are fundamentally powerless due to their dire need for economic development and job creation as well as their exclusion from extra-local decision-making processes (Mohai and Saha 2006; Lichter and Brown 2011; Pellow 2016). Yet, as David Pellow (2016, 381) points out, "the rural dimensions of environmental justice studies have long been present, but generally only in the background, rarely foregrounded, centered, or taken seriously as a social, ecological, cultural, economic, and political category that shapes [environmental justice] struggles every day."

THE PHYSICAL ENVIRONMENT

The term *environmental hazards* brings many different ideas of pollution to mind. This section provides an overview of four physical environment issues—energy resource development, agriculture, climate change, and

waste facility siting—that affect the invironmental conditions of vulnerable rural populations, including community and individual health. The
industries discussed in this section are overwhelmingly located in rural
places, meaning they affect rural residents not only through proximity
and exposure but also through occupational conditions because a larger
share of rural people are employed in mining and agriculture industries compared to urban residents (McGranahan 2003; Bureau of Labor
Statistics [BLS] 2014).

ENERGY RESOURCE DEVELOPMENT

When considering the environmental and human health impacts of
energy development, the extraction of fossil fuels has received the majority of attention from scholars and activists alike. Rural areas that have
experienced a great deal of energy development—such as coal mining,
natural gas extraction, and petroleum drilling—may be known as "energy
sacrifice zones" or "places that are exploited for the purpose of supplying cheap fossil fuels and electricity to power the world's growing energy
demands" (Harlan et al. 2015, 137). From extraction to processing to handling waste by-products, different types of energy resource development
are linked to negative environmental and human health consequences for
residents and employees.

One particular type of energy resource development often connected
to rural environmental (in)justice is mountaintop removal, a surface-
level coal mining process by which coal seams running through the
upper portion of a mountain are mined by blasting and removing all
of the overlying rock and soil to create a level work surface (Bell 2016;
U.S. Energy Information Administration 2015). This type of energy
extraction is largely concentrated in the region of central Appalachia
(West Virginia, southwest Virginia, and eastern Kentucky and
Tennessee), which is predominantly rural and has high rates of poverty
and unemployment (Partridge, Betz, and Lobao 2013; Tallichet 2014).
Mountaintop removal, in addition to the traditional underground coal
mining that also is concentrated in this region, has contributed to invironmental health degradation through increased instances of intense
flood events, soil erosion and landslides, water contamination, and
air and noise pollution (Bell 2016). When compared to the rest of the
United States, the coal-mining subregions of Appalachia in particular
are plagued by higher rates of chronic illness, birth defects, cancer, and

mortality, even after controlling for the lower socioeconomic indicators of these subregions (Hendryx 2008, 2011; Ahern et al. 2011).

Coal production in central Appalachia is linked to negative inviron-mental consequences through waste impoundments in which hazard-ous wastewater and slurry are stored behind hazardous dams. These impoundments are more likely to be located near neighborhoods with higher rates of poverty and unemployment (Greenberg 2016). History has documented several instances of impoundment dam failure in which coal slurry floods have killed hundreds of people, left thousands more home-less, and utterly destroyed local ecosystems and drinking water sources (Erikson 1976; Morrone and Buckley 2011). In addition to the effects on general population health, coal extraction in this region is inextri-cably linked to particular occupational health issues, such as coal work-ers' pneumoconiosis (CWP), commonly known as black lung. This is a chronic, and often fatal, lung disease caused by the long-term inhala-tion of dust generated in coal production, rates of which have unexpect-edly risen in recent years among central Appalachian miners (Centers for Disease Control and Prevention [CDC] 2012b).

Other forms of energy development also have been linked to det-rimental environmental and human health conditions. Several studies have found that residential proximity to natural gas wells may be asso-ciated with a heightened prevalence of skin, neurological, gastrointes-tinal, and respiratory conditions through exposures to air and water contaminants (Bamberger and Oswald 2012; Steinzor, Subra, and Sumi 2013; Rabinowitz et al. 2015). Fossil fuel extraction is not the only type of energy development with negative implications for vulnerable rural people and places. Proximity to nuclear power plants and ura-nium mining are associated with increased risk of cancer, birth defects, and hereditary illnesses in neighboring communities through environ-mental contamination and radiation exposure (Vakil and Harvey 2009; Malin 2015). Hydroelectric dams have been linked to compromised invironmental health through dam failure and flooding, loss of food security, increased exposure to vector-borne and water-related diseases, and reservoir-induced seismicity (Lerer and Scudder 1999). Several such dams are located throughout rural America, some in very close proxim-ity to vulnerable areas such as Native American reservations and the controversial Grand Coulee Dam in Washington, the largest electric power-producing facility in the United States (U.S. Energy Information Administration 2016).

AGRICULTURE

Agricultural production processes also pose consequences for the invironmental conditions of rural populations. One prominent focus of research has been on the impacts of pesticide use in industrial agriculture on farmworkers and surrounding agricultural communities. Although pesticides vary widely in their human toxicity, many used in U.S.-based agriculture contribute to both acute short-term illnesses and chronic long-lasting illnesses, such as cancer, reproductive and developmental problems, endocrine disruption, respiratory disorders, and immune system depression (Harrison 2011, 31). The estimated number of total pesticide poisonings annually in the United States is around 300,000, with Latino populations being more commonly affected (Carolan 2016). Farmworkers, predominantly those who are low-wage, nonwhite, and without access to health care, are exposed to pesticides routinely through mixing and applying pesticides to crops and during ongoing planting, maintenance, and harvesting of crops (Carolan 2016). Due to job insecurity and financial pressures to work rapidly, farmworkers also tend to underreport exposure-related illnesses, delay decontamination and treatment practices, and only selectively use protective equipment in the field (Snipes et al. 2009; Thierry and Snipes 2015).

The issue of exposure to toxic pesticides does not stop at the edge of the field; exposure continues for farmworkers and their families as they eat pesticide-contaminated foods from their place of work and carry home pesticides on their clothing (Carolan 2016). Exposure is also an issue for communities neighboring industrial agriculture operations by way of pesticide drift, which occurs when pesticides move (via wind or water) from the area in which they were applied to nearby localities and people (Harrison 2011; Guthman and Brown 2016). Just like the issue of farmworker exposure, the communities that fall victim to pesticide drift are often impoverished, nonwhite, immigrant populations, largely in California where industrial production of fruits and vegetables still relies heavily on the use of pesticide additives (Harrison 2008). In addition to pesticides, other agricultural contaminants can affect environmental and human health. Fertilizer runoff results in nutrient pollution of surface and ground water, which is connected to skin irritation, stomach or liver illness, respiratory problems, and neurological effects (EPA 2016b). Drinking water containing nitrates, a particular compound found in fertilizers, is linked to a serious and often fatal health condition in infants known as blue baby syndrome (EPA 2016b).

Another agricultural issue that negatively affects the invironmental conditions of low-income, rural communities is concentrated animal feeding operations (CAFOs), which are a specific type of large-scale industrial agriculture facility that raises animals in very dense populations for the human consumption of meat, eggs, or milk and whose waste comes into contact with the local water supply (Hribar 2010). The invironmental issues associated with CAFOs concern the amount of manure they produce, which is known to contain a variety of contaminants that negatively affect water and air quality, and consequently nearby residents. These contaminants include excessive nutrients (e.g., nitrogen and phosphorus), animal-borne pathogens such as *E. coli*, growth hormones, antibiotics, and chemical additives (Hribar 2010). They have been connected to a variety of chronic respiratory, gastrointestinal, and neurological illnesses, as well as to more acute conditions of skin/eye irritation and joint/muscle pain (Wing and Wolf 2000). Several studies have shown that CAFOs (and their ill effects) are more likely to be concentrated near rural communities with a higher prevalence of low-income and racial/ethnic minority populations (Wing and Wolf 2000; Wing, Cole, and Grant 2000; Donham et al. 2007). CAFO workers, who are even more drastically exposed to these invironmental hazards, are also made up primarily of low-income and racial/ethnic minority workers, who are predominantly Hispanic and foreign-born (Mitloehner and Calvo 2008). More than 25 percent of CAFO workers develop a range of respiratory diseases, and exposure to high concentrations of bio-aerosols has been linked to organic dust toxic syndrome, a condition that affects more than 30 percent of workers in the swine industry alone (Donham et al. 2007).

CLIMATE CHANGE

Climate change and human health are intrinsically linked in the invironment. Human-induced climate change is associated with increases in extreme temperatures and precipitation (Fischer and Knutti 2015). The National Institute of Environmental Health has issued concerns about a number of health illnesses that could increase as a result of extreme temperatures and precipitation. These include asthma, allergies, cancers (via increased ultraviolet radiation), cardiovascular issues (via heat stress and air quality), water-borne disease, and weather/heat related morbidity and mortality (Berko 2014; Portier et al.

2010). Similar findings are reported by the Intergovernmental Panel on Climate Change (IPCC). The IPCC's 2014 report links climate change to negative health effects via extreme temperatures, flooding and storms, and ultraviolet radiation. These weather changes lead to increased heat-induced illness and death, air pollutant–induced illness, as well as increases in morbidity and mortality due to food- and water-borne diseases.

These invironmental impacts are not evenly distributed across the United States. For instance, rural counties experienced the highest rates of cold-related mortality and flood-storm-lightning-related mortality from 2006 to 2010 (Berko 2014). This may be the product of the types of occupations and recreational activities available in rural counties as well as distance to trauma centers. In addition, severe weather changes affect rural livelihoods because unpredictable growing seasons raise issues of food and occupational insecurity, especially for those employed in the agricultural sector. Environmental risks are not determined by climate alone, but also by a rural community's ability to adapt (Gutierrez and LePrevost 2016; Davidson, Williamson, and Parkins 2003). Rural communities that experience increases in severe weather are dependent on fire departments and emergency medical services teams that are volunteer-based. Depressed places have weaker safety nets and deteriorating infrastructure and may be unable to meet the needs of people during natural disasters.

Finally, many rural communities are centered around tourism, which is being affected by climate change. Rural communities are already disproportionally more vulnerable due to a lack of occupational diversity (EPA 2011; Adger, Lorenzoni, and O'Brien 2009), and depressed or unstable economic conditions will undoubtedly affect rural people's health and well-being by restricting their access to positive health behaviors (e.g., healthy foods) as well as access to health care. These challenges in tourism-based communities are exacerbated by the affects of climate change. For example, estimates show that unstable snowfalls and increased overall temperatures will negatively affect winter sport tourism in the decades ahead unless communities actively use adaptation strategies (Scott, McBoyle, and Mills 2003). Adaptation and mitigation policies and strategies are needed to prepare rural communities (Jensen 2009) for invironmental changes. Coupled with climate change mitigation, this will be essential in supporting the environmental and human health of low-income rural communities.

WASTE FACILITY SITING

The 1980s and 1990s were a period of realization of the invironmental inequalities associated with hazardous waste and dumping. This was also the era when environmental justice literature began substantiating the gross inequalities of hazardous waste dumping. The EPA (2016c) defines hazardous waste as "a waste with properties that make it dangerous or capable of having a harmful effect on human health or the environment. Hazardous waste is generated from many sources, ranging from indus-trial manufacturing process wastes to batteries and may come in many forms, including liquids, solids, gases, and sludges." Facilities that pro-duce, store, or dispose of hazardous waste are more likely to be located in low-income and rural areas. Research suggests that rural America has become a dumping ground for urban America (Lichter and Brown 2011). For example, Bullard (2000) found that hazardous waste facilities were disproportionately located in rural minority communities in the South. Similar studies on other types of waste facilities have found waste sites are more likely to be located in working-class communities, in communi-ties with larger shares of minorities, and in low population density areas (Davidson and Anderton 2000; Kearney and Kiros 2009; Atlas 2002). Public and private agencies have targeted Native American reservations as well—populations plagued by generations of socioeconomic vulner-ability and lagging improvements in disease treatment—to act as sites for the storage and disposal of hazardous nuclear waste (Randel 2001; Brook 1998). The unequitable distribution of these facilities is a manifestation of decades of distributive injustices when inclusivity of all voices in the policy process was not prioritized.

The strategic placement of waste facilities in low-income, minority, and indigenous rural communities can have profound invironmental affects on health disparities. The health implications of living or work-ing around hazardous waste sites are extensive (Brender, Maantay, and Chakraborty 2011). For example, risk of brain cancer among children is higher for those whose mothers lived within one mile of industries that were listed on the Toxic Release Inventory during pregnancy (Choi, Shim, Kaye, and Ryan 2006). Reproductive outcomes and, in particular, chro-mosomal abnormalities, including neural tube defects and heart defects, have been linked to a mother's residential proximity to hazardous waste landfill sites (Vrijheid et al. 2002; Croen et al. 1997). Residence near waste sites has been linked to higher rates of diabetes in New York State

(Kouznetsova et al. 2007) even after controlling for other determinants of diabetes including smoking status, diet, exercise, and income. For the Native American tribes' land targeted for nuclear and hazardous waste storage and disposal, the physical environmental risks to the health of these populations exacerbates their already elevated risks of certain types of cancers, which have been found in regional analyses (Weaver 2010; White et al. 2014; Hoffman et al. 2014). The health implications of living or working near hazardous waste, coupled with the fact that these waste sites are disproportionality located in rural and low-income communities, require a new approach to determining where and how waste is disposed as well as investment in mitigating the current environmental and human health consequences of hazardous waste.

THE HEALTH CARE ENVIRONMENT

The invironmental relationships between environmental hazards and the health of low-income populations in rural America is mediated by the level of access to quality health care. Lack of access to care can be explained by many factors, including financial and geographic barriers (Comber, Brunsdon, and Radburn 2011). This section discusses the state of rural health care, including how and to what extent federal health care reform has improved access to quality care in low-income rural America to be able to treat the health consequences of environmental hazards.

The financial barriers to accessing health care have been at the center of national discourse in the past decade. The Patient Protection and Affordable Care Act (ACA) sought to expand access to insurance to low-income populations to rid economically vulnerable populations of this barrier. The Medicaid expansion component of the ACA was a key part of the health care reform package. It sought to create equal access to Medicaid—including among childless adults. Prior to expansion, eligibility for Medicaid varied drastically by state, both in terms of income eligibility thresholds and whether childless adults were eligible. The Supreme Court's 2012 ruling on the *National Federation of Independent Business v. Sebelius* resulted in states having the ability to refuse to expand Medicaid. Nearly half of states opted out of Medicaid expansion in 2014. In these states, there is what is called a "coverage gap." The coverage gap represents those individuals who make too much to qualify for Medicaid but too little to afford insurance through the newly created health insurance marketplaces, even with federal tax credits. According to the Kaiser Family

Table 11.1 Average County-Level Percent Insured by Metropolitan Status and Whether the County Is in a State That Expanded Medicaid, 2013–2014

Types of counties	Average county-level percent insured, 2013		Average county-level percent insured, 2014	
	Expanded Medicaid	Did not expand Medicaid	Expanded Medicaid	Did not expand Medicaid
Completely rural	80.00	75.96	86.55	79.37
Medium nonmetro	81.22	75.88	86.78	78.73
Large nonmetro	81.75	77.47	86.86	80.28
Medium metro	82.32	78.37	87.50	81.29
Large metro	84.88	79.64	89.03	82.57

Source: Author's analysis of Small Area Health Insurance Estimates for 2013–2014 from U.S. Census Bureau (2015).

Foundation, "nearly two-thirds of uninsured people in rural areas live in a state that is not currently implementing the Medicaid expansion" (Newkirk and Damico 2014).

The county-level health insurance coverage rate for rural and urban counties in states that did and did not expand Medicaid is presented in table 11.1. In 2013, before Medicaid expansion, counties in states that would eventually choose not to expand Medicaid already lagged behind in terms of county-level health insurance coverage rates. On January 1, 2014, when Medicaid expansion was rolled out, nearly half of state leaders chose not to participate. Although nearly all counties in all states experienced increases in coverage rates from 2013 to 2014, the disparity between counties in states that did or did not expand Medicaid has increased. Other state and county-level factors explain why states that would eventually opt out of Medicaid had lower rates of county-level coverage to begin with, but Medicaid expansion exacerbated these disparities, leaving behind states whose leaders had chosen not to expand. Moreover, across both years and among both counties in states that did and did not expand Medicaid, the coverage rates in nonmetro and rural counties continue to lag behind those of metro counties. Therefore, we can expect that rural and nonmetro counties will continue to lag behind but even more so in states that did not expand. Vulnerable residents in these counties who potentially face the health consequences of more prevalent environmental hazards will continue to face financial barriers in accessing care.

Rural residents also face geographic barriers in accessing health care, and this also is tied to state Medicaid expansion decisions. Residents in rural areas face longer distances to primary care physicians (Chan, Hart, and Goodman 2006). This is the result not only of the wider disbursement of the rural population but also due to lower per capita levels of physicians and surgeons in rural areas (Rosenblatt 2000; Thompson et al. 2005). Exacerbating this issue is the accelerating rate of hospital closures in rural America (Hsia and Shen 2011), which leads to greater travel distances for rural residents seeking care. The rate of rural hospital closures has been higher in states that did not expand Medicaid (Kaufman et al. 2015). In part, this is explained by the fact that in states that did not expand Medicaid, hospitals are experiencing a higher rate of uncompensated care costs. Uncompensated care costs are accrued by hospitals and physicians when caring for uninsured patients or patients who are not able to pay their bills. Uncompensated care costs reached $50 billion in 2013 (Assistant Secretary for Planning and Evaluation [ASPE] 2015). Costs have begun to decline, but the decline is significantly larger in states that expanded Medicaid (ASPE 2015). In rural areas, where hospitals struggle with lower profitability, revenue, and utilization, high rates of uncompensated care can increase their risk of closure (Kaufman et al. 2015). Rural hospital closure rates exacerbated by state decisions not to expand Medicaid leave many rural residents with larger geographic barriers when deciding whether to seek care. The low-income rural populations in the states that did not expand Medicaid continue to struggle in accessing quality health care due to financial and distance barriers. The risk these barriers pose is that rural residents will receive less preventive and primary care, which is essential for improved community health and reduced health care spending (Institute of Medicine [IOM] 2003, 2009). Together, as part of the invironment, environmental risks, geography, and socioeconomic indicators help to explain the degree to which these rural residents can access care and live a healthy life (McMichael 2013).

Environmental hazards and lower access to care in rural communities are related to and compounded by poor health outcomes for rural residents. For example, not having health insurance is associated with not receiving primary and preventive care (CDC 2012a; Tejada et al. 2013) and thus being diagnosed at later stages of illnesses, which is more costly and more likely to be terminal (Wilper et al. 2009; IOM 2009). In addition, socioeconomic, demographic, and geographic characteristics of rural areas put residents at greater health disadvantages. For example, research demonstrates that rural health behaviors (e.g., smoking, diet, activity levels) are associated with elevated risks of chronic health illnesses such as diabetes, obesity, cancer, and chronic obstructive pulmonary disease (COPD) in rural communities (Eberhardt and Panuk 2004; Hartley 2004; Meit et al. 2014). These factors, added to the elevated health risks associated with environmental hazards discussed earlier, are evidence of the invironmental disadvantage rural communities and people face.

LOOKING FORWARD

Strategic action and planning is taking place at the federal level to address the invironmental concerns raised in this chapter. The EPA is currently the chair of an Interagency Working Group on Environmental Justice (EJ IWG), which facilitates Executive Order 12898: Federal Actions to Address Environmental Justice in Minority Populations and Low-Income Populations (EPA 2016d). Federal agencies involved in this working group are attempting to address issues that affect the invironmental well-being of vulnerable communities, including low-income and rural communities. In addition, the EPA is crafting a 2020 Action Agenda: a five-year strategy for "deepening environmental justice progress in the EPA's programs to improve the health and environment of overburdened communities; working with partners to expand [their] positive impact in overburdened communities; [and] demonstrating progress on significant national environmental justice challenges" (EPA 2016e).

Programs are beginning to address the health care needs of low-income rural populations. Broadly speaking, Medicaid and the Children's Health Insurance Program (CHIP) provide health insurance to low-income adults and children in the United States, although, as previously stated, the degree to which Medicaid is available varies by state. Several programs specifically target underserved regions, including rural areas, with an increased supply of health care professionals. The National Health Service Corps (NHSC) places thousands of primary health care providers in underserved communities each year and provides scholarships and loan repayment programs to physicians who join. This and other programs, such as the United States Public Health Service Commissioned Corps (PHSCC), are beginning to fill some of the health care access gaps in rural America. Yet thousands of underserved communities and frontier areas, many of which are rural, fall within the health professional shortage areas or medically underserved areas (U.S. Department of Health and Human Services 2016).

CONCLUSION AND IMPLICATIONS

This chapter has examined some of the environmental hazards facing low-income rural communities in the United States and considered the implications on the health status of those rural communities and residents. Low-income rural communities have borne a disproportionally large share of environmental burdens. An invironmental approach acknowledges the consequences of environmental hazards that lead to socioeconomic, environmental, and biological instability in low-income rural communities—particularly in communities that lack a health environment that is accessible to all. Unstable occupational and physical environments, met with unstable or incomplete social and health infrastructures, create a recipe for higher risks of morbidity and mortality for vulnerable populations.

It is important to acknowledge the rural environmental hazards that have not been discussed in this chapter, such as forestry and deforestation, lead and other heavy metal exposure, petrochemical factories, and food deserts (see chapter 10). These environmental hazards also pose significant consequences for rural communities. This chapter focused on four realms of hazards at the forefront of rural environmental justice literature and particularly on distributive justice and the distribution of environmental "bads." Just as the distribution of environmental bads is inequitable, so is the distribution of environmental "goods." A great deal of research has focused on what is called environmental privilege (Pellow and Brehm 2013), an area that can equally inform future efforts toward justice. Rural populations are more likely to be exposed to environmental hazards, but they are also less able to address or alleviate these situations procedurally or politically because of a lack of financial resources and education, language barriers, and legal status (Walker 2012; Taylor 2014; Pellow 2016). Moreover, low-income rural populations often lack the resources and capital to escape residential or occupational environmental hazards. Together these limitations leave rural populations as sitting ducks, unable to affect or change their invironmental situation.

Researchers studying environmental injustices continue to face methodological challenges. In particular, data limitations affect our knowledge—and therefore policy and practice—around rural environmental justice. The lack of data and the challenges to collecting data on both rural health and the environment make it difficult to substantiate the invironmental links between environmental hazards and health outcomes. Linking chemicals to individual and community health is extremely difficult. Chemicals can be transmitted through soil, water, and air and can take decades, if not centuries, to decompose. Humans are exposed to chemicals in many ways, and in most cases people are more likely to be exposed to a mixture of chemicals than to just one chemical, making it difficult to narrow down a "who done it" for chemicals (De Rosa et al. 1996). Missing data in many federal data sets further exacerbates the ability of researchers to substantiate relationships. As a result, most of the rural environmental justice studies that do exist are regional or community case studies, making it difficult to compare, validate, and draw wider conclusions.

Despite recent advancements to incorporate environmental justice values in policy and regulatory processes, rural America continues to bear the invironmental consequences of these environmental hazards amidst a health care context that lags behind in accessibility. Rural residents face greater financial and geographic barriers in accessing primary and emergency care due to lower levels of physicians, accelerated rates of hospital closures and consolidations, and lower rates of insurance coverage. Interdisciplinary research is needed to better understand the connections between health status and environmental hazards, as well as how the rural health care context mediates or exacerbates that relationship. The environmental justice movement first began nearly three decades ago in Warren County, North Carolina, and it has made monumental strides in shedding light on and advocating for environmental justice. It is the responsibility of current and future generations to continue that work. For low-income rural American communities to no longer be treated as the dumping ground for America, all voices—low-income, minority, and indigenous—must be part of the solution toward equitable burdens and benefits in the interconnected and interdependent relationship between our environment and our individual lives.

Case Study: The Environment and Health

Michael Hendryx

Appalachia is a forested, mountainous region of the eastern United States extending from southern New York to northern Mississippi. It is home to about 25 million people, about 52 percent of whom live in rural settings. Within Appalachia are three subregions: northern, central, and southern Appalachia. To some degree each region has had its own history and its own developmental successes and struggles. This case study focuses on central Appalachia and addresses the complex interplay between rural poverty in this subregion and the environmental affects of its long-standing dependence on coal.

According to the Appalachian Regional Commission (ARC), Appalachia has a poverty rate of about 17 percent compared to 15.4 percent for the nation at large. Of the region's 420 counties, 203 (48 percent) are classified into lower levels of economic development (what ARC calls either "at-risk" or "distressed") based on measures of income, employment, and poverty relative to the United States as a whole. Within central Appalachia, which includes the Appalachian counties of Kentucky, North Carolina, Tennessee, Virginia, southern Ohio, and most of West Virginia, this figure rises from 48 percent to 66 percent.

Central Appalachia also has a long-standing economic dependence on coal, in particular a form of surface coal mining called mountaintop removal. Mountaintop removal takes place in the steep terrain of central Appalachia in eastern Kentucky, southern West Virginia, western Virginia, and northern Tennessee. It involves clear-cutting forests and using explosives and heavy machinery to remove up to hundreds of feet of rock and soil to reach coal seams. This activity occurs in proximity to populated communities. The rock and soil, called overburden, is dumped into adjacent valleys, permanently burying headwater streams. Research has shown that the quality of surface waters emerging from mountaintop mining areas is severely impaired. The use of explosives and machinery for coal extraction, processing, and transportation also has raised concerns among local residents about air quality affects.

Epidemiological investigations have documented that the people of Appalachia who live where coal mining takes place are at elevated risk for a variety of health problems. Among these health problems are higher rates of total mortality, cancer, cardiovascular and respiratory illness, and poor birth outcomes including birth defects. To some extent these health problems result from poor socioeconomic conditions in the region and to behavioral problems that often coincide with low socioeconomic status. Smoking rates in mining communities are higher than regional averages, for example, as are obesity rates. However, the published studies show that people in communities where mountaintop removal is practiced have significantly elevated risks for these poor health outcomes even after statistical adjustment for other risks including smoking, poverty, obesity, educational attainment, age, and sex.

Another set of studies has begun to document that environmental quality in rural mountaintop mining communities is impaired compared to rural control communities that don't have mining. Significantly higher levels of ultrafine particulate matter is in the ambient air in mining versus control communities, with evidence that particulate matter in mining communities contains silica, organic compounds, and other chemicals that are known to be harmful to health. One laboratory study demonstrated that dust collected from the ambient air in rural mining communities, but not dust from rural nonmining communities, caused changes to human lung cells indicative of cancer development and progression. These studies illustrate that environmental health issues are not confined to urban environments, and that rural populations also face environmental threats from human activities.

In one sense, studies on mining's public health affects have treated poverty and other traditional socioeconomic and behavioral risks almost as "nuisance" variables, as confounds to be measured and controlled in statistical models. Once this is done, we see that people in mountaintop mining communities still have poorer health outcomes that cannot be explained by the traditional indicators. At least some of this disparity seems to be environmentally related. But in another sense, it is important to understand that poverty and mountaintop removal are connected, and that poverty is not simply a variable to be set aside or controlled. When data on where mountaintop removal takes place is combined with the most recent poverty data from the Appalachian Regional Commission for the years 2009–2013, the poverty rate is 22.1 percent in the counties within the four states where mountaintop removal takes place, compared to 18.8 percent for other Appalachian areas in those same four states. Mountaintop removal uses explosives and machinery to efficiently extract large amounts of coal without the need for extensive manual labor, and the number of miners needed per ton of coal extracted is less for this method than for others. The practice of mountaintop removal also comes with opportunity costs; it destroys the landscape, degrades roads, pollutes air and water, contributes to poor public health, and therefore discourages alternative economic development. If a worker isn't fortunate enough to have one of the few relatively well-paying mining jobs, there isn't much else to choose from.

To address the problem of poverty in rural central Appalachia, it is apparent that economic diversification is needed that reduces the area's coal dependence. This would have benefits both in terms of improved environmental conditions and, over time, improved economic conditions. To paraphrase Einstein, "Insanity is doing the same thing over and over and expecting a different result." More coal mining will not change the economic conditions that it created in the first place. Deliberate investments in education, adult retraining, and alternative business development are urgently needed.

REFERENCES

Adger, Neil, Irene Lorenzoni, and Karen L. O'Brien. 2009. *Adapting to Climate Change: Thresholds, Values, Governance.* Cambridge, MA: Cambridge University Press.

Ahern, Melissa, Michael Hendryx, Jamison Conley, Evan Fedorko, Alan Ducatman, and Keith J. Zullig. 2011. "The Association Between Mountaintop Mining and Birth Defects Among Live Births in Central Appalachia, 1996–2003." *Environmental Research* 111(6):838–46.

Assistant Secretary for Planning and Evaluation. 2015. "Insurance Expansion, Hospital Uncompensated Care, and the Affordable Care Act." Department of Health and Human Services. https://aspe.hhs.gov/sites/default/files/pdf/139226/ib_Uncompensated Care.pdf.

Atlas, Mark. 2002. "Few and Far Between? An Environmental Equity Analysis of the Geographic Distribution of Hazardous Waste Generation." *Social Science Quarterly* 83(1):365–78.

Bamberger, Michelle, and Robert E. Oswald. 2012. "Impacts of Gas Drilling on Human and Animal Health." *New Solutions: A Journal of Environmental and Occupational Health Policy* 22(1):51–77.

Bell, Michael. 2012. *An Invitation to Environmental Sociology.* Thousand Oaks, CA: Sage.

Bell, Shannon. 2016. *Fighting King Coal: The Challenges to Micromobilization in Central Appalachia.* Cambridge, MA: MIT Press.

Berko, Jeffrey, Deborah Ingram, Shubhayu Saha, and Jennifer Parker. 2014. "Deaths Attributed to Heat, Cold, and Other Weather Events in the United States, 2006–2010." National Health Statistics Report. Washington, DC: Centers for Disease Control.

Brender, Jean D., Juliana A. Maantay, and Jayajit Chakraborty. 2011. "Residential Proximity to Environmental Hazards and Adverse Health Outcomes." *American Journal of Public Health* 101(S1):S37–52.

Brook, Daniel. 1998. "Environmental Genocide." *American Journal of Economics and Sociology* 57(1):105–13.

Brulle, Robert J., and David N. Pellow. 2006. "Environmental Justice: Human Health and Environmental Inequalities." *Annual Review of Public Health* 27:103–24.

Bullard, Robert Doyle. 2000. *Dumping in Dixie: Race, Class, and Environmental Quality*, vol. 3. Boulder, CO: Westview Press.

Bureau of Labor Statistics. 2014. "National Census of Fatal Occupational Injuries in 2014 (Preliminary Results)." Washington DC: U.S. Department of Labor. http://www.bls .gov/news.release/pdf/cfoi.pdf.

Carolan, Michael. 2016. *The Sociology of Food and Agriculture*, 2nd ed. London, UK: Routledge.

Centers for Disease Control and Prevention. 2012a. "Cancer Screening: United States, 2010." *Morbidity and Mortality Weekly Report* 61(3):41.

———. 2012b. "Pneumoconiosis and Advanced Occupational Lung Disease Among Surface Coal Miners—16 States, 2010–2011." https://www.cdc.gov/mmwr/preview /mmwrhtml/mm6123a2.htm.

Chan, Leighton, L. Gary Hart, and David C. Goodman. 2006. "Geographic Access to Health Care for Rural Medicare Beneficiaries." *Journal of Rural Health* 22(2):140–46.

Choi, Hannah S., Youn K. Shim, Wendy E. Kaye, and P. Barry Ryan. 2006. "Potential Residential Exposure to Toxics Release Inventory Chemicals During Pregnancy and Childhood Brain Cancer." *Environmental Health Perspectives* 114(7):1113–18.

Comber, Alexis J., Chris Brunsdon, and Robert Radburn. 2011. "A Spatial Analysis of Variations in Health Access: Linking Geography, Socio-Economic Status and Access Perceptions." *International Journal of Health Geographics* 10(1):1.

Croen, Lisa A., Gary M. Shaw, Lisa Sanbonmatsu, Steve Selvin, and Patricia A. Buffler. 1997. "Maternal Residential Proximity to Hazardous Waste Sites and Risk for Selected Congenital Malformations." *Epidemiology* 8(4):347–54.

Davidson, Debra J., Tim Williamson, and John R. Parkins. 2003. "Understanding Climate Change Risk and Vulnerability in Northern Forest-Based Communities." *Canadian Journal of Forest Research* 33(11):2252–61.

Davidson, Pamela, and Douglas L. Anderton. 2000. "Demographics of Dumping II: A National Environmental Equity Survey and the Distribution of Hazardous Materials Handlers." *Demography* 37(4):461–66.

De Rosa, Christopher T., Barry L. Johnson, M. Fay, H. Hansen, and Moiz M. Mumtaz. 1996. "Public Health Implications of Hazardous Waste Sites: Findings, Assessment and Research." *Food and Chemical Toxicology* 34(11):1131 38.

Donham, Kelley J., Steven Wing, David Osterberg, Jan L. Flora, Carol Hodne, Kendall M. Thu, and Peter S. Thorne. 2007. "Community Health and Socioeconomic Issues Surrounding Concentrated Animal Feeding Operations." *Environmental Health Perspectives* 115(2):317–20.

Eberhardt, Mark, and Elsie Pamuk. 2004. "The Importance of Place of Residence: Examining Health in Rural and Nonrural Areas." *American Journal of Public Health* 94(10):1682–86.

Environmental Protection Agency. 2011. "Iowa Climate Change Adaptation & Resiliency Report." https://www.epa.gov/sites/production/files/documents/iowa_climate _adaptation_report.pdf.

———. 2016a. "Environmental Justice." https://www.epa.gov/environmentaljustice.

———. 2016b. "Nutrient Pollution—The Effects: Human Health." https://www.epa .gov/nutrientpollution/effects-human-health.

———. 2016c. "Hazardous Waste." https://www.epa.gov/hw/learn-basics-hazardous-waste.

———. 2016d. "Federal Interagency Working Group on Environmental Justice." https://www.epa.gov/environmentaljustice/federal-interagency-working-group-environmental-justice-ej-iwg.

———. 2016e. "EJ 2020 Action Agenda." https://www.epa.gov/environmentaljustice/ej-2020-action-agenda.

Erikson, Kai T. 1976. *Everything in Its Path*. New York: Simon & Schuster.

Fischer, Erich M., and Reto Knutti. 2015. "Anthropogenic Contribution to Global Occurrence of Heavy-Precipitation and High-Temperature Extremes." *Nature Climate Change* 5(6):560–64.

Greenberg, Pierce. 2016. "Disproportionality and Resource-Based Environmental Inequality: An Analysis of Neighborhood Proximity to Coal Impoundments in Appalachia." *Rural Sociology*. doi: 10.1111/ruso.12119.

Guthman, Julie, and Sandy Brown. 2016. "Whose Life Counts: Biopolitics and the 'Bright Line' of Chloropicrin Mitigation in California's Strawberry Industry." *Science, Technology & Human Values* 41(3):461–82.

Gutierrez, Kristie S., and Catherine E. LePrevost. 2016. "Climate Justice in Rural Southeastern United States: A Review of Climate Change Impacts and Effects on Human Health." *International Journal of Environmental Research and Public Health* 13(2):189.

Hanson, Randel D. 2001. "Half Lives of Reagan's Indian Policy: Marketing Nuclear Waste to American Indians." *American Indian Culture and Research Journal* 25(1):21–44.

Harlan, Sharon, David Pellow, J. Timmons Roberts, Shannon Bell, William Holt, Joane Nagel. 2015. "Climate Justice and Inequality." In *Climate Change and Society: Sociological Perspectives*, ed. Riley E. Dunlap, Robert J. Brulle. New York: Oxford University Press.

Harrison, Jill. 2008. "Lessons Learned from Pesticide Drift: A Call to Bring Production Agriculture, Farm Labor, and Social Justice Back into Agrifood Research and Activism." *Agriculture and Human Values* 25(2):163–67.

———. 2011. *Pesticide Drift and the Pursuit of Environmental Justice*. Cambridge, MA: MIT Press.

Hartley, D. 2004. "Rural Health Disparities, Population Health, and Rural Culture." *American Journal of Public Health* 94(10):1675–78.

Hendryx, Michael. 2008. "Mortality Rates in Appalachian Coal Mining Counties: 24 Years Behind the Nation." *Environmental Justice* 1(1):5–11.

———. 2011. "Poverty and Mortality Disparities in Central Appalachia: Mountaintop Mining and Environmental Justice." *Journal of Health Disparities Research and Practice* 4(3):6.

Hoffman, Richard M., Jun Li, Jeffrey A. Henderson, Umed A. Ajani, and Charles Wiggins. 2014. "Prostate Cancer Deaths and Incident Cases Among American Indian/Alaska Native Men, 1999–2009." *Journal Information* 104(S3).

Hribar, Carrie, and Mark Schultz. 2010. "Understanding Concentrated Animal Feeding Operations and Their Impact on Communities." Bowling Green, OH: National Association of Local Boards of Health. https://www.cdc.gov/nceh/ehs/docs/understanding_cafos_nalboh.pdf.

Hsia, Renee Yuen-Jan, and Yu-Chu Shen. 2011. "Rising Closures of Hospital Trauma Centers Disproportionately Burden Vulnerable Populations." *Health Affairs* 30(10):1912–20.

Institute of Medicine. 2003. "A Shared Destiny: Community Effects of Uninsurance." http://www.nap.edu/catalog/10602.html.

———. 2009. America's Uninsured Crisis: Consequences for Health and Health Care, 60–63. Washington, DC: National Academies Press.

Intergovernmental Panel on Climate Change. 2014. "Human Health: Impacts, Adaptation, and Co-Benefits." In *Climate Change 2014: Impacts, Adaptation, and Vulnerability*, chap. 11. http://www.ipcc.ch/report/ar5/wg2/.

Jensen, Jennifer K. 2009. Climate Change and Rural Communities in the US. *Rural Policy Research Institute*. http://www.rupri.org/Forms/Climate_Change_Brief.pdf.

Kaufman, Brystana G., Sharita R. Thomas, Randy K. Randolph, Julie R. Perry, Kristie W. Thompson, George M. Holmes, and George H. Pink. 2015. "The Rising Rate of Rural Hospital Closures." *Journal of Rural Health* 32(1): 35–43.

Kearney, Greg, and Gebre-Egziabher Kiros. 2009. "A Spatial Evaluation of Socio Demographics Surrounding National Priorities List Sites in Florida Using a Distance-Based Approach." *International Journal of Health Geographics* 8(1):1.

Kouznetsova, Maria, Xiaoyu Huang, Jing Ma, Lawrence Lessner, and David O. Carpenter. 2007. "Increased Rate of Hospitalization for Diabetes and Residential Proximity of Hazardous Waste Sites." *Environmental Health Perspectives*, 75–79.

Lal, Pankaj, R. Janaki, R. Alavalapati, and Evan D. Mercer. 2011. "Socio-Economic Impacts of Climate Change on Rural United States." *Mitigation and Adaptation Strategies for Global Change* 16(7):819–44.

Lerer, Leonard B., and Thayer Scudder. 1999. "Health Impacts of Large Dams." *Environmental Impact Assessment Review* 19(2):113–23.

Lichter, Daniel T., and David L. Brown. 2011. "Rural America in an Urban Society: Changing Spatial and Social Boundaries." *Annual Review of Sociology* 37:565–92.

Malin, Stephanie A. 2015. *The Price of Nuclear Power: Uranium Communities and Environmental Justice*. New Brunswick, NJ: Rutgers University Press.

McGranahan, David A. 2003. "How People Make a Living in Rural America." In *Challenges for Rural America in the Twenty-First Century*, ed. David L. Brown and Louis E. Swanson, 135–51. University Park: Pennsylvania State University Press.

McMichael, Anthony J. 2013. "Globalization, Climate Change, and Human Health." *New England Journal of Medicine* 368(14):1335–43.

Meit, Michael, Alana Knudson, Tess Gilbert, Amanda Tzy-Chyi Yu, Erin Tanenbaum, Elizabeth Ormson, Shannon TenBroeck, Alycia Bayne, and Shena Popat. 2014. "The 2014 Update of the Rural-Urban Chartbook." Rural Health Reform Policy Research Center. https://ruralhealth.und.edu/.../2014-rural-urban-chartbook-update.pdf.

Mitloehner, F. M., and M. S. Calvo. 2008. "Worker Health and Safety in Concentrated Animal Feeding Operations." *Journal of Agricultural Safety and Health* 14(2):163–87.

Mohai, Paul, and Robin Saha. 2006. "Reassessing Racial and Socioeconomic Disparities in Environmental Justice Research." *Demography* 43(2):383–99.

Mohai, Paul, David Pellow, and J. Timmons Roberts. 2009. "Environmental Justice." *Annual Review of Environment and Resources* 34:405–30.

Morrone, Michele, and Geoffrey Buckley. 2011. "Introduction: Environmental Justice and Appalachia." In *Mountains of Injustice: Social and Environmental Justice in Appalachia*, ed. Michele Morrone and Geoffrey L. Buckley. Columbus, OH: Ohio University Press.

Newkirk, Vann, and Anthony Damico. 2014. "The Affordable Care Act and Insurance Coverage in Rural Areas." The Kaiser Family Foundation. http://kff.org/uninsured /issue-brief/the-affordable-care-act-and-insurance-coverage-in-rural-areas.

Partridge, Mark D., Michael R. Betz, and Linda Lobao. 2013. "Natural Resource Curse and Poverty in Appalachian America." *American Journal of Agricultural Economics* 95(2):449–56.

Pellow, David N. 2016. "Environmental Justice and Rural Studies: A Critical Conversation and Invitation to Collaboration." *Journal of Rural Studies* 47(A):381–86.

Pellow, David N., and Hollie Nyseth Brehm. 2013. "An Environmental Sociology for the Twenty-First Century." *Annual Review of Sociology* 39:229–50.

Portier, Christopher J., Kimberly Thigpen Tart, Sarah R. Carter, Caroline H. Dilworth, Anne E. Grambsch, Julia Gohlke, Jeremy Hess, et al. 2010. "A Human Health Perspective on Climate Change: A Report Outlining the Research Needs on the Human Health Effects of Climate Change." Research Triangle Park, NC: Environmental Health Perspectives, National Institute of Environmental Health Sciences.

Rabinowitz, Peter M., Ilya B. Slizovskiy, Vanessa Lamers, Sally J. Trufan, Theodore R. Holford, James D. Dziura, Peter N. Peduzzi, et al. 2015. "Proximity to Natural Gas Wells and Reported Health Status: Results of a Household Survey in Washington County, Pennsylvania." *Environmental Health Perspectives* 123(1):21.

Randel, H. 2001. "Half Lives of Reagan's Indian Policy: Marketing Nuclear Waste to American Indians." *American Indian Culture and Research Journal* 25(1):21–44.

Rosenblatt, Roger A. 2000. "Physicians and Rural America." *Western Journal of Medicine* 173(5):348.

Scott, Daniel, Geoff McBoyle, and Brian Mills. 2003. "Climate Change and the Skiing Industry in Southern Ontario (Canada): Exploring the Importance of Snowmaking as a Technical Adaptation." *Climate Research* 23(2):171–81.

Snipes, Shedra Amy, Beti Thompson, Kathleen O'Connor, Bettina Shell-Duncan, Denae King, Angelica P. Herrera, and Bridgette Navarro. 2009. "Pesticides Protect the Fruit, but Not the People: Using Community-Based Ethnography to Understand Farmworker Pesticide-Exposure Risks." *American Journal of Public Health* 99(S3):S616–21.

Steinzor, Nadia, Wilma Subra, and Lisa Sumi. 2013. "Investigating Links Between Shale Gas Development and Health Impacts Through a Community Survey Project in Pennsylvania." *New Solutions: A Journal of Environmental and Occupational Health Policy* 23(1):55–83.

Tallichet, Suzanne E. 2014. "Got Coal? The High Cost of Coal on Mining Dependent Communities in Appalachia and the West." In *Rural America in a Globalizing World*, ed. Conner Bailey, Leif Jensen, and Elizabeth Ransom, 279–95. Morgantown: West Virginia University Press.

Taylor, Dorceta. 2014. *Toxic Communities: Environmental Racism, Industrial Pollution, and Residential Mobility*. New York: NYU Press.

Tejeda, Silvia, Julie S. Darnell, Young I. Cho, Melinda R. Stolley, Talar W. Markossian, and Elizabeth A. Calhoun. 2013. "Patient Barriers to Follow-Up Care for Breast and Cervical Cancer Abnormalities." *Journal of Women's Health* 22(6):507–17.

Thierry, Amy Danielle, and Shedra Amy Snipes. 2015. "Why Do Farmworkers Delay Treatment After Debilitating Injuries? Thematic Analysis Explains If, When, and

Why Farmworkers Were Treated for Injuries." *American Journal of Industrial Medicine* 58(2):178–92.

Thompson, Matthew J., Dana Christian Lynge, Eric H. Larson, Pantipa Tachawachira, and L. Gary Hart. 2005. "Characterizing the General Surgery Workforce in Rural America." *Archives of Surgery* 140(1):74–79.

U.S. Census Bureau. 2015. "Small Area Health Insurance Estimates, 2013–2014." http://www.census.gov/did/www/sahie/index.html.

U.S. Department of Health and Human Services. 2016. "Health Resources and Services Administration: Shortage Areas." https://datawarehouse.hrsa.gov/topics/shortageAreas .aspx.

U.S. Energy Information Administration. 2015. "Coal Production Using Mountain-top Removal Mining Decreases by 62 Percent Since 2008." http://www.eia.gov /todayinenergy/detail.cfm?id=21952.

——. 2016. "Washington: Profile Overview." http://www.eia.gov/state/?sid=WA.

Vakil, Cathy, and Linda Harvey. 2009. "Human Health Implications of Uranium Mining and Nuclear Power Generation." Safe Drinking Water Foundation. https://www.safewater.org/PDFS/reportlibrary/HumanHealthImplications UraniumNuclear.pdf.

Vrijheid, M., Helen Dolk, B. Armstrong, L. Abramsky, F. Bianchi, I. Fazarinc, Ester Garne et al. 2002. "Chromosomal Congenital Anomalies and Residence Near Hazardous Waste Landfill Sites." *The Lancet* 359(9303):320–22.

Walker, Gordon. 2012. *Environmental Justice: Concepts, Evidence and Politics.* New York: Routledge.

Weaver, Hilary N. 2010. "Native Americans and Cancer Risks: Moving Toward Mul-tifaceted Solutions." *Social Work in Public Health* 25(3–4):272–85.

White, Arica, Lisa Richardson, Chunyu Li, Donatus Ekwueme, and Judith Kaur. 2014. "Breast Cancer Mortality Among American Indian and Alaska Native Women, 1990–2009." *American Journal of Public Health* 104(S3):S432–38.

Wilper, Andrew, Steffie Woolhandler, Karen Lasser, Danny McCormick, David Bor, and David Himmelstein. 2009. "Health Insurance and Mortality in US Adults." *American Journal of Public Health* 99(12):2289–95.

Wing, Steve, Dana Cole, and Gary Grant. 2000. "Environmental Injustice in North Carolina's Hog Industry." *Environmental Health Perspectives* 108(3):225.

Wing, Steve, and Susanne Wolf. 2000. "Intensive Livestock Operations, Health, and Quality of Life Among Eastern North Carolina Residents." *Environmental Health Perspectives* 108(3):233.

CHAPTER 12

Education and Information

Catharine Biddle and Ian Mette

Child poverty remains one of the greatest obstacles to educating youth today, with the largest proportion of American children living in poverty located in rural areas (Brown and Schafft 2011; Iceland 2006). Schools, as the chief publically funded social institution responsible for children's development, are often championed by the media and policy makers alike as being the primary engine of future social equality (Gerstl-Pepin 2006). What remains unacknowledged in this paradigm, however, is that schools across the United States are often unintended contributors to perpetuating inequality through practices that disproportionately target marginalized and impoverished youth (Noguera 2003). This marginalization begins with the assumption by schools and policy makers that poverty is a universal phenomenon that is both constant (one either is poor or is not) and aspatial (there is no difference in the experience of childhood poverty across urban and rural contexts). In reality, research on poverty throughout the United States suggests that as many as 65 percent of Americans take advantage of welfare benefits by the time they are 65 (Ludwig and Mayer 2006; Rank and Hirschl 2002) and that poverty as a lived experience is a diverse and highly contextualized phenomenon (Blank 2005; Sherman 2014). Factors such as the size of one's community, whether one attends a rural or urban school, the network of social services, and the willingness of people to use them dictate much about the experience of childhood poverty across contexts (Blank 2005; Sherman 2009, 2013, 2014).

Contextual differences also play a role in local perceptions of the promise of education to create social equality in a community. Depending on the geographic, social, and economic needs of a community, the meaning ascribed to the skills, knowledge, and aspirations cultivated by schools may develop differently (Budge 2006, 2010). The meaning and implications of a "college and career ready" federal agenda for education, for example, might be read in divergent ways by urban areas where postsecondary training and colleges are located in the community itself versus rural areas where few such opportunities are available locally (Corbett 2007; Wright 2012). The implications of such an agenda for each community, therefore, differ: urban and suburban youth may enjoy the benefits of postsecondary training while staying firmly connected or even continuing to live within their communities, whereas rural youth often must leave their communities and local support systems to pursue such opportunities (McDonough, Gildersleeve, and Jarskey 2010). With such an example, it is possible to see how the notion that "all of America's youth must go to college" might evoke differing responses from people in different places.

The implications of such contextual differences for rural schools in understanding and meeting the needs of students and their families experiencing poverty are explored in this chapter. Rural schools are often closely linked to the communities they serve, both as one of the few local social institutions and as a site of intergenerational connection and community pride (Lyson 2002). However, as part of a national system of public education, rural schools find themselves subject to extralocal educational priorities and mandates that impede their ability to serve their communities well (Biddle and Schafft 2016; Sipple and Killeen 2004). These competing priorities can lead rural communities to ask difficult questions of their schools, such as how education will fulfill its promise locally and, perhaps more important, whose purposes education really serves (Schafft 2010). Rural schools' responses to these questions, as well as their ability to adequately serve the needs of their poorest students, are bound up in a complex web that includes the legacy of American antipoverty policies of the twentieth century, governmental responses to the current economic and financial ethos and system, and schools' obligation to shoulder the burden of performance-based accountability reporting mandated by twenty-first-century educational reforms.

To understand these complexities, the relationship between childhood poverty, education, and youth development is described across contexts, and the formal mechanisms that schools have inherited for addressing and responding to poverty are explained. School funding mechanisms may disadvantage rural schools, and the bias against rural environments in the design of federal and state education policy is described.

The cumulative effect of these issues on the resulting organizational capacity of rural schools to effectively meet the unique needs of their communities and, in particular, the needs of students and families experiencing poverty is explored. The chapter concludes with a discussion of counternarratives and the possibility that rural school innovations can address childhood poverty and community economic development. Contemporary policy developments that may enhance or constrain this responsiveness are also addressed.

AN OVERVIEW OF CHILD POVERTY AND SCHOOL SERVICES

The effects of childhood poverty on social, emotional, physical, and health development are profound and affect the development of individuals living in poverty throughout their life span (Jones and Sumner 2011). Children who experience ongoing and persistent poverty are more likely to have negative health effects due to a lack of adequate nutrition (Korenman and Miller 1997), and they may experience a lack of access to adequate health and social services (Hanson, McLanahan, and Thomson 1997). Moreover, the ability for parents to invest in the development of their child, including but not limited to instilling the value of education, making informed health decisions, and passing along knowledge about making wise financial decisions, is also affected by poverty (Duncan and Brooks-Gunn 2013). What results is a cycle of reinforcement that can lead to intergenerational poverty, reinforcing a common misconception among Americans that poverty is due to a lack of work ethic or moral values rather than being a cycle reinforced by social and economic conditions (Sullivan 2011; Swanson 2001). Poor children are three times more likely not to complete high school, are twice as likely to have a teen pregnancy, and will earn upward of 40 percent less in mean family income (Corcoran 2009).

Childhood poverty also has a significant impact on brain development. Although there is no discrepancy in cognitive ability among socioeconomic and racial groups of American infants (Ferguson 2007), children who experience persistent poverty are negatively affected in their IQ as well as verbal communication, and they score lower on achievement tests (Smith, Brooks-Gunn, and Klebanov 1997). However, environment greatly influences the ability of children experiencing poverty to fully maximize their genetic intellectual ability (Berliner 2006). In addition, childhood poverty, specifically the lack of exposure to early childhood education and the inability for parents to provide adequate health and social services early in life, negatively affects classroom behavior and increases the likelihood of behavioral maladjustment (Lipina and Colombo 2007). What results is a negative impact on the well-being of children living in poverty, which creates a domino effect on learning and creates education gaps.

FEDERAL MEASURES TO ADDRESS ISSUES ASSOCIATED WITH CHILDHOOD POVERTY

The evolution of both educational policy and formal school services to address childhood poverty has been intimately tied to federal social policy. Over the past fifty years, the United States has attempted to broadly address socioeconomic inequities through a variety of policy measures. Starting with President Lyndon Johnson and the War on Poverty in 1964, an assortment of antipoverty policies were proposed to address changing global economies, labor markets, and education and health care systems (Cancian and Danziger 2009). These policies included creation of programs such as Medicaid, Medicare, and Head Start, as well as the expansion of benefits provided through Social Security (Danziger and Haveman 2001), all of which were aimed at reducing childhood poverty. As a result, from the 1960s through 2010, states throughout the rural South, once considered the most impoverished region of the United States, reduced poverty rates by more than half (see figure 12.1). Only a few states, including California, Michigan, Nevada, New York, and Oregon, saw poverty levels increase during this time span.

Although impressive and important, antipoverty policies and their influence on reducing childhood poverty had their greatest impact prior to 1970, after which their effect began to diminish. From 1960 to 1969, poverty rates for children under eighteen dropped from 26.5 percent to an all-time recorded low of 13.8 percent (U.S. Census Bureau 2010); from 1970 onward, a widening gap began to emerge between the percentage of Americans living in poverty and the percentage of American children under eighteen living in poverty (see figure 12.2). Moreover, as a result of gender wage inequity, 44 percent of children living in female headed households are now living in poverty as opposed to 11 percent in married couple households (Cancian and Reed 2009; Haskins 2012). The reality is that in the United States today, almost one-third of children will experience poverty at some point in their life, with 29 percent of those living in

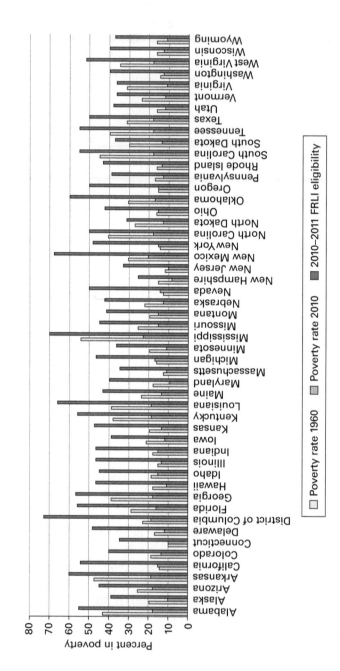

Figure 12.1   Change in poverty rates in the United States from 1960 to 2010.

Source: Adapted from Poverty Rates by County, 1960–2010, U.S. Census Bureau (2010a) and NCES free and reduced lunch rate eligibility (2012).

Legend: Poverty rate 1960 · Poverty rate 2010 · 2010–2011 FRLI eligibility

Y-axis: Percent in poverty

States (top to bottom): Wyoming, Wisconsin, West Virginia, Washington, Virginia, Vermont, Utah, Texas, Tennessee, South Dakota, South Carolina, Rhode Island, Pennsylvania, Oregon, Oklahoma, Ohio, North Dakota, North Carolina, New York, New Mexico, New Jersey, New Hampshire, Nevada, Nebraska, Montana, Missouri, Mississippi, Minnesota, Michigan, Massachusetts, Maryland, Maine, Louisiana, Kentucky, Kansas, Iowa, Indiana, Illinois, Idaho, Hawaii, Georgia, Florida, District of Columbia, Delaware, Connecticut, Colorado, California, Arkansas, Arizona, Alaska, Alabama

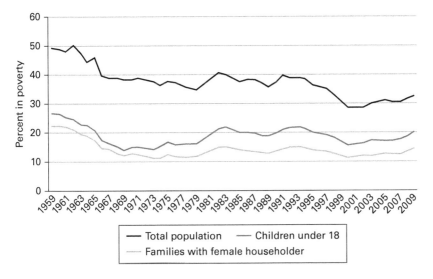

Figure 12.2   Segments of American population living in poverty.

Source: Adapted from *Income, Poverty, and Health Insurance Coverage in the United States: 2009*, U.S. Census Bureau (2010b).

rural places compared to 21 percent in urban areas (O'Hare 2009). As a result, there has been increasing pressure on schools, particularly in rural places, to address the host of developmental and social issues associated with increased numbers of children experiencing poverty (Berliner 2006).

Since the 1960s, an evolving patchwork of federal and state policies has been crafted to leverage the daily contact schools have with poor children to mitigate or ameliorate the developmental and cognitive effects of living in poverty. Perhaps none has been more profound than Title I, part of the Elementary and Secondary Education Act (ESEA) of 1965. Born from the same political efforts of the Johnson administration's War on Poverty, the purpose of Title I was a "national commitment to help educate economically and educationally disadvantaged children" (Jennings 2001, 1). The federal government disburses funds to state agencies of education, which in turn distribute these funds to schools serving economically disadvantaged populations of children. The introduction of Title I funds as a financial support for schools in the 1960s was the first time the federal government systematically provided funding for education in the United States, and over the past few decades this has led to increasing federal involvement and oversight in education (Kaestle and

Smith 1982). The most recent and perhaps farthest reaching examples of this oversight are the accountability measures for schools that were introduced as part of the reauthorization of ESEA, also known as No Child Left Behind.

Another important federal intervention effort to help reduce the impacts of childhood poverty, specifically the impact on homeless youth, is the McKinney-Vento Homeless Assistance Act. First authorized in 1987, the McKinney-Vento program ensures that homeless children remain enrolled in their school despite changes to their residential status, and it requires the school to provide transportation to school from wherever the children are living (U.S. Department of Education 2004). In 2000, over 580,000 American children grades K–12 were served by the McKinney-Vento program, and more than 19,000 preschool students were served as well (U.S. Department of Education 2006). These services attempt to minimize the impact of housing insecurity on children's education by eliminating the disruption of services and learning loss that accompanies transitions between different schools. It is difficult to measure the number of homeless in rural places, in part because rural homelessness often takes the form of doubling-up with family or friends or staying in substandard housing, but available studies indicate that the rural homeless are more likely to be families with children than the homeless in urban or suburban areas, reinforcing the importance of this program for remote and rural districts (U.S. Department of Housing and Urban Development 2013).

One of the most recognizable federal programs that helps address poverty in schools is the National School Lunch Program, which provides free meals to students with a family income at or below 130 percent of the poverty level and reduced price meals to students with a family income between 130 and 180 percent of the poverty level (National Center on Education Statistics 2015). The belief undergirding this intervention is that when children come to school hungry they are unable to learn. The National Center for Education Statistics (2015) reports varying levels of free or reduced-price lunch (FRPL) usage by state and locale.

Although all of these federally funded services are designed to take advantage of the daily contact between children experiencing poverty and schools, it can be challenging for rural schools in particular to fulfill the intention of these policies in practice. For example, 70 percent of qualifying families in urban areas enroll their children for free and reduced price lunches, but only 63 percent of qualifying rural families enroll their children in this program (Carson 2015). Stigma around social assistance in small communities may play a role in depressing the use of these programs for eligible families in a way that is different from larger, urban settings (Sherman 2009). It is imperative for schools to reach out to families to identify their eligibility and ensure services for their students, but rural schools face additional challenges because of their constrained organizational capacity in the face of diminishing school funding and school policy mandates. In the following sections, the pressure that inequitable school funding and the invisibility of rural school's unique needs in state and federal policy making is discussed.

THE EFFECTS OF SCHOOL FUNDING ON RURAL SCHOOLS AND POOR FAMILIES

Schooling in the United States, unlike many other countries, historically has been a highly decentralized system that relies on state monies and local financial support, often in the form of property taxes, to fund local public schools (Baker, Sciarra, and Farrie 2014). As a result, the local economy has a profound effect on the funding a school receives and, in turn, the capacity of that school to provide educational amenities and services to its students (Tyack 1972). Pockets of concentrated poverty within the United States, such as communities where poverty exceeds 20 percent or even 30 percent of the population, can translate into both a reduced ability for local municipalities to fund their schools and an increased need for higher-cost school services (Dayton 1998; Massey 1996). These services include special education, English language learning support, supplemental services (such as after-school tutoring), and coordination of services for transient students (Baker et al. 2014).

Such concentrated disadvantage has been exacerbated for many rural places in the last fifty years as their local economies have increasingly become tied to the global economy. This has resulted in the outsourcing of jobs to other countries, the introduction of megastores that outcompete locally owned businesses through competitive global supply chains, and the restructuring of companies to be less bound to a particular location so that they can shift geographically and be more responsive to changes in global markets (Goetz and Swaminathan 2006; Urry 2005). Some rural communities have found viable alternative means of sustaining the local economy, but for others these changes have meant increasingly constricted local opportunities for work, the introduction of economic uncertainty, and, in some cases, complete economic collapse (Sherman 2009, 2014). Since the 2008 recession, employment has continued to rebound more slowly in rural areas than in urban areas (U.S. Department of Agriculture 2015). These realities, in turn, affect local migration patterns of both adults and young people in search of work and devalue local property as the community becomes less attractive to potential newcomers (Lyson 2002). Together, these factors contribute to chronic declining enrollments of students in schools across rural America (Schwartzbeck 2003; Jimerson 2007).

STATE-LEVEL FUNDING INEQUITY

These changes have more recently become compounded by pressure on some state education agencies to be increasingly fiscally conservative when it comes to funding public amenities and services. In 2015, thirty-one states provided less school funding per student than prerecession levels. For fifteen of these states, the difference exceeded 15 percent of the pre-2008 funding levels (Leachman, Albares, Masterson, and Wallace 2016). As state agencies tighten their belts in response to fiscal political pressure, greater pressure is placed on local communities to make up the gap in funding state and federally mandated school services and in meeting the basic educational needs of students in their schools. However, the economic capacity of many of these communities often has been eroded by the realities of the global economic system far beyond the control of local residents. As a result, some rural communities have to consider closing their schools due to an inability to fund them, which has devastating effects on community vitality and can reinforce patterns of economic decline and marginalization (Lyson 2002).

Even prior to these more recent budget cuts, the existing mechanisms for state provision of funds to local schools had been accused of having an unfair bias against small and rural schools. To understand these claims, it is important first to understand how state agencies of education provide funding to schools. Equity in school funding can be understood as existing along two equally important dimensions: the *overall level of funding* allocated to public schooling for the whole state and the *distribution* of that funding (Baker et al. 2014). To determine distribution of funds, states create a funding "formula," typically based on the number of students served by a school (Imazeki 2007). Structured differently in each state, these formulas may provide similar per pupil funding to all districts with varying needs (referred to as "flat" funding), greater funding to districts with higher concentrations of students in poverty, or less funding to districts with higher concentrations of poor students (Baker et al. 2014). Although regressive funding systems that provide less money to districts with greater need might appear counterintuitive, these funding systems often occur when overall state funding to districts is low and no cap is placed on local spending. This allows rich districts with high property values and affluent citizens to outspend poorer districts that are without these economic advantages.

School districts with high concentrations of poverty often suffer in this system. Nationally, thirty-four states employ funding formulas that provide either flat funding to districts or provide less state and local funding to districts with higher concentrations of poverty (Baker et al. 2014). However, rural districts with high concentrations of poverty are often doubly disadvantaged by state funding formulas, which rely on enrollment numbers for total allocation. As enrollments decline and they receive fewer funds, rural schools are still responsible for the many mandated costs associated with maintaining a public school and associated student services, in addition to costs unique to these schools, such as higher transportation costs (Jimerson 2007). The result is often budget cuts to teaching positions in subject areas such as art, physical education, or music, which are not subject to state standardized tests. Conversely, budget reductions may occur through the defunding of amenities such as libraries, sports teams, or support services. These differences have not gone unchallenged by rural districts, however. In 2011, rural plaintiffs brought eight active cases with constitutional challenges to state school funding inequity across the United States, and twenty-seven out of thirty-two such cases in previous years were brought by rural plaintiffs as well (Dayton 1998; Strange 2011).

FEDERAL FUNDING INEQUITY

A small portion of the funding schools receive consists of federal financial support in the form of Title I funds, which schools are entitled to if they serve qualifying populations of students. Other federal funds are disbursed through competitive grants directly to districts or to state education agencies (Rural School and Community Trust 2011). Rural schools face several unique challenges in competing for federal grant monies. First, many rural school districts maintain a relatively small number of district-level staff, so their capacity to identify and write proposals for such grant money is more limited than that of larger districts in suburban and urban areas that typically employ more educators (Johnson, Mitchell, and Rotherham 2014). Second, grant programs, like school funding formulas, often disburse funds based on the number of students in a district rather than on the stated need, so rural districts may end up with grants that are too small to cover their intended purpose (National Education Association 2015).

The compounded effect of local economic conditions and both state and federal funding inequities affects the organizational capacity of rural schools to effectively address issues associated with childhood poverty in rural communities. As a result, rural schools may find that strategies that work for suburban or urban schools to better combine and leverage financial resources remain unrealistic in their communities (Dayton 1998). The pressure to employ such strategies has increased in recent years, however, because federal and state oversight has increased.

URBAN-CENTERED EDUCATIONAL POLICY AS FEDERAL PRACTICE IN EDUCATION

Since the 1960s, the federal role in America's traditionally decentralized education system has increased. The introduction of ESEA in 1964 and Title I funds for schools serving low-income populations brought about this increase in federal power (Welner and Chi 2008). Liberal policies of the 1960s aimed to increase social equity among Americans, but release of the commissioned report *A Nation at Risk* in 1983 spurred a shift in federal priorities. American educational performance was framed as being key to overall global U.S. economic competitiveness (Schafft 2010). Policy makers began increasingly to focus their interventions in education on maintaining and expanding global U.S. economic power (Au 2010). This interest coincided with a shift in economic policy toward a neoliberal schema that placed increasing value on the strength of the free market and individual consumer choice, rather than state regulation, to drive economic prosperity and growth (Harvey 2005).

Over the past thirty years, these neoliberal economic policies have influenced education policy by increasingly positioning education as an individual good rather than a collective one meant to develop human capital that could respond to the liquidity and rapid mobility of an increasingly global economy (Bauman 2001). As a result, educational reforms have focused on promoting market-based competition between schools and school choice, increasing standardization of curriculum, and big data (Ball 2004; Au 2010; Schafft 2010). Recent policies, such as No Child Left Behind and Race to the Top, have ostensibly been designed to promote equity and quality education for low-income youth, but they were conceptually designed based on urban and suburban settings. The complex relationship of rural places and neoliberal economic agendas has meant that these programs have struggled to fulfill their promise in rural schools (Jimerson 2007; Schafft 2010).

THE IMPLICATIONS OF NO CHILD LEFT BEHIND AND RACE TO THE TOP FOR THE RURAL POOR

With the introduction of No Child Left Behind (NCLB) in 2001, the federal government mandated that states implement accountability measures that influenced the assessment of students, qualifications for teachers, and funding and restructuring for low-performing schools (Irons and Harris 2007). The premise was that a more centralized accountability structure would force states to give greater attention to equity between populations that were ignored or marginalized in the past, particularly low-income students and students with special needs (Welner and Chi 2008). To support these efforts, NCLB placed new reporting and data management responsibilities on districts, provided requirements for whom districts could hire, and graded district performance in large part on annual state tests measuring student performance in math and reading (Linn, Baker, and Betebenner 2002).

These requirements placed additional burdens on all school districts and were particularly challenging for many rural districts (Jimerson 2005a, 2005b; Hodge and Krumm 2009). The highly qualified teacher provision of NCLB, which requires teachers to have a bachelor's degree, a teaching license, and demonstrable knowledge of each subject area taught, disrupted shared staffing arrangements in already hard to staff schools and reduced definitions of "teacher quality" to degree requirements rather than skill or expertise in working with the unique needs of students in rural contexts (Brownell, Bishop, and Sindelar 2005; Eppley 2009; Hodge and Krumm 2009). If schools failed to make adequate yearly progress (AYP) and meet the benchmarks for proficiency in reading and math set out by the law in 2002, they were labeled as failing schools and were subject to additional requirements. Some of these requirements, such as the provision of supplemental educational services for low-income students, were well meaning but difficult for rural schools to implement without the rich network of private providers available in urban areas (Barley and Wegner 2010; Jimerson 2005b); others, such as the opportunity for school choice for students in failing schools, were almost impossible for districts to shoulder in the face of shrinking budgets and remote locations (Jimerson 2005b).

Recognizing the difficulties for districts associated with these accountability measures, the Obama administration used the opportunity presented by the large allocation to the American Recovery and Reinvestment Act in 2009 to create the Race to the Top competition and School Improvement Grants programs (U.S. Department of Education 2015). These incentive-based programs opened competitive grants up to both states and school districts. To be competitive for these funds, however, states had to agree to a series of policy conditions, including teacher evaluation systems tied in part to student test scores, the founding and expansion of charter schools in their states, and specific reconstitution or reform practices in the lowest performing 5 percent of schools in the state (McGuinn 2011).

These programs, too, were difficult for rural states and school districts to use to their advantage. Many rural states have been hesitant to introduce legislation allowing charter schools in the face of already declining student enrollments due to the hollowing out effect this might have on districts' ability to continue to serve a diversity of students in small communities (Clancy 2015). Value-added models of teacher evaluation that rely on evaluating teacher performance through measuring increases in student test scores may be unfair to rural teachers or teachers with a high number of mobile or transient students whose small class sizes mean that the student performance from year to year might vary widely (Corcoran 2010; Goetz 2005). In addition, the models required by Race to the Top and School Improvement Grants for reform among the bottom 5 percent of schools were premised on dense populations supporting flat or increasing student enrollment and robust labor markets for educators—qualities that most rural districts simply do not have (Mette 2013). It is no wonder, then, that out of the states that received the initial and second round Race to the Top funds, only three out of twelve states were predominantly rural and none had high concentrations of rural poverty (Rural School and Community Trust 2010).

These federal policies are two examples of the ways in which current trends in reform often favor urban and suburban school districts that support larger student bodies and thus have a larger budget to respond to reform initiatives (Baker et al. 2014). Marginalized populations in rural places under such a system may be doubly disadvantaged because they are repositioned as a liability in a system of resource scarcity and ill-fitting policy (Schafft, Killeen, and Morrissey 2010). Rural places, with less population, also often have little political economy to advocate for change. As a result, the organizational capacity of rural schools to address the needs of their most vulnerable populations are often constrained.

EFFECT OF URBAN-CENTERED SCHOOL FUNDING AND POLICY REGIMES ON RURAL SCHOOLS

Funding and political biases have played an important role in shaping the organizational capacity of rural schools to meet the economic and educational needs of rural communities and, in particular, the unique needs of poor children and families in those communities (Corbett 2007; Schafft 2010). Low funding levels overall and a funding distribution system based on population density create a context of scarcity in which individual funding priorities have a greater impact than in contexts of plenty, and neoliberal educational policies affect what schools are forced to designate as priorities in the first place. The combined effects of scarcity and an increased federal role in determining local education agency priorities translates into a constrained ability of rural school systems to make choices that are responsive to the unique needs of their communities and their schools' families. In particular, rural schools may find it more difficult to recruit and retain educators who understand their community needs, to provide special services that meet the needs of their learners, and to give nuanced messages to young people about their future prospects both within and outside their rural community.

TEACHER LABOR MARKETS AND SCHOOL SERVICE PROVISION

Historically, recruiting trained teachers to rural areas always has been difficult. With the professionalization of teaching, the necessity of teaching credentials, and the centralized location of many teacher training institutes (formerly called normal schools) within cities, rural school reformers in the early twentieth century often lamented the difficulties of convincing newly trained educators to move to rural places without the attractions of urban life (Biddle and Azano 2016). The necessity of offering lower salaries than those in urban or suburban districts combined with the remote or distant locations of many rural schools make rural teaching posts less attractive to new teachers today (Schwartzbeck 2003).

Retention of rural educators can be difficult as well because rural teaching posts often entail a greater diversity of responsibility while at the same time being more isolated than teachers in other contexts. Rural teachers are more likely to be teaching multiple subjects or teaching outside of their content area (Eppley 2009), yet rural teachers often have fewer opportunities to attend professional development courses that would enable them to supplement and enhance their existing skills (Howley and Howley 2005). Generally, frequent contact with other educators through professional development or strong district-level networks provides teachers with opportunities to discuss, compare, and improve their teaching practice based on the insights of others (Snow-Gerono 2005). Without these opportunities, rural educators may feel they have to reinvent the wheel to solve every problem of practice they face (Howley and Howley 2005). This professional isolation can lead to poor morale or to a sense of helplessness in the face of organizational and community challenges, particularly in areas of concentrated economic disadvantage (Schlichte, Yssel, and Merbler 2005). As a result, teachers may be attracted to geographic areas with higher salaries and fewer challenges. These staffing and infrastructural issues, as well as budgetary concerns and the impact of policy on school priorities, result in fewer course offerings, particularly in advanced-level courses, as well as a stricter emphasis on testable skills such as reading, math, science, and writing (Bouck 2004; Khattri, Riley, and Kane 1997).

THE RELATIONSHIP BETWEEN SCHOOLING, YOUTH ASPIRATIONS, AND OUT-MIGRATION IN RURAL PLACES

One of the most complex aspects of the relationship between rural schools and rural communities is the role of the school in encouraging youth out-migration from rural places (Gibbs and Cromartie 1994; McLaughlin, Shoff, and Demi 2014). Public schools are tasked with the responsibility of developing youths' skills, or human capital, to serve the needs of both local and national economic and civic growth (Corbett 2015). However, the evolving nature of the U.S. economy, with its decreased emphasis on manufacturing and other forms of labor and increased focus on service and technological innovation, means that secure future employment now requires higher levels of education than were needed in the past (Petrin, Schafft, and Meece 2014). As a result, the necessity of higher education and postsecondary training has never been more important than it is today. However, the dearth of opportunities to receive this training within or near rural communities means rural youth often must leave their communities to continue their education (Wright 2012). Although it is hoped that youth who leave their communities to complete their education will return, limited job opportunities in their hometowns are available for students with such training or higher education to use the skills they have gained (Petrin et al. 2014).

This reality creates an ambivalence among many educators as to how to approach their engagement with the aspirations of rural youth. For many, the economic decline and low-wage opportunities available in rural communities mean that encouraging any aspiration other than college-going does not seem to be in any individual student's economic best interest (Budge 2010). However, in other places, this ambivalence is born from the sometimes rapidly changing economic contexts that characterize some rural places today (Corbett 2007). The dynamism of many industries and their globalized approach to managing their industrial portfolios mean that rapid cycles of boom and bust may create unrealistic hope for youth that lucrative, long-term labor opportunities that appear overnight in their communities are a sustainable path for a future in their hometowns (Schafft and Biddle 2014, 2015). Although educators acknowledge that these industries might allow young people the opportunity to gain experience and earn large amounts of money, many wonder whether these short-lived windfalls will lead to sustainable future employment or saving for other opportunities in the future (Schafft et al. 2014).

In either case, rural schools are in the difficult position of playing a role in who stays and who leaves their communities. Carr and Kefalas (2009) suggested that schools intentionally encourage high-achieving students to leave the community by investing energy and resources in their success while ignoring the development of the lower-achieving students who ultimately end up staying and becoming the remaining population of the area. However, Petrin and colleagues (2014) suggest that, in fact, student perceptions of local economic conditions play a far greater role in determining whether high achievers ultimately return to their communities.

CONCLUSION

The institutional capacity of rural schools to address the needs of vulnerable and economically disadvantaged children and families in their communities is severely constrained by a political system that ignores the unique needs of rural places, an economic system that positions youth as mobile human capital disembedded from the places where they grew up, and a school funding system that distributes funds on the basis of numbers and not need. This combination of factors can give rise to an ethos among educators that poverty is a problem beyond their reach (Dutro 2010). Many express powerlessness in the face of an eroded organizational capacity, already overburdened trying to meet the demanding needs of federal and state accountability measures (Schafft, Killeen, and Morrissey 2010).

In December 2015, the Every Student Succeeds Act (ESSA) was passed, which reauthorized the Elementary and Secondary Education Act of 1965. ESSA attempts to eliminate some of the more punitive measures for failing schools introduced in both No Child Left Behind and Race to the Top (U.S. Department of Education 2015). It is unclear, however, what, if any, changes this will mean for rural schools around their capacity to more effectively address the unique needs of children experiencing poverty. The law does financially support the expansion of the Promise Neighborhoods program, an approach to school–community partnerships and wraparound services that aims to ensure that all children "have access to great schools and family and community support that will prepare them to attain an excellent education and successfully transition to college and a career" (U.S. Department of Education 2015). However, even in the rhetoric surrounding these promising practices, it is clear that the philosophical positioning of youth as labor for a global economy has not changed, and schools will still be held accountable to that vision of educational purpose with, in the words of U.S. Secretary of Education, "new and smarter tests" (Duncan 2015). Fundamentally, the pressure to teach to standardized tests and encourage students to pursue careers and further education outside their communities will likely still limit the ability of rural schools to be responsive to their unique community needs.

There is hope, however, because some rural districts across the country are engaging in innovative school–community partnerships designed to address the unique needs of vulnerable rural families and children. Examples in all areas of community life are evident. In Pennsylvania, a district superintendent worked with a local broadband company to ensure that high-speed Internet access is available at an affordable price not only for the school but for local families in their homes (Schafft, Alter, and Bridger 2006). In Wyoming, taxes on profits from mineral and petroleum extraction fund public education across the state at a rate of per pupil funding second only to Massachusetts (Bake et al. 2014). In the borderlands of rural Texas, the Llano Grande Center was founded by Mexican American youth and public school teachers to give youth an opportunity to conduct action research within their communities and school to find new ways of doing school reform at a local level (Guajardo et al. 2006). In rural Vermont, Unleashing the Power of Partnership for Learning tackles similar community and school reform issues in New England schools by building the capacity of youth and teachers to do action research together (Biddle 2015). In Cody-Kilgore, Nebraska, a youth business class built and now runs a community grocery school for local families—the only such amenity within forty miles of the town (Rural Schools Collaborative 2015).

What remains to be seen, however, is the extent to which these individual grassroots partnerships are capable of inspiring and maintaining a focus on meeting the needs of economically vulnerable families in rural places as they enhance opportunities for learning through youth leadership experience and project-based learning that inform the future citizens of these rural locations. Within the current political and financial context, it is too easy for schools to overlook or ignore the needs of these students, or worse, to see them as a liability in the face of mandates and fiscal constraint. However, it is imperative for schools, districts, and state education agencies to maintain their focus on meeting the needs of economically vulnerable families in rural places for the long-term health of these communities.

Case Study: Education, Economic Disadvantage, and Homeless Students in Pennsylvania's Marcellus Shale Gas Region

Kai A. Schafft

The Marcellus Shale play is a natural gas–bearing geologic formation a mile below the earth's surface. Underlying about two-thirds of mostly rural Pennsylvania, and extending into parts of West Virginia, New York, Ohio, and Maryland, geologists have long recognized that the

Marcellus formation contained significant amounts of natural gas. However, it wasn't until technological developments in the 2000s created conditions for the economically feasible large-scale commercial extraction of shale gas that the Marcellus Shale and other similar "unconventional" natural gas reservoirs[1] began to be actively developed. By 2007, unconventional natural gas extraction in Pennsylvania had begun in earnest, and by the end of 2016, the Pennsylvania Department of Environmental Protect well count "spud" data showed there were more than 10,000 unconventional gas wells across the shale gas regions of the state.

Much of this so-called boomtown development has taken place in mostly rural areas that have experienced years of economic contraction with few anticipated prospects for economic development. For example, by the middle of 2010, when the shale gas boom was near its peak, just one of the fifty wealthiest school districts in Pennsylvania had experienced any unconventional gas drilling, with only a single well. By contrast, of the fifty *poorest* school districts, eighteen had shale gas development with a total of 364 wells (Kelsey et al. 2012). New workers and industrial activity raised expectations of economic benefits for local people and communities, hopes reinforced by gas industry advocates and enthusiastic pronouncements from the Pennsylvania governor's office (Schafft and Biddle 2015).

Schools experienced these local changes in a number of different ways. The expectation among many administrators was that enrollments would rise, which was a development to be welcomed by many given historical trends of enrollment decline in much of the Marcellus region. This did not happen, however, because the majority of out-of-state workers did not necessarily intend to relocate to Pennsylvania permanently, and those with families, for the most part, tended to leave their families behind. What teachers and administrators *did* notice, however, was an uptick in homeless students, even in school districts in which homelessness had not occurred in recent memory.

A superintendent from a heavily drilled county on the New York border explained:

> At my school I've seen the impact, I think, mostly in housing. I find that the people who are coming from mostly Texas and Oklahoma and the adults are just working on sites. They might be here a couple of months and then they are gone. . . . Rentals of apartments and housing

have skyrocketed so our own native people who tend to be fairly transient, moving from one place to another, can't find anywhere to live. This is the first year, I've been in education for thirty-five years, this is the first year I've ever known of some of my students being homeless. In fact, I have a family that has been evicted and they have to be out today and they don't have anywhere to go. Also a lot of these gas people bring fifth wheels or, uh, campers, and families are living in campers so we have a family with two or three kids and they're living in the camper, which I can't even imagine.

Homelessness represents an indicator of extreme social need. For educators, student homelessness is additionally a concern because of the disruption it poses to the social and academic lives of students. This disruption often results in academic underachievement and increased risk of dropping out. For schools and administrators, homelessness and student mobility also can result in significant administrative, education, and record-keeping challenges (Killeen and Schafft 2015).

Many educators noted the new incidence of homeless students whose families had been priced out of rental housing, and superintendents began to talk about a second group of technically homeless students sometimes referred to as the "Hummer homeless," students of gas worker families temporarily residing in the district in recreational vehicles and driven to school in their parents' Humvee. Although living in households with an income far above the poverty line, nonetheless these students were classified as homeless according to federal guidelines because of their residence in a temporary or nonstandard dwelling. Although an apocryphal story, it neatly encapsulates the frustration and contradictions felt by many administrators, especially as other longer-term residents found themselves priced out of local rental housing, unable to secure housing assistance, and making do by couch surfing and temporarily doubling-up with friends and other family members.

In public discourse, natural resource development is often equated with local economic development, despite a growing body of "resource curse" scholarship suggesting the underwhelming or even negative long-term local economic outcomes of such development (e.g., James and Aadland 2011; Matz and Renfrew 2015). What is less well recognized, however, are the uneven social and economic outcomes of boomtown development that occur not only in the midst of rapid development but often precisely *because* of that development. Rural poverty often is described according to its "invisibility," even though poverty in the United States has historically been concentrated in non-metropolitan areas (Brown and Schafft 2011; Tickamyer 2006). The economic insecurities accompanying rural boomtown development are all the more invisible because they occur in the context of an economic boom. As local institutions central to communities, schools can provide an important lens for understanding the economic and demographic impacts of community change, such as boomtown development and the seemingly paradoxical creation of new forms of poverty and inequality in the midst of rapid localized economic expansion.

[1] "Unconventional gas reserves" refers to gas contained *within and throughout* geologic formations such as shale and sandstone. Because the gas is trapped in the geological formation, gas extraction typically relies on the use of horizontal drilling into the geology and the use of hydraulic fracturing to break apart the geology and free the gas so it can flow to the surface for extraction (Wilber 2012).

REFERENCES

Au, Wayne. 2010. "The Idiocy of Policy: The Anti-Democratic Curriculum." *Critical Education* 1(1):1–16.

Baker, Bruce, David G. Sciarra, and Danielle Farrie. 2014. "Is School Funding Fair? A National Report Card." Education Law Center. http://www.schoolfundingfairness.org/National_Report_Card_2014.pdf.

Ball, Stephen J. 2004. "Education for Sale! The Commodification of Everything?" King's Annual Education Lecture. http://nepc.colorado.edu/files/CERU-0410-253-OWI.pdf.

Barley, Zoe A., and Sandra Wegner. 2010. "An Examination of the Provision of Supplemental Educational Services in Nine Rural Schools." *Journal of Research in Rural Education* 25(5):1–13.

Bauman, Zygmunt. 2001. *Liquid Modernity*. New York: Wiley.

Berliner, David C. 2006. "Our Impoverished View of Educational Research." *Teachers College Record* 108(6):949–95.

Biddle, Catharine. 2015. "Communities Discovering What They Care About: Youth and Adults Leading School Reform Together." PhD dissertation, Pennsylvania State University, University Park, PA.

Biddle, Catharine, and Amy P. Azano. 2016. "Constructing the Rural School Problem: A Century of Rurality and Rural Education Research." *Review of Research in Education* 40(1):298–325.

Biddle, Catharine, and Kai A. Schafft. 2016. "Educational and Ethical Dilemmas for STEM Education in Pennsylvania's Marcellus Shale Gasfield Communities." In *Reconceptualizing STEM Education: The Central Role of Practices,* ed. Richard Duschl and Amber Bismack, 205–15. New York: Routledge.

Blank, Rebecca M. 2005. "Poverty, Policy, and Place: How Poverty and Policies to Alleviate Poverty Are Shaped by Local Characteristics." *International Regional Science Review* 28(4):441–64.

Bouck, Emily C. 2004. "How Size and Setting Impact Education in Rural Schools." *The Rural Educator* 25(3):38–42.

Brown, David L., and Kai A. Schafft. 2011. *Rural People and Communities in the 21st Century: Resilience and Transformation.* Malden, MA: Polity Press.

Brownell, Mary T., Anne M. Bishop, and Paul T. Sindelar. 2005. "NCLB and the Demand for Highly Qualified Teachers: Challenges and Solutions for Rural Schools." *Rural Special Education Quarterly* 24(1):9–15.

Budge, Kathleen. 2006. "Rural Leaders, Rural Places: Problem, Privilege, and Possibility." *Journal of Research in Rural Education* 21(13):1–10.

——. 2010. "Why Shouldn't Rural Kids Have It All? Place-Conscious Leadership in an Era of Extralocal Reform Policy." *Education Policy Analysis Archives* 18(1):1–26.

Cancian, Maria, and Sheldon Danziger. 2009. "Changing Poverty and Changing Antipoverty Policies." In *Changing Poverty, Changing Policies*, ed. Maria Cancian and Sheldon Danziger, 1–31. New York: Russell Sage Foundation.

Cancian, Maria, and Deborah Reed. 2009. "Family Structure, Childbearing, and Parental Employment: Implications for the Level and Trend in Poverty." In *Changing Poverty, Changing Policies*, ed. Maria Cancian and Sheldon Danziger, 92–121. New York: Russell Sage Foundation.

Carr, Patrick, and Maria Kefalas. 2009. *Hollowing Out the Middle: The Rural Brain Drain and What It Means for America.* Boston: Beacon Press.

Carson, Jessica A. 2015. "Many Eligible Children Don't Participate in School Nutrition Programs: Reauthorization Offers Opportunities to Improve." Carsey Institute Brief No. 85. https://carsey.unh.edu/publication/child-school-nutrition-programs.

Clancy, Kaitlyn. 2015. "States Without Charter Schools Are Falling Behind." The Heartland Institute. https://www.heartland.org/policy-documents/research-commentary-states-without-charter-schools-are-falling-behind.

Corbett, Michael. 2007. *Learning to Leave: The Irony of Schooling in a Coastal Community.* Halifax, Nova Scotia: Fernwood Press.

——. 2015. "Rural Education: Some Sociological Provocations for the Field." *Australian and International Journal of Rural Education* 25(3):9–25.

Corcoran, Mary. 2009. "Mobility, Persistence, and the Consequences of Poverty for Children: Child and Adult Outcomes." In *Understanding Poverty*, ed. Sheldon H. Danziger and Robert H. Haveman, 127–161. Cambridge, MA: Harvard University Press.

Corcoran, Sean P. 2010. "Can Teachers Be Evaluated by Their Students' Test Scores? Should They Be? The Use of Value-Added Measures of Teacher Effectiveness in Policy and Practice." Education Policy for Action Series. Annenberg Institute for School Reform at Brown University. http://files.eric.ed.gov/fulltext/ED522164.pdf.

Danziger, Sheldon H., and Robert Haveman. 2001. "Introduction: The Evolution of Poverty and Antipoverty Policy." In *Understanding Poverty*, ed. Sheldon H. Danziger and Robert H. Haveman, 1–24. Cambridge, MA: Harvard University Press.

Dayton, John. 1998. "Rural School Funding Inequities: An Analysis of Legal, Political, and Fiscal Issues." *Journal of Research in Rural Education* 14(3):142–48.

Duncan, Arne. 2015. "Excerpts from Education Secretary Arne Duncan's Prepared Remarks at the Learning Forward Conference," December 8. http://www.ed.gov/news /press-releases/excerpts-education-secretary-arne-duncan%E2%80%99s-prepared -remarks-learning-forward-conference-today-dec-8.

Duncan, Greg J., and Jeanne Brooks-Gunn. 2013. "Family Poverty, Welfare Reform, and Child Development." *Child Development* 71(1):188–96.

Dutro, Elizabeth. 2010. "What 'Hard Times' Means: Mandated Curricula, Class-Privileged Assumptions, and the Lives of Poor Children." *Research in the Teaching of English* 44(3):255–92.

Eppley, Karen. 2009. "Rural Schools and the Highly Qualified Teacher Provision of No Child Left Behind: A Critical Policy Analysis." *Journal of Research in Rural Education* 24(4):1–11.

Ferguson, Ronald F. 2007. *Toward Excellence with Equity: An Emerging Vision for Closing the Achievement Gap*. Cambridge, MA: Harvard Education Press.

Gerstl-Pepin, C. I. 2006. "The Paradox of Poverty Narratives: Educators Struggling with Children Left Behind." *Educational Policy* 20(1):143–62.

Gibbs, Robert M., and John B. Cromartie. 1994. "Rural Youth Outmigration: How Big Is the Problem and for Whom?" *Rural Development Perspectives* 10(1):9–16.

Goetz, Stephan J. 2005. "Random Variation in Student Performance by Class Size: Implications of NCLB in Rural Pennsylvania." *Journal of Research in Rural Education* 20(13):1–8.

Goetz, Stephan J., and Hema Swaminathan. 2006. "Walmart and County-Wide Poverty." *Social Science Quarterly* 87(2):211–26.

Guajardo, Francisco, Delia Pérez, Miguel A. Guajardo, Eric Dávila, Juan Ozuna, Maribel Saenz, and Nadia Casaperalta. 2006. "Youth Voice and the Llano Grande Center." *International Journal of Leadership in Education* 9(4):359–62.

Hanson, Thomas L., Sara McLanahan, and Elizabeth Thomson. 1997. "Economic Resources, Parental Practices, and Children's Well-Being." In *Consequences of Growing Up Poor*, ed. Greg. J. Duncan and Jeanne Brooks-Gunn, 190–238. New York: Russell Sage Foundation.

Harvey, David. 2005. *A Brief History of Neoliberalism*. Toronto, Canada: Oxford University Press.

Haskins, Ron. 2012. "Combating Poverty: Understanding New Challenges for Families." Testimony to the United States Senate Committee on Finance. http://www.brookings .edu/research/testimony/2012/06/05-poverty-families-haskins.

Hodge, C. Lynn, and Bernita L. Krumm. 2009. "NCLB: A Study of Its Effect on Rural Schools: School Administrators Rate Service Options for Students with Disabilities." *Rural Special Education Quarterly* 28(1):20.

Howley, Aimee, and Craig B. Howley. 2005. "High-Quality Teaching: Providing for Rural Teachers' Professional Development." *The Rural Educator* 26(2):1–5.

Iceland, John. 2006. *Poverty in America: A Handbook*. Los Angeles: University of California Press.

Imazeki, Jennifer. 2007. "School Funding Formulas: What Works and What Doesn't? Lessons for California." Center for California Studies. http://www.csus.edu/calst /government_affairs/reports/School_Funding_Formulas_Final.pdf.

Irons, E. Jane, and Sandra Harris. 2007. *The Challenges of No Child Left Behind.* New York: Rowman & Littlefield Education.

James, Alex, and David Aadland. 2011. "The Curse of Natural Resources: An Empirical Investigation of U.S. Counties." *Resource and Energy Economics* 33:440–53.

Jennings, John F. 2001. "Title I: Its Legislative History and Promise." In *Title I: Compensatory Education at the Crossroads,* ed. Geoffrey D. Borman, Samuel C. Stringfield, and Robert E. Slavin, 1–24. Mahwah, NJ: Lawrence Erlbaum.

Jimerson, Lorna. 2005a. "Special Challenges of the 'No Child Left Behind' Act for Rural Schools and Districts." *The Rural Educator* 26(3):1–4.

——. 2005b. "Placism in NCLB—How Rural Children Are Left Behind." *Equity & Excellence in Education* 38(3):211–19.

——. 2007. "Slow Motion: Traveling by School Bus in Consolidated Districts in West Virginia." Rural School and Community Trust. http://www.ruraledu.org/user_uploads /file/docs/slow_motion_wvbusdes.pdf.

Johnson, Lars, Ashley Mitchel, and Andrew J. Rotherham. 2014. "Federal Education Policy in Rural America." Rural Opportunities Consortium of Idaho. http://www .rociidaho.org/wp-content/uploads/2015/01/ROCI_2014FedEdPolicy _FINAL_0115.pdf.

Jones, Nicola A., and Andy Sumner. 2011. *Childhood Poverty, Evidence and Policy: Mainstreaming Children in International Development.* Portland, OR: Policy Press.

Kaestle, Carl, and Marshall Smith. 1982. "The Federal Role in Elementary and Secondary Education, 1940–1980." *Harvard Educational Review* 52(4):384–408.

Kelsey, Timothy, Willian Hartman, Kai A. Schafft, Yetkin Borlu, and Charles Costanzo. 2012. "Marcellus Shale Gas Development and Pennsylvania School Districts: What Are the Implications for School Expenditures and Tax Revenues?" Penn State Cooperative Extension Marcellus Education Fact Sheet.

Khattri, Nidhi, Kevin W. Riley, and Michael B. Kane. 1997. "Students at Risk in Poor, Rural Areas: A Review of the Research." *Journal of Research in Rural Education* 13(2):79–100.

Killeen, Kieran, and Kai A. Schafft. 2015. "The Organizational and Fiscal Implications of Transient Student Populations in Urban and Rural Areas." In *Handbook of Research in Education Finance and Policy,* ed. Helen F. Ladd and Edward B. Fiske, 623–63. New York: Routledge.

Korenman, Sanders, and Jane E. Miller. 1997. "Effects of Long-Term Poverty on Physical Health of Children in the National Longitudinal Survey of Youth." In *Consequences of Growing Up Poor,* ed. Greg. J. Duncan and Jeanne Brooks-Gunn, 70–99. New York: Russell Sage Foundation.

Leachman, Michael, Nick Albares, Kathleen Masterson, and Marlanna Wallace. 2016. "Most States Have Cut School Funding and Some Continue Cutting." Center on Budget and Policy Priorities. http://www.cbpp.org/sites/default/files/atoms/files /12-10-15sfp.pdf.

Linn, Robert L., Eva L. Baker, and Damian W. Betebenner. 2002. "Accountability Systems: Implications of Requirements of the No Child Left Behind Act of 2001." *Educational Researcher* 31(6):3–16.

Lipina, Sebastían J., and Jorge A. Colombo. 2007. *Poverty and Brain Development During Childhood: An Approach from Cognitive Psychology and Neuroscience*. Washington, DC: American Psychological Association.

Ludwig, Jens, and Susan Mayer. 2006. "'Culture' and the Intergenerational Transmission of Poverty: The Prevention Paradox." *The Future of Children* 16(2):175–96.

Lyson, Thom A. 2002. "What Does a School Mean to a Community? Assessing the Social and Economic Benefits of Schools to Rural Villages in New York." *Journal of Research in Rural Education* 17(3):131–37.

Massey, Douglas S. 1996. "The Age of Extremes: Concentrated Affluence and Poverty in the Twenty-First Century." *Demography* 33(4):395–412.

Matz, Jacob, and Daniel Renfrew. 2015. "Selling 'Fracking': Energy in Depth and the Marcellus Shale." *Environmental Communication* 9(3):288–306.

McDonough, Patricia M., R. Evely Gildersleeve, and Karen M. Jarsky. 2010. "The Golden Cage of Rural College Access: How Higher Education Can Respond to the Rural Life." In *Rural Education for the Twenty-First Century: Identity, Place, and Community in a Globalizing World*, ed. Kai A. Schafft and Alecia Youngblood-Jackson, 191–209. University Park: Pennsylvania State University Press.

McGuinn, Patrick. 2011. "Stimulating Reform: Race to the Top, Competitive Grants and the Obama Education Agenda." *Educational Policy* 26(1):136–59.

McLaughlin, Diane K., Carla Shoff, and Mary-Ann Demi. 2014. "Influence of Perceptions of Current and Future Community on Residential Aspirations of Rural Youth." *Rural Sociology*, 79(4):453–77.

Mette, Ian. 2013. "Turnaround as Reform: Opportunity for Change or Neoliberal Posturing?" *Interchange* 43(4):317–42.

National Center for Educational Statistics. 2015. "Concentration of Public School Students Eligible for Free or Reduced-Price Lunch." http://nces.ed.gov/programs/coe/indicator_clb.asp.

National Education Association. 2015. "Rural Schools." http://www.nea.org/home/16358.htm.

Noguera, Pedro. 2003. *City Schools and the American Dream: Reclaiming the Promise of Public Education*. New York: Teachers College Press.

O'Hare, William. 2009. "The Forgotten Fifth: Child Poverty in Rural America." Carsey Institute. http://scholars.unh.edu/cgi/viewcontent.cgi?article=1075&context=carsey.

Petrin, Robert A., Kai A. Schafft, and Judith L. Meece. 2014. "Educational Sorting and Residential Aspirations Among Rural High School Students: What Are the Contributions of Schools and Educators to Rural Brain Drain?" *American Educational Research Journal* 51(2):294–326.

Rank, Mark R., and Thomas A. Hirschl. 2002. "Welfare Use as a Life Course Event: Toward a New Understanding of the U.S. Safety Net." *Social Work* 47(3):237–48.

Rural School and Community Trust. 2010. "High Poverty Rural Districts Largely Left Out of Race to the Top." http://www.ruraledu.org/articles.php?id=2551.

——. 2011. "What Is Title I Funding?" http://www.formulafairness.com/title1.

Rural Schools Collaborative. 2015. "Cowboy Grit Inspires a Rural Community in Nebraska." http://ruralschoolscollaborative.org/stories/cowboy-grit-inspires-a-rural-community-in-Nebraska.

Schafft, Kai A. 2010. "Conclusion: Economics, Community, and Rural Education: Rethinking the Nature of Accountability in the Twenty-First Century." In *Rural Education for the Twenty-First Century: Identity, Place, and Community in a Globalizing World*, ed. Kai A. Schafft and Alecia Youngblood-Jackson, 275–289. University Park: Pennsylvania State University Press.

Schafft, Kai A., Theodore R. Alter, and Jeffrey C. Bridger. 2006. "Bringing the Community Along : A Case Study of a School District's Information Technology Rural Development Initiative." *Journal of Research in Rural Education* 21(8):1–10.

Schafft, Kai A., and Catharine Biddle. 2014. "School and Community Impacts of Hydraulic Fracturing Within Pennsylvania's Marcellus Shale Region, and the Dilemmas of Educational Leadership in Gasfield Boomtowns." *Peabody Journal of Education* 89(5):670–82.

——. 2015. "Opportunity, Ambivalence, and Youth Perspectives on Community Change in Pennsylvania's Marcellus Shale Region." *Human Organization*, 74(1):74–85.

Schafft, Kai A., Leland Glenna, Brandn Green, and Yetkin Borlu. 2014. "Local Impacts of Unconventional Gas Development Within Pennsylvania's Marcellus Shale Region: Gauging Boomtown Development Through the Perspectives of Educational Administrators." *Society & Natural Resources*, 27(4):389–404.

Schafft, Kai A., Kieran Killeen, and John Morrissey. 2010. "The Challenges of Student Transiency for Rural Schools and Communities in the Era of No Child Left Behind." In *Rural Education for the Twenty-First Century: Identity, Place, and Community in a Globalizing World*, ed. Kai A. Schafft and Alecia Youngblood-Jackson, 95–114. University Park: Pennsylvania State University Press.

Schlichte, Jacqueline, Nina Yssel, and John Merbler. 2005. "Pathways to Burnout: Case Studies in Teacher Isolation and Alienation." *Preventing School Failure: Alternative Education for Children and Youth* 50(1):35–40.

Schwartzbeck, Terri Duggan. 2003. "Declining Counties, Declining School Enrollments." American Association of School Administrators. http://aasa.org/uploadedFiles/Policy_and_Advocacy/files/DecliningCountiesandEnrollment.pdf.

Sherman, Jennifer. 2009. *Those Who Work, Those Who Don't: Poverty, Morality, and Family in Rural America*. Minneapolis: University of Minnesota Press.

——. 2013. "Surviving the Great Recession: Growing Need and the Stigmatized Safety Net." *Social Problems*, 60(4):409–32.

——. 2014. "Rural Poverty: The Great Recession, Rising Unemployment, and the Under-Utilized Safety Net." In *Rural America in a Globalizing World: Problems and Prospects for the 2010s*, ed. Conner Bailey, Leif Jensen, and Elizabeth Ransom, 523–42. Morgantown: West Virginia University Press.

Sipple, John W., and Kieran Killeen. 2004. "Context, Capacity, and Concern: A District-Level Analysis of the Implementation of Standards-Based Reform in New York State." *Educational Policy* 18(3):456–90.

Smith, Judith R., Jeanne Brooks-Gunn, and Pamela K. Klebanov. 1997. "Consequences of Living in Poverty for Young Children's Cognitive and Verbal Ability and Early School Achievement." In *Consequences of Growing Up Poor*, ed. Greg. J. Duncan and Jeanne Brooks-Gunn, 132–89. New York: Russell Sage Foundation.

Snow-Gerono, Jennifer L. 2005. "Professional Development in a Culture of Inquiry: PDS Teachers Identify the Benefits of Professional Learning Communities." *Teaching and Teacher Education* 21(3):241–56.

Strange, Marty. 2011. "Finding Fairness for Rural Students." *Phi Delta Kappan* 92(6):8–15.

Sullivan, William M. 2011. "Interdependence in American Society and Commitment to the Common Good." *Applied Developmental Science* 15(2):73–78.

Swanson, Jean. 2001. *Poor-Bashing: The Politics of Exclusion*. Toronto, Canada: Between the Lines.

Tickamyer, Ann R. 2006. "Rural Poverty." In *Handbook of Rural Studies*, ed. Paul Cloke, Terry Marsden, and Patrick Mooney, 411–26. London, UK: Sage Publications.

Tyack, David B. 1972. "The Tribe and the Common School: Community Control in Rural Education." *American Quarterly* 24(1):3–19.

U.S. Census Bureau. 2010. "Income, Poverty, and Health Insurance Coverage in the United States: 2009." https://www.census.gov/prod/2010pubs/p60-238.pdf.

U.S. Department of Agriculture. 2015. "Rural America at a Glance." http://www.ers.usda.gov/media/1952235/eib145.pdf.

U.S. Department of Education. 2004. "Education for Homeless Children and Youth Program." http://www2.ed.gov/programs/homeless/guidance.pdf.

——. 2006. "Report to the President and Congress on the Implementation of the Education for Homeless Children and Youth Program Under the McKinney-Vento Homeless Assistance Act." http://www2.ed.gov/programs/homeless/rpt2006.doc.

——. 2015. "Every Student Succeeds Act." http://www.ed.gov/essa.

U.S. Department of Housing and Urban Development. 2013. "The 2013 Annual Homeless Assessment Report to Congress." http://www.hrsa.gov/advisorycommittees/rural/publications/homelessnessruralamerica.pdf.

Urry, John. 2005. "The Complexities of the Global." *Theory, Culture & Society* 22(5):235–54.

Welner, Kevin Grant, and Wendy C. Chi. 2008. *Current Issues in Education Policy and the Law*. Charlotte, NC: Information Age Publishing.

Wilber, T. 2012. *Under the Surface: Fracking, Fortunes, and the Fate of Marcellus Shale*. Ithaca, NY: Cornell University Press.

Wright, Christina. 2012. "Becoming to Remain: Community College Students and Postsecondary Pursuits in Central Appalachia." *Journal of Research in Rural Education* 27(6):1–11.

CHAPTER 13

Crime, Punishment, and Spatial Inequality

**John M. Eason, L. Ash Smith, Jason Greenberg,
Richard D. Abel, and Corey Sparks**

INTRODUCTION

In the social sciences, the link between poverty and crime is well established. The relationship has been fortified by decades of sociological research and is fundamentally reciprocal. At the level of both the individual and the neighborhood, poverty exacerbates one's likelihood of experiencing crime; and encounters with the criminal justice system, in turn, worsen the socioeconomic condition of people and communities. The goal of this chapter is, first and foremost, to explore the ways in which crime influences poverty—and vice versa—in rural America.

It is important to note that the majority of literature exploring the causes and consequences of crime has been conducted within the realm of *urban* sociology. Many of our empirical crime statistics are collected from urban areas, and many of the theoretical foundations for our understanding of crime also emerge from the urban literature because criminal activity is generally more common in metropolitan areas, which are more heavily populated and policed than are rural regions. This chapter translates what we know about crime and punishment in low-income metropolitan communities to poor *rural* America.

The chapter begins with a summary of findings from criminologists who have studied poverty, crime, and punishment across the rural–urban continuum in recent years. In addition to laying the groundwork for what is already known, this overview illustrates the gaps in our knowledge and the need for a comprehensive framework linking rural poverty and crime. This framework is provided by adapting Donnermeyer and DeKeseredy's concept of the *square of crime* to rural communities. In essence, the square of crime suggests that multiple, interlocking, criminogenic actors (i.e., the public, the state, the offender, and the victim) interact to produce elevated rates of criminal activity in certain neighborhoods. Each corner of the square is supported with relevant theoretical postulations and empirical data on crime in impoverished rural communities. In addition, Sampson's (2012) theory of the *neighborhood effect,* which invokes a community's characteristics, such as its socioeconomic condition and level of residential segregation, is used to better understand the elements of spatial disadvantage and poverty that contribute to crime in rural America.

Having laid the conceptual foundation, the chapter then describes three noteworthy trends regarding the rise in homicide, incarceration, and prison construction in rural regions. Trends in these phenomena have gained considerable attention in recent years, popularizing scholarship in the field of rural criminology. Building on the research of these criminologists, several factors are common to rural areas: (1) certain violent crimes, such as murder, have *increased* in rural America even as they decrease in urban America; (2) rural towns that are disproportionately poor, black, and rural suffer from targeted policing and higher rates of incarceration; and (3) the *prison boom* (and the consequent problem of prisoner reentry) has linked the economies of rural places inextricably to the well-being of the local prison. The chapter concludes by describing the implications for the future of the rural poor on the basis of our understanding of crime and punishment in low-income communities in rural America.

CRIME AND PUNISHMENT ACROSS THE RURAL–URBAN CONTINUUM

Much of our knowledge of crime and punishment concerns *urban* America; for example, in urban areas concentrated disadvantage is a predictor of neighborhood murder rates (Sampson, Raudenbush, and Earls 1997), mass imprisonment (Mauer 2006; Pattillo, Weiman, and Western 2004; Travis, Western, and Redburn 2014; Wacquant 2001), and prisoner reentry (Rose and Clear 1998). These well-established social facts are based on national trends (Mauer 2006; Pattilloet al. 2004; Travis et al. 2014) or findings from select urban neighborhoods in a single city (Sampson et al. 1997; Sampson and Loeffler 2010; Sampson 2012), and they are often assumed to represent urban areas exclusively. As a result, rural poverty and spatial inequality *across* the rural–urban continuum are often left out of the conversation surrounding crime and punishment.

There is a dearth of comparative scholarship on crime in rural versus urban communities, and it is not known, for instance, whether incarceration rates differ between urban and rural areas. It is known that crime rates, across the rural–urban continuum, are consistently higher in high-poverty counties. Moreover, when studying crime across the continuum, ways in which the criminal activity of urban areas affects that of rural regions must be considered. For instance, criminologists expect that the impetus for rising substance abuse and gang activity in rural regions can be attributed to the trafficking of drugs from urban areas into rural communities. This might explain, in part, why the sale and abuse of methamphetamine is so high in rural communities (Garriott 2011).

Some types of crime are more likely to occur in rural than in urban areas of the United States. For example, organized rings of livestock, grain, and equipment thieves are more common in rural regions (Weisheit, Falcone, and Wells 2005). Many criminal activities related to wildlife (e.g., animal poaching) and agriculture (e.g., crop and timber thefts) are unique to rural regions. Other criminal activities that are more likely to occur in rural regions include violent crimes such as homicide, rape, and assault among acquaintances rather than strangers (Weisheit, Falcone, and Wells 1994).

Beyond the types of crimes themselves, crime *reporting* also varies along the urban–rural continuum. This is due to cultural differences in victimization perspectives. It should be noted that no statistically significant differences in the percentage of violent victimizations reported to police exist for rural versus urban poor areas (Truman and Langton 2015). However, some criminologists theorize that cultural features of rural communities might lead to lower rates of crime reporting in general (violent and nonviolent crimes included). These cultural components include "informal social control among citizens, a mistrust of government, and a reluctance to share internal problems [with outsiders]" (Weisheit et al. 1994). Part of the reluctance to involve outsiders may involve perspectives of personal protection and higher gun ownership among rural residents. Although handgun ownership is only 7 percent higher in rural areas than in urban ones, gun ownership overall in rural communities is nearly triple that of urban areas.

Differences in crime and punishment among rural and urban areas also concern agencies of the state, such as local law enforcement and the courts. The central policing organization in rural areas tends to be the sheriff's department, whereas in urban areas it is the municipal police (Weisheit,

Falcone, and Wells 1995). Police departments in rural areas tend to be underresourced in comparison to those in urban communities, with "lower budgets, less staff, less equipment, and fewer written policies to govern their operations" (Weisheit et al. 1994, 1). In rural regions, nearly half of the local police departments have less than a dozen sworn officers; over 90 percent have fewer than fifty officers (Weisheit et al. 1995). Nonetheless, rural law enforcement officials tend to be more highly respected by the public than police officers in urban regions (Weisheit et al. 1994). Finally, rural courts—in comparison to urban courts—are less formal and more flexible, potentially leading to greater racial differences in criminal sentencing (Weisheit et al. 1995). These facts all speak to how the challenges rural communities face regarding crime and punishment are related to urban challenges yet may differ greatly in type and scope (see Duhart 2000).

WHERE DOES POVERTY FIT?

Though rural and urban regions experience some dissimilarities in crime and punishment, crime and poverty are intricately related in all communities—rural and urban alike. The *criminalization of poverty* refers to the way in which low-income individuals are drawn into the criminal justice system at higher rates when compared to middle- and high-income individuals. This phenomenon has been documented with respect to the criminalization of extreme poverty and homelessness (Prather 2010; Dolan and Carr 2015); the problem of debtor's prisons and unaffordable bail fines and court fees, which disproportionately plague indigent criminal defendants (American Bar Association 2016); the criminalization of the welfare system, which injures poor recipients of public assistance (Gustafson 2009); and the issues of the school-to-prison pipeline and probation profiteering, which likewise target low-income individuals and communities (Dolan and Carr 2015).

Individuals in poor households are more likely to suffer violent victimization, irrespective of whether they are located in rural, suburban, or urban areas (figure 13.1). For the rural poor, 38.8 per 1,000 individuals are likely to suffer a violent crime at some point in their lives, versus 43.9 for every 1,000 urban poor individuals. Crime rates are higher both among urban individuals generally and among the urban poor than among rural individuals or the rural poor (Truman and Langton 2015). In rural regions, the difference between rates of violent victimization among low- and high-income individuals is especially pronounced (figure 13.2).

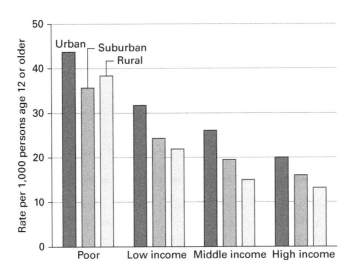

Figure 13.1 Rate of violent victimization, by poverty level and location of residence, 2008–2012.

Source: Reprinted from the Bureau of Justice Statistics, "Special Report: Household Poverty and Nonfatal Violent Victimization, 2008–2012."

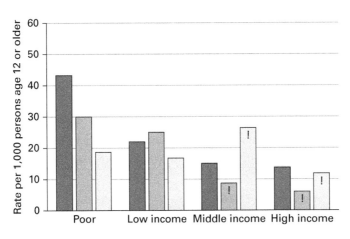

Figure 13.2 Rate of violent victimization, by poverty level and race, Rural counties, 2008–2012.

Note: "!: Interpret with caution; estimate based on 10 or fewer sample cases, or coefficient of variation is greater than 50%" (quoted from p. 5 of the Bureau of Justice Statistics "Special Report").

Source: Figure reprinted from the Bureau of Justice Statistics, "Special Report: Household Poverty and Nonfatal Violent Victimization, 2008–2012."

Although crime rates in rural counties have generally been lower than those of urban communities, both experience greater rates of crime in high-poverty areas (Weisheit et al. 1994), and the effect of poverty on crime is less pronounced in rural than in urban areas (Weisheit, Falcone, and Wells 2005).

The link between poverty and crime has long been understood as mutually reinforcing (Weisheit et al. 1995), especially in rural areas. For instance, Arthur (1991) found that poverty and measures thereof (e.g., rates of unemployment and use of public aid) were highly correlated with not only property crimes but also violent crimes in rural Georgia. In addition, measures of income inequality are consistently positively correlated with crime rates over time, and a rise in median household income is associated with lower or declining levels of crime over time (Deller and Deller 2011). These examples powerfully illustrate the *neighborhood effect*, whereby a consensus behavior—or set of characteristics at the neighborhood-level—affects residents' behaviors at the individual level (Sampson 2012). Thus, if the broader community experiences a drop in median household income or a rise in income inequality, this may influence an individual's likelihood of becoming a victim (or perpetrator) of a crime in that community. Similarly, elevated rates of crime may contribute to the poverty of the neighborhood through lowered property values, for instance. The relationship between poverty and crime is often bidirectional, and it is difficult to cleanly tease apart which "causes" the other. As such, it is important to note that causation should not be assumed to go *only* from poverty to crime (or crime to poverty).

The theory of the *square of crime* (figure 13.3) is useful in explaining why crime and poverty are so heavily interrelated. Developed by criminologists Joseph Donnermeyer and Walter DeKeseredy, it states that

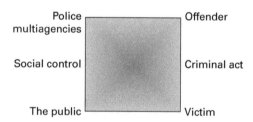

Figure 13.3 The "square of crime."

Source: Reprinted from Joseph Donnermeyer and Walter DeKeseredy's "Toward a Rural Critical Criminology."

crime in any community involves the mutual interaction of multiple stakeholders. There are four primary actors, each of whom comprises a corner of the square: the victim, the offender, the public, and the state (i.e., law enforcement and the courts). Criminogenic features of a neighborhood therefore include both the area's *structural traits* (its police agencies and the attitudes of the public) and *individual-level characteristics* (the attributes of potential victims and offenders). The former engage in social control, preventing (or exacerbating) the likelihood of criminal activity occurring in a given context. The latter are those directly involved in the criminal act itself (i.e., the perpetrator and the victim). Crime in any context, but especially in rural poor America, cannot be understood in the absence of any one of these four actors.

The literature on the police and the public and their respective interactions with crime and punishment help to further explain the *social control* aspects of crime in rural poor areas. Specifically, predictors of crime in rural regions include the area's structural features, such as informal social control mechanisms and cultural feelings within the community. Deller and Deller (2011, 126) found that cultural norms in rural regions, such as that crime is a "personal matter," discourage rural victims from seeking the involvement of "outsiders," such as law enforcement officials; crime victims may instead prefer to deal with the problem themselves and with other in-group members of their neighborhood (Deller and Deller 2011). The attention to the in-group and the exclusion of the law enforcement out-group may lead to lower rates of crime reporting and increased victim vulnerability.

This perspective is rooted in *social disorganization theory*, which is the notion that "structural factors influence social networks which in turn influence social control" (Deller and Deller 2011, 123). By this theory, a structural factor, such as the spatial dispersion and geographic isolation of a rural community, may enhance residents' notions of an in-group versus an out-group. The *in-group* refers to those individuals viewed as belonging within the community, and the *out-group* consists of community outsiders. Ideas about who does (and who does not) belong in a community's social network may in turn influence the ways in which crimes are handled within that community. Thus, criminal activity might be considered local law enforcement's prerogative if the police are part of the in-group social network. But if the police are viewed as community outsiders, residents may view crime as a personal matter to be handled privately among themselves and without the aid of local law enforcement officials. Illustrating the square of crime, the victim, the public, and the agencies of the state all interact *interdependently* through social disorganization theory; these groups collectively discourage victims from seeking state assistance due to the public feelings about crime and the cultural beliefs of the community.

In line with social disorganization theory, a lack of resources in rural poor areas—such as underfunded public schools and a lack of possibilities for social mobility—leads to fewer opportunities for "prosocial (i.e., less criminal, less deviant) behavior" among individuals in low-income rural communities (Donnermeyer et al. 2006, 208). This deficiency of opportunity, moreover, occurs for two individual-level actors: the offender and the victim. A lack of resources both feeds antisocial behavior among criminal offenders and enhances the "vulnerability" of potential victims (Mawby and Yarwood 2011, 78). That is, to combat the view that their rural hometown is resource-dearth, some rural residents may seek to "maintain an idyllic representation of rural life" (77). Enacting this "rural idyll," residents may leave doors unlocked, elevating their risk of becoming a victim of a crime (78). Further, at the public level, residents in rural communities tend to be culturally less fearful of crime compared to residents of urban areas; this, too, may lead to lax security in rural households, aggravating one's risk for becoming a victim of criminal activity (Weisheit et al. 1995).

Public perceptions such as these are an essential informal form of social control that may reduce (or heighten) one's risk for experiencing crime in rural communities. Public perceptions that have this controlling influence on crime offer an example of *collective efficacy*. Collective efficacy is the ability to control the behavior of groups and individuals within a community. This control is a central form of social capital involved in mitigating the predictive power of neighborhood disadvantage and poverty on crime (Sampson et al. 1997). For instance, living in a community where neighbors help each other out tends to motivate new residents to be vigilant against crime, whereas living in a high-crime area where neighbors keep to themselves makes an individual more likely to be a victim of crime. Neighborhoods with higher measures of collective efficacy are better at tamping down crime than neighborhoods with comparable levels of disadvantage and less collective efficacy. With collective efficacy in mind, the square can be extended as a type of neighborhood effect in rural communities.

An additional neighborhood-level criminogenic concern for rural poor communities relates to the gendered dynamic of economic displacement. Some rural criminologists, such as Donnermeyer and DeKeseredy (2008), have asserted that a *"crisis of masculinity"* exists among poor males in the United States today (14). This crisis primes them for committing greater acts of violence in both the private and the public sector. Low-income men in postindustrial rural regions experiencing economic displacement (e.g., through the loss of a family farm or a local economic recession) may no longer view social mobility and the American Dream as realistically attainable. Lacking the ability to claim masculinity through the traditional breadwinner role, some low-income rural men may turn to male-on-female violence and substance abuse. Some scholars attribute the rise in interpersonal crimes in rural America to this gendered phenomenon (Donnermeyer and DeKeseredy 2008). Worse still, male-on-female violence is a structural issue in rural poor regions, invoking the state actors of the square of crime. That is, police in rural regions are less likely to intervene in domestic violence situations than those in urban areas (Weisheit et al. 1995).

Some criminologists have posited that youth experience a similar cultural crisis due to a lack of economic opportunities. Youth may be at a higher risk for substance abuse and criminal activity in impoverished rural communities if they feel "stuck" in their local towns and are unable to find a job to support independence from their parents (Mawby and Yarwood 2011, 78). If the period during which they remain dependent on their families is too prolonged, young people may experience a delayed transition to adulthood and an increased risk of delinquent behavior (Rutherford 2002). This is both a structural concern and an individual-level impetus for the offender to commit crimes in rural regions, again demonstrating the interdependence of actors in the square on crime.

Finally, one last feature of crime in poor rural America concerns patterns of substance addiction and abuse. Rates of substance abuse in rural areas are generally akin to those of small and large metropolitan areas, but certain substances are more regularly abused in rural areas. For instance, binge alcohol use by youths aged twelve to seventeen is more common, as is cigarette smoking and smokeless tobacco use. Other substances are abused at a lower rate in rural than urban areas; these include underage alcohol use, illicit drug use, and illicit drug or alcohol dependence

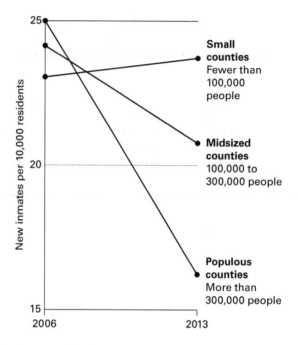

Figure 13.4   A growing divide: people in rural areas are much more likely to go to prison than people in urban areas, a major shift from a decade ago.

Source: Adapted from Keller and Pearce's "This small Indiana county sends more people to prison than San Francisco and Durham, N.C., combined. Why?"

(Substance Abuse and Mental Health Services Administration 2014). In recent years, substance abuse (especially heroin) has been so prevalent in rural areas that it has led to an increase in rates of prison admissions in rural regions. In the early 2000s, individuals in rural, suburban, and urban communities were equally likely to be incarcerated. Due to drug arrests today, individuals in rural counties are "50 percent more likely to go to prison" than those in larger, more urban areas (Keller and Pearce 2016; figure 13.4).

Rates of incarceration for drug offenders in recent years may be higher in rural areas due to structural features of urban regions. For instance, it has been argued that the prison overcrowding prevalent in urban counties encourages urban judges to offer probationary sentences instead of jail time. Such an extent of prison overcrowding is not present in rural correctional facilities; thus, probationary sentences are employed with less regularity. Similarly, urban areas may be more resource-rich in terms of their ability to combat substance abuse and addiction outside the context of the criminal justice system—a service many rural counties are not equipped to provide (Keller and Pearce 2016). This disparity of resources represents a consequence of *spatial inequality*; that is, the unequal allocation of resources across spatial scales (or places). In this way, substance abuse is not only an offender-level issue but one concerning state agencies (e.g., a lack of state-run facilities to combat addiction) and structural issues of inequality faced by rural America.

Overall, issues relevant to the criminalization of poverty in rural communities may be summarized using the intersectional "square" of crime. The square of crime suggests that criminal activity involves multiple stakeholders: the offender, the victim, the agencies of the state (e.g., the police), and the public at large (Donnermeyer and DeKeseredy 2008). Several aspects of crime in rural areas are mutually determinative aspects of crime, involving both structure and individual actors: rates of violent victimization, social disorganization theory and the "outsider" problem, the informal social control of organic solidarity, a lack of resources and the rural idyll cultural image, the crisis of masculinity and issue of youth dependence, and substance abuse problems. The criminalization of poverty in rural communities essentially relies on the interdependence and mutual interaction of these varied stakeholders, leading to a prevalence of crime—and lack of resources to successfully combat it—in impoverished rural communities.

This section has shown the importance of the neighborhood effect and context for understanding how broader structural factors may affect crime at the level of the individual. Some aspects of context (e.g., poverty and inequality) affect crime in similar ways across the rural–urban continuum, but other aspects are unique to rural America. These issues of context that affect crime and punishment concern three nascent crime trends in rural areas: rising murder rates, mass imprisonment, and the prison boom. The following sections explore these phenomena, as well their implications for the future of crime and punishment in rural America.

TRADING PLACES?: MURDER RATES ACROSS THE RURAL–URBAN CONTINUUM

The first trend concerns homicide rates across the rural–urban continuum. For the first time in decades, the United States witnessed a decline in murder as part of the crime drop of the 1990s (figure 13.5). Despite the

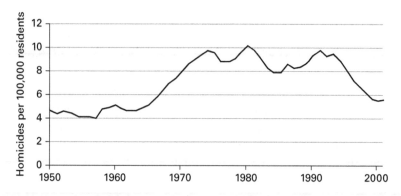

Figure 13.5   For the first time in decades, the United States witnessed a decline in murder as part of the crime drop of the 1990s.

Source: Levitt (2004), based on FBI Uniform Crime Report data.

broad policy and theoretical implications of murder for all communities, the debate over the "great" crime drop of the 1990s has been centered on deterrence in cities—specifically, on the role of active and intentional criminal justice policy in reducing urban violent crime. For example, many argue that improved policing, mass incarceration, gun control, and reduction of open-air drug markets were key determinants in reducing the murder rate (Blumstein and Wallman 2006; Zimring 2011). Tactics believed to cut crime include increasing police officers, data-driven patrols based on geographic information system (GIS) analysis, stop-and-frisk, zero-tolerance, and community policing. Economic growth and shifting demographics (e.g., aging baby boomers) were also believed to be important factors in reducing murder (Blumstein and Wallman 2006).

Zero-tolerance and other police practices of locking up citizens for small offenses such as panhandling or drug possession grew out of the War on Drugs and have contributed to mass imprisonment and, ultimately, the prison boom (Martin and Price 2016). Despite stop-and-frisk resulting in more people being locked up for petty offenses for longer periods, from the zero-tolerance policies perspective, aggressive and over policing was a huge success in reducing crime in urban areas. Because these policies were widely heralded as making cities safe (Zimring 2011), many rural communities imported these practices with very little question (McQuade 2016). However, the effect of zero-tolerance policing policies on rural crime may be negligible (McQuade 2016), highlighting the importance of context for understanding crime trends. If the policy prescriptions credited for the crime drop were taken at face value, we would not only continue aggressive policing but also expand zero-tolerance policing tactics like stop-and-frisk that many argue (Gelman, Kiss, and Fagan 2005; Meares 2014) are thinly veiled forms of racial profiling. Scholars (Gelman et al. 2005; Meares 2014) also find that these policies lock up people for longer sentences on increasingly petty offenses. In fact, aggressive and over policing may contribute to rising incarceration in rural communities, fueling the construction of new jails (Pragacz 2016). Martin and Price (2016) assert that these policies ultimately contribute to rising levels of imprisonment nationwide. As it stands, the United States is the world leader in imprisonment, with well over 2 million Americans presently incarcerated.

Though debates on the causes and consequences of the "great" crime drop continue, the universality of this trend is rarely disputed. Levitt (2004) is not alone in claiming that "the drop of crime in the 1990s affected all geographic areas and demographic groups" (167). But was the crime bust really universal? There are several important reasons to explore this question. First, some areas may not have experienced any decline in murder rates. Second, some explanations for the crime drop may have substantial boundary conditions. That is to say, the context of murder in urban northern places could vary drastically from that in rural southern places. It is important to explore whether the precipitous decline of murder during the 1990s was universal across all U.S. census places. According to the U.S. Department of Commerce, a U.S. census-designated "place" is defined as "the statistical counterparts of incorporated places [that] are delineated to provide data for settled concentrations of population that are identifiable by name but are not legally incorporated under the laws of the state in which they are located." Recent empirical advances in the study of rural U.S. census places enables a better understanding of how context shapes crime and punishment across rural and urban communities. Although homicides declined in the largest U.S. cities, the crime drop of that period was not universal.

In general, victimization rates for violent crime are higher in urban (22.2 per 1,000 people) than in rural (18.3 per 1,000 people) counties; incidences of murder/manslaughter are likewise greater in urban (4.7 per 100,000 people) than in rural (3.0 per 100,000 people) counties (Office for Victims of Crime 2016). Nonetheless, Weisheit, Falcone, and Wells (2005) demonstrate that seventeen of the thirty counties with the highest murder rate were rural in 2000. This means that the majority of high murder rate counties are not anchored by a large urban city. Many of the highest murder rates during this period were in smaller, less densely populated communities.

Lee, Maume, and Ousey (2003) found that homicide rates are consistently higher in U.S. counties with greater socioeconomic disadvantage and concentrated poverty.[1] However, they note that concentrated poverty is a significant predictor of homicide only in urban areas; for rural counties, socioeconomic disadvantage is the key determinant (Lee et al. 2003). Further, Barnett and Mencken (2002) examine the impact of poverty and a lack of resources on crime in rural areas. Defining resource-deficient counties as those with high unemployment, poverty, income inequality, or a large number of female-headed households, they find that "resource disadvantage" is positively associated with both property crimes and violent crimes (e.g., homicide). Murder also is concentrated in high-poverty, rural counties (Lee and Ousey 2001; Light and Harris 2012), but little is known about the specific concentration of crime in rural towns and neighborhoods. To be more precise, there are few empirical tests of neighborhood effects as a predictor of murder across the rural–urban continuum—a system differentiating nonmetropolitan counties by proximity to metro areas and degree of urbanization from metropolitan counties by the size of their metro area. In this section, novel data is used to investigate incidents of murder between 1970 and 2000 across rural, suburban, and urban U.S. census places. Ultimately, these data show that the context of rural communities matters in determining national murder trends.

Although homicides declined in the largest U.S. cities between 1980 and 2000, the trend was far from universal across spaces and demographics. In contrast to the precipitous decrease in urban murders during the great crime decline, suburban and rural communities witnessed a marked *increase* in murder. Although concentrated disadvantage cannot be definitely stated as the cause, there is a strong link between rising crime/violence and deprivation. Thinking about the violence across the rural–urban continuum unearths the acute, compounded, and chronic effects of disadvantage and allows the mapping of new geographies of poverty.

Before mapping murder trends, let's consider the data and methods used to measure murder rates across time and space. The analysis spans 1980 to 2000 using data from the FBI's Uniform Crime Report, U.S. decennial census data, and county- and state-level demographics from the University of Kentucky Center for Poverty Research. How context

Table 13.1 Fixed Effect Negative Binomial Regression Predicting Murders 1980–2000

Variables	(IRR/z-Ratio)	(IRR/z-Ratio)
Year	.995 (–7.76)	.995 (–7.74)
Year*rural (Beale code)	1.00 (9.17)	
Year*micropolitan		1.00 (8.63)
Controls	Yes	Yes
Wald Chi-square	2,488.27***	2,480.74
N	106,196 (5,635)	106,196 (5,635)

Source: Federal Bureau of Investigations Uniform Crime Report, 1980–2000.

Note: Exposure set to LN (population); controls include: % black, % Hispanic, % female-headed households, poverty rate, unemployment rate, % population living in same household 5+ yrs, % owner occupied housing, % vacant housing.

* $p<0.05$, ** $p<0.01$, *** $p<.001$.

influences crime in rural places is broadly examined, but the analysis deals specifically with the role of racial stigma and concentrated disadvantage in increasing murder rates among rural communities.[2]

The analysis (see table 13.1) reveals that murder rates in urban areas declined overall between 1980 and 2000, but the homicide rate increased across U.S. census places by region, state, nonmetropolitan U.S. census place, as well as across key demographic dynamics (e.g., poor blacks) representative of concentrated disadvantage. In comparing nonmetropolitan areas, rural areas have experienced even greater increases in their homicide rates than suburban places. By delving deeper into these trends, huge variations are seen within the rural, suburban, and urban contexts. Figure 13.6 shows the maximum (upward bound) and minimum (lower bound) murder rates, and the graph line is the regression fit mean of the murder rate from 1980 to 2000 in rural U.S. census places. The figure demonstrates that, over this period, the average murder rate rose across all rural U.S. census places.

In investigating the relationship between rural poverty and murder, disadvantage is a stronger predictor of murder outside of urban areas over time. To clarify further, in contrast to the common belief that the decrease in violent crimes such as murder has been a universal trend since the 1990s, the murder rates in rural communities with higher levels of concentrated disadvantage have been rising. The maximum and minimum murder rates are shown in figure 13.7, and the graph line shows the regression fit mean of the murder rate from 1980 to 2000 in rural U.S. census places that are at least 50 percent African American.

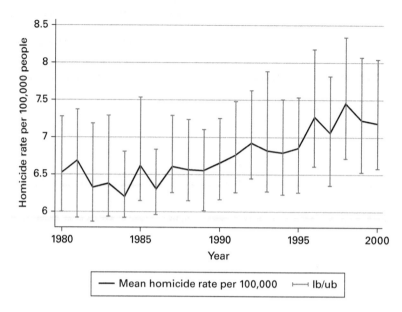

Figure 13.6   Homicide rates for rural U.S. census places, 1980–2000.

Source: Federal Bureau of Investigations, Uniform Crime Report, 1980–2000.

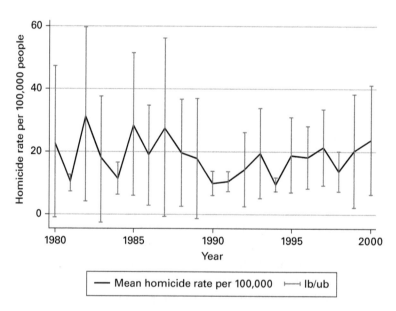

Figure 13.7   Homicide rates for rural U.S. census places 1980–2000, majority Black.

Source: Federal Bureau of Investigations, Uniform Crime Report, 1980–2000.

Some areas may not have experienced any decline in murder, but murder is a commonplace outcome in U.S. census places with higher levels of concentrated disadvantage. A central theoretical implication of these findings is that the relationship of spatial inequality to crime in rural communities must be reconsidered. For this reason, further examination of rural crime studies is needed, but the neighborhood effect across and within places also needs to be extended because violent crime is one of the most important outcomes of racial and economic stratification (e.g., Sampson 2012; Peterson and Krivo 2010).

Although roughly fifteen years have passed since the release of these data from the Uniform Crime Report, national crime and murder rates remain low. However, incarceration rates continued to rise until they leveled off after 2010. Sociologist Bruce Western (2006) shows that this rise in incarceration took place despite a decrease in crime. This is evidenced by the way in which incarceration continually rises, until it peaks at 2.4 million annually after 2010. The crime drop also did not have much to do with the number of citizens under state supervision, and the number of U.S. citizens on parole, probation, and other forms of supervision now totals more than 7 million annually.

The ripple effects of misguided policing strategies such as stop-and-frisk travel beyond mass imprisonment as they give way to increased prisoner reentry (Wodahl 2006; Eason, Zucker, and Wildeman 2017) and the construction of new prison facilities—the majority of which are being constructed in rural communities (Eason 2010, 2017). Continuing these policies and practices means more for disadvantaged rural communities than just building more prisons. Rural communities are experiencing not only increased murder rates but also an expansion of the criminal justice system through aggressive policing (McQuade 2016) and the construction of new jails (Pragacz 2016). The reach of punishment into rural communities also occurs along color lines, and research shows that the disproportionate rates of imprisonment for African Americans are higher in rural communities (Eason et al. 2017). This pattern of higher rates of minority contact with the criminal justice system in rural communities makes sense given that rural communities often have more traditional values and may be more culturally repressive. In fact, some would argue that differences in the public's perception and tolerance for crime explain the different homicide rates across rural and urban America. The next section considers how spatial inequality and context are linked to incarceration rates.

IMPRISONMENT ACROSS THE RURAL–URBAN CONTINUUM

The oversight of rural communities in studies of crime and punishment occurs in part because mass imprisonment is conflated with the prison boom. *Mass imprisonment* refers to the warehousing of 2 million U.S. citizens, whereas the *prison boom* describes the massive expansion of prison construction—from 511 prisons to 1,663 in just over thirty years. Though explorations of the relationship between imprisonment and prison building are still young, it is clear that the marked increase in prisoner reentry is a direct result of mass imprisonment. Like murder and prisoner reentry, mass imprisonment is often characterized almost exclusively as an urban phenomenon. Many studies continue to link crime and punishment to the importance of urban neighborhoods (Sampson 2012), thus expanding our knowledge on the spatial and racial contours of urban communities and punishment (Pattillo et al. 2004; Wacquant 2001; Western 2006). We know far less about the link between spatial inequality and crime in rural neighborhoods. The northern, urban-centered view of crime and punishment is so dominant that it renders rural communities virtually invisible and is a key reason rural communities remain underinvestigated.

But the relevance of the prison boom to rural communities cannot be overstated. Today the majority of prisons are constructed in nonmetropolitan U.S. census places, whereas less than a third of prisons had been built in rural areas before the 1980s (Huling 2002). More recently, some rural counties, especially those with high rates of unemployment, "actively lobby" for the construction of new prisons in their area to achieve economic development (Weisheite et al. 1995, 86). Though there is some debate over whether the prison boom has led to economic gains in rural regions (see, e.g., Huling 2002), the preponderance of recent scholarship suggests that it has not. For instance, King, Mauer, and Huling (2003) analyzed seven rural counties over a twenty-five-year period. They found no statistically significant differences in the economic trends for rural counties with prisons versus those without them. Prisons are hailed as a potential fix for economically depressed rural communities because of the jobs they have the potential to create, but local residents are not necessarily qualified for these positions. As such, rates of unemployment and per capita income are roughly the same for rural communities with a correctional facility and those without one (King et al. 2003). Thorpe (2014) found that building new prisons in economically disadvantaged rural areas has not effectively lowered poverty in those counties.

In fact, these so-called development projects (Huling 2002) not only fail to produce economic growth in a locality but may actively *hurt* the community. Thorpe (2014) argues that they uphold racial systems of domination by "link[ing] the perceived economic stability and political power of lower-class, rural whites to the continued penal confinement of poor, urban blacks" who are incarcerated in rural facilities in majority-white areas (17). This is especially important insofar as prisoner reentry is concerned. John Eason (2012, 2017) has studied rural *prison towns*—that is, nonmetropolitan municipalities that have secured and constructed a federal, state, or private prison. Eason finds that they both *receive* prisoners (through building new facilities and taking in new inmates from elsewhere) and *produce* them (via prisoner reentry). Thus, rural prison towns may be hurt by the vast prison construction and export of urban criminals to rural communities.

Ultimately, many (Eason 2010; Gilmore 2007; Schlosser 1998; Lawrence and Travis 2004; Weisheit et al. 1995) agree that there are strong connections between socioeconomic disadvantage in rural communities and the prison boom. There is less consensus on whether the prison boom is the result of disadvantage or a cause of disadvantage. The prevailing view is that the prison boom is primarily a function of northern, urban, mass imprisonment (Schlosser 1998). However, one of the authors of this chapter, penologist John Eason (2017), demonstrates that rural communities build prisons not simply for jobs but to manage their poor reputations. In fact, southern rural spatial inequality (concentrated disadvantage) at the U.S. census place is a key driver of the prison boom (Eason 2010, 2017). Eason (2012) also argues that if rural concentrated disadvantage is measured at the appropriate spatial scale—that is, on the level of the town and the neighborhood—it can explain a host of other crime and punishment phenomena, including criminal activity and mass imprisonment.

The link between crime and mass imprisonment remains the subject of debate. Some scholars, such as Bruce Western (2006), argue that mass imprisonment is unrelated to rising crime rates. Others, such as Steven Levitt (2004), argue that imprisonment deters crime. Even so, mass imprisonment and reentry remain grossly underinvestigated topics in rural communities. How does spatial inequality shape the contours of ex-convicts reentering life in rural America? What is the link between concentrated disadvantage, crime, and criminal justice in rural America? To answer these questions, the theoretical rationale behind mass imprisonment must be explored.

Imprisonment, like all punishment, is a form of social control. In an effort to explain the U.S. imprisonment rate, Blumstein and Cohen (1973) posit the theory of the *stability of punishment*. They argue that crime is not only functional and natural in society but that it will "be maintained at a specific level" and remain constant over time (198). This thesis builds on sociologist Émile Durkheim's (1984) assertion that crime is "normal" and "part of all healthy societies." From this perspective, punishment is a form of boundary maintenance. Based on this assertion, Blumstein and Cohen (1973) propose a behavior-punishment distribution in considering the imprisonment rate as a measure of punishment from 1930 to 1970. Their analysis provides evidence that imprisonment rates in the United States during this period support the stability-of-punishment thesis. Although they later retracted this position in the face of increasing rates of U.S. imprisonment, the central question posed in this line of inquiry lingers: If societies accept crime as natural and functional, should there be a natural and functional level of punishment? Since Blumstein and Cohen's time, scholars have argued that the primary reasons for increased imprisonment are conflicts of race and class.

According to *conflict theory*, mass imprisonment is a strategy to manage surplus labor. From a racial threat perspective, on the other hand, mass imprisonment is a means of social control for black and Latino populations. Mass imprisonment is not only considered a backlash to a specific form of racial threat—the civil rights movement—but a product of the racially biased War on Drugs (Alexander 2010; Mauer 2006; Tonry 2011; Western 2006). To many, the War on Drugs is the most important driver of mass imprisonment and the fivefold increase in the U.S. prison population since 1970 (Alexander 2010; Mauer 2006; Tonry 2011; Western 2006). Although these theories provide plausible explanations for past trends in imprisonment, they do not tell the entire story.

Hawkins (1987) raises questions about the utility of racial threat and conflict perspectives in explaining racial differences in punishment. He argues that the conflict and racial threat perspectives oversimplify the nexus of race and punishment and must be reworked. Along this same line, one can question whether mass imprisonment is simply a backlash to the civil rights movement or whether mass imprisonment can be reduced to a by-product of the War on Drugs. These factors play an important role in determining mass imprisonment, but the spatial and temporal differences in these two factors alone cannot account for increased punishment given the magnitude and longevity of this phenomenon.

For instance, the civil rights movement took place primarily in the urban South. Aside from the dubious ability and desire of government actors to sustain a backlash against the civil rights movement over time, if mass imprisonment is indeed a response to the movement, then there should be increased racial disparities in imprisonment in the South. However, Hawkins and Hardy (1989) establish that, since 1970, the largest increases in the disparate rate of incarceration for African Americans versus whites took place outside of the South. Moreover, Western (2006) found that during the era of mass imprisonment the disproportionate rate of imprisonment between black and white males that has existed since the convict-leasing system decreased slightly during the late 1990s. Although racial disparities still abound in the criminal justice system, this empirical evidence suggests that race cannot be the only factor in mass imprisonment. Therefore, like other incarnations of racial threat and the conflict theory, the civil rights backlash and the War on Drugs hypotheses are oversimplified explanations for mass imprisonment.

Rather than attempt to theorize mass imprisonment, the more important question raised here is whether this empirical evidence sheds light on differences in mass imprisonment across rural and urban places. Convicted criminals are not likely to be incarcerated near the places they commit crimes; in fact, urban dwellers are often transported to rural prisons to serve their sentences. As for rural prisoners, there is no reason to believe that they are more likely to serve out their sentences near their homes either. As such, the community housing the imprisoned has more to do with local economies than with social attitudes toward crime.

Given that mass imprisonment disproportionately affects poor communities of color, one must ask whether there are disproportionate rates of mass imprisonment for people of color in rural areas. Using Eason, Zucker, and Wildeman's (2017) framing of the rural communities as a producer of prisoners to investigate the contribution of rural concentrated disadvantaged to mass imprisonment, data from the Project on Arkansas Imprisonment, Reentry, and Health Disparities (PAIRHD) was surveyed. PAIRHD is an effort to examine the socioeconomic changes and health outcomes associated with imprisonment and prison reentry across towns in Arkansas. Overall, the project examines the incidence of health outcomes in Arkansas as a function of U.S. census place characteristics, imprisonment, and reentry rates.[3]

To understand trends in imprisonment across Arkansas towns over time, admissions rates were examined. Figure 13.8 shows the annual rate

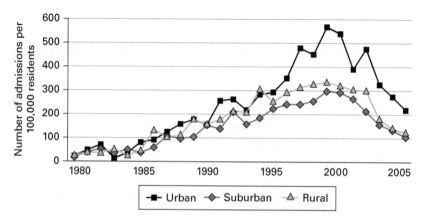

Figure 13.8   ADOC prison admissions by U.S. census place.

Source: John M. Eason. 2015. "Project on Arkansas Imprisonment, Reentry, and Health Disparities." Compiled from data from the Arkansas Department of Health, the Arkansas Department of Corrections, and the U.S. Census Bureau. Available via the author.

of admission across rural, suburban, and urban places for the Arkansas Department of Corrections (ADOC) from 1980 to 2005. Given that Arkansas is a predominantly rural state, Little Rock dominates the admissions trend for urban areas. In examining the trends in admission across rural, suburban, and urban U.S. census places, prison admissions into ADOC rose steadily from 1980 to 1995. During this period, there is not significant variation across rural, urban, and suburban communities; on average, admissions ranged between two hundred and three hundred admissions to ADOC per 100,000 residents. However, after 1995 the rate of admissions from urban U.S. census places in Arkansas outpaced that of suburban and rural communities, increasing to the highest point measured between 1980 and 2005 at nearly six hundred admissions per 100,000 residents by 1999. After 1993, rural areas began to outpace suburban areas in ADOC admissions, eventually peaking in 1999 at more than 300 admissions per 100,000 residents.

Again, using admissions rates, racial differences in imprisonment are mapped across Arkansas over time. Figure 13.9 shows the annual rate of admission by race for ADOC from 1980 to 2005. The disproportionate rate of imprisonment for African Americans compared to whites has been consistent over time in admissions to ADOC, but the gap increased steadily from 1980 to 1998. In 1980, the rate of admissions to ADOC for African Americans was more than seven times that of whites. By 1990, the

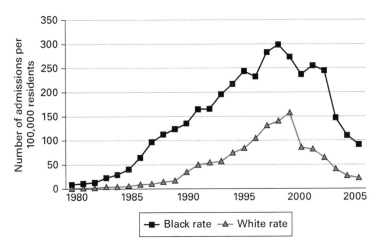

Figure 13.9 Total ADOC prison admissions rates by race.

Source: John M. Eason. 2015. "Project on Arkansas Imprisonment, Reentry, and Health Disparities." Compiled from data from the Arkansas Department of Health, the Arkansas Department
of Corrections, and the U.S. Census Bureau. Available via the author.

rate of admissions for whites had increased twenty-eightfold from 1980.
Over this same period, the rate of African American admissions increased
by more than fifteen times compared to 1980, closing the disproportionate rate of incarceration between African Americans and whites to 3.85 by
1990. By 2000, the rate of admissions for African Americans and whites
reached its pinnacle, and the rate of disproportionate admissions also
increased, with African Americans being nearly seven times as likely as
whites to be admitted to ADOC. This section demonstrates the salience of
rural communities in understanding the varied contours of mass imprisonment. The next sections consider the importance of rural communities'
structures and spatial contexts to the prison boom and prisoner reentry.

PLACING THE PRISON BOOM

The prison boom has reshaped the landscape of punishment in rural
America (Lawrence and Travis 2004; Eason 2017). Although prison proliferation disproportionately affects rural communities, we are only now
beginning to explore the causes and consequences of this phenomenon. If
laid end to end, the prisons built during the boom would cover nearly six
hundred square miles. Most of this acreage is in rural communities, and
nearly 70 percent of prisons were built in nonmetropolitan communities.

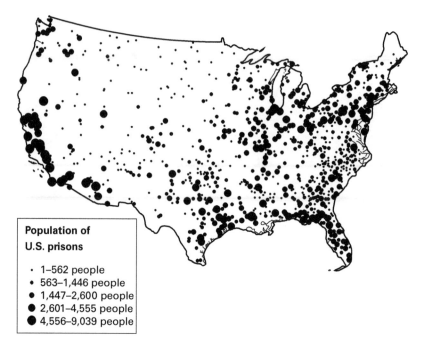

Figure 13.10   U.S. prison proliferation, 2010.

Source: Eason 2016.

For comparison, this landmass is about half the acreage of Rhode Island. Figure 13.10 shows all U.S. prison facilities in 2010 according to size and location. Many larger prisons are located in, or near, urban areas, but there are also many large prisons in rural areas. An accurate count of the number of prisoners held in rural prisons cannot be provided, but a conservative estimate is that 1.3 million prisoners are held in rural prisons annually. This estimate was derived using a subsample of facilities that include the average daily population of the prison in 2010.

Furthermore, the facilities sampled support an average daily population of 758 prisoners and 231 staff. Despite the vast amount of attention given to private prisons in the popular discourse, fewer than 10 percent of all facilities operate under private contracts. In analyzing the location of the entire population of U.S. prisons, roughly 81 percent are run by state governments; the remaining 9 percent are federal. Only about 1 percent of all U.S. census places builds a prison in any period.

Currently there are over 400,000 corrections officers, about one-third of whom are black or Latino (Ward 2006). The fact that prisons

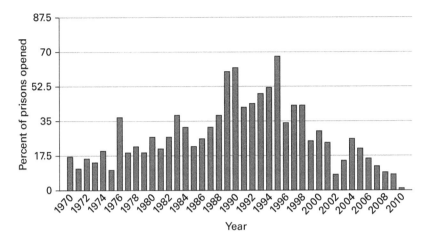

Figure 13.11   U.S. prison boom, 1970–2010.

Source: Eason 2016.

employ more than 100,000 corrections officers of color complicates the narrative of punishment as only contributing to racial inequality. Further complicating how we understand the racial landscape of prison building, penologist John Eason (2010) studied spatial inequality and found that during the height of the prison boom in the 1990s, prison building was a result of concentrated racial and economic disadvantage in U.S. census places. Eason argued that the essential local determinants of prison building in rural U.S. census places were the size of the black and Hispanic populations, the poverty level, and the total population of the community. Furthermore, during the height of the prison boom, the South was more likely than any other region to build a prison. Because of the prison boom, the prison, an undeniably stigmatized institution, is indelibly linked to the political economy of depressed rural communities of color (Eason 2012, 2017). Though the prison boom (figure 13.11) has reshaped the rural landscape, the contours of prison towns' demographic characteristics across the entire prison boom period have not yet been mapped. This section uses data from the Prison Proliferation Project (Eason 2016) to expand on Eason (2010) and explore town-level correlates of prison building.

The Prison Proliferation Project[4] includes novel data on prison building, allowing a comparison of predictors across different periods of the prison boom. A thumbnail sketch describes rural towns that built prisons versus those that did not. This is followed by an overview of national trends in prison building across different periods of the prison boom, paying particular attention to the role of spatial inequality. U.S. census place poverty rates and the residential segregation dissimilarity index are used as predictors of prison building. Certain trends are consistent across all periods of the prison boom. For instance, the South is the most dominant across all periods, with roughly 45 percent of all prisons in the prison boom period built in this region. The percent of residents living below poverty and percent black is higher in towns that received prisons than in those that did not across all periods of the prison boom. In addition, residential segregation was a strong predictor of prison building in the 1990s and 2000s across the nation and in the South.

During the 1970s and 1980s, trends in towns that built prisons and those that did not were relatively stable. For instance, prison-building towns had roughly 8 percent more black residents than towns that did not build prisons, and prison towns were only slightly poorer, with roughly 2 percent more of the population living below poverty. In the 1990s and 2000s, however, these trends shifted with increases in poverty, percentage of black residents, and residential segregation becoming strong predictors of prison building. These trends provide evidence of the power of concentrated disadvantage in U.S. census places in predicting prison building. This evidence provides further support for considering context and the neighborhood effect when trying to better understand crime and punishment in rural America. The problem of rural reentry for rural poverty is especially relevant in this context given the boom in prison construction in rural America.

RETHINKING RURAL REENTRY

What about prisoner reentry? Each year nearly 800,000 formerly incarcerated individuals leave prisons to return home (Carson and Sabol 2012). There are fewer social services and health care organizations for prisoners reentering in rural areas than in urban regions (Wallace, Eason, and Lindsey 2015). The return is more than a singular event; prisoner reentry is a process that reshapes neighborhoods, institutions, families, and individuals (Miller 2014). The concentration effects of prison reentry produce a host of negative outcomes for urban neighborhoods (Clear, Waring, and Scully 2005). Reentering prisoners suffer many challenges, such as barriers to employment, poor access to safe and affordable housing, and obstacles to health care. Despite the catalog of scholarship mapping the effects of reentry on urban communities, little is known about how prisoner reentry affects rural communities (Wodahl 2006). Given that prisoner reentry has lasting and meaningful effects on communities, it is important to understand how reentry affects rural communities. How does spatial inequality shape the contours of ex-convicts reentering life in rural America? Specifically, what are the effects of concentrated disadvantage and racial composition on reentry across the rural–urban continuum?

Again, data from PAIRHD is used to examine rates of reentry across nonmetropolitan and metropolitan counties. The reentry data consist of approximately 118,000 reentries (not individuals) between 1990 and 2008, across 541 U.S. census places and seventy-five counties in the state of Arkansas. Figure 13.12 provides a preliminary analysis, illustrating the constant increase in reentry rates in Arkansas between 1990 and 2008

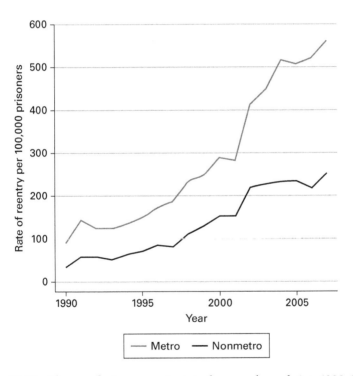

Figure 13.12 **The rate of prisoner reentry into the general population, 1990–2008.**

Source: John M. Eason. 2015. "Project on Arkansas Imprisonment, Reentry, and Health Disparities." Compiled from data from the Arkansas Department of Health, the Arkansas Department of Corrections, and the U.S. Census Bureau. Available via the author.

across metropolitan and nonmetropolitan counties. Once again, Little Rock dominates the trend in reentry for urban areas because Arkansas is predominantly a rural state.

During this period, there is significant variation in reentry trends among metropolitan and nonmetropolitan communities. Metropolitan communities have a reentry rate of more than 500 per 100,000 residents, whereas nonmetropolitan areas have a rate of just over 200 per 100,000 residents. This analysis provides only a very cursory description of trends; it warrants a deeper analysis segmenting the nonmetropolitan communities into suburban versus rural areas. Furthermore, future analyses need to focus on characteristics of concentrated disadvantage within U.S. census places. In any case, it is clear that many elements of context—a community's rurality, percent black, poverty level, and degree of concentrated disadvantage—matter for explaining trends in the prison boom, mass incarceration, and prisoner reentry in rural America.

CONCLUSION

Context, spatial inequality, and poverty within and across U.S. census places are important in determining key crime and punishment outcomes in rural America. Using the square of crime theory, poverty is criminalized through the interdependent actions and beliefs of a multiplicity of actors, both at the individual level (i.e., the victim, the offender) and beyond (i.e., the public, the state). First, place matters with reference to three recent trends in rural crime. To this point, the downward trend in murder is far from universal across spatial scales and place-level demographics. More specifically, although there has been a downward trend in murder across U.S. cities, rural communities effectively traded places with their urban counterparts and have witnessed an increase in homicide rates in recent years. Second, rural rates of prisoner reentry and incarceration have likewise increased over time. Finally, using novel data on the U.S. prison boom, towns with higher levels of poverty, larger black populations, and greater residential segregation were more likely to build a prison in the 1990s and 2000s.

Given what is known about the mutual reinforcement of poverty and crime in the United States, the findings of this chapter have serious implications for the future of rural America. If we continue to direct our preventative resources and public attention to curtailing crime in urban regions alone, we stand to neglect rural poor indivdiuals and communities. If inequality continues to rise in the United States, with more and more prisons being built in economically depressed rural communities, crime and punishment may remain entrenched in impoverished regions of rural America.

Ultimately, the findings of this chapter illustrate the importance of taking into account context when discussing crime and punishment. Neighborhood-level poverty rates matter, but so, too, do measures of spatial inequality, racial composition, and place along the rural–urban continuum. Overall, this chapter suggests that if rural, low-income communities experience a continued growth in poverty and spatial inequality, the varied actors within the square of crime may continue to interact in unique ways—fueling not only crime and punishment but also exacerbating socioeconomic disadvantage for the rural communities and people of the United States.

Case Study: Violence Against Women in America's Heartland

Walter S. DeKeseredy and Amanda Hall-Sanchez

Within criminological and sociological circles, rural American communities are well known for experiencing myriad social problems, especially poverty and high levels of unemployment. Much less is known, however, about violence in these areas. In fact, rural crime has ranked among the least studied topics in criminology (Donnermeyer and DeKeseredy 2014). This selective inattention is now being addressed mainly by a growing international cadre of critical criminologists. They view the major causes of crime as the unequal class, racial/ethnic, and gender relations that control our society. To date, one such group of scholars in particular has contributed the bulk of empirical, theoretical, and policy work on criminological issues in rural communities. These are feminists who study intimate violence against women, and we are active members of this cohort. Feminism is defined as "a set of theories about women's oppression and a set of strategies for change" (Daly and Chesney Lind 1988, 502).

Feminist research on violence against rural women quickly exploded on the scene in the latter part of the last decade, with much of the U.S. work being done in the rural Appalachian part of southeast Ohio. This case study is based on this region and spans ten years in which rich, in-depth interviews were conducted with fifty-five women who were assaulted in ways few of us could possibly imagine when they wanted to leave, were trying to leave, were in the process of leaving, or finally left their male partners.

The women who revealed their stories were all at great risk of being killed. In fact, regardless of where women live in the United States, women who are separated run a sixfold increase of being murdered (DeKeseredy and Schwartz 2009; Ellis, Stuckless, and Smith 2015). Using aggregate National Crime Victimization Surveys (NCVS) from 1992 to 2009, Rennison, DeKeseredy, and Dragiewicz (2012) found that a higher percentage of rural divorced/separated women are victims of rape/sexual assault than are urban divorced/separated women. In addition, rural separated women are victims of intimate rape/sexual assault at significantly higher rates than their suburban and urban counterparts. Rennison, DeKeseredy, and Dragiewicz (2013) also found that rural divorced and separated women are victimized by other types of violence at rates exceeding those of their urban and suburban counterparts.

Interviews conducted since 2003 and up to 2013 provide further support for the empirically informed claim by Rennison et al. (2012, 2013) that separation/divorce assault is a major problem in rural American communities. The most important themes that stood out were male peer support, men's patriarchal dominance and control, men's consumption of violent and racist pornography, and membership in the all-male hunting subculture, which also involved male peer support. This concept is defined as the attachments to male peers and the resources that these men provide that encourage and legitimate woman abuse.

In addition to these risk factors, interviews revealed that the system of social practices that dominates and oppresses rural and urban women alike operates differently in rural places. For example, the masculization of the rural, the dominance of man and mankind over women and nature, is represented as natural and unproblematic (Carrington, Donnermeyer, and DeKeseredy 2014). Furthermore, whereas many men in urban areas (usually males of color) report adversarial relationships with police, men who abuse women in rural communities are more likely to be friends with and be protected by criminal justice officials.

This case study also confirmed what other scholars in the field are finding. For instance, there is widespread acceptance of violence against women and community norms prohibiting victims from seeking social support. Moreover, compared to urban women, rural women have fewer social support resources, and those available cover large geographic areas. Rural women face additional barriers, including geographic and social isolation and inadequate (if any) public transportation. Another factor exacerbating rural women's troubles is being uninsured; rural women are less likely to be insured than are urban and suburban women.

Popular films, documentaries, news stories, and television shows may portray rural women as weak, unintelligent, seductive, or strong, but only rarely do they focus on male-to-female violence in rural communities. Sadly, this research, and studies done by a few other scholars, show that numerous rural women continue to suffer in silence, and those interviewed in this case study constitute just the tip of the iceberg.

NOTES

1. *Concentrated disadvantage* is in general a key predictor of negative neighborhood outcomes such as crime—not only for violent crimes, such as homicide. For instance, living in a community in which residents are exposed to violence (hearing gunshots) makes people more likely to live in fear. Similarly, living in a high-crime area where neighbors keep to themselves increases the likelihood that someone will be the victim of crime.

2. The key dependent variable is annual murder rate at the U.S. census place, and key independent variables include year, population size, percent urban population, race, poverty, residential segregation, and foreign- or native-born status. Other controls include percent vacant housing, owner-occupied housing, and party of state government. Residential segregation, percent black, poverty, and vacant housing are commonly used in the neighborhood effects literature to measure concentrated disadvantage. A fixed-effects regression was used with robust clustered standard errors around FIPS-place level to parse out the effects within and between geographic locations.

3. The first data set consists of individual inmate reentry records from the Arkansas Department of Corrections (ADC) between 1990 and 2008. Address data are included in the ADC data, allowing inmates to be geocoded to communities after release. The second data set consists of U.S. census and county-level data related to new incidents of HIV annually between 1990 and 2011, the density of community organizations collected from annual county and zip code business pattern census data between 1990 and 2010, and structural census covariates associated with socioeconomic and demographic characteristics of residents collected from the 1990, 2000, and 2010 decennial census. U.S. census and county-level segregation data is created using block-group census data on race and ethnicity from decennial censuses. The index of dissimilarity

is included for all pairs of whites, blacks, and Hispanics. The P^* isolation index is included for each of these three groups as well.

In 1997, the Standard Industrial Classification (SIC) code system used to classify types of businesses was replaced with the North American Industry Classification System (NAICS). The NAICS system was developed under supervision by the Office of Management and Budget and was a collaborative effort between the United States, Canada, and Mexico. Although SIC and NAICS codes are not strictly comparable, and the NAICS system has evolved over time, it is possible to establish near comparability in broad classifications of industry (e.g., farming/forestry, mining, construction, retail, finance). All SIC and NAICS codes have been recoded to the 2007 NAICS system; the latest system developed during the study period. Additionally, the county-level census data set includes rural–urban continuum codes (i.e., Beale codes) obtained from the U.S. Department of Agriculture.

The data were originally constructed so that each individual sentence received an entry. That is, individuals who entered prison on a single date for multiple sentences were counted by the number of sentences. This means that an individual who entered prison after being convicted of four counts of a crime was counted four times. Because the focus of this study is the number of prison admissions, the data needed were adjusted to reflect only admissions. As such, the data were collapsed to reflect only the number of entries for an individual on a given date. Even if a person entered prison on a single date for ten different crimes, that person was still only counted once.

4. These data were augmented and merged with Geolytics' decennial U.S. Census demographic and economic data using GIS software resulting in a data set with every U.S. census place from 1970 to 2000 normalized to 2000 decennial boundaries (N=25,150) and 1,663 prisons spread across all fifty states. Unlike most data on prisons, these data are not a sample of prisons or towns—the data set includes every adult prison facility and every municipality in the United States. These data were then merged with files containing U.S. state-level economic and program transfer data covering the years 1980 to 2011 as maintained by the University of Kentucky Center for Poverty Research (UKCPR). The UKCPR data include such state-level predictors as party affiliation of the governor and both chambers of the legislature, as well as state-level demographic, poverty, and employment variables. The data are additionally delineated along the rural–urban continuum according to the Beale Rural-Urban Classification Codes (RUCC). The RUCC designates the degree of rurality (9 the most rural) or urbanity (1 the most urban) for each census location in every period of the analysis, with 1974, 1983, 1993, and 2003 as designated years for determining rural–urban classifications. Because of the potential for prison populations to tip the RUCC designation from rural to urban, 1974 was used as a baseline for this analysis.

To this end, data were obtained from several sources including the *2010 Directory of Adult and Juvenile Correctional Departments, Institutions, Agencies, and Probation and Parole Authorities* and the Inter-University Consortium for Political and Social Research data holdings. The latter includes a listing of the 1,600-plus U.S. prison facilities by latitude and longitude coordinates, U.S. census place, name of facility, and year of facility construction. The directory is regarded as the "gold standard" of prison locations by a contact at the United States Bureau of Prisons. The location of each facility was verified using the Coding Accuracy Support System, a location verification system used by institutions such as the United States Postal Service, and each case was reconciled multiple times. This extensive process was used to ensure the accuracy of facility locations within each U.S. census place along with the corresponding year it opened. However, only residential segregation measures to 1990 and 2000 were available for this analysis.

REFERENCES

Alexander, Michelle. 2010. *The New Jim Crow: Mass Incarceration in the Age of Color-blindness*. New York: New Press.

American Bar Association, Commission on Homelessness & Poverty. 2016. "Criminalizing Poverty: Debtor's Prison in the 21st Century." http://www.americanbar.org/content/dam/aba/publications/litigation_committees/childrights/16-06-20-CE1606FSS-course-materials.authcheckdam.pdf.

Arthur, John A. 1991. "Socioeconomic Predictors of Crime in Rural Georgia." *Criminal Justice Review* 16(1):29–41.

Barnett, Cynthia, and Carson F. Mencken. 2002. "Social Disorganization Theory and the Contextual Nature of Crime in Nonmetropolitan Counties." *Rural Sociology* 67(3):372–93.

Blumstein, Alfred, and Jacqueline Cohen. 1973. "Theory of the Stability of Punishment, A." *Journal of Criminal Law & Criminology* 64: 198.

Blumstein, Alfred, and Joel Wallman. 2006. *The Crime Drop in America*, rev. ed. New York: Cambridge University Press.

Carrington, Kerry, Joseph F. Donnermeyer, and Walter S. DeKeseredy. 2014. "Intersectionality, Rural Criminology, and Re-imaging the Boundaries of Critical Criminology." *Critical Criminology* 22(4):463–477.

Carson, Ann E., and William J. Sabol, W. 2012. "Prisoners in 2011." Bureau of Justice Statistics, NCJ 239808. https://www.bjs.gov/content/pub/pdf/p11.pdf.

Clear, Todd R., Elin Waring, and Kristen Scully. 2005. "Communities and Reentry: Concentrated Reentry Cycling." In *Prisoner Reentry and Crime in America*, ed. Jeremy Travis and Christy Visher. New York: Cambridge University Press, 179–208.

Daly, Kathleen, and Meda Chesney-Lind. 1988. "Feminism and Criminology." *Justice Quarterly*, 5(4), 497–538.

DeKeseredy, Walter, and Martin Schwartz. 2009. *Dangerous Exits: Escaping Abusive Relationships in Rural America*. New Brunswick, NJ: Rutgers University Press.

Deller, Steven C., and Melissa W. Deller. 2011. "Structural Shifts in Select Determinants of Crime with a Focus on Rural and Urban Differences." *Western Criminology Review* 12(3):120–38.

Dolan, Karen, and Jodi L. Carr, 2015. "The Poor Get Prison: The Alarming Spread of the Criminalization of Poverty." Report by the Institute for Policy Studies. http://www.ips-dc.org/wp-content/uploads/2015/03/IPS-The-Poor-Get-Prison-Final.pdf.

Donnermeyer, Joseph F., and Walter DeKeseredy. 2008. "Toward a Rural Critical Criminology." *Southern Rural Sociology* 23(2):4–28.

——. 2014. *Rural Criminology*. London: Routledge.

Donnermeyer, Joseph F., Pat Jobes, and Elaine Barclay. 2006. "Rural Crime, Poverty, and Community." In *Advancing Critical Criminology: Theory and Application*, ed. Walter S. DeKeseredy and Barbara Perry. Lanham, MD: Lexington.

Duhart, Detis T. 2000. "Urban, Suburban, and Rural Victimization, 1993–98." Bureau of Justice Statistics, NCJ 182031. https://www.bjs.gov/content/pub/ascii/usrv98.txt.

Durkheim, Émile. 1984. *The Division of Labor in Society.* New York: Free Press.

Eason, John M. 2010. "Mapping Prison Proliferation: Region, Rurality, Race, and Disadvantage in Prison Placement." *Social Science Research* 39(6):1015–28. doi: 10.1016/j.ssresearch.2010.03.001.

——. 2012. "Extending the Hyperghetto: Toward a Theory of Punishment, Race, and Rural Disadvantage." *Journal of Poverty* 16(3):274–95.

——. 2016. "Prison Proliferation Project." http://www.johneason.com/prison-proliferation/.

——. 2017. *Big House on the Prairie: Rise of the Rural Ghetto and Prison Proliferation.* Chicago: University of Chicago Press.

Eason, John M., Danielle Zucker, and Christopher Wildeman. 2017. "Mass Imprisonment Across the Rural-Urban Interface." *Annals of the American Academy of Political and Social Science.*

Ellis, Desmond, Noreen Stuckless, and Carries Smith. 2015. *Marital Separation and Lethal Domestic Violence.* New York: Routledge.

Garriott, William. 2011. *Policing Methamphetamine: Narcopolitics in Rural America.* New York: NYU Press.

Gelman, Andrew, Alex Kiss, and Jeffrey Fagan. 2006. "An analysis of the NYPD's Stop-and-Frisk Policy in the Context of Claims of Racial Bias." *Journal of the American Statistical Association* 102(479):813–823.

Geolytics CensusCD 1970. 2010. East Brunswick, NJ: GeoLytics, Inc.

Geolytics CensusCD 1980 in 2000 Boundaries. 2010. East Brunswick, NJ: GeoLytics, Inc.

Geolytics CensusCD 2000. 2010. East Brunswick, NJ: GeoLytics, Inc.

Gilmore, Ruth Wilson. 2007. *Golden Gulag: Prison, Surplus, Crisis, and Opposition in Globalizing California.* Berkeley: University of California Press.

Gustafson, Kaaryn. 2009. "The Criminalization of Poverty." *Journal of Criminal Law and Criminology* 99(3):643–716.

Hawkins, Darnell F. 1987. "Beyond Anomalies: Rethinking the Conflict Perspective on Race and Criminal Punishment." *Social Forces* 65(3):719–745.

Hawkins, Darnell F., & Kenneth A. Hardy. 1989. "Black-White Imprisonment Rates: A State-by-State Analysis." *Social Justice* 16(4[38]):75–94.

Huling, Tracy. 2002. "Building a Prison Economy in Rural America." In *Invisible Punishment: The Collateral Consequences of Mass Imprisonment,* ed. Marc Mauer and Meda Chesney-Lind. NY: New Press.

Keller, Josh, and Adam Pearce. 2016. "This Small Indiana County Sends More People to Prison Than San Francisco and Durham, N.C., Combined. Why?" *New York Times,* September 2. http://www.nytimes.com/2016/09/02/upshot/new-geography-of-prisons.html?_r=0.

King, Ryan S., Marc Mauer, and Tracy Huling. 2003. "Big Prisons, Small Towns: Prison Economics in Rural America." The Sentencing Project. http://www.sentencingproject.org/wp-content/uploads/2016/01/Big-Prisons-Small-Towns-Prison-Economics-in-Rural-America.pdf.

Lawrence, Sarah, and Jeremy Travis. 2004. "The New Landscape of Imprisonment: Mapping America's Prison Expansion." Urban Institute. http://www.urban.org /UploadedPDF/410994_mapping_prisons.pdf.

Lee, Matthew R., Michael O. Maume, and Graham C. Ousey. 2003. "Social Isolation and Lethal Violence Across the Metro/Nonmetro Divide: The Effects of Socioeconomic Disadvantage and Poverty Concentration on Homicide." *Rural Sociology* 68(1):107–31.

Lee, Matthew R., and Graham C. Ousey. 2001. "Size Matters: Examining the Link Between Small Manufacturing, Socioeconomic Deprivation, and Crime Rates in Nonmetropolitan Communities." *Sociological Quarterly* 42(4):581.

Levitt, Steven D. 2004. "Understanding Why Crime Fell in the 1990s: Four Factors That Explain the Decline and Six That Do Not." *Journal of Economic Perspectives* 18(1):163–190.

Light, Michael T., and Casey T. Harris. 2012. "Race, Space, and Violence: Exploring Spatial Dependence in Structural Covariates of White and Black Violent Crime in US Counties." *Journal of Quantitative Criminology* 28(4):559–86.

Martin, William G., Joshua M. Price. 2016. *After Prisons?: Freedom, Decarceration, and Justice Disinvestment*. London: Lexington.

Mauer, Marc. 2006. *Race to Incarcerate*, 2nd ed. New York: New Press.

Mawby, Rob I., and Richard Yarwood. 2011. *Rural Policing and Policing the Rural: A Constable Countryside?* Burlington, VT: Ashgate.

McQuade, Brendan. 2016. "From the Carceral Leviathan to the Police State: Policing Decarceration in New York State." In *After Prisons? Freedom, Decarceration, and Justice Disinvestment,* ed. William Martin and Joshua Price, chap. 3. Washington, DC: Rowman & Littlefield.

Meares, Tracey L. 2014. "The Law and Social Science of Stop and Frisk." *Annual Review of Law and Social Science* 10:335–352.

Miller, Reuben Jonathan. 2014. "Devolving the Carceral State: Race, Prisoner Reentry, and the Micro-Politics of Urban Poverty Management." *Punishment & Society* 16(3):305–35.

Office for Victims of Crime. 2016. "Urban and Rural Crime." https://ovc.ncjrs.gov /ncvrw2016/content/section-6/PDF/2016NCVRW_6_UrbanRural-508.pdf.

Pattillo, Mary, Bruce Western, and David Weiman, eds. 2004. *Imprisoning America: The Social Effects of Mass Incarceration*. New York: Russell Sage Foundation.

Petersilia, Joan. 2003. *When Prisoners Come Home: Parole and Prisoner Reentry*. New York: Oxford University Press.

Peterson, Ruth D., and Lauren J. Krivo. 2010. *Divergent Social Worlds: Neighborhood Crime and the Racial-Spatial Divide*. New York: Russell Sage Foundation.

Pragacz, Andrew J. 2016. "Is This What Decarceration Looks Like? Rising Jail Incarceration in Upstate New York." In *After Prisons? Freedom, Decarceration, and Justice Disinvestment,* ed. William Martin and Joshua Price, chap. 5. Washington, DC: Rowman & Littlefield.

Prather, Sarah McKenzie. 2010. "The Criminalization of Homelessness." UNLV Theses, Dissertations, Professional Papers, and Capstones. http://digitalscholarship.unlv.edu /cgi/viewcontent.cgi?article=1010&context=thesesdissertations.

Rennison, Callie Marie, Walter S. DeKeseredy, and Molly Dragiewicz. 2012. "Urban, Suburban, and Rural Variations in Separation/Divorce Rape/Sexual Assault: Results from the National Crime Victimization Survey." *Feminist Criminology* 7(4):282–97.

——. 2013. "Intimate Relationship Status Variations in Violence Against Women: Urban, Suburban, and Rural Differences." *Violence Against Women* 19(11):1312–30.

Rennison, Callie Marie, Molly Dragiewicz, and Walter S. DeKeseredy. 2013. "Context Matters: Violence Against Women and Reporting to Police in Rural, Suburban, and Urban Areas." *American Journal of Criminal Justice*, 38(1):141–59.

Rose, Dina R., and Todd R. Clear. 1998. "Incarceration, Social Capital, and Crime: Implications for Social Disorganization Theory." *Criminology* 36(3):441–80.

Rutherford, A. 2002. *Growing Out of Crime: The New Era*. Winchester, UK: Waterside.

Sampson, Robert J. 2012. *Great American City: Chicago and the Enduring Neighborhood Effect*. Chicago: University of Chicago Press.

Sampson, Robert J., and Charles Loeffler. 2010. "Punishment's Place: The Local Concentration of Mass Incarceration." *Daedalus* 139(3):20–31.

Sampson, Robert J., Stephen W. Raudenbush, and Felton Earls. 1997. "Neighborhoods and Violent Crime: A Multilevel Study of Collective Efficacy." *Science* 277(5328):918.

Schlosser, Eric. 1998. "The Prison-Industrial Complex." *Atlantic* 282(6):51.

Substance Abuse and Mental Health Services Administration. 2014. "Results from the 2013 National Survey on Drug Use and Health: Summary of National Findings." NSDUH Series H-48, HHS Publication No. (SMA) 14-4863. Rockville, MD: Substance Abuse and Mental Health Services Administration. https://www.samhsa.gov/data/sites/default/files/NSDUHresultsPDFWHTML2013/Web/NSDUHresults2013.pdf.

Thorpe, Rebecca. 2014. "Urban Divestment, Rural Decline and the Politics of Mass Incarceration." *The Good Society* 23(1):17–29.

Tonry, Michael. 2011. *Punishing Race: A Continuing American Dilemma*. London: Oxford University Press.

Travis, J. 2005. *But They All Come Back: Facing the Challenges of Prisoner Reentry*. Washington DC: The Urban Insitute.

Travis, Jeremy, Bruce Western, and Steve Redburn, eds. 2014. *The Growth of Incarceration in the United States: Exploring Causes and Consequences*. Washington, DC: National Academies Press.

Truman, Jennifer L., and Lynn Langton. 2015. Criminal Victimization, 2014. U.S. Department of Justice, Office of Justice Programs, *Bureau of Justice Statistics* Revised September 29, 2015.

Wacquant, Loïc. 2001. "Deadly Symbiosis: When Ghetto and Prison Meet and Merge." *Punishment and Society* 3 (1):95–134.

Wallace, Danielle, John M. Eason, and Andrea M. Lindsey. 2015. "The Influence of Incarceration and Re-entry on the Availability of Health Care Organizations in Arkansas." *Health & Justice* 3(1):1.

Ward, Geoff K. 2006. "Race and the Justice Workforce." In *The Many Colors of Crime: In-equalities of Race, Ethnicity, and Crime in America*, ed. Ruth Peterson, Lauren Krivo, and John Hagan, 67–90. New York: New York University Press.

Weisheit, Ralph A., David N. Falcone, and L. Edward Wells. 1994. "Rural Crime and Rural Policing," National Institute of Justice, U.S. Department of Justice. https://www.ncjrs.gov/pdffiles/rcrp.pdf.

——. 1995. "Crime and Policing in Rural and Small-Town America: An Overview of the Issues." Research Report for the National Institute of Justice, U.S. Department of Justice. https://www.evawintl.org/Library/DocumentLibraryHandler.ashx?id=464.

——. 2005. *Crime and Policing in Rural and Small-Town America: An Overview of the Issues.* Long Grove, IL: Waveland Press.

Western, Bruce. 2006. *Punishment and Inequality in America.* New York: Russell Sage Foundation.

Wilkinson, Kenneth. 1984. "A Research Note on Homicide and Rurality." *Social Forces* 63(2):445–52.

Wodahl, Eric J. 2006. "The Challenges of Prison Reentry from a Rural Perspective." *Western Criminological Review* 7(2):32–47.

Zimring, Franklin E. 2011. *The City That Became Safe: New York's Lessons for Urban Crime and Its Control.* New York: Oxford University Press.

PART V

Programs, Policy, and Politics

Part V details the accomplishments and shortcomings of antipoverty policies in addressing poverty in rural America. The first two chapters underscore the need for policy makers to recognize that particular features of rural areas mandate policy solutions tailored to these features. The final chapter reprises the theme of the book and answers two questions: Why is rural poverty neglected, and what is to be done?

Chapter 14, "The Safety Net in Rural America," reviews the extent to which current policies reduce income poverty in rural and urban America. It reveals that safety net programs significantly reduce poverty, but even so leave between 6 and 7 million rural residents in poverty. Uniform federally funded and administered social insurance and welfare programs do the most to reduce rural poverty. Programs jointly funded by federal and state governments whose design and implementation have devolved to the states, such as the TANF block grant, have been less successful. Consequently, the chapter warns that reforms that would devolve even more responsibility on the states could worsen poverty for rural Americans.

Chapter 15, "The Opportunities and Limits of Economic Growth," argues that rural areas "suffer from some basic structural features that constrain the ability of economic development efforts to reduce poverty." For instance, low population density, few industries in rural areas, and a growing population in urban (but not rural) areas all account for market issues in rural America. The author argues that community-based solutions are more effective at alleviating rural poverty because they combine profit motives with social objectives and better invoke the voice of the community. Market-based strategies alone are not enough, however.

Foundations and government resources are needed to expand funding for these antipoverty solutions.

Chapter 16, "Politics and Policy: Barriers and Opportunities for Rural Peoples," restates the goal of the text: to rectify the pervasive lack of serious scholarly attention to the issue and to bring this neglect to the attention of students, scholars, the public, and policy makers who often display deep ignorance of the issue. The chapter broadly summarizes the lessons brought to light and focuses on two questions. Answers to the first question—Why is rural poverty neglected?—are found in demographic issues (such as the relatively small size of the rural population, its obscurity, and its demographic composition); pervasive myths of idyllic self-sufficiency; the lack of specific policy to address rural issues, especially rural poverty; and the embedment of the roots of rural poverty in formal social institutions including the role of the state, faith-based institutions, and the legal system. To answer the second question—What can be done?—a four-part prescription going into the future is offered: be aware that the problems of poverty exist as part of larger structures of stratification, inequalities, and power dynamics; refine and extend the diagnosis of the problems; encourage and support more and better research; and, most of all, strive for better policy and programs tailored to meet the specific needs of rural people and places.

CHAPTER 14

The Safety Net in Rural America

Jennifer Warlick

INTRODUCTION

After declining rapidly during the 1960s, rural poverty has proven to be stubbornly persistent. This chapter examines the role the U.S. *social safety net*—a catchall for government programs designed to relieve hardships of poverty—plays in the reduction of rural poverty and how popular proposals might alter its antipoverty effectiveness. Specifically considered is how the most important safety net programs, excluding those addressing health care needs, reduce poverty rates. The reductions in poverty reported in this chapter are based on the supplemental measure of poverty (SPM), an alternate measure developed by the Census Bureau in the late 1990s to correct problems in the methodology used to determine poverty thresholds and family resources (see chapters 2 and 3). The SPM is preferred when measuring the impact of safety net programs on the level of poverty because it has more comprehensive definitions of the resources available to families and their monetary needs than does the official poverty measure (OPM) (Short 2014). When applied historically, the SPM shows a more pronounced decline in rural poverty between 1967 and 2014 than does the Census Bureau's official measure (Nolan et al. 2017), and this decline is sufficiently great to overturn the conventional wisdom that rural poverty has been greater than urban poverty over the past fifty years. These results stem largely from the controversial cost-of-living adjustment in the SPM. This adjustment may cause the antipoverty effects reported in the next section to be overstated for rural families and understated for urban families. The appendix to this chapter provides more information about the implications of using the SPM.

Certain characteristics of rural America simultaneously generate the need for assistance and lower the effectiveness of antipoverty programs. For example, remote locations, the absence of affordable public transportation, and nondiversified local economies place rural residents at a disadvantage when seeking education, skills training, work experience, and employment in stable, full-time jobs with living wages and benefits. In turn, the likelihood of low-wage employment and underemployment is higher, as is the need for public assistance. Ironically, many of these same factors make it difficult for rural residents to establish their eligibility for, apply for, and receive assistance from safety net programs (Tickamyer and Henderson 2010, 2011; Allard and Cigna 2008). Rural residents also are likely to live in relatively poor states where economic conditions and social and political conditions limit public assistance.[1]

This chapter considers the implications of these factors for building effective safety net programs in rural America. It begins by reporting estimates of the effects of the most important safety net programs on rural poverty in 2013. A comparison of the antipoverty effectiveness of these programs in rural areas relative to urban America follows, illuminating the vulnerabilities of rural people and places that account for the observed differences. Next comes a summary of research by Tickamyer and Henderson (2010, 2011) about the particular problems that resulted from implementation of the Temporary Assistance for Needy Families (TANF) program in Appalachian Ohio in the late 1990s and 2000s. This research reviews the negative consequences of devolving authority for assistance programs to state and local governments. The chapter concludes by considering the implications of current proposals that would follow the TANF model and consolidate federal funds for housing assistance, nutritional programs, and social services into block grants to the states, and devolve to them greater authority for the design, implementation, and administration of safety net programs (Ryan 2014).

THE ANTIPOVERTY EFFECTIVENESS OF SAFETY NET PROGRAMS IN RURAL AMERICA

The national SPM poverty rate in 2013 was 15.5 percent. Across age groups, the SPM was highest for children under eighteen, at 16.4 percent, and lowest for people sixty-five and older, at 14.6 percent. The SPM was higher for residents of urban areas (15.9 percent) than rural areas (13.2 percent). This relationship is the same for all age groups.

Would these poverty rates have been higher in the absence of safety net programs? Which of the programs have the greatest antipoverty effectiveness overall? Are they equally effective for different age groups and for rural versus urban residents? To answer these questions, this section reviews the evidence about the antipoverty effectiveness of the ten most important safety net programs in terms of total expenditures and the number of beneficiaries, with the exception of medical assistance programs (Medicare, Medicaid, and State Child Health Insurance Program) and Pell education grants (Tanner 2012; Falk 2012).[2] Their salient features are presented in table 14.1. Estimates of their impact on poverty are presented in table 14.2.

The cell entries in table 14.1 are found using a two-step procedure. First, the poverty rate without cash value of the benefits distributed by the respective program is calculated. For this calculation, only the benefits from the program in question are zeroed out. The resulting poverty rates are shown in table 14.3 (see appendix).

Second, the difference between the poverty rate with and without the program is divided by the poverty rate without the program. For example, zeroing out Social Security benefits would raise the SPM for the total population from 15.5 percent to 24.1 percent. The difference of 8.6 percentage points divided by 24.1 is 0.373. It follows that the percent reduction in the SPM attributable to Social Security is 37.3. This percentage change also represents the probability that a specific program will lift a poor individual across the poverty threshold.

Reviewing table 14.2, we see that *all* of the programs bring about some reduction nationwide in the number of people who are counted as poor. The exception to this result is the population sixty-five years and older. For this population, the last four rows of the last column show zero reduction. These cells represent the percentage by which means-tested programs targeting families with children—child support received, Temporary Assistance for Needy Families (TANF), General Assistance (GA),[3] and the Special Supplemental Nutrition Program for Women, Infants, and Children (WIC)—decrease poverty among the elderly. Few people sixty-five years and over are eligible for these programs. Thus, it is not surprising to see that they have zero impact on SPM poverty rates for the elderly. Overall, the numbers in table 14.2 constitute a resounding yes to our first question. Poverty rates for all groups would be higher in the absence of safety net programs.

Table 14.1 Program Characteristics of Social Insurance and Means-Tested Programs for Low-Income Families

1	2	3	4	5	6	7	8	9	10	11
Program (year of enactment)	Funding source	Administering agency	Target population	Forms of assistance	Apply online	Total expenditures (billions of 2012 dollars)	Recipients in 2012 (millions)	Average spending per recipient (2012 dollars)	Maximum benefit (% of poverty threshold)	Eligible population participating (%)
OASI (1935)	FICA payroll tax	SSA	Retired workers and survivors	Cash	Yes	$725	44.8	$12,200	1 person: 290% 2 persons: 340%	96%
SSDI (1935)	FICA payroll tax	SSA	Disabled workers and their dependents	Cash	Yes	$596	10.6	$13,300	1 person: 290% 2+ persons: 340%	—
EITC (1975)	Federal general revenues	IRS	LIᵃ working families with children	Cash	Yes	$55	25.2	$2,200	23%	79%
ACTC (1997)	Federal general revenues	IRS	LI working families with children	Cash	Yes	$28	21.0	$1,300	6%	—
SNAP (1964)	Federal/state general revenues	FNS and state agencies	LI households	EBT card for food purchases only	In 42 states	$79	44.7	$1,800	31%	83%
SSI (1972)	Federal general revenues	SSA	LI aged, blind, and disabled persons	Cash	No	$49	7.8	$6,300	Singles: 75% Couples: 80%	58% (elderly only)
Housing assistance (1937)	Federal general revenues	Rural housing service, USDA	LI families	Subsidized rental units	No	$39	4.8	$8,000	—	25%
UI (1935)	Employer tax	State/federal government	Unemployed workers	Cash benefits	Yes	$93	7.8	$5,200	Varies by state ranging from 18% (LA) to 56% (MA)	—

School lunch (1946)	Federal general revenues	FNS/USDA	LI children	Meals	No	$11.6	31.6	$365	—	40%
TANF (1996)	Federal/state general revenues	Designated executive agency in each state	Needy families with children	Cash and services	No	$18	—	—	Varies by state ranging from 10% (MI) to 48% (NY)	
WIC (1966)	Federal general revenues	FNS/USDA	LI women, infants, and children at nutritional risk	Food and services (education, counseling, referrals)	No	$7	9.7	$700	—	43%

Sources:

Columns 1–5: Spar 2011; UI: Col. 7, Carrington 2013; Col. 10.

Column 6: Internal Revenue Service 2016; Social Security Administration 2016c; Food and Nutrition Service 2015b. 2015c; Housing assistance, Wiki 2016.

Columns 7–9: Social Security Administration 2016d; Congressional Budget Office 2013; Housing assistance: Cowan 2016 and Hernandez 2014; UI: Whitraker and Isaacs 2014 (Col. 7); School Lunch: Food and Nutrition Service 2013; WIC: Johnson et al. 2013.

Column 10: All but the OASI and SSDI percentages are for a single-parent with two children: Social Security Administration 2016e, 2016f; U.S. Census Bureau 2016; Center on Budget and Policy Priorities 2016, 2015, 2014; Spar 2011; fileunemployment.org, 2013; and Stone and Chen 2104.

Column 11: Only 4 percent of individuals aged 62–84 in 2010 will never receive Social Security benefits (Whitman. Reznik, and Shoffner 2011); EITC and ACTC: Internal Revenue Service 2016; SSI: McGarry and Shonei 2015; TANF: Brown 2010; Housing Assistance: Poethig 2016; SNAP: Food and Nutrition Service 2015a; WIC: Smith 2016.

Note: The terms *urban* and *rural* follow the classifications in the Current Population Survey (CPS). The CPS defines rural or nonmetropolitan (the two terms are used interchangeably) as all counties outside of urban core-based areas that are not economically integrated with them. There are two types of core-based areas: metropolitan (50,000 or more people) and micropolitan (10,000–50,000 people). Urban and metropolitan are also interchangeable terms.

[a] All target populations other than OASI, SSDI, and UI are low-income (LI) populations. The highest income allowable for eligibility is frequently 185 percent of a family's poverty threshold (Spar 2011).

[b] The percentages for the EITC, ACTC, and SNAP are for families of three: 2 adults, 1 child.

Table 14.2 Percent Reduction of SPM Poverty Rates Owing to Inclusion of Selected Safety Net Programs, 2013

	Total U.S.	All people		Children 0–17		Nonelderly adults 18–64		Elderly adults 65+	
		Urban	Rural	Urban	Rural	Urban	Rural	Urban	Rural
Social Security	35.7	33.2	49.6	10.1	17.8	20.2	33.5	70.5	78.6
Refundable tax credits	15.8	15.9	14.8	28.1	25.9	11.7	11.5	1.3	0.8
SNAP	9.4	9.1	11.4	14.6	15.4	6.5	10.3	5.6	4.5
SSI	7.7	7.0	10.8	5.6	7.1	7.1	12.1	9.6	8.0
Housing subsidies	6.1	6.5	4.3	8.2	5.9	4.8	3.7	8.5	1.6
UI	4.3	4.2	5.0	5.1	4.7	3.7	4.4	1.9	1.6
Child support received	3.1	3.0	4.3	5.6	7.7	1.9	2.2	0.7	0.0
School lunch	3.1	3.0	3.6	6.6	5.9	1.9	2.2	0.7	0.0
TANF/GA	1.9	1.9	2.2	2.9	3.4	1.3	1.5	0.0	0.0
WIC	1.3	1.2	2.2	2.3	2.7	0.6	1.5	0.0	0.0

Sources: The *Total U.S.* column is from Short 2014. The other columns are based on data in Council of Economic Advisors (2015). All of the calculations in the table use data from the Bureau of Labor Statistics (2014).

PROGRAMS THAT RELIEVE POVERTY

Which programs have the greatest antipoverty effectiveness? The programs in table 14.2 are listed in order of the size of their effect (largest to smallest) on the SPM poverty rate. The rank order is the same for the total population and for the urban population.[4] The rank order for the rural population is similar with only one exception: housing assistance falls to sixth place and unemployment insurance (UI) rises to fifth place.

Social Security tops the list, lifting 6 million rural residents out of poverty[5] and reducing the SPM poverty rate for rural Americans by almost half (49.6 percent).[6] Funded through payroll taxes, Social Security provides monthly benefits to retired adults as well as disabled adults and surviving immediate relatives of workers who die while covered by the program; the size of the benefit received is dependent on lifetime earnings taxed and number of years worked. The reduction in poverty is greatest for elderly adults (78.6 percent), followed by nonelderly adults (33.5 percent), and then children (17.8 percent). This ordering reflects the eligibility rules of Old Age and Survivors Insurance (OASI) and Social Security Disability Insurance (SSDI), the effects of which are combined in table 14.2. As table 14.1 shows, OASI covers a vast population—all workers in covered employment and their dependents—and 96 percent of eligible elderly adults nationwide either do or will receive OASI. Nonelderly adults receive SSDI benefits only if disabled. Table 14.1 indicates that the number of OASI recipients was four times greater than the number of SSDI recipients in 2013. Children receive benefits as survivors of covered workers or because a parent receives SSDI.

A second feature of Social Security that explains its dominance in reducing poverty is that its benefits are higher on average than benefits from means-tested programs. The largest program in the federal budget ($905 billion), accounting for almost one-quarter of federal spending in fiscal year 2016 (Congressional Budget Office [CBO] 2016), Social Security paid benefits to 55 million people in 2012 who received an annual average of $13,100 (CBO 2013). Nearly 45 million retired workers and the survivors of workers received average benefits of $12,200, and almost 11 million disabled workers received benefits that averaged $13,300.[7]

In contrast, nationwide the Supplemental Security Income (SSI) program, which provides monthly stipends to low-income people who are aged, blind, or disabled, paid the *highest* average cash transfer among means-tested programs at $6,300 (nearly $7,000 less than the average Social Security benefit), and its recipient population was only 7.8 million in 2012 (see table 14.1). The earned income tax credit (EITC) and the additional child tax credit (ACTC), both refundable tax credits allowing qualifying families to reduce their tax liability or receive tax refunds, reached 25 and 21 million families, respectively, but the average annual benefits of these programs were only $2,200 and $1,300. The average housing assistance voucher was $8,000, but the population served by this program was small, not quite 5 million (CBO 2013; Social Security Administration 2016d).

Several features of Social Security explain its higher benefits. First, Social Security benefits are intended to replace earnings of workers in covered employment (96 percent of all workers) and are based on average lifetime earnings.[8] In contrast, means-tested programs target families that can demonstrate lowness of income and supplement their resources so that they may meet minimal basic needs: food, clothing, shelter, medical insurance, and the expenses associated with working. Another important difference is the public's perception that Social Security benefits are earned whereas means-tested benefits are not. Recipients view Social Security benefits as an annuity purchased with their payroll taxes (FICA). Means-tested benefits are funded from state and federal general revenues, and even though many people who receive them paid income taxes in better times, means-tested benefits are viewed as handouts. Their maximum levels are kept low to avoid undermining personal responsibility and creating dependency. In addition, means-tested benefits are more likely to vacillate with downturns in economic conditions and policy swings related to elections.

Although means-tested programs with their smaller target populations and lower average benefits cannot match the antipoverty effectiveness of Social Security programs, they are nonetheless important sources of support. How do they stack up in reducing poverty among the rural population? Table 14.2 shows that the combination of the EITC and ACTC, the refundable portion of the child tax credit (CTC), rank first among rural children and nonelderly adults, reducing poverty by 25.9 percent and 11.5 percent, respectively. Not unexpectedly, they have a negligible impact on the elderly, few of whom house children. Created in 1975, the EITC has grown from a small, tentative program to the largest means-tested cash transfer program, distributing $55 billion in 2011 to 25.2 million recipients, mostly families with children who received an average refund of

$2,200. Legislation creating CTC followed two decades later. The ACTC provided an average refund of $1,300 to 21 million families at a cost of $28 billion in 2011. Nearly four of five eligible families, representing one of every three rural taxpayers, claimed these refunds, which increased their income by an average of 13 percent (Durst and Farrigan 2011).

The Supplemental Nutrition Assistance Program (SNAP) ranks second in poverty reduction for children but third for nonelderly and elderly adults. Formerly known as food stamps, SNAP provides monthly benefits to low-income individuals and families that can be used to purchase food. Although SNAP is the most far-reaching poverty assistance program in terms of expenditures and recipients ($79 billion and 45 million in 2012), its average annual benefits per household are relatively modest at $1,800. Overall, SNAP lifts 800,000 rural residents out of poverty.

The SSI program ranks second for rural nonelderly and elderly adults, reducing poverty by 12.1 percent and 8.0 percent, respectively. SSI replaced the state programs of Aid to the Aged, Aid to the Blind, and Aid to the Permanently and Totally Disabled in 1972. Unlike the previous state programs, children with disabilities are eligible for SSI, and it ranks fourth among means-tested programs for rural children, reducing their SPM rate by 7.1 percent, or about half of the reduction owing to SNAP. SSI established a nationally uniform, maximum monthly cash benefit across all states, eliminating state variation, but left open the option for states to increase this maximum with state-funded supplements. It is important to note (see table 14.1) that the maximum benefits levels under SSI are relatively generous, at 75 percent and 80 percent of the poverty thresholds for single individuals and couples, respectively.

The antipoverty rankings of the remaining programs vary by age group for the rural population. Child support received ranks third for children, reducing poverty by 7.7 percent, followed by housing subsidies and the School Lunch Program, at 5.9 percent each. Unemployment insurance (UI), combined benefits from TANF and GA programs, and the WIC program reduced poverty among rural children by 4.7 percent, 3.4 percent, and 2.7 percent, respectively. The reduction in the SPM rate for nonelderly adults owing to the last six programs in table 14.2, housing subsidies through WIC, ranges from 4.4 percent to 1.5 percent. UI ranks above housing subsidies for this subgroup.[9] Finally, housing subsidies and UI reduce the SPM rate for elderly rural residents by a modest 1.6 percent each.[10]

In addition to reducing the number of people living in poverty, the programs in table 14.2 also have profound effects on deep poverty (those living at or below 50 percent of the poverty line). The Council of Economic Advisors (2015) estimates that Social Security and SNAP reduce deep poverty among rural children by one-half and nearly one-third, respectively.

Although the focus has been on the individual effects of the programs in table 14.2, in reality many families receive assistance from more than one program. The Council of Economic Advisors (2015) found that without OASI, SSDI, EITC, SNAP, and other programs, poverty among rural children would have been 70 percent higher over the period 2009 to 2011.

Finally, it should be noted that this analysis has focused on changes in only one dimension of poverty: resource (income) poverty. A significant body of research documents the long-term benefits for the healthy physical, cognitive, social, and emotional development of children who receive benefits from safety net programs (Council of Economic Advisors 2015; Furman and Ruffini 2015; Center on Budget and Policy Priorities 2014). For example, research shows that SNAP participation leads to healthier children who are more likely to graduate from high school and become self-sufficient earners in adulthood (Hoynes, Schanzenbach, and Almond 2016).

THE RELATIVE ANTIPOVERTY EFFECTIVENESS OF SAFETY NET PROGRAMS ACROSS RURAL AND URBAN AMERICA

This section compares the effects of safety net programs on poverty in urban and rural America, thereby calling attention to characteristics that are distinctly rural. The relative antipoverty effectiveness of the programs can be found by comparing the percentage changes in the SPM for the urban and rural populations in table 14.2. This exercise reveals that eight of the ten programs reduce poverty by a greater percentage in rural areas than in urban areas. Alternately stated, the probability that a rural resident will be lifted out of poverty by these eight programs is greater than the corresponding probability for an urban resident. Only refundable tax credits and housing subsidies have a greater impact in urban areas. In rural areas, four programs reduce the SPM by at least 10 percent: without Social Security, refundable tax credits, SNAP, and SSI, the SPM would be 49.6 percent, 14.8 percent, 11.4 percent, and 10.8 percent higher, respectively. Only Social Security (33.2 percent) and refundable tax credits

(15.9 percent) generate double-digit percentage changes in the SPM for urban areas. Although their impact is much smaller, UI, the School Lunch Program, TANF, and WIC all have greater antipoverty effects in rural areas.

THE EFFECT OF PLACE ON POVERTY PROGRAMS

What do we know about rural places and rural populations that might explain why safety net programs reduce poverty more in rural America? Chapter 1 explained that the rural population is older than that of urban America and is aging at an accelerated rate. All else being equal, programs targeting the elderly, such as OASI, and SSI, would serve a higher proportion of the rural population. It is also true that populations in rural counties typically have higher rates of disability than urban counties: 7.6 percent versus 4.2 percent of adults (Bishop and Gallardo 2011). Ruffing (2015a) identifies four factors that elevate the percentage of a state's population that receives disability benefits: low-rates of high school completion; an older workforce; relatively fewer immigrants; and an economy based on forestry, certain types of mining, utilities, construction, and manufacturing. These characteristics describe the rural places of industrial Midwest states and many southern and Appalachian states. It follows that higher percentages of the population in these states receive disability benefits from either SSDI or SSI. West Virginia leads the nation in the percentage of its population that receives SSDI, SSI, or both, at 12.5 percent, followed by Alabama (11.0 percent), Arkansas (10.7 percent), and Mississippi (10.7 percent). These higher rates of receipt, in turn, may explain the greater antipoverty effectiveness of SSDI (combined with OASI) and SSI in rural states.

Place-based factors also may explain the greater effectiveness of SNAP in reducing poverty levels in rural America. Using county-level data, Slack and Myers (2012) found higher-than-average SNAP participation rates in clusters of counties in southern Appalachia, the Mississippi Delta, and along the border between Mexico and the United States. Persistent poverty, depressed economic conditions and stagnant labor markets, and low levels of investments in public institutions and infrastructure characterize these geographic clusters and explain their greater reliance on SNAP. This greater reliance, in turn, may explain the greater reduction owing to SNAP among rural residents (11.4 percent) than among urban residents (9.1 percent).

Distressed economies also may be the key to the greater antipoverty effectiveness of the EITC and ACTC. Rural families are more likely to be working in low-wage jobs than other poor families, and a higher percentage of rural children than urban children live in low-wage families. Consequently, the percentage of all families living in rural areas who received EITC was about 4 percentage points higher in 2013 (Council of Economic Advisors 2015). Rural families have a higher rate of EITC receipt in forty-two states, especially in the South and Southwest where rural families also receive higher credits on average (O'Hare and Kneebone 2007). The Council of Economic Advisors (2015) reports that rural children also are more likely to live in a single-parent household or in a home with a disabled parent, boosting the impact of child support received and the federal disability programs (SSDI and SSI) on rural child poverty.

A CLOSE-UP OF TANF

Temporary Assistance for Needy Families is the safety net's primary cash assistance program for needy families. Given this status, it is surprising that it has so little impact on poverty, rural or urban. Table 14.2 shows that overall TANF reduces poverty by only 1.9 percent. Its impact in rural America is slightly higher at 2.2 percent, tying it for bottom rank with WIC. This section takes a closer look at TANF to understand why the primary cash assistance program has so little impact. This examination is facilitated by in-depth research conducted in rural Ohio (Tickamyer and Henderson 2010, 2011). It reveals obstacles that undermine the effectiveness of welfare programs in rural places.

The Personal Responsibility and Work Opportunity Reconciliation Act (PRWORA) of 1996 created TANF to replace Aid to Families with Dependent Children (AFDC) as the primary cash assistance program for low-income families. In contrast to the federally funded and administered EITC, CTC, and SSI programs, PRWORA devolved to the states responsibility for achieving the goals stated in the long title of the act: to restore the American family, reduce illegitimacy, control welfare spending, and reduce welfare dependency. The last goal is generally understood to mean decreasing caseloads. To achieve these goals, PRWORA embraced radical changes in the federal/state partnership that existed under AFDC. Specifically, PRWORA capped block grants from the federal government, replaced state/federal matching entitlements, imposed work requirements, and limited the number of years a family could participate over its lifetime. The specifics of program design—including allocation of the block grants between cash assistance, social services, and other strategies to encourage more work and less dependence—were devolved to the states (Committee on Ways and Means 2014). For reasons described next, these changes led to a deepening of poverty among the poorest families and greater reliance on programs providing in-kind assistance, such as SNAP and housing vouchers.

WHY TANF FAILED RURAL FAMILIES

Devolving policy control to states and localities disadvantages those experiencing poverty in rural locations for multiple reasons. Remoteness, isolation, and perhaps poverty of place present unique obstacles difficult to overcome on a limited budget. Tickamyer and Henderson (2010, 2011) provide specific evidence of these outcomes in their study of the implementation of TANF in Appalachian Ohio. When PRWORA devolved responsibility for the design, implementation, and administration of programs to assist needy families to the state, Ohio devolved its responsibilities to its counties. Facing distressed economies, extremely rural and isolated poor counties were unable to meet the demands of the Ohio Works First program (helping families achieve financial independence through work). On the rare occasion that a job opening was found and filled, lack of supportive infrastructure such as transportation and child care jeopardized the stability of employment.[11] Officials in rural areas argued unsuccessfully for greater discretion to allocate funds to address poverty of place through local economic development and job generation, and to direct transfers to families, instead of addressing personal employment barriers to prepare residents for jobs that did not exist. The consequences of welfare reform for Appalachian Ohio were increases in unemployment compensation receipt and SNAP use (as families failed to satisfy the work conditions of TANF and were sanctioned off), and decreases in social insurance benefits (unemployment benefits) and work-conditioned tax transfers (EITC and CTC).

It is important to note that attempts to tailor assistance to each family's needs reduced the share of TANF block grants distributed *as cash* welfare grants from 70 percent to 26 percent nationwide (Schott, Pavetti, and Floyd 2015) and increased reliance on the delivery of social services throughout states, including poor rural areas where spatial distance complicates and disrupts their delivery. Social service providers must meet face to face with recipients at agency offices or at clients' homes, but remoteness and isolation both create physical barriers between clients and providers and reduce local capacity where budgets are determined by the number of people served without regard to the average cost of serving them.[12]

CONCLUDING OBSERVATIONS

This chapter has shown that U.S. safety net programs substantially reduce and ameliorate poverty among rural Americans. Taken together, the top ten safety net programs lifted 9 million rural residents, including 1.6 million children, out of poverty in 2013 (Council of Economic Advisors 2015). Even so, nearly 7 million rural residents, including 1.5 million children, continue to live in poverty. Clearly there are some actions that, if taken, could improve the effectiveness of public assistance to the rural poor: improving the adequacy of benefit levels, increasing accessibility, and raising participation. These are not independent goals. For example, actions to increase the adequacy of benefits may make participation more desirable.

Nationwide the role of direct cash transfers such as TANF for families with children has diminished over the past thirty-five years, both in terms of the number receiving benefits and in the purchasing power of those benefits. Since 1979, 82 percent of families with children in poverty received assistance from AFDC, TANF's predecessor. In 1996, the year PRWORA passed, this percentage was down to 68 percent, and by 2010 participation had fallen to 27 percent. The number of families in extreme poverty receiving TANF benefits declined by 58 percent. Over the same period, the real purchasing power of TANF benefits decreased by 20 percent because states did not adjust maximum benefits for increases in the general prices of goods and commodities. In contrast, poverty thresholds were raised to account for inflation. Consequently, the number of states with maximum TANF benefits below 25 percent of the poverty thresholds rose from zero in 1994–1995 to 25 in 2009–2010 (Trisi and Pavetti 2012). The average TANF-to-poverty ratio is lowest, below 20 percent, in the southern states that are home to the greatest number of persistently poor counties. Lower benefits explain the greater depth of poverty.

WHY BENEFITS STAY LOW

The explanation of low benefits lies with policy design, which is driven by political, social, and economic institutions. The history of exclusionary and discriminatory policies in the South largely accounts for low benefit levels there. Conservative political philosophies, such as the neoliberal perspective on poverty, promote self-sufficiency through work and prescribe very low maximum benefits to prevent dependency (Dixon 2012). The weak economies of many rural states contribute to the lowness of benefits as well. Tax revenues rise and fall with states' per capita incomes, and states with the lowest per capita incomes cannot afford generous benefits. Introducing devolutionary policies (such as the TANF block grant) into this context was a recipe for underfunded programs that could not overcome the spatial challenges of rural areas, such as the lack of public transportation, day care facilities, and services for the elderly and disabled. Proposals to block grant additional programs and devolve more responsibility to the states, such as those in the House Budget Committee's report "Expanding Opportunity in America" (Ryan 2014), would do additional damage to low-income families in rural America if they became law.

"Expanding Opportunity in America" also recommends extending work requirements in SNAP to all nonelderly, able-bodied adults, not just to those without dependents as is currently the law. Similar to block granting, the burden of this extension would be felt most strongly in rural areas where there are fewer work opportunities and higher costs of working, such as transportation and child care.

PARTICIPATION RATES

Low participation rates, defined as the percentage of eligible people enrolled, also stymie the effectiveness of welfare programs. Welfare programs cannot help eligible people who do not enroll in them. This includes 57 percent of eligible families nationwide who do not enroll in TANF (Brown 2010).[13] Participation rates are low when the costs of participating outweigh the benefits. This imbalance is more likely to occur in states with low maximum benefits. Factors commonly cited as increasing costs include travel expenses, complex application procedures, unawareness of program benefits, and stigma associated with receiving welfare (Brown 2010; Food and Nutrition Service 2015a; Internal Revenue

Service 2016; McGarry and Shonei 2015; Smith 2016; Sherman 2006, 2009, 2013; Warlick 1982).

Increasing participation will be difficult in rural America because the costs and benefits of participation are intertwined. Consider how insufficient public transportation interacts with application procedures to limit access to benefits among rural Americans. Applicants to SSI, TANF, SNAP (in eight states), and WIC must visit local welfare offices to submit required paperwork (SSI—Social Security Administration 2016c; TANF—U.S. Department of Health and Human Services 2016; SNAP—Food and Nutrition Service 2015b; WIC—Food and Nutrition Service 2015c). Even when enrollment can be accomplished online—as is the case for refundable tax credits and SNAP in forty-two states— rural residents may be at a disadvantage due to lower levels of connectedness to the Internet.[14] Addressing public transportation problems without simplifying and assisting applicants with the enrollment process, or vice versa, will solve only half the problem. Moreover, investments in transportation or communications infrastructure could require dramatically increasing budgetary outlays for safety net programs at the expense of benefit adequacy or investments in education and health care, which are contributors to rural poverty in their own right (see chapters 11 and 12).

THE FUTURE OF POVERTY PROGRAMS

Resisting greater devolution of responsibility to the states is a necessity. It is also a defensive strategy. In contrast, proactive strategies include federal subsidization of benefits, or perhaps the much bolder remedy of federalizing programs using the model of SSI. When SSI replaced the state programs of Aid to the Aged, Aid to the Blind, and Aid to the Permanently and Totally Disabled in 1972, it established nationally uniform, maximum monthly cash benefits across all fifty states at 75 percent and 80 percent of the poverty thresholds for single individuals and couples, respectively (Center for Budget and Policy Priorities 2014). Although the uniform benefit eliminated state variation for basic benefits, SSI left open the option for states to increase this maximum with state-funded supplements. In 2015, forty-four states and the District of Columbia supplemented the basic federal benefit (Social Security Administration 2016a), bringing benefits even closer to poverty lines. In contrast, in 2009–2010, no state's maximum TANF-to-poverty threshold was 75 percent or above, and only three states were in the 50–74 percent range (Trisi and Pavetti 2012). Although passage of similar legislation establishing a nationally uniform TANF benefit seems unlikely in the current political climate, the antipoverty effectiveness of SSI does underscore the potential of federally funded and administered programs to raise the adequacy of benefits and participation rates relative to state funded and administered programs, and hence the effectiveness of means-tested programs in the poorest states. Unless Americans, rural and urban alike, find the political will to enact these or similar proactive measures, there is little reason to think that safety net programs will reduce rural poverty below current levels.

Appendix: Trends in Rural and Urban Poverty Using the Supplemental Poverty Measure

This appendix examines the implications of substituting the supplemental poverty measure (SPM) for the official poverty measure (OPM) when tracing poverty rates for rural and urban America through time and measuring the antipoverty effectiveness of safety net programs. Four important conclusions are illustrated in figures 14.1 through 14.4.

Figure 14.1 compares poverty rates as reported by the Census Bureau for rural America from 1967 to 2014 using the SPM and the OPM (Short 2014). This figure reveals two important findings. First, similar to the OPM, the SPM shows a marked decline in poverty since the late 1960s. Second, this decline has been greater than is commonly understood. According to the OPM measure, rural poverty was only 14 percent lower in 2014 than in 1967 (21 percent versus 18.1 percent). In contrast, the SPM shows a decline four times greater than the OPM—59 percent—as the poverty rate fell from 32.2 to 13.2 percent.

Third, substituting the SPM for the OPM alters trends in relative poverty between rural and urban America. Figure 14.2 plots annual SPM poverty rates for rural and urban America back to 1967 and reveals that poverty rates for rural America have fallen below those in metropolitan areas since 1994 (Nolan et al. 2017; Short 2011). The conventional wisdom based on the OPM is that rural poverty rates have consistently exceeded urban rates since 1959 (Economic Research Service 2015).

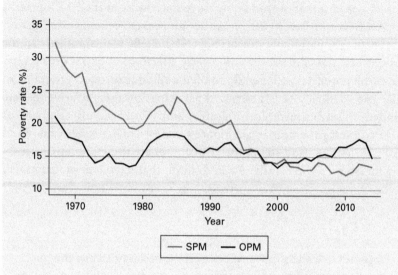

Figure 14.1   SPM and OPM rural poverty rates, 1967–2014.

Source: Bureau of Labor Statistics, Current Population Survey 2014.

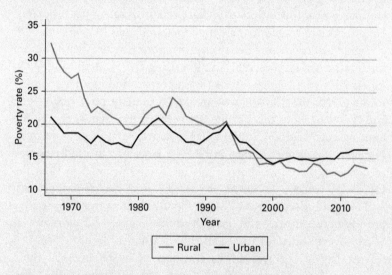

Figure 14.2   SPM rural and urban poverty rates, 1967–2014.

Source: Nolan, Waldfogel, and Wimer 2017.

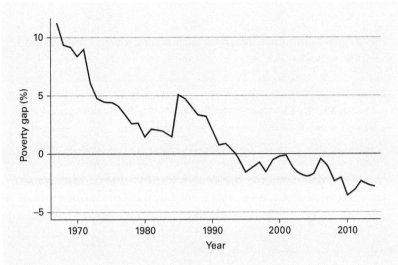

Figure 14.3 Rural-urban poverty gap, 1967–2014.

Source: Nolan, Waldfogel, and Wimer 2017.

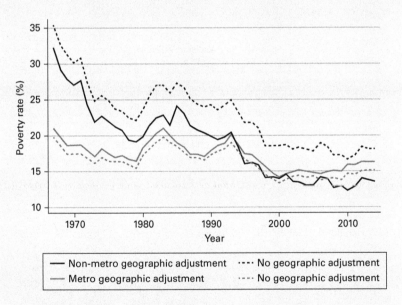

—— Non-metro geographic adjustment	···· No geographic adjustment
—— Metro geographic adjustment	···· No geographic adjustment

Figure 14.4 Rural and urban SPM poverty trends, with and without geographically adjusted thresholds.

Source: Nolan, Waldfogel, and Wimer 2017.

Figure 14.3 illustrates this point slightly differently. The line traces the difference—or the *poverty gap*—between rural and urban SPM rates between 1967 and 2014. It shows that the gap has been negative since 1994.

Fourth and finally, changes in the rural–urban poverty gap depend in large part on the SPM's controversial adjustment of poverty thresholds, which reflect geographical differences in the cost of living as measured by the price of housing (see chapter 2). Figure 14.4 illustrates this outcome by presenting two versions of the SPM. The solid lines trace poverty rates as measured by the SPM with the cost-of-living adjustment and are labeled "geographic adjustment"; the dashed lines trace the version of the SPM that omits the cost-of-living adjustments and are labeled "no geographic adjustment."

Clearly the level of rural poverty relative to urban poverty is dependent on which SPM measure is employed. Comparison of the geographically adjusted SPM leads to the conclusion that rural

Table 14.3 SPM Poverty Rates Zeroing Out Individual Programs, 2013

	Total	All		Children 0–17		Nonelderly adults 18–64		Elderly adults 65+	
		Urban	Rural	Urban	Rural	Urban	Rural	Urban	Rural
Social Security	24.1	23.8	26.2	18.8	17.4	19.8	19.7	51.1	58.8
Refundable tax credits	18.4	18.9	15.5	23.5	19.3	17.9	14.8	15.3	12.7
SNAP	17.1	17.5	14.9	19.8	16.9	16.9	14.6	16.0	13.2
SSI	16.8	17.1	14.8	17.9	15.4	17.0	14.9	16.7	13.7
Housing subsidies	16.5	17.0	13.8	18.4	15.2	16.6	13.6	16.5	12.8
UI	16.2	16.6	13.9	17.8	15.0	16.4	13.7	15.4	12.8
Child support received	16.0	16.4	13.8	17.9	15.5	16.1	13.4	15.2	12.6
School Lunch	16.0	16.4	13.7	18.1	15.2	16.1	13.4	15.2	12.6
TANF/GA	15.8	16.2	13.5	17.4	14.8	16.0	13.3	15.1	12.6
WIC	15.7	16.1	13.5	17.3	14.7	15.9	13.3	15.1	12.6

Sources: The *Total U.S.* column is from Short (2014). The other columns are from the Council of Economic Advisors (2015). All of the calculations in the table use data from the Bureau of Labor Statistics, Current Population Survey, Annual Social and Economic Supplement (2014).

poverty was greater than urban poverty until 1994, but it has been less every year since then (Council of Economic Advisors 2015). Comparison of the nongeographically adjusted SPM challenges this conclusion: rural poverty lies everywhere above that for urban poverty.

The adjustment for geographical variations in the cost of housing has one final noteworthy implication: it most certainly biases the estimates of the antipoverty effects of safety net programs presented in the body of the chapter. Because housing is less expensive in rural areas on average, the adjustments lower the poverty thresholds for rural families relative to urban families. All else being equal, before accounting for transfers, fewer rural families will fall under the thresholds than when using the OPM. It follows that smaller levels of transfers are needed to lift rural families across the lower thresholds and out of poverty in the absence of the cost-of-living adjustments. The reverse is true for urban families: larger transfers are required to lift them across higher thresholds. A fixed distribution of benefits will have greater effects on rural poverty than on urban poverty. Thus, the effects reported should be regarded as upper-bound estimates in rural areas and lower-bound estimates in urban areas. That is, the antipoverty effects of assistance programs actually may be lower in rural areas and higher in urban areas than was reported.

NOTES

1. The Economic Research Service (2015) reports that the nonmetro/metro poverty rate gap has historically been largest for the South, which was home to a disproportionately large percentage (43 percent) of the U.S. nonmetro population over the period 2010 to 2014.

2. The Current Population Survey asks households about their participation in these ten programs. The Census Bureau reports on their antipoverty effectiveness in its annual report on the supplemental poverty measure. For the report on poverty in 2013, see Short (2014).

3. General Assistance is a state funded and administered program offered by twenty-five states and the District of Columbia to very low income people without minor children who are not eligible for any other public assistance programs. The primary target group is disabled people who do not qualify for SSI. GA benefits are low and eligibility is frequently time limited. The number of GA programs has declined by a third since 1989, and the maximum benefit levels in most of the states with GA programs are lower now than they were in 1998 (Schott and Hill 2015).

4. Note that the overall reduction in the SPM rate is not equal to the sum of the individual reductions because some families receive benefits from multiple programs. Taken singly, no one program may lift the family out of poverty, but when combined, they do carry the family across the poverty threshold. The last program to be added to the total would receive credit for this feat, but the ordering of the programs for a single family is arbitrary (Sherman and Trisi 2015).

5. Author's calculation based on the poverty rates in the case study and statistics in Short (2014).

6. The program commonly referred to as Social Security after the legislative act that created it is comprised of multiple programs, each targeting a different population. Here the focus is on Old Age and Survivors Insurance (OASI) and Social Security Disability Insurance (SSDI), the two programs with the greatest number of recipients. Health insurance for elderly people, Medicare, is also a component of Social Security. The expenditure and recipient numbers in table 14.1 and the text are for OASI and SSDI.

7. The Center on Budget and Policy Priorities (2016) estimates that OASI lifts 40 percent of the elderly out of poverty annually. This is due in part to the importance of OASI as a retirement source of income. OASI accounts for at least half of the total income of 61 percent of elderly recipients and for 90 percent or more for a third of elderly beneficiaries.

8. Benefits are calculated with a progressive formula. Thus, replacement rates decline as average wages increase. On average, benefits replace about 50 percent of earnings for low earners (defined as 45 percent of the average wage), 39 percent for average earners, and 33 percent for high wage earners (160 percent of the average wage) (Center on Budget and Policy Priorities 2016).

9. Unemployment Insurance is a social insurance program, and, like OASI and SSDI, it does not explicitly target low-income Americans. Instead UI insures American workers against periods of unemployment. It is funded by a special tax levied on employers that is deposited to state trust funds.

10. Two housing assistance programs directly target low income rural residents: the Single Family Housing Direct Loan Program and the Very Low-Income Rural Housing Repair Loan and Housing Assistance Grants Program. Very low income is defined as less than 50 percent of median family income in the rural area where they reside, and low income is 50–80 percent of median family income. Both programs were authorized by the Housing Act of 1949 with the goal of assisting low-income households in obtaining adequate but modest, decent, safe, and sanitary dwellings and related facilities in rural areas. Only elderly households are eligible for the Very Low-Income Rural Housing Repair Loan and Housing Assistance Grants Program. Approximately 7,000 elderly households received loans and grants averaging $770 for total expenditures of $5.4 million in FY 2013. Total loans from the Single Family Housing Direct Loan Program equaled $50.1 million (Cowan 2016). Another 170,000 families with limited to moderate incomes purchased loans and grants, and 286,000 received rental assistance (Hernandez 2014).

11. Tickamyer, Henderson, White, and Tadlock (2000, 189) find that reliable, affordable transportation is a "major problem for the rural poor, 57 percent of whom lack automobiles and 66 percent of whom live in places without reliable public transportation."

12. One barrier is physical: seniors and disabled people often cannot drive, or may find it difficult to use public transportation, to get to offices (Food Research and Action Center 2004).

13. Participation rates in the major means-tested programs vary nationwide from a high 83 percent for SNAP (Food and Nutrition Service 2015a) to a low of 40 percent for TANF (Brown 2010). The participation rate for EITC is 79 percent (Internal Revenue Service 2016); among the elderly 58 percent of eligible people participate in SSI (McGarry and Shonei 2015); and 43 percent of eligible mothers with young children are enrolled in WIC (Smith 2016).

14. Although 84 percent of all American adults now have access to the Internet, connectedness is lower for Americans with specific characteristics, including being black (78 percent) or Hispanic (81 percent), living in a home with less than $30,000 annual income (74 percent connectedness), having less than a high school degree (66 percent connectedness), being sixty-five years or older (58 percent connectedness), and living in a rural community (78 percent connectedness) (Perrin and Duggan 2015). These are the characteristics of many rural residents, and they confound communications between program administrators and clients.

REFERENCES

Allard, Scott W., and Jessica Cigna. 2008. "Access to Social Services in Rural America: The Geography of the Safety Net in the Rural West." RUPRI Rural Poverty Research Center Working Paper No. 08–01.

Bishop, Bill, and Roberto Gallardo. 2011. "The Geography of Disability." Daily Yonder, November 30. http://www.dailyyonder.com/geography-disability/2011/11/30/3619/.

Brown, Kay E. 2010. "Temporary Assistance for Needy Families: Implications of Changes in Participation Rates." General Accountability Office, GAO-10-495T. http://www.gao.gov/products/GAO-10-525.

Bureau of Labor Statistics. 2014. "Current Population Survey." Annual Social and Economic Supplement.

Carrington, William. 2013. "The Unemployment Insurance System." Congressional Budget Office. https://www.cbo.gov/publication/44041.

Center on Budget and Policy Priorities. 2014. "Introduction to the Supplemental Security Income (SSI) Program." Revised February 27. http://www.cbpp.org/research/introduction-to-the-supplemental-security-income-ssi-program.

——. 2015. "Chart Book: Accomplishments of the Safety Net." http://www.cbpp.org/research/poverty-and-inequality/chart-book-accomplishments-of-the-safety-net.

——. 2016. "Policy Basics: Top Ten Facts About Social Security." http://www.cbpp.org/research/social-security/policy-basics-top-ten-facts-about-social-security.

Committee on Ways and Means, U.S. House of Representatives. 2014. *2012 Green Book: Background Material and Data on the Programs Within the Jurisdiction of the Committee on Ways and Means*, 18th ed. Washington, DC: U.S. Government Printing Office.

Congressional Budget Office. 2013. "Growth in Means-Tested Programs and Tax Credits for Low-Income Households."

———. 2016. "CBO's 2016 Long-Term Projections for Social Security: Additional Information." December 2015. https://www.cbo.gov/publication/52298.

Council of Economic Advisors. 2015. "Opportunity for All: Fighting Rural Child Poverty." The White House. https://obamawhitehouse.archives.gov/sites/default/files/docs/rural_child_poverty_report_final_non-embargoed.pdf.

Cowan, Tadlock. 2016. "An Overview of USDA Rural Development Programs." Congressional Research Service Report.

Dixon, John. 2012. "On Being Poor-by-Choice: A Philosophical Critique of the Neoliberal Poverty Perspective." Poverty & Public Policy 4(2):1–19.

Durst, Ron, and Tracey Farrigan. 2011. "Federal Tax Programs and Low-Income Rural Households." Economic Information Bulletin, No. 76(May):iii. Washington, DC: Economic Research Service, U.S. Department of Agriculture.

Economic Research Service. 2015. "Rural Poverty and Well-Being: The Geography of Poverty." Washington, DC: U.S. Department of Agriculture.

Falk, Gene. 2012. "Low-Income Assistance Programs: Trends in Federal Spending." Congressional Research Service.

Fileunemployment.org. 2013. "Unemployment Benefits Comparison by State." http://fileunemployment.org/unemployment-benefits-comparison-by-state.

Food and Nutrition Service. 2013. "National School Lunch Program Fact Sheet FY 2012." https://www.fns.usda.gov/sites/default/files/NSLPFactSheet.pdf.

———. 2015a. "Reaching Those in Need: Estimates of State Supplemental Nutrition Assistance Program Participation Rates in 2012—Summary." Washington, DC: U.S. Department of Agriculture. https://www.fns.usda.gov/snap/reaching-those-need-estimates-state-supplemental-nutrition-assistance-program-participation-rates.

———. 2015b. "Supplemental Nutrition Assistance Program (SNAP): SNAP Application and Local Office Locators." http://www.fns.usda.gov/snap/snap-application-and-local-office-locators.

———. 2015c. "WIC How to Apply." Washington, DC: U.S. Department of Agriculture. https://www.fns.usda.gov/wic/wic-how-apply.

Food Research and Action Center. 2004. "A Guide to the Supplemental Security Income/Food Stamp Program Combined Application Projects." Report of the Food Research and Action Center.

Furman, Jason, and Krista Ruffini. 2015. "Six Examples of the Long-Term Benefits of Anti-Poverty Programs." https://obamawhitehouse.archives.gov/blog/2015/05/11/six-examples-long-term-benefits-anti-poverty-programs.

Hernandez, Tony. 2014. "Rural Housing Service." Statement before the Subcommittee on Agriculture, Rural Development, Food and Drug Administration, and Related Agencies Committee on Appropriations, U.S. House of Representatives. April 4.

Hoyne, Hilary, Diane Whitmore Schanzenbach, and Douglas Almond. 2016. "Long-Run Impacts of Childhood Access to the Safety Net." American Economic Review 106(4):903–34.

Internal Revenue Service. 2016. "EITC and Other Refundable Credits: Statistics for Tax Returns with EITC." www.eitc.irs.gov.

Johnson, B., B. Thorn, B. McGill, A. Suchman, M. Mendelson, K. L. Patlan, B. Freeman, R. Gotlieb, and P. Connor. 2013. "WIC Participant and Program Characteristics 2012." Prepared by Insight Policy Research under Contract No. AG-3198-C-11–0010. Alexandria, VA: U.S. Department of Agriculture, Food and Nutrition Service.

McGarry, Kathleen, and Robert F. Schoeni. 2015. "Understanding Participation in SSI." Ann Arbor, MI: University of Michigan Retirement Research Center Working Paper WP 2015–319. http://www.mrrc.isr.umich.edu/publications/papers/pdf/wp319.pdf.

Nolan L., J. Waldfogel, and C. Wimer. 2017. "Long-term Trends in Rural and Urban Poverty: Insights Using a Historical Supplemental Poverty Measure." Forthcoming in *Annals of the American Academy of Political and Social Science*.

O'Hare, William, and Elizabeth Kneebone. 2007. "EITC Is Vital of Working-Poor Families in Rural America." Fact Sheet No. 8 (Fall). Durham, NH: Carsey Institute. http://scholars.unh.edu/cgi/viewcontent.cgi?article=1031&context=carsey.

Perrin, Andrew, and Maeve Duggan. 2015. "Americans' Internet Access: 2000–2015." Pew Research Center. http://www.pewinternet.org/2015/06/26/americans-internet-access-2000-2015/.

Poethig, Erika. 2016. "One in Four: America's Housing Assistance Lottery," Metrotrends Blog, Urban Institute. http://www.urban.org/features/housing-assistance-matters-initiative.

Ruffing, Kathy A. 2015. "Geographic Pattern of Disability Receipt Largely Reflects Economic and Demographic Factors." Center on Budget and Policy Priorities, January 9. http://www.cbpp.org/research/geographic-pattern-of-disability-receipt-largely-reflects-economic-and-demographic-factors.

Ryan, Paul [Chairman] and House Budget Committee Majority Staff. 2014. "Expanding Opportunity in America." Committee on the Budget: U.S. House of Representatives, July 24.

Schott, Liz, and Misha Hill. 2015. "State General Assistance Programs Are Weakening Despite Increased Need." Center on Budget and Policy Priorities. http://www.cbpp.org/research/family-income-support/state-general-assistance-programs-are-weakening-despite-increased.

Schott, Liz, Ladonna Pavetti, and Ife Floyd. 2015. "How States Use Federal and State Funds Under the TANF Block Grant." Center on Budget and Policy Priorities. http://www.cbpp.org/research/family-income-support/how-states-use-federal-and-state-funds-under-the-tanf-block-grant.

Sherman, Arloc, and Danilo Trisi. 2015. "Safety Net More Effective Against Poverty Than Previously Thought." Center on Budget and Policy Priorities. http://www.cbpp.org/research/poverty-and-inequality/safety-net-more-effective-against-poverty-than-previously-thought.

Sherman, Jennifer. 2006. "Coping with Rural Poverty: Economic Survival and Moral Capital in Rural America." *Social Forces* 85(2):891–913.

——. 2009. *Those Who Work, Those Who Don't: Poverty, Morality, and Family in Rural America*. Minneapolis: University of Minnesota Press.

——. 2013. "Surviving the Great Recession: Growing Need and the Stigmatized Safety Net." *Social Problems* 60(4):409–32.

———. 2011. "The Research Supplemental Poverty Measure: 2010." U.S. Census Bureau, Current Population Reports, P60–241. https://www.census.gov/prod/2011pubs/p60-241.pdf.

———. 2014. "The Supplemental Poverty Measure: 2013." U.S. Census Bureau, Current Population Report, P60–254. https://www.census.gov/library/publications/2014/demo/p60-251.html.

Slack, Tim, and Candice A. Myers. 2012. "Understanding the Geography of Food Stamp Program Participation: Do Space and Place Matter?" *Social Science Research* 41:263–75.

Smith, Kristin. 2016. "Fewer Than Half of WIC-Eligible Families Receive WIC Benefits." Carsey Institute, National Issue Brief No. 102. http://scholars.unh.edu/carsey/278/.

Social Security Administration. 2016a. "Annual Report of the Supplemental Security Income Program." https://www.ssa.gov/oact/ssir/SSI16/index.html.

———. 2016b. "Annual Statistical Supplement: Highlights." April 2016.

———. 2016c. "SSI: How Do I Apply." https://www.ssa.gov/disabilityssi/ssi.html.

———. 2016d. "Statistical Tables." https://www.ssa.gov/oact/STATS/.

———. 2016e. "What Is the Maximum Social Security Disability Benefit Payable?" https://faq.ssa.gov/link/portal/34011/34019/article/3735/what-is-the-maximum-social-security-retirement-benefit-payable.

———. 2016f. "What Is the Maximum Social Security Retirement Benefit Payable?" https://faq.ssa.gov/link/portal/34011/34019/article/3735/what-is-the-maximum-social-security-retirement-benefit-payable.

Spar, Karen. 2011. "Federal Benefits and Services for People with Low Income: Programs, Policy, and Spending, FY2008–FY2009." Congressional Research Service.

Stone, Chad, and William Chen. 2014. "Introduction to Unemployment Insurance." Center on Budget and Policy Priorities. http://www.cbpp.org/research/introduction-to-unemployment-insurance.

Tanner, Michael D. 2012. "The American Welfare State: How We Spend Nearly $1 Trillion a Year Fighting Poverty—and Fail." Cato Institute, Policy Analysis No. 694. https://www.cato.org/publications/policy-analysis/american-welfare-state-how-we-spend-nearly-$1-trillion-year-fighting-poverty-fail.

Tickamyer, Ann R., and Debra A. Henderson. 2010. "Devolution, Social Exclusion, and Spatial Inequality in U.S. Welfare Provision." In *Welfare Reform in Rural Places: Comparative Perspectives,* ed. Paul Melbourne, 41–59. Bingley, UK: Emerald Group Publishing Limited.

———. 2011. "Livelihood Practices in the Shadow of Welfare Reform." In *Economic Restructuring and Family Well-Being in Rural America,* ed. Kristin E. Smith and Ann R. Tickamyer, 274–94. University Park, PA: Pennsylvania State University Press.

Tickamyer, Ann R., Debra A. Henderson, Julie Anne White, and Barry L. Tadlock. 2000. "Voices of Welfare Reform: Bureaucratic Rationality Versus the Perceptions of Welfare Participants." *Affilia* 15(2):173–92.

Trisi, Danilo, and LaDonna Pavetti. 2012. "TANF Weakening as a Safety Net for Poor Families." Center on Budget and Policy Priorities. http://www.cbpp.org/research/tanf-weakening-as-a-safety-net-for-poor-families.

U.S. Census Bureau. 2016. "Poverty Thresholds." https://www.census.gov/data/tables/time-series/demo/income-poverty/historical-poverty-thresholds.html.

U.S. Department of Health and Human Services. 2016. "Office of Family Assistance." http://www.acf.hhs.gov/ofa/help.

Warlick, Jennifer L. 1982. "Participation of the Aged in SSI." *Journal of Human Resources* 17(2):236–60.

Whitman, Kevin, Gayle L. Reznik, and Dave Shoffner. 2011. "Who Never Receives Social Security Benefits?" *Social Security Bulletin* 71:17–24.

Whittaker, Julie M., and Katelin P. Isaacs. 2014. "Unemployment Insurance: Programs and Benefits." Congressional Research Service. http://digitalcommons.ilr.cornell.edu/key_workplace/1233/.

Wiki. 2016. "How to Apply for HUD Housing." http://www.wikihow.com/Apply-for-HUD-Housing.

CHAPTER 15

The Opportunities and Limits of Economic Growth

Gary Paul Green

For several decades, policy makers have relied on economic growth as the principle strategy for alleviating poverty. Based on a premise that "a rising tide lifts all boats," economic growth promises to create jobs, raise wages, and improve opportunities for the poor. Economic growth also has the capacity to unleash innovation and entrepreneurship, which can contribute to job and income growth as well. Proponents of the economic growth model have stressed the limited success of government programs in the past in reducing poverty (Murray 1984).

This emphasis on economic development stands in stark contrast to previous efforts to reduce poverty. Poverty programs in the United States have historically focused on providing social services such as housing, food, and child care to low-income families. At various times in history, religious organizations and nonprofit organizations have taken a lead role in these programs, but the responsibility has fallen largely to state and federal governments (O'Connor 1999). These programs provide low-income households with a social safety net that is critical to building opportunities for economic mobility.

This chapter examines two important questions relating to this transition from providing social services to promoting economic growth as the response to poverty. First, how effective is job growth in lifting workers out of poverty? Theoretically, job growth should reduce unemployment and poverty for a couple of reasons. New jobs can create opportunities for the unemployed and the poor. Competition for workers raises wages and improves opportunities for low-wage workers. Economic growth creates new markets that provide incentives for entrepreneurship, which opens new opportunities for low-wage workers. These benefits of economic growth, however, are dependent on several conditions that may not be met in many rural areas today. In addition, it should be recognized that policies promoting job growth tend to be individualistic in nature—they are not directed toward poor places. Workers are assumed to be mobile and will move to places where job growth is occurring.

The second question concerns whether community-based approaches to economic growth are any more effective than traditional economic development strategies (such as offering tax incentives and subsidies) in lowering unemployment and poverty rates and raising wages. For most rural communities, economic development strategies involve efforts to attract or retain businesses in the area. These place-based approaches can be distinguished from strategies that emphasize community-owned and controlled institutions. Community-based economic development attempts to minimize external control of the local economy and maximize the benefits for residents. A growing number of localities, for example, have created community development financial institutions, such as microenterprise loan funds or regional workforce development networks, to reduce unemployment and poverty. Although these activities promote economic development, community-based strategies have social objectives as well. A distinguishing characteristic is that they have mechanisms directed toward the poor and disadvantaged in specific places. In other words, it is not assumed that markets will reduce poverty and inequality without institutional change. By incorporating social goals, these strategies attempt to overcome some of the inherent weaknesses of markets in the fight against poverty.

This chapter examines the opportunities and limits of promoting economic growth as a means of fighting poverty with a focus on how the context in rural areas may limit the benefits of economic growth for the rural poor. Next, the potential and limits of community-based economic development approaches to alleviate rural poverty are assessed. Microenterprise loan funds are widely used to promote entrepreneurship as a pathway out of poverty. Workforce development programs attempt to prepare unemployed and disadvantaged workers for local jobs. Tourism is frequently touted as an effective way for rural communities to create new jobs. Finally, the potential and limits of these community-based development efforts in rural areas are examined.

THE EVOLUTION OF PLACE-BASED POVERTY PROGRAMS

Beginning in the progressive era, community practitioners attempted to counteract poverty by providing comprehensive approaches to social service delivery in neighborhoods. Progressives were concerned with the high rates of immigration and the resulting social disorganization found in urban areas. They believed the rapid rates of immigration at the turn of the twentieth century were contributing to the lack of social integration and urban social problems. The goal of community intervention was to better integrate the poor into the larger society and build a sense of collective efficacy rather than change the structural conditions that were creating the social problems. These efforts focused on providing child care, job training, and language programs to the poor through neighborhood organizations.

Franklin Roosevelt's New Deal shifted the emphasis on poverty alleviation to federal programs promoting home ownership and government-supported employment, such as the Works Progress Administration (Green and Haines 2015). Through a variety of direct relief programs, the federal government also provided stimulation to the economy. Policy makers recognized the weaknesses of local efforts to ameliorate the high rates of poverty and unemployment generated by the Great Depression. Although some critics have charged that the New Deal effectively squashed social unrest and protected the interests of the capitalist class, there is agreement that it established a social safety net for the poor, especially among the elderly, through the establishment of the Social Security program in 1935 (Piven and Cloward 1971). The New Deal programs were directed at individuals, but the social welfare programs were implemented at the local level. This decision to implement social policy through poor places reflected the political reality that the administration needed the support of southern Democrats to pass much of the New Deal legislation (Green and Haines 2015).

Lyndon Johnson's War on Poverty placed more emphasis on local control and public participation in poverty programs. The Community Action Program (CAP), for example, required the "maximum feasible participation" of residents in designing and implementing programs affecting their area (Moynihan 1969). In addition, CAP allocated resources to nonprofit organizations in communities to provide job training and social services. Local officials were opposed to these programs because they were unable to control how these resources were used. Although the War on Poverty has been criticized for failing to eliminate poverty, it did introduce innovative strategies for engaging the public in poverty programs and made important advancements in reducing poverty.

The Clinton administration used federal tax incentives and grants to improve the business climate in selected poor neighborhoods and communities. The Empowerment Zones/Enterprise Community (EZ/ EC) initiative, however, also provided support for job training, child care, and transportation to assist residents seeking jobs. This initiative, originally proposed under the Reagan administration, directly linked improvements in the business climate with poverty reduction in impoverished neighborhoods and communities. Although it prioritized economic development in places, it also provided important social services (and job training) to poor communities. Evaluations of the effectiveness of the EZ/ EC initiatives, however, suggest they had mixed effects (Pitcoff 2000).

One of the Obama administration's key place-based poverty programs, the Promise Zone initiative, was modeled after a program in Harlem that provides a wide range of services that focus on the well-being of children. It went beyond the tax incentive programs established by the Clinton administration. The program provided funds for neighborhood revitalization, especially street lighting and removing abandoned buildings. In addition, the programs focused on support for pre-K and early college programs. Each location had a plan for development that is supported with tax breaks for businesses, job training, AmeriCorps volunteers, and improved service provision.

This brief review points to the evolution of place-based poverty programs from service provision to economic development. The idea that economic development is the best tool to fight poverty has become firmly entrenched in federal, state, and local policy. This transformation is part of the broader resurgence of neoliberalism (Harvey 2005). Neoliberal strategies typically involve cutting government expenditures and using market mechanisms to solve social, economic, and environmental problems. There continues to be considerable debate, however, on whether these strategies can adequately address inequality and poverty (Blank 1997). Conversely, many analysts also doubt that place-based economic development approaches are the appropriate mechanism for addressing poverty (Dreier 2015; Lemann 1994).

As state and local governmental deficits have increased over the past few decades and many regions have suffered relatively high long-term unemployment rates, municipalities have intensified their efforts by providing economic development incentives as a means of increasing government revenues, jobs, and income as well as reducing poverty and unemployment. The next section briefly reviews the literature on the opportunities and limits of economic development as a strategy for reducing rural poverty.

THEORETICAL FOUNDATIONS OF THE
ECONOMIC GROWTH MODEL

Economic theory suggests that demand-side labor market policies have a potential to reduce poverty and unemployment, primarily through job creation and competition for workers. Some of the underlying assumptions of the economic growth model are examined next, and weaknesses of this theory when applied to addressing poverty, especially in rural areas, are evaluated.

Per economic theory, localities are in competition with each other to attract capital and people. Local governments are assumed to be rational actors that pursue economic development for the benefit of the entire community (Ramsay 1996). Federalism deters localities from redistributive policies and assumes that they can be more efficiently administered at the state and national levels (Peterson 1981).

Another assumption underlying the economic growth model is that businesses and residents are perfectly mobile and will choose to locate in places that offer them their preferred mix of services and taxes. Localities that attract new residents or businesses increase government revenue, which allows them to provide more services or reduce taxes. In addition, job growth provides new opportunities for the poor and the underemployed. Even if employed workers take many of the jobs that are created, unemployed workers in the region benefit from old jobs that open. In addition, job growth theoretically generates competition among employers for workers. This competition should lead to wage growth, which also can pull the working poor out of poverty. If localities lose businesses or population, they must raise taxes to maintain the existing level of services. This process of raising taxes can lead to more population and business losses, and the poor and unemployed are left with fewer job opportunities. The economic growth model is depicted in figure 15.1.

Government policies promoting economic development rely heavily on tax breaks, subsidies, and other incentives to attract businesses or to retain them in the locality. Much of the debate regarding these policies concerns whether these incentives are necessary to influence business location decisions. One critique is that subsidies have little or no influence on business location decisions. Research suggests that factors such as proximity to markets and labor productivity are much more important than taxes and other incentives in business location or expansion decisions (Green, Fleischmann, and Kwong 1996; Lobao, Jeanty, Partridge,

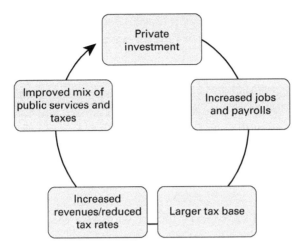

Figure 15.1   The economic growth model.

and Kraybill 2012). Thus, many businesses receive tax breaks when they would have located in the area without them.

One important factor influencing the relationship between economic growth and poverty is how local governments fund their economic development activities. If local governments reduce expenditures for education and social services to provide incentives for businesses, residents and businesses may migrate to other places (Bartik 1991). Thus, this strategy may have negative consequences for low-income and unemployed workers. For example, many communities use tax increment financing (TIF), which freezes taxes on businesses that expand or locate in a specific area. These programs often have a negative impact on schools and other services that are funded primarily through property taxes (Hicks, Faulk, and Quinn 2015).

It is also important to consider the net benefits and costs of economic development incentives (Green et al. 1996). As competition for jobs has increased over the past few decades, rural communities are offering more incentives to attract new firms. There is concern in many communities that this hypercompetition for capital has resulted in more costs than benefits. The jobs created do not make up for the lost government revenue and the decline in social services for the poor.

Research on the effects of job growth on local unemployment is somewhat mixed. In one of the most frequently cited studies on the benefits of tax breaks on unemployment, Bartik (1991) estimates that a state and local business tax reduction of 10 percent would increase business activity in an area by 2.5 percent. Increased business activity results in more job opportunities and ultimately lowers the unemployment rate. Bartik (1991) concluded that a 1 percent increase in local employment reduced the long-run local unemployment rate by 0.1 percent and raised the labor force participation rate by 0.1 percent. This analysis of urban areas suggests that the net benefits are greater than the costs for most economic development policies. More recent evidence suggests that job growth may have a stronger impact in rural counties with high rates of poverty (Partridge and Rickman 2005; Partridge, Rickman, and Li 2009).

Other studies have found a limited impact of economic growth on poverty or unemployment because growth redistributes rather than creates jobs (Logan and Molotch 1987). In other words, job growth in one region comes at the expense of jobs in other regions. Although local poverty rates may decline locally, the aggregate poverty rate does not change.

Even at the local level, economic growth may have a negligible effect on unemployment and poverty. Summers et al. (1976) reviewed the research on new plant locations in small towns and concluded that on average previously unemployed workers take fewer than 10 percent of jobs created in these settings. In-migrants or workers who already have jobs take most of the new jobs that are created. Many of the job vacancies may be filled by workers willing to commute long distances and are not interested in moving closer to their job. Hout, Levanon, and Cumberworth (2011) also found that employers are reluctant to hire long-term unemployed workers because of perceived outdated skills, which means they do not employ local workers who have been unemployed for a long period. In a more recent analysis on this issue, however, Betz and Partridge (2012) found that migration over the past fifteen years has been less responsive to employment opportunities in rural areas. This would suggest that local unemployed and low-income workers would benefit from job creation.

Economic growth may fail to generate benefits for the unemployed or poor because of a skills mismatch (Gibbs, Swaim, and Teixeira 1998). A skills mismatch can occur when the skills demanded by employers do not match well with the skills of workers in the area (Kain 1992). Lack of transportation may limit the ability of job seekers to find and obtain available jobs. In urban areas, racial residential segregation is a major contributor to the spatial mismatch between the inner city and suburbs. Most of the unemployed and poor live in the inner city, but they do not have access to the jobs being created in the suburbs. In rural areas, residential segregation is less the issue, but commuting distances and lack of public transportation may present obstacles for job seekers.

Second, job seekers may lack the skills required by local employers. Economic development efforts, for example, may successfully attract employers to the region, but the new jobs do not match the skills available in the local workforce. Or the skills demanded by employers may be changing more rapidly than the workforce's skills due to technological advancements. On average, rural residents have lower levels of human capital (e.g., education and job training) than do urban residents (Lichter, Beaulieu, Findeis, and Teixeira 1993; Marre 2015). Often job openings for skilled workers remain unfilled. Employers also discuss the lack of "soft" skills among workers as a serious obstacle to hiring workers (Moss and Tilly 2003). Examples of soft skills might include the ability to work in teams or interpersonal skills required to deal with customers.

Finally, training and educational institutions may not be preparing workers for the types of jobs available in the region. Training programs require enough students to efficiently offer an educational or training setting. Equipment necessary for training may require a scale that is not available in many rural areas. The response by workers in many rural communities is to migrate to urban areas where they may be able to get a better return on their investment in education and training.

Economic growth potentially creates job openings for low-income and unemployed workers and places pressure on employers to raise wages. In practice, however, there are many institutional reasons these policies may have a limited impact on poverty and unemployment. Firms in industries with global markets face pressures to keep wages to a minimum. The lack of unions in most rural areas also reduces the bargaining power of workers in these settings.

The empirical evidence suggests that labor demand policies can potentially overcome some of these obstacles by more carefully targeting resources to workers and employers (Bartik 2001). First, subsidies to employers should focus on hiring unemployed workers in the local labor market. Many communities have adopted "first source" incentives to ensure that jobs created through subsidies first benefit local workers who need jobs. Often these incentives will require that new positions be created to satisfy the requirement.

Second, to be effective, subsidies should be targeted to areas with high unemployment rates. Many states offer incentives to businesses to locate anywhere in the state. Typically, these businesses will not locate in areas with high unemployment.

Third, subsidies may more effectively reduce unemployment and poverty if they are directed to small businesses and nonprofit agencies. These employers tend to be less mobile than corporations recruited to the area and may generate more long-term benefits for low-income and unemployed workers (Brown, Hamilton, and Medoff 1990).

COMMUNITY-BASED ANTIPOVERTY PROGRAMS

Rural communities have relied heavily on the traditional tools of economic development, such as industrial recruitment activities, to create demand for workers. There is growing concern that these efforts are largely ineffective for most communities. Thus, many economic development practitioners in rural areas have turned to alternative strategies. Community development financial institutions, for example, direct financial resources to communities or borrowers who may have difficulty gaining access to loans from traditional institutions. Workforce development programs focus on preparing unemployed workers for the labor force. As extractive industries have declined in many rural areas, economic development efforts have turned to amenity-based development to promote job opportunities. These projects focus directly on ensuring that the poor will benefit from the economic development activity. Some of the strengths and weaknesses of each of these approaches are addressed in the following sections.

COMMUNITY DEVELOPMENT FINANCIAL INSTITUTIONS

Rural businesses and residents often lack access to financial capital. They suffer from disinvestment as traditional financial institutions reinvest local assets to other more profitable or less risky locations. There may be several reasons for capital markets to operate in this manner in rural areas (Green and Haines 2015). First, rural credit markets tend to lack competition. For example, small towns typically cannot support more than one or two banks. With little or no competition, financial institutions face less pressure to serve the needs of the community (especially low-income residents) or to take more risk.

Second, financial institutions often lack adequate information about loan applicants. Financial institutions tend to rely on signals that do not necessarily reflect the risk of the applicant. With inadequate information, lenders tend to take less risk. This can be especially disadvantageous for rural borrowers because the loan decisions are increasingly made in urban areas. Removing the decision making from rural communities means that lenders have even less informal information about applicants and will take less risk.

Third, there continues to be concern that financial institutions may discriminate against minority and women applicants. Rejection rates are much higher for minorities and women than for other loan applicants (Squires and O'Connor 2001). There are fewer alternative sources of credit for women and minorities in rural areas.

In response to these limitations in rural credit markets, several localities have created community development financial institutions (CDFIs) designed to improve access to credit for women, minorities, and the poor. These institutions build assets that can be used for education, home ownership, or small business development (Sherraden 1991). The most common loan funds are microenterprise loan funds, community development credit unions, and community development banks. These institutions do not focus exclusively on profits but inject a social element into their decision-making processes as well. In this regard, CDFIs' financial assets are not treated strictly as commodities, so they will be available to residents.

MICROENTERPRISE LOAN FUNDS

Microenterprise loan funds are designed to address the difficulties entrepreneurs and small businesses face in gaining access to debt capital. These businesses seldom borrow from traditional banks and lending institutions. Microenterprise loan funds especially promote entrepreneurship among women and minorities who face more obstacles in rural labor markets (Tigges and Green 1994). Although the amount varies, microenterprise loan funds make very small loans to purchase equipment or supplies for a business, such as a sewing machine to start a dressmaking business or a snow blower to begin a snow removal service.

Some microenterprise loan funds have adopted the principles used by the Bangladeshi Grameen Bank. The Grameen Bank is famous for peer group lending practices that make loans to small groups of women (five to eight members) and then rotate the loan around to different members when it is repaid. This practice establishes peer pressure to repay loans and helps to provide social support to entrepreneurs. The Grameen Bank has a loan loss rate of approximately 2 percent, which is extremely low for a loan fund ("Grameen Bank at a Glance" 2015).

One example of a successful rural microenterprise loan fund is the Four Bands Community Fund on the Cheyenne River Reservation in rural western South Dakota (Dewees and Sarkozy-Banozczy 2010). The 501(c)(3) nonprofit organization provides small business loans. Applicants must complete business training and may receive technical assistance for their businesses. The education and training that are required are essential pieces to the success of these funds and to poverty alleviation on reservations. By providing alternative sources of funding, the poor and unemployed find alternatives to wage employment in these poor rural areas.

Rural microenterprise loan funds face several constraints. Most funds are not large enough to become self-sustaining, so they must rely on foundations and governments to continually fund their activities. It is much easier to achieve the necessary scale and become self-sustaining in urban areas where there is a higher density of borrowers. Few recipients of microloans graduate to commercial banks, so the borrowers remain dependent on microenterprise loan funds (Dewees and Sarkozy-Banozczy 2010). This pattern limits the ability of microenterprise loan funds to reach additional entrepreneurs and have a broader impact on rural development (Green and Haines 2015).

Regulations or public policies also can create obstacles for microenterprise loan funds. In many states, entrepreneurial earnings count against income limits for receiving public aid. This means that entrepreneurs risk losing their aid, such as health care, if they earn too much from their business. In addition, entrepreneurs frequently must obtain a business license, which can be a difficult obstacle to overcome for a newly established business. Health regulations can serve as a major obstacle for microenterprises, especially for those in the food industry. Requiring businesses to meet industry standards for production may prove to be too costly for many small businesses and farms.

Overall, there is a great deal of potential with microenterprise loan funds in rural development. They are constrained, however, by the low density of borrowers in most rural areas. Relatively few of these microenterprises expand to employ additional workers, which may limit their impact on poverty. Developing loan funds across a broader region may be an effective way to overcome the limits of population density in rural areas. Overall, microenterprise loan funds offer an alternative for many rural poor people who have very little access to traditional financial institutions (Ager 2014).

COMMUNITY DEVELOPMENT CREDIT UNIONS

Community development credit unions (CDCUs) operate like other credit unions, except they have a geographic or associational bond in areas where most members are low-income residents. There are approximately 400 CDCUs in the United States. These institutions limit their investments to local areas where their customers live.

An example of a CDCU is the Lac Courte Oreilles Federal Credit Union (LCOFCU) located in Hayward, Wisconsin (Dewees and Sarkozy-Banoczy 2010). The LCOFCU offers a wide variety of financial products, including savings accounts and loans. Credit products are offered only to tribal members as alternatives to predatory lending institutions in the area. In addition to the lending programs, the LCOFCU provides financial education classes and credit counseling to borrowers. The credit union features several loan programs that improve access to credit for borrowers who may not have much collateral or have a poor credit history.

In most cases, CDCUs operate as intermediaries between low-income borrowers and social investors. Social investors are interested in supporting efforts to improve access to capital in areas that have limited access to conventional sources of capital. Thus, they tend to be more limited in their operations and are dependent on the social investment funds for resources. Most CDCUs are in urban areas where there is a higher density of potential borrowers than in rural areas. CDCUs typically provide small consumer loans and small business loans.

COMMUNITY DEVELOPMENT BANKS

Like other CDFIs, community development banks serve as an intermediary between social investors (such as foundations and individuals) and poor neighborhoods and communities. These banks, however, tend to focus on housing loans, although some also do a substantial amount of lending to businesses.

One of the most touted community development banks was the Southern Development Bancorporation, which was located in rural Arkansas. This bank was modeled after the successful South Shore Bank in Chicago (Taub 1988). The bank became engaged in a wide variety of activities beyond lending. Much of their activity was related to development efforts in the Delta region, which has had historically high poverty rates.

Community development banks have had limited success (Taub 1988). The lack of social investment funds supporting them has been a major limitation. It may be easier to see the reasonable returns on investing in housing in urban areas where there may be more of a market. It may be more difficult to do this type of housing development in rural areas because of the low demand.

Overall, community development financial institutions address many of the weaknesses of rural credit markets and focus on the social needs of rural communities. These institutions direct assets to low-income residents who may be locked out of the conventional financial system. It is safe to say that CDFIs have been more successful in urban areas because of the scale and population density available in urban settings. Businesses relying on these sources of credit still face other structural disadvantages that these institutions cannot address.

One of the major limitations of CDFIs is that most are unable to become self-sufficient and therefore rely on foundations and social investors for continual financial support. This dependence has two important consequences. First, it means that funds are limited and do not come close to being able to fully address the problem of rural poverty. Second, dependence on external sources of finance may constrain the efforts of these institutions to address a broad set of needs in poor communities and to challenge the local power structure (Stoecker 1997). Dependency on external sources of funding, therefore, may constrain the activities of advocacy groups, especially their community organizing efforts.

WORKFORCE DEVELOPMENT

Over the last few decades, practitioners and policy makers have recognized that workforce development is integral to economic development. Workforce development is more than just job training, however. It involves a wide range of activities from orientation to the work world to placement, as well as mentoring and follow-up counseling and crisis intervention. This approach to job training tends to be more holistic than most government training programs, and it provides a stronger linkage to local employers.

One of the primary reasons workforce development has been emphasized in rural areas is the persistent gap in educational attainment between urban and rural areas. Part of the gap can be explained by the demographic differences between rural and urban populations: rural areas have a much older population, and these workers tend to have less education (Beaulieu and Mulkey 1995). The gap in education, however, persists for even younger workers. Rural schools often lack the resources available in urban areas. In addition, the returns on investment in education and training are lower in rural than in urban areas (Gibbs et al. 1998). This means there is less of an incentive for rural residents to invest in additional education and training.

A second reason for the rise in interest in workforce development is because rural employers provide very little job training (Green 2007). Rural employers tend to demand a less-skilled workforce, which is reflected in the lower wages in the workforce. Manufacturing jobs in rural areas tend to demand more routine skills that do not require much education or specific job training (Green 2007).

Workforce development networks are intended to overcome some of the weaknesses inherent in rural labor markets. First, workforce development networks address one of the key issues facing low-wage workers— job information (Holzer 1996). Most unemployed and low-wage workers rely primarily on family and friends for information about available jobs. In addition, most workers find jobs through family or friends that are employed by the firm that is hiring them. One of the problems with these informal channels of information is that job seekers are disadvantaged (in terms of wages and benefits) compared to those who use more formal channels. This is especially the case for minority job seekers (Green, Tigges, and Diaz 1999). Workforce development networks provide more formal sources of information for low-wage and unemployed workers, which improves their likelihood of finding good jobs.

Second, workforce development networks provide a stronger linkage between workers' skills and those demanded by local employers. This is one of the key differences between workforce development networks and government job training programs that have been administered in the past. Government programs are not strongly tied to local demand. Research suggests that the types of jobs most available to poor and unemployed workers tend to require "soft" skills rather than extensive math or reading skills (Bartik 2001). This is especially true for jobs that require interaction with customers or coworkers. Workforce development networks often promote training programs that build these types of skills through direct interaction with employers.

Third, workforce development networks also address some of the obstacles to employer-provided training. Employers are often reluctant to provide training to workers because they fear they will lose their investment when a worker takes a job elsewhere. It is in the interest of most employers to provide job training to increase productivity, but it is not in the interest of individual employers to take the risk of training workers and losing them to other employers. Workforce development networks address this collective action problem by bringing together employers with common training needs. By collaborating, employers overcome their collective action problem and generate a sufficient scale to efficiently provide training programs. One example is the plastics industry in central Wisconsin, which identified some common training needs and worked with the technical colleges and high schools to provide the training (Green 2007).

Finally, workforce development networks may provide workers with increased opportunities for occupational mobility. In many instances, employers provide few opportunities for workers to move up within their firm because they recruit workers with more advanced skills outside the firm. The result is higher turnover rates among low-skilled workers. In addition, employers may face difficulty in finding qualified workers. Workforce development networks can address these problems by establishing career ladders within a region. Low-skilled workers are encouraged to stay with their employer to receive additional job training. After they receive the training, they can obtain better paying jobs with employers participating in the network. This arrangement benefits low-wage employers because they can reduce their turnover rate and retain workers for a longer period. Employers demanding more skilled workers benefit because they gain access to this skilled workforce in the region. Employees benefit because they obtain additional training while holding onto their job (Mitnik and Zeidenberg 2007).

These workforce development networks can be established in several different ways in rural areas, and each has its own advantages and disadvantages (Harrison and Weiss 1998). In some cases, a single community-based organization is responsible for providing social services, job training, placement, and counseling. PathStone is an example of a sole provider model that provides workforce development services for immigrants in rural New York. This model has the advantage of providing a holistic approach to address the needs of low-income workers. In addition to job training, it provides clothing, transportation, and health care to migrant workers.

A more common way of organizing workforce development networks is to establish industrial clusters. Firms in the same industry can organize training and apprenticeship programs with educational institutions in a region. The advantage of the clusters is that they can identify common needs and build apprenticeship and training programs with educational institutions. One example is the 2+2+2 program established through the Wisconsin Plastics Valley Association. The foundation of the program is a plastics youth apprenticeship program for high school students in the region. After graduating, credits can be applied toward an associate's degree with one of the regional technical colleges. This degree prepares students for the more skilled positions in the plastics industry. Finally, workers can transition to a bachelor's degree program at the University of Wisconsin-Stout or the University of Wisconsin-Platteville to pursue a degree in engineering that focuses on plastics industry technology (Green 2007).

A third model is the hub-spoke employment training networks with a community-based organization as the central node linking employers, local governments, and training institutions. One example of a hub-spoke training network is the Mid-Delta Workforce Alliance, which has been operating in several rural counties in Mississippi and Arkansas since 1994. The alliance focuses primarily on providing workforce development services for low-skilled employees. The alliance identifies and mobilizes workforce development resources and establishes collaborative efforts at the local level. It has been actively involved in job shadowing programs, school-to-work programs, and other activities designed to improve job training in the region (Green 2007).

Although workforce development programs address some of the limitations in labor markets, it is difficult to overcome the structural weaknesses in rural labor markets. Workforce development primarily influences the supply side of the labor market while largely ignoring the demand side. Examples of demand-side policies include public employment programs or incentives (e.g., tax credits) for employers to hire disadvantaged workers. Bartik's (2001) review of the empirical literature on demand-side policies suggests that these programs may have a stronger effect on hiring disadvantaged workers than do supply-side approaches. Demand-side approaches, however, are seldom used in the United States (especially in rural areas). Supply-side approaches are more consistent with the broader cultural values of American individualism. Ideally, labor market policies would incorporate both demand- and supply-side elements.

The lack of job opportunities in rural areas contributes to the "brain drain" from which so many rural communities suffer. Firms located in rural areas tend to be late in the profit/product cycle, which means that the industries have routinized production and have less need for skilled workers. Similarly, rural labor markets are often "thin," which means that there are few jobs in each occupational category. These structural characteristics have the effect of reducing the competition for workers in these jobs and depressing wage levels (Green 2012). It is difficult for workforce development efforts to counter these structural obstacles in rural areas.

Finally, rural labor markets often lack intermediaries, such as unions, that improve wages and benefits. Unions have been shown to have a positive effect on wages and benefits (Mischel 2012). The low population density is probably the major reason for the lack of intermediaries.

AMENITY-BASED DEVELOPMENT AND TOURISM

Rural economies have historically been dependent on the extraction of natural resources, such as agriculture, forestry, mining, and fishing. Technological advancements and structural changes in extractive industries have reduced employment in these industries. In the 1960s and 1970s, low-wage manufacturing facilities moved into rural areas (Summers et al. 1976). Globalization and technological changes have contributed to the loss of manufacturing jobs in many rural areas, especially in those industries that face competition from developing countries.

Today, the service sector accounts for a growing proportion of jobs in rural areas. One of the major growth areas in the service sector is the expansion of tourism, recreation, and retirement opportunities in rural areas. In many rural communities, retirement income has become the economic base for these localities (Bishop and Gallardo 2011). This shift in the economic base of rural communities signifies a transformation from viewing natural resources as commodities to be extracted for external markets to a source of consumption for tourism, recreation, and retirement (Power 1988). Natural amenities have been shown to be a major factor in rural population change (Hunter, Boardman, and Saint Onge 2005; McGranahan 1999). Promotion of tourism is often used to address income inequality and poverty in rural communities, especially pro-poor tourism (Deller 2010; Scheyvens 2011). Jobs in the tourism industry typically do not require much training and can provide opportunities for workers with little job experience (Reeder and Brown 2005).

Amenity-based development efforts in rural areas face several obstacles. Natural amenities are highly income elastic, which means that high-income residents are willing to pay a higher price for living in the area. High-amenity regions tend to be less affordable, especially in terms of housing, for low-income residents. Low-income workers must commute long distances to work in these communities. Amenity-based development can produce a form of rural gentrification. Although this strategy generates new jobs, it may be more difficult for the poor to live in the community because of changes in the housing market. Local strategies are needed to ensure that affordable housing is available in these markets.

Jobs in the tourism and recreation industries tend to provide low wages, few benefits, and limited opportunities for economic mobility (Marcouiller, Kim, and Deller 2004). Many of the jobs in these industries are part-time or seasonal. Like most other industries in the service sector, tourism development tends to generate more income inequality in rural areas (Marcouiller et al. 2004).

There also is evidence that tourism-dependent communities often face more fiscal stress (Keith, Fawson, and Chang 1996). The high level of fiscal stress is probably because many of the natural amenities that draw tourists are public goods—they are available to everyone—but only residents must maintain them. Local governments may find that the costs exceed the benefits in supporting these amenities. One of the results is that social services may be limited, and the poor may have access to fewer resources.

Overall, amenity-based development, especially tourism, is the basis for economic development in many rural areas today. Tourism has become one of the largest industries in the world. A basic contradiction in amenity-based development is that job and population growth may destroy the key to economic development—the quality of the environment. Especially in areas with a fragile environment, any population or employment growth can threaten the natural amenities that are so attractive. Ironically, it typically is the recent migrants, rather than long-term residents, in rural areas who are often more supportive of more restrictive land use and environmental policies.

Finally, this discussion has suggested that there is often a tension between extraction activities and amenity-based development in resource-dependent communities. Over the past decade, many rural areas have experienced a boom, especially in gas shale development, that has generated many new jobs (Mason, Muehlenbachs, and Olmstead 2015). These regions have experienced significant population and income growth. One of the concerns about economic booms in resource-rich regions is that exports of resources may have a negative effect on the rest of the economy (what is referred to as the Dutch disease). The poor may benefit from some of the jobs created through extractive activities, but the costs of labor and other factors of production may drive out other economic activity that may benefit the poor. In addition, mining activities generally last for a relatively short period and leave regions dependent on these resources in a worse position once the resources are depleted (Power 1988). It is possible to balance extractive activities with amenity-based development, but it is a delicate equilibrium to maintain.

CONCLUSIONS

Rural areas continue to suffer from some basic structural features that constrain the ability of economic development efforts to reduce poverty. In some regions, rural communities continue to be dependent on a few industries, especially the extractive sector. This sector is extremely vulnerable to major shifts in markets and to new technology. Rural regions are often at a competitive disadvantage in the global market. For the past two decades, rural population growth has significantly lagged growth in urban areas (Kusmin 2014). Without major investments by federal and state governments in basic services, such as education and health care, population and jobs will concentrate in urban areas. This situation may leave behind the most disadvantaged rural residents who are less mobile.

Some of the primary community-based strategies that rural communities have employed to promote more opportunities for the poor have been described. It is doubtful that community-based antipoverty approaches will ever be able to overcome the structural forces facing disadvantaged communities. Yet these efforts are more likely to increase the participation of the poor in decisions affecting their community and yield significant benefits to residents.

An underlying issue to consider is whether economic development strategies that are ultimately based on job growth can ever be an effective approach to address poverty. Some analysts believe that neoliberal strategies are the fundamental cause of inequality and poverty, which makes them illogical choices as antipoverty mechanisms.

There are two important responses to this criticism of neoliberalism. First, these critiques assume that government programs are the only alternative for progressive change. There appears, however, to be very little public support for increasing the role of government, especially for programs related to rural poverty. The proportion of the population in rural areas continues to decline, and there is very little political support to shift resources to these issues.

Second, the key to many community-based economic development strategies is that they combine the profit motive with social objectives. The goal is not to maximize profits at all costs but to achieve social goals as well. Community development financial institutions are especially illustrative there. They must turn a profit to survive (and to provide resources to other residents), but they attempt to do this while serving local, low-income residents. These models usually do not have the resources to address all the need in rural areas. Foundations, social investment funds, and government resources are needed to expand these alternatives in rural areas.

This discussion about the limits of economic development as a strategy to reduce rural poverty raises some larger issues about the future of rural areas. Some economists have argued that the poor in rural areas choose to live in these communities and are making a trade-off between wages and noneconomic benefits to live in a rural community (e.g., easier access to outdoor recreation) (see Roback 1988). This argument implies that poverty is a choice rather than a consequence of social processes. It ignores the fact that poverty is often intergenerational and that children in poor families are more constrained in their choices (Sharkey 2013). It ultimately means that we need to find ways of providing a stronger safety net across rural areas to ensure that rural residents have the same choices urban residents have.

Finally, much of the discussion surrounding economic development and poverty focuses on job creation. We need to remember that many of the rural poor are underemployed (Young 2012). Additional low-wage jobs may have little or no effect on moving people out of poverty. Policies designed to address the issue of working poverty in rural areas must focus simultaneously on the supply and the demand side of local labor markets. These policies must focus on new pathways for building the high road in rural areas.

REFERENCES

Ager, Caplan M. 2014. "Communities Respond to Predatory Lending." *Social Work* 59:149–56.
Bartik, Timothy J. 1991. *Who Benefits from State and Local Economic Development Policies?* Kalamazoo, MI: W. E. Upjohn Institute for Employment Research.
———. 2001. *Jobs for the Poor: Can Labor Demand Policies Help?* New York: Russell Sage Foundation.
Beaulieu, Lionel J., and David Mulkey. 1995. *Investing in People: The Human Capital Needs of Rural America.* Boulder, CO: Westview Press.

Betz, Michael, and Mark Partridge. 2012. "Country Road Take Me Home: Migration Patterns in Appalachian America and Place-Based Policies." *International Regional Science Review* 36:267–95.

Bishop, Bill, and Roberto Gallardo. 2011. "Rural Counties More Dependent on Social Security." *Daily Younder.* http://www.dailyyonder.com/rural-more-dependent-social-security/2011/10/31/3578/.

Blank, Rebecca. 1997. "Why Has Economic Growth Been Such an Ineffective Tool Against Poverty in Recent Years?" In *Poverty and Inequality: The Political Economics of Redistribution*, ed. J. Neill, 27–41. Kalamazoo, MI: W. E. Upjohn Institute for Employment.

Brown, Charles, James Hamilton, and James Medoff. 1990. *Employers Large and Small.* Boston: Harvard University Press.

Deller, Steven. 2010. "Rural Poverty, Tourism, and Spatial Heterogeneity." *Annals of Tourism Research* 37:180–205.

Dewees, Sarah, and Stewart Sarkozy-Banoczy. 2010. "Investing in the Double Bottom Line: Growing Financial Institutions in Native Communities." In *Mobilizing Communities: Asset Building as a Community Development Strategy*, ed. Gary Paul Green and Ann Goetting, 14–47. Philadelphia, PA: Temple University Press.

Dreier, P. 2015. "Philanthropy's Misguided Ideas for Fixing Ghetto Poverty: The Limits of Free Markets and Place-Based Initiatives." *Nonprofit Quarterly.* http://nonprofitquarterly.org/2015/03/19/philanthropy-s-misguided-ideas-for-fixing-ghetto-poverty-the-limits-of-free-markets-and-place-based-initiatives/.

Gibbs, Robert M., Paul L. Swaim, and Ruy Teixeira, eds. 1998. *Rural Education and Training in the New Economy: The Myth of the Rural Skills Gap.* Ames, IA: Iowa State University Press.

"Grameen Bank at a Glance." 2015. http://www.grameen-info.org/grameen-bank-at-a-glance/.

Green, Gary Paul. 2007. *Workforce Development Networks in Rural Areas: Building the High Road.* Cheltenham, United Kingdom, and Northhampton, MA: Edward Elgar.

——. 2012. "Rural Jobs: Making a Living in the Countryside." In *International Handbook of Rural Demography*, ed. Laszlo Kulcsar and Katherine Curtis, 307–18. New York, NY: Springer.

Green, Gary P., Arnold Fleischmann, and Tsz Man Kwong. 1996. "The Effectiveness of Local Economic Development Policies in the 1980s." *Social Science Quarterly* 77:609–25.

Green, Gary Paul, and Anna Haines. 2015. *Asset Building and Community Development*, 4th ed. Thousand Oaks, CA: Sage.

Green, Gary Paul, Leann M. Tigges, and Daniel Diaz. 1999. "Racial and Ethnic Differences in Job Search Strategies in Atlanta, Boston and Los Angeles." *Social Science Quarterly* 80:263–78.

Harrison, Bennett, and Marcus Weiss. 1998. *Workforce Development Networks: Community-Based Organizations and Regional Alliances.* Thousand Oaks, CA: Sage.

Harvey, David. 2005. *A Brief History of Neoliberalism.* New York: Oxford University Press.

Hicks, Michael, Dagney Faulk, and Pam Quirin. 2015. *Some Effects of Tax Increment Financing in Indiana.* Muncie, IN: Center for Business and Economic Research, Ball State University.

Holzer, Harry. 1996. *What Employers Want: Job Prospects for Less-Educated Workers.* New York: Russell Sage Foundation.

Hout, Michael, Asaf Levanon, and Erin Cumberworth. 2011. "Job Loss and Unemployment." In *The Great Recession*, ed. David B. Brusky, Bruce Western, and Christopher Wimer, 59–81. New York: Russell Sage Foundation.

Hunter, Lori, Jason Boardman, and Jarron Saint Onge. 2005. "The Association Between Natural Amenities, Rural Population Growth, and Long-Term Residents' Economic Well-Being." *Rural Sociology* 70:452–69.

Kain, John. 1992. "The Spatial Mismatch Hypothesis Three Decades Later." *Housing Policy Debate* 3:371–92.

Keith, John, Christopher Fawson, and Tsangyao Chang. 1996. "Recreation as an Economic Development Strategy: Some Evidence from Utah." *Journal of Leisure Research* 28:96–107.

Kusmin, Lorin. 2014. "Rural America at a Glance." Economic Brief EB-26. Washington, DC: U.S. Department of Agriculture, Economic Research Service.

Lemann, Nicholas. 1994. "The Myth of Community Development." *New York Times*, January 9.

Lichter, Daniel, Lionel J. Beaulieu, Jill Findeis, and Ruy Teixeira. 1993. "Human Capital, Labor Supply, and Poverty in Rural America." In *Persistent Poverty in Rural America*, ed. Rural Sociological Society Task Force on Persistent Rural Poverty, 39–67. Boulder, CO: Westview Press.

Lobao, Linda, P. Wilmer Jeanty, Mark Partridge, and David Kraybill. 2012. "Poverty and Place Across the United States: Do County Governments Matter to the Distribution of Economic Disparities." *International Regional Science Review* 35:158–87.

Logan, John R., and Harvey L. Molotch. 1987. *Urban Fortunes: The Political Economy of Place.* Berkeley: University of California Press.

Marcouiller, David W., Kwang Koo Kim, and Steven C. Deller. 2004. "Natural Amenities, Tourism, and Income Distribution." *Annals of Tourism Research* 31:1031–50.

Marre, Alexander. 2015. "Rural Education." Washington, DC: U.S. Department of Agriculture, Economic Research Service. http://www.ers.usda.gov/topics/rural-economy-population/employment-education/rural-education.aspx.

Mason, Charles F., Lucija A. Muehlenbachs, and Sheila M. Olmstead. 2015. *The Economics of Shale Gas Development.* Washington, DC: Resources for the Future.

McGranahan, David A. 1999. "Natural Amenities Drive Rural Population Change." Agricultural Economic Report No. 781. U.S. Department of Agriculture, Food and Rural Economics Division, Economic Research Service.

Mischel, Lawrence. 2012. "Unions, Inequality, and Faltering Middle-Class Wages." Economic Policy Institute. http://www.epi.org/publication/ib342-unions-inequality-faltering-middle-class/.

Mitnik, Pablo A., and Matthew Zeidenberg. 2007. *From Bad to Good Jobs? An Analysis of the Prospects for Career Ladders in the Service Industries.* Madison, WI: Center on Wisconsin Strategy.

Moss, Philip, and Chris Tilly. 2003. *Stories Employers Tell: Race, Skill, and Hiring in America.* New York: Russell Sage Foundation.

Moynihan, Daniel P. 1969. *Maximum Feasible Misunderstanding: Community Action in the War on Poverty.* New York: Free Press.

Murray, Charles. 1984. *Losing Ground: American Social Policy 1950–1980*. New York: Basic Books.

O'Connor, Alice. 1999. "Swimming Against the Tide: A Brief History of Federal Policy in Poor Communities." In *Urban Problems and Community Development*, ed. Ronald Ferguson and William Dickens, 77–138. Washington, DC: Brookings Institution Press.

Partridge, Mark, and Dan Rickman. 2005. "High Poverty Nonmetropolitan Counties in America: Can Economic Development Help?" *International Regional Science Review* 28:415–40.

Partridge, Mark, Dan Rickman, and Hui Li. 2009. "Who Wins from Local Economic Development? A Supply Decomposition of U.S. County Employment Growth." *Economic Development Quarterly* 23:13–27.

Peterson, Paul E. 1981. *City Limits*. Chicago, IL: University of Chicago Press.

Pitcoff, Winton. 2000. "EZ'er Said Than Done." *Shelterforce Online* 112. http://www.shelterforce.com/online/issues/112/EZEC.html.

Piven, Francis Fox, and Richard A. Cloward. 1971. *Regulating the Poor: The Functions of Public Welfare*. New York: Vintage.

Power, Thomas M. 1988. *The Economic Pursuit of Quality*. Armonk, NY: M. E. Sharpe.

Ramsay, Meredith. 1996. *Community, Culture, and Economic Development: The Social Roots of Local Action*. Albany, NY: State University of New York Press.

Reeder, Richard J., and Dennis M. Brown. 2005. "Recreation, Tourism and Rural Well-Being." Economic Research Service Report No. 7. Washington, DC: U.S. Department of Agriculture, Economic Research Service.

Roback, J. 1988. "Wages, Rents, and the Quality of Life." *Journal of Political Economy* 90:1257–77.

Scheyvens, Regina. 2011. *Tourism and Poverty*. New York: Routledge.

Sharkey, Patrick. 2013. *Stuck in Place: Urban Neighborhoods and the End of Progress Toward Racial Equality*. Chicago: University of Chicago Press.

Sherraden, Michael. 1991. *Assets and the Poor: A New American Welfare Policy*. New York, NY: M. E. Sharpe.

Squires, Gregory D., and Sally O'Connor. 2001. *Color and Money*. Albany, NY: State University of New York Press.

Stoecker, Randy. 1997. "The CDC Model of Urban Redevelopment: A Critique and an Alternative." *Journal of Urban Affairs* 19:1–22.

Summers, Gene F., Sharon D. Evans, Frank Clemente, E. M. Beck, and Jon Minkoff. 1976. *Industrial Invasion of Nonmetropolitan America: A Quarter Century of Experience*. New York: Praeger.

Taub, Richard P. 1988. *Community Capitalism*. Boston, MA: Harvard Business School Press.

Tigges, Leann M., and Gary P. Green. 1994. "Small Business Success Among Men- and Women-Owned Firms in Rural Areas." *Rural Sociology* 59:289–310.

Young, Justin R. 2012. *Underemployment in Urban and Rural America, 2005–2012*. Durham, NH: Carsey Institute, University of New Hampshire.

CHAPTER 16

――――

Politics and Policy

BARRIERS AND OPPORTUNITIES FOR RURAL PEOPLES

Ann R. Tickamyer, Jennifer Sherman, and Jennifer Warlick

This book presents compelling evidence of the significance of rural poverty in the United States. The persistence, pervasiveness, and severity of poverty across populations, communities, and institutions that make up the heart of rural America has been demonstrated. Comparisons have been drawn with poverty in urban locales, and the causes and consequences of poverty that are distinctly rural and those that are not have been addressed. It has not been suggested that rural poverty is worse than other forms and locations of poverty, although in some places and some times that is certainly the case. It is not a contest to see where it is most extreme or who suffers more; it is plenty serious enough regardless of how others fare. This book seeks to rectify the pervasive lack of serious scholarly attention to rural poverty and to bring this neglect to the attention of students, scholars, the public, and policy makers who often display deep ignorance of the issue. Clear, evidence-based analysis has been presented that neither overdramatizes nor ignores the existence of problems. Both approaches are all too common. Colleagues in the United Kingdom sometimes refer to the "rural idyll," by which they mean the romanticization of rural landscapes so that they are seen as an escape from the problems of modern life (Bell 2006; Cloke, Goodwin, Milbourne, and Thomas 1995). This is in sharp contrast to the grim pictures of rural life as backward and disadvantaged implicitly seen in both popular accounts and studies with a development focus (Lyson and Falk 1993; Milbourne 2004). Even insider accounts with a sympathetic view paint a bleak picture of dysfunction and false consciousness among the rural working class and poor (Frank 2005; Vance 2016). Neither approach realistically addresses the problems of rural people and places.

WHY IS RURAL POVERTY NEGLECTED?

Two questions arise: Why are the problems of rural poverty so pernicious? and Why do they receive so little attention? The answers are closely intertwined. First are the demographic issues. The rural population is much smaller than the urban population, less than 20 percent of the nation's total, and despite swings from decade to decade, most recently it is declining. Equally significant, rural poverty is too often hidden in "flyover" country. It is easier to ignore the issues of people and places that are out of sight and out of mind of the media and other opinion makers than when they are visible on a daily basis as is the case of large urban centers. Nevertheless, approximately 50 million people live in places classified as rural, areas that compose the vast majority of the U.S. land mass, and a substantial proportion of them are poor. Furthermore, some of these populations represent demographic categories that remain in the shadows and too often receive the short end of the stick, such as immigrants (both documented and undocumented), Native Americans, other racial and ethnic minorities, and single mothers and their children. Typically, these groups are worse off in rural places than their urban counterparts. Finally, an unfortunate feedback loop develops in many places with the lack of economic opportunity leading to increased out-migration and brain drain, leaving behind many of the most vulnerable. The chapters in part III focusing on vulnerable populations and part IV focusing on community and societal institutions provide detailed accounts and examples of how these groups fare and the structures and processes implicated.

Second, as alluded to above, many myths about rural life are outdated, outmoded, or just plain wrong. The rural idyll views rural communities as peaceful retreats from urban crime and chaos, where families can pursue fulfilling subsistence-oriented lifestyles. Although there are lush pastoral landscapes in rural America, agriculture does not make up the basis for the economy in most places, nor is it the source of most rural livelihoods. Yet myths persist that rural residents should be able to overcome financial hardships and reduce deprivation by gardening and similar agrarian self-provisioning activities. Even if possible for more than the occasional household, this would represent a bandage on the massive economic trauma documented in this book. At the same time, rural communities often exhibit strengths in the form of physical amenities and capital that transcend limited services and employment. Mythical strengths and weaknesses do little to address the realities of the rural poor.

Third, as discussed elsewhere (Tickamyer and Smith 2011), there is a lack of specific policy to address rural issues in general and rural poverty in particular. There are agricultural policies, trade policies, economic development policies, natural resource policies, and so on that affect rural America. Some have targets that are primarily rural, such as agricultural policy, but none are focused on the specific problems of rural lives and livelihoods. As has been documented extensively, even the most far-reaching poverty assistance program—the Supplemental Nutrition Assistance Program (SNAP, formerly food stamps)—originated primarily as an agricultural support mechanism rather than either a poverty or a rural policy. Poverty policy is almost uniformly national in formulation and scope and largely responsive to beliefs about urban problems (Rose and Baumgartner 2013). Information below the national level on poverty policy and programs focuses on the states and rarely looks specifically at rural conditions. One of the most respected compendiums of poverty policy and programs barely mentions "rural" in over four hundred pages and fourteen chapters of analysis (Cancian and Danziger 2009). To the extent that federal efforts consider rural conditions in policy, they may hurt the rural poor as much as they help. For example, incorporating geographic differences in the cost of living in poverty measures, although seemingly beneficial in formulating a more realistic view of what is a poverty income, has been critiqued for misrepresenting the real costs of rural residence. Accounting for lower housing costs but not including transportation needs or scarcity of services reinforces the view that rural life is necessarily less expensive and less likely to have real hardships for its poor.

The U.S. Department of Agriculture and its various units, especially the Economic Research Service (2016), go a long way to provide information and analysis of socioeconomic conditions and policies that affect rural communities and populations. However, here too the greatest emphasis is on commodities, production, and the rural economy. Important issues of relevance to understanding rural poverty, such as food insecurity, are reported mainly as an indirect, albeit welcome, by-product of agricultural policies and programs.

Fourth, some of the problems of rural poverty are embedded in the formal institutions that serve communities, families, and individuals, and here too understanding of rural conditions takes a back seat to the problems of their urban counterparts. As described in part IV, issues of the adequacy of rural schools, housing, food security, the economy, health care, and more in serving their stakeholders are often unique to rural populations and locales. Although the major institutions linked to problems of poverty have been covered, in some ways this book has barely skimmed the surface of the institutional obstacles and failures, and other issues deserve scrutiny. For example, it is popular to think that poverty should be addressed by faith-based institutions, but as reported in myriad news accounts (cf. Fanger 2013; Ferret 2016; Van Biema 2009), many rural churches are in decline with consequent problems for common outreach programs, such as food pantries and housing assistance. There is little research on how this has affected the rural poor or the role of religious institutions in the economic fortunes of rural communities at this time. Similarly, churches, schools, the family, clubs, and voluntary organizations are purveyors of both cultural standards and material assistance, and they have much to say about who is worthy and who is not, who is included in the life of the community and who is not, and similar labels that may determine the difference between making it or not.

Another area that deserves greater attention is the legal system and disparities in its application across place. We are more used to thinking about social locations such as race, class, and gender as flashpoints in creating legal and judicial inequities and injustices, but spatial location is also relevant, and it intersects with social categories. As this is being written, the news is filled with the outrageous actions of representatives of the criminal justice system, primarily in poor urban minority communities but in rural areas as well. As Pruitt shows in the case study accompanying chapter 5 that illustrates the legal pitfalls and obstacles encountered by a poor Native American single mother in the rural West, the judicial system can be indicted for its failure to understand rurality and the ways this affects the poor.

The role of the state also could have separate coverage. There is a large amount of research on the actions of governments, but much less on government's impact on rural places. The effects of government policies and programs on rural places pervade the analysis in every chapter. Alternative approaches could focus on the explicit actions of government at every level, taking on such issues as the capacity of local governments, the comparative ability to influence policy between urban and rural places, the corruption often found in remote rural civic organizations and state agencies designed to serve the poor, the political agency (or its lack) of rural residents, the disempowering effects of social structures and organizations

BARRIERS AND OPPORTUNITIES FOR RURAL PEOPLES 443

on the poor, or the rise and influence of neoliberalism and its spinoffs. All of these topics are touched upon in these chapters, but none is brought together in one account.

Perhaps the rise and influence of neoliberalism and its spinoffs is especially worthy of further investigation because neoliberalism has set the terms of public policy and political discourse for the last several decades. It includes the push for deregulation, privatization, and reduction in spending for social services and public goods, all with negative consequences across social sectors but particularly problematic for the poor. One corollary of the neoliberal agenda, the emphasis on devolution, has been particularly consequential for the rural poor. The focus on devolution of the welfare provision from the federal government to state and local communities that accompanied the sweeping welfare reform of the 1990s meant that there is great unevenness in policies, programs, and capacities to address the needs of the rural poor and, incidentally, much less ability to evaluate their effectiveness across place (Tickamyer, White, Tadlock, and Henderson 2007; Tickamyer and Smith 2011). Here, too, national and urban policies and statistics dominate, with information on rural America either swamped by them or reported in smaller studies and accounts that do an admirable job of providing local context but make it hard to generalize.

This last point is both a strength and a challenge. The diversity of rural America across all empirical and analytic categories makes it difficult to discuss the issues of rural people and places in a uniform way. The reasons for rural poverty vary by geography, demography, history, and political economy. Attention to context and nuance in the best of case studies create compelling accounts that go far to provide in-depth descriptions and explanations of both the causes and consequences of rural poverty. Studies such as those conducted by Duncan (2015) and Sherman (2009 and chapter 8) are superb models of this approach. It is the triumph of "little data" over the allure of big data, necessary because large-scale representative data for rural places are in short supply. Nevertheless, the diversity of rural landscapes obscures the extent of real deprivation and need.

WHAT IS TO BE DONE?

The first task has been accomplished by this book. This is the first comprehensive account of rural poverty in more than twenty years, and it is one of the very few uncovering the facts of rural poverty and exploring all of its ramifications. Diagnosing the problems, however, leaves us hungry for solutions, and these are harder to come by. The complexity of the mix of politics, policy, and public opinion makes it difficult to argue that quick fixes are possible. Perhaps the last item—popular beliefs—is the most unyielding and makes the others more difficult. To the extent that the poor are seen as responsible for their own problems through laziness, lack of initiative, and poor life choices—popular themes that have dominated beliefs about poverty even in the face of contrary evidence—barriers to addressing poverty realistically and objectively will be hard to overcome. There is a very large literature studying poverty policies and programs and a great deal of knowledge about what works and what doesn't and under what circumstances. However, many of the policies that might be put in place are politically unfeasible; many programs that exist are punitive, unrealistic, or lacking in resources. This goes double for rural poverty whose visibility is lacking for all the reasons previously discussed.

Despite knowing a lot about rural poverty, we really need to know more. That requires not just a desire on the part of researchers to conduct studies but on support for consistent, reliable, and regular data collection for rural people and places. Because of smaller population sizes, many public and private data sources have poor rural representation. Even the most comprehensive official sources such as the Census Bureau have substituted a five-year cycle for collecting data for the smallest communities. The American Community Survey (ACS) that now substitutes for the Census long form takes five years to acquire full information on places smaller than 20,000 people. Other technical measures to preserve confidentiality of respondents means that rural geography sometimes is distorted or eliminated in reporting survey results (U.S. Census 2016), and generally, information useful for human service provision is limited (Strong et al. 2005). At the same time, big data from a variety of new sources, including commercial interests such as supermarket scanner data, mean that there are exciting new avenues of data acquisition to explore. Finally, it is imperative to keep the kinds of case studies and qualitative work referenced throughout this book coming to capture the deep understanding of rural life and livelihoods that only they can provide.

Conceptually, it is important to be aware that the problems of poverty exist as part of larger structures of stratification, inequalities, and power dynamics. Poverty can be defined as a condition but also as part of larger social processes of sorting and allocating resources to individuals, families, households, communities, and regions. These inevitably entail power relations of domination and subordination. Poor people suffer from lack of income to meet their needs, but also from lack of power to influence policy and the distribution of public goods. Poor places similarly are often the result of spatial inequalities fostered by larger social and economic policies that drain resources and constrain development. The poverty found in poor rural regions such as the Mississippi Delta, Appalachia, Indian reservations, and the colonias of the Southwest reflect inequalities and exploitation at the intersections of both people and place. Poverty and inequality are not synonymous, but they are intimately related and mutually reinforcing, which has been demonstrated throughout this book.

At the same time, it would be wrong to think there hasn't been important progress or that people, both individually and collectively, can't make a difference. We live in a time of great and fast-moving change on every front, including numerous changes for the better for rich and poor alike. The reduction in poverty rates from when we first began to measure them is a clear illustration of improvement. Many more could be cited. There may be a long way to go, and new problems emerge all the time, but that shouldn't negate the very real progress made. Social scientists of all stripes often focus on the structure end of the agency–structure continuum discussed in chapter 4. The result is a tendency to lose track of the ability of individuals to make a difference, for policy and programs to improve life conditions, and for both small and large acts to add up to change the world.

So what can be done? The short answer is to continue the struggle for better knowledge, better understanding, better data, better research, and most of all better policy and programs tailored to meet the specific needs of rural people and places. Many of the chapters in this book discuss specific measures that can go a long way toward assisting rural populations and communities in poverty. Whether it is jobs, food security, access to health care, housing, child care, education, or infrastructure needs, it is critical to recognize that rural America has unique challenges and circumstances. Policies and programs, whether universally devised or specifically formulated for rural places, must recognize that context and place matter when devising strategies and implementing change. None of this can happen without understanding, commitment, and effort, and thus the challenge is to bring attention to these issues. This book is one small contribution to that effort. At a much larger level, one heartening development in 2011 was the creation of the White House Rural Council (2016) to "address challenges in Rural America" and charged with responsibility for both creating new initiatives and coordinating across multiple agencies and programs. Perhaps at last the United States will have a high-visibility forum from which to specifically promote rural policy and its implications for poverty. Thus, the long answer is the same—pursuit of knowledge, understanding, data, and policy—with the recognition that these are not easy goals that can be achieved quickly but are part of larger political struggles.

REFERENCES

Bell, David. 2006. "Variations on the Rural Idyll." In *Handbook of Rural Studies*, ed. T. Marsden, P. Cloke, and P. Mooney, 149–60. Thousand Oaks, CA: Sage.

Cancian, Maria, and Sheldon Danziger, eds. 2009. *Changing Poverty, Changing Policies.* New York: Russell Sage Foundation.

Cloke, Paul, Mark Goodwin, Paul Milbourne, and Chris Thomas. 1995. "Deprivation, Poverty and Marginalization in Rural Lifestyles in England and Wales." *Journal of Rural Studies* 11(4):351–65.

Duncan, Cynthia M. 2015. *Worlds Apart: Poverty and Politics in Rural America,* 2nd ed. New Haven, CT: Yale University Press.

Economic Research Service. 2016. "About ERS." U.S. Department of Agriculture. http://www.ers.usda.gov/about-ers.aspx.

Fanger, Amanda. 2013. "Rural Churches Struggle for Survival." *Dakotafire.* http://dakotafire.net/newspapers/rural-churches-struggle-for-survival/3688/print/.

Ferrett, Rob. 2016. "Decline of the Midwestern Rural Church?" Wisconsin Public Radio, February 5. http://www.wpr.org/decline-midwestern-rural-church.

Frank, Thomas. 2005. *What's the Matter with Kansas? Howe Conservatives Won the Heart of America.* New York: Henry Holt.

Lyson, Thomas A., and William W. Falk, eds. 1993. *Forgotten Places: Uneven Development and the Loss of Opportunity in Rural America.* Lawrence: University Press of Kansas.

Milbourne, Paul. 2004. *Rural Poverty: Marginalization and Exclusion in Britain and the United States.* London, UK: Routledge.

Rose, Max, and Frank R. Baumgartner. 2013. "Framing the Poor: Media Coverage and U.S. Poverty Policy, 1960–2008." *Policy Studies Journal* 41(1):22–53.

Sherman, Jennifer. 2009. *Those Who Work, Those Who Don't: Poverty, Morality, and Family in Rural America.* Minneapolis: University of Minnesota Press.

Strong, Debra A., Patricia Del Grosso, Jigar Bhatt, Shannon Phillips, and Kate Scheppke. 2005. "Rural Research Needs and Data Sources for Selected Human Services Topics. Volume 2: Data Sources." Final Report. Mathematica Policy Research, Inc. https://aspe.hhs.gov/sites/default/files/pdf/139381/volumes-1-and-2.pdf.

Tickamyer, Ann R., and Kristin Smith. 2011. "Conclusions." In *Economic Restructuring and Family Well-Being in Rural America*, ed. K. Smith and A. Tickamyer, 336–46. University Park: Pennsylvania State University Press.

Tickamyer, Ann R., Julie White, Barry Tadlock, and Debra Henderson. 2007. "Spatial Politics of Public Policy." In *The Sociology of Spatial Inequality*, ed. Linda Lobao, Gregory Hooks, and Ann R. Tickamyer, 113–39. New York: SUNY Press.

U.S. Census. 2016. "SIPP (Survey of Income and Program Participation) 2008 and 2014 Users' Guide." http://www.census.gov/programs-surveys/sipp/guidance/users -guide.html.

Van Biema, David. 2009. "A Rural Exodus." *Time* 173(5):44–45.

Vance, J. D. 2016. *Hillbilly Elegy: A Memoir of a Family and Culture in Crisis*. New York: HarperCollins.

White House Rural Council. 2016. "About the Rural Council." The White House. https://www.whitehouse.gov/administration/eop/rural-council.

CONTRIBUTORS

Richard D. Abel is a doctoral student in the Department of Sociology at Texas A&M University and recipient of the Dr. Howard Kaplan Memorial Assistantship.

Catharine Biddle is assistant professor of educational leadership at the University of Maine. Her research investigates the relationship between education and rural sociology; she has explored ways in which schools can address issues of social inequality. Her recent publications include "Implementing Middle School Youth-Adult Partnerships: A Study of Two Programs Focused on Social Change" (2015) and "Opportunity, Ambivalence and the Purpose of Schooling in Pennsylvania's Marcellus Shale Region" (2015).

Raeven Faye Chandler is a PhD candidate in rural sociology and demography at Pennsylvania State University's College of Agricultural Sciences. Her main research interests revolve around health and immigration.

Alisha Coleman-Jensen is a sociologist with the Food Assistance Branch of the U.S. Department of Agriculture's Economic Research Service where she examines household food security in the United States. She is the lead author of the USDA's annual report on household food security.

Walter S. DeKeseredy is Anna Deane Carlson Endowed Chair of Social Sciences and Director of the Research Center on Violence at West Virginia University. He is the author of *Abusive Endings: Separation and Divorce Violence against Women* (2017) and *Violence against Women in Pornography* (2016).

John M. Eason is assistant professor in the Department of Sociology at Texas A&M University. His research examines crime and punishment in relation to spatial demographics. He is the author of *Big House on the Prairie: Rise of the Rural Ghetto and Prison Proliferation* (2017).

Danielle Ely is a research assistant at Pennsylvania State University. She studies rural sociology and demography.

Elyzabeth W. Engle is a dual-title PhD candidate in Rural Sociology and Human Dimensions of Natural Resources and Environment at Pennsylvania State University. Her research interests include place-based community development, regional food systems, and human-environment interactions.

Gary Paul Green is professor of community and environmental sociology at the University of Wisconsin-Madison. He is an expert in economic sociology. He is the co-author of *Asset Building and Community Development* (2011) and co-editor of *Mobilizing Communities: Asset Building as a Community Development Strategy* (2010).

Jason Greenberg is assistant professor of management at the NYU Stern School of Business where his research focuses on economic and organizational sociology. His recent publications include "Activist Choice Homophily and the Crowdfunding of Female Founders" (2016) and "The Strength of Weak Ties in MBA Job Search: A Within-Person Test" (2016).

Amanda Hall-Sanchez is an assistant professor of criminal justice in the Department of Social Sciences at Fairmont State University. Her current teaching and research interests include intersectional analyses of violence against women; feminist, critical, and rural criminologies; sexualities and LGBTQ+ communities; and women's experiences with incarceration. Her recent publications include "Adult Pornography and Violence against Women in the Heartland: Results from a Rural Southeast Ohio Study" (2017).

Rosalind P. Harris is a member of the Rural Sociology Faculty in Community and Leadership Development, part of the College of Agriculture, Food, and Environment and the Department of Sociology at the University of Kentucky. She is also affiliate faculty in Appalachian Studies and in Gender and Women's Studies. Her publications include "Geographies of Resistance within the Black Belt South" (2017).

Jill Ann Harrison is an associate professor of sociology at the University of Oregon. Her research focuses on the local effects of globalization, deindustrialization, and environmental change. She is the author of *Buoyancy on the Bayou: Shrimpers Face the Rising Tide of Globalization* (2012).

Mark H. Harvey is associate professor of sociology at Florida Atlantic University. He specializes in social inequality; the political economy of space; and race, class, and gender. His publications include "Consensus-Based Community Development, Concentrated Rural Poverty, and Local Institutional Structures: The Obstacle of Race in the Lower Mississippi Delta" (2013) and *Welfare Reform in Persistent Rural Poverty: Dreams, Disenchantments, and Diversity* (2006).

Michael Hendryx is professor of applied health science in the School of Public Health at Indiana University. His work has appeared in the *International Journal of Environmental Health Research*, *Environmental Science and Policy*, the *British Journal of Cancer*, *Environmental Science and Technology*, and elsewhere.

Leif Jensen is Distinguished Professor of Rural Sociology and Demography at Pennsylvania State University's College of Agricultural Sciences. His research interests lie in social stratification, demography, and economic development. His publications include *Rural America in a Globalizing World* (2014) and "Climatic Conditions and Human Mortality: Spatial and Regional Variation in the United States" (2016).

Kenneth M. Johnson is a senior demographer at the Carsey School of Public Policy and professor of sociology at University of New Hampshire. He is an expert in demographic trends and population redistribution in the United States and was selected in 2016 for the prestigious Andrew Carnegie Fellowship. His numerous publications include "Diverging Demography: Hispanic and Non-Hispanic

Contributions to U.S. Population Redistribution and Diversity" (2016) and "Demographic Trends in Nonmetropolitan America: 2000 to 2010" in *Rural America in a Globalizing World* (2014).

J. Celeste Lay is associate professor of political science at Tulane University. Her research focuses on American political behavior, political socialization, and public policy. She is the author of *A Midwestern Mosaic: Immigration and Political Socialization in Rural America* (2012).

Ian Mette is assistant professor in educational leadership at the University of Maine. He specializes in school reform policy and has authored works such as "School Turnaround: A Rural Reflection of Reform on the Reservation and Lessons for Implementation" (2016) and "Poverty, Privilege, and Political Dynamics within Rural School Reform: Unraveling Educational Leadership in the Invisible America" (2016).

Kathleen Miller is the academic programs director at the Harry S. Truman School of Public Affairs at University of Missouri. She has worked as a program director for the Rural Policy Research Institute on subjects pertaining to rural economic development. Her recent publications include "County Level Resilience and Vulnerability Index" (2015) and "A Critical Review of Rural Poverty Literature: Is There Truly a Rural Effect?" (2005).

Shannon M. Monnat is assistant professor of rural sociology, demography, and sociology at Pennsylvania State University. Her research interests lie at the intersection of demography, sociology, and public health. She has published articles such as "The Great Recession and America's Geography of Unemployment" (2016) and "The New Destination Disadvantage: Disparities in Hispanic Health Insurance Coverage Rates in Metropolitan and Nonmetropolitan New and Established Destinations" (2016).

Lisa R. Pruitt is Martin Luther King, Jr. Professor of Law at the University of California Davis. She specializes in feminist legal theory and the intersection of law and rural livelihoods. Her recent publications include "Protecting People, Protecting Places: What Environmental Litigation Conceals and Reveals about Rurality" (2016) and "Welfare Queens and White Trash" (2016).

Danielle Christine Rhubart is a sociologist and demographer with a focus on environmental sociology, population health, and spatial inequality. She received her PhD in rural sociology with a dual title in demography from Pennsylvania State University.

Kai A. Schafft is associate professor in the Education Policy Studies Department at Pennsylvania State University. His work focuses on rural development, spatial inequality, and the relationship between the wellbeing of rural schools and the communities they serve. He has published more than seventy articles, book chapters, and reports on a variety of rural issues.

Jennifer Sherman is associate professor in the Department of Sociology at Washington State University. Her research consists of studying families in rural communities and how their choices are influenced by spatial and cultural contexts. She has authored books such as *Those Who Work, Those Who Don't: Poverty, Morality, and Family in Rural America* (2009).

Tim Slack is associate professor in the Department of Sociology at Louisiana State University. He specializes in economic and spatial inequality and has published articles including "How Did the Great Recession Impact the Geography of Food Stamp Receipt?" (2014) and "Work in Rural America in the Era of Globalization" in *Rural America in a Globalizing World* (2014).

Kristin Smith is a family demographer at the Carsey School of Public Policy and research associate professor of sociology at University of New Hampshire. Her research focuses on women's labor force and family policy. Relevant publications include *Economic Restructuring and Family Well-Being in Rural America* (2011), "Exploring the Spatial Wage Penalty for Women: Does It Matter Where You Live?" (2013), and "Changes in Wives' Employment When Husbands Stop Working: A Recession-Prosperity Comparison" (2010).

L. Ash Smith studies sociology, poverty, and public policy at the University of Notre Dame.

Corey Sparks is associate professor in the Department of Demography at the University of Texas at San Antonio. He specializes in spatial and statistical demography. His published articles include "An Examination of Disparities in Cancer Incidence in Texas Using Bayesian Random Coefficient Models" (2015) and "An Application of Bayesian Methods to Small Area Poverty Rate Estimates" (2014).

Barry Steffen is a social science analyst at the U.S. Department of Housing and Urban Development, where he has coauthored numerous reports on housing needs for Congress and publications on assisted housing programs and health.

Brian Thiede is assistant professor of rural sociology, sociology, and demography at Pennsylvania State University's College of Agricultural Sciences. He explores the relationship between demographic trends and economic development in publications such as "The Great Recession and America's Geography of Unemployment" (2016) and "America's Working Poor: Conceptualization, Measurement, and New Estimates" (2015).

Ann R. Tickamyer is professor of rural sociology at Pennsylvania State University's College of Agricultural Sciences specializing in spatial inequality and rural poverty. Her publications on rural poverty include *Economic Restructuring and Family Well-Being in Rural America* (2011) and "Gender Justice, Climate Change, and Sustainable Development in Indonesia" (2014).

Jennifer Warlick is associate professor of public policy and economics at University of Notre Dame, College of Arts and Letters. She is an expert in antipoverty policy and has published numerous studies on income maintenance policy and the measurement of poverty. She is also the founding and current director of Notre Dame's Poverty Studies and Interdisciplinary Minor.

Bruce Weber is professor emeritus of applied economics at Oregon State University. In the early 2000s he co-directed the RUPRI Rural Poverty Research Center, and from 2003 to 2015 he was director of the OSU Rural Studies Program. His research focuses on rural poverty, upward mobility, and economic inequality. He is the coeditor of *Rural Wealth Creation* (2014) and *Rural Dimensions of Welfare Reform* (2002).

Sarah Whitley is a member of the clinical faculty of sociology at Washington State University. She specializes in the sociology of education, poverty, qualitative methodologies, rural/urban sociology, social inequality, and stratification. Her recent publications include "Changing Times in Rural America: Food Assistance and Food Insecurity in Food Deserts" (2013).

Emily J. Wornell is research assistant professor at Ball State University, working with the Center for Business and Economic Research and the Rural Policy Research Institute. She has published articles including "Gender Justice, Climate Change, and Sustainable Development in Indonesia" (2014).

INDEX

Page numbers in italics indicate figures or tables.

discouragement, underemployment and, 242, 252*n*3

distributive justice, 301

diversity: growth, 13, 14; in new economy, 237–38; nonmetropolitan minority population distribution, 2010, *20*; nonmetropolitan population by race/Hispanic origin, 2010, *21*; racial and ethnic, 239; in rural America, 19–22

divide and rule tactic, 158

domestic violence, 357

Donnermeyer, Joseph, 349, 354, 357

doubling-up, housing insecurity and, 281

Dragiewicz, Molly, 378

drinking water, 304

dropout rates, 31, 341

drugs: abuse, 219, 351, 357; open-air markets, 360; War on Drugs, 360, 368

Duncan, Cynthia, 42, 209, 443

Durkheim, Émile, 368

earned income tax credit (EITC), 249, 396, 400, 411*n*13

Eason, John, 367, 369, 373

EBT cards. *See* electronic benefit transfer cards

Economic Research Service (ERS): food insecurity and, 259; role of, 6, 26, 45, 57, 59, 409*n*1, 441; unemployment rates and, 190

economy, 42; amenity-based development and tourism, 432–34; American Economic Association, 29; ASEC, 74–75, 82*n*1; booms, 433; Bureau of Agricultural Economics, 43; casinos and, 159; community-based programs and, 424–32; in context, 231, 247–49, 416–17; Council of Economic Advisors, 398, 400; demographic change and restructuring of, 239–40; development of, 91–95; diversity in new, 237–38; education and, 95,

239–40, 339–42; with employment hardship in 2000s, 240–47; farming and, 11–12; gender inequality and, 96–97; globalization and, 232–33, 250–52; Great Depression, 1, 22, 34–35, 418; Great Recession, 23–24, 42, 94, 97, 118, 123–30, 244; growth model, *421*; homeless students with education and, 339–42; immigrants and, 195–96; with industrial-occupational composition, 233–37; manufacturing counties and, 13, 14, 16; Office of Economic Opportunity (OEO), 38, 154; old and new, separation of, 232–33; place-based programs and, 417–19; Scientific Charity movement and, 34; status by county, 1960, by, *44*. *See also* social capital

education: advanced, 216, 217, 219; in context, 322–24, 338–39; dropout rates, 31, 341; with economic disadvantage and homeless students, 339–42; economy and, 95, 239–40, 339–42; ESEA, 327–28, 332, 338; ESSA, 338; federal funding inequity and, 331–32; federal measures with child poverty and, 325–29; Indian Education and Self-Determination Act (1975), 154; inequality with, 428–29; National Center for Education Statistics, 328; National School Lunch Program and, 267–68, 328, 397; NCLB, 328, 333–35, 338; Pell grants for, 391; reform, 335–36; with school funding and families, 323, 329–30; with schooling, youth aspirations, and out-migration, 336–37; with school services and child poverty, 324–25; state-level funding inequity and, 330–31; teacher labor markets and school service provision with, 335–36; with urban-centered policy as federal practice, 332–33; with urban-centered school funding and policy regimes, 335